# Social Psychology in Christian Perspective

## EXPLORING THE HUMAN CONDITION

## Angela M. Sabates

IVP Academic

An imprint of InterVarsity Press
Downers Grove, Illinois

*InterVarsity Press*
*P.O. Box 1400, Downers Grove, IL 60515-1426*
*ivpress.com*
*email@ivpress.com*

*InterVarsity Press® is the book-publishing division of InterVarsity Christian Fellowship/USA®, a movement of students and faculty active on campus at hundreds of universities, colleges, and schools of nursing in the United States of America, and a member movement of the International Fellowship of Evangelical Students. For information about local and regional activities, visit intervarsity.org.*

*Scripture quotations, unless otherwise noted, are from the New Revised Standard Version of the Bible, copyright 1989 by the Division of Christian Education of the National Council of the Churches of Christ in the USA. Used by permission. All rights reserved.*

*While all stories in this book are true, some names and identifying information in this book have been changed to protect the privacy of the individuals involved.*

*Cover design: Cindy Kiple*
*Cover image: ©DrAfter123/iStockphoto*
*Interior design: Beth McGill*

*ISBN 978-0-8308-3988-9 (print)*
*ISBN 978-0-8308-6641-0 (digital)*

*Printed in the United States of America* ♾

*InterVarsity Press is committed to ecological stewardship and to the conservation of natural resources in all our operations. This book was printed using sustainably sourced paper.*

**Library of Congress Cataloging-in-Publication Data**

Sabates, Angela M., 1962-
  Social psychology in Christian perspective : exploring the human condition / Angela M. Sabates, Ph.D.
    pages cm.
  Includes bibliographical references.
  ISBN 978-0-8308-3988-9 (casebound : alk. paper)
  1. Christianity—Psychology—Textbooks. 2. Social psychology—Textbooks. 3. Psychology and religion—Textbooks. 4. Psychology—Philosophy—Textbooks. I. Title.
  BR110.S23 2012
  302—dc23

                                                                                        2012038555

| P | 22 | 21 | 20 | 19 | 18 | 17 | 16 | 15 | 14 | 13 | 12 | 11 | 10 | 9 | 8 | 7 | 6 | 5 | 4 | 3 | 2 |
|---|----|----|----|----|----|----|----|----|----|----|----|----|----|---|---|---|---|---|---|---|---|
| Y | 38 | 37 | 36 | 35 | 34 | 33 | 32 | 31 | 30 | 29 | 28 | 27 | 26 | 25 | 24 | 23 | 22 | 21 | 20 | | |

In loving memory of my sister,
Vivian Sabates, whose untimely death as a college student
was a main impetus in my search for faith and brought me,
in unexpected ways, to the writing of this text.

*Trust in the L*ORD*, and do good.*

**Psalm 37:3**

# Contents

Preface . . . . . . . . . . . . . . . . . . . . . . . . . . . . . . 19

Acknowledgments. . . . . . . . . . . . . . . . . . . . . . . . 21

**1 SOCIAL PSYCHOLOGY**
*METHODS AND ASSUMPTIONS* . . . . . . . . . . . . . . . 23

What Is Social Psychology? . . . . . . . . . . . . . . . . . 23

How Do Psychologists Study Social Behavior? . . . . . . . . 27

What Are Some Common Findings
in Social Psychology?. . . . . . . . . . . . . . . . . . . . . 32

Is There a Positive or Negative Focus in
Social Psychology Research? . . . . . . . . . . . . . . . . . 32

What Are Some Advantages and Disadvantages
of the Empirical Approach?. . . . . . . . . . . . . . . . . . 37

How Do Social Psychologists Interpret Their Findings?
A Look at Evolutionary Psychology. . . . . . . . . . . . . . 39

How Does the Evolutionary Approach
Generate Hypotheses? . . . . . . . . . . . . . . . . . . . . 46

What of the Naturalist View of Humans? . . . . . . . . . . 47

So Far . . . . . . . . . . . . . . . . . . . . . . . . . . . . . 50

Questions to Consider . . . . . . . . . . . . . . . . . . . . 51

Key Terms . . . . . . . . . . . . . . . . . . . . . . . . . . . 51

**2 WHAT HAS CHRISTIANITY TO DO WITH
SOCIAL PSYCHOLOGY?** . . . . . . . . . . . . . . . . . . . 53

Why Is One's View of the Human Condition
So Important?. . . . . . . . . . . . . . . . . . . . . . . . . 53

Is It Valid to Integrate Christian Ideas with a
Scientific Understanding of Social Interaction?. . . . . . . . 55

How Does One Integrate Christian Ideas with
Social Psychology? . . . . . . . . . . . . . . . . . . . . . . 57

What Do Creation, Fall and Redemption Suggest
to Us About Social Behavior? . . . . . . . . . . . . . . . . . .   60

What of Creation and Human Social Interaction? . . . . . .   62

   Imago Dei . . . . . . . . . . . . . . . . . . . . . . . . . . . . .   62

   Creation and Community . . . . . . . . . . . . . . . . . . .   63

      Community and the Relational Self . . . . . . . . . .   64

      Community and Other-Centeredness . . . . . . . . .   66

      The Relational Self and Other-Centeredness
      as God's Image . . . . . . . . . . . . . . . . . . . . . . . .   67

      Limited Beings in Community . . . . . . . . . . . . . .   69

What of the Fall and Human Social Interaction? . . . . . . .   70

What of Redemption and Human Social Interaction? . . . .   73

What Else Distinguishes the CFR Approach
from a Naturalist Model? . . . . . . . . . . . . . . . . . . . . .   75

How Is the Empirical Approach Relevant to
a Christian View of Persons? . . . . . . . . . . . . . . . . . . .   76

So, What of Hypotheses and Interpretations? . . . . . . . . .   78

How Else Can We Get a More Balanced View of Humans?
A Look at Positive Psychology. . . . . . . . . . . . . . . . . . .   80

What About Possible Limitations of the CFR Approach? . . .   84

So Far . . . . . . . . . . . . . . . . . . . . . . . . . . . . . . . . . . .   85

Questions to Consider . . . . . . . . . . . . . . . . . . . . . . . .   87

Key Terms . . . . . . . . . . . . . . . . . . . . . . . . . . . . . . . . .   87

3  THE SELF IN A SOCIAL WORLD . . . . . . . . . . . . . . .   88

Why Study the Self? . . . . . . . . . . . . . . . . . . . . . . . . . .   88

Are Current Notions of the Self Consistent with a
Biblical Perspective? . . . . . . . . . . . . . . . . . . . . . . . . .   90

Self-Perception and Self-Concept:
*How Do We Know Ourselves?* . . . . . . . . . . . . . . . . . . .   92

Is Our Self-Concept Multifaceted?. . . . . . . . . . . . . .   95

Is Self-Concept Only Descriptive?. . . . . . . . . . . . .   96

Are We Always Consciously Aware of Our Self-Concept?. .   97

Do Ideas of the Self Vary Across Cultures? . . . . . . . .   97

Self-Esteem: *How Well Do We Like Ourselves?* . . . . . . .   98

Is Self-Esteem a Unitary Concept?. . . . . . . . . . . . .   99

Is Higher Self-Esteem a Good Thing?. . . . . . . . . . .   100

How Much Do We Strive to Maintain Our Self-Esteem?. .   102

How Do Social Comparisons Affect Our Self-Esteem? . .   104

What Implications Does a Christian View of
Self-Esteem Have for Research? . . . . . . . . . . . . . .   106

Just How Relational Is the Self?. . . . . . . . . . . . . . .   109

Are There Gender Differences in Our Intrinsic
Relational Nature?. . . . . . . . . . . . . . . . . . . . . .   113

A Christian View of Our Intrinsic Relational Nature . . .   114

The Self in Action: *How We Present Ourselves to Others*. . .   115

Just How Self-Centered Are We? . . . . . . . . . . . . . . .   115

Are Self-Serving Tendencies Universal?. . . . . . . . . .   118

Self-Presentation. . . . . . . . . . . . . . . . . . . . . . .   120

Both Self-Seeking *and* Intrinsically Relational? . . . . . .   122

Self-Regulation . . . . . . . . . . . . . . . . . . . . . . .   127

Self-Regulation from the CFR View . . . . . . . . . . . .   132

So Far . . . . . . . . . . . . . . . . . . . . . . . . . . . . .   135

Questions to Consider . . . . . . . . . . . . . . . . . . . .   136

Key Terms . . . . . . . . . . . . . . . . . . . . . . . . . . .   136

**4 SOCIAL PERCEPTION AND SOCIAL COGNITION**
*Understanding Others and Our Social World* . . . .   138

What Is Social Cognition? . . . . . . . . . . . . . . . . . .   138

How Accurate Are Our Perceptions?. . . . . . . . . . . . . 140

Bounded Rationality and a Christian View of Humans . . . 142

The Importance of Evaluating When Perceiving Others. . . 143

    Evaluating Moral Character . . . . . . . . . . . . . . 144

    Evaluating Nonverbal Cues. . . . . . . . . . . . . . . 146

    Evaluating Behavior. . . . . . . . . . . . . . . . . . . 149

    Warm or Cold?. . . . . . . . . . . . . . . . . . . . . . 149

    Web-Based Social Cognition. . . . . . . . . . . . . . 152

    How Organized Are Our Evaluations of Others? . . . . . 153

Purpose of Social Cognition: *Naturalist and CFR Views*. . . 154

Strategies for Social Perception and Cognition . . . . . . . 156

    Categorization . . . . . . . . . . . . . . . . . . . . . . 156

    Attributions . . . . . . . . . . . . . . . . . . . . . . . 158

    Covariation and Attributions . . . . . . . . . . . . . . 164

    Heuristics. . . . . . . . . . . . . . . . . . . . . . . . . 166

    Affect . . . . . . . . . . . . . . . . . . . . . . . . . . 168

    Additional Biases in Social Cognition. . . . . . . . . . 170

        Narratives . . . . . . . . . . . . . . . . . . . . . 171

        Hindsight Bias . . . . . . . . . . . . . . . . . . . 172

        Primacy and Recency Effects . . . . . . . . . . . . 172

        Illusion of Control . . . . . . . . . . . . . . . . . 174

        The Rosy View . . . . . . . . . . . . . . . . . . . 174

        Counterfactual Thinking: "What If?" . . . . . . . . 176

        Illusory Correlations . . . . . . . . . . . . . . . . 178

        Confirmation Bias . . . . . . . . . . . . . . . . . 179

The (In)Accuracies of Social Cognition:
*Bounded Rationality and a Christian View* . . . . . . . . . 181

    Accuracy Revisited . . . . . . . . . . . . . . . . . . . 182

Limits to Accuracy: *Bounded Rationality* . . . . . . . . . 185

A Christian View of Accuracy and Its Limitations . . . . 186

So Far . . . . . . . . . . . . . . . . . . . . . . . . . . 188

Questions to Consider . . . . . . . . . . . . . . . . . . 188

Key Terms . . . . . . . . . . . . . . . . . . . . . . . . 189

## 5 SOCIAL INFLUENCE
### *CONFORMING GROUPS AND OBEDIENT INDIVIDUALS* . . . . 191

What Is Social Influence? . . . . . . . . . . . . . . . . . 191

What Is a Group? . . . . . . . . . . . . . . . . . . . . . 192

The Prevalence of Group Membership and Conformity . 193

Groups and Other Social Psychological Concepts . . . . . 194

An Evolutionary View of Groups . . . . . . . . . . . . . 195

A Christian Perspective of Groups . . . . . . . . . . . . 195

Intragroup Processes . . . . . . . . . . . . . . . . . . . 197

Brainstorming . . . . . . . . . . . . . . . . . . . . . . 197

Deindividuation . . . . . . . . . . . . . . . . . . . . . 199

Social Loafing . . . . . . . . . . . . . . . . . . . . . . 201

Social Facilitation . . . . . . . . . . . . . . . . . . . . 202

Group Polarization and Risky Shift . . . . . . . . . . . 204

Groupthink . . . . . . . . . . . . . . . . . . . . . . . . 206

Intergroup Relations . . . . . . . . . . . . . . . . . . . 208

In-Groups vs. Out-Groups . . . . . . . . . . . . . . . . 208

Intergroup vs. Interpersonal Competition . . . . . . . . 209

Groups and Christianity . . . . . . . . . . . . . . . . . 210

Conformity . . . . . . . . . . . . . . . . . . . . . . . . 211

Prevalence of Conformity . . . . . . . . . . . . . . . . 212

Is Conformity Inherently Productive or Destructive? . . . 214

Why Conform?. . . . . . . . . . . . . . . . . . . . . . 215

Classic Studies of Conformity . . . . . . . . . . . . . . 216

Factors Influencing Conformity. . . . . . . . . . . . . . 217

    Group Size. . . . . . . . . . . . . . . . . . . . . . . 217

    Perceived Loss of Freedom. . . . . . . . . . . . . . . 219

    Moral Convictions . . . . . . . . . . . . . . . . . . . 220

    Minority vs. Majority Influence. . . . . . . . . . . . . 221

Social Contagion. . . . . . . . . . . . . . . . . . . . . 224

Christianity and Conformity. . . . . . . . . . . . . . . 226

Obedience . . . . . . . . . . . . . . . . . . . . . . . . . 228

    What Factors Contribute to Obedience? . . . . . . . . 228

    A Classic Study and Its Variants: Milgram and Others . . . 229

    A Christian View of Obedience Research. . . . . . . . . 233

So Far . . . . . . . . . . . . . . . . . . . . . . . . . . . 234

Questions to Consider . . . . . . . . . . . . . . . . . . 234

Key Terms. . . . . . . . . . . . . . . . . . . . . . . . . 235

**6 ATTITUDES AND PERSUASION**

*YET MORE EXAMPLES OF SOCIAL INFLUENCE* . . . . . . . . 237

Attitudes. . . . . . . . . . . . . . . . . . . . . . . . . . 238

    What Are Attitudes?. . . . . . . . . . . . . . . . . . . 238

    How Do We Form and Change Attitudes? . . . . . . . . 240

    What Is the Content of Attitudes? . . . . . . . . . . . . 243

    What Functions Do Attitudes Serve? . . . . . . . . . . 244

    Are We Always Aware of Our Attitudes? . . . . . . . . 245

    How Are Attitudes Related to Behavior? . . . . . . . . 248

    How Do Attitudes Bias Social Perception? . . . . . . . . 255

    CFR View and Attitudes . . . . . . . . . . . . . . . . 255

Persuasion: *Changing Attitudes* . . . . . . . . . . . . . . . . . . 259

  When Does Persuasion Work? . . . . . . . . . . . . . . . 261

  Dual-Process vs. Unimodal Theories of Persuasion . . . . 262

  What Other Factors Affect the Likelihood of Persuasion? . . 265

  How Is Gender Related to Persuasion? . . . . . . . . . . 266

  How Do Emotions Affect Persuasion? . . . . . . . . . . 268

  What Are Some Strategies Used in Persuasion? . . . . . . 269

    The Foot-in-the-Door Phenomenon . . . . . . . . . 269

    Low-Ball Technique . . . . . . . . . . . . . . . . 270

    Door-in-the-Face Phenomenon . . . . . . . . . . . 270

  CFR View and Persuasion . . . . . . . . . . . . . . . 271

  So Far . . . . . . . . . . . . . . . . . . . . . . . . . . 273

  Questions to Consider . . . . . . . . . . . . . . . . . . 274

  Key Terms . . . . . . . . . . . . . . . . . . . . . . . . 274

**7 AGGRESSION** . . . . . . . . . . . . . . . . . . . . . . 276

  What Is Aggression? . . . . . . . . . . . . . . . . . . . 277

  What About Verbal Aggression? . . . . . . . . . . . . . 278

  How Does Scripture Define Aggression? . . . . . . . . . 280

  Religious Extremists and Aggression . . . . . . . . . . . 284

  Sexual Violence . . . . . . . . . . . . . . . . . . . . . 285

  What Are Some Biological Explanations of Aggression? . . 288

    Prefrontal Cortex . . . . . . . . . . . . . . . . . 288

    The Amygdala . . . . . . . . . . . . . . . . . . . 289

    Serotonin . . . . . . . . . . . . . . . . . . . . . 290

    Behavioral Genetics . . . . . . . . . . . . . . . . 290

    A Brief Comment on Biological Explanations
    of Aggression . . . . . . . . . . . . . . . . . . . 293

Evolutionary Psychology Perspectives of Aggression. . . . . 294

Psychosocial Explanations of Aggression . . . . . . . . . . 295

    Personality Variables . . . . . . . . . . . . . . . . . . . . 299

    Self-Esteem. . . . . . . . . . . . . . . . . . . . . . . . . . 302

    Gender and Aggression. . . . . . . . . . . . . . . . . . . . 303

    Developmental Sequence of Aggression. . . . . . . . . . 304

Family Factors Related to Aggression . . . . . . . . . . . . 305

    Parenting style. . . . . . . . . . . . . . . . . . . . . . . . . 305

    Physical abuse . . . . . . . . . . . . . . . . . . . . . . . . 306

Situational Factors Related to Aggression . . . . . . . . . . 307

    Aggressive Cues . . . . . . . . . . . . . . . . . . . . . . . 307

    Temperature . . . . . . . . . . . . . . . . . . . . . . . . . 308

    Crowding. . . . . . . . . . . . . . . . . . . . . . . . . . . . 309

    Violent Media . . . . . . . . . . . . . . . . . . . . . . . . 309

Is Aggression Getting Worse?. . . . . . . . . . . . . . . . . . 312

How Can We Reduce Violence?. . . . . . . . . . . . . . . . . 313

    Social-Cognitive Approaches. . . . . . . . . . . . . . . . . 314

    Prosocial Models and Norms. . . . . . . . . . . . . . . . . 314

    International Peace Efforts . . . . . . . . . . . . . . . . . . 315

A Christian View of Reducing Aggression:
*Humanizing and Forgiveness* . . . . . . . . . . . . . . . . . 316

    Humanizing . . . . . . . . . . . . . . . . . . . . . . . . . . 317

    Forgiving. . . . . . . . . . . . . . . . . . . . . . . . . . . . 321

    Forgiveness and Humanizing After Genocide . . . . . . . 322

    Forgiveness and Humanizing in Everyday Life . . . . . . 325

So Far . . . . . . . . . . . . . . . . . . . . . . . . . . . . . . 326

Questions to Consider . . . . . . . . . . . . . . . . . . . . . 327

Key Terms. . . . . . . . . . . . . . . . . . . . . . . . . . . . 327

## 8 PREJUDICE, STEREOTYPES AND DISCRIMINATION    329

Some Relevant Questions and Key Terms . . . . . . . . . .    330

Categorization  . . . . . . . . . . . . . . . . . . . . . . .    333

Why Study Prejudice, Stereotypes and Discrimination? . . .    334

Who Are the Usual Targets of Prejudice,
Stereotypes and Discrimination? . . . . . . . . . . . . . .    336

    The Obese  . . . . . . . . . . . . . . . . . . . . . . . .    337

    The Elderly . . . . . . . . . . . . . . . . . . . . . . . .    338

    Those Who Are Ill or Disabled. . . . . . . . . . . . . .    339

    Gender  . . . . . . . . . . . . . . . . . . . . . . . . . .    340

How Do Victims of Prejudice, Stereotypes and
Discrimination Respond? . . . . . . . . . . . . . . . . . .    342

Other Relevant Factors. . . . . . . . . . . . . . . . . . .    342

    Approaches Emphasizing Individual Differences . . . . .    343

    Prejudice as a Self-Esteem Enhancer? . . . . . . . . . .    346

    Social-Cognitive Processes in Prejudice  . . . . . . . . .    347

Religiosity and Prejudice. . . . . . . . . . . . . . . . . .    351

Is Prejudice Inevitable?. . . . . . . . . . . . . . . . . . .    360

Racial Reconciliation: *Is There Hope?* . . . . . . . . . . .    367

So Far . . . . . . . . . . . . . . . . . . . . . . . . . . . .    372

Questions to Consider . . . . . . . . . . . . . . . . . . .    373

Key Terms . . . . . . . . . . . . . . . . . . . . . . . . . .    373

## 9 PROSOCIAL BEHAVIOR
### *HELPING* . . . . . . . . . . . . . . . . . . . . . . . . . .    375

Why Study Helping? . . . . . . . . . . . . . . . . . . . .    376

Key Terms and Complex Motives. . . . . . . . . . . . . .    378

Whom Do We Tend to Help the Most?. . . . . . . . . . .    380

    A Just World . . . . . . . . . . . . . . . . . . . . . . .    380

Those Who Are Similar to Us . . . . . . . . . . . . . . 382

Those Whom We Like . . . . . . . . . . . . . . . . . 384

Those Whom We Find Attractive . . . . . . . . . . . 385

Kin and Other Close Folks . . . . . . . . . . . . . . . 387

Whom Do We Help: *A Christian Perspective* . . . . . . . 389

When Do We Tend to Help? . . . . . . . . . . . . . . . . 389

Emergency Situations . . . . . . . . . . . . . . . . . 389

Everyday Helping Situations . . . . . . . . . . . . . . 396

Geographical Area . . . . . . . . . . . . . . . . . . . 397

Mood . . . . . . . . . . . . . . . . . . . . . . . . . 398

Empathy . . . . . . . . . . . . . . . . . . . . . . . 400

A Christian View of Empathy and Helping . . . . . . . 400

Who Is Most Likely to Offer Help? . . . . . . . . . . . . 403

Gender . . . . . . . . . . . . . . . . . . . . . . . . 403

Social Exchange Theory . . . . . . . . . . . . . . . 404

An Altruistic Personality? . . . . . . . . . . . . . . . 406

Religiosity . . . . . . . . . . . . . . . . . . . . . . 407

Social Norms for Helping . . . . . . . . . . . . . . . . 409

Reciprocity Norm . . . . . . . . . . . . . . . . . . . 410

Social Responsibility Norm . . . . . . . . . . . . . . . 411

Obedience as Other-Centeredness . . . . . . . . . . . . . 411

How Can We Increase Helping Behavior? . . . . . . . . . 412

Information . . . . . . . . . . . . . . . . . . . . . . 412

Prosocial Role Models . . . . . . . . . . . . . . . . . 413

Reducing Ambiguity . . . . . . . . . . . . . . . . . . 413

Complex Motives for Helping: *Two Views* . . . . . . . . . 414

Naturalism and Helping . . . . . . . . . . . . . . . . 417

Altruism as Other-Centeredness . . . . . . . . . . . . 421

Christianity and Altruism. . . . . . . . . . . . . . . . . . . 423

Questions to Consider . . . . . . . . . . . . . . . . . . . . 425

Key Terms. . . . . . . . . . . . . . . . . . . . . . . . . . . 426

## 10 INTERPERSONAL ATTRACTION AND RELATIONSHIPS
### *WHO LIKES WHOM AND WHEN AND WHY?*. . . . . . . . . . 427

The Relevance of Relationships and
Interpersonal Attraction. . . . . . . . . . . . . . . . . . . 427

Physical Proximity: *Love Thy Neighbor* . . . . . . . . . . . 429

Why Is Proximity So Powerful? . . . . . . . . . . . . . . 432

When Might Proximity Not Result in Liking? . . . . . . . 433

A Christian View on Proximity and Attraction . . . . . . 435

Similarity: *Do We Like People Who Are Like Us?* . . . . . . . 437

Is Similarity Always Real or Also Just Perceived? . . . . . 439

What About Similarity and Marriage? . . . . . . . . . . . 439

Why Is Similarity So Powerful? . . . . . . . . . . . . . . 442

Do We Tend to Like Others Who Look Like Us? . . . . . 443

Does Similarity Always Lead to Attraction? . . . . . . . . 444

A Christian View on Similarity . . . . . . . . . . . . . . 445

Physical Attractiveness: *Do We Tend to Like
Beautiful People?* . . . . . . . . . . . . . . . . . . . . . . . 446

What Is "Beautiful"? . . . . . . . . . . . . . . . . . . . . 448

Is the Physical Attractiveness Stereotype a
Self-Fulfilling Prophecy? . . . . . . . . . . . . . . . . . . 449

Is Physical Attractiveness Always a Good Thing? . . . . . 450

Is the Physical Attractiveness Stereotype Universal
and Always So Strong? . . . . . . . . . . . . . . . . . . . 451

Social Exchange Theory: *Relationships and Reciprocity* . . . . 452

The Power and Meaning of Relationships:
*A Christian View Revisited*. . . . . . . . . . . . . . . . . . 454

Questions to Consider . . . . . . . . . . . . . . . . . . . . . 457
Key Terms . . . . . . . . . . . . . . . . . . . . . . . . . . . 458

Glossary . . . . . . . . . . . . . . . . . . . . . . . . . . . . 459
References . . . . . . . . . . . . . . . . . . . . . . . . . . . 478
Image Credits and Permissions . . . . . . . . . . . . . . . . 552
Author Index . . . . . . . . . . . . . . . . . . . . . . . . . 553
Subject Index . . . . . . . . . . . . . . . . . . . . . . . . . 564

# Preface

For many years, I have wondered about the connections between the Christian faith and what the science of psychology suggests to us about the nature of human social interaction. Numerous readings and conversations with colleagues, friends, family, students and even strangers have all helped me to gain greater insight into these connections. The discussions in this text reflect in large part the "unwitting collaboration" that these many sources have participated in with me. How fitting it seems that this text on social psychology, whose very emphasis is social interaction, should be largely the result of the interactions I have had with many fellow humans. In places where it seems I may have erred or misunderstood these sources, I assume full responsibility.

In addition to my many readings and conversations with others, I have observed, as no doubt you have as well, the capacity that we humans have to both love one another generously and to act selfishly. I have always been intrigued by this tension. Until recently, most of the readings in social psychology, as well as in the field at large, have seemed to focus primarily on our selfish and errant ways. Along with many other Christian scholars, I sensed that this relative neglect of our potential for goodness must be based on a set of assumptions regarding the nature of humans. Indeed, the assumptions of naturalism and reductionism, which pervade our field not only in terms of methodology but also focus of study, are unlikely to look for and find data that are consistent with the view that people are created for good, are fallen, but may yet be redeemed. These Christian assumptions have the potential to expand the range of questions that social psychology explores as well as the possible explanations of the data. Assuming a researcher is using the same scientific rigor that the field commands, such broadening of the range of inquiry and explanations has the potential to provide a more robust understanding of social interaction.

The views presented in this text are meant to add to, not conclude, this process of integration. These views provide one way in which Christian thought can both contribute to, and be enlightened by, the existing and growing body of data in social psychology. Central to this endeavor is the acknowledgment that humans were created with the capacity to partake in God's redemptive plan for one another. How we do this, and what circumstances and factors facilitate or hinder this process, is one of the main questions social psychology could potentially explore. In this way, social psychologists would study, to borrow loosely the language of British philosopher Alasdair MacIntyre (2007), not only "human nature as it happens to be" but also "human nature as it is when it realizes its *telos*, i.e., purpose." Thank you for being willing to consider together with me one way in which this exploration can take place.

ANGELA M. SABATES

# Acknowledgments

Many sincere thanks are due to my colleague C. Eric Jones, who was instrumental in the original thinking and editing for this text, especially for the first few chapters. Our shared zeal for understanding how Christian principles relate to the field of social psychology was often an inspiration to me, refining my thinking. I also wish to thank colleagues at Bethel University from various fields of study; each helped me understand different facets of human functioning, sometimes praying for me, encouraging me or prodding me along the way: Juan Hernandez of Biblical and Theological Studies, Michael Dreher of Communication Studies, Earleen Warner of the Bethel Library and Karen Tangen of the Business Department. From my own department of psychology, I thank Joel Frederickson, who was one of the readers of the original proposal and gave many helpful suggestions. Thanks to my dear friend and colleague Lucie Johnson, who has also been a very helpful encourager and editor of chapter drafts. I cannot count the number of hours she and I have spent in local coffee shops talking about ways to consider how Christian thinking relates to the field. Many students from Bethel and Palm Beach Atlantic University read earlier chapter drafts and gave helpful suggestions from the student's view; thank you all! I also very much appreciate the encouragement and helpful suggestions of anonymous reviewers, who later revealed themselves to me as Darlene Hannah of Wheaton College and Peter Hill of Biola University. Thank you also to Gary Deddo, the ever-patient editor at InterVarsity Press, who saw the potential of this project from its inception, and to David Congdon, the IVP editor who helped bring this book to its completion. I owe many thanks to my friends and neighbors, who often asked about the book and earnestly said they wanted to read it despite my warnings that it is a textbook. I owe special thanks to my parents, who, gratefully, never gave up on my efforts despite the many missed deadlines. Special thanks to my mother, who read earlier drafts and suggested that I reconsider certain wording that would likely be incomprehensible to the average student. I wish also to thank my daughter, Sveta, and step-daughter, Heather, who both understood the importance of this project for me and were patient whenever I told them I had to sit in front of the computer for hours on end to write "the book." They are glad it is done! I wish to offer special thanks to my much-beloved husband, Jeff Berryhill, whose tender love for me, razor-sharp editing, endless encouragement and patience are some of the most cherished gifts God has granted me. And, of course, I acknowledge much appreciation to God for his love, grace and wisdom.

# 1

## Social Psychology

*Methods and Assumptions*

*The heavens are telling the glory of God;*
*and the firmament proclaims*
*his handiwork.*

**PSALM 19:1**

### WHAT IS SOCIAL PSYCHOLOGY?

Imagine that you are on a road trip with several friends. The four of you have been looking forward to this break after a long school year. The trip starts off with everyone in a happy mood, singing along to the songs on the radio, each of you privately basking in the wonders of your friendship with your delightful travel companions. You can't imagine a time when you would not be such great friends. Midway through the trip, the car suddenly runs out of gas. "No problem," you say, trying to keep the upbeat mood alive in the midst of this setback. "We can just stand out here by the side of the road and motion to other drivers. I'm sure we can get some help in no time."

After about one hour of failed attempts to get help from the passing drivers—who, you're convinced, seem to speed up as they pass you by—it is getting very hot outside. You notice that the mood of your group has changed; you have begun to lose patience and started blaming each other for not ensuring that the car had enough gas to begin this journey.

You then collectively decide that it is time to start walking toward the nearest gas station, but which way should you walk? Some of you say that you should risk going forward in the direction of your trip, assuming that you will pass a gas station before long; others of you say that you should walk in the other direction, where you know for certain that you had passed a gas station about two miles ago. Should you all walk together, or should one of you stay by the car just in case a nice driver stops to help sometime soon?

In the midst of trying to resolve this dilemma, what do you think will happen in the group? Will you increase your mutual efforts to maintain group cohesion, or will the group become increasingly argumentative? Will all members of the group be equally likely to help resolve the group's dilemma ("we're all in this together"), or will some member(s) be more lax, allowing the rest to do most of the work? Will one of you emerge as the group leader and be able to persuade the others of the best course of action? Will your perceptions of one another be altered due to the stress of the situation? And, by the way, why didn't any of those drivers who passed by stop to help?

The seemingly infinite number of potential answers to the above questions demonstrates how human social behavior is arguably among the most complex of all phenomena in science. This complexity often leads to great difficulty when trying to describe, explain and predict various aspects of social behavior. The intricate connection of many personal and situational factors produces the behavior that we observe. The field of social psychology is one attempt at understanding this complexity.

*Social psychology* is the scientific study of human social interaction, including our perceptions of one another and of social situations. This field is concerned with understanding a broad range of features, including how we persuade one another, how individuals interact within groups, what circumstances lead to both productive and destructive social behavior, and so on. In short, social psychology attempts to explore social influence. Allport (1924), whose definition of social psychology is one of the oldest and most often cited, suggested just how powerful social influence can be when he clarified the idea that this influence is due not only to the result of the actual presence of others, but also to the implied or *imagined* presence of others. To better understand the goals of the field, consider just a few of the many questions that social psychologists explore:

- Why aren't our behaviors always consistent with our professed attitudes?
- Under what circumstances are we most likely to be persuaded?
- When and whom are we most likely to help?
- How reliable are eyewitness testimonies?
- How do we form impressions of political candidates?
- Are racism and prejudice really declining, or are we just getting better at hiding them?
- Who is attracted to whom, and why?

The relevance of such topics makes the study of social psychology important not only for researchers, but also for the public at large. The findings of social psychology are often applied to real-life dilemmas. For example, research findings about what factors contribute to group violence can be particularly helpful for public officials and community members who are concerned about rioting or gang violence in the schools. Similarly, knowing what factors may impair an eyewitness's accuracy in recalling the events of a crime is helpful both for the police who question such witnesses as well as for jury members' assessments of an eyewitness account in the courtroom.

Specifically for students, the findings of social psychology research can be especially relevant as one considers all the social interactions and dynamics that occur during college life. Surely almost all college students, for example, would be interested in knowing what factors contribute to interpersonal attraction. (By the way, for those of you who are interested, there is more on this in the last chapter.)

Figure 1.1 presents the way in which some of the major areas of research in social psychology are discussed in this text. Also included are just a few relevant questions typically asked in those areas of research. Note how extensive the field is, and also be aware that the different areas are interrelated, each significantly interacting with the others.

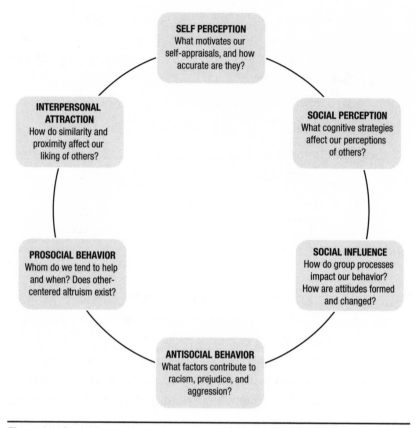

**Figure 1.1. Social Psychology: Research and Sample Questions**

So far, the empirical research in social psychology has helped provide a greater understanding of the many influences on human social behavior. This text will explore that relevant research, which has indeed added much to our understanding of how humans interact. In addition, this text will explore how the field of social psychology can be enriched when one considers related ideas that stem from a Christian understanding of both the human condition and the ultimate purposes for social interactions. More specifically, it is proposed that if we consider the perspective that humans were created in God's image for relationship with him and others, we could arrive at a richer understanding of human social interaction than if we only used the current naturalist assumptions of social psychology; and further, that Christian ideas of persons are a legitimate and valid starting point for social psychology research. This Christian approach to social psychology will be fully discussed in chapter two.

This first chapter will focus on the empirical method that social psychologists use to study human interactions, the assumptions that have guided those research efforts and the possible implications of those assumptions. Naturalism, the assumption that is most prevalent in social psychology research, will be reviewed. For the sake of simplicity, *naturalism* refers to the belief that reality comprises material substance, and that the immaterial (e.g., God, soul, mind, etc.) either does not exist or is irrelevant to empirical investigation because it cannot be measured. The view of humans that emerges from this naturalist stance will also be discussed in this chapter. An understanding of such assumptions and their implications helps us understand the possible strengths and limitations of such an approach to the understanding of human social interaction.

Bear in mind that naturalism in psychology is not a new idea. For example, psychologist and philosopher William James noted in his 1890 textbook, *Principles of Psychology,* that psychology was on the naturalistic track, and for the sake of its progress as a science it should be allowed to continue as such. Many historical major theorists in psychology (e.g., Freud, 1929; Skinner, 1971) as well as more contemporary theorists (e.g., Buss, 2005; Tooby & Cosmides, 2003) have likewise espoused a naturalistic view of humanity.

## How Do Psychologists Study Social Behavior?

Since social psychologists employ traditional scientific research methods to study human social interaction, it is important to review some of the basic strategies used in the field. This approach to research is based on *empiricism*, which is a key component of the scientific method. Empiricism focuses on gathering evidence through observations and seeks to obtain a more objective understanding of the topic of study than is possible through random, unstructured observations or intuitions.

To illustrate how social psychologists use the scientific approach, let us consider the example of how they explore helping behavior, a prominent topic in the field. The scientific process often begins with a broad research question such as: What variables affect a person's propensity to help others? From the research question, specific hypotheses are generated. A *hypothesis* is a testable statement that proposes a possible explanation or prediction of some phenomenon or event. Through it, one gives an educated guess about the answer to the research question. To be "testable" in this context means that the validity of the statement can be tested using the experimental method. A hypothesis may include a prediction. For example, researchers may propose that a person is less likely to help others if that person is in a hurry or has some other pressing appointment waiting. So, the experimenters would then test their hypothesis by manipulating the time-pressure variable to see if it has the predicted effect of lessening the chances of helping. In this way, they are exploring cause-effect relationships.

Along with specific hypotheses, social psychologists also develop theories. *Theories* are general explanations based on a large amount of data. Theories provide frameworks from which to understand the various empirical observations and also generate additional hypotheses. They help to organize the myriad research findings by suggesting how they fit into a more cohesive, larger picture. One example of a theory in social psychology is known as *social role theory*. Originally proposed by Eagly (1987), this theory arose as an effort to unify the many empirical observations of the apparent differences in the social behavior of males and females (e.g., levels of aggression, types of helping behavior, etc.). According to this theory, the sex differences seen in social behavior are largely the result of the gender roles that have been ascribed to men and women. Thus, for example, this theory proposes that society's emphasis on males being strong and virile helps explain why males are more likely than females to perform acts of helping that are of a chivalrous or heroic nature (Eagly & Crowley, 1986). In this way, social role theory attempts to provide an overarching framework within which to understand one particular aspect of social behavior.

To review, the scientific process entails the following steps:

1. Begin with a question (usually based on some observations of social behavior).

2. Form a hypothesis (like an educated guess that attempts to answer at least part of the research question).

3. Test the hypothesis (collect data and analyze it).

4. Interpret the results (Do they support your hypothesis? Are they consistent with other empirical observations or theories of social behavior?).

5. Communicate the results.

6. Numerous consistent observations lead to the formulation of theories, which also generate new hypotheses.

Remember that *formulating good hypotheses* and *interpreting the results* in as accurate a way as possible are two main processes necessary for a successful scientific approach. Like other scientists, social psychologists generate hypotheses and systematically test these by making observations in a variety of ways. Psychologists observe social interactions in many different contexts, including both laboratories and real-life social settings such as malls, street corners, political rallies, parties, and so on. You may have even been an unwitting subject in one of those types of studies!

Overall, there are two major types of research in psychology: experimental and correlational. As noted above, the *experimental* approach seeks to explore cause-and-effect relationships between variables by manipulating one or more variables to see what effect that has on another variable or set of variables. The following are examples of the experimental approach.

- **Laboratory experimentation.** You will likely recall from your earlier studies that lab experiments most often involve the manipulation of some (independent) variable(s) to assess its/their effect(s) on another (dependent) variable or set of variables. When social psychologists study helping behavior using this experimental method, they might vary the difficulty of the specific task of helping or the time constraints involved (independent variables) in order to assess how these factors affect the likelihood that the subjects will help (dependent variable).

- **Field experiments.** In these types of studies, social psychologists conduct experiments in natural settings. As with lab experimentation, the researcher will manipulate some independent variables to see how they affect helping, but this time the experiment takes place in a natural setting such as at a mall or school yard instead of in a lab. This type of experiment might involve, for example, the researcher varying the gender or age of the "person in need" to see how these factors affect the likelihood of helping.

In addition to the experimental approach, the second main type of research in psychology is *correlational.* These types of studies explore how variables co-vary without implying anything about cause and effect. Remember that "correlation does not imply causation"—in other words, two variables could co-vary strongly without one necessarily "causing" the other. Consider, for example, the relationship between gender and helping. A number of researchers (e.g., Huston, Ruggiero, Conner & Geis, 1981) have found that on helping tasks that require great physical strength and the potential of danger to the self, males are generally more likely to offer help. In this case there is a positive correlation between gender and helping with tasks that require great physical strength: as the strength required increases, the chances that the helper will be male increase as well. This does not mean that gender itself actually "causes" helping; the positive relationship simply means that males are more likely to help if the task requires more physical strength (perhaps because of a third variable, i.e., males tend to be taller and stronger than females). Now consider the following examples of studies where the correlational approach may be used:

- **Naturalistic observations.** In these types of studies, social psychologists attempt to observe how human social interaction takes place without any direct experimental intervention. For example, if studying helping behavior this way, a social psychologist might simply stand on a corner of a major intersection or in an airport lobby and look for how people respond to anyone who might genuinely be in need for any reason. Here the experimenter may try to see how the gender of the person in need correlates with the chances of receiving help.

- **Surveys.** Surveys ask direct questions of persons, often about their own behaviors, attitudes or opinions. They are most often used in correlational research. For example, subjects might be asked what sort of person (older vs. younger, male vs. female, etc.) they think they would be most likely to help. The experimenter may then correlate age and gender of the respondents with the type of person they think they would be most likely to help. They would be able to assess, for example, whether gender is related to the likelihood of helping older vs. younger people or whether no significant relationship exists among the variables.

Another important way in which psychologists study social behavior and cognitions is through the use of *content analysis*. This approach is often used when researchers are looking for themes or specific types of content in written text, verbal interactions or media images. There are different ways in which content analysis can be performed. It involves many steps, often including coding the content and quantifying the data for analysis. For example, suppose researchers were interested in exploring the incidence of sexual images in persuasive television ads. First the researchers would identify what qualifies as a sexual image (e.g., scanty clothing, suggestive language or looks, etc.). The researchers would then decide on a representative sample of television ads to watch. Then they would observe the number of times such images were used in the ads, coding each incidence. These data could then be analyzed to look for trends (e.g., overall prevalence of sexual images, time of day in which sexual images are most prevalent, etc.). Many applications of content analysis are possible. Consider, for example, how researchers could analyze political speeches for specific persuasive tactics, investigate racist content in magazine ads, look for indications of marital contentment in conversations between spouses, and so on.

Table 1.1. Empirical Approaches Most Often Used by Social Psychologists

| Experimental | Correlational |
|---|---|
| **1. Lab experiments:** manipulate variables in a controlled setting. | **1. Naturalistic observations:** observe social behavior in real-life settings without manipulating variables. |
| **2. Field experiments:** manipulate variables in a more natural setting | **2. Surveys:** ask direct questions to look for relationships among variables. |

Remember that all of the above-noted ways of studying social behavior use an empirical approach, which is considered to be one of the hallmarks of any scientific endeavor. Asking good questions (hypotheses) and interpreting the results in the most accurate way possible are two key components of a successful empirical approach.

## WHAT ARE SOME COMMON FINDINGS IN SOCIAL PSYCHOLOGY?

Now that you have reviewed the major types of empirical research used in social psychology, we can look at what that research has found. As of the writing of this text, the field of social psychology has been studying human social interaction for over seventy-five years. The data obtained from these studies have provided very useful information regarding general tendencies in social behavior. And, as noted earlier, many of these findings have been applied to various real-life settings. You will see as you read through this text that, especially when the results are considered collectively, there are several very interesting patterns that emerge. Listed here are two of these patterns, which are found quite consistently in research in the U.S. and across several other cultures. Note that these are especially relevant to the discussions in this text and will be discussed in more detail in a later section.

**People often tend to act in a self-serving manner** (e.g., Campbell & Sedikides, 1999; Miller & Ross, 1975). These findings suggest that humans most often seek to maximize their own personal advantage in their interactions with others.

**Humans appear to have an intrinsically relational (social) nature** (e.g., Baumeister & Leary, 1995; Leary & Cox, 2007). These findings suggest that humans have what is called a "fundamental" need to belong, which means that social connectedness is an essential part of our very being.

## IS THERE A POSITIVE OR NEGATIVE FOCUS IN SOCIAL PSYCHOLOGY RESEARCH?

In addition to these two patterns of findings, another interesting pattern can be seen in the focus of much social psychology research. If you consider the sorts of questions that social psychologists have most commonly asked, their emphasis has generally been about how things go *wrong* in human social behavior. This emphasis on asking questions about problems in social interaction began after the horrors of the Holocaust during World War II, after which social psychology began its main thrust in research. During the 1940s, '50s and '60s, social psychologists studied a number of important questions regarding the potentially destructive effects of social interaction. Many of these studies looked at how obedience, social perception and conformity can lead to devastating consequences and also at how we commonly misperceive one another. Following are just a few of the questions asked by the earlier researchers:

- How does large-scale propaganda encourage hatred for the "enemy" (e.g., WWII propaganda) (Jowett & O'Donnell, 1992)?

- How does frustration lead to aggression (e.g., Miller et al., 1941)?

- How does an "authoritarian personality" encourage anti-Semitic prejudice (Adorno, Frenkel-Brunswik, Levinson & Sanford, 1950)?

- How can people be persuaded to form a quick, false impression of another based on limited information (e.g., Kelley, 1950)?

- How are individuals compelled to follow group norms despite personal convictions or perceptions (e.g., Asch, 1951)?

- How do authority figures convince others to obey their orders to perform aggressive acts on another (e.g., Milgram, 1963)?

Thus, as noted in the *APA Monitor Online* (1999), "the period after World War II was one of searching for problems for social psychologists." This approach made sense in light of the devastating effects of World War II and the subsequent Korean and Vietnam Wars, as well as the difficult conflict that surrounded race issues in the U.S. One could argue that the types of questions that were asked reflected the historical context and also seemed to focus on and presume a primarily negative perspective of human social relations. The image of humans that emerges from this kind of research, whether or not intended, is one of a quite vulnerable being, most often inclined toward errors in perception and almost inevitably manipulated by the social situation. These characteristics make sense in light of how the historical context prompted the questions that were most often asked. From that perspective, the results seem accurate and they help us to better understand the atrocities of the wars and the racial conflict.

Has the focus of research questions in social psychology continued to emphasize what goes wrong as opposed to what also goes right in our dealings with one another? And have you begun to wonder whether reading this textbook is likely to make you depressed about the human condition? As you will see, the relatively negative view of human social interaction still lingers in the field. Nevertheless, recent efforts have begun to look more closely at the human potential for positive social interaction, including exploring compassion, forgiveness and accuracy in social perception.

The emerging field of *positive psychology,* which focuses on exploring human strengths and virtues and increasing subjective, community and institutional well-being, is having an impact on the traditionally negative view of humans that social psychology presented (e.g., Seligman & Csikszentmihalyi, 2000; Gable & Haidt, 2005). As noted by Seligman, Parks and Steen (2004), positive psychology aims to be a "balanced field that integrates research on positive states and traits with research on suffering and pathology . . . a psychology that concerns itself with repairing weakness as well as nurturing strengths, . . . and a psychology that concerns itself with reducing that which diminishes life as well as building that which makes life worth living" (p. 1380). Gable and Haidt (2005) likewise call for "an understanding of flourishing to complement our understanding of despair" (p. 103).

The positive psychology movement has important implications for research in social psychology. For example, researchers are now exploring more positive aspects of social behavior, such as the positive role of group behavior and the possible empathy-related factors in helping behavior.

Despite the impact of the positive psychology movement, the negative bias in social psychology still prevails. For example, citing the *Psychological Abstracts* from the end of the nineteenth century to the year 2000, Bierhoff (2002) notes that compared with the study of prosocial behavior (e.g., helping, altruism, etc.), social scientists have concentrated much more on the study of antisocial behavior (e.g., aggression, discrimination, etc.). In fact, he notes as one example that the topic of aggression was ten times more likely to be studied than was prosocial behavior, no matter which year is considered within that time span.

Examples of this negative bias in social psychology will be seen throughout much of the research reviewed in this text. Using helping behavior as an example, you will see that while at first glance the topic of helping behavior seems optimistic enough, you will not get very far in that chapter before you realize that the findings are not very encouraging. In fact, the whole area of helping research in social psychology first began as the result of the highly publicized crime in which neighbors allegedly did not intervene when they heard Kitty Genovese's cries for help while she was being stabbed to death outside of her New York City apartment. As you will read in chapter nine, the validity of this claim that the neighbors were apathetic has been questioned by later researchers (Manning, Levine & Collins, 2007). Nevertheless, the presumed apathy of the neighbors prompted researchers Latané and Darley (1970) to begin the study of helping by asking why people do *not* help. Since that initial study, much of the focus in the helping research has been on impediments to helping such as time constraints (Darely & Batson, 1973), dissimilarity between the helper and the one needing help (Schroeder, Penner, Dovidio & Piliavin, 1995; Cialdini, Brown, Lewis, Luce & Neuberg, 1997), and so forth.

With relatively few exceptions, social psychologists have not traditionally focused their research efforts on the many commonplace instances in which people *do* help. Nor have they generally focused on instances when people have made greatly self-sacrificing efforts to help, as in the case of those who risked their own lives to help the Jews during World War II. In fact, the notion that humans are even capable of other-centered helping is not widely supported by researchers. Note that if a scientist starts from the bias of uncovering impediments to helping, then questions about what prompts both everyday helping as well as grand heroic incidents of helping might be seen as either uninteresting, inconsequential or the exception.

Why brothers aren't allowed to perform surgery together.

Source: http://www.webdonuts.com/2012/04/brothers/

**Figure 1.2.**

The above discussion does

not mean to suggest, of course, that social psychologists always neglect to study what goes right in social interactions. In fact, in the past decade, there has been a significant increase in studying more constructive, pro-social interactions, as you will see. Still, one common assumption that underlies much of the research on social behavior is that humans are essentially self-centered beings who pursue positive social interaction with self-serving goals (Sedikides & Strube, 1997). Thus, it is not yet clear whether the *primary* focus of the field will continue to be problems in social functioning and interpreting the social processes that "look good" (e.g., altruism) as ultimately self-serving.

This is all very interesting, you may say, but how does the seemingly negative focus of social psychology's hypotheses affect our ability to get an accurate picture of human social interaction? After all, maybe the things that go wrong in our interactions with others just make for more interesting research than do those things that go right. In addition, social psychologists have accurately demonstrated and helped us understand many things that we can all observe go wrong in our everyday social interactions. So, in that way, the relatively negative image of human social interaction that results from these research questions may indeed be well-founded. And many of the things observed by social psychologists are readily evident in everyday life. For example, you have probably observed that attitudes of racism and prejudice are often prevalent and seem quite difficult to eradicate. You may have also observed that we tend to form first impressions quite quickly based on little information about the person. And those first impressions can often be wrong, yet we are often resistant to change them, even in the face of contrary evidence. And when others confront us with the errors of our thinking, is the usual tendency for us to embrace the other and thank them profusely for correcting our ways, or do we tend to get defensive about what we believe is true, even when presented with evidence to the contrary? Furthermore, haven't we all witnessed and indeed ourselves emphasized self-interest in at least *some* of our dealings with others?

The following chapters certainly provide a very sobering look at what can indeed go wrong in our interactions. In fact, in chapter after chapter, you will see that the view of humans that emerges is often a rather depressing one. If you had to summarize what social psychology findings currently tell us about humans in a single sentence, you could say something like the following: "Mostly self-seeking creatures who simultaneously crave social connections, humans generally overestimate the accuracy of their many error-filled social perceptions, even in the face of contrary evidence." Not a very promising picture, is it? Still, it certainly seems true enough, at least on the surface.

Suppose all those things noted above are true of us to a degree. But what if this negatively toned focus leads to an incomplete picture of humans and our social interactions? Let's return to this question in the next chapter when we can explore in more depth what a Christian view of persons could contribute to our understanding of human social interaction.

## WHAT ARE SOME ADVANTAGES AND DISADVANTAGES OF THE EMPIRICAL APPROACH?

Since social psychology research employs the empirical approach, understanding the benefits and potential drawbacks of such an approach can be helpful when interpreting research findings. The rigor of the empirical approach offers numerous benefits toward our understanding of human social interaction. First, it requires testable hypotheses, which help to guard against unfounded "hunches" that are often inaccurate. Second, it allows for the systematic collection of empirical support for or against any particular theory or hypothesis, facilitating explanations and predictions of social behavior. So, for example, research in the two areas of social perception and groups can be compared with relevant research findings in the area of helping to explore how social perception strategies along with group behavior influence the likelihood of helping. New research findings can help inspire later hypotheses and ultimately theories. In short, the systematic nature of the empirical approach offers us a way to gather pieces of evidence that build on each other and help to form increasingly well-developed and accurate ideas regarding human social interaction.

The findings of social psychology have certainly increased our understanding of human social interaction. Yet there are understandably some limitations to the empirical approach of social psychology, just as there are limitations to *all* efforts to investigate any phenomenon.

One potential limitation of the empirical approach is what Molden and Dweck (2006) refer to as "generalized principles of thought and action," which are the focus of social science research. Despite the benefits of this approach, the results actually describe only the "average person," and thus tell us nothing about any particular individual or how they are likely to respond in a given social setting. Suppose, for example, that you read a very compelling study that found a significant tendency for the subjects to be more aggressive after they were provoked by the experimenter. As tempting as it might be, you could not then assume that you—or any specific individuals you know, for that matter—are more likely to be aggressive if provoked. This is true even if numerous studies replicated the results of that first study; you just can't tell how any one individual will act based on the average actions of the respondents in the study.

Another limitation of the scientific approach is noted by Myers (2005) and relates to a broader issue. Psychology, like all the other sciences, cannot tell us about the meaning and purpose of human life or the ultimate goals or moral ideals toward which we should be striving as we live in community. For example, social psychologists (e.g., Dovidio, Eller & Hewstone, 2011) have been able to describe the conditions in which individuals who make conscious efforts to interact with racially diverse others express less racist ideologies than do those who live more segregated existences. Suppose that social psychologists may also observe that less racist attitudes are associated with less violence and discriminatory behavior among the races. They may also be able to demonstrate that those who are racist and carry out discriminatory acts also report on questionnaires that they are not as happy as those who are not racist. Thus, all things being equal, the outcomes are better for everyone if they live in a racially integrated society that makes deliberate attempts at racial reconciliation.

But apart from the better practical outcomes (e.g., peaceful coexistence, more pleasant interactions, greater levels of self-reported happiness, etc.), on what other basis could science then tell us that to love people of all races is itself the "right" or "virtuous" aim? Science could help us to reach those goals once they have been deemed beneficial, but it has no basis for determining those ultimate goals in the first place.

That is generally the purview of religious, philosophical or other moral traditions and standards.

Let's say we agree that despite all that science can tell us, it cannot tell us about the ultimate meaning or goals of human social interaction and that that is indeed not the task of science. Then consider the following questions: If discovering the ultimate purposes of human social interaction is not the task of science, does that necessarily mean that these ultimate aims are not relevant when interpreting the results of the scientific findings? Furthermore, does this necessarily mean that these ideas about ultimate purposes are not relevant to the formulating of the scientist's questions (i.e., hypotheses)? Recall that generating good hypotheses and explaining research findings in the most accurate way possible are both considered to be integral components of the scientific process. Let's see what social psychologists say about this.

### How Do Social Psychologists Interpret Their Findings? A Look at Evolutionary Psychology

Like other scientists, social psychologists use theories and other related assumptions and observations when interpreting the data obtained through the empirical method. Remember that theories provide organizing frameworks to make sense of the data. Historically, social psychologists have not usually developed metatheories (large unifying theories) to explain social behavior broadly. In fact, Schaller, Simpson and Kenrick (2006) note that one of the main criticisms of social psychology is that it has traditionally consisted of a "long list of interesting, but unrelated, phenomena" (p. 8).

Nevertheless, social psychology has developed alongside several major movements within the field that influenced the thinking of many social psychologists. One of these movements is *behaviorism,* which emphasizes learning principles such as rewards and punishment. Another orientation is the *cognitive approach,* which emphasizes how people think about the social world and their social interactions. The cognitive approach is still often used in social psychology to explore many social phenomena such as how mental shortcuts affect our social perception, how people develop attitudes, and so on.

It is important to note that regardless of the diversity of perspectives in psychology, naturalism has been a common underlying assumption in the majority of research. Working primarily within this framework of naturalism, social psychologists over the last two decades have continued to look for ways to unify the field of psychology so that the diverse findings may be more coherent. One of the most prominent proposals for a metaexplanation of social psychology research findings has been that of *evolutionary psychology* ("EP"; e.g., Barkow, Cosmides & Tooby, 1992; Buss, 1995, 2000, 2005). Tooby, Cosmides and Barrett (2005) emphasize the importance of evolutionary theory to the field of psychology by stating that "studying psychology and neuroscience without the ana-

lytical tools of evolutionary theory is like attempting to do physics without mathematics" (p. 18). Though evolutionary psychology is certainly the most prevalent metatheory in the field, it is yet unclear whether it can help unify psychology (Confer et al., 2010; Derksen, 2005).

The EP perspective assumes that humans are the products of the evolutionary process proposed by Charles Darwin (1859, 1871). As believed to be the case with all other species, this process originated through randomness and chance, and natural selection determined which features of human behavior, cognition and emotion survived. As espoused by most evolutionary psychologists, humans are thus seen as the products of a natural process whose origin is chance. From this view, human behavior is best explained as the result of psychological mechanisms that exist because they were in some way advantageous for the survival of our primal ancestors.

EP as it has been presented in the psychological literature generally has naturalism as one of its major assumptions. Recall that naturalism refers to the idea that all of reality is the product of natural processes and that the supernatural is either false, unknowable or not inherently different from natural phenomena or hypotheses (Kolak, 1997). From the vantage point of naturalist evolutionary psychology, ideas regarding human social interaction that emerge from religious traditions would be considered at best irrelevant.

If a researcher supports the evolutionary psychology perspective, does that also mean that he or she must necessarily endorse a naturalist worldview that there was no designer or intent in the origin of life or that all of reality consists solely of natural matter? Not at all! For example, the notion of *theistic evolution,* which is accepted by many Jewish, Muslim and Christian individuals, is based on the idea that God is the originator of life and that to varying degrees he designed the process of evolution to achieve his intents and purposes for all species. There are many scientists who espouse a specifically Christian theistic approach to evolutionary theory.

Buss (1999) notes that one important strength of the EP approach is that it explains all behavior in terms of both *ultimate* and *proximate* causes. *Ultimate* causes refer to those evolutionary factors such as natural selection and the environment of our primal ancestors that explain *why* some behavior exists or occurs. Thus, this is why any behavior or emotion (e.g., anger and aggression, etc.) that increased our primal ancestors' survival and reproductive advantage persists. *Proximate* causes refer to more recent factors such as genetics, behavioral reinforcement and developmental history that explain *how* we eventually develop and display specific behaviors. Ward and Siegert (2002), using the example of child sexual abuse, note that evolutionary psychology does not propose a rigid determinism. That is, the EP view does *not* support genetic determinism, nor does it propose that we are not able to change our actions. Liddle and Shackelford (2011) additionally note that just because EP seeks to study and explain many types of selfish behavior does not mean that it advocates such behaviors.

According to EP, the primary drive for individual survival and reproductive advantage are reflected in the tendency toward self-seeking behavior that would help ensure these goals. Liddle and Shackelford (2011) offer one example of this assumption when discussing motives for altruism toward related others. They explore why we often make great sacrifices to help some related others more than others by referring to the underlying assumption of kin selection. "The reason that the costs of altruism are offset when helping genetic kin is that the altruist is bene-fitting from someone with whom he or she shares genes. Thus, the ben-eficiary's reproductive success is a means by which the altruist can rep-licate his or her genes. But if the genetic kin cannot reproduce or is otherwise limited reproductively, the costs are not offset to the same degree, and one might thus expect altruistic behavior to decrease" (p. 129). The authors thus argue that research supports the assumption that lack of reproductive advantage is the main reason why humans are less likely to care for related others who are elderly or ill than we are for those who are healthy and fertile (Fitzgerald & Colarelli, 2009).

EP also maintains that differences in social behavior between indi-viduals arise from the fact that humans learn from one another (Boyd & Richerson, 2005). A culture is one prominent place in which this learning occurs. Cultural groups can perpetuate certain beliefs, and this information accumulates over time. Thus, the sort of information that different cultures foster can lead to different beliefs and behaviors be-cause others in the local environment have them.

Tooby and Cosmides (1992) note that EP sees culture as one of the most important aspects of human nature. The EP approach assumes that cul-tures evolved because during hominid evolution, our ancestors adopted new social arrangements that helped individuals. For example, all cultures use social exchange and cooperation (e.g., favors between friends, giving gifts, etc.) between two or more individuals for mutual benefit. Tooby and DeVore (1987) state that successful social exchange was critically important for hominid evolution. The early social arrangements also helped the group by maintaining group cohesion in the face of group competition.

As noted earlier, according to EP, generally speaking, whatever we see in our current social interactions is believed to be the result of behaviors that were beneficial for the survival of our ancestors. In other words, traits, emotions, social behaviors, and so on are all adaptations that re-sulted from the process of natural selection and still linger. EP theorists also note, however, that many human adaptations that were helpful for our ancestors' environment may not be adaptive in our current environment and may thus lead to destructive ends, including a compromise of our survival. For example, humans may be predisposed to eat fatty foods because this helped our ancestors survive during times when food was scarce. Currently, however, that way of eating often leads to obesity, heart disease and early death.

Tooby and Cosmides (2005) review another related and fundamental premise of EP, which is that the brain is a physical system that functions like a computer whose circuits are designed to generate behavior that is appropriate to your environmental circumstances. Different neural circuits are specialized for solving different adaptive problems. So, in the context of human social interaction, the various so-called *mental modules* in your brain are activated to respond to the specific demands of the social context in a way that is most beneficial for your survival and that of your biological descendants (Hagen, 2005). That is important because then your descendants would be able to pass on your shared genes to successive generations.

As a side note, Hardcastle and Stewart (2002) argue that the bias in neuroscience to consider brain functions as highly localized in specific areas of the brain is not well supported by actual brain research. So while it is true that certain parts of the brain are associated with specific functions, there is far more evidence that specific brain functions are integrated throughout the brain instead of being restricted to highly defined areas (Cabeza & Nyberg, 1997; Buller & Hardcastle, 2000). Regardless, many social psychologists who use the EP approach still refer to mental modules (or so-called psychological mechanisms) in their explanation of social behavior.

As noted by Cosmides and Tooby (1995), social psychologists with an EP view seek to understand the universal, evolved architecture that we all share by virtue of being humans. They further note that the genetic basis for the architecture of the human brain and resultant cognitive capacities are universal, creating what is called by some the *psychic unity of humankind*. This concept refers to how all members of the human species share the same basic, adaptive cognitive capacities and resultant general tendencies in social behavior.

The EP perspective holds that a consistent tendency in humans' social nature would be expected, though allowances would be made for cultural and situational variation in how those tendencies are expressed. For example, Fessler (2004) notes that the EP approach acknowledges that universal human characteristics, such as emotions, may all be the same but be expressed differently in different societies. Hence the fair amount of consistency seen in human social behavior when one looks at the collective findings of the social psychology research would be of no surprise from the evolutionary standpoint. It should be noted, however, that though this consistency in human inclinations would make sense given that we are all part of the same species, there is still disagreement among some evolutionary psychologists regarding whether a consistent human nature even exists (Caporael, 2001).

Among EP theorists, this perspective is presumed relevant to our responses in different social situations (e.g., whether we perceive another as friend or foe, whether or not we help, to what degree we conform to a particular group's demands, whether we obey another or are persuaded by another, etc.). For each of these social situations, an evolutionary psychologist might argue that our responses depend on our brain's capacity to activate the correct mental module that evolved to address that specific kind of social situation, to assess the survival benefit of the range of possible responses, and to then respond accordingly. Indeed, well-known evolutionary psychologist David Buss (1995) has noted that many of the issues related to our ancestors' survival and reproductive capacity are social in their very nature because they entailed interactions among people. Likewise, Brewer and Caporael (1990) argue that many of the behaviors we see in the social world (such as cooperation, loyalty, fear of social exclusion, etc.) have as their origin the idea of the cooperative group, which may have been the primary survival strategy of our ancestors.

Incidentally, it is important to note that evolutionary psychologists do not generally make the claim that current social behavior is primarily the result of *present* concerns for survival. For example, a researcher with the EP approach would not necessarily suggest that you joined that sorority or fraternity so that you would not be killed on Saturday night;

or that you joined that basketball team just so you could avoid the possible dangers that would occur in your life if you didn't join the team. Instead, the focus is on discovering ways in which current social behaviors reflect psychological mechanisms that evolved so that our ancestors could enhance their chances of survival. So, going to the movies with your friends this weekend might emanate from a strategy of group bonding that our ancestors found helpful for survival. Despite this distinction between ultimate and proximal causes, EP still emphasizes explanations of the origins of social behaviors in terms of their adaptive value. This point will be further discussed in chapter two.

Remember the two overall general findings of social psychology research—namely, both our generally self-seeking behavior and our apparent need to relate to others? From the EP perspective, these general findings make sense because they would have been beneficial for our ancestors' survival. This is logical, isn't it? All things being equal, if you look out for your own best interests and that of your biological relatives, you and your family are less likely to be killed. In this way, not only do you survive, but you have a better chance of the continuation of your genetic line of successors. Similarly, with regard to our apparently intrinsic relational nature, it is difficult to survive if you are not a member of some group(s), because group membership greatly increases the likelihood that members will care for and protect each other. And who can deny that survival is indeed an important consideration for virtually everyone? Just consider all the great lengths that people go to in order to recover from medical illness.

As for the instinct to reproduce, don't most people become parents, and don't all cultures consider fertility an asset? The EP view has thus gained much ground as of late as an explanatory model for social psychology research findings as well as a major source of hypothesis generating.

Using the concise set of principles of the EP view, one can systematically explain a wide range of social behaviors. In an effort to identify this broad range of topics studied by evolutionary psychologists, Webster, Jonason and Orozco (2010) reviewed the publication trends of the prominent EP journal, *Evolution and Human Behavior* (and its predecessor, *Ethology and Sociobiology*) from 1979 to 2008. Their results indicated that despite its diverse topics of study, evolutionary psychology has focused on a core group of topics such as human social and sexual behavior, (facial) attractiveness, kinship, and altruism. Additionally, the researchers noted that in the last decade, there seems to be a shift toward studying topics related to sex, sex differences, faces, attraction and morality.

Interestingly, several social psychologists have more recently suggested that some social interaction does not seem to be about survival as the end aim. Baumeister and Bushman (2007), for example, have stated that there is something fundamentally relational about people that is inherent in their cultural nature. Leary and Cox (2007) have similarly argued that our relational social behavior is of an importance that far surpasses the goal of survival and seems to aim for higher-level meaning. It is not made clear by these authors, however, how using a naturalist perspective as a starting point accounts for these observed desires for higher meaning. By contrast, as shall be seen in the following chapter, a Christian perspective of humans, whether or not based on evolutionary principles, can help account for this observed need for higher-level meaning and purpose. This is because a Christian view of persons as presented here is based on the presupposition that humans were created in God's image precisely for higher-order purpose—namely, to love God and to live in loving community with others.

## HOW DOES THE EVOLUTIONARY APPROACH GENERATE HYPOTHESES?

Thus far you have seen some ways in which the EP view addresses one key component of the empirical method: the interpretation of the data. But how does this approach also generate testable hypotheses? Buss (1995) clarifies that evolutionary psychology has many different levels of theory and specific hypotheses/predictions. Buss argues that at one level is evolutionary theory itself, which is not directly testable and, he says, is "like a law and is assumed to be true" (p. 3). But then there are middle-level evolutionary theories that produce more specific and testable hypotheses. For example, Trivers (1971) first proposed the theory of *reciprocal altruism*, which attempts to explain why it is that people sometimes help others even when helping comes at great personal cost. Trivers proposed that altruism evolved because the helper may be in a situation one day where he or she may need help. Thus that person would expect help from the one he or she helped before.

From the theory of reciprocal altruism has emerged the hypothesis that people will be more likely to cooperate and help each other out if they sense that the other is behaving likewise. But if the person detects that the other is cheating, then cooperation and altruism will decrease. This has been tested using the prisoner's dilemma studies (e.g., Pruitt, 1967), which will be described in chapter nine in regard to helping behavior.

Other specific hypotheses from the evolutionary psychology approach involve the nature of the psychological mechanisms that drive human behavior. For example, Buss (1995) considers the common finding that men on average do much better than do women on tasks of spatial abilities that involve mental rotation and map reading. Silverman and Eals (1992) argued that these are the particular forms of spatial ability that would have facilitated skill at hunting, which our primal ancestral males focused on. Females, by contrast, focused on gathering. Based on this assumption, Silverman and Eals proposed that women would excel more at certain types of spatial tasks that would have been very beneficial for gathering, such as object memory and location memory. Other testable hypotheses include how humans make cost-benefit analyses in different situations involving romantic relationships (Sedikides, Oliver & Campbell, 1994).

## WHAT OF THE NATURALIST VIEW OF HUMANS?

Any major theory or viewpoint in psychology assumes certain things to be true of the human condition. As previously noted, and as will be further discussed in the following chapter, the EP view of humans can be in some ways quite consistent with a Christian view of personhood. Remember that supporting an evolutionary view of humans does not necessitate endorsing a naturalist worldview. Nevertheless, the EP view presented in most of social psychology research is generally based on a naturalist view of reality. In this section, we will look at what sort of view of humans logically emerges from a naturalistic worldview.

A naturalist view of humans generally sees people as concerned ultimately with self-interests. A naturalist approach does not have any real basis for a sense of purpose or meaning to human life as distinct from other animals. This is vaguely reminiscent of Freud's (1929) comment that he could not understand why people kept asking about the meaning of human life and not asking the same question about the meaning of a dog's life. Thus, from this view, even though it is true that humans may have certain abilities (e.g., the capacity for language, abstract thinking and meaningful relationships) that distinguish us from other species, with regard to our significance, we are not otherwise in any logical or significant sense different from our fellow lions, for example. This is especially true of an evolutionary approach that assumes *only* random evolutionary processes and all species sharing the same ultimate goal of survival and reproductive advantage. Stewart-Williams (2011), for example, noted: "There is no reason to think that there is a teleological answer to the question of why we are here; there is only a historical one" (i.e., evolution).

Table 1.2 reviews some of the main assumptions of a naturalist view of personhood as discussed above. Consider some potential negative and positive implications of each of these assumptions. How is each relevant to human social interaction? Remember that supporting an evolutionary view of humans does not necessitate a naturalist worldview.

Table 1.2. Naturalist Assumptions of Personhood

| Social Phenomena | Explanation |
|---|---|
| Origin of human life | Randomness and chance events precipitated human life. |
| Self-seeking tendencies | Originate from the primary drive for survival and reproductive advantage; we relate to others in a primarily self-seeking way; even seemingly other-centered actions are generally considered ultimately self-centered. |
| Intrinsic relational nature | The drive to relate to others leads to many advantages (e.g., increased subjective well-being, social prestige, increased chances of survival, etc.). Our relational nature is thus ultimately only an inherent part of our nature because it is instrumental toward the achievement of other goals. |
| Value, dignity of persons | No specific basis for this apart from cultural, religious, and other moral traditions. |
| Ultimate goals (teleology) of social interactions | Survival and reproduction; other self-seeking and group-seeking motives (e.g., self-fulfillment, social advantage, etc.) |

"So what's the big deal?" you may ask. "What if humans are just the result of natural processes and we have no real ultimate purpose beyond survival?" In fact, it may just be an illusion for us to go about life thinking that we have some special dignity or worth. You may furthermore argue that it is easier to understand social relations as the result of such random natural processes where survival is the ultimate purpose, because at least that theory is succinct and clear. Nevertheless, the lack of any consistent basis for the dignity and worth of humans has a number of important implications for the application of social psychology research.

From a naturalist view, there is also no ultimate ethical perspective for how humans should treat one another in social interactions. After all, if humans are ultimately just animals with special advanced thinking and language capabilities, on what foundation (apart from survival of the species) would a naturalist approach logically distinguish or advocate one way of social conduct from another? This idea that moral values regarding our interactions with each other and the world at large are not based on any transcendent moral standards was further suggested by Harvard biologist E. O. Wilson (1975). He once proposed that the time may be right for "ethics to be removed temporarily from the hands of the philosophers and be biologicized" (p. 562).

As noted earlier in this chapter, the scientific method of social psychology does not have any consistent source for making ethical claims because it intends to be a *descriptive* approach instead of a *prescriptive* approach. A naturalist view may be able to describe to some extent what happens in social interactions, but it cannot really prescribe what *should* happen in social interactions among humans unless the data point to specific behaviors and attitudes that may result either in destructive ends—in other words, any compromise of our potential for survival—or in a positive end such as increased subjective well-being. This is a limitation of science that is commonly acknowledged and thought to be perfectly consistent with the definition and proper goals of science.

Despite this limitation, it is probably safe to assume that at least the overwhelming majority of social psychologists would agree with certain ethical concepts such as the notion that racism, hostile aggression and the unwillingness to help when we are able are wrong. In fact, social psychologists also routinely conclude from their findings how the data can be relevant to solving such problems in the broader social context. Consider the example of prejudice and racism. Numerous social psychologists have focused their research efforts on investigating factors related to the propensity for prejudice and ways to ameliorate this negative social phenomenon (e.g., Anderson, 2010; Brewer, 1999; Dovidio, Glick & Rudman, 2005). Whenever social scientists explore how the findings of empirical research can be applied to real-life circumstances, they must move from a more pure scientific endeavor to one that necessarily entails value judgments and interpretations that are not inherent to the data.

## SO FAR . . .

This chapter has reviewed the goals of social psychology as a field of study. In addition, there has been a review of the empirical approach, along with its strengths and drawbacks. The prevailing naturalist premise in the field was also described, along with its implications, especially for a view of personhood. Evolutionary psychology—which often, but not necessarily, proposes a naturalist assumption about reality—was also discussed. After reading this chapter, hopefully you have a more thorough understanding of how a scientist's view of reality has significant implications for the sorts of questions researchers ask as well as the sorts of interpretations of the findings that are considered.

As you read through the text, it is important to keep in mind that the processes of both forming hypotheses and interpreting data may be greatly influenced by particular biases of the researcher. Even though researchers are trying to be as objective as possible, they must interpret and organize the scientific findings. At that level of analysis, it is impossible to refrain from at least some measure of personal bias despite one's best efforts to remain objective. For that reason, it is essential that researchers understand their own underlying assumptions about the human condition and what those assumptions imply for the research process. Hopefully as you read this text, you will become more attuned to your own worldview and assumptions about personhood and better grasp the implications of these for your understanding of social psychology research questions and findings.

The next chapter will explore a possible alternative to a naturalist view of human social interaction. Specifically, a Christian view of personhood is presented in which humans are seen as beings who were created for good, are fallen, but are still capable of being redeemed. As you will see throughout this text, some assumptions and interpretations of social behavior may be shared by both a Christian approach and a naturalistic approach. At other times, some fundamental differences exist. Now let us join together to explore where these different assumptions lead us as we try to understand the complex nature of human social interaction.

## QUESTIONS TO CONSIDER

1. On what basis could a naturalist view of persons inspire hope for more positive human social interaction? When might a naturalist view lead to more distressing views of the potential in human interactions?

2. How self-seeking do you think humans are? On what do you base your opinion?

3. If you were a researcher who held an explicitly Christian theist evolutionary perspective, would your assumptions regarding possible motives for social behavior differ in any way from those of an EP approach that holds naturalist premises? If so, how?

## KEY TERMS

*behaviorism*
*cognitive approach*
*content analysis*
*correlational approach*
*empiricism*
*evolutionary psychology*
*experimental approach*
*field experiments*
*hypothesis*
*lab experimentation*
*naturalism*

*naturalistic observations*
*positive psychology*
*proximate cause*
*psychic unity of humankind*
*social psychology*
*social role theory*
*surveys*
*theistic evolution*
*theories*
*ultimate cause*

# 2

# What Has Christianity to Do
# with Social Psychology?

*For we are what he has made us,*
*created in Christ Jesus for good works,*
*which God prepared beforehand*
*to be our way of life.*

EPHESIANS 2:10

## WHY IS ONE'S VIEW OF THE HUMAN CONDITION SO IMPORTANT?

Have you ever sat with friends debating ideas regarding what people are like? One friend may claim that "people just can't be trusted," or another may say, "Given a chance, humans will stab you in the back." Yet another may argue that "people can be trusted until they give you a reason not to trust them." Or maybe you have heard such generalizations about the opposite gender. These are powerful assumptions about humans that help shape the way we interact and what we expect of one another. In fact, it's interesting to see how vehement people get when defending their views of humans. We tend to conjure up or collect all sorts of examples that seem to confirm our preexisting biases, and we do not generally give these ideas up easily. In fact, until such conversations arise, we may not even be fully aware of how deeply entrenched our views are.

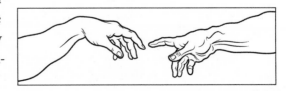

Many authors (e.g., Evans, 1979; Van Leeuwen, 1985; Holmes, 1992) have noted that a perspective of human nature is an important element in every worldview. As you have already read, whether or not social psychologists acknowledge some underlying theory of human nature, such a theory nonetheless exists for all researchers and pervades their thinking regarding the types of questions they ask, the manner in which they ask them, and the conclusions they ultimately draw from their observations.

As discussed in chapter one, the most prominent assumption about humans that social psychologists currently propose is based on naturalism. Recall that naturalism in this context refers to the idea that reality comprises material substance only, and that if the immaterial (e.g., God, soul, etc.) does exist, it is either irrelevant to scientific investigation or else not measurable, and hence unimportant. As already noted, this view of the human condition pervades research in terms of hypothesis generation as well as interpretation of the data. This chapter will explore an alternative to the naturalist perspective; namely, one possible Christian understanding of persons and its relevance to our understanding of human social interaction.

Because of the primary role that one's view of the human condition plays in both everyday social life as well as in scientific inquiry, a Christian perspective of social behavior should include an exploration of a Christian view of the human condition. In addition, it is important to explore ways in which these assumptions are consistent with, and also different from, the prevailing naturalist understanding of persons in social psychology.

In order to lay the groundwork for a discussion of the specific Christian approach that is presented in this text, several related points will first be discussed. First, we will explore whether it is even reasonable or valid to consider the role of ideas that emanate from a religious tradition—in this case, Christianity—in *any* scientific endeavor. Second, we will look at a possible way to integrate Christian ideas of humans with the scientific study of social psychology. This approach focuses on using a view of humans that is theocentric, or God centered.

The subsequent sections will specify the approach that is used in this text, which emphasizes the core, orthodox Christian concepts of creation, fall and redemption and how these relate to our higher call for community, our intrinsically relational nature and our capacity for other-centeredness. Then, there will be a discussion of one key implication of a Christian view of persons; that is, its potential to broaden the types of hypotheses that are generated and the types of interpretations of the data that are made in social psychology research. Finally, there will be a discussion of possible limitations to a Christian view of humans as a starting place for the empirical study of social behavior. Let us now begin with a discussion of whether Christian ideas are even relevant to the scientific endeavor.

## Is It Valid to Integrate Christian Ideas with a Scientific Understanding of Social Interaction?

The practice of incorporating theological assumptions into the empirical method is not widely supported by the scientific community. Quite often, revelation knowledge is generally not considered relevant to the scientific process. Like any other science, social psychology is most often defined as an empirical account of the natural world that is restricted, both in its subject matter and its conclusions, to the natural world. This definition is consistent with the position of the U.S. National Academy of Science, which resolved in 1988 that "religion and science are separate and mutually exclusive realms of human thought whose presentation in the same context leads to misunderstanding of both science and religion" (as cited in Johnson, 2002, p. 44).

Some modern scientists argue that science is what yields facts and hence real knowledge, while religion yields values, which are not considered knowledge. So if an argument or explanation for human behavior emerges from outside of science (e.g., from a religious tradition), then many researchers would disregard it. Thus, research in the field of psychology, as in all of the other sciences, has largely ignored any potential role of theological insights regarding human behavior.

Within the church, there are also concerns regarding the integration of Christian ideas with scientific investigations. Since the beginning of Christianity, people of faith have wrestled with the question of how to relate to the ideas that emerge from the culture at large. So many different opinions have been offered regarding whether it is logical and valid to integrate faith and reason, that it is not possible to review these all here. For many, science and faith are not asking the same questions, so they should be considered independent entities. For others, science and faith can inform one another, thus an understanding of how they might relate can increase our understanding of both.

The Christian perspective of humans that is presented in this text assumes that social psychology research can help enrich our understanding of humans as God's creation and tell us much about the nature of human social interaction. Likewise, it is assumed that a Christian view of persons can provide legitimate questions and interpretations of the research findings. The views presented here are but one way of addressing the relationship between Christian ideas and social psychology, and it is like all other views in its inability to fully describe all truth about such a complex subject as social behavior.

There are many Christian scholars whose ideas are consistent with the premises of this text. McGrath and McGrath (2007), for example, argue that Christian scholars can challenge science to consider as valid any theory that adequately explains the data. Further, they propose that "science and religion offer possibilities of cross-fertilization" (p. 37). In other words, since the Scriptures were never intended to be an exhaustive manual on the nature of human behavior, we can learn a lot from the findings of psychological research.

Philosopher Alvin Plantinga (1994) likewise proposes that in trying to understand ourselves and our world it is not logically necessary to engage in a science that is narrowly defined by naturalist premises. He argues that it is possible from a Christian perspective to take into account *all* that we know, including such things as the fact that human beings were created by God in his image, that they have fallen into sin, and so forth. Plantinga notes that these truths could play an important role in our understanding of topics such as aggression and altruism, which are both a major research focus of social psychologists. The idea again is that along with the scientific method as a valid empirical approach for the social sciences, theological assumptions may be as plausible, and potentially more valid, than naturalistic ones, and as such, they should be considered rather than excluded.

The view presented in this text is also consistent with that of Sawatsky (2004), who notes that scholarship is not only the pursuit of truth, but also the pursuit of wisdom. In the case of monotheistic religious perspectives (e.g., Christian, Muslim and Jewish), wisdom is grounded in God. For a Christian, wisdom includes things such as love of God and neighbor, fear of God, humility, and so forth. This wisdom has much relevance to our understanding of how human social interactions are, can be and should be.

Sawatsky (2004) further notes that for a Christian, integration is not only about the relationship between faith and reason. He refers to Paul's passage in 1 Corinthians 13:13, in which Paul says that in addition to faith, *hope* and *love* are also core aspects of Christian identity. When considering the role of these three virtues from the standpoint of social psychology, *love* is manifested in other-centered social interaction, *hope* can be grounded in the belief that such social interaction is possible, and *faith* can remind us that humans are created in God's image with the potential for other-centered social behavior and redemption.

Finally, keep in mind, as W. R. Miller (2005) notes, that attempts to understand the human condition and ways to improve human welfare do not originate in the field of psychology. There is a long tradition of religious and philosophical perspectives that precede psychology. These traditions have made significant contributions to our understanding of the ways in which humans interact and what these interactions suggest regarding the human condition. These ideas have been largely ignored in the field of psychology. Miller notes, "Perhaps in the decades ahead, it will become clearer just how much we have been missing" (p. 25).

## How Does One Integrate Christian Ideas with Social Psychology?

Even if one agrees in theory with the possibility of exploring the relationship of Christian ideas of persons and social psychological principles, how does one do this on a practical level? The answer to this question varies widely among Christian scholarly circles. In fact, a primary difficulty with the integration of Christian ideas and science is simply the definition of integration. For example, an entire special edition of the

*Journal of Psychology and Christianity* (Summer, 1996) was devoted to exploring different approaches to the integration of faith and the academic discipline of psychology. In the opening article, Eck (1996) noted that the only thing that all of the writers of the articles could agree upon was that the exact definition of integration could not be agreed upon! During the writing of this text, the Christian Association of Psychological Studies (CAPS) devoted its annual conference to exploring the nature of the integrative process and hosted a very spirited debate.

In this text, the controversies surrounding integration as well as the relative merits and shortcomings of *any* approach are acknowledged. It is not the goal of this text to resolve questions or issues related to the process of integration. Still, assuming that integration is a worthwhile— indeed, necessary—endeavor, each chapter will explore how a Christian view of humans may be relevant for the specific research topics covered therein. Thus, which aspects of a Christian view of persons will be emphasized varies by chapter.

As noted in chapter one, two essential components of a successful scientific endeavor include hypothesis generation and interpretation of research findings. The Christian approach presented in this text emphasizes these two essential components. In the individual chapters, the nature of the specific research topic will determine to some extent which of the two is emphasized. In the case of *generating new hypotheses*, various chapters will explore how starting from a Christian view of persons as created in God's image could lead to a broader range of plausible hypotheses and potentially different results than does the current naturalist view of persons. Given the Christian premise that we are participants in God's redemptive plan for each other, hypotheses related to how individuals and groups can act in specifically redeeming ways would be a greater focus of research. For example, Maehr (2005) suggests that more research efforts explore hypotheses regarding how religion can be a significant motivational force. Additionally, given that forgiveness plays such an important role in increasing the chances of positive outcomes (e.g., reducing retaliatory aggression), Magnuson and Enright (2008) have proposed an initial model regarding ways in which a church can be a forgiving community. Wade (2010) also notes that more research should test hypotheses about whether explicit or implicit forgiveness approaches are more effective. Baumeister (2005) likewise suggests that psychologists need to research ways in which the Judeo-Christian view of will can act as a source of promoting social responsibility and virtuous action.

In the case of *interpreting the data,* Hill (2005) notes that the authority of Scripture cannot just be claimed, but rather its explanatory power must be demonstrated "on psychology's terms." Consider an example regarding how a scientist would interpret behavior that appears other-centered (e.g., altruistic acts). Because both naturalist and Christian views of persons acknowledge the self-centered tendencies in social behavior, there are cases in which both would explain those data in similar ways. For example, there may be evidence that the appearance of kindness served some other obviously self-centered goal (e.g., political or social advantage). Other cases of altruism may be interpreted differently by naturalist versus Christian assumptions. This is because a Christian view of humans includes acknowledging the potential for genuinely other-centered actions. This is consistent with what Batson and Shaw (1991) call a "pluralism of motives": some self-centered and others genuinely other-centered, as well as a mixture of both. By contrast, the naturalist view will find apparently other-centered behavior as ultimately self-seeking. In these cases, then, a Christian view of persons would increase the possible explanations of the data and in many cases better fit the data.

Van Leeuwen (2002) specifies another central issue related to how one interprets the data from social psychological research. She notes that beginning with naturalist premises leads a researcher to interpret common behaviors (e.g., greed, gender differences in social behavior) as "natural"—in other words, stemming from our natural state of being. Van Leeuwen says that many psychologists disregard the fact that these social behaviors reflect human fallenness, not an inescapable way of being.

Having asserted that a Christian view of persons allows for the possibility of other-centered behavior, let's now look more closely at what an orthodox Christian view would claim about human nature, the human condition and their implications for human social interaction.

## WHAT DO CREATION, FALL AND REDEMPTION
## SUGGEST TO US ABOUT SOCIAL BEHAVIOR?

Briefly, the view presented here is based on the premise that God exists, he created humans in his image for good, this goodness has been corrupted by sin, and he has established a means for restoration through Christ and the continuing presence of the Holy Spirit. Human social interaction thus reflects our created goodness, our corrupted condition, and functions, potentially, within God's redemptive plan. These points will be discussed in more detail later in this section. Much of what this approach proposes may be familiar to you, as it is in many ways consistent with a mainline, orthodox Christian view of humans. This view is also consistent with the approach used by Alister McGrath (2006), who says that a theoretical model does not have to try to prove that God exists or that he created us in his image. Rather, a model could "presuppose God's existence so that revelation provides an interpretive framework within which nature can be understood" (p. 7). Hence, this text is *not* an attempt to prove God's existence via the empirical approach. Rather, it begins with the assumption that God exists, and then we see where that assumption leads us when we observe and interpret social behavior.

Thus, the approach being proposed begins with the assumption of "God along with nature" as opposed to the naturalist assumption of "no God"—in other words, "nature alone." McGrath and McGrath (2007) further note that there are demonstrations in the natural world of the coherence of belief in God, and that our beliefs may be shown to be *justifiable* without our having demonstrated that they are *proven.*

One helpful way to frame this discussion about a Christian view of persons is to consider the common Christian constructs of creation, fall and redemption. The concept of *creation* can help us understand humans' potential for positive social interaction and capacity for other-centeredness, the way God intended things to be. The concept of the *fall* will provide the contextual basis for discussing both the negative social interactions found so frequently in social psychology as well as for discussing this Christian approach's concept of the fallen human condition. The term *redemption,* though best illustrated in Christ's sacrificial death and resurrection, also applies to God's provision for good to yet be accomplished in this world, even through positive social interaction. It is this latter aspect of redemption that this text uses as the focus of a Christian view of social psychology.

Since the concepts of creation, fall and redemption are so central to this approach, for the sake of simplicity, it will be referred to as the *CFR approach* of human social interaction. According to this view, the concepts of creation, fall and redemption are interrelated. So, for example, redemption is related to the human potential for goodness just as creation is, and so forth. Yet these concepts are discussed here independently first to clarify how they are used in this text.

A brief review of the basics may be helpful: The CFR approach assumes that God exists, he created humans in his image for relationship with him and with others, and social relationships are one primary way in which God works out his redemptive plan. From this view, the nature and purpose of social relationships—namely, living in loving community—are key components of the purposes of God. Hence, the topics covered in social psychology are very important for our understanding of the human condition. And, as Sawatsky (2004) notes, such knowledge has the potential to help us understand and celebrate God's creation and also to participate in God's work of restoring and transforming the world, which is what the Christian is called to do.

It should be noted that other Christian authors (e.g., Vitz, 1997; Jones & Butman, 1991) have discussed additional and equally important facets of human nature that are not focused upon here (e.g., the holistic view of persons' body and soul, the nature of human agency/will, etc.). The assumptions of the CFR approach, however, are principally concerned with an exploration of human social interaction that is most relevant to the social psychology research that has been conducted thus far. It should also be emphasized again that the CFR view presented here is but one of a number of possible Christian perspectives on the human condition. In this text, the terms *CFR approach* and *a Christian view* are sometimes used interchangeably. But this is not meant to imply that the CFR view represents the only correct Christian perspective of the human condition.

Before specifying the details of the Christian view of persons presented in this text, it would be helpful to see a brief outline of the main points of this approach:

- All humans are created in God's image and thus possess the ability to relate to others in loving, other-centered ways.

- Humans are also created with an intrinsically relational nature, just as God is a relational being. The purpose of humans' relational nature is to live in loving, other-centered community that God desires.

- Humans are created as finite, limited beings. Thus, even if there were no sin, we would still have limitations inherent in our ability to accurately perceive and respond to social situations.

- Humans have a fallen condition that results in a tension between sin and the ability to engage in other-centered concern.

- God works redemptively with humans such that, despite the limitations of sin, humans can still live in generally loving, other-centered relationships.

## WHAT OF CREATION AND HUMAN SOCIAL INTERACTION?

*Imago Dei.* Somewhere, somehow, God created humans. Think carefully for a moment about this very familiar orthodox Christian idea: God as our Creator. Why did he create us? What was his intent for us? All of God's creation reflects his glory in some way or other, and the Scriptures explicitly state that humans were created in God's image (Genesis 1:26). "There is something about the way God is that is like the way we are" (Moreland & Rae, 2000, p. 157). What does that reality enable us to do? What does that imply about our nature and our potential in social interaction? Many theologians have disputed this central tenet of the Christian faith, and following is a brief review of some of those basic ideas. Table 2.1 summarizes the discussion that follows.

Since humans are created in God's image, this implies many things about our responsibilities, our potential and our privileges with regard to social interaction. Indeed, with that special status come significant responsibilities and implications for our social functioning, including the command to love God and others with our whole hearts and minds (Mt 22:37-40); to love one another as he has loved us (Jn 13:34); to love our enemies (Mt 5:44); to care for widows and orphans (Jas 1:27); to act justly and to love mercy and to walk humbly with God (Mic 6:8); and the list goes on.

This text cannot explore the full range of what theologians have said it means to have been created in God's image. That would include, among other things, a lengthy discussion of numerous attributes presumed to be true of God such as will, creativity, rationality, and so on. These attributes are not only related to what God intends for human social interaction, but also emanate from the very nature of his being, which all humans share by virtue of our having been created in his image. Instead, as noted earlier in this section, the focus here will be more broadly on two specific categories of the attributes of humans that seem most relevant to social psychology: our intrinsically relational nature and our capacity for virtuous other-centeredness.

Note that as was mentioned earlier, the CFR view also assumes that humans were created as limited, finite beings. These limitations are not the result of sin, but rather a reflection of the reality that we are lesser beings than God.

**Table 2.1. Social Beings as God Created Us**

| |
|---|
| ***Highest end:*** relationship with God and with others (community) |
| ***Means to that end:*** |
| • Intrinsic relational nature defined as desire for connection to others, etc. |
| • Capacity for other-centeredness (kindness, compassion, humility, altruism, love, integrity, etc.) |

***Creation and community.*** As Grenz (1994) notes, the belief that God created the world logically elicits questions regarding God's intentions for his created world. Grenz and many others (e.g., McMinn & Campbell, 2007) have argued that the ultimate goals of God include several things that are inextricably interwoven. The first of these is the fellowship between humans and God. Related to this is the goal of the relationship among humans, and the relationship between humans and the broader created world (e.g., the natural world). In other words, the notion of *community* is essential to understanding God's purposes for creation, is at the heart of the biblical narrative and has much relevance for our contemporary social world. More specifically, Grenz adds that community is crucial because it arises out of the very essence of God as Trinity—meaning, God enters into relationship with creation, and also is internally relational within the Godhead. The one God of the Bible is the fellowship of Father, Son and Holy Spirit (O'Collins, 1999). From this communal nature of the Trinity stems the communal nature of the humans who were created in his image.

As already noted, an integral part of a Christian understanding of humans is the belief that to live in loving community with God and others is the ultimate aim of life. Consider one well-known instance of scriptural support for the idea that community with God and others is a higher-order goal. In Matthew 22:37-40, the Pharisees, the chief religious sect of that day, had tried to test Jesus by asking which was the greatest commandment in the Law. Christ answered: "'Love the Lord your God with all your heart, and with all your soul, and with all your mind.' This is the greatest and first commandment. And a second is like it: 'You shall love your neighbor as yourself.' On these two commandments hang all the law and the prophets."

As noted earlier, social psychology research focuses on the relationship among people, and this text will do likewise. The CFR view obviously has much to say about the relationship between humans and God, but that will not be a primary focus here.

What would be some of the general characteristics of community if one considered what God's intentions for it might look like? In order to answer this question, we must first consider humans, who are the principal agents in this loving community. The CFR approach assumes two major characteristics of humans that are essential parts of what it means to live in community: an *intrinsically relational nature* and the *capacity for other-centeredness,* both of which will be discussed in the following sections. Further questions that will be addressed include: What does it mean from a practical standpoint to live in community as God intended, and what do we need to accomplish this? What social psychological concepts are relevant to this specific objective?

*Community and the relational self.* You have probably heard of the idea of people living in community. It is often discussed and conjures up many common images such as a friendly neighborhood or a close-knit group of friends or coworkers who help each other out, or perhaps a city or town where the people work collaboratively on various projects or initiatives. The word *community* also makes one think of how the various members have a sense of belonging and reciprocity, a sense of give-and-take.

An intrinsically relational nature draws us toward relationship with others in the first place. To be intrinsically relational means that humans are innately driven to connect with others, and that our sense of identity and purpose is significantly affected by our relationships with others (Evans, 2005). Orthodox Christianity assumes that social interactions and community are an integral part of God's redemptive process. That is, as McFadyen (1990) points out, our relationships with others help both form and transform us. He further notes that our social relations are one primary way in which God works to bring about our redemption and sanctification. Vitz (1997) likewise argues that an integral part of a Christian concept of personhood is interdependence—mutual and freely chosen care for each other. Theologian Miroslav Volf (2006) similarly suggests that as part of a community, the individual is constantly being shaped by the others with whom they are in relationship, but still the individual retains the freedom (to varying degrees) to decide how these relationships will affect them.

Various scriptural examples of the importance of the social nature of humans are seen in descriptions of the self throughout both the Old and New Testaments. These examples demonstrate the integral role of group membership in forming self-identity. For example, a basic component of the ancient Israelites' concept of their identity is defined by their membership in a particular group with a specific ethnic heritage. In the New Testament, Paul likewise claims to be a "Hebrew born of Hebrews," (Phil 3:5) also demonstrating a self-concept that is intimately related to group identity. It is interesting to note how biblical descriptions of humans further reinforce our inherently social nature beyond ethnic considerations by implying some relationship between humans and God or humans with each other (e.g., "joint heirs with Christ" [Rom 8:17]; part of "a royal priesthood" [1 Pet 2:9]; members of the body of Christ [1 Cor

12:27], etc.). In addition, all of the Ten Commandments have to do either with our relationship to God or to other people. Thus, the prime importance given to the relational side of humans is seen all throughout the Scriptures. In fact, a primary understanding of what it means to be Christian emphasizes our relationship with God and with other people.

In sum, consistent with the naturalist understanding of humans, the CFR approach assumes that humans are intrinsically social or relational, suggesting that social interactions and relationships are an integral part of every facet of our identity and life experience. Indeed, it suggests that our relational nature is the core aspect of our being, within and through which all else about our nature is expressed.

*Community and other-centeredness.* In addition to the importance of the relational nature of humans, another essential component of loving community has to do with how God created humans to be able to live in such community. From an orthodox Christian view of humans, God is love, and that is why we can love. This is an important point because the CFR approach assumes that possessing some of the characteristics of God (along with and through his grace) is what enables humans to live in the sort of community that God intended.

Thus, a researcher with the CFR approach would also assume that in order for loving community to be possible, humans must possess the ability to engage in some measure of genuine *other-centered behavior* in order to carry out God's will for relationships. To act in other-centered ways includes things such as considering the needs of others before our own and acting fairly and justly, even when doing so may incur great personal expense. It should be noted that this approach does not necessarily assume that humans are acting purely selflessly in any given social act, as uncovering the complete underlying motives for a single act is not possible. The CFR approach, however, provides a logical starting point for contending that true other-centeredness can be, to varying degrees, one of the motives for positive social behavior. This is because from this view, humans are created in God's image, and as such, we share in his goodness.

The CFR approach does not assume that the needs of the self should never be considered when making decisions in various social contexts. Indeed, a Christian view of persons assumes that life presents a constant tension between the need for self-concern and other-centered concern. The Scriptures urge us to "love your neighbor as yourself" (Mk 12:31) and also "to lay down" our lives for others (Jn 15:13). Christ demonstrates our tremendous worth as persons to God. Thus, while the Bible provides numerous references to the command to love others and deny oneself, there is also reference to caring for oneself. This delicate balance between concern for self and other-centered concern depends very much on the specific social context as well as God's direction. As Fritz (1998) notes, communion with others is not the same thing as "unmitigated communion," which is an unhealthy self-neglect and overinvolvement with others. Many times, self- and other-centered concern work in a sort of coaction, as when love for one's own child heightens one's propensity to donate to a charity for needy children. Regardless, the CFR approach does assume that focusing on the needs of others is an essential component of a loving community, and that humans can be expected to display self-sacrificial behavior that to varying degrees demonstrates genuine care for others.

God's intent is for us to engage in universal love and compassion. This divine command to love is not referring to a superficial, transient or necessarily joyful feeling of love (Evans, 2006). In fact, this other-centered love can be quite difficult, at times necessitating separation, as in cases where forgiveness does not lead to reconciliation (Worthington, 2003). Thus, manifestations of other-centered love may vary depending on the specific social situation.

Both Christians and naturalists often agree regarding the duty of universal love. But, as Evans (2006) notes, a naturalist view cannot explain what the origin of the command for mutual regard is apart from self-serving and group-serving goals. The naturalist perspective could thus encourage love and regard because of a shared humanity. A Christian view would encourage universal love because of a shared humanity that is created in God's image.

*The relational self and other-centeredness as God's image.* Now, let us consider again some other connections between our intrinsic relational nature and our potential for other-centeredness. As noted earlier, the CFR approach assumes that relationships are a major source of our sense of self, our sense of purpose and meaning in life, our decisions about what conduct is appropriate, and so on. This is consistent with the findings of social psychologists (e.g., Baumeister & Leary, 1995) who argue that a sense of belongingness is a fundamental human need. In addition, many other psychologists (e.g., Erikson, 1959; Buss, 2003) have likewise argued that humans are intrinsically social in nature.

So if social psychologists have already declared that humans are intrinsically relational beings, how does a Christian perspective add anything unique? Batson (1990) offers a compelling observation here. He noted that while social psychologists may claim that humans are naturally social beings, researchers also consistently interpret this social nature as a product of our ultimate goals of survival, self-preservation, or some other self-serving end such as self-fulfillment and increased subjective well-being. From that standpoint, Batson argues, humans would not really be intrinsically *social* beings, but rather intrinsically *egocentric* beings underneath it all.

In contrast, a researcher who holds the CFR perspective would propose that humans, by virtue of having been created in God's image, have an intrinsic relational nature that includes a genuine capacity for other-centered care. And again, while the CFR approach acknowledges that self-centered reasons can be the cause of some of our seemingly other-centered behaviors, it also maintains that there can be many behaviors that are prompted by a true other-centeredness that is characteristic of what it means to live in community, and these other-centered motives should be considered when generating hypotheses and interpreting data.

Suppose you agree with the basic tenets of the Christian view of persons described above. You may still rightly ask if it makes sense to consider humans in relation to God if social psychology is concerned with humans in general, not Christians in particular. This is a fair question. After all, with the exception of research that is specifically aimed at exploring how people of faith might perceive a certain social psychological issue (e.g., helping behavior, prejudice and racism), the research includes subjects of all (or no) religious tradition. The CFR approach nevertheless assumes that it is indeed fair and relevant to apply a Christian understanding of persons to all of humanity because it assumes, as the Scriptures note, that it is all *humans,* not only *Christians,* who are created in God's image. Thus, whether or not one believes in God does not determine whether one possesses the essential features of what it means to be human. One could well argue that God's grace is needed to be able to live according to what the optimal community could be like, but that is not the point here. The focus is instead on the human *potential* for expressing other-centeredness as a function of having been created in God's image for communal living. Indeed, you may know some people who are not professing Christians who are nicer than some of the Christians you know!

To review, the sort of loving community that the CFR approach refers to would include many of the same attributes of the triune God such as unity and mutual love and regard. A researcher with the CFR approach would assume that since we are created in God's image to fulfill our individual contributions to the community, we are both intrinsically relational and also capable of more goodness than might be suggested by the current negative focus of much of social psychology research. Recall that we are here discussing how God *created* us to be. Thus, from this Christian perspective, humans should possess in their nature the capacity for other-centeredness (e.g., compassion, empathy, altruism), which ultimately serves to create and maintain the life of the community.

*Limited beings in community.* In addition to having been created with an intrinsically relational nature that enables us to live in other-centered community, humans were also created as finite beings. Our finite nature concerns our mortality, but even more than that, it concerns our status in relation to God: we are far less than him. The limitations that are part of our finite nature are an intentional part of God's created order. God says in the Scriptures: "As the heavens are higher than the earth, so are my ways higher than your ways and my thoughts than your thoughts" (Is 55:9). The sorts of limitations that we are here exploring are not the result of sin; they were intentionally created by God. These God-ordained limitations are an important consideration for our understanding of human social interaction. We cannot, despite our most noble efforts, perfectly perceive and respond to our social world, even if we had no biases or sinful motives. As will be discussed in the social perception chapter (chap. 4), for example, while humans have an impressive ability to accurately perceive others, we also have cognitive limitations that impede our ability to see others clearly (Gigerenzer & Selten, 2002).

There are several implications as we consider the God-ordained limitations in humans. First is the need for humility. As Phelps (2004) notes, proper acknowledgment of one's cognitive limitations can help reduce pride, as these limitations emphasize the glory and power of God in contrast to his limited creation. Humility is also called for as we consider the potential for error in our perceptions of others and of social situations. Awareness of our limitations further challenges us to have a great sense of humility regarding our attempts to study the rich complexity of human social behavior. This includes being ever ready to acknowledge the limitations of any approach, including the empirical method.

In addition to encouraging humility, our awareness of human limitations also challenges us to be more appreciative of the interdependence of humans. As already noted, we are created to live life together. We are dependent on one another for a more accurate understanding of our social world, and this interdependence is inherent in our created being, irrespective of sin.

## WHAT OF THE FALL AND HUMAN SOCIAL INTERACTION?

From the perspective of the CFR approach, then, we are limited beings created in God's image for community, with the necessary relational nature and potential for other-centeredness that would result in such community. But that sounds a bit too easy, doesn't it? If God created humans and saw that all he created was "good" (Gen 1), then why is it that humans can be capable of so many variations in social behavior, apparently ranging from one extreme of loving kindness to the other extreme of aggressive and hateful acts? Have you ever wondered about the tensions inherent in your own motivations for a single act? This idea of the broad range of potential social behaviors as well as the complexity of motivations for single interactions is a central concern for social psychology and brings us to the orthodox Christian view of the fall.

In the previous sections, you read about how God designed things to be, but the harsh reality is that despite what God intended, humans are actually capable of quite a bit of savage aggression, hatred and self-centeredness. From an orthodox Christian perspective, such negative behavior began after the fall. Whether one interprets the Scriptures literally to mean that Adam and Eve actually ate the forbidden apple (Gen 3), or whether one sees the story as symbolic, the point is the same: God had good intentions for us humans that were distorted by sinful, willful disobedience. And depending on where you live and your own life experience (and how often you watch the nightly news), you may be quite tempted to accept that this is where the story ends: humans are barely more than savage animals who, if left to their own devices, would always seek their own gain at the expense of others. Contemplating the fallen state of humanity is indeed a sobering task.

Remember that until recently, social psychology focused on what goes wrong in social interactions. From a Christian approach, one could argue that the results of these studies (e.g., the prevalence of racism and aggression) are a strong reminder of the fallen human condition and have done much to elaborate on the specific ways in which negative social behavior reflects the fallen state of humans. The naturalist's human generally has as the ultimate goal some self-serving or group-serving social advantage, may demonstrate significant compromises of integrity in exchange for social acceptance, display errors in social perception, show humans as prone to denigrating the out-group, and the list goes on.

With this emphasis on the fallen condition of humans, what would social psychologists say about humans' intrinsic social nature and the capacity for virtue? Well, if social interactions ultimately serve some self-seeking goal, then as mentioned earlier this chapter, our relational nature is a means to an end, the end here being either survival or some other mediating social advantage. Similarly, behavior that appears to be other-centered is actually fundamentally self-serving in some way, hence social psychology's focus on research questions that explore the self-seeking, error-prone characteristics of humans and the interpretations that result from this limited view of humans. The picture that emerges is one of a mostly self-centered being with lots of ulterior motives and a tendency to be rather easily influenced by the group. And that is where the story ends. Or is it?

The CFR approach maintains that although the naturalist view seems accurate in describing certain aspects of social behavior, it is limited in scope because it has no logical basis for assuming the inherent potential for goodness in the fallen human being. This limitation of naturalism results from neglecting to consider the fact that humans are created in the image of God and are part of an unfolding story. In contrast, a Christian view holds that when explaining social behavior we must take into account not only the impact of the fall of humanity but also the impact of the image of God, even though that image has been corrupted. As theologian Reinhold Niebuhr (1941) proposed, a Christian perspective of human nature can adequately hold this tension, while most other theories seem to either excessively exalt or else denigrate humans. Kilner (2010) further notes that the Scriptures do not support the notion that the fall totally corrupted the image of God in us, although there is much controversy regarding this issue. Table 2.2 reviews some of the main similarities and differences between a naturalist and a Christian view of the fallen human being.

Table 2.2. The Fallen Social Being: Naturalist and Christian views

|  | CFR tenets | NEP tenets |
|---|---|---|
| **Highest end** | Relationship with God and with others (community) | Generally self-seeking goals such as survival, reproductive advantage, or some other social advantage |
| **Means to that end** | *Intrinsic relational nature* that both longs to connect with others in healthy, loving ways and also with the capacity to engage in destructive, self-seeking goals in relation to others | *Intrinsic relational nature* that is in some way beneficial for the person or his/her group. |
|  | *Capacity for other-centeredness* (e.g., kindness, compassion, humility, altruism, love, integrity, etc.) along with capacity for sin, i.e., both other-centered and self-centered | *Capacity for other-centeredness:* generally seen as ultimately self-serving in some way (e.g., altruism that serves some underlying self-serving motive[s]). |

Thus, from the CFR view, the fallen human condition entails both our capacity to act in other-centered, Godlike ways and also to act in negative, self-seeking ways. This tension may at first glance sound very much like the perspective of social psychology from the naturalist view. After all, social psychologists have not claimed that humans are incapable of apparently other-centered social behavior. But as noted in table 2.2, a naturalist approach often begins with the premise that social behavior ultimately reflects behavior that emanates from a fundamentally self-seeking tendency. For example, consider the perspective of researchers who endorse both naturalism and the evolutionary psychology model. From this view, the social behavior that we observe has endured because it was at one time advantageous for the survival and genetic advantage of our primal ancestors. A Christian researcher who is not a naturalist and yet supports the evolutionary model would instead likely argue that while both survival and reproductive advantage were, and may often continue to be, key motivators of social behavior, there are other higher-purpose motives for social behavior, which emanate from God's creation of humans with the capacity to love and honor one another's personhood.

## WHAT OF REDEMPTION AND HUMAN SOCIAL INTERACTION?

So far in this exploration of a Christian understanding of humans as it relates to social interaction we have been looking at the crucial role played by both our creation in God's image and our fallen condition. An orthodox Christian view holds that though God allowed the possibility of the fall, he also provided for redemption, which operates on different levels, including personal salvation and the redeeming potential of social processes. Since social psychology attempts to explore social behavior as it exists in the natural world around us, the CFR approach likewise focuses its concern for redemption on other-centered relationships. This focus should help us better see the hope that Sawatsky (2004) brings to our attention.

The CFR approach proposes that one way to consider redemption within the context of social psychology may be to think about our purpose for studying social psychology to begin with. Ultimately, as McFadyen (1990) would suggest, research that increases knowledge of our social vulnerabilities and inclinations can help us to contribute to the transforming of each other and ourselves as we seek to grow to be more like Christ. So, for example, applied social psychology research that explores how racist attitudes are formed and maintained can help us to work toward ways to reform those attitudes, a view shared by both naturalist and Christian premises about humans. A Christian view presents us with the reality that such change is possible and helps inform the strategies we might undertake (e.g., repentance, forgiveness) to achieve racial reconciliation. Consequently, considering how the various concepts in this text may apply to one's own life could help in the continuous process of transformation and sanctification.

According to the CFR approach, another reason for hope is related to the more optimistic alternative hypotheses and interpretations of the data that are possible from a Christian perspective of the human condition. As previously discussed, until more recently the hypotheses generated by a naturalist approach have been fairly narrowly defined in terms of what tends to go wrong in social interactions. This may be one reason why the potential other-centeredness of humans is not as evident in the research. In addition, historically, the explanations of the data (e.g., altruism research) have not allowed for a sufficient consideration of other-centered motives in humans.

Of course, one may rightly argue that just because the Christian approach to understanding the human condition is more hopeful than a naturalist one does not mean that the Christian view is more valid per se. Conducting social psychology research from a Christian view of persons requires that our hope must be tempered with realism. That is, hope regarding the potentially redeeming nature of social interaction must also acknowledge the brokenness of humankind. We are, in essence, exploring the similarities and differences between what MacIntyre (2007) called "human nature as it happens to be" versus "human nature as it is when it realizes its *telos*, i.e., purpose." A challenge in this text is to explore ways in which the relatively more hopeful view of the human condition may be borne out in the research.

In order to clarify the discussions in future chapters, consider again some of the major similarities and differences in assumptions regarding the human condition as proposed by Christian and naturalist approaches.

Table 2.3 summarizes these differences. Note that while there is not unanimous agreement among all social psychologists who espouse either the naturalist view or the Christian view of persons here described, the points noted in this table may be considered commonly espoused elements of each. In noting the differences between the two perspectives, be sure to notice similarities such as the acknowledgment of self-seeking motives.

**Table 2.3. Christian Theistic and Naturalist Ideas**

| Phenomenon | Christian Tenets | Naturalistic Tenets |
|---|---|---|
| **Life origin** | Life created by God in some way (including possibly through evolutionary processes); humans created in his image. | Life created by impersonal, natural process. |
| **Purpose of life** | Community with God and others. | Driving force is generally seen as survival and reproductive advantage or other self- or group-centered pursuits such as self-fulfillment and happiness that result from a presumably other-centered way of life. |
| **Self-seeking tendencies** | Primarily a reflection of our brokenness; can also work alongside other-centered concern toward legitimate ends. | Ultimately seen as originating from the primary drive for survival; protecting oneself increases chances of many positive social outcomes. |
| **Fundamental need for social relatedness and inclusion** | Primary way in which humans are drawn together and achieve the ultimate goal of community. Also can aid survival and lead to subjective well-being, though these are not seen as the primary goals. | Increases the chances of social inclusion, which enhances survival or other self-seeking goals such as subjective well-being. |
| **Optimal social functioning (Morality)** | Humans were created with an innate capacity for other-centeredness in order to achieve God's intents for creation. Morality also provides many advantages to self and group. | Optimal social functioning (e.g., integrity, generosity, compassion, etc.) seen as having been adaptive at some point for our ancestor's survival or other benefits. |

## WHAT ELSE DISTINGUISHES THE CFR APPROACH FROM A NATURALIST MODEL?

Beginning with the above-noted assumptions about a Christian view of humans means that the CFR approach is emphasizing a *theocentric* (God-centered) approach and considering that as compared to social psychology's *anthropocentric* (human-centered) approach to understanding humans. An anthropocentric approach regards humans as the central element and involves interpreting reality exclusively in terms of human values and experience (Cameron, 2005). This is the perspective of traditional social psychology, which makes observations about human behavior and tries to limit its conclusions about persons to the data collected. It would be consistent with the approach of any of the human sciences and is also considered to be essential if one is working within the most prominent definition of the sciences, which is concerned only with the natural realm.

A theocentric approach, by contrast, emphasizes that God is the central aspect to our existence and is our ultimate concern such that human behavior is interpreted in the light of what we can understand about God's purposes and intents. The CFR approach is based on a theological anthropology: humans understood in relation to God. This assumption is based on the scriptural truth that God has created us for his glory (Is 43:7).

Why a theological anthropology? As Cameron (2005) notes, such an approach could help increase our understanding of the human experience because it involves a reciprocal process. That is, when seeking the meaning of human experience, we direct attention to God, in whose image we have been created. Then, inquiring further and understanding more about the nature of God and his purposes, we can deepen our understanding of the nature of humans who were created in his image.

## How Is the Empirical Approach Relevant to a Christian View of Persons?

So far you have read about the basics of the CFR approach as well as the legitimacy of using Christian assumptions of persons in the empirical study of human social behavior. What does this theocentric view of humans have to say about the empirical approach? It should be reiterated that a focus on the theocentric approach to understanding humans and the intents and purposes of social interaction does not in any way disregard the scientific method used by social psychology, which focuses on human experiences and behavior alone. In fact, the CFR approach sees the rigor of the scientific approach as an important tool for understanding certain aspects of humanity within a social psychological perspective. Though the Scriptures provide us with many general descriptions of human inclinations, they do not specify the intricacies of social behavior in the way that social psychology research can.

One example where the Scriptures give a general description of human behavior can be seen in the many admonitions against harsh, unfair judgments of others (e.g., Mt 7:1-3; Rom 2:1; Jas 4:11), which suggest that there is a human tendency toward such unfair judgment. Social psychological research can help us understand specific ways in which such judgments might take place in everyday social interaction. One example is the *fundamental attribution error* (Jones & Harris, 1967), which is the tendency to explain behavior in terms of internal dispositions or personality traits of the other person, discounting the influence of situational factors. From this view, if a cashier acts rudely to you, you may quickly assume that she is a rude person instead of considering that she may just be having a bad day. This is but one example of how the specificity of the scientific method can enhance our understanding of the general descriptions of humans presented in the Scriptures.

The CFR approach assumes that the Scriptures have their own authority with regard to the nature and condition of humans and thus do not have to be empirically tested to be considered truth. Nevertheless, remember as McGrath and McGrath (2007) note, the enduring descriptions of humans that the Scriptures provide can be shown to be coherent, plausible and a good source of hypothesis and explanation in the empirical method. This is true despite the limitations of the empirical approach, including, as W. R. Miller (2005) notes, the reality that "God cannot be controlled as an independent variable" (p. 32).

Van Leeuwen (1985) argued that the empirical approach used in psychology dehumanizes people because it is a method based on the natural sciences that views humans as relatively passive objects of study rather than as active participants capable of exercising choice. Van Leeuwen suggested that psychology should use more human sciences approaches and be more open to ideas regarding the human condition that emanate from philosophical and religious traditions.

The CFR view acknowledges the above-noted limits of the empirical approach and proposes that a Christian view of humans can address some of these concerns. For example, as noted earlier, a Christian view of personhood begins with an assumption about the dignity, worth and potential of humans, resulting in a broadening of plausible hypotheses and interpretations of the data. A researcher working from a CFR view certainly acknowledges the value of studying particular aspects of the person (cognitive, physiological, etc.) and the ability of such processes to inform our view of humans. Yet, when social psychology focuses on the study of behavior instead of the study of personhood, the human is reduced to a mere sum of the complex interplay among the various facets of our being. W. R. Miller (2005) notes that such a reductionist way of studying and interpreting humans is like "studying the brush-strokes and hues on a canvas, without appreciating the art itself, never mind the artist" (p. 293). Miller suggests that the field "needs both a microscope and a telescope"—meaning, we need to study both the particulars of our being, always with the coherent view of the human person in mind. Thus far, the naturalist "big picture" of humans ironically continues to reduce humans instead of considering them as holistic beings with a purpose, as the CFR view does.

## SO, WHAT OF HYPOTHESES AND INTERPRETATIONS?

Throughout the discussions so far in chapters one and two, it has been stressed that a key to any successful scientific endeavor is the capacity to generate plausible hypotheses and interpretations of the data. It has also been proposed that the CFR approach can offer a broader range of legitimate hypotheses and interpretations than can a model based on naturalist claims. But it should be noted that just because the CFR approach can do so does not necessarily mean that it is a more *valid* approach than another competing view. Indeed, one could offer any number of ridiculous hypotheses and interpretations, as you may have observed on occasion in everyday social life. Thus, in this text, the goal is to explore how a Christian view of humans can demonstrate a logical coherency and a relevance to the data such that our understanding of human social interaction is enriched.

As you read about the vast array of research topics in social psychology that are presented in this text, you will note that the ways in which Christian ideas of humans are relevant to hypotheses and interpretations of data will vary depending on the specific social psychological concept under study. Thus, apart from assuming the main tenets of the CFR approach listed earlier in this chapter, this text will not present a single focus of integration for each area of research. Instead, as you go through the chapters you will see that at times Christian ideas of the human condition may be especially relevant to a specific concept in the chapter (e.g., the need for realistic appraisals of self-esteem in order to achieve positive social functioning). At other times, the biblical notion of other-centeredness may be especially relevant to the whole concept under study (e.g., how the biblical mandate to forgive can reduce aggression or how the created human is capable of other-centered altruism). And in still other cases, the CFR view that humans were created as limited beings may help expand our understanding of some research findings (e.g., the consistent finding that despite our relative accuracy in social perception, that accuracy is limited). Regardless of the focus of integration in each chapter, the CFR view, when compared to the naturalist view, will be able to consider the so-called pluralism of motives that Batson and Shaw (1991) note is a more accurate portrayal of the complexity of human social interaction.

Table 2.4 presents examples of how the CFR view will be applied to the various topics from each chapter in this text. Note that the integration attempts presented here are obviously not an exhaustive list of possible connections between a Christian view of humans and the research in social psychology. In addition, note that the topics chosen for this text represent some of the major areas of study in social psychology. But because of space limitations, other topics, especially those that deal with applied social psychology, are not covered here (e.g., conflict and peacemaking, social psychology in the courtroom). Some of the important aspects of those applied topics have been included in the larger discussions within each chapter where possible.

One additional point is necessary to understand as you look at this table and continue to read this text. Just because some of the naturalist and Christian assumptions regarding the human condition are different does not mean that a Christian view of personhood cannot be informed by the existing empirical research. This is because, as many have noted (e.g., Worthington, 2010), God's truth comes from many sources. There is thus no necessary conflict between truths revealed by experimental means and scriptural revelation about personhood. Used properly, each can be a valuable source of information about the nature and functioning of humans. An understanding of either can help inform an understanding of the other, and together, a richer understanding of humans can be developed.

Table 2.4. Examples of Integration

| Social Psychological Concept(s) | Possible Integrative Issues |
|---|---|
| The Self | The importance of a biblical view of realistic self-esteem in relation to positive social outcomes; the created relational nature of humans as a basis for challenging the (almost) exclusive belief in the primacy of self-seeking tendencies of humans |
| Social Perception | The potential for accuracy in social judgment as part of God's redemptive plan; the basis for limitations in social perception in relation to both sin as well as intended limitations of humans as created beings |
| Social Influence: Groups and Conformity | The positive potential of group processes; examining factors related to resistance to conformity pressures, as well as the positive aspects of conformity |
| Social Influence: Attitudes and Persuasion | The importance of explicit and implicit attitudes from a biblical view; alternative explanations of apparent moral hypocrisy |
| Antisocial Behavior: Aggression | Biblical ideas of aggression; the integral role of the biblical commands of humanizing and forgiving others in reducing aggression |
| Antisocial Behavior: Racism and Prejudice | Other-centeredness as the basis for the potential to reduce prejudice; role of repentance and forgiveness in efforts to reduce hatred between groups |
| Prosocial Behavior and Helping | A biblical view of the human potential for both altruism and egocentrism |
| Interpersonal Attraction and Relationships | Relevance of the divine command to love others for building community and interpersonal relationships |

## HOW ELSE CAN WE GET A MORE BALANCED VIEW OF HUMANS? A LOOK AT POSITIVE PSYCHOLOGY

Suppose you agreed with the primary premises of the CFR view of humans, but you were still disinclined to think that using a Christian view of persons is a valid way to proceed. Where else could you look for ways to obtain a more balanced view of humans? You may recall in chapter one the brief discussion of the movement known as *positive psychology*. Those research efforts focus on the conditions and processes that contribute to the optimal functioning of individuals, groups and institutions (Seligman, 2002; Seligman & Csikszentmihalyi, 2000). Topics routinely studied in positive psychology include such character strengths and virtues as compassion, humility, perseverance, kindness, empathy, creativity and integrity. This certainly sounds positive enough.

In further stressing the need for a more positive psychology, Gable and Haidt (2005) note that the current "focus on prejudice overlooks the process of acceptance, a focus on conflict ignores how compromises are forged, and a focus on bias misses the many instances of accuracy and the circumstances that surround it" (p. 104). So, you may be wondering: What if social psychology just added more studies having to do with positive social behavior and virtues? Wouldn't that be enough to address the above-noted concerns regarding social psychology's limited view of humans? Such an approach has already begun in the field and could indeed broaden social psychology's view of humans, thereby enhancing our understanding, especially of the positive potential of social interaction.

From the perspective of the CFR approach, there are some limitations with relying on the positive psychology movement to give us a more balanced view of humans. These limitations have to do with the problems inherent in beginning with the naturalist premises that currently pervade the field. That is, if humans are seen as the products of a totally natural, undirected reality, then it is likely that self-seeking motives will still prevail when it comes to the types of hypotheses that are generated and the sorts of interpretations that are made of the data.

Indeed, the majority of positive psychology research is focused on hypotheses that explore what virtues are related to personal benefits such as high levels of life satisfaction and subjective well-being. Seligman, Parks and Steen (2004), for example, along with their recommendation that psychology should study strengths and virtues, note that psychology should also develop interventions that can help people become "lastingly happier" (p. 1379).

The CFR model acknowledges the contributions of an approach that helps us understand the benefits of other-centered behavior. But a key difference between a naturalist approach and a Christian approach to that understanding has to do with the role of virtue. It seems from the positive psychology view that virtues are seen as a means to an end. Specifically, virtuous behavior is seen as a way to the "good life," which includes subjective well-being, happiness and a sense of greater purpose and meaning. By contrast, a Christian view sees virtue itself as the end or goal, especially because this is one primary ingredient of loving relationships.

From a Christian view, one may argue that happiness is a good thing and that we can find more ways to increase self-fulfillment. But the CFR approach would not see happiness or self-fulfillment as a primary goal. For example, being kind and compassionate to someone whom you consider to be perpetually annoying does not necessarily lead to happiness. But it is important because obedience to God's commands to love one another is important.

Consider the example of forgiveness. There are numerous commands in the Scriptures to forgive one another (e.g., Mt 18:21-22). This is an absolute command. The Scriptures do not refer to forgiving so that you can feel good afterward, nor do they mention how self-fulfilled you might feel as a result. Forgiveness may indeed lead to such positive ends, but it can also often be a long, painful process. Even though greater life satisfaction may result from forgiving another, from the CFR view this may be seen as the byproduct of this specific obedience to God, not the ultimate aim itself. Thus, research based on Christian premises of humans would be more inclined than would a naturalist approach to investigate questions having to do with circumstances that elicit more genuine other-centered behaviors.

With regard to a limited range of interpretations of the data, the positive psychology approach still relies heavily on naturalist assumptions, especially those of a naturalist approach to evolutionary theory (Buss, 1999; Massimini & Delle Fave, 2000). Consequently, prosocial behaviors such as helping behavior that is extended to unrelated others and even jeopardizes one's own survival is often interpreted as some variation of the survival motive and/or some other self-seeking motive (e.g., Kruger,

2001), as well as resulting from cognitive strategies that we use to "fool" ourselves that the cost of helping another is not really that significant (McGuire, 2003). From that view, other virtuous behaviors such as integrity and modesty would likewise be interpreted as having primarily (or often exclusively) underlying self-seeking motives.

In addition to a relatively narrow range of possible hypotheses and interpretations of the data that result from simply combining a naturalist evolutionary approach with positive psychology, there is another limitation to that approach in terms of its ability to help us better understand human social interaction. This limitation relates to how the naturalist view would explain what optimal social functioning looks like. Held (2004), for example, states that the most daunting task for positive psychology involves defining what actually is positive and also distinguishing the ambiguous line between *describing* something as good and *prescribing* it as good.

How would social psychologists make this distinction in order to inform the public of ways to make things better? What does "better" or "optimal" mean in this context? As stated earlier, this is difficult to do if one does not begin with the premise that there are transcendent moral virtues that serve a teleological purpose. Nevertheless, Diener and Suh (1997, as cited in Gable & Haidt, 2005) suggested researchers could look for the following when deciding what is positive or valuable: (1) the choices people make regularly, (2) how people judge how satisfying or pleasant some choice is, and (3) a value system or cultural norms.

These sound like reasonable criteria for determining what is a good way for social interactions to proceed. But in reality, these three criteria are sometimes in agreement and other times are not. So, for example, think about a situation in which a group of people feel just fine (and even happy) engaging in aggressive or otherwise offensive acts of prejudice. This would be one example of how personal choices are discrepant with cultural norms. Or think of times when all three criteria are consistent, but the resultant behavior is still not "good"; when what people choose and how they judge those choices are consistent with some cultural value system but those choices are clearly not other-centered (e.g., slavery in the early U.S.).

As already noted, here a Christian foundation has a clear advantage over a naturalistic view in explaining what is good social functioning. This is because a Christian understanding about positive social interaction relies on the wisdom presented in the enduring tradition of the Scriptures. Even though we are unable to fully adhere to, or fully understand, God's laws and intentions due to our created limitations and our fallen condition, this does not change God's revealed laws of moral conduct. By contrast, psychology's aim is to describe our social interactions, but it cannot provide any consistent ethical guideline for how we should relate to one another. Even in cases where social psychological findings are used to help solve social problems (e.g., racism, prejudice, aggression), psychology does not provide any consistent moral standard upon which it decides that these types of behaviors are wrong. Consequently, as difficult as this may be to imagine, a behavior like racism that is currently viewed as destructive could one day be perceived in more positive ways if social norms and personal feelings change regarding the matter, or if benefits for group survival are discovered.

## What About Possible Limitations of the CFR Approach?

In discussing possible limitations of the naturalist view, one must also be aware of possible limitations and criticisms of the CFR approach. For one thing, while the CFR approach can explore to what degree it seems consistent with the data, it cannot really "prove" anything about its central assumption that God exists and that he created us in his image. In this way, the CFR approach is similar to the naturalist approach, which cannot prove its primary assumption of naturalistic origins. Both paradigms are limited to generating hypotheses and explanations and exploring how well the current research seems to be consistent with their assumptions about the origins of human life and its primary motives and purposes.

Another possible and related limitation of the CFR view is that while it assumes that humans are capable of genuinely other-centered as well as self-centered motives, it is difficult to accurately assess underlying motives from observable behavior. In addition, a single social behavior can be the result of many intervening steps. For this reason, it is important to emphasize again that this approach will focus on how consistent its assumptions appear to be with the data, not on whether or not it can "prove" that genuinely other-centered motives exist.

Furthermore, just as scientists who use a naturalist premise exhibit bias in their research, Christian scholars also have biases that affect our interpretations of Scripture and our resultant views of the human condition. One must thus be careful, as Worthington (2010) notes, when using a "filter approach" that presupposes the authority of Scripture regarding human behavior. This is because we may have misunderstood the relevant Scripture(s) and thus based our assumptions on false premises. To reduce this type of error, we must be deliberate about pursuing as accurate a reading of Scripture as possible, taking into consideration appropriate exegetical processes. Although the CFR view is historically sound and does present a coherent understanding of persons, any endeavor, including the one presented in this text, has the possibility of error. Thus, the effort presented here of integrating scriptural teaching with social psychological research is understood to be a part of an ongoing process rather than the final word on the matter.

## So Far . . .

This chapter has reviewed one possible alternative to the naturalist model of humans that is so prominent in the field of social psychology. This Christian view is based on the core beliefs of Christian orthodoxy: creation, fall and redemption. This CFR approach is based on the assumption that God exists and that he created humans as relational and loving beings for community. A Christian view of persons also sees that our potential for other-centered concern is impeded to varying degrees because we were created as limited beings and we live in a fallen condition. In spite of these limitations, humans are capable of partaking in God's redemptive plan, especially as this redemption is expressed in social interactions and community.

Remember that according to the naturalist (and naturalist evolutionary) view, the primary motivations for social behavior are self- and group-seeking. On the other hand, a Christian view of personhood acknowledges the self-seeking potential of humans yet involves a much broader range of possible motivations and potential for social inter-action. The view presented in this text suggests that despite the differences in underlying assumptions about persons, both the naturalist and Christian approaches share many common observations about social behavior and have the capacity to contribute to a more comprehensive understanding of human behavior.

Remember that wherever the naturalist assumptions of evolutionary theory are mentioned, this text is not primarily concerned with whether evolutionary theory itself is correct. The main concern here is instead with the naturalist premise itself. Social psychology has a long history of using naturalism as an underlying premise. It is only recently that evolutionary psychology has become one of the main exemplars of naturalism in the field. Furthermore, in this discussion of the limits of naturalism, the goal is not to discount the contributions that naturalist social science has made nor to discount the contributions of evolutionary psychology's explanations per se. The focus is rather on the naturalist and Christian theist presuppositions regarding humans, which could be expressed as "nature alone" vs. "God along with and through nature," respectively. Whatever method God might have chosen to create humans could be considered beside the point for this discussion.

Because the evolutionary approach is becoming more prominent in social psychology, many of the following chapters will discuss evolutionary psychology's (EP) proposals and interpretations of the topic of focus. Consequently, many times the terms *naturalism* and *EP* will be used together in the same discussion. But remember that one cannot assume that any particular social psychologist who uses the EP approach is by definition a naturalist. Nevertheless, the manner in which evolutionary psychology is generally expressed in the literature assumes only the existence of the natural realm. Remember that evolutionary psychology acknowledges both ultimate causes (those that were beneficial for the survival and reproductive advantage of our ancestors) and proximate causes (those that are more recent, such as genetic and socio-cultural influences). You will soon notice that over the past decade especially, psychologists have also begun to pay more attention to hypotheses related to productive social behavior (e.g., virtue).

When comparing the assumptions of a naturalist view with a Christian view of persons, the question is not which set of assumptions can be proved—neither can be. Rather, the interesting thing is what research questions and interpretations of findings they share in common and which they don't. In cases where there are differing explanations of the data, we seek both the explanation that best fits the evidence and the one that adds more understanding of the topic. This is the sort of explanation that Lipton (2004) calls not just the "likeliest," but the "loveliest."

## Questions to Consider

1. What do you think are some advantages and disadvantages of broadening the range of hypotheses and interpretations of the data that the CFR approach suggests?

2. Besides an intrinsically relational nature and the capacity for other-centeredness, can you think of other attributes that would be important to possess in the pursuit of community?

3. Suppose you were a researcher who held both a CFR view as well as a Christian theist evolution view. How might your understanding of the role of the survival instinct differ from a naturalist view? (Consider from a Christian view the question "Survival to what end?")

4. Can you think of additional specific ways in which the CFR approach may offer hope for more positive social behavior? How might this hope be expressed in research efforts?

## Key Terms

*anthropocentric approach*
*CFR approach*
*creation*
*fall*
*fundamental attribution error*
*imago Dei*
*redemption*
*theocentric approach*

# 3

# The Self in a Social World

*O LORD, our Sovereign, . . . what are
human beings that you are mindful of them,
mortals that you care for them?*

**PSALM 8:1, 4**

## WHY STUDY THE SELF?

Imagine one of your professors turning to you in the middle of a lecture
and proclaiming with due authority in front of the whole class that you fit
the average profile of a serial killer. Depending on the situation, you may
interpret this as funny, offensive or just plain stupid. What is the basis for
your reaction? On some level, you must know instantaneously that you
are not, in fact, a serial killer (assuming, as I am, that you do not engage
in serial homicide). But who goes around life thinking consciously about
this feature of their identity? How often in casual conversation, or in a
classic pickup line, have you heard a fellow student tell you about their
major, where they are from, and then suddenly say, "And, by the way, I am
not a serial killer"? Yet on some level, we know this about ourselves so
definitively that we are ready to defend our reputations in this matter if
the occasion arises. How is it that we "know" something about ourselves
and in some cases never really think about it consciously? This is but one
example of how pervasive and influential our self-concept is.

It may seem strange at first glance that most social psychology textbooks, whose main purpose is to explore the *interpersonal* level of be-

havior, include a chapter on the self toward the beginning of the text. Nevertheless, beginning with a closer look at the different aspects of the self actually makes sense. For example, since social behavior could arguably be described as the interaction among and between different collections of selves, then understanding more about this concept would be especially important. For one thing, it could reveal a lot about the human condition and how it is expressed in social interaction. In addition, knowledge of the self can help us better understand its relationship to all of the other social psychological concepts such as group influence, social perception, helping and others that will be discussed in later chapters.

From the perspective that all individuals were created in God's image, the self constitutes an important part of our created being. This area of research, then, can help us explore the complexity of the human condition, including its potential for both self-centered and other-centered motives.

It is important to remember that the different concepts in social psychology (group influence, persuasion, etc.) are ultimately all interrelated and their effects are reciprocal. Thus, having a separate chapter on the self is not meant to obscure the relationship of the individual with the social context. This point will be clearer once you begin to understand more fully the role of the self in the various aspects of social functioning as you go through the text.

As Leary (2007) notes, social psychology research on the self has been quite broad, encompassing different emphases ranging from concepts related to self-perception to concepts related to emotional processes such as self-esteem enhancement and self-conscious motives. In general, regardless of the research focus, the questions mostly emphasize understanding how social interactions help define, develop and alter the self and how the self is motivated in light of those relationships. As with all of the concepts studied by social psychologists, the various questions regarding the self are interrelated.

This chapter will focus on the following main areas of research on the self:

- Self-concept and self-esteem
- The relational tendencies of the self

- How the self is presented to others (self-serving tendencies)

- Strategies for self-regulation

In addition, this chapter will explore possible implications of a Christian view of persons specifically for research in the area of self-esteem as well as in the area of our relational tendencies and how these are related to our apparent self-serving tendencies. As you will see, there is a vast array of research findings about the self, so it is not possible to discuss the full range of relevant research implications from a Christian perspective. Nevertheless, this chapter will explore how the above-noted areas of research are related to the concepts of creation, fall and redemption in order to see how these connections may contribute to a better understanding of the apparent motives and tendencies of the self. Note that the Christian view presented in this text sees the self as an integral part of the created person.

## ARE CURRENT NOTIONS OF THE SELF CONSISTENT WITH A BIBLICAL PERSPECTIVE?

Before we begin to discuss specific areas of research on the self and the possible implications for that research from a Christian view, it is important to resolve one potential concern: the relevance of biblical notions of the person. The image of humans that is presented in the Scriptures appears to have most to do with an individual's relationship to God and to others. As Duvall (1998) notes, the word *self* or *ego* does not exist in the New Testament account of persons. Instead, words such as *pneuma* (spirit), *kardia* (heart) and *psyche* (soul) are used. So, do these biblical notions of self even resemble the definition of self that modern social psychologists use? Are we even studying the same construct?

Recall that the Scriptures were written during premodern times, when it was customary to see the self as an integral part of a much larger whole, including the cosmos and the supernatural. By contrast, in modern times, ideas about the self include such individual concepts as autonomy and an increasing belief in naturalistic origin. Consequently, can the Scriptures even speak to our modern understanding of, and seeming preoccupation with, self-awareness and self-fulfillment?

Consistent with premodern ideas, the self is represented in the Scriptures as intimately related to one's ethnic group, to God and to others in general. Do the Scriptures, then, allow for self-concept apart from one's relationship with God and others? It appears that there are examples where individuals, with God's help, examine their hearts in order to acknowledge and know who they are (e.g., Ps 139:24; Mt 13:15). But these examples are ultimately most concerned with self-examination that leads to an acknowledgment of accountability and the need for repentance, not greater self-awareness as we currently understand it. There is awareness of the self, though not as an end in itself.

From a Christian (specifically CFR) perspective, nevertheless, one could argue that even though ideas regarding the self have significantly changed across time, the substance of the human condition has not. Humans have always been relational and were created for good, though this potential has been compromised by the fall and can yet be redeemed. Thus, one can see the different definitions of the self across time as manifestations of larger philosophical movements or shifts within the overall cultural context rather than actual changes in the essence of the person. For example, consider a culture within the modern West that has a predominantly naturalistic worldview and, consequently, perceptions of the self that are naturalistic as well. But if that same culture were to experience a change in philosophical orientation decades later, its ideas about humans would change accordingly. In this case, it would be the notion of self, rather than the human condition itself, that changes over time.

The current postmodern perspective of the self could be considered a good example of the changing philosophical notions of the self. In postmodern thinking, the very concept of a core self is being questioned. That is, some researchers (e.g., Foucault, 1977; Gergen, 1991) contend that humans have no consistent, central self, but rather a variety of social selves that are presented at various times as the situation warrants. This does not mean that we merely alter our self and behavior depending on the circumstances but rather that no true self even exists; instead, we have a collection of possible selves. From this view, the concept of self as an autonomous, self-reliant individual is merely a construction that was conceived in a particular time and place (specifically, the Western world since the Renaissance; Middleton & Walsh, 1995). This recent perspective would then result in significant changes in the way that culture sees (and studies) humans.

As noted above, despite these trends in perceptions of the self, one who maintains the CFR approach would assume that the human condition has not really changed, even though perceptions of the self have changed. From this view, then, considering the implications of a biblical view of personhood for the research on the self is a logical endeavor. This is because the self is a central part of the created human being and thus reflects the human condition as seen in social interaction. But before exploring the relevance of a Christian view of persons for this area of research, let us begin by looking at what the research says regarding how we come to know and evaluate ourselves.

## SELF-PERCEPTION AND SELF-CONCEPT:
### *How Do We Know Ourselves?*

Before you continue to read this section, think for a moment about four or five characteristics of yourself. What words did you use to describe yourself: easygoing? uptight? sociable? intelligent? How did you know that those descriptors applied to you? There are many cues we look to in order to better understand ourselves and form our self-concept as well as our sense of self-esteem. Regardless of the avenue we choose, social psychologists emphasize the importance of self-knowledge through interactions with others. For example, one way in which we come to know who we are is through the seemingly nonsocial process of *introspection* or self-observation. This is the process whereby people look inward and examine their own thoughts, feelings and motives. However, even this apparently independent method of self-examination has some basis in social interaction.

Consider one example of how introspection is social in nature. Suppose you took a long walk to have some time for personal reflection about your identity. What is the basis for the content of your thoughts? How did you even come up with the terms that you examine during your introspection? On what basis do you decide that one term better describes you than does another term? Did you, as Bem (1972) suggested, observe your own behavior in order to infer what your characteristics are? Did you form your opinions about yourself based on what you think others think of you, in a process Cooley (1902) called the *looking glass self*? Has someone else either told you outright or implied that those words apply to you? Did you think about how you compare with others in different ways to come up with these ideas? These are some of the types of questions with which social psychologists are concerned when attempting to understand how we come to form our *self-concept*, an organizing set of ideas or schemas about who we think we are.

The idea of the self has prompted much research by psychologists who are interested in identifying what constitutes self-awareness as a constant, basic feature of human personality. Brewer (1991) noted that this research on the structure and function of the self has traditionally been a "highly individuated" concept. That is, the focus was on understanding the internal structures and differentiation of the self-concept rather than on the connection of the self to the external world (i.e., to others). More recently, increasing attention has been paid by social psychologists to the social identity part of the self—that is, the part of self-concept that deals with one's relation to others.

According to social psychologists, our self-concept includes a lot of different information, including the roles that we play, our gender, our profession, our membership in various groups and our relatively enduring personality traits (Deaux, Reid, Mizrahi & Ethier, 1995; Markus & Wurf, 1987). Our concept of self includes what are called *self-schemas*, or beliefs about the self that organize and guide the processing of information that is relevant to the self. Yet, as Tesser, Wood and Stapel (2006) note, our self-concept is not just a series of cognitions about who we think we are. Rather, as we will also see in the section on self-esteem, it has significant implications for how we process information, what we remember, the goals we pursue and how we relate to others. Thus, there is a motivational aspect of self-concept that is dynamic in that it plays a significant role in how we interact with the social world around us.

One way in which we attempt to form our self-concept is through the process of *social comparison*, which involves, as the name suggests, comparing ourselves with others in order to have a clearer sense of who we are and how we feel about ourselves. Originally proposed by Festinger (1954), the theory of social comparison has undergone significant revisions since then. Suls, Martin and Wheeler (2002), for example, talk about *upward social comparisons* and *downward social comparisons*. Upward social comparison occurs when individuals compare and associate themselves with others whom they perceive in some way as socially better. In this type of comparison, people can look really good in their own eyes by considering themselves one of the successful group. In downward comparison, by contrast, an individual would compare their own situation with that of others who are deemed to be less fortunate in some way. This has the effect of making one's own situation seem far better off.

Both upward and downward comparisons are proposed to be ways in which we can enhance our self-concept and self-esteem. So, if you compare your own academic abilities with those of the brightest students on campus, you can convince yourself that you possess many of the same attributes and feel a lot smarter. You can also feel a lot smarter by comparing your own abilities with those of students who continually struggle their way through classes. Either way, you come out looking smarter (at least in your own eyes). The person(s) with whom you choose to compare yourself can greatly influence the outcome of your self-appraisal.

Source: http://www.webdonuts.com/2012/04/paper/

**Figure 3.1.**

Aside from personal reflection and social comparisons, how else do we solidify a sense of self? Some researchers (Klein, Rozendal & Cosmides, 2002) have sought to explore the neuropsychological sources of self-concept. Specifically, these researchers have investigated the relationship between self-concept and memory. These efforts have focused on how knowledge of the self is represented and retrieved from memory. *Computational models* suggest that self-knowledge is represented in specific events and behaviors involving the self. According to this view, a person decides whether a characteristic is self-descriptive by consulting a library of personal memories and computing an answer from whatever episodes are activated (Smith & Zarate, 1992). For example, if you are trying to decide whether the word *rude* describes you, you would search your memory for social situations you have been involved in and quickly survey these to see if your behavior was, in your estimation, rude.

By contrast, *abstraction models* suggest that self-knowledge consists of summary representations that have been abstracted from events and behaviors involving the self. For example, you would know something about yourself (e.g., that you are friendly) by accessing a database of previously computed summary representations (Klein & Loftus, 1993). This would be a kind of overall summary, or the gist of your ideas about yourself.

Klein et al. (2002) propose that self-concept involves a number of different components. From their comparisons of individuals with neurological impairments to those with no impairments, the authors concluded that self-concept includes knowledge of facts about one's own life, a sense of personal agency and ownership (the belief that "I" cause my own thoughts and actions), and the ability to self-reflect. These researchers propose that understanding each of the above and the relationship among them will provide a more accurate understanding of how we come to know ourselves. For example, the authors note that the various components of the self are interrelated, such that one component of the self (e.g., knowledge of facts of one's own life) affects the functioning of another component of the self (e.g., a sense of personal agency).

*Is our self-concept multifaceted?* One important question about self-concept has to do with whether it is one definitive entity, or whether self-concept is better understood as a collection of numerous discrete aspects. For example, Shavelson, Hubner and Stanton (1976) developed a multifaceted model of self-concept in which general self-concept was divided into specific domains (e.g., social, physical, academic). This model has generated much research (e.g., Byrne, 1996) that suggests that rather than a general, overall idea, our concept of self is more accurately perceived as consisting of multiple domains. For example, imagine a classmate who describes himself as having good social relationships and simultaneously describes himself as less intelligent than the average student. In this case, the individual would be considered to have a positive social self-concept, but a low academic self-concept.

Some researchers (e.g., Brewer & Gardner, 1996; Sedikides & Brewer, 2001) propose that self-concept is more accurately seen as composed of three separate systems, each with its own properties and motivations. From this view, we see our *individual self* in terms of our unique traits and dispositions; we see our *relational self* in terms of our close, interpersonal relationships; and we see our *collective self* in terms of our relationships with larger groups. Brewer and Chen (2007) suggest that each part of the self has its own social tension that seeks to be resolved, as noted in table 3.1. According to Brewer and Chen, these tensions result in conflicts at each level, and one must achieve some optimal balance between these conflicting motives for defining self in relation to others. Furthermore, feeling satisfied or secure in one area of relatedness does not necessarily mean that a person will feel satisfied with their social self at the other level.

**Table 3.1. Components of Self-Concept**

|            | Characteristics | Social Tension |
|------------|-----------------|----------------|
| **Individual** | Self-conceptions formed from personal characteristics | Definitions of unique characteristics of the self VERSUS those of the others with whom we are in relationship |
| **Relational** | Aspects of the self-concept that are shared with relationship partners and define the person's role or position within close interpersonal relationships | The need for autonomy VERSUS the need for intimacy with specific others |
| **Collective** | Self-conceptions that result from inclusion in large social groups as well as contrasting the group to which one belongs (i.e., the in-group) with relevant out-groups | Belonging and inclusion in the group VERSUS the need for separation and personal distinctiveness |

Source: Brewer & Chen, 2007; Sedikides & Brewer, 2001

*Is self-concept only descriptive?* As if the debate about whether self-concept is one-dimensional or multidimensional were not complex enough, yet another controversy in self-concept research has to do with whether self-concept is only descriptive (it simply describes who you think you are), or whether it also has an evaluative component (it includes your evaluation of the different aspects of your definition of yourself). Some researchers consider the term *self-esteem* as the evaluative component of self-description, and use the term *self-concept* for descriptive components of self-perception. But others (e.g., Shavelson, Hubner & Stanton, 1976; Marsh, 1993) have argued that self-concept is both evaluative and descriptive. In other words, these researchers suggest that one's self-concept includes general information about who we are (e.g., our roles), as well as our feelings about how well we think we are doing in each area of our lives. So, according to this view of self-concept, you could describe yourself as a college sophomore and also evaluate how you compare intellectually with that class of students. These two assessments would then be considered vital components of your self-concept according to the multidimensional model.

**Are we always consciously aware of our self-concept?** Everyone is concerned at some time or other about his or her identity or self-concept. Nevertheless, our level of conscious awareness about our identity varies depending on the situation. For example, many studies (e.g., Snyder, 1987; Schlenker & Weigold, 1990) suggest that you may be more aware of yourself and your actions when you are in a situation in which you are trying to impress others or otherwise encourage them to have a particular perception of you. The motivation to maintain a conscious level of self-awareness may be less when you are not attempting to impress anyone. Imagine, for example, a situation in which you have been driving for about an hour on a long and boring highway and are not trying to impress anyone. In that case, unless you are deliberately involved in self-reflection, you are not usually acutely aware of the various elements that constitute your self-concept. (You may, in fact, often be tempted while driving on a highway to speculate about your concept of your fellow drivers!) But consider a situation in which you are about to meet for the first time your soon-to-be in-laws. Most people would understandably become at least a bit self-conscious and make some efforts to be ingratiating and to gain approval. This will be discussed in more detail in a later section regarding self-monitoring.

**Do ideas of the self vary across cultures?** Are Western ideas regarding self-concept universal? Do non-Western cultures have different ideas and emphases regarding the different elements of self-concept and the self in general? For example, when defining the self, does it make a difference whether we live in a more *sociocentric* or *egocentric* culture? These terms have traditionally been used by researchers (e.g., Shweder & Bourne, 1984; Triandis, 1995) to refer to the difference between *collectivism* versus *individualism*. Sociocentric (collectivist) cultures and subcultures—such as Japan, China and Bali, and groups such as the Amish—stress that individual identity is primarily dependent on group membership, particularly membership within the extended family (Castillo, 1997; Geertz, 1973). In these groups, individual interests are often subordinated to the good of the collective whole. Social obligations are considered of utmost importance. By contrast, egocentric (individualist) cultures, which are mostly in the industrialized West, more often emphasize personal freedom and autonomy; dependence is generally seen as a weakness (Castillo, 1997). In addition, these cultures more often stress that social relationships are voluntary associations that can be broken at will.

So, given the above descriptions, we would expect that individuals in egocentric cultures would tend to define themselves in more individualistic ways, while the self-concept of those from sociocentric cultures would be more intertwined with interpersonal relationships. Interestingly, more recent research on the distinction between collectivist and individualist cultures suggests that this distinction is not as clear as traditionally thought (Brewer & Chen, 2007). For example, while individuals from non-Western cultures may tend to define themselves more explicitly as part of a group (e.g., a caste), it seems that people of all cultures are motivated to pursue both close personal relationships as well as connections to larger social circles and to incorporate these relationships in various ways as part of their self-identity.

## Self-Esteem: *How Well Do We Like Ourselves?*

Almost anywhere in the news these days, you can hear about the dangers of low self-esteem in children and adults. Think about how many problems are blamed on low self-esteem. Why did a child beat up other children on the playground? His problem must be low self-esteem. Why did a child cheat on an exam? Maybe she has low academic self-esteem.

Why is that classmate of yours rude? He must feel bad about himself and is taking it out on everyone else. And so forth. Such explanations about the alleged powers of low self-esteem are plentiful.

Interestingly, Baumeister, Tice and Hutton (1989) actually found that the average self-esteem score for Americans is usually quite high, often by more than a standard deviation above the midpoint of the scale. Thus, they conclude that this raises serious doubts about the notion that the social ills of American society are caused by widespread low self-esteem. And yet, the idea has lingered. But before we elaborate on that, let us consider what researchers mean by the term *self-esteem* and explore just how powerful it is.

***Is self-esteem a unitary concept?*** Self-esteem is one of the most commonly researched topics in social psychology and is another important part of how we define ourselves. Although self-esteem is generally conceptualized as one of the most important parts of the self-concept, there is much controversy about the exact definition of the term *self-esteem*. (Incidentally, have you noticed how much disagreement there is among researchers regarding the definition of the concept they are studying?) Some researchers (e.g., Rosenberg, Schooler & Schoenbach, 1995) argue that self-esteem refers to an individual's overall positive evaluation of the self, and that it consists of two distinct dimensions: *competence* (i.e., one's sense of being capable) and *worth* (one's sense of personal worth and value; Gecas & Schwalbe, 1983).

Other researchers (e.g., Marsh, 1993) have expressed a concern with the tendency to consider self-esteem as a global, consistent feature of self-concept. In other words, just as self-concept appears to be multifaceted, these researchers argue that the concept of self-esteem is multifaceted and subject to change depending on the immediate situation, one's mood, recent experiences and memories of recent events. This argument holds that self-esteem appears to be more accurately described in terms of different domains and experiences. For example, one could have a different evaluation of one's academic ability after just having failed an exam as opposed to a situation in which one has just gotten the highest grade in the class on an exam. In addition, one could have a relatively high academic self-esteem, but a relatively lower social self-esteem.

Researchers also generally agree that self-esteem has an affective component. In other words, higher self-esteem "feels good" and is related to feelings of pride and competence. In contrast, lower self-esteem is related to feelings of shame and inadequacy. Heatherton and Polivy (1991) also found that ego threats can produce negative state self-esteem, leading to negative affect. For example, in one study, they had students take part in a puzzle task. In the failure condition, after ten minutes, the experimenter entered the room and asked the subjects, "Haven't you finished yet?" and told them that they had not done very well. The experimenter then took the puzzle away from the subject and proceeded to solve the puzzle in under twenty seconds. Subjects in this condition were more likely to experience a decrease in both affect and state (temporary) self-esteem.

***Is higher self-esteem a good thing?*** In 1986, the governor of California, George Deukmeijian, funded a large project that entailed many efforts aimed at investigating whether increasing self-esteem would reduce different types of problems such as aggressive behavior, teen pregnancy and other social problems. The task force published a report edited by Mecca, Smelser and Vasconcellos (1989, as cited in Baumeister et al., 2003). In the preface, Smelser noted, "Many, if not most, of the major problems plaguing society have roots in the low self-esteem of many of the people who make up society" (p. 1). But the findings did not support the hopes of the task force, which had to acknowledge the very low correlations between self-esteem and every outcome measured in the project. In addition, the task force noted that no direct causal relationship could be established between self-esteem and destructive behavior.

Still, for decades, one of the reasons why social psychologists have studied self-esteem is because it has been associated with many positive outcomes for the individual and the society as a whole. For example, efforts to raise the self-esteem of school-aged children have been associated with decreased rates of risky behavior such as drug use and delinquency (e.g., King, Vidourek, Davis & McClellan, 2002). Nevertheless, in actuality, there is a lot of controversy regarding this widespread belief that higher levels of self-esteem help reduce the likelihood of negative behavior. Emler (2001), for example, reviewed the literature on self-esteem and concluded that relatively low self-esteem is a risk factor for such things as depression, suicide attempts, teenage pregnancy, eating disorders and victimization by bullies, but that even in these cases, low self-esteem was only one of many factors that predisposed a person to get involved in these behaviors. In addition, Emler noted that contrary to widespread belief, the data suggest that relatively low self-esteem is *not* a significant risk factor for delinquency, violence toward others, drug use, educational underachievement or racism.

One possible problem with the assumption that higher self-esteem leads to better outcomes is that researchers have generally been focusing on self-esteem as a *cause* rather than as a *result* of positive social behavior. It seems, instead, that it is positive, productive behavior that might be more likely to result in higher levels of self-worth. Consider the example of school performance. Does increasing students' self-esteem lead them to do better in school, or is it more likely for diligent academic work and resultant good grades to lead to better self-esteem? Skaalvik and Hagtvet (1990, as cited in Baumeister et al., 2003) followed six hundred Norwegian schoolchildren—one group in third grade, the other in sixth—for one and a half years. They measured self-esteem and academic performance both at the beginning of the study and at the end. Students who did well in school over the year were more likely to have higher self-esteem the next year than did those students who did not perform well academically. In addition, high self-esteem did not lead to performing well in school. In fact, sixth graders with high global self-esteem tended to have lower academic achievement in seventh grade.

There is one problem with this assumption that higher levels of self-esteem lead to better social outcomes: the potentially negative effects of excessive levels of self-esteem, especially those that border on what Bushman and Baumeister (1998) call "excessive self-love," or narcissism. This is associated with many negative behaviors: racist attitudes, risky behaviors such as drunk driving or driving too fast, resisting positive social pressures from adults and peers, and physically aggressive behavior such as school shootings.

In one of their studies, Bushman and Baumeister (1998) had subjects write essays and then be given written feedback that had been allegedly written by another participant. The feedback was either positive ("Great essay, no comment") or, in the ego-threat condition, negative ("This is one of the worst essays I have ever read"). Then subjects took part in a competitive timed reaction test, where the subjects competed against the alleged other participant. Whoever pushed the button the slowest received a loud blast of noise. Subjects got to choose which level of noise the other participant got. Consistent with the finding that excessively high levels of self-esteem (i.e., narcissism) can increase the likelihood of aggression, overall, subjects who had scored high on a narcissism scale delivered louder blasts of noise to their competitors regardless of the type of feedback they had received. In the ego-threat condition, subjects who scored highest on narcissism delivered the loudest noise.

This song isn't really special to me, but it does provide a wonderful showcase for my voice.

**Figure 3.2.**

Thus, while attempts to raise self-esteem levels in some cases may result in positive effects such as improved interpersonal relationships, raising self-esteem levels certainly does not provide a major deterrent or cure for social ills, and may actually inadvertently contribute to them. Rosenberg, Schooler and Schoenbach (1989), for example, found that the relationship between self-esteem and behavior is often reciprocal. In their study of 1,886 adolescent males, they found that low self-esteem can lead to delinquent behavior and also that delinquent behavior can increase subsequent self-esteem.

*How much do we strive to maintain our self-esteem?* Suppose classmate A rather nicely and diplomatically told classmate B that he did not think she was as smart or as attractive as she thought she was.

You can imagine any number of different responses from classmate B. Overall, do you suppose she would readily embrace these conclusions, even thanking her classmate for being so honest with her and helping her readjust her own self-perceptions? Maybe, but to what degree in general do people seek to maintain a positive self-image rather than seek accurate information? According to most research efforts, this happens quite a bit, though for differing reasons.

There has been a consistent finding that people often seek to maintain their self-esteem and that if threats to their self-image occur, they often seem to go to great lengths to repair it. Leary and Downs (1995) explored this finding and proposed the *sociometer theory* to help explain the apparent connection between self-esteem and our perceptions of others' reaction to us. According to this theory, the self-esteem system monitors the social environment and looks for cues (often at an unconscious level) of rejection or exclusion and alerts the person by way of negative affect, which in this case refers to lowered self-esteem. Leary et al. (1995) found that feelings about oneself are very sensitive to perceptions of rejection or acceptance. In fact, the correlations were so high that the researchers noted, "For all practical purposes, self-feelings were a proxy for perceived exclusion" (p. 523).

Leary et al. (1998) later found that the relationship between self-esteem and perceived social exclusion or inclusion was most strong at moderate levels of rejection or acceptance. So, if you were at a party and felt moderately rejected or excluded by others, then according to the sociometer theory, you would likely experience at least a temporary (state) decrease in self-esteem. But if, as the night progressed, the group totally rejected you and excluded you from conversation, there would be no significant additional negative effect on your self-esteem level. Similarly, if you experienced excessive inclusion, that would not have any additional effect on self-esteem than would moderate inclusion. Leary et al. suggest several possible reasons for these findings, noting among them that perhaps such extreme reactions to us may be perceived as less credible. In either case, Leary et al. maintain that self-esteem functions to protect the person against social rejection and exclusion. So, according to these researchers, it is not self-esteem itself that a person is trying to maintain; rather, it is the desire to be socially included that is the more compelling motivation.

The attempt to enhance one's self-esteem was also noted in an interesting series of studies by Haslam et al. (2005). They found that subjects rated themselves as more "human" than others when taking into consideration positive qualities such as openness and interpersonal warmth. Interestingly, subjects also saw themselves as more human than others in terms of possessing negative emotionality as well. So, for example, subjects tended to report that they had more of the innate emotion of anger than did others. The authors noted that this apparent propensity to see oneself as somehow "more human" than another could help explain how people dehumanize others and justify their own aggressive actions, as will be discussed in the chapter on aggression (chap. 7).

Other social psychologists (e.g., Crocker, 2002) have expressed different concerns concerning the degree to which Americans appear to be consumed by efforts to enhance their self-esteem, especially when these efforts are based on meeting criteria set by others for what makes a person worthwhile. Crocker argues that our many efforts at self-esteem enhancement may be frustrated because they are based on unreliable and inconsistent responses from others. Crocker notes that this instability of responses from others has the ironic effect of actually decreasing self-esteem and has negative effects on one's mental health. So, according to this view, depending so much on others' approval does not have the intended effect of raising our self-esteem. In fact, it often just makes us exhausted!

***How do social comparisons affect our self-esteem?*** As noted earlier in the discussion of upward and downward social comparisons, self-esteem is often affected when we compare our own attitudes, opinions, characteristics or abilities to those of others. Many researchers have investigated specific domains in which social comparisons take place. One relatively frequent area of interest has been related to how comparisons regarding physical attractiveness affect one's self-evaluation. For example, Morse and Gergen (1970) studied the effect of others' appearance on participants' self-esteem during a job interview. Self-comparison with a person whose appearance was neat resulted in a decrease in self-esteem, whereas self-comparison with a person whose appearance was untidy resulted in an increase in self-esteem.

Other studies also suggest that an individual's self-evaluation may be significantly affected by the perceived physical attractiveness of others with whom one comes into contact. For example, Cash, Cash and Butters (1983) found that women who had assessed photographs of attractive women rated themselves lower in self-esteem than did women who had assessed photographs of ordinary-looking women. Wheeler and Miyake (1992) also found that physical attractiveness is one of the primary dimensions in social comparisons.

Overall, since researchers have not agreed on issues such as the exact definition of self-esteem or whether high self-esteem is an asset, it should be no surprise that there is a lack of a coherent model of self-esteem. Research in this area has instead been very diverse, representing a variety of different aspects of the concept. Cast and Burke (2002) outline the different directions that research on self-esteem has taken. First, self-esteem has been investigated as an *outcome,* with the focus being on processes that enhance or inhibit self-esteem (e.g., Coopersmith, 1967; Harter, 1993). This first line of research has provided such a variety of possible self-esteem enhancement strategies that some researchers have called this collection of strategies the "self-zoo" (Tesser, Martin & Cornell, 1996). These self-esteem enhancement strategies generally fall under three classes of mechanisms for increasing self-esteem: processes related to social comparison (e.g., Tesser, 1988), processes related to maintaining consistency between our behaviors and attitudes in order to reduce threats to self-esteem (Festinger, 1957), and processes that involve self-affirmation (Steele, 1988). Table 3.2 summarizes the different research approaches to self-esteem.

**Table 3.2. The "Self Zoo": Different Ways to Conceptualize Self-Esteem**

| | |
|---|---|
| **Self-esteem enhancement strategies** | "I feel better/worse about myself depending on whom I use as a comparison group." <br> "I feel better about myself when my interpretations of my actions are consistent with my beliefs about myself." <br> "I am a worthwhile person . . . I can do this . . . My life has meaning," etc. |
| **Self-esteem as a motive** | "I will try to diminish that other person so that I can maintain my positive sense of self." |
| **Self-esteem as a buffer** | "I just experienced this difficulty, but I know I am strong enough to overcome it." |

Second, researchers have investigated self-esteem as a *motive*—that is, the tendency for people to behave in ways that maintain or increase self-esteem; more specifically, the tendency to present oneself to others in the best possible light, as noted in studies of self-enhancement (e.g., Kaplan, 1975; Tesser, 1988). A third focus in self-esteem research has investigated self-esteem as a *buffer* from experiences that are harmful or threatening. For example, Thoits (1994) investigated how higher levels of self-esteem can help individuals respond to trauma in more healthy ways than can individuals with lower levels of self-esteem. Cast and Burke (2002) note that little effort has been done to integrate these three research streams into a coherent model of self-esteem.

Given the confusion regarding the degree to which high self-esteem is associated with negative social outcomes, several researchers have noted that investigating the distinction between high and low self-esteem may not be the most valid approach. Kernis (2003), for example, suggests that there is a difference between *optimal self-esteem* and high self-esteem. A person with optimal self-esteem is realistic and honest regarding their own strengths and relative weaknesses. Kernis notes that optimal self-esteem is stable and genuine. In contrast, high self-esteem itself can be fragile, depending on how defensive it is. Using this distinction between optimal and high self-esteem, Kernis argues that we can better understand why high self-esteem is often associated with negative social behavior because those cases would be indicative of a fragile, defensive self-esteem as opposed to an optimal level of self-esteem.

***What implications does a Christian view of self-esteem have for research?*** As noted previously in this chapter, Baumeister et al. (2003) recount the self-esteem movement that took place over several decades, beginning in the 1970s. This movement involved numerous psychologists investigating the positive outcomes of high self-esteem and proposing school and community-wide initiatives all across the U.S. You may recall that these programs, although certainly well-intended and with their own merit, have been largely unsuccessful. Raising self-esteem levels is not generally significantly related to any positive social outcome, and in some cases can actually have detrimental effects (Forsyth & Kerr, 1999). In fact, the intuitive notion that high self-esteem leads to positive social outcomes also has the potential to inadvertently create "excessive self-love," which is related to many negative social outcomes such as racism and aggression (Bushman & Baumeister, 1998).

While many psychologists have since reconsidered whether enhanced self-esteem really leads to positive social outcomes, endorsement of this idea remains strong for the public at large. One example of this is the National Association for Self-Esteem (NASE), whose goal is to "promote awareness of and provide vision, leadership and advocacy for *improving the human condition* through the enhancement of self-esteem" (NASE, 2000, as cited in Baumeister et al., 2003; italics added). Thus, the idea that higher self-esteem is a causal factor for positive social behavior does not quickly fade away.

A Christian view of persons can offer insight into the mixed value of self-esteem in social relations. This is because the CFR approach has a different starting point for research on self-esteem. In the Scriptures, two seemingly opposing messages are given regarding our self-worth. On the one hand, we are commanded to "love your neighbor as yourself" (Mk 12:31), implying the importance of self-regard. On the other hand, we are told numerous times to deny the self (e.g., Mt 5:40; Mt 16:24) and "not to think of yourself more highly than you ought" (Rom 12:3), implying the need for humility. What then would be a Christian perspective of self-esteem if the Scriptures say both to value the self and others and to beware of the dangers of a grandiose sense of self? And how would this perspective specifically guide research on this topic?

McGrath and McGrath (1992) suggest that healthy self-regard emanates from an understanding of Christ's redemption for us and from our identity as God's adopted children in relation to others. They further note that this helps to keep us "properly recognizing our self-worth without falling into self-worship" (back cover). They point to a tension between humility and pride, with humans having a general tendency toward pride.

The CFR approach to self-esteem rests on the mandate Scripture presents to us regarding a delicate and crucial balance between self- and other-regard (i.e., "love your neighbor as yourself"). From that perspective, one could hypothesize that healthy self-worth is inextricably connected to recognizing the worth in others. Thus, efforts to elevate self-esteem without also encouraging esteem for others would be expected to create a fragile basis for self-worth or a level of self-centeredness that is contrary to positive social interactions. Thus, research efforts could investigate the effects of encouraging *both* self-esteem alongside esteem for others.

A researcher who holds the CFR view of the human condition would not likely expect that social ills can be significantly reduced by increasing self-esteem. One would instead assume, based on the fallen condition of humans, that increasing self-esteem without also encouraging regard for others is often accompanied by increasing pride and the problems that pride engenders. Indeed, Baumeister, Tice and Hutton's (1989) finding that so many Americans report an elevated self-esteem would not be surprising from a Christian view. After all, one enduring warning from Scripture is how easy it is for humans to fall prey to "excessive self-love," an increased sense of entitlement, and unhealthy and even more defensive levels of high self-esteem, consistent with the research of Bushman and Baumeister (1998).

To review, beginning with a concern regarding the human tendency toward pride, a researcher holding the CFR view would not be likely to suggest that social ills are caused primarily or significantly by low self-esteem or that social ills can be significantly reduced by increasing self-esteem. Instead, a focus for research could be more on developing programs that encourage honest appraisals of one's strengths and weaknesses in conjunction with encouraging positive regard for others. The CFR approach would also suggest more research in the area of pride and its effects on social behavior. In addition, it would be interesting to continue to explore how a healthy self-esteem can be a *result,* rather than a cause, of positive social behavior.

It is helpful to remember that when discussing the different research emphases that emerge from a naturalist and a Christian view of humans, one must consider some of the similarities as well. Note, for example, how some of the research noted earlier in this chapter appears to be consistent with that proposed by a Christian view of persons. Note especially Kernis's (2003) idea about the fragility of high self-esteem and the need for more stable self-esteem based on realistic views of the self, and Leary's (2006) argument that more research about pride is needed.

In addition to the implications for research, knowledge of the potentially destructive effects of fragile high self-esteem could be helpful for everyday social life. After reading this research, I started to notice in my own community the prevalence of messages that encourage excessive self-regard. At the local YMCA, for example, there is a large banner that reads, "Be your own hero." A student of mine recently recounted how teachers in her high school district were no longer allowed to use red pen to correct or edit student papers be-

cause red ink may wound students' self-esteem. Teachers are instead encouraged to use green ink, which is more "neutral" and presumably less offensive. Everywhere one can see the glorifying of students' accomplishments (e.g., bumper stickers that read, "My child is an honor student at . . ."). Many such seemingly innocent messages suggest that we are not fully aware of the fragility of self-esteem that only glorifies the self without encouraging honest self-reflection. Both research and a

**Figure 3.3.**

Christian view of the human condition encourage us to beware of the potential social ills that result from such excessive self-love.

## JUST HOW RELATIONAL IS THE SELF?

In the preceding sections, you read about the broad and complex study of self-concept and self-esteem. Many of the cited studies demonstrated the importance of interpersonal relationships and the perceived evaluations that others have of us as an integral part of our self-evaluation. You have probably noticed that people seem to differ in the degree to which they want to relate to others. Some may thrive by seeking out many relationships, while others may be just as happy relating to fewer friends. Do we have evidence that humans are nevertheless intrinsically social beings despite these individual differences in personality style? And if so, just how compelling is the degree to which we seek to maintain social connectedness?

Baumeister and Leary (1995) suggest that the need for social connection is so strong and central to our being that they refer to it as the *fundamental need to belong.* In their exhaustive review of the literature, they argue that this need for close interpersonal relationships is characterized by two main features. First, there is the need for frequent personal contacts or interactions with the other person. Baumeister and Leary noted that ideally, these interactions would be mostly pleasant, or free from conflict. Second, they note that these relationships need to be perceived as potentially continuing into the future and also characterized by concern and stability. The authors also comment on how the research indicates the ease with which people everywhere seem inclined to form social relationships in the absence of any ulterior motives or special prompting. People further show resistance and distress when breaking bonds with others.

Additionally, Baumeister and Leary note how the lack of such close relationships results in significant negative consequences for both emotional and physical functioning. They cite other researchers (e.g., Ainsworth, 1989; Axelrod & Hamilton, 1981; Bowlby, 1989; Buss, 2003) who contend that the desire to form and maintain social bonds is advantageous from an evolutionary standpoint because close relationships provide both survival and reproductive benefits.

What current social phenomena in the modern West do you think most obviously show humans as social beings? I would answer with little hesitation: cell phones and Facebook! I am constantly amazed at the apparently unquenchable desire for interconnection that Facebook generates and satisfies. And as for cell phones, I am further impressed with the speed and frequency with which my students text each other (sometimes, regrettably, during class). When I asked one of my students why he always felt the need to keep his cell phone on, he noted gravely, "What if I missed an important life-or-death message?" He was unfazed by my comments regarding the very low probability with which such messages occur.

Brewer and Gardner (1996) and Brewer (2007) also agree that the research overwhelmingly provides support for the intrinsic relational nature of humans. Nevertheless, they argue that most often the researchers erroneously lump together the concepts of close interpersonal relationships and connections with larger social groups. Brewer (2007) proposes that close relational ties (what she prefers to call "bonding") are not the same as the ties we have with larger social networks, which she refers to as "belonging." She notes that researchers use these terms interchangeably as though they mean the same thing, but she argues from the evolutionary perspective that the two have different adaptive functions. Specifically, close personal relationships have a wide range of benefits for both people, including mutual concern and attention. By comparison, connections with larger social groups can extend the range of benefits to include things like the sharing of resources and greater potential for mutual protection (Caporael, 1997).

Baumeister and Leary's (1995) hypothesis that lack of close social connections results in significant emotional and physical consequences is consistent with another area of research that explores what happens when we are socially excluded. Williams (2003), in explaining the feeling of being ostracized, encourages the reader to imagine what it feels like to be ignored or dismissed, to have others go about their business as though we didn't exist. Think about that in your own life. How have you responded when friends, relatives or acquaintances have purposely excluded you from some activity or otherwise ignored you?

Eisenberger, Lieberman and Williams (2003) demonstrated that feelings of rejection and ostracism affect the brain in much the same way as does physical pain. They hooked up subjects to functional MRIs and asked them to play a virtual ball-tossing game from which the subjects were eventually excluded. The researchers measured self-reported distress during both the exclusion period as well as the period in which subjects were engaged in the game. They found that distress was correlated with changes in the areas of the brain that are also affected by physical pain—the anterior cingulate cortex and the right ventral prefrontal cortex. So compelling is the effect of rejection!

Other authors (e.g., Williams, Forgas and von Hippel, 2005) likewise discuss the devastating effects of social ostracism. In addition, they discuss how once excluded, individuals perceive and respond to their social environments differently. They note that the research on reactions to ostracism is mixed. While some researchers (e.g., Lakin & Chartrand, 2005) have found that people who are ostracized often engage in prosocial acts such as kindness and helpfulness, other researchers (e.g., Gaertner & Iuzzini, 2005; Twenge et al., 2001) have shown that ostracism often leads to antisocial behavior such as violent reactions. In either case, the research indicates that ostracism has significant effects on our subsequent social behavior, once again suggesting the power of social inclusion and connectedness.

It may seem obvious why ostracism has potentially negative consequences for one's survival and social advantage, but what if experimenters could manipulate the conditions so that the subject could actually *benefit* from being ostracized? Would that diminish the negative effects of ostracism? This is the question that vanBeest and Williams (2006) attempted to explore in their creative experiment using a variation of the computer game *Cyberball*. This game involves three players who interact virtually by tossing a ball back and forth between them on their respective computer screens. The subjects were not aware that the other two "players" on the screen were actually not human subjects at all, but rather simulated actors programmed to respond in certain ways. In the inclusion condition, the subjects received one-third of the tosses. In the exclusion condition, the subjects received only two tosses and then never received another toss and simply watched the other two players toss the ball back and forth between each other. Some subjects lost money while being included, and others gained money while being excluded. The results indicated that after the *Cyberball* game was over, the subjects were much more satisfied and happy when they were included than when they were excluded, regardless of whether they were in the gain or loss condition. So in this case, being included was of prime importance, even if it meant losing money.

Several studies of children ages six to eleven also demonstrated the tendency to go to significant lengths to help ensure inclusion and favorable ratings from others (Banerjee, 2002). In these studies, the children were asked to describe themselves either while alone in a room or while in front of an audience. Of the children who were faced by an audience, the older ones chose self-descriptors that they believed were consistent with what the audience preferred. Banerjee suggests that this is an attempt to avoid rejection by making efforts at being perceived in the most positive light possible.

So, all things considered, the research generally provides support for the idea that humans are intrinsically relational beings. Interestingly, Leary (2007) proposes that the relational nature of humans is so compelling that even efforts at self-enhancement (such as self-esteem-boosting efforts) may be seen as "efforts to obtain material or interpersonal outcomes, such as to establish, maintain, and protect one's relationships with other people" (p. 234).

Further, the research suggests the consistent finding that if you feel wanted and socially included by your peers, you are more likely to feel good about yourself. This may be one reason why social situations that seem so outwardly destructive may have such appeal for some people. A gang or cult member, for example, may decide that it is far better to risk dying as part of a group than to live a life that is lonely.

***Are there gender differences in our intrinsic relational nature?*** As noted in the above discussion, the relational nature of humans has been found in crosscultural studies and thus seems to be universal. But could the two genders differ in the degree to which they are relationally oriented? Have you heard the stereotype that females are much more relational creatures than are males? What does the research show? Do males in fact define themselves and behave in a less relational way than do women? It seems that in general, the answer is no, but what does seem to differ between the two genders are the *types* of relationships that are emphasized.

Seeley et al. (2003) reviewed the literature on gender differences in self-definition and social connectedness. They note that in general research suggests that both men and women report close interpersonal/relational bonds as being more important than collective bonds (larger group connections). But one interesting difference did occur. That is, while men and women both tend to emphasize and define themselves via close social relationships, once beyond that initial similarity, men tend to emphasize larger group affiliations more than do women (Baumeister & Sommer, 1997; Gabriel & Gardner, 1999).

In two studies, Seeley et al. (2003) asked men and women to consider a group that was important to them and to take a group attachment scale. The results indicated that for women, the extent to which she was relationally attached, or felt close, to a fellow group member was sufficient to explain the importance of the group for her. But for the men, the importance of the group depended on the extent of both the relational and collective attachment.

*A Christian view of our intrinsic relational nature.* The finding that humans are intrinsically relational is of course consistent with both a naturalist and a Christian view of humans. Both views include the reality that humans engage in social relationships for some sort of self-gain. Nevertheless, each of these views proposes different explanations for these findings. These different explanations reflect a different starting point with respect to the primary motives for our relational nature. As noted in the previous section, the naturalist view proposes primarily (and often exclusively) self-serving motives for our relational nature (enhance self-esteem, avoid social ostracism, etc.). From the CFR view, our relational nature is an integral part of our created being, enabling us to partake in God's redemptive plan, and includes the potential for other-centered motives as well as self-centered motives.

The research we will look at in the following section suggests that humans appear to be quite self-serving. This research on self-centered tendencies seems at first quite discrepant with the intrinsically relational nature of humans that we just discussed. That is, how can humans both crave connection with others and yet ultimately be most concerned with themselves? Interestingly, as we will see at the end of the next section, more recent research has suggested that humans have a greater capacity than once thought to engage in other-centered concern in interpersonal relationships. Thus, the discussion regarding humans' other-centered potential will follow the next section so that we can consider together these recent findings.

### THE SELF IN ACTION: *HOW WE PRESENT OURSELVES TO OTHERS*

*Just how self-centered are we?* Recall a time in class when the professor handed back an exam in which many of the students did not do well. Can you remember the students' responses? If those responses were like most students', they probably included things like: "This was not a fair test!" or "The test questions were unclear." Later among themselves, students are likely to perpetuate the impression that the professor is impossibly difficult. Students are often much more likely to say things like those rather than to admit that they did not study enough, that they had difficulty understanding some of the concepts or that they tried to cram in all the information the night before the exam. Conversely, imagine a situation in class where all the students did well on an exam. How many of them would cite the reason for their success as the easiness of the test? Indeed, in this case the students would be more likely to take credit for their good grades.

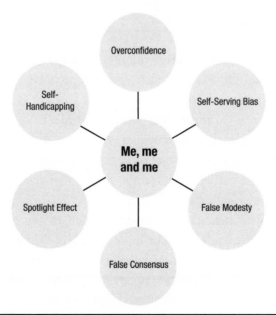

**Figure 3.4. Just How Self-Serving Are We?**

This tendency to take personal credit for our successes and to blame external factors for our failures is known as the *self-serving bias* (Campbell & Sedikides, 1999; Chan et al., 1998; Sedikides et al., 1998). This general tendency is seen in many different situations that involve social relations, and more generally reflects a strong tendency to present ourselves in the most favorable light possible. In fact, in one instance where research participants were informed about the self-serving bias, they still rated themselves as less frequently self-serving in their judgments than is the average person (Friedrich, 1996)!

Along with the example of the self-serving bias, other self-serving tendencies are also evident in the research; for example, our tendency to rate ourselves as "better than average." Myers and Ridl (1979) argue that in most of our comparisons of self with others, we have a "superiority complex." This is evident even when it is known that it is a statistical impossibility for the majority to be better than the average because the average reflects the majority! For example, most drivers, even those who have been hospitalized for accidents, believe themselves to be safer and more skilled than the average driver (McKenna & Myers, 1997).

Another common finding in social psychological research about the self is the dynamic of *false consensus*. This is another example of our self-centered tendencies. False consensus involves an overestimation regarding how much others agree with our opinions/ideas (e.g., Krueger & Clement, 1994). If you are honest, you can probably recall at least a time or two when you were genuinely amazed that not everyone agreed with your opinion on something that seemed like it should be so "obvious" to everyone. Political campaign seasons are an excellent time to observe false consensus. I often observe on campus how members of the different political parties often cannot believe that anyone would vote for the opposing candidate.

Self-serving tendencies also are manifested in the *overconfidence effect,* which is the tendency to be more confident than accurate in our judgments (Dunning, Griffin, Milojkovic & Ross, 1990). This is sometimes referred to as *belief perseverance.* For example, researchers have found that people are generally overly confident about the accuracy of their impressions and attitudes, even to the point of being reluctant to consider evidence that clearly contradicts our initial impressions (Festinger, Riecken & Schachter, 1956; Ross & Lepper, 1980). Consider as one example of this phenomenon the impact of first impressions. Have you ever been in a situation where your opinion of someone eventually became quite different than was your initial impression of them? How easy was it to change your mind about that person? Often, changing first impressions is quite difficult, even with contrary evidence.

This tendency toward overconfidence is especially powerful when ambiguous information is presented; people tend to interpret it as confirmation of their previously held beliefs (Lord, Ross & Lepper, 1979). As we will review in later chapters, one potential danger of this overconfidence is that there is much more error in our perceptions than we care to admit.

Another example of our self-centered tendencies may be seen in what is called the *self-reference effect*. This is our tendency to process efficiently information that is related to the self. When we think about something in relation to ourselves, we tend to remember it better (e.g., Symons & Johnson, 1997). For example, many students study class material more effectively by relating it to personal experience.

And yet another way in which our self-serving tendencies are seen is in our tendency to imagine that if we are so self-focused, then others are as interested in our lives as we are and that others notice even small details of our behavior or emotions. This appears to be a lifelong concern for us. For example, several developmental psychologists (e.g., Piaget & Inhelder, 1969; Elkind, 1976) describe concepts such as the *imaginary audience*, or *spotlight effect*, where some adolescents can become so self-conscious that they think everyone is watching their every move. While these examples may at first appear as the tendency of those who are much younger and less mature than the average college student or adult, this tendency actually continues to varying degrees throughout life.

To assess the development of the spotlight effect, Frankenberger (2000) had both adolescents (aged 14-18) and adults (aged 20-89) complete sub-scales of the adolescent egocentrism, self-consciousness and interpersonal reactivity scales. After splitting adults into younger (19-30), middle (31-59) and older (60+) subgroups, the results showed no significant difference between adolescents and younger (19-30) adults with regard to egocentrism. Thus, the results suggest that concerns with an imaginary audience are not confined to adolescence. In reality, we agonize over things about ourselves that others may hardly notice or soon forget.

*Are self-serving tendencies universal?* So far, our discussion of self research has indicated that we are generally self-focused, self-enhancing and fairly convinced that others are as interested in us as we are in ourselves. The question remains, however, whether this generally self-serving tendency found in Western egocentric cultures is also applicable to individuals in non-Western, sociocentric cultures. One aspect of this self-serving tendency that is related to this discussion is that of self-enhancement, which involves all efforts to present oneself in a positive light (e.g., taking credit for successes and denying failures). The findings of many social psychological studies (e.g., Markus & Kitayama, 1991) have suggested that the self-enhancement tendency is a basic motivating factor for the self in egocentric cultures, but not in sociocentric cultures.

For the purposes of our discussion, let us first focus on the Japanese as an example of a sociocentric culture. In a review of many studies of the Japanese, Kitayama, Takagi and Matsumoto (1995) noted that the Japanese do not generally exhibit a self-serving bias. Takata (1987) also reported that the Japanese tend to demonstrate a "modesty bias" whereby they accept negative feedback concerning themselves as more valid than they do positive feedback. Westerners, as we have already discussed, generally tend to emphasize their successes, while the Japanese tend to emphasize self-criticism, or failure.

One way to interpret this discrepancy between Americans' self-enhancement and the Japanese's apparent modesty is to suggest that the Japanese are naturally more inclined to be modest and thus less self-enhancing. This interpretation implies that in this respect the general nature, or underlying disposition, of the Japanese differs from those of their Western counterparts.

A more careful look, however, reveals that despite all the cultural differences, the underlying nature of the Japanese can be seen as equally self-serving and self-concerned as that of Americans. For example, the Japanese are members of a culture that has traditionally perceived the self as interdependent—in other words, more socially connected and thus generally restrained to maintain social harmony. Their apparent modesty, then, can arguably be construed as a way in which to present themselves in the most positive way in light of their culture's expectations (Heine, Takata & Lehman, 2000). In addition, a culture's attempts to restrain self-aggrandizement imply their acknowledgment that this is a strong tendency that needs to be suppressed. With these points in mind, it becomes more evident how the underlying self-enhancing nature of both Americans and Japanese can arguably be considered the same, though each is manifested differently as a function of cultural rules.

Gaertner, Sedikides and Chang (2008) likewise found the tendency toward self-enhancement in a group of undergraduate students at three Taiwanese universities. They gave the subjects self-enhancement surveys that included both collectivist and individualist traits, and asked the subjects to rate themselves in comparison to their peers. The results indicated that the Taiwanese students were as self-enhancing as were their Western counterparts. But one main difference is that the Taiwanese students tended to self-enhance most on the items that were specifically more highly lauded in collectivist cultures (e.g., respectful, compliant, self-sacrificing).

Incidentally, it should be noted that the majority of studies comparing sociocentric cultures to egocentric cultures have historically focused on comparing either the Japanese or the Chinese with people of Western cultures (primarily the U.S.). More recent studies have looked at other cultures as well. For example, Kurman (2001) studied two sociocentric cultures, the Singaporean-Chinese and the Israeli Druze, and compared these with the egocentric culture of Israeli Jews. Kurman argued against the idea that the interdependent self, which is found in sociocentric cultures, lacks self-enhancement as an intrinsic quality. In one study Kurman found that the Druze are collectivist and yet exhibit less modesty and more self-enhancement than did the Singaporeans. In a second study, Kurman's findings suggested the possibility that "when requirements for modesty are less internalized and modesty is lower, the self-enhancement motive can function more freely" (p. 1714). In other words, it seems that if a culture does not restrain the self-serving bias, then that tendency is likely to be expressed, regardless of what type of culture it is.

Myers (2005) further notes research that suggests that people worldwide are privately self-enhancing. The self-serving bias has been noted among Dutch high school and university students, Belgian basketball players, Indian Hindus, Japanese drivers, Australian students and workers, Chinese students, Hong Kong students and sports writers, and French people of all ages.

*Self-presentation.* As if it were not enough to view ourselves in favorable ways, the research suggests that we also act to enhance the way that others see us. One way in which we commonly do this is known as the process of *self-presentation,* also known as *impression management,* and is accomplished in some very clever ways (Jones, 1990, as cited in Kenrick, Neuberg & Cialdini, 2002). Self-presentation involves trying to control the impressions people have of us. To understand this, imagine a time when it really mattered to you what another person or group of people thought of you. For example, have you ever seen a fellow student speaking to a new love interest and been amused by the alteration in their voice, posture and mannerisms? What is the purpose of these changes? Obviously it is to impress the other. (Either that or it is the result of extreme nervousness!) You may have experienced a similar situation when going on a job interview, dressing and acting in ways that you otherwise may not in everyday life.

As Snyder (1980) explains, there are significant differences in the extent to which people can and do control their self-presentation. One way in which we do this is through the process of *self-monitoring*—being attuned to one's public image and adjusting one's actions according to the needs of the situation. High self-monitors are especially in tune with the perceived demands of the situation, and will often change their behavior to be in compliance with those demands. Snyder argues that actors and trial lawyers are especially high self-monitors. Low self-monitors, by contrast, are less inclined to alter their behavior to follow social pressures, so their behaviors often match their real attitudes. Jones and Baumeister (1976) concluded that those who engage in a lot of self-monitoring prefer to interact with those whose behaviors and words reflect their true feelings. In this way, the high self-monitor does not have to expend a lot of energy in deciphering others' words and actions. Most of us are somewhere in the middle in terms of self-monitoring.

Another self-serving tendency is a strategy known as *false modesty*, which is the tendency to disparage the self in the presence of others with the intent of presenting a favorable self-image (Gibson & Sachau, 2000). For example, how often do you hear a star athlete or accomplished musician or researcher say outright: "All of my success is due to my own talents alone." Or: "The only person I have to thank is myself." On the contrary, you usually hear mildly self-deprecating comments such as: "By myself I could not have accomplished this work" or: "This work is best presented as a collaborative effort. There is no way I could have achieved this by myself." While some of the credit given to others certainly reflects sincere attempts to acknowledge their contributions, often these types of comments hint at a less sincere humility. You can imagine any number of possible reasons for this tendency. In some ways, modesty is charming and certainly much more appealing than is self-aggrandizement. You can well imagine your friends' responses to you if all you did was go around claiming how great you are all the time.

False modesty can also often result from the desire to have others flatter us. For example, when an adolescent girl proclaims in front of her friends that she feels fat and unattractive, what is the usual response? Her friends will most likely respond by telling her that she is not really *that* overweight and that she is in fact very attractive. In any case, it appears that we are aware that modesty, whether false or not, presents a much more positive image of us to others than would overt pride.

Several interesting studies (Essock-Vitale & McGuire, 1985) have demonstrated other ways in which people engage in self-enhancing ways to manage the impression others have of them. These researchers found that subjects boastfully reported more frequent personal helping experiences as helper than as recipient. In this way, they enhanced their self-image and presented socially desirable appearances because they could appear both helpful and less vulnerable.

Another way in which we can manage the impressions that others have of us is through a strategy known as *self-handicapping*. This is when we actually sabotage our efforts at success by creating roadblocks that lessen our chances of success (Berglas & Jones, 1978). In this way, we protect our self-image with behaviors that create an excuse for later failure. For example, imagine a student who is concerned about the difficulty of an upcoming exam. For three days prior to the exam, he manages to find all sorts of errands to run and offers to drive a few friends to the airport at all hours of the day and night. In this way, he makes it virtually impossible for himself to study adequately for the exam. When he does poorly on the test, he saves face by explaining to his friends that he did not do well because he had so little time to study.

Academic procrastination is a very common example of self-handicapping. Urdan and Midgley (2001) give examples of self-handicapping among students. They note the oft-heard complaints: "I could have aced the test, but I put off studying until the last minute." Or: "I could have gotten a good grade in this course, but I spent a lot of time with my friends last semester" (p. 115). The authors note that these are strategies intended to save face, or to avoid seeming stupid. You may have experienced procrastination in your own studies and perhaps caught yourself saying something like, "I have been so busy over the past few weeks, I really didn't have time to study for this test!" In this way, you can blame your lack of studying for your failure. Another example of the self-handicapping strategy may be a young man or woman who is afraid of having unsuccessful relationships yet keeps dating those who are rude and inconsiderate. In this way, when the relationship fails, he or she can insist that it was not their fault but rather yet another confirmation of how unreliable the opposite sex can be.

Thus, in general, the above research suggests numerous different ways in which we exhibit self-serving tendencies. In general, these tendencies serve to increase our self-esteem, increase the chances that others will look upon us favorably, and otherwise manage the impression others have of us to suit our goals. Attempts at self-monitoring, self-presentation and overall impression management all seem to serve these aims. For example, self-presentation strategies can boost our self-esteem because the more people like us, the better we feel about ourselves (Leary et al., 1995). Similarly, self-monitoring can increase the chances that we will be socially included.

**Both self-seeking and intrinsically relational?** The studies discussed in this chapter have presented compelling support for the assumption that humans are intrinsically relational beings. Remember that these findings are consistent with both a naturalist perspective and a Christian view of persons. Recall, however, that what differs between these two views are the presumed origin and functions of this relational nature. Taylor and Gonzaga (2006), in describing a naturalist EP perspective of relationships, claim, "Humans, like many other primate species, have adapted group living and deep investment in social bonds as a primary solution to the problems of survival and reproduction" (p. 211). To illustrate this point, the authors note all the life-saving roles that relationships serve, including how strong social support has an equal or greater impact on health compared to well-established predictors of health such as smoking and lipid levels. Thus, according to Taylor and Gonzaga, "the absence of social ties is toxic for health" (p. 211).

From a Christian view, survival may certainly be considered a strong motivator and consequence of social interconnectedness. Yet a Christian approach suggests that the intrinsic relational nature of humans is at the very core of our created being and serves the other higher-order goals of relationship with God and others. It makes sense that consistent social relationships result in many personal benefits, and the lack of strong social support often has devastating practical consequences. From a Christian view, it is also true that social relationships are an end goal themselves because they are an expression of God's created order, his own relational nature and his redemptive plan. From a Christian view, then, humans have a strong survival instinct, but the drive for connectedness is just as fundamental.

Remember that along with this apparent social nature, researchers have consistently found many self-seeking tendencies in human social interaction. Examples of this self-centered nature are seen in concepts such as the self-serving bias, self-presentation strategies and many self-esteem enhancement strategies. How are these findings reconcilable with a presumably social nature? That is, how can humans be both deeply relational *and* deeply self-centered? In order to explore this question, we must first consider whether a naturalist approach has a logical basis for finding a relational nature in humans as a higher-order goal.

Just how social can humans really be from a naturalist view? Batson (1990), as noted in the previous chapter, provides a helpful discussion of this question. He presents a review of the literature, which suggests that humans seem ultimately to care mostly, if not exclusively, for themselves. Batson further notes that there is a general belief in the field that we value others instrumentally; that is, we tend to care for their welfare usually to the degree that it affects ours. He states the general interpretation in the research that "our behavior may be highly social; our thoughts may be highly social; but in our hearts, we live alone. . . . We are social egoists" (p. 336).

Despite the apparent increase in interest regarding the higher-order purposes of social relationships (e.g., Leary, 2007), the recent research continues to exemplify social psychology's focus on the self-seeking tendencies of humans. For example, Fehr and Fischbacher (2003) argue that in the case of altruism, the experimental evidence indicates that two major motives for seemingly other-centered acts such as al-truism are reputation formation and strong reciprocity, or the expec-tation of something in return. In addition, as noted in the previous chapter, even more recent research efforts in the positive psychology movement ironically point toward egocentric, ultimately self-centered motives such as self-fulfillment for seemingly other-centered be-haviors. For example, virtues such as forgiveness, compassion and co-operation are generally presented in the literature with a focus on their impact on the individual's subjective well-being as a primary goal (McCullough, Bellah, Kilpatrick & Johnson, 2001; Sagiv & Schwartz, 2000; Seligman, 2002, respectively).

Thus, a naturalist approach consistently emphasizes the self-seeking tendencies of humans. This focus is consistent with a naturalist evolu-tionary approach that reduces the ultimate explanation for social be-havior to natural selection and adaptations for survival at the virtual exclusion of other possible explanations of human social behavior. From this view, humans are functionally "social" yet social egoists at heart. This social egoism drives even behavior that appears genuinely other-centered. It would be difficult to argue otherwise using a naturalist premise of the human condition.

The CFR view likewise acknowledges our capacity for social egoism, but also recognizes the capacity for other-centeredness that can be expressed in social interactions. Related to this assumption is that in our social relations, humans, created in God's image, experience tension between a fallen nature and the redemptive capacity for other-centeredness. Thus, as previously noted, a researcher with the CFR view has a logical starting point for the assumption that the self can have both self-centered and other-centered motives. Before we begin to discuss support for the idea of the potential for genuine other-centeredness, let us review briefly the research findings that are consistent with the Christian idea of fallenness.

As seen throughout our discussion regarding the research findings about the self, there is nothing like a close look at human social conduct to humble even the best of us. Recall that in general, the research findings suggest that people tend to behave in self-centered ways. For example, research suggests that people generally like to think nice thoughts about themselves (e.g., Campbell & Sedikides, 1999), often go to great trouble to defend their kind thoughts about themselves (e.g., McKenna & Myers, 1997), tend to be overly confident (e.g., Ross & Lepper, 1980), and often think that others are as interested in them as they are in themselves (e.g., Elkind & Bowen, 1979). In addition, when presenting themselves to others, people often engage in at least mildly deceptive ploys to appear in the most positive light possible (e.g., Gibson & Sachau, 2000). It also is interesting, and almost comical in a way, to see how self-serving tendencies are manifested in a propensity to see selfishness in others and not in ourselves (e.g., Friedrich, 1996). Studies consistently show that humans have a significant capacity for self-centeredness.

If we stopped with the research as briefly reviewed above, we would leave this chapter with a rather depressing view of the self. But what of the human capacity for other-centered social interaction? After all, from a Christian view, other-centered behaviors and motives *are* an end goal in and of themselves, as they are the way in which we have right relationship with others.

According to the CFR view of persons, the human tendency to long for interaction with others, barring any significant pathology that would preclude it, is inescapable and can be considered in and of itself a virtuous, or godly, way of being. Nevertheless, our inherent social need can be distorted and exhibited in some very unhealthy, self-seeking ways as evidenced in the research. For example, much of the literature on the self reveals that one's self-perception is affected by others to a very significant degree. This finding alone would be consistent with our God-given social nature. But note what else the research shows: humans are often overly susceptible to the impressions of others, and in many cases one could so desperately seek the approval of others to the extent that one is inclined to self-present in at least mildly deceptive ways just to obtain that approval (e.g., Snyder, 1980) or else to avoid shame for failure (e.g., Berglas & Jones, 1978). In addition, as noted in Crocker's (2002) research, people are often so driven to enhance self-esteem based on others' inconsistent expectations that this effort often results in increased stress as well as a self-concept that may be fragile and subject to many fluctuations.

Starting from a Christian perspective allows for the possibility that there are many instances in which self-seeking motives are not dominant. This is because other-centeredness is a necessary component of loving community. Yet, as we've just seen, humans seem to have a tendency to act in very self-serving ways. If this were the only substantial mode of being, then loving community would be a very difficult, if not impossible, goal. But is the self necessarily as consistently self-seeking as the research seems to show?

More recent research regarding self-serving tendencies seems consistent with the CFR view that humans can, and often do, act in other-centered ways. For example, Gaertner et al. (2008) propose that the amount of self-centeredness depends on whether we are talking about the individual, relational or collective self. Recall that the *individual self* consists of self-schemas based on personal characteristics, the *relational self* is based on close, interpersonal relationships, and the *collective self* is based on one's relationship with the group. Gaertner et al. note that humans seem to do many apparently unselfish, and indeed self-sacrificing, things on the interpersonal level. But in relation to larger groups, individuals seem less inclined to act in other-centered ways. The researchers thus conclude that there is an "implication for a quieter ego." That is, individuals are much more likely to subdue their selfish tendencies in relation to others than research has suggested since that research has not generally distinguished between different levels of the self. The authors note that a "quieter ego" has numerous benefits, including a greater propensity to help others and a decrease in the tendency to take credit for success and deny blame for failure.

The Gaertner et al. (2008) findings are consistent with the CFR view regarding the other-centered potential in humans. As Jones and Butman (1991) note, "humans experience compound and conflicting motivations, . . . which are seldom pure and never simple" (pp. 55-56). Future research could investigate more closely the conditions under which individuals are likely to override their own self-interests for the good of another and use this information to explore ways in which this concern for others can be modeled and taught.

## SELF-REGULATION

Now that we have discussed self-identity, our relational nature, and our apparent self- and other-centered tendencies, let us turn our attention to another major area of research: self-regulation. *Self-regulation* is the process of exercising control over one's impulses and being able to alter one's behavior in accordance with either internal or external standards or goals (Baumeister & Vohs, 2004). Following rules and inhibiting some desire in exchange for delayed gratification are examples of self-regulation or self-control. Self-regulation implies some measure of volition, or will. Though the concept of choice was considered an integral component of experimental social psychology at its inception (e.g., Lewin, 1952), after the emergence of behaviorism and its emphasis on observable behavior, social psychologists became increasingly disinterested in the study of the will. Later with the cognitive movement, social psychologists again began demonstrating concern about the concept of deliberate choice (Iyengar & Lepper, 2002).

Until more recently, social psychologists had not explored human free will as a potential causal agent because such a force was either not believed to exist (e.g., Bargh, 1990, 1999) or because it was thought that such a concept would be impossible to explore using the empirical method of study (e.g., Kuhl & Koole, 2004) or because compared to automatic processes it was seen to be rather useless (Bargh, 1999). Nevertheless, in more recent research in social psychology, there has been a greater interest regarding whether humans actually can exert their will and if so, to what degree and under which circumstances.

As noted by Bargh (2004), existential questions such as consciousness and human freedom are no longer just within the domain of philosophy; rather, "they have finally become traceable through scientific methods" (p. 394). Because of this increased interest and research regarding the will, you would be more likely to see this concept discussed in more detail in future social psychology textbooks.

Given the pattern of controversy among social psychologists regarding just about every concept related to the self, it should be no surprise that they have not come to an agreement regarding the capacity of humans to deliberately choose their thoughts, actions and attitudes. In general, the conflict surrounding the will is expressed in a few different ways. Some researchers (e.g., Wegner & Wheatley, 1999) disagree as to whether the will even exists at all or is an illusion largely the result of unconscious, automatic processes. A second way of looking at will reduces it to the physiological patterns we see in the brain—for example, activity in the frontal lobe when what appears to be will is being exercised. Thus, from this perspective, no independent will exists.

A recent line of research proposes that the will is in fact an independent entity that can be studied just like we can study aggression, intelligence and self-esteem (Kuhl & Koole, 2004). This perspective does not discount the role of the brain in the capacity to exercise one's will, but its proponents argue that just because physiological factors can be identified that affect and help explain how the will works does not mean that you have the complete picture of what the will is.

Vohs, Baumeister and Ciarocco (2004) note that self-regulation is an integral part of self theory and also has significant practical implications. Self-control, of course, has many benefits and is one of the most important factors that make it possible for human beings to live peaceably.

In addition, self-regulation is involved in many activities that are considered essential for healthy living (e.g., eating right, stopping smoking, etc.). Furthermore, there is a universal tendency for cultures to require self-regulation and punish its failures, even though cultures may differ as to what impulses must be regulated and when or what failures to self-regulate can be tolerated.

Carver and Scheier (1981, 1998) emphasize the idea of goals in their understanding of self-regulation. They argue that goals are an essential part of life, and without them, the risk for death is significantly higher than for those who have goals. If goals are obstructed, then individuals with a high level of subjective well-being will substitute other goals or else find alternate paths to achieve the goal (Showers & Ryff, 1996, as cited in Carver & Scheier, 1998). For example, Beck, Brown and Steer (1989) conducted a longitudinal study of individuals who had been hospitalized for depression. The subjects took a depression scale and a hopelessness scale at the beginning of their hospital stay. Subjects who had reported higher levels of hopelessness were much more likely to have committed suicide ten years post-hospitalization than were those who reported lower levels of hopelessness.

Baumeister, Muravin and Tice (2000) also review some of the literature regarding self-control. They reiterate Barkley's (1997) claim that self-control is for the ultimate long-term benefit of the individual. In addition, they argue that self-control is analogous to a muscle that, when overused, gets tired. So, the authors note that while self-control may be beneficial in the long run, it can be very costly and arduous in the short run. From this view, humans have a limited capacity to exert self-control. So, if self-control is required for an extended time, or the individual squanders their self-control with frivolous living, then he or she is likely to experience deficits in self-control in other areas of life.

One theory that explores whether the self can determine to act in ways that are not consistent with situational determinants is known as *self-determination theory* (SDT; Deci & Ryan, 1985, 1995). This theory suggests that humans have three innate psychological needs: *autonomy, competence* and *relatedness* (Deci & Ryan, 1991). Autonomy is characterized by an individual's need to feel that they are the origin of their actions, and it includes the concept of choice. Competence is characterized by a sense of proficiency and the perception of being effective in the things we do. Relatedness is characterized by the desire to experience a feeling of belonging and to be socially connected.

SDT proposes that the extent to which the above-noted three fundamental needs are met provides a description of an individual's motivational state. There are four motivational states, ranging from most self-determined to least self-determined. The most desirable level of motivation on this continuum is *intrinsic motivation,* thought to exist when an individual chooses to engage in an activity for its own sake or for the satisfaction derived from the activity itself rather than from an external reason or reward (Ryan, Kuhl & Deci 1997). After several intervening stages, the theory proposes the final level of motivation represented on the continuum, called *amotivation,* when individuals lack both intrinsic and extrinsic motivation to act, maybe because of a poor self-image, a poor image of the activity, or lack of interest, time or knowledge.

According to self-determination theory, one's motivation can be increased through a process referred to as *internalization,* in which individuals can choose to adapt to and accept values and behaviors that are not intrinsically appealing at first, especially as autonomy, relatedness and competence increase. For example, there are some students who are not exceptionally motivated to study apart from the grades they might receive. Suppose that one of those students began to feel more *competent* in her performance in a physics class as a result of excellent instruction. Imagine that she also gained an increasing sense of *autonomy* that resulted from her improvement in science skills and the resultant lessened need for tutoring. Also imagine that she began to make new friends who loved science, and they welcomed her warmly into the group (*relatedness*). According to SDT, this student would likely become motivated to study for sheer love for the material itself as opposed to the grades per se. (Strange as that may seem, it actually can happen!) Table 3.3 illustrates the main components of self-determination theory.

**Table 3.3. Self-Determination Theory and Motivation**

| Type of Motivation | Motivational Process | Example | Christian Considerations |
|---|---|---|---|
| Amotivation | No intent or desire to act. | "I have no interest or desire to change my racist thinking." | Under what circumstances might one's desire for external rewards be considered mature motivation? |
| External Regulation | Perform behavior to receive reward or satisfy some external demand. | "I have to avoid making racial slurs because I would get in trouble with my boss. And if I act as though I am not racist, my coworkers will commend me." | |
| Introjected Regulation | Behavior is performed, but not perceived as one's own. | "I guess if everybody else is talking about this 'diversity' issue, I should act as though it's important." | Living in community can encourage conformity to righteous living even when we are conflicted about our own views on the behavior. Is this motivation to conform necessarily "lesser than" intrinsic motivation, as suggested by SDT? |
| Regulation Through Identification | Behavior is personally important but is contingent on some external reward. | "I guess these diversity issues are important after all. And it's great that I also get acknowledged at work for my efforts at exploring multiculturalism." | |
| Integrated Regulation | Regulations are adopted into one's value system, but is still somewhat contingent on external rewards. | "I really believe in the value of diversity. And I also like being included in the "in-group" at work that is active in this effort!" | |
| Intrinsic Motivation | Motivation is internally generated; highest level of motivation. | "I believe that regard for dissimilar others is important in its own right. I will further the cause of diversity even if I am ostracized by my friends and relatives!" | How might the motivation that stems from a desire to follow God's divine command to love be related to intrinsic motivation? |

Deci & Ryan, 2002; Johnson, 2011.

Eric Johnson (2011) offers a Christian view of self-determination theory. He notes that the theory emphasizes the self, yet neglects to focus on the relational nature of self-control. Specifically, Johnson insists that from a Christian view, the capacity for self-regulation is a gift from God to help one serve others rather than primarily to help oneself. As will be discussed in more detail later, both a naturalist and Christian view of self-determination acknowledge benefits to self and others. A key difference between these two views is the primary function of self-determination.

Overall, despite the ongoing controversies, Baumeister (2005) notes that the empirical research provides much evidence for the existence of self-regulation and will. He stresses that the longstanding deterministic mindset of psychologists can be dangerous, as it may incline people who believe that self-restraint is nonexistent to act accordingly. As an example, Baumeister notes a study (Vohs & Schooler, 2003) in which the participants read one of several different messages regarding whether human will exists. Those who read the essay that claimed that no free will exists were more likely to cheat on a test that was administered to them than were the students who had not read that message. Imagine the many possible negative social implications of such a deterministic mindset ("I couldn't help but hit her"; "I was overcome by the desire to steal that shirt"; "I simply can't make better choices about relationships"; "I just have to overdrink because that is what college students do"; etc.).

Thus, contrary to the historically deterministic mindset of many social psychologists, the promising potential of self-control is now receiving much attention from social researchers (e.g., Tangney, Baumeister & Luzio Boone, 2004). Many of these studies have found high correlations between self-control and a wide variety of positive outcomes such as higher academic grades, interpersonal success, less pathology, better adjustment and so on. Self-control certainly seems like a very important virtue.

## Self-Regulation from the CFR View

From a Christian view of the human condition, the capacity to self-regulate is essential to our understanding of both individual and group accountability. This view assumes that in order to move toward the ultimate goal of loving community with God and others, an individual must be able to exert a measure of self-restraint and make choices that are good for others as well as for oneself. In addition, an individual must have the ability to be deliberate about the importance of engaging in other-centered social behavior that is often at odds with self-centered interests. The CFR view thus supports the notion of will that was articulated by Jones and Butman (1991): a Christian view of persons does not imply that we can act totally without restraint or influence on our will, but we still have a measure of the capacity to self-regulate as well as the responsibility to do so. As noted in the previous section, more recent research supports this belief in both the reality of human will as well as its potential.

While the CFR view assumes the presence of some measure of will, the focus of this approach for the purposes of this text concentrates on the relational and other-centered potential of humans, and not on the human will per se. Nevertheless, as Jones and Butman (1991) note, in order for humans to serve "as agents of reconciliation and renewal in human relationships," we must be able to make conscious, deliberate choices. Our choices are no doubt influenced, to varying degrees, by the interplay of our physiology, environment and past experiences. Nevertheless, from a Christian view, we act with at least a "limited freedom."

The moral implications of human will are significant. Both a Christian view of persons and, more recently, a naturalist view support the reality that human will exists. Both acknowledge, as Evans (2005) emphasizes, that without self-control, morality is not possible. Yet, of course, morality does not only include the ability to exercise one's will to choose rightly. One must be able to discern what "rightly" means in a given social context. Sometimes, those choices are clear. For example, imagine a situation in which someone rudely drives her car in front of another on the highway. In this case, while one may be tempted to retaliate, most drivers do not act so aggressively. (Unless of course you are in a major city such as Miami, Florida, where my family lives; they constantly tell me of stories of road rage being acted out!) In many cases in life, however, the choice may not be so clear or so easy to make. Many moral situations require the rightful distinction between exercising one's will to act in other-serving ways versus acting in a way that is primarily self-centered, and discerning the proper tension between the two.

At present, the social psychology research from a naturalist perspective still emphasizes the self-seeking goals (e.g., personal happiness and personal success) that can be achieved through self-control. A Christian view agrees that these personal goals are important and valuable. Beyond these personal benefits of self-control, social psychologists who support both a naturalist and Christian view would agree that exercising one's will to engage in seemingly other-centered behavior such as helping and restraining one's inclinations toward racist thinking are also valuable and necessary. There is one important distinction between the naturalist and Christian views of self-control, however. This distinction has to do with the potential and necessity of other-centered behavior. At present, social psychologists who use a naturalist view seem to be emphasizing the human capacity for self-control as the highest virtue. Self-control is, as Baumeister (2011) stated, "as close to penicillin as psychology is going to get" for curing social ills. (Wait: didn't we hear this type of claim before with regard to the potential of high self-esteem?) What happens to this capacity for self-control if the personal benefits that it affords are not possible or forthcoming? For what reason would an individual then persevere with self-control? Why choose to restrain some impulse if there is no guarantee that doing so will ever pay off?

From a Christian view, as Evans (2005) notes, the answer to these questions is based on the reality that self-control is not the ultimate virtue. Instead, submission to God's leading is of fundamental importance. Self-control may indeed be the penicillin for many social ills, but submission to God's command for other-centered love is the highest call of the Great Physician. Self-control is often a means to the end of submission to God. But this submission is a relational choice that transcends the particular situation. So we choose to forgive another not because of its benefit to self or even to other, but because of relationship with God. Indeed, Galatians 5:23 includes self-control as a fruit of the Spirit.

Past research has helped us better understand what circumstances tend to be related to people acting in seemingly other-centered ways. Despite the contributions of such research, it generally presupposes primarily (and often exclusively) self-centered motives. Future research could expand on the current self-control findings by exploring the process individuals go through to make deliberate self-sacrificing decisions that are related to participation in meaningful community. It would be interesting to investigate whether belief in a moral code enacted by a relational God results in a more enduring self-control when personal gains are not assured.

## SO FAR . . .

As the previous discussions demonstrate, both naturalist and Christian perspectives acknowledge the importance of the self and its development through social interactions. Both Christian as well as naturalist researchers who support an evolutionary model begin with the assumption that the self is an evolved construct whose ability to self-reflect and interact with others served specific adaptive purposes for our primal ancestors, and the maintenance of these behaviors harkens back to that time (Kurzban & Aktiptis, 2006; Sedikides, Skowronski & Dunbar, 2006). As noted in the previous chapter, a Christian view certainly acknowledges the innate drive for survival as part of our created nature. But from a Christian view, survival in this life is not an ultimate value. A distinguishing feature of the Christian approach is that it considers the self as part of a created being, and regardless of the method of its creation by God, its ultimate goals are loving relationship with God and others. In order to accomplish these ultimate ends, humans are endowed with an intrinsically relational nature and an innate capacity for genuine other-centeredness, even in this imperfect, fallen state. A realistic view of oneself is essential in this process, as is the acknowledgment of how the self is grounded in its relationship with others.

In addition, the CFR view considers human will as one of the important factors that makes meaningful community possible. Human will needs to be understood as part of God's created order and its most rightful expression as the result of submission to God's leading.

Understanding the characteristics, meaning and purpose of the self is an essential part of understanding human social interaction. This will become clearer as you read the following chapters. Notice for each topic how the intrinsically relational nature of humans is expressed. Also look for how the delicate tension between self-centered and other-centered tendencies will be reflected in all of the various social psychological concepts discussed. Also consider the relevance of human will in social interaction.

## QUESTIONS TO CONSIDER

1. Imagine that you are a researcher who holds the CFR view. What possible explanations would you propose for the finding that people seem inclined to compare themselves with others? Can you think of ways in which this tendency reflects both the way God created us *and* our fallen condition?

2. Even though the CFR approach assumes that humans have a tendency toward pride due to our fallen condition, this view would not necessarily hold that pride is an inevitable consequence. Based on what you know so far about the CFR approach, why is this so? In what ways might this compare to a naturalist view of humans as ultimately and inevitably self-seeking?

3. Do you think there are times when any of the specific self-enhancing strategies discussed in this chapter could be considered a way of acting in an other-centered fashion?

4. Imagine that you have conducted a study of a particular social behavior that entails great personal sacrifice on the part of the subjects. What criteria would you use to discern the degree to which the motives of your subjects are either self- or other-centered, or a mixture of both?

5. What observations have you made of the relational nature of humans at present?

## KEY TERMS

*abstraction models*
*amotivation*
*belief perseverance*
*collective self*
*collectivism*
*computational models*
*downward social comparison*
*egocentric*
*false consensus*

*false modesty*
*fundamental need to belong*
*individual self*
*individualism*
*internalization*
*intrinsic motivation*
*introspection*
*looking-glass self*
*optimal self-esteem*
*overconfidence effect*
*relational self*
*self-concept*
*self-determination theory*
*self-esteem*
*self-handicapping*
*self-monitoring*
*self-presentation/impression management*
*self-reference effect*
*self-regulation*
*self-schemas*
*self-serving bias*
*social comparison*
*sociocentric*
*sociometer model of self-esteem*
*spotlight effect*
*upward social comparison*

# 4

## Social Perception and Social Cognition

*Understanding Others and Our Social World*

*For now we see in a mirror, dimly, but then
we will see face to face. Now I know only in part;
then I will know fully, even as I
have been fully known.*

1 CORINTHIANS 13:12

### WHAT IS SOCIAL COGNITION?

When I am in an airport or some other public place, I like to people watch. I don't just look at the people walking by and say to myself such simple comments as, "Oh, there goes a man" or "There goes a child." I don't simply notice the observable facts as I see them. Rather, I am more inclined to form impressions of the people, even conjuring up stories to myself about their lives, when I haven't even spoken a word to them!

What information do you focus on when forming impressions of others? You may well have surmised that there are many factors that influence our impressions: physical attractiveness, age, gender, non-verbal cues, salient physical characteristics (e.g., a visible physical disability), social surroundings, your personal motives and so on. What cues do you look for when trying to assess social situations? Are you generally conscious of the process, or do you suddenly become aware that you had formed some opinion? How often have your initial impressions been accurate? How willing are you to have your initial impressions challenged? These are some of the questions that social psychologists have explored as they research the area of social perception.

Formally, *social perception* has to do with perceiving and understanding others. *Social cognition,* on the other hand, has to do with how we use cognitive strategies such as schemas to process and apply social information. For simplicity of wording, in this chapter the term *social cognition* will refer to both the process of perceiving others and the cognitive strategies we use for understanding our broader social world. Social perception and social cognition are intimately related and together are involved in all the specific social interactions that are covered in the remaining chapters. For example, social cognition is involved when one makes a prejudiced judgment of another or when deciding whether or not to help someone (e.g., "Is this person deserving of my help?" or "Would I endanger my own life by helping this person?").

You may ask why a separate chapter on social cognition is needed. Consider its potential to significantly affect our responses, future behavior and choices. In some instances, our perception can mean the difference between life and death (e.g., when perceiving another potentially aggressive person) or simply the risk of embarrassment (when speaking out in social psychology class). Obviously, the ability to correctly understand our social world is essential not only for survival, but also for quality of life. On the average day, social cognition mostly involves our understanding of others with whom we routinely come into contact but may also include our interpretation of the actions or intentions of political candidates, potential love interests or suspicious-looking persons on campus. Thus, social cognition is integral to our social functioning, and you will see examples of it throughout this text. But here the focus will be specifically on some of the most commonly used strategies for comprehending our complex social world and the inherent biases, strengths and limitations of these strategies. So, this chapter will focus on the types of information acquired and the many specific strategies we use for understanding our social world, while other chapters will focus on what happens as a result of that social appraisal (e.g., help or don't help; discriminate or don't discriminate; follow the group or don't; etc.).

## HOW ACCURATE ARE OUR PERCEPTIONS?

As you will read in this chapter, the research overall suggests that global evaluations of others generally happen quickly and with little information, and we tend to be overly confident in our perceptions even when faced with contrary evidence. How accurate are these perceptions of our social world? You will see that although researchers historically focused on the many systematic cognitive errors we make, more recent research in the field of cognitive psychology has suggested that humans are actually quite capable observers and interpreters of their social environment, albeit in imperfect ways.

And yet on a practical level, we see many examples of misperception, as when people who believed they had accurately perceived another person end up in a relationship with devastating consequences. Or consider how sometimes we make accurate assessments of others, while at other times we rush to judgments of racism or misplaced hate. How do we understand this apparent tension between humans' ability to adequately understand their social world while also at times making great errors that result in such negative outcomes? This question has been explored more recently by cognitive and social psychologists (e.g., Gigerenzer & Selten, 2002) who have studied the concept known as *bounded rationality*, which was first proposed by Simon (1956).

Bounded rationality means that humans are limited by a lack of time or cognitive space to develop optimal solutions or judgments. Instead, as Gigerenzer and Selten (2002) suggest, decision makers simplify the information they perceive or consider when trying to arrive at a rational decision or assessment about a social situation. They try to arrive at a rational judgment from that limited information, and the end result is what is called a *satisficer* or satisfactory solution that is good enough as an alternative to pursuing the optimal answer. In this respect, even when trying to make rational decisions regarding other individuals or about specific social situations, our brains are limited (bounded) in terms of the amount of information to which we can attend, and we try to make the best judgments based on that limited information.

Bounded rationality is a useful way to think about the cognitive limitations that make social cognition so complex. On the one hand, it assumes that we are able to perceive accurately enough to maintain a fairly well-ordered social life. On the other hand, it helps explain why we make so many errors, specifically because we cannot attend to all the relevant information necessary to have the optimal correct judgment each time. So, when engaging in social cognition, we save cognitive energy by using so-called fast and frugal strategies, such as heuristics, which will be discussed in this chapter. We use these strategies because we simply do not have the time or capacity to consider every single bit of information that would be necessary to arrive at a perfect assessment. Sometimes these strategies result in perceptions that are accurate enough; other times, the strategies result in errors with major consequences.

The concept of bounded rationality relates to the interesting discrepancy between how we perceive ourselves and how we perceive others. For example, remember the self-serving tendencies discussed in the previous chapter? According to that research, we tend to cut ourselves slack, especially when we attribute the causes of our failures to outside influences. In contrast, the research on social cognition suggests that while perceiving others, we are not as likely to afford that kind of grace. In addition, take note of the overconfidence that pervades our

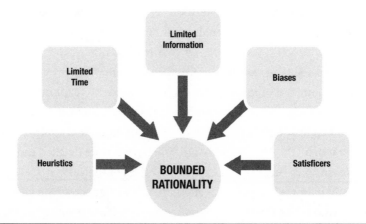

**Figure 4.1. Bounded Rationality**

sense of accuracy in our social perceptions, and recall the overconfidence effect noted in the self chapter. At face value, these errors seem to emerge from self-centered motives. But is that the whole story? Perhaps some of these seemingly self-centered errors are related to bounded rationality. We will return to that possibility toward the end of the chapter.

## BOUNDED RATIONALITY AND A CHRISTIAN VIEW OF HUMANS

The finding that humans are inescapably limited (bounded) in their capacity to thoroughly consider all relevant information is consistent with a Christian view of humans as finite beings. Specifically from the CFR approach, recall that though humans are created in God's image, we simply cannot process information to the same degree that God can. Consequently, we can make errors including distortions or misjudgments of others and of our social life in general, even when we are not trying to do so and we don't have any ulterior motive. As will be reinforced later in this chapter, our limited ability to accurately perceive others is not only due to the fallen human condition, but is indeed an integral part of our created nature. Knowing this limitation, we are challenged to take great care to learn how we might reduce the incidence of misperceptions that lead to destructive social consequences (e.g., socially excluding or aggressing against marginalized groups) and to act with humility about the possible errors in our perceptions.

As noted earlier, we are able to be rather accurate in our perceptions. How is our capacity for accurate social cognition related to the tensions between self- and other-centeredness inherent in the human condition? That is, how much does our capacity to express other-centered concern relate to our ability to rightly perceive the other and his/her circumstance? How does bounded rationality relate to sin? In order to explore these questions, let us focus our integration discussion in this chapter on the relationship between bounded rationality and the human condition from a CFR approach. The end of the chapter will have a more detailed discussion of these tensions. But let's first explore examples of the various specific processes and biases inherent in our attempts to understand our social world.

Note that while the various strategies we use for social cognition are discussed in different sections, this does not mean that these are mutually exclusive. In fact, the many different strategies we use for understanding our social world interconnect in many ways.

To sum up, remember that this chapter will explore:

- the many different conscious or unconscious strategies we use to understand our social world,

- the relative strengths and limitations of these strategies, and

- the tension between accurate social judgments and bounded rationality and the implications of this tension from a Christian view of personhood.

## THE IMPORTANCE OF EVALUATING WHEN PERCEIVING OTHERS

Before we begin to explore specific information and strategies that we use to understand others and our social world more broadly, it is important to note the significant role that evaluation plays when we are engaged in social cognition. Recall that in the previous chapter on the self, self-perception includes both self-concept and self-esteem, factors that each include an evaluative component. To evaluate the self, questions such as the following are typically asked: How attractive am I? How smart am I? How capable am I of performing well on this task? And so forth. This evaluative process is also involved when we are trying to perceive others. Wojciszke (2005) notes that a basic function of social cognition is an evaluative process that helps us discern between potentially harmful and potentially beneficial others. Thus, when trying to understand others, we rate them on various evaluative factors, such as their level of warmth, competence, trustworthiness and moral values. In addition, many researchers (e.g., Bargh, 1997; Dijksterhuis & Bargh, 2001; Zajonc, 2000) note that these evaluative processes often happen automatically, intuitively and outside of our conscious awareness. This is known as *automatic processing*. This is distinguished from *effortful processing*, which entails careful and conscious deliberation (Bargh, 1997).

Since initial impressions happen so quickly, can we tell what sorts of information people generally look to when making these fast evaluative assessments? Clearly, the information we are attuned to varies with the specific social circumstance. For example, if you were going to make a decision regarding which surgeon to choose for a significant upcoming surgery, you would likely be especially interested in information about the surgeon's competence. In this case, your perceptions would likely be based on effortful processing. By contrast, if you were trying to decide whether to go on one date with an attractive class member who just asked you out, you may not be so interested in that person's level of academic competence but instead focus on their physical attractiveness, sense of humor or ability to be easygoing. In this case, your processing might be more automatic as you form a quick initial impression of whether you like the person or not.

*Evaluating moral character.* The information we look for when first meeting others varies depending on the social circumstance, but a number of researchers have suggested that perceivers focus the greatest attention on information related to the other's values or moral character, especially when compared to other information such as level of competence. DeBruin and Van Lange (2000, as cited in Baron & Byrne, 2003), for example, conducted a study in which they gave subjects information about their partner for a mixed-motive game. This is a game in which, as in real life, there are pressures to both cooperate and compete with one's opponent. The participants were given written information regarding their partner's values and traits, which was either positive (e.g., this person is considerate and helpful) or negative (e.g., this person is inconsiderate and not helpful), and then about the partner's level of competence, either positive or negative. The participants took significantly more time reading over the information regarding their partner's values and traits when compared to reading information about the other's competence. This suggested a greater interest in the partner's values rather than the partner's competence.

In addition, participants took longer reading information that suggested negative values in the partner than they did when reading information that suggested positive values in the other. And after receiving negative information about the opponent's values, subjects spent less time reading information about that person's competence. This suggests the power of negative information about another, consistent with the *negativity effect,* where negative information more strongly influences our evaluations than does comparably extreme positive information (Cacioppo & Berntson, 1994; Fiske, 1980; Kanouse & Hansen, 1971). Ito, Cacioppo and Lang (1998) further demonstrated that negative information seems to register more strongly in the brain itself. They showed subjects negative, positive and neutral pictures, and found that subjects' brains experienced more pronounced evoked potentials (stimulation) when processing the negative photos.

The finding that we pay especially close attention to negative information about others is related to what was noted earlier about the importance of rating others' moral character. A single negative piece of information about the other's moral character can carry great weight in our perception of them and possibly alert us to risks. Wojciszke's (2005) research suggests that when forming global impressions of others, we tend to perceive the other's behavior in mostly moral terms. He further demonstrated that impressions and emotional responses to others seem to be more strongly based on perceived morality as compared with perceived competence. In an earlier series of studies, Wojciszke, Bazinska and Jaworski (1998) showed that when gathering information to form a global impression of another, perceivers were more interested in knowing about morality traits than competency traits. In addition, when later asked to recall their perception of the other, participants were more likely to remember morality traits than competency traits. When subjects were given a description of a fictitious character and were asked to develop a global impression of the person, participants tended to pay more attention to the characteristics related to the person's moral character as opposed to the characteristics related to the person's competency.

As noted earlier, the focus of our perceptions varies depending on the goals of the assessment. Nevertheless, the research suggests that on average, we are very concerned with the moral character of others as an overarching framework for developing impressions of them. Think of the example of the surgeon noted above. If you assessed that the surgeon is the most competent you had yet met, but you also learned that he or she tends to gamble away the family's money, that single bit of information may be enough to encourage you to pursue another physician. Similarly, our assessment of others' moral character helps us choose our friends, our romantic interests and potential spouses, employees and so on.

*Evaluating nonverbal cues.* Nonverbal cues such as facial expression, eye contact, tone of voice, hand gestures, body posture and physical appearance often command our attention when we are looking for information by which to assess others. These cues are important both when forming first impressions and when interpreting another's later behavior. In this section, the focus will be on the following specific nonverbal cues: eye contact (especially direction of eye gaze), facial gestures (especially smiling) and physical attractiveness.

Senju and Johnson (2009) note the importance of what is called the *eye contact effect,* which refers to how eye contact elicits activity in the parts of the brain related to social interaction. The direction of eye gaze (direct vs. averted), especially, is an important factor related to our perceptions of others. Macrae et al. (2002) review some of the research that indicates the importance of eye gaze as a variable in our interpretation of others. This social phenomenon begins in infancy, when infants prefer to look at the eyes rather than any other part of the face, and infants as young as four months old can discriminate between staring and averted eyes (Morton & Johnson, 1991; Vacera & Johnson, 1995, as cited in Macrae et al., 2002). This pattern continues into adulthood, and our ability to assess the nonverbal language of the eyes plays a crucial role in our social cognitions. Direct eye gaze can indicate both negative (e.g., potentially aggressive) as well as positive (e.g., romantic attraction) social information, and our perceptions in these cases influence our understanding of, and behavior toward, the other person.

Bradely et al. (2001) also note the importance of facial expression, specifically either smiles or frowns, in our perceptions of others. This is consistent with the work of Willis and Todorov (2006), who demonstrated that subjects took only 100 milliseconds to make trait inferences about faces they were shown. Bradely et al. cite the research of Winkielman, Zajonc and Schwarz (1997), who demonstrated the speed with which facial expression and affect can influence judgments. In these studies, subliminal priming was used to elicit an affective response to a target. Subjects were "primed" by being exposed to a smiling face, a frowning face or a neutral polygon presented for an interval that was so brief (1/250 of a second) that subjects could not even recognize or recall the stimulus later. After the subject was exposed to the stimulus, an ideograph was presented for two seconds. An *ideograph* is a symbol or character that represents an idea or object, such as that used in the Chinese written language. Then the subjects rated whether or not they liked the ideograph. The results indicated that for those ideographs that were preceded by smiling faces, the liking ratings were significantly higher than for those preceded by either neutral or frowning images. This priming effect was lasting, as was seen in a second session, where ideographs primed by the opposite "face" were not effective because the effect of the first priming had remained. This finding is consistent with what Berridge and Winkielman (2003) call "unconscious liking."

Some researchers have also found that not only subliminal smiles but also observable smiles can affect our judgment of others in rather profound ways. La France and Hecht (1995), for example, explored the possibility that transgressors who smile might be judged more leniently than those who do not. The researchers were also interested in whether the type of smile might produce different degrees of leniency. Subjects were asked to judge a case of possible academic misconduct and were shown a photograph of a female target either displaying a neutral expression, a sincere smile, a false smile or a miserable smile. The results indicated that overall, the smiling faces received more leniency than did nonsmiling faces, although they were not seen as less guilty. The type of smile was not significantly related to the amount of leniency given to the target. In addition, the researchers found that the variable that best explained this smile-leniency effect was the perception that the target was trustworthy.

Thus, as you might have expected, smiles are a good asset. They can influence our judgments of each other, boosting our chances of being well-perceived. But sometimes, of course, smiles can be upsetting; you would not, for example, want to see a professor smiling just after seriously criticizing your research paper. And certainly in other cases, a smile may be deemed annoying or insincere. But overall, smiling is more likely to lead to favorable impressions of others than are frowning or neutral expressions.

Facial expressions can, of course, be misinterpreted. These misinterpretations can lead to funny, embarrassing or otherwise unexpected consequences. Once, for example, a friend who was confiding in me noted how she appreciated the intense look on my face, which suggested I had been very attentive to her plight. Moments after she said this, I vomited from a case of food poisoning. The intense expression I had was actually due to nausea!

One last nonverbal cue (though not a behavioral one) to discuss is perceived level of physical attractiveness. Are beautiful people more likely to be perceived as having other positive qualities such as kindness, integrity and competence than are less attractive individuals? The short answer is yes, quite a bit, though not always. Researchers (Dion, Berscheid & Walster, 1972) have referred to this phenomenon as the *physical attractiveness stereotype,* or the belief that what is beautiful is good. This stereotype will be discussed in more detail in chapter ten on attraction, along with some of its limitations and qualifications (e.g., Eagly et al., 1991). For now, it is interesting to note how social cognition can often be significantly influenced by another's perceived beauty.

There are obviously many other nonverbal cues we "read" to form impressions of others. For example, body posture, tone of voice and hand gestures are also commonly observed nonverbal cues. In addition, Chaplin et al. (2000) showed that a firm handshake was associated with positive perceptions, especially for women, and they concluded that a firm handshake may be a form of self-promotion for women.

Clearly, accurately reading nonverbal cues also serves an important role in the building of community. For example, caring for others who have needs and concerns sometimes involves being able to discern subtle cues in the inflection of the other's voice or in a fleeting facial expression. This ability to "read" one another has more recently been impacted by the increasing use of technology for communication. For example, Rovai (2001) investigated how a sense of community can be encouraged in online classes, which have quickly become quite popular. Online classes at present most often involve communication through text and generally do not include video or audio cues. Many times, the professor and the students never actually meet. Thus, nonverbal cues like facial expressions and tone of voice, which we typically use to perceive others, are only indirectly available. In these cases, Rovai notes that a sense of community can be developed in these classes by increasing the amount of online communication between professor and students (e.g., regular feedback) and having students partake in regular discussions online.

***Evaluating behavior.*** Along with the more subtle or passive types of nonverbal cues we use to form impressions of others, more active or obvious behavioral cues are another important source of information for social cognition. We watch others' behavior for clues in order to form impressions of their motives, personality and so on. For example, Smith and Zarate (1992) note that we observe what are known as behavioral *exemplars,* or concrete examples of behaviors. We also make *abstractions,* or mental summaries, based on repeated observations of those behaviors. There is also *abstract trait knowledge,* in which we associate the behavior with some particular trait. Research suggests that we rely on these various sources of information at different times. Budesheim and Bonnelle (1998), for example, found in their studies that although abstract trait knowledge generally served as the basis for causal judgments, behavioral exemplars were used if they were easily accessible and participants were motivated to engage in effortful processing. For example, if you are highly motivated to assess someone accurately, then you would be more likely to pay close attention to specific behaviors that person engages in to draw your conclusions about them.

Some research suggests that when we are trying to explain another's current behavior, we retrieve examples of that person's past behavior from memory; other research indicates that we develop abstract trait knowledge when making such judgments. For example, when we first meet someone we may infer personal traits from the specific behaviors or exemplars we observe. But when we have had repeated interactions with that person, we can gather observations we have made of them across time and form impressions based on abstractions or mental summaries (Budesheim & Bonnelle, 1998; Karlsson, Juslin & Olsson, 2008).

***Warm or cold?*** So far in this section, we have been looking at how we use nonverbal cues, eye contact, physical attractiveness and larger behavioral cues when forming impressions of others. Is there evidence that we also form impressions of others based on single observed personality traits? In a series of classic studies, Asch (1946) explored this question and proposed that the *warm-cold variable* was an example of a personality trait that significantly affects our initial perceptions of others. The warm-cold variable reflects whether a person is described as loving, affectionate and caring or cold, distant and aloof. Think about the possible ways this descriptor might affect your impression of someone. Would you be more inclined to assume that a warm person also possesses other positive qualities as well, especially compared to someone whom you perceive as "cold"?

In one experiment, Asch gave two groups of subjects an identical list of adjectives that supposedly described an individual. The only difference between the two lists was that in one list the person was labeled as "warm," while in the other list, "cold" was used. When compared with the subjects who were presented the "cold" list, those with the "warm" list later described the individual with more positive descriptors from a list of paired opposites (e.g., honest or dishonest). Kelley (1950) later demonstrated how a preconceived notion of a person as warm or cold affects not only one's initial perception of the other, but also affects the likelihood that you are inclined to interact with that other person. In this experiment, students who were given biographies of a guest speaker in advance were more likely to rate him more favorably after the lecture if the biography included the word *warm* instead of *cold*. In addition, those students in the warm condition were more likely to interact with the guest professor during a twenty-minute discussion that followed the lecture.

Other studies have investigated alternative aspects of the warm-cold variable. Widemeyer and Loy (1988), for example, showed that the warm-cold variable affected students' perceptions of an alleged guest lecturer, and this effect held regardless of the students' major and gender. Specifically, the professor who was described as "warm" in the biography was rated as having many more positive personality characteristics than the professor who was labeled "cold." For example, the warm professor was deemed more effective as an instructor, less hostile, less irritable and more humane than his cold counterpart. Cuddy, Fiske and Glick (2008) further demonstrated that the warm-cold variable, along with one's perception of another's competence, are principal factors underlying every group stereotype studied across cultures. Additionally, Wojciszke, Bazinska and Jaworski (1998) demonstrated that the warm-cold variable, along with perceived competence, together account for the largest amount of variance (82%) in people's evaluation of social behavior. We should all, then, hope that others describe us as warm rather than cold!

Interestingly, recent studies by Williams and Bargh (2008) demonstrated that even *physical* sensations of warmth or cold can significantly influence the perception of relational warmth or coldness in another person. In the first study, unsuspecting subjects were asked by a confederate of the experiment to hold a cup of coffee for her while they walked together to the lab. The coffee was either hot or iced. When they arrived in the lab, the subjects read a description of a stranger and then had to rate the stranger on ten different personality traits. The results showed that those who held the hot cup judged the target person as being "warmer" (i.e., more caring) than did those who held the cold cup. In a second study, subjects were given instructions asking them to evaluate a

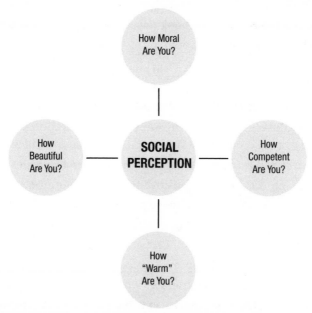

**Figure 4.2. Some Questions We Ask in Social Perception**

therapeutic pad that was either hot or cold. Later, when the subjects were given a small reward for their participation (either a bottle of Snapple or a dollar voucher for the local ice-cream shop), those who touched the warm pad were more likely to give the reward to a friend rather than keep it for themselves. Williams and Bargh conclude that we generally make warm/cold judgments very quickly and automatically. Figure 4.2 summarizes the different cues we look for when perceiving others.

*Web-based social cognition.* As noted earlier, the growing use of technology has led to increasing research exploring the manner in which various social psychological phenomena are enacted in the cyber world. For example, which cues online are used to form initial impressions of others? Weisbuch, Ivcevic and Ambady (2009) explored this question. They introduced individual university students to another "participant," who was actually a female confederate. The confederate and subject were asked to get to know each other by asking questions. The experimenter then left the room and returned after four minutes had passed. After a debriefing session, the participant was asked for permission to download his/her Facebook page. This page was then seen by other participants, who were asked to rate the target person (the one who had presented their Facebook page) with regard to likeability, the extent to which the judge would want to be friends with the target person, the extent to which the target person seemed attractive and the extent to which the target person seemed trustworthy.

The findings suggest that there is some consistency between first impressions formed in response to observations made in the real world and impressions based on information found on webpages. As noted earlier, a person's perceived expressivity (e.g., smiling) generally creates a positive first impression. In this study positive first impressions both in the real world and online indicated that those persons who showed nonverbal expressivity were given positive ratings. The authors conclude that though there are many qualitative differences between real-life social interactions and online interactions, it appears that both real-world and online perceivers use some of the same strategies when making first impressions.

Hancock and Dunham (2001) also explored how computer-mediated communication affects how we form impressions of another's personality. They had subjects participate in either a face-to-face interaction with a partner, or else a computer-mediated conversation in real time with an online partner. Subjects were then asked to rate the others' personality traits. The researchers found that those who rated an online partner made less detailed but more intense personality descriptions of their partners than did those who interacted face-to-face. The authors suggest that the more limited online cues regarding the other person may take on a more powerful meaning than if you had nonverbal cues to take into consideration when assessing another. Imagine, for example, you were rating the personality traits of a fellow student whom you had not previously met. Now suppose that you noticed that the student had left you a message regarding when to meet, and that message was full of spelling errors. When you actually meet, you may also notice that the student seems rushed and busy, as suggested by her rate of speech, glances at her watch and shifts in her chair. You may interpret the misspellings as the result of that students' busy schedule. But if you had only interacted with that student via text online and had not been able to observe her nonverbal cues, you may interpret those misspellings as evidence of carelessness and lack of regard for the importance of the meeting.

***How organized are our evaluations of others?*** Given the broad range of information available for perceiving others, it would seem that our chances are quite high of becoming confused with the various inputs. How well do we keep all the verbal, nonverbal and other behavioral cues straight in our minds in order to form a coherent evaluation of others? Hamilton, Katz and Leirer (1980) suggest that the various items of information we use when perceiving others are organized into a coherent cognitive representation. This organization of information, the researchers contend, facilitates later retrieval. They conducted a series of experiments in which subjects were shown a list of fifteen sentence predicates, each describing a specific behavior (e.g., "... took his dog for a walk" and "... watched a movie on TV"). Half of the subjects were told that this was an experiment on impression formation, and they should try to develop an impression of the person described by those predicates. The other half were told that this was a memory experiment, and they would be asked afterward to recall as many of the predicates as possible. Across three experiments, the subjects who were told it was an "impression study" had significantly higher recall for the predicates than did the memory group. This suggests that the impression subjects unknowingly organized the discrete bits of information into memory in a more effective way than the memory group did. Similarly, you may have noticed that grouping class material into more meaningful chunks helps you to better recall the information than if you simply memorized by rote a long string of seemingly unrelated material.

## PURPOSE OF SOCIAL COGNITION: *NATURALIST AND CFR VIEWS*

As noted in the chapter thus far, we use a wide variety of information to perceive others. We watch what others say, what they do and how they look to develop impressions that ultimately lead to a coherent synthesis of the other person. We are engaged in a constant process of noting, evaluating and drawing conclusions. We generally do this quickly and automatically, and we are often quite confident in our perceptions. This process entails error, as it is impossible to accurately perceive all the relevant information. And yet, on most occasions, we seem to be accurate enough in our perceptions to get along in our social world.

As we look at the social cognition research discussed so far, we see that the intrinsic relational nature of humans, included in both the naturalist and CFR perspectives, is supported. That is, social cognition is an inherently relational process. Other people's relational behavior influences our perceptions of them; likewise, our perceptions often influence their relational behavior. There is a closely intertwined feedback loop between social perception and social relationships.

We have also seen from the social cognition research that people place a high priority on judging each other's moral character. From an evolutionary view, the high priority people place on judging others' moral character makes sense from a survival standpoint. Cosmides and Tooby (1989, 1992), for example, hypothesized that the human brain has evolved a module that was adapted through the process of natural selection in order to facilitate the detection of individuals who are likely to act in egotistical manners and thus be unlikely to reciprocate or cooperate. From this view, the ability to detect another's integrity has implications for one's likelihood of survival. An evolutionary approach to social cognition also acknowledges that accurate social cognition enables many important prosocial behaviors (e.g., helping) to occur. Yet the primary focus of this research has reflected the naturalist view regarding how accuracy enhances self-protection and other social advantages. Haselton and Funder (2006), for example, noted that the human brain has evolved to perceive others with enough accuracy to at least promote survival and reproductive advantage. We can, for instance, make surprisingly accurate judgments regarding another's personality and likelihood of cheating us following very brief observations of the other. Given how important these types of judgments are for selecting future mates and friends, it would make sense that our brains have developed the mechanisms to judge these characteristics.

From a Christian view of persons, the naturalist focus on survival and other social gains as the primary origin and purpose of social cognition may have logical merit, but it is overly reductionist. To begin, remember the human potential for other-centeredness that is a central part of the CFR view of persons. From this view, social cognition plays a major role in not only self-protection and social gain, which are of course important, but also in the redemptive work of God in our own lives as well as those of others. The ability to perceive others—their feelings and intentions, their needs and so on—is necessary to fulfill God's purposes of community and of other-centered engagement and care. Furthermore, rightly perceiving each other is an essential part of the process of accountability, which often serves to enhance meaningful community. As the research in this chapter will further demonstrate, humans' capacity to perceive others is often more accurate than researchers had traditionally thought. This is not surprising from a Christian view of persons, which assumes that God created people with the tools for meaningful relationships, including adequate social cognition.

In the following section, you will read about additional types of strategies we use when perceiving others. Consider examples of each in your own life.

## STRATEGIES FOR SOCIAL PERCEPTION AND COGNITION

To review, we have seen that people use a broad range of information when perceiving others. This can include nonverbal information such as facial gestures and physical appearance, in addition to judgments of the other's moral character as well as specific concrete behaviors. We organize this information and form cohesive overall impressions of others. Now that we have reviewed some of the specific types of information we use to perceive our social world, let us look at the strategies we use to incorporate that information to form impressions and evaluations. Notice in the remainder of the chapter how the various strategies discussed can save us time and cognitive effort as we strive to move toward efficiency in our social perceptions.

*Categorization.* Suppose you are at a party where your new love interest also happens to be. Now suppose you had confided in a roommate about your new infatuation and learned that your roommate knows that person. Later that evening, you see your friend talking with your new love interest. You are initially pleased, figuring that maybe your roommate is complimenting you. But half an hour later you notice that they are still talking and laughing joyfully. You begin to question what is going on. Is your friend flirting with your new interest? Is he/she blabbing about your affections for that person? Can you really trust your friend? Is he/she still your friend, or has he/she become your betrayer or competitor?

This process of perceiving what groups another belongs to is known as *social categorization,* and it occurs on a daily basis. Macrae et al. (2002) note that when trying to understand others, we advance the process by relying on categorical thinking. Certainly categorical thinking can be efficient, because instead of having to perceive the details of others' individual attributes, proclivities and so on, we can use generic, category-based beliefs (stereotypes) to guide our dealings with them (Allport, 1954; Bodenhausen & Macrae, 1998; Macrae & Bodenhausen, 2000, as cited in Macrae et al., 2002). This type of categorizing thus saves times and cognitive effort and helps us bring order to an otherwise apparently chaotic social world.

When are we most likely to categorize others? Recall that others' facial expressions (e.g., angry vs. neutral) evoke immediate responses to them. It turns out that this feature also facilitates our categorization of that person. Specifically, based on the facial expression of the other, the perceiver tends to categorize him or her as friend or enemy, or as harmless or potentially harmful. This makes sense, doesn't it? After all, if your professor showed up for the first day of class with a scowl on her face, you might immediately wonder if she can be categorized as a fair grader or a nice person. You might wonder similar things about a date who shows up at your door with a friendly smile or a menacing frown.

To further explore the influence of facial expressions on our categorizing of others, Bradley et al. (2001) had subjects view pictures with different emotional and neutral content. They found that the strongest reactions (e.g., emotional arousal, skin conductance responses, cardiac deceleration) occurred when participants viewed pictures depicting threat. These faces would then be more likely to be categorized as enemies.

Recall that eye contact, and specifically eye gaze, is an important prompt for forming social judgments. Eye gaze can even affect the categorizing of another's gender. Macrae and Bodenhausen (2000), for example, asked subjects to view pictures of both male and female faces, presented one at a time, on a computer screen. Subjects were asked to identify as quickly as possible whether the person in the picture was male or female. Some of the pictures were presented with a full-face direct gaze, some with a three-fourths-face direct gaze, others with a lateral averted gaze (looking off to one side) and some with their eyes closed. The results indicated that subjects more quickly categorized the gender of faces with a direct gaze (whether full face or three-fourths-face) than of those faces that had averted glances or eyes closed. These results suggest the importance of eye gaze direction for our everyday construal of others.

Trying to classify others also often includes distinguishing whether the other is part of our own group (the in-group) or part of another (the out-group). Perdue et al. (1990) reviewed research (e.g., Hamilton & Trolier, 1986) regarding how the process of social categorization includes this type of distinguishing. People often come to believe that in-group members (us) are similar to them in ways that are unrelated to the specific criterion used for categorization (e.g., Spears, Doosje & Ellemers, 1997). So, if you met a new friend who is the same age and major as you, you might classify that person as part of the in-group and begin to make assumptions that he/she also agrees with you on other issues such as political views.

Perdue et al. also note that when categorizing others, the language we use to describe them is a major determinant of our perceptions. For example, words such as *we, us, ours, they* and *theirs* tell us something about the in-group or out-group status of people and thus have a significant influence on our perception of them. In both the group chapter (chap. 5) and the prejudice chapter (chap. 8), the impact of these in-group and out-group categories will be discussed.

The process of categorization thus brings order and efficiency when we perceive others and makes our social world more manageable. Gilbert et al. (1988) note that categorizing is one of the most common strategies we use to understand others, and often it happens outside of our conscious awareness. While there are benefits to categorizing, significant errors can occur, with potentially profound negative effects on our assessment of others. For example, categorizing a person from a different race than our own as a member of the "out-group" often results in prejudice. In the following sections, we will look at some other common strategies for social cognition and review both the benefits and drawbacks of these strategies.

*Attributions.* In everyday life, we don't just attempt to classify people into different groups. We also make inferences about the *causes* of others' behavior, our own behavior and all sorts of social happenings. These causal assumptions are called *attributions.* When we attribute a particular behavior or circumstance to a cause, we are going beyond merely observing and concluding that something has happened to understanding *why* it happened. Why was that man aggressive? Why did she say that to me? Why did I not answer back? Why does that person keep ignoring my really funny remarks? The impact of our answers to these sorts of questions suggests the importance of causal inferences in social cognition, especially when we are trying to understand the motives for another person's actions.

Many people claim that they have a good sense of what motivates or causes another's behavior. They might say something like, "I am a good judge of character. I can always tell if a person is being up-front." Despite these claims, it is often more difficult than we may think to interpret others' actions. Just think about what we have to do to figure someone out: we have to make assumptions about invisible constructs such as motives, intentions or character from visible behaviors that we can observe. This can get tricky; we can never measure directly the various motives of another (nor of ourselves, for that matter). We can, of course, make reasonable deductions about another's character, especially those whom we have gotten to know very well over the years. But even if we observe a consistent pattern in their behavior, can we be sure about what motivates it? Would the same motives apply to all people whom we have seen act in the same way?

Gilbert and Malone (1995) review three decades of research on what are known as *attribution theories:* theories that explore how people try to understand others by making causal explanations—or, as Kelley (1973) describes it, how we answer the question "why?" Gilbert and Malone state that while attribution theories differ in terms of their focus, they all explore how we distinguish between internal and external causes for others' behaviors and decide to which of these we should attribute the other's conduct (Fishbein & Ajzen, 1975; Bem, 1972; Hilton & Slugoski, 1986; Jones & Davis, 1965; Kelley, 1967; Medcof, 1990; Reeder & Brewer, 1979; Trope, 1986, as cited in Gilbert & Malone, 1995). In this context, *internal forces* refer to character and disposition, while *external forces* refer to situational variables such as time frame, peer pressure and so on.

Whether we attribute another's behavior to internal or external causes can have major consequences. For example, suppose your roommate accidentally stepped on the homemade cookies you had left on a dish on the floor. If you assumed it was because something tripped him or her (external force), then you might be inclined to accept his or her apologies while being disappointed at the loss of your scrumptious dessert. But if you assumed that your roommate stepped on the cookies because of their selfish or envious disposition (internal force), you may be less inclined to accept an apology and instead feel free to get angry.

When exploring the different ways in which we attribute causes to our own behaviors versus the behaviors of others, Jones and Nisbett (1971, 1972) describe an "asymmetry" of attribution, which they labeled the *actor-observer hypothesis*. In other words, when we try to explain our own behavior, we often emphasize situational or external causes. In contrast, when we try to explain the behavior of others, we emphasize internal or dispositional traits. Often, as noted in chapter three on the self, this works to our advantage. For example, if both you and your classmate responded harshly toward a particular professor, you would likely be especially aware of the possible situational causes of your behavior (e.g., midterm exams and the stress they cause). Yet, when observing another (in this case, a classmate), the person becomes the focus of our attention, and this presumably leads to our judgments of their character or disposition as the central cause of their actions.

Studies supporting the actor-observer asymmetry have been conducted numerous times, and the concept has widely been referred to as an integral aspect of the social condition of humans (e.g., Aronson, 2002). In one classic study (Jones & Harris, 1967), participants were asked to read speeches written by fellow college students that either favored or were opposed to Fidel Castro, the Communist leader of Cuba. The participants were told that the writer of the speech had free choice about the matter or else that the writer had been instructed on which position to take (no choice). Interestingly, they made attributions about the writer's position, regardless of whether they believed the writer had been told to take that pro-Castro stance. Students made negative attributions about the speech writer even when told that the speech writer was required to write in favor of Castro. This suggests that the subjects did not weigh the situational pressures as much as would be reasonable to do.

Another early study (Ross, Amabile & Steinmetz, 1977) of the actor-observer asymmetry involved basketball players who were randomly assigned to shoot free throws in either a well-lighted gym (favorable conditions) or a badly lighted gym (unfavorable conditions). On average, subjects rated those players who shot in the badly lighted gym to be poorer players than those assigned to the well-lighted court. This occurred despite the subjects' knowledge of the unfair advantage the players received in the well-lighted gym.

Closely related to the research on the actor-observer asymmetry is research on a concept known as the *fundamental attribution error* (FAE;

Ross, 1977; Ross & Nisbett, 1991). This refers to the tendency to explain others' behavior using internal attributions (e.g., character, personality or disposition) as opposed to external attributions (e.g., environmental/ situational influences). The FAE can occur when only a single behavior has been observed and situational factors are clearly influencing the behavior. Ross and Nisbett further state that people "assume a person has traits corresponding directly to the type of behavior that was exhibited" (p. 88).

To understand the FAE, imagine that you are in a long line at the campus bookstore. Suddenly, the student in front of you reaches the cash register and announces to the cashier in a harsh tone: "It's about time you got to me! I have been waiting forever! Hurry up!" What would you think about her at that point? Would you be likely to empathize with her, assuming that her behavior is due to stress from final exams, or would you consider her rude? According to the fundamental attribution error, your response to the above situation will likely be to think that the young woman's behavior is the result of her selfish, rude or egocentric personality. This explanation would take precedence over the possibility that she is in a hurry and feels pressured by the time constraints.

Gilbert and Malone (1995) describe a similar concept known as *correspondence inference bias,* or the tendency to infer that the actions of an actor correspond to or indicate stable personal characteristics. Gilbert and Malone note that this inference is susceptible to error because "when one infers the invisible from the visible, one risks making a mistake" (p. 21). Despite its connection with the FAE, the latter has received much more attention in the literature.

You could probably imagine both positive and negative outcomes of the FAE. Like categorization, attributing others' behavior to internal traits can serve as an efficient mental shortcut to facilitate our perception of others. This saves time and cognitive energy. But errors that can result from this strategy often lead to undesirable consequences. For example, one could perceive the plight of marginalized groups such as AIDS victims as the result of that group's internal dispositions (e.g., disregard for propriety, irresponsible behavior), and in doing so assign more personal responsibility for the disease than may be warranted. In this example, the FAE is similar to what is known as the *just-world phenomenon*

(Lerner, 1966, 1980; Montada & Lerner, 1998), which refers to assumptions that others "get what they deserve" and underestimations of the relevance of situational factors that may have contributed to or caused people's difficult circumstances.

Are there elements of the Christian faith that may incline us to engage in the fundamental attribution error? Li et al. (2012) suggested that a theological emphasis on the soul may incline Christians to more readily blame another for their actions. This is because believing that everyone possesses an individual soul that is accountable before God increases the belief in individual accountability, hence the greater propensity for making dispositional rather than situational attributions. Li et al. hypothesized that because the Protestant tradition places more emphasis on the inward state and beliefs of the individual (including the soul) than does the Catholic tradition, the Protestant subjects would be more inclined to make internal attributions about both moral and immoral actions that were presented in short scenarios. In a series of studies in which subjects' belief in the soul was primed (e.g., subjects being asked to write essays arguing in favor of the belief in the soul), Protestant subjects were significantly more likely than were Catholic subjects to make internal attributions regarding the subject presented in the moral scenario.

The findings of Li et al. may have important implications for Christians. Suppose, for example, that belief in a soul is indeed shown to be a significant motivator for making internal attributions. This knowledge could be used to help encourage Christians to be more cautious about jumping to conclusions about the reasons for others' actions. Nevertheless, as Li et al. acknowledge, further research in this area would need to assess religiosity with more precise measures. In addition, future research would need to explore how belief in a soul may be related to making both accurate (rightly discerning) and inaccurate (unduly harsh) internal attributions, and how the tension between the two presents a significant challenge for many believers.

So, what conclusions might we draw from the attribution research presented so far? Overall, the findings suggest a relatively self-centered approach to making attributions. Let's consider the example of how we tend to explain negative behavior. First, the research suggests that we

are often focused on finding self-serving ways to attribute our own negative behaviors to environmental causes. Sound familiar? This is consistent with the self-serving bias you read about in the last chapter.
Second, we appear more likely to attribute others' negative behaviors to
their own disposition, while underemphasizing possible situational
variables that might be impacting that behavior. This difference in the
way we make attributions about our own versus others' negative behaviors reflects a self-seeking way of understanding the complex motives for social behavior. It also reminds us of the scriptural admonitions
against harsh judgments of others, especially as these judgments tend to
downplay our own sin (Mt 7:3-5). The actor-observer difference arguably illustrates an important bias in social cognition and helps explain our propensity to make the sorts of quick evaluations against
which the Scriptures give so many warnings. But are the research
findings as consistent as they appear at first glance?

Despite the contributions of the attribution research noted in the previous discussion, there are some inconsistencies in the data. For example, though there seems to be overwhelming evidence for the actor-
observer bias, a meta-analysis of 173 studies revealed that this concept is
actually not well supported by the literature (Malle, 2006). In fact, Malle
found that "a large number of studies that found no or even opposite
evidence had never entered the scientific discourse, the qualitative reviews, or the textbooks" (p. 491). Why might the actor-observer bias not
be as prevalent a phenomenon as previously thought? Malle and his
colleagues think that to distinguish only between person variables and
situational variables as the causes of behavior is too simplistic. They
have instead developed an attribution model they call the *folk-
conceptual theory of explanation* (Malle, 1999, 2004; Malle et al., 2000;
O'Laughlin & Malle, 2002, as cited in Malle, 2006). This model proposes
that if one examines people's attributions for everyday behaviors, it becomes apparent that they do not attribute those behaviors to simple
person-versus-situation terms. Instead, their explanations are often embedded in a complex folk-conceptual framework, which includes as a
central element distinctions between intentional and unintentional behavior (Buss, 1978; Malle, Knobe & Nelson, 1997; White, 1991). People

explain intentional behaviors very differently from unintentional behaviors, and they apply a variety of explanation modes to intentional action beyond the classic person-situation dichotomy (Malle et al., 2000).

Malle et al. do not deny that actor-observer differences in explanations of behavior occur, but rather that these differences have more to do with the different types of events the actor and observer are describing (e.g., actions vs. experiences), the modes of explanation and even the specific language used to express these explanations. So, according to this view, the differences are more complex than a simple actor-observer difference based mostly on making internal vs. external attributions. And in further considering the related fundamental attribution error (FAE), Malle et al. argue that when people make attributions about another person's behavior, they are not trying to explain that behavior per se but rather trying to determine whether that behavior is characteristic of the person. Furthermore, the FAE has to do with trait inferences from behavior, whereas the actor-observer asymmetry concerns overall explanations of behavior.

*Covariation and attributions.* Kelley (1967, 1973) also explored factors involved in attributions regarding another's behavior. He proposed the *covariation model,* which states that a person will associate a particular behavior with an apparent cause that covaries with it. In other words, a behavior is attributed to events or conditions that appear at the same time (see table 4.1).

**Table 4.1. Kelley's Covariation Model**

| Possible Causes of Behavior | | | |
|---|---|---|---|
| | **Person** | **Object** | **Situation** |
| Factors affecting attribution for the observed behavior | *consensus* (How similar is this person's behavior to that of most others in that situation?) | *distinctiveness* (Is the individual's behavior unique to that situation, or does it occur across situations?) Low distinctiveness means that the person behaves similarly in all situations, and high distinctiveness means that the person only shows the behavior in certain situations. | *consistency* (Is the person's behavior the same the next time the situation occurs?) |

**Internal attribution** (cause of behavior attributed to the person): If consensus and distinctiveness are low, and consistency is high. **External attribution** (cause of behavior attributed to the environment): If consensus, distinctiveness, and consistency are all high.

Source: Gilovich et al., 2006; Kelley, 1950, 1967, 1973

To better understand Kelley's covariation model, let us consider an example. Many years ago, I had a neighbor who screamed at my roommates and me if our trash can was even slightly on his side of the shared driveway. (I hasten to add that this situation with the trash can happened maybe three times in the two years we were neighbors.) The neighbor's aggressive response surprised me, and I confess that I could not resist forming a negative impression of this man. Based on the covariation model, my negative impression formed because I attributed his behavior to internal causes. That is, I attributed his screaming to a personality flaw (internal attribution) rather than to the misplaced trash can or other life stressors (external attribution).

According to Kelley's model, I attributed the neighbor's behavior to internal causes because of the low consensus, low distinctiveness and high consistency I observed in his behavior. With regard to low *consensus,* I would have observed that this neighbor's behavior was not the same as others' behavior in this context: most other neighbors would probably not have screamed at us. As for low *distinctiveness,* I observed that the neighbor's behavior was similar in other situations: he often refused to say good morning to us and also was often rude to his wife. Thus, there was nothing distinctive about the screaming. And finally, the neighbor's behavior had high *consistency,* because he was rude to us each time the trash was left on his side of the driveway.

Note that I was not conscious of the process of making internal attributions of this man's screaming behavior, nor did I sit at the kitchen table with my roommates, reviewing Kelley's criteria to make a psychologically sound conclusion. Kelley assumed that causal attributions typically happen in an automatic, unconscious manner, though upon conscious reflection, one can recognize these three types of distinctions.

A number of studies have provided support for the covariation model. Yet others (e.g., Malle, 1999) have suggested that the model is too simplistic, as we often do not have access to all three kinds of information when we are judging the cause of another's behavior.

Regardless of which process is used to describe the way we understand our social world, we have seen that errors occur in our perceptions. What remedies are there for these errors? A number of attribution theorists (e.g., Jones & Davis, 1965; Kelley, 1967; Stewart et al., 2010) have developed possible strategies for avoiding impulsive overgeneralizations about another's motives. First, we should be mindful not to attribute another's behavior to any single causal agent. Second, we should practice being more deliberate in considering the impact of possible environmental factors on others' behaviors. Certainly, these cautions do not suggest that one needs to dismiss the potential relevance of personal accountability as a motivator of behavior. Instead, we are reminded of the delicate balance that often exists in making social judgments. These specific cautions are especially helpful for Christians when discerning sin in others, as well as in ourselves.

*Heuristics.* Another strategy for social cognition consists of "mental shortcuts" known as *heuristics.* These are shortcuts we use to interpret social situations when we don't have enough time or information to process all the details. Heuristics save us much-needed time and cognitive energy. Often, the heuristic leads to accurate perceptions, but other times, heuristics lead to errors in judgment. Consider one example. Imagine that you have just seen broad media coverage of an airplane accident. Two days later, you are asked what you think the chances are of being involved in an airplane crash. In this case, you might tend to think it is more likely than if you had not seen that news coverage. This is an example of the *availability heuristic,* which has to do with judging the probability of some event from the ease with which information about it is brought to mind (Tversky & Kahneman, 1974). The more easily we recall something, the more likely we are to think that it is more likely to happen and more dangerous than something we don't recall but is actually objectively more likely to happen. For example, after the 9/11 attacks in New York City and Washington, D.C., many Americans likely thought the probability of a terrorist attack on U.S. soil was greater than was the probability of an American developing colon cancer. In fact, the probability of developing colon cancer was (and remains) much higher. In the case of the availability heuristic, an individual disregards or underestimates the base rate (i.e., actual statistical frequency) of an event or situation, sometimes leading to overresponding and other times to underresponding. In the case of some medical conditions such as colon cancer, this can result in a dangerous underestimation of likelihood and a failure to take adequate precautions.

Related to the availability heuristic is the process known as *priming*, which occurs when information becomes more available in your memory as you are exposed to it. For example, suppose your school held a week-long racial reconciliation workshop for students. During this time, you heard many stories about racial incidents that have occurred on your campus. Then suppose that the following week, you and your friends are talking about your perceptions of racial incidents in the community surrounding your campus, and you all agree that there must be many such occurrences. This perception may be due to the ease with which racial incidents come to your mind after having spent a week hearing about them. When exploring the strong potential effect of priming, some researchers (e.g., Bargh & Pietromonaco, 1982) have suggested that priming can often occur outside of our conscious awareness (*automatic priming*).

Tversky and Kahneman (1974) noted another heuristic, which addresses such questions as: What is the probability that object A belongs to class B? What is the probability that event A originates from process B? And so forth. When answering such questions, people typically rely on the *representativeness heuristic*. In this heuristic, individuals rate the likelihood that A belongs in category or group B based on how much A resembles B. For example, suppose that you were told about a woman who loves to read, is methodical, and is also introverted and soft-spoken. Then you were asked to judge the likelihood that she is a librarian versus the likelihood that she is a nurse. Using the representativeness heuristic, you would be more likely to guess that she is a librarian despite the fact that there are many more nurses than librarians. In this case, as Tversky and Kahneman suggested, you would be ignoring important information such as the higher base rate of nurses as compared to that of librarians.

Another process related to the above-noted heuristics is known as the *anchoring effect*, which is the tendency to rely too much on (or to "anchor") your decisions or judgments on one specific trait or piece of information. For example, Tversky and Kahneman (1974) asked subjects to guess the percentage of African nations that were members of the United Nations.

Before guessing, one group was asked, "Was it more than 45 percent?" The other group was asked, "Was it more or less than 60 percent?" The results indicated that those in the first group (45 percent) guessed lower values than did those in the second group. This suggests that the single bit of information given to them significantly affected the subjects' perception by anchoring their responses with a reference point.

*Affect.* The heuristics discussed so far have focused on how we make sense of our social world through strategies related to the way we think. But what about the importance of *affect* in understanding our social world? Affective responses have to do with a feeling state regarding the "goodness" or "badness" of some stimulus. These reactions help guide judgments or decisions, and they typically occur quickly, automatically and sometimes outside of our conscious awareness (Zajonc, 1980). Zajonc was among the first to explore the power of our affective responses, stating, "We do not just see 'a house': We see a handsome house, an ugly house, or a pretentious house" (p. 154). He adds, "We sometimes delude ourselves that we proceed in a rational manner and weigh all the pros and cons of the various alternatives. But this is probably seldom the actual case. Quite often 'I decided in favor of X' is no more than 'I liked X'. . . . We buy the cars we 'like', choose the jobs and houses we find 'attractive', and then justify these choices by various reasons" (p. 155).

Slovic et al. (2002) likewise argue for the importance of affect in guiding judgments and decisions. Specifically, they propose that people use an *affect heuristic* to make judgments. According to this view, when making judgments and decisions regarding a specific situation or person, we consult an "affect pool" that contains all the positive and negative responses that we have consciously or unconsciously associated with the specific social situation.

Sherman, Kim and Zajonc (1998) explored the effect of priming subjects with positive or negative affective cues by asking subjects to study Chinese characters and their English meanings. Half of the meanings were positive (e.g., "beauty"), while half were negative (e.g., "disease"). Then participants were given a test of these meanings. After this, subjects performed a task in which they were asked their preference from a pair of Chinese characters. Characters with a positive meaning were preferred 70 percent of the time.

Next, the same characters were presented with neutral meanings (e.g., "chair," "sheet"), and subjects were told that these were the "true" meanings. Subjects were again asked to choose from each pair of characters. Despite having learned the new meanings, the characters that had been initially paired with positive meanings still were generally preferred.

Mellers et al. (1992) suggest that the more precise the affective impression, the more powerful its effect on decision making. For example, how positive would your initial impression of a potential date be if all you knew was that she/he was intelligent? What if all you knew was that she/he can be obnoxious?

Numerous studies have demonstrated the importance of affect in guiding decisions. For example, Hsee and Kunreuther (2000) found that subjects would be more willing to pay for insurance for a "beloved" antique clock that cannot be repaired versus another one for which the person has "no special feeling." Hsee and Menon (1999) likewise found that subjects were more willing to buy a warranty on a car they had just purchased if it was a beautiful convertible versus if it was an ordinary-looking station wagon. This was true even if the expected repair expense and cost of the warranty was the same for both cars.

Lowenstein et al. (2001) suggest that the power of affect to influence our judgment or response also depends on how important the outcome is. When the stakes are high, people tend to size up the situation with an all-or-nothing affective response. Thus, actual probability would have very little effect on one's judgment or behavior. For example, upon hearing that one has cancer, it would matter little that the likelihood of dying from cancer is actually quite low. In this case, the person would be more likely to concentrate, at least initially, on the daunting possibility of dying. Likewise, if one were faced with the news that one's child had been involved in a car accident, the immediate response would likely be a strongly affective one (e.g., fear, dread), despite the fact that the incidence of fatalities or serious injuries is quite small for car accidents. In either case, the affective response is very strong and contributes significantly to one's preferences and behavior. Thus, Lowenstein et al. conclude that in cases where the stakes are high, people are more sensitive to *possibility* than to *probability*.

Alhakami and Slovic (1994) also demonstrated the strong relationship between affect and perceived risk/benefit of an activity (e.g., using pesticides). They found that perceived benefits and risks of an activity were related to the strength of positive or negative affect associated with that activity. If a person likes an activity, they are more inclined to judge the risks as low and the benefits as high; if they dislike the activity, they are more likely to judge the opposite—high risk and low benefit. Thus, in addition to our *thoughts* about something, our *feelings* also have a significant impact on our judgments about it.

It is possible that affect is also related to the biases in probability and frequency seen in the availability heuristic. Specifically, Lichtenstein et al. (1978) suggest that availability works not only through ease of recall, but also because remembered and imagined images are associated with some affect. For example, these researchers explored why the frequencies of highly publicized, yet less probable, causes of death (e.g., accidents, homicides and cancer) were relatively overestimated, while underpublicized, yet more probable, causes (e.g., diabetes, stroke, asthma) were underestimated. The researchers suggest that the highly publicized causes of death are more affectively charged—that is, more sensational—and this may account both for their prominence in the media and their relatively overestimated frequencies.

Thus, it appears that affective responses are closely linked to the cognitive strategies (e.g., heuristics, attributions) we use for social cognition. This combination of cognitive and affective responses significantly affects the way we perceive others and social situations in general. Given that affect can be such a powerful contributor to our social perceptions and decision making, it should be no surprise that we can be quite vulnerable in response to efforts to manipulate our affective responses. We also should recognize our own influence on others when we present emotional appeals in an effort to persuade them or otherwise influence their decisions. Similarly, this finding of the strong connection between affect and social cognition is an important consideration for spiritual transformation in Christians (Hill, 2002). We will look more closely at this in the persuasion chapter (chap. 6).

**Additional biases in social cognition.** So far in this chapter, you have read about the various specific ways in which we try to understand our social world, including the speed with which we form initial impressions of others, the importance of evaluation in that process, the different nonverbal cues we look for to make those assessments and the specific mental shortcuts we use to assess social situations and make decisions. Those processes highlight our tendency to use strategies that save us cognitive time and energy but sometimes lead to errors in social cognition. So far in this discussion, the major focus has been on how we perceive other people. The following sections will instead focus more on biases in the way we perceive social situations in general.

You will recall that the processes we use for perceiving others and for perceiving events are related to each other. So in the following sections, note the connections with the previously noted strategies.

*Narratives.* How we understand our social interactions can be affected by a number of factors. Baumeister and Newman (1994), for example, suggest that we use a *narrative approach* when trying to understand our life events. According to this view, we construct narratives, or stories, about events and think about them in affective terms, usually in a way that reveals a self that is positive and competent. As Mitchell and Thompson (1994) note, all these events have different components that are combined into an overall summary evaluation. We could, for example, change, forget or reconstruct various components of the experience, and these changes would alter the overall evaluation of the event.

The specific components of our social world that we focus on also affect our overall evaluation of an experience. For example, if your beloved announces that he/she is going to break up with you, your response to that news could vary, depending on your focus. If you choose to focus on the possibility that you were both too young to be involved in such a serious relationship and you can now explore other possible relationships, or that now you have some time to travel independently, you might have a more positive perception of the breakup. But if your focus is on how miserable the process will be of ending this relationship and restructuring your life without your beloved, your response is likely to be more negative. Obviously, in real life, most such important situations are not so simplistic, and we often experience ambivalence. Nevertheless, the research suggests that our focus plays an important role in our perception of events.

*Hindsight bias.* You may have heard of the phrase "the Monday-morning quarterback." That is the person who says what the coach or players should have done in the game, after the outcome is already known. Or perhaps you have experienced a friend commenting that she "knew it all along" that you would be accepted by the graduate school of your choice. Maybe your professor has just gone over a complex math problem, and after you see the answer, you think to yourself, "Of course! I could have gotten that!" These are all examples of the *hindsight bias*, which is also known as the "I-knew-it-all-along" phenomenon. This is the tendency to believe, once the outcome is known, that you could have foreseen it.

The early work of Fischhoff (1975) investigated whether people tended to be more confident regarding their judgment of information if they had not known the correct answer versus if they had been told the correct answer ahead of time. Subjects were given historical scenarios (e.g., the nineteenth-century war between the British and Gurkhes of Nepal). In the *foresight condition,* subjects had to give confidence ratings for four possible outcomes without knowing which of them had actually occurred. In the *hindsight condition,* subjects were told the actual outcome and then asked to state their hypothetical confidence had they not been told the actual outcome. Subjects with hindsight were significantly more confident about the actual outcome.

Hoffrage, Hertwig and Gigerenzer (2000) cite numerous studies that have found support for the hindsight bias in a diverse range of situations. These include political events (Fischhoff & Beyth, 1975; Pennington, 1981), medical diagnosing (Arkes et al., 1981), outcomes of scientific experiments (Slovic & Fischhoff, 1977) and economic decisions (Bukszar & Connolly, 1988). It seems everyone is an "expert" after they know the outcome!

*Primacy and recency effects.* Many times, we must draw conclusions about social situations or persons on the basis of information that is acquired over time. The information that is available early in this process is often weighted more heavily than is information that is obtained later on. This is known as the *primacy effect,* which is based on the early work in memory by Ebbinghaus (1885). This effect results in the early information taking on a disproportionate importance, and increasing the chances that it will be remembered more than will later information (Lingle & Ostrom, 1981). Opinions formed early in a process can thus have a significant effect on information that is gathered later, which is often interpreted in a way that supports one's initial impression (Nisbett & Ross, 1980; Webster, 1964). The primacy effect may be related to *belief perseverance,* in which once a belief or opinion is formed, it can be very resistant to change, even in the face of contrary evidence (Freedman, 1964; Ross & Lepper, 1980).

Also related to the primacy effect is the *recency effect,* which is the tendency for individuals who are asked to recall a list of words or information to start with the items at the end of the list, which are fresh in one's memory. Taken together with the primacy effect, memory seems best for early items and later items in a list or sequence, as compared to items in the middle of the list.

Primacy and recency effects can influence a broad range of social judgments. For example, a number of studies (e.g., Anderson & Hubert, 1963; Jones & Goethals, 1972) found that primacy effects can influence impression formation. When Asch (1946) presented a series of adjectives describing a person, the first adjectives were found to have more impact on impressions than did the later adjectives. When adjectives with more positive meaning were given first followed by words with less positive meaning, the participants tended to rate that person more positively. Yet, when the order was reversed, participants tended to judge the target person less positively. Thus, the same words used to describe a person could yield very different ratings of that person depending on the order in which the words are presented. Birnbaum (1974), however, found that when using words with strong negative meanings, the negative words seem to overwhelm the positive descriptions of the target person, whether they are presented first or last. This finding is consistent with the negativity bias noted earlier this chapter.

Another example of the influence of the primacy and recency effects on our social perceptions is seen in the political campaign process. Political candidates routinely invest the most amount of money on campaigning toward both the beginning and end of the campaign, with the hope that voters will consider these messages the most salient and remember them. Likewise, if you are initially reluctant to help an elderly family member, but then spend several months helping out, then at the end get tired and start to complain, the person might not as easily recall all the help you gave them during that intervening time.

*Illusion of control.* Sometimes the way we perceive social situations involves the error of thinking that we have more control over a situation or outcome than is objectively the case. This is known as the *illusion of control* and even happens in games of chance (Langer, 1975). In a series of classic studies, Langer demonstrated how the illusion of control is at work in gambling situations. In one study, subjects played a card game of chance with an opponent who either seemed nervous and clumsy or with an opponent who seemed confident. As predicted, the subjects overestimated the likelihood of winning against the nervous opponent, despite the reality that the game's outcome was due to chance. Subjects overestimated their own ability to outwit their opponent.

The illusion of control has been linked to the positive effects of optimism on mental health. Presson and Benassi (2003), for example, found that higher levels of depressive symptoms are associated with *lower* levels of the illusion of control. Alloy and Clements (1992) investigated the effects that the susceptibility of the illusion of control has on immediate emotional reactions to failure in a lab as well as to actual negative life events. Their results suggested that subjects who were more susceptible to the illusion of control tended to experience less immediate negative mood following the lab failure, less discouragement after real-life negative events, and less depressive symptoms a month later after a high number of negative life events.

Presson and Benassi (1996) conducted a meta-analysis of fifty-three studies of the illusion of control. They found an interesting link between hindsight bias and the illusion of control in these studies. Specifically, there were larger effect sizes with subjects' perception of their ability to *predict* outcomes versus subjects' perception of their ability to *control* outcomes.

*The rosy view.* Despite all the media coverage regarding the prevalent rates of depression in the U.S., a significant amount of research (e.g., Diener & Diener, 1996) suggests that in general, most people report being happy and have an optimistic view of life, thinking that they are more likely than the average person to experience positive life events and less likely to experience negative events (Shepperd, Ouellette & Fernandez, 1996). This so-called *optimism bias* is pervasive. In fact, in many cases, people tend to be optimistic both before a life experience (*rosy prospection*) as well as afterward when recalling that experience (*rosy retrospection;* Mitchell et al., 1997). This is true even when the experience of the actual event is negative. Mitchell et al. note that it is not that people don't enjoy their experiences, but rather that relative to their before and after ratings, the enjoyment of the intermediate experience is less.

Rosy prospection and rosy retrospection can both significantly affect the way we perceive social life events. Bartlett (1932, as cited in Mitchell et al., 1997) suggests that remembering involves active reconstruction, and this reconstruction is often significantly different from the truth of the experience. This rosy view varies with the situation. For example, there are some life experiences that we consider to be too painful to either anticipate with joy or recollect later as rosy in any way. Nevertheless, even in extremely frustrating situations, people often recall the incidents that happened with a much rosier view than when they were going through the process.

Mitchell et al. (1997) investigated the rosy view by assessing subjects' anticipation of, actual experiences in and later recollection of various life events: a trip to Europe, a Thanksgiving vacation and a three-week bicycle trip to California. All three studies supported their hypothesis that expectations of personal

This isn't so bad . . . last year I was Mary's donkey.

**Figure 4.3.**

events are often more positive than the actual experience during the event itself, and subsequent recollection of that event is more positive than the actual experience.

A personal example of rosy retrospection occurred in the spring semester of 2001, when I took a group of students to study with me in London. When we were getting ready to come back to the States, one of those students went to a local post office in London to mail some boxes back home. She returned to our flat a few hours later, sweating and huffing. She spoke endlessly about the rude post office staff and the long lines and waiting she endured. Several years later, as we were reminiscing about the trip, she laughed aloud and asked me if I remembered how "funny" that incident was. I could hardly believe my ears: was this the same young woman who had just a few years earlier complained bitterly about that very experience? Think about your own experiences with rosy retrospection; what possible reasons might you have to remember some difficult trials with such fond recollection?

*Counterfactual thinking: "What if?"* One winter morning, shortly after I dropped off my kids at school, a car came up quickly behind me on the icy Minnesota road. The driver slammed into the passenger side of my car and caused my car to spin out of control, but fortunately I made it to the side of the road without causing further accidents. The man in the passenger seat of the other car motioned to me to remain seated, implying that they would get out to survey the damage. Instead, they suddenly sped away before anyone was able to get their correct license plate number, and I was left with my car totaled.

After recovering from the initial shock and calling the police, I became furious that anyone would commit a hit-and-run accident. My feelings and perceptions about that event over the next week, however, varied with my focus and my imagined alternative outcomes to that accident. What if the children had still been in the car at the time of the accident? They both sat on the passenger side and, given the degree of damage to those doors, would certainly have been hurt. And if the other car had hit me even harder, I could have been hurt as well. When I concentrated on those outcomes, my perception of the event included a sense that I had been "lucky" despite the difficulties involved.

This process of imagining alternative outcomes to past or present events or situations is known as *counterfactual thinking*, literally, "contrary to the facts" (Byrne, 1997; Kahneman & Tversky, 1982; Roese, 1997). It is something that we do fairly routinely. Kasimatis and Wells (1995) note that nearly everyone generates counterfactual thoughts, regardless of intellectual or verbal skills. In what specific ways have you imagined what might have been: What if your parents had never met, or what if you had not signed up for that course where you found your favorite subject, or what if you had chosen to go to the restaurant on the night that there was a shooting? Counterfactual thinking also includes regret: If only I had studied harder. If only I had not taken that book that didn't belong to me. And so forth. As Douglas Hofstadter (1979) indicated, "Think how immeasurably poorer our mental lives would be if we didn't have this creative capacity for slipping out of the midst of reality into soft 'what ifs'!" (p. 643).

Several researchers (e.g., Markman et al., 1993; Roese, 1994, as cited in Epstude & Roese, 2008) distinguish between two possible types of imagined alternative outcomes. *Upward counterfactuals* are involved when one imagines a better outcome than actually occurred. This usually doesn't end with your feeling happy about the circumstance. *Downward counterfactuals* have to do with imagining worse outcomes than actually occurred. In these cases, one generally feels better about the outcome that actually did occur.

Related to the distinction between upward and downward counterfactuals is the *functional theory of counterfactual thinking*, reviewed by Epstude and Roese (2008). According to this view, counterfactual thinking serves the function of managing and coordinating ongoing behavior. Roese (1997), for example, notes that counterfactual thinking can have an affective purpose by making us feel better (e.g., imagining a far worse outcome than was actually the case—downward counterfactuals). He notes that counterfactual thinking can also help improve future performance when one imagines a possible better outcome that could happen if behavior were different (upward counterfactuals). Epstude and Roese note that counterfactual thoughts are typically activated by a failed goal. These thoughts specify what one might have done differently to have achieved that goal (Markman et al., 1993; Roese, Hur & Pennington,

1999). From this view, counterfactual thinking may be a useful and even necessary component of behavior regulation. So, if you had just failed an exam due to lack of studying, you might imagine what could have happened if you had adequately studied, conclude that you would have done better had you studied and perhaps study more the next time.

Despite the potential for counterfactual thinking to improve future performance, Mandel and Lehman (1996) note some possible difficulties with this type of thinking. One possible problem occurs when people focus on some controllable choice they made (controllable antecedent) that is not really of value for determining the outcome across cases. Mandel and Lehman give the example of saying to oneself, "The accident would not have occurred if only I had taken a different route." While this may be technically true in this one instance, the reality is that one could encounter a careless driver at *any* intersection (and also that one cannot know in advance where careless drivers will be). Thus, unrealistic regret may be a potentially devastating consequence of counterfactual thinking. Mandel and Lehman suggest that it would be more productive to concentrate on antecedents that are both controllable and related to your target outcome.

*Illusory correlations.* Have you ever noticed how many things in life seem to co-vary (i.e., happen at the same time)? For example, have you ever sworn that it rains every time you have just washed your car? Or have you had that uncanny experience of reading ahead for a class only to later discover that the professor has just chosen to delete that reading for this semester? You are convinced that reading ahead for class is associated with a higher chance that your professor will cancel that reading assignment. A very common occurrence in social cognition is that, as we try to make sense of our social world, we commonly assume meaningful correlations between events or situations. The reality is that many of these things that appear to be related are not statistically related at all or not to any significant degree. These thoughts are known as *illusory correlations,* which are the perception of a relationship between two variables when in actuality there is at best only a minor relationship between the two, or when no relationship exists at all (Chapman & Chapman, 1967). People sometimes assume that because two events occurred together at one point in the past, one event must have caused the other.

Illusory correlations are especially common for infrequent events, which are generally more easily remembered than are more frequent events. Because infrequent events are relatively more easily remembered, they seem more significant, and when judging their covariance with another event, we tend to disproportionately weight them.

Hamilton (1981) suggests that both positive and negative stereotypes are a good example of illusory correlations. People tend to assume that certain groups and traits occur together, and frequently overestimate the strength of the association between the two variables. Hamilton explains that when perceiving a target person from a social category, overestimations of the occurrence of negative behavior associated with that social group lead to negative stereotypes of that individual target person. Conversely, he gives an example of how a positive stereotype may result from an illusory correlation. For example, someone may hold the mistaken belief that all people from small towns are extremely kind, and when meeting a very kind person, the immediate assumption might be that the person is from a small town. This happens despite the lack of evidence that kindness is related to city population.

*Confirmation bias.* As you recall reading in the previous chapter, *confirmation bias* refers to looking for evidence that supports your initial claim. Nickerson (1998) notes that confirmation bias refers to a variety of phenomena, all of which include an inappropriate supporting of hypotheses or beliefs whose truth is in question. Nickerson further notes that confirmation bias usually occurs in less conscious ways than when one is deliberately trying to find evidence (e.g., a legal inquiry). Yet this presumed line between deliberate analysis of evidence versus unconsciously weighting some piece of evidence more than others is a fine one to draw.

Nickerson reviewed the literature regarding the different components of confirmation bias. This research suggests that people tend not to seek, and perhaps even to avoid, information that would challenge their initial hypotheses or beliefs, to give undue weight to confirmatory evidence, and to devalue negative, disconfirming evidence (Koriat, Lichtenstein & Fischhoff, 1980; Pyszczynski & Greenberg, 1987, as cited in Nickerson, 1998). Woods, Matterson and Silverman (1966) noted this in the so-called *medical student syndrome*. After learning about a specific illness and its symptoms, the student may look for those symptoms in his or her own body, thus increasing the chances that they will find them even if they are within normal limits. I warn my students of this every time I teach Abnormal Psychology.

Confirmation bias may lead to many errors in perception of others and of social situations. One area in which this bias may be relevant is in the development of stereotypes. As noted earlier, stereotypes often involve believing that certain specific behaviors are more common among certain groups of people (gender, racial group, ethnic group, age group, etc.). These correlations between group and behavior may or may not be accurate. Nevertheless, once you are convinced that members of a specific group behave in certain ways, you are likely to seek and find evidence to support that belief and oppose evidence that contradicts it.

Table 4.2 summarizes some of the benefits and drawbacks of the various social cognition strategies outlined in the preceding sections. Think about some possible examples of each of these in your own life. What other risks and benefits can you see as you engage in each of these strategies or biases?

Table 4.2. Examples of Benefits and Limitations of Some Social Perception Strategies

|  | Benefits | Drawbacks |
|---|---|---|
| Counterfactual thinking | Can cause us to imagine ways in which we could do things differently (better) the next time | Can cause us to condemn ourselves for past mistakes; can give us the illusion that things would have turned out better if only we hadn't made the choices we did. |
| Rosy retrospection | Can enhance mood and help us keep past experiences in perspective. | Can cause us to minimize negative information from the past that should be a focus of our current attention. |
| Representativeness heuristic | Can help us make quick and often accurate assumptions about someone when we have little time to process. | Can cause us to make hasty generalizations about others and may lead to negative biases/prejudices. |
| Availability heuristic | Can alert us to probable outcomes, especially when we have little time to process the different possibilities. | Can cause us to overestimate how probable something really is. |
| Affect heuristic | Spontaneous, strong emotions can lead us to discern correctly when they are a response to hidden issues that are obscure to our conscious awareness. | Can cause us to make erroneous conclusions about others and about social situations, especially when the affect is strong or easily elicited. |

## THE (IN)ACCURACIES OF SOCIAL COGNITION: *BOUNDED RATIONALITY AND A CHRISTIAN VIEW*

The discussions in this chapter highlight the complexity of social cognition, both in terms of motivating factors and of consequences. It can be unsettling to consider the important implications of our social judgments, especially when we understand how quickly many of these judgments occur. Consider the variety of important decisions that result from our perceptions: Whom will our friends be? Whom will we hire? Whom might we hate? Whom will we blame? Will we perceive a certain situation as beneficial or destructive? The list goes on and on.

The ability to make wise decisions about others and about our social world in general is based in large part on our ability to make accurate social judgments. Yet, the research discussed throughout this chapter suggests that the accuracy of our perceptions can be significantly reduced in many cases due to a number of reasons. For example, recall the *speed* with which we make many of these judgments. The discussions so far have demonstrated that we often save cognitive space and time by using mental shortcuts to estimate probabilities or to make causal attributions.

The accuracy of our social judgments can also be reduced by *competing motives,* such as a desire for heightened self-esteem, control and cognitive consistency (Pyszczynski & Greenberg, 1987). As one example, at times accuracy may not be as highly valued as the need to make oneself look good, as when a person deliberately judges another as incompetent, thereby elevating one's own status in comparison. Sometimes those competing motives are not conscious, yet they still impact the accuracy of our judgments. You have seen in this chapter the human proclivity toward efficiency in our judgments: how can we make the most accurate perceptions in the shortest amount of time possible, using the least amount of cognitive resources?

Source: http://www.webdonuts.com/2012/04/favor/

**Figure 4.4.**

When trying to understand social cognition from a Christian view of persons, it is helpful to review two specific aspects of social judgments. First, as noted earlier in this chapter, the CFR view holds that despite the seemingly endless errors in our social judgments, humans should be capable of a higher degree of accuracy than the research has suggested until recently. This is because the ability to accurately perceive others is an essential component of our ability to engage in meaningful, loving community. If our social perceptions mostly comprised error, we would be very limited in our ability to respond to others in loving ways because we would have a very difficult time judging the needs of others or responding to social situations.

In addition to the CFR view that humans are capable of a significant amount of accuracy in social judgments, a second principle has to do with the *limits* of our ability to be accurate. Knowledge of the factors that affect our social judgments can help us understand the human condition from a Christian view. Of prime importance is the consistent finding that while errors in social cognition can be reduced, they are to some degree unavoidable. Even if we were able to identify every single error in our perceptions, we would be unable to totally eradicate faulty perceptions. This is not fatalistic thinking; it is a realistic appraisal of humankind and is consistent with the CFR view of humans as finite beings.

In this section, then, let us consider the research in social cognition from the CFR view of humans as capable of accurate judgments but unable to avoid inaccuracies. To this end, let us first consider the historical research bias toward finding errors in perception and the more recent attention being given to perceptual accuracy and the potential benefits of heuristics. Next, research regarding the limits of accuracy will be discussed with a focus on the concept of bounded rationality. Finally, possible ways in which a Christian view of persons is relevant to both of these lines of research will be discussed.

*Accuracy revisited.* As noted earlier, the accuracy of our social judgments has wide-ranging implications for day-to-day situations and for major events in our lives. All of the areas of social interaction that are discussed throughout this text (e.g., helping behavior, stereotypes, group behavior) are significantly influenced by the ways in which we assess social cues. It comes as no surprise, then, that researchers have studied the types of biases and systematic errors we make in our social cognition (e.g., Gilovich, 1991; Nisbett & Ross, 1980; Jost & Kruglanski, 2002). These findings have been very helpful for increasing our understanding of some of the specific ways errors in judgment occur and also ways to help remediate these errors.

As Jussim (2005) notes, however, researchers have traditionally shown much less interest in the *accuracy* of our social judgments. The idea that we are actually capable of considerable accuracy in our social judgments (e.g., Funder, 1999) has only more recently gained significant attention. Jussim (2005) argues that accuracy research is essential if one is interested in correcting systematic errors.

More recent research in the area of social cognition has suggested that humans' capacity for accuracy in social perceptions is higher than traditionally thought. But the concept of accuracy itself has been a controversial one. On what basis, for example, do we define accuracy? To what degree is it based on actual objective criteria or on the subjective perception of an individual with specific goals and motives? Jussim (2005) provides an extensive review of the literature on accuracy in social cognition. He refers to this accuracy as *probabilistic realism*. The word *realism* in this context refers to the belief that there exists an objective reality that is independent of our perceptions. *Probabilistic* refers to the fact that most criteria and social beliefs are probabilistic, not absolute. Jussim gives the example of children who have a high IQ. Those children have a high probability of doing well in school, but there is no guarantee that they will do so. In addition, if you believe the political candidate that you voted for is the best one for the job, you do not also have to logically believe that he or she will always make the right choice. Thus, Jussim argues that "accuracy is rarely all or none; it is usually a matter of degree" (p. 5). Thus, flawed and imperfect as we may be, we can come to know reality at least much of the time.

Jussim (2005) further states that accuracy and bias can coexist, and that certain biases can in fact enhance accuracy. For example, in a study of college students, those who relied most on stereotypes (biases) regarding categories of students ("preppy," "hippies") who chose to live in different residential halls were most accurate in their judgments regarding particular individual residents (Brodt & Ross, 1998, as cited in Jussim, 2005). Similarly, Diekman et al. (2002) suggest that beliefs about whole populations are usually, though not always, at least moderately accurate. Ryan (2002) further notes that when assessing accuracy, we must be careful to note what level of analysis we are engaged in. For example, accuracy in perceptions of large populations may differ from accuracy of perceptions of smaller groups and of individuals. Absolutist stereotypes, which involve the belief that all members of a particular group have some specific attribute, are almost always inaccurate.

Thus, as Jussim (2005) suggests, a balanced understanding of both accurate and inaccurate biases is helpful in working toward a reduction of systematic errors in social cognition and the potential consequences of those errors (e.g., discrimination, racism). Certain biases that are accurate may seem politically incorrect or offensive. For example, the bias that African American males of a certain age group are more likely than males of the same age from other ethnic backgrounds to be engaged in violent crimes is true statistically (Hagan, Krivo & Peterson, 2006). The acknowledgment of this information can help us discover the sources of this crime and help ameliorate them.

Another more recent line of research addressing accuracy in social cognition emphasizes the advantages of *heuristics*. Recall that these are mental shortcuts we use in our social judgments. These help us to make sense of our social world. When faced with uncertain events (e.g., the likelihood that a candidate will be elected), we tend to rely on a limited number of heuristic principles that reduce the complexity involved when we are trying to assess probabilities. Earlier work (e.g., Tversky & Kahneman, 1974) suggested that these heuristics were often full of error. More recent research, however, has emphasized the potential accuracy of heuristics. Heuristics have been referred to as "fast and frugal" strategies that are part of what Gigerenzer et al. (1999) say constitute an "adaptive toolbox" that evolution has built in the human mind for specific types of inference and reasoning (Cosmides & Tooby, 1992; Payne et al., 1993, as cited in Todd & Gigerenzer, 2007). According to this view, heuristics often lead to accuracy because they are the result of the adaptive processes of evolution, culture and learning. These forces have shaped human minds to be rational by relying on simple decision heuristics that give us both speed and accuracy in specific environments.

Green and Mehr (1997, as cited in Gigerenzer, 2008) demonstrated one example of the benefits of heuristics. The researchers worked with physicians in a hospital where the intensive care unit was overcrowded. This overcrowding was due to the physicians cautiously assigning patients who were suspected to have heart disease to the intensive care unit. The researchers developed a heuristic consisting of a "fast and frugal decision tree" that enabled physicians to more accurately predict heart attacks than when using complex decision strategies.

Obviously, errors in perception can occur if individuals use heuristics in inappropriate environments. Yet, Todd and Gigerenzer (2007) note that these errors are examples of the boundaries of a mechanism's ecological *rationality* rather than its irrationality. *Ecological rationality* has to do with statements such as "Heuristic A is more frugal or accurate than is Heuristic B in Environment X." "When mind and world fit together, the evolved capacities, building blocks and simple heuristics in our adaptive toolbox can guide us to make good choices in a fast and frugal manner" (p. 208). In further emphasizing the potential accuracy of heuristics, Gigerenzer (2008) argues that heuristics are not always "second-best" strategies, and in fact can often result in more accurate judgments than can more complex decision strategies.

**Limits to accuracy: Bounded rationality.** So, social cognition entails error, but it also has much more potential for accuracy than has traditionally been thought. How, then, does accuracy get distorted? The concept of *bounded rationality* may help us better understand how this occurs. Recall that the concept of bounded rationality, introduced at the beginning of this chapter, (Simon, 1956; Gigerenzer & Selten, 2002) refers to the reality that we are limited (bounded) in our decisions because we do not have the time or cognitive capacity to always achieve optimal solutions or judgments. Instead, we simplify the information we look for when trying to arrive at a decision or assessment of a social situation, and from that limited information we try to make a rational judgment. Thus, as you may recall, the end result is that many decision makers become what are called *satisficers,* accepting a satisfactory solution that is good enough for our purposes rather than finding the optimal answer. In this respect, even when trying to make rational decisions regarding other individuals or about specific social situations, our brains are limited in terms of the amount of information to which we can attend, and then we try to make the best judgments based on that limited information.

Bounded rationality is a useful way to think about the cognitive limitations that make social cognition so complex. On the one hand, it assumes that we are able to perceive accurately enough to maintain a fairly well-ordered social life. On the other hand, it helps explain why we make errors, specifically because we cannot attend to all the relevant information necessary to have the optimal correct judgment each time. So, we save cognitive energy by using the so-called fast and frugal strategies, such as heuristics. We use these strategies because we simply do not have the time or capacity to consider every single bit of information that would be necessary to arrive at a perfect assessment. Sometimes these strategies result in perceptions that are accurate enough; other times, the strategies result in significant errors in perception.

*A Christian view of accuracy and its limitations.* When considering the potential for accuracy in social judgments, a Christian view of persons can begin by considering the purpose(s) of social cognition. As noted earlier, the CFR view holds that humans are created by God with the potential for other-centeredness, which necessitates an adequate amount of accuracy in our social perceptions. As already stated, accuracy serves to enable us to discern the needs of others and also enables us to make wise, godly decisions in a wide variety of social settings.

Proposing that accuracy in social judgments primarily serves to enable us to engage in other-centeredness does not discount other important reasons for accuracy. For example, many researchers have argued that a main purpose for accuracy in social judgments is that it enhances our chances of survival and social gains. This is especially true when we can perceive who is deceiving us or who intends to harm us. Clearly, if we did not have enough accuracy in our perceptions, socially and otherwise, we would almost certainly die because we would not be able to discern danger. The survival value of accurate social judgments does not conflict with a Christian view of persons. Nevertheless, once again we see the difference in emphasis between a naturalist and a CFR view. Specifically, the CFR view proposes that survival is an important, though not ultimate, motive for humans. Our capacity to be other-centered and accurate in our perceptions of others may lead us to act on their behalf and at times jeopardize our own survival.

Even though humans are capable of a significant amount of accuracy in social judgments, the research clearly suggests that we are inescapably limited (bounded) in the capacity to consider all relevant social cues. As noted earlier, these limits are consistent with a Christian view of humans as finite beings with a need to be humble about ourselves. Phelps's (2004) example of human memory as reliable and efficient as well as error prone and limited can be instructive here. As noted in chapter two, Phelps suggests that in addition to errors that occur as the result of sin, some of "the limits seen in human cognition are inherent and purposeful in God's creation of finite beings rather than the result of sin or moral evil." Phelps further states that proper acknowledgment of one's cognitive limitations can help prevent pride, as they emphasize the glory and power of God in contrast to his limited creation. From this view, human cognition is capable of much accuracy, and the distortions that do occur in our social judgments exist both because of sin and also because of our good, limited, creaturely nature. This is consistent with the concept of bounded rationality.

There are several possible research emphases that a Christian view of humans could suggest regarding social perception and cognition. First, it would be helpful to investigate how people perceive destructive social conditions as a function of hope, cynicism and apathy. In other words, is a person who has hope for redemptive work to occur more likely to consider simultaneously the realistic gravity of the situation as well as the hope for change than would someone who is either cynical or apathetic? And how might these differences in perspective also mediate one's likelihood of participating in that specific redemptive work?

Another research direction could include a greater focus on individuals who appear to have particularly good social cognition and investigate how the specific strategies those people use may be used to teach others. This would be more than simply assessing accuracy on various perceptual tasks (e.g., visual perception tasks), but rather would also include more closely studying those whose life in general seems to exemplify good discernment and judgment in a variety of contexts.

An interesting idea to ponder is whether, if there were no sin, there would not be painful social interactions. But this is not necessarily the case. Some interactions might still be painful due to misperceptions. Even if one had more humility, empathy and openness with regard to their social judgments, they would still make mistakes. Perhaps, then, one sign of other-centeredness is the willingness to humbly acknowledge one's own limited capacity to perceive instead of harshly judging another's.

## So Far . . .

The research in social cognition presents an image of humans as efficient, reasonably accurate, yet also prone to error in our social judgments. The research also suggests a tendency to judge others rather quickly. Many of our social judgments help us organize the complexity of our social world. Yet many times, we hold fast to our impressions despite evidence that contradicts our judgments.

From a Christian view, we can readily see the tension between self- and other-centered motives in the processes we use to form social judgments. In addition, from both naturalist and Christian views, we can see the vital role that accuracy in social judgments plays in a well-functioning social world. We must recognize both our potential for accuracy as well as our vulnerability to distortion in social cognition; both are relevant to our understanding of all the social processes discussed in the remainder of this text. Consider, for example, in the following chapter on conformity and obedience, the role that social judgments play in our willingness to be influenced by others.

## Questions to Consider

1. Do you think that the same error in social cognition could be at one time due to sin and at another to the inherent limitations of a limited created being and other times to both? If so, how would we know the difference?

2. In what ways might the goals of studying perceptual accuracy from a naturalist view be similar and different than from a Christian view?

3. What is your understanding of the hope regarding social cognition that a Christian view of persons offers? What might this view neglect to consider?

## KEY TERMS

*abstract trait knowledge*
*abstractions*
*actor-observer hypothesis*
*affect*
*affect heuristic*
*anchoring effect*
*attribution theories*
*attributions*
*automatic priming*
*automatic processing*
*availability heuristic*
*belief perseverance*
*bounded rationality*
*confirmation bias*
*correspondence-inference bias*
*counterfactual thinking*
*covariation model*
*downward counterfactuals*
*ecological rationality*
*effortful processing*
*exemplars*
*external forces*
*eye contact effect*
*folk-conceptual theory of explanation*
*functional theory of counterfactual thinking*
*fundamental attribution error*
*heuristics*
*hindsight bias*
*ideograph*
*illusion of control*

*illusory correlations*
*internal forces*
*just-world hypothesis*
*medical student syndrome*
*negativity effect*
*optimism bias*
*physical attractive stereotype*
*primacy effect*
*priming*
*probabilistic realism*
*recency effect*
*representative heuristic*
*rosy retrospection*
*satisficer*
*social categorization*
*social cognition*
*social perception*
*upward counterfactuals*
*warm-cold variable*

# 5

# Social Influence

*Conforming Groups and Obedient Individuals*

*Do not be conformed to this world,*
*but be transformed by the renewing of your minds,*
*so that you may discern what is the will of God—*
*what is good and acceptable and perfect.*

**ROMANS 12:2**

## WHAT IS SOCIAL INFLUENCE?

Everywhere you look in our social world, you can see the powerful effect that humans have on each other. Consider all the people who have influenced your own beliefs, attitudes and behaviors. What about your own impact on others? All of these are examples of *social influence,* the process by which individuals alter each other's attitudes, feelings and behaviors as a result of their interaction. Research in the area of social influence covers a broad range of issues such as conformity, obedience, group processes, persuasion and attitudes. Arguably, every topic that social psychologists study involves some measure of social influence. As you have already seen in this text, the degree of influence we can have on one another is significant and sometimes staggering. Since social influence is so powerful and it can be used for both positive and destructive ends, understanding the factors that are relevant to it is of utmost importance.

The first part of this chapter will focus on group processes, which are a key to how a lot of social influence occurs, especially conformity. This chapter will also explore the concept of obedience as one of the many responses to social influence as well as the integral role of conformity and obedience within God's redemptive plan.

## WHAT IS A GROUP?

There is some controversy regarding the nature of a group. For example, is a group a distinct entity apart from the individuals it comprises (the group is greater than the sum of its parts)? Or is it true that "there is no psychology of groups which is not entirely or essentially a psychology of individuals" (F. Allport, 1926, p. 4)? In this text, it is assumed that group processes represent the forces inherent in the condition of the individual humans in the groups, hence both the productive and destructive potential of groups.

I'm sorry, Rev. Greer, sir, but the board just vetoed your proposal to increase defense spending.

**Figure 5.1.**

Levine and Moreland (2006) offer a helpful way to conceptualize groups and how they help fill different individual needs. Acknowledging that a group consists of two or more individuals, they review the literature regarding the various key characteristics of groups, including cohesiveness, communication, influence and interdependence. As an alternative to focusing on these characteristics, Moreland (1987) instead suggests that we think of *groupiness,* or social integration, which is the degree to which sets of people freely interact in a wide range of experiences, have a shared history and expect future interaction. From this view, a family or group of friends would have a high degree of groupiness, whereas a group in a theater has a low degree of groupiness. This way of categorizing provides a more general description that takes into account many characteristics of groups as noted above.

A definition of groups also entails considering how groups fulfill certain needs for individuals. Levine and Moreland (2006) review this research (e.g., Baumeister & Leary, 1995; Forsyth, 1999) and suggest the following key needs that groups fulfill:

- Survival (mutual protection, fighting against enemies, etc.)

- Psychological needs (e.g., avoid loneliness, exert power and influence, etc.)

- Informational needs (e.g., help members evaluate their opinions)

- Identity needs (provide a collective basis for beliefs about oneself— "We are Minnesota Vikings fans," "We are poets," etc.)

Thus, a group varies with respect to certain essential characteristics (e.g., cohesiveness) as well as the degree and type of personal needs it fulfills (e.g., security or identity). It is also interesting to note that one could feel a deep sense of connectedness with others whom one has just met simply by virtue of being perceived as being members of a common group (e.g., racial group). For example, if you are traveling abroad and meet a fellow native of your country of origin, you could instantly feel a sense of connection with that person than would usually occur between members of a longstanding group who have known each other a long time. In addition to the purposeful nature of groups, group membership is part of the richness of life.

*The prevalence of group membership and conformity.* Group membership is inevitable. Every single person belongs to a variety of groups by virtue of their age, gender, geographic location, profession, racial and ethnic origins, and so on. In fact, our identity is based largely on group membership (remember this from the chapter on the self?). Our identification and interaction with the various groups to which we belong vary, of course. Clearly, for example, you are typically much more aware of and interactive with your family and friends than you would be with groups to which you belong simply because you fit the category of that group (e.g., redheads or left-handers). You may have observed that in informal social settings, groups seem to naturally emerge even when there are no previously agreed-upon criteria for group membership.

The inevitability of group membership raises some interesting questions regarding the purpose of groups. Some groups (e.g., sports teams) have clearly defined purposes, while others are more by chance (e.g., an audience in a theater). Groups are one of the most powerful entities in human social interaction. As history and your own observations have doubtless shown, groups can be powerful forces for the good and the bad.

***Groups and other social psychological concepts.*** As you read this chapter, keep in mind the close connection between the concept of a group and the other social psychological principles presented in this text. For example, consider the research on the self. A group is a collection of selves, and thus we can logically expect that group behavior reflects to some degree the tendencies and potentials seen in individuals. As one example, consider how the self-serving bias can be amplified in the group context, resulting in a *group-serving bias*. Taylor and Doria (1981) showed that groups tend to make favorable attributions for their own successes and downplay the favorable qualities and successes of other groups. This is related to the research on *social perception:* groups must also perceive each other and make attributions about each other's motives and intents. As with individual social perception, one group's ability to accurately perceive another is limited, as suggested by the concept of *bounded rationality,* which you read about in the previous chapter. As you will see in the remaining chapters, group behavior also has important implications for research in prejudice, helping and so on. In short, as with all other social psychological concepts covered in this text, this separate chapter on groups should not lead us to believe that group behavior is independent of the social tendencies inherent in it.

*An evolutionary view of groups.* Brewer and Caporael (2006) review the research regarding evolutionary perspectives toward groups. They note that humans are dependent on collective knowledge and cooperation for our very survival. Boinski and Garber (2000) note how for evolving hominids, finding food, defending oneself and others, and moving across a landscape were largely group processes. More successful groups survived. In addition, so would individuals who were more suited for group living, thus the shift toward cooperative groups.

Brewer and Caporael (2006) point to our hairless, relatively weak bodies and our extended infancy as evidence that we are not suited for individual survival or even for survival in small family units. This produces what they call *obligatory interdependence* (Caporael & Brewer, 1995). From this view, the researchers argue that the longstanding debate in social psychology regarding the potential for other-centered concern (altruism) versus inherent self-centered concern is a false either-or dichotomy. They argue instead that the concept of obligatory interdependence helps explain how other-centered concern can be exhibited. They offer the example of a parent in a group demonstrating concern for another parent's children. Brewer and Caporael note that this concern is not associated with genetic relatedness, but rather with the fact that survival of one's offspring depends on the community. Thus, the children that a parent looks out for will be more likely to help that parent's own children later on, thereby increasing the chances of survival of one's offspring. Looking more closely at Brewer and Caporael's understanding of other-centered concern, one can see how the researchers seem to suggest that self-centered concern (in this case, concern for the future of one's own children) is still the primary motivator of humans, even when they demonstrate concern for others.

*A Christian perspective of groups.* The survival value or other values discussed above that some groups provide for us certainly can be an essential reason for their existence. Yet the fact that people persistently form groups even when there is no pressing need would seem to support a central tenet of both the naturalist and the CFR view of personhood: the intrinsically relational nature of humans. Aside from the groups that naturally form (e.g., race, ethnicity) and those that form for specific, practical reasons (e.g., sports teams, classes), why do we actually seek out group involvement in other social contexts where to be a member of a group does not seem "necessary"? Indeed, why do we sometimes go to great lengths to be accepted by different social groups? As we have seen in the previous chapters, the drive for social inclusion is very powerful. In the context of efforts at group membership, the desire for social inclusion is especially pronounced.

From the CFR view of humans, one main reason why the intrinsic relational nature of humans exists both at an interpersonal level as well as on a group level is because we are made for community. This is an "obligatory interdependence" of a relational sort, and groups help us fulfill our relational nature by providing community. This community purpose of groups suggests the significant potential of groups to work in redemptive ways at larger societal levels that would not be possible from an individual or interpersonal perspective. Consider the biblical writings, where the main themes often are not about how God works with the individual, but rather with large groups (twelve tribes of Judah, the church as the body of Christ, etc.). People operated collectively. We are both intrinsically relational and intrinsically affiliative. In biblical times, as in the present, God's redemptive work is often played out on a large scale within the context of groups. For example, efforts toward racial reconciliation take place largely in groups and between them. A group most often accomplishes together what a single individual cannot do.

The redemptive potential of groups would be great if all group members were other-centered. But from a Christian view of persons that acknowledges the inherent tensions between self- and other-centered tendencies, a group has a unique and incomparable ability to express this tension. As you read through this chapter, you will see that group behavior is often not optimal nor positive. On the one hand, the group can offer its individual members important counterbalances to self-deception, yet a group has its own potential for self-deception and destructive processes. This should not surprise us, given the vulnerabilities of the human condition. But a group's potential for destructive or evil processes is not the whole story. You will also read about ample evidence of groups' potential for other-centered processes. Interestingly, recently social psychologists are focusing more on the positive outcomes of group behavior and processes, as you will see later in this chapter.

Thus, from a Christian view, on the one hand, groups are meant to be a significant part of God's redemptive plan. On the other hand, groups can, and often do, perform less than optimally. They also have the capacity to perform the grossest acts of evil. Both the good and destructive potential of groups are often the result of conformity within the group. Nevertheless, as you will see, the research in this area does not generally support the notion of individual group members who are mindless automatons, falling prey to the group's dynamics. Instead, as you will see, the impact of group processes on individual behavior is far more complex.

Following are some discussions regarding specific group processes. Note how these include a significant degree of social influence.

### INTRAGROUP PROCESSES

Important processes and dynamics *within* the group are called *intragroup processes*. These are the focus of the current discussion. At the end of the chapter, we will look more closely at *intergroup* (between-group) *processes*. As noted earlier, groups have a productive potential, yet group processes can also result in deficient or destructive group behavior. Think about how the tension between self- and other-centered tendencies is reflected in the group processes described below.

**Brainstorming.** Suppose that the president of your college invited students to generate ideas to improve campus life. Do you think that you would be able to come up with more creative ideas alone or as part of a group of other students? As is the case in the complex world of human social interaction, the answer depends. Like individuals, groups have an amazing ability to generate creative solutions. One way in which this can occur is through the process of *brainstorming*, which consists of generating as many ideas or solutions as possible and generally refraining from evaluating them until the generating process is complete. The goal is to present numerous possible solutions, thereby increasing the chances of obtaining high-quality possibilities.

The intuitive appeal of brainstorming seems obvious, but researchers Brown and Paulus (2002) suggest that it is not always as effective as one might expect. For example, they cite the research of Sutton and Hargadon (1996) that finds evidence for the effectiveness of collaboration for problem solving. Yet at times brainstorming is counterproductive, leading to *less* generation of solutions. They also cite Paulus, Larey and Ortega (1995), who demonstrated that groups often overestimate their effectiveness at providing solutions. Paulus et al. note that brainstorming in groups can result in a reduction of idea generation due to what is called *production blocking.* This blocking of ideas happens because individual group members have to wait their turn to provide their answers, thus possibly getting distracted or inattentive due to concentrating on one's own train of thought so as not to forget it. *Social loafing,* which you will read about in a later section, also diminishes the productivity of a group brainstorming session, as individual members may let others do most of the work.

So, how can the effectiveness of brainstorming be increased? Brown and Paulus (2002) suggest that group brainstorming is most effective when it increases the memory associations that individual group members make. For example, imagine again your college president asking for ways to improve campus life. Suppose that you live on campus, and the idea of improved parking had not occurred to you. But then, Brown and Paulus suggest, if a commuter student expresses concerns about parking on campus, you might be primed to remember how your parents had had a difficult time finding parking the last time they were visiting the campus. Thus, your associative memory made a link that it would otherwise not have made. This is an example of how a group can facilitate solutions by fostering memory connections.

Brown and Paulus (2002) also suggest other ways to improve brainstorming, specifically increasing idea generations and reducing inhibition of responses:

- use a combination of individual and group brainstorming within a single session.

- have group members write their answers instead of speaking them, with each member reading the others' responses and giving their own response thereafter. This is referred to as *"brainwriting"* (Paulus & Yang, 2000).

- use computers to present a significant number of potential solutions to each individual member.

*Deindividuation.* Sometimes individuals in crowds or mobs do dangerous or aggressive things that they would not otherwise do alone. One reason why this may occur is the process of *deindividuation,* which refers to a loss of self-awareness and self-evaluation. This loss often results in non-normative behavior or risk taking and disinhibition. Postmes and Spears (1998) review some of this research. Festinger, Pepitone and Newcomb (1952) were among the first to describe the effects of deindividuation, noting that when an individual group member is anonymous within the group, there is a reduction in inner restraints and a greater likelihood to engage in behaviors they might not otherwise do. What is it about deindividuation that produces these results?

Initial research on deindividuation suggested that being *anonymous* was sufficient to produce disinhibition. So, a person whose identity was not known to the group could get away with doing antinormative things without being punished. The early research suggested inconsistent results regarding the effects of anonymity. Subsequent revisions of deindividuation theory have instead focused on *reduced self-awareness* as the defining feature of deindividuation (e.g., Diener, 1980). Decreased self-awareness happens when attention is drawn away from the self, and consequently self-evaluation and conscious deliberation of one's actions is hindered. This reduced self-awareness would then contribute to risk taking and violation of normative behavior.

Other researchers have focused on *collective group norms* as the primary defining influence for those who feel deindividuated. For example, Johnson and Downing (1979) had participants become anonymous by wearing masks and overalls like those of the Ku Klux Klan or nurses' uniforms. They delivered shocks more when dressed in Ku Klux Klan outfits than when dressed as nurses, whose norms would be nonviolent. This finding suggests how groups are sensitive to normative cues associated with the social context.

So if one is a member of a group or crowd, is there a significant chance of experiencing anonymity, a decreased self-awareness and resultant antinormative behavior, or transgressing social norms? Not exactly. A meta-analysis of sixty studies of deindividuation showed overall little support for this proposal, and in some studies actually found contrary evidence (Postmes & Spears, 1998). This meta-analysis did show support for the hypothesis that large groups are more likely than are smaller groups to produce deindividuation effects, yet these effect sizes are small.

One interesting finding in the Postmes and Spears meta-analysis is consistent with the *Social Identity Model of Disinhibition Effects* (SIDE model; Reicher, 1984, 1987; Reicher et al., 1995), which distinguishes between the group's norms and more general social norms. From this view, deindividuating settings do not lead to anonymity or a loss of personal identity. Instead, these situations help foster a more social or collective identity, meaning more identification with the group and its norms. As Postmes and Spears (2002) note, a person who is deindividuated is less aware of the personal self and more in tune with the group's norms. Thus, even if the group's behavior seems irrational or disinhibited to outsiders, the behavior makes sense to the group members, who do not see themselves as acting mindlessly.

Reicher (1987) offers an example of the SIDE model. Imagine that you are in a crowd that is protesting cruelty to animals. In this case, your attention would be focused on the shared concern for the animals (i.e., your identification with the group norms). If an opposing group (e.g., police) acts toward the crowd "as though it were one"—by, for instance, blocking their way—the SIDE model would predict that your strong allegiance to the group's values and norms would make you more likely to adhere to the group's behavior; in this case, possibly plowing through the police line.

The research on deindividuation thus does not suggest that humans necessarily become mindless robots in the context of group settings where violence or other antinormative behavior occurs. Rather, the research seems more consistent with the notion that individuals are actually "hyper aware" of the group's values and act accordingly. In that case, the norms of the group prevail over individual and general social norms, so the person's behavior is more intentional and deliberate than traditional deindividuation theory suggested. In any case, the research does suggest that group values can be very powerful.

***Social loafing.*** Most students recognize this story: you are part of a group project for class, and one or several of the members are slacking off, not doing their part of the work. Or maybe *you* are the one who slacked off. Does being part of a group enhance or inhibit performance and teamwork? Once again, the short answer is: it depends. Often, groups work more efficiently than do individuals. But other times, persons in groups do not perform to their individual potential (Laughlin, 1980). This is *social loafing*, or the tendency to work less as group size increases.

Latané, Williams and Harkins (1979) investigated social loafing in two experiments that involved shouting and clapping. In both experiments, participants shouted and clapped louder when they were alone than when they were with others. Thus, individual efforts were reduced when individuals perceived that others were doing the work. Research in organizational contexts further suggests that social loafing is related to decreased group performance, increased absenteeism, decreased group satisfaction and decreased group cohesiveness (Duffy & Shaw, 2000).

In some cases, social loafing has no significant implications. For example, imagine that you are involved in a car wash sponsored by your dorm to raise money for new carpet for the dorm. If you slack off a bit because there are lots of other students doing hard work washing cars, your individual contribution may not significantly impair the end result (notwithstanding the implications for your individual integrity). But sometimes, the effects of social loafing can result in very destructive or unproductive consequences, or even endangerment of another.

Given the potential harm that social loafing can do, researchers have been interested in finding ways to reduce social loafing. They have suggested several factors that increase individual effort:

- when individual contributions to the goal are identifiable (Williams, Harkins & Latané, 1981, as cited in Kenrick, Neuberg & Cialdini, 2002). This is one of the reasons that when I assign group projects, I always assign a greater grade to the individual efforts and require students to specify what part of the research they did.

- when the task is meaningful to the individual group members.

- when the group is cohesive (e.g., a group of friends vs. a group of strangers).

- when the project is presented as a challenge rather than a problem to solve (Shepperd & Taylor, 1999).

*Social facilitation.* You have just learned that social loafing refers to how group members may slack off when others are present. How else does the presence of others in a group affect our performance on tasks? This depends on a number of factors. Zajonc (1968, 1980) proposed the *mere presence effect.* From this view, the mere presence of others increases arousal, or drive, which results in an increase in dominant (well-learned) responses. From this view, if you are a good singer, then the presence of an audience would enhance your performance. In addition, the mere presence effect predicts that in general, on simple tasks, public audiences facilitate performance, while performance on complex problems performed in the presence of others tends to decrease.

According to Williams, Harkins and Karau (2003), the exact ways in which the mere presence of others leads to social facilitation (i.e., the dominant response) is yet unclear. For example, some have argued that the presence of others is distracting and thus affects attention, hence the poorer performance on complex tasks (Baron, 1986). Others (e.g., Cottrell, 1972) have argued that the presence of others acts as a signal that our performance will be evaluated or that we will be in competition with others. Evaluation apprehension then may result, and this apprehension could either increase or decrease our performance, depending on the degree to which our dominant responses lead to correct completion of the task at hand. Williams, Harkins and Karau conclude that the research thus far has only resulted in a "bare beginning" of understanding how the mere presence of others leads to evaluation apprehension and how this affects our performance. This is because many of the experiments have failed to include conditions that systematically examine the various sources of evaluation (the experimenter, the self, coactors, etc.). Hence, we can only reasonably state that the presence of others seems to impact our performance in some way that is either conducive to better performance or hinders our performance, and this effect depends on the difficulty of the task, its relevance and importance to us, and the source of the evaluation.

There is an interesting line of research regarding how the presence of others may lead to stereotype thinking. Lambert et al. (2003) investigated this, proposing a counterintuitive hypothesis. Traditionally, as you will read in the prejudice chapter (chap. 8), while in the presence of others people will often refrain from expressing negative stereotypes of racial or ethnic groups. In part, this is due to the effects of social desirability—wanting to be perceived well by others. Lambert et al. considered stereotypes as a type of dominant response and hypothesized that the presence of others can actually *increase* the likelihood that a person will openly express a stereotype. This is because stereotypes are well learned and habitual, just like other dominant responses (Devine, 1989; Fazio, 1995; as cited in Lambert et al., 2003).

In one experiment, Lambert et al. told participants that they would see pairs of pictures, a face and then either a picture of a gun or hand tool. The faces were four white and four black, both male and female for each race. Participants were told they had to respond to the second picture by identifying it as a gun or hand tool, that the task would measure both speed and accuracy, and that they had to respond quickly. Participants were told that their responses were either confidential or that they would be asked to share and discuss their responses with the other participants in the testing room. Anticipating public awareness increased, not decreased, the tendency for participants to use their stereotypic attitudes toward Blacks. This was especially true among participants who were high in social anxiety. This finding was interesting, given that by definition, socially anxious individuals have a great concern about doing or saying something wrong in public. A second experiment replicated these findings. Lambert et al. note that more research is needed regarding how the presence of others may result in socially undesirable behaviors or attitudes.

Thus, the presence of others in group contexts can have divergent effects on our performance. In some cases, social loafing occurs. In other cases, the presence of others enhances our well-learned responses. In yet other cases, the presence of others can reduce our performance by distracting us or causing us to feel apprehension regarding others' evaluation of us, or even lead to negative thinking about others. How else can others influence us?

*Group polarization and risky shift.* Suppose that you are talking with a group of peers regarding something about which you feel moderately strongly. Have you ever noticed that your opinion about the issue may become more pronounced after talking with the group who also hold that opinion? Perhaps you felt so worked up after the discussion that you felt like taking to the streets with a banner for your cause? This intensification of one's initial opinion after group discussion is referred to as *group polarization* (Moscovici & Zavalloni, 1969; Myers & Lamm, 1975). Group polarization generally involves moderate tendencies/opinions in a given direction that become more extreme in the same direction.

The process of group polarization can result in shifts in decisions, whereby the group's decisions are sometimes more risky than the individuals' (*risky shift*), or less risky than the individuals' (*cautious shift*; Brown, 1965, 1974). Isenberg (1986) notes two major explanations that have been proposed for why decision shifts occur: *social comparison processes* and *persuasive argumentation*. In the case of social comparison, since humans have a tendency to want to be well perceived by others, they often assess what others are thinking or feeling and try to appear in the best light possible. So, for example, suppose you were involved in a group discussion about feminism. According to the social comparison view, you would try to gauge the group's average position regarding feminism and try to appear even more feminist (or less, if the group leans in that direction) than average. Since most group members would be inclined to do the same social comparison process, the group's overall reported opinion would shift to a more extreme point.

An alternative explanation for decision shifts in groups involves persuasive argumentation. From this view, group discussion will cause an individual to shift their attitudes or behaviors in a given direction to the extent that the discussion presents compelling arguments favoring that direction (Burnstein & Vinokur, 1975, 1977, as cited in Isenberg, 1986).

Thus, a group may or may not shift to a riskier position if the arguments presented in the group discussion are not especially novel and persuasive (Kaplan, 1977).

In addition to social comparison and persuasive arguments as sources of decision shifts in groups, is it possible that group decision shifts occur as the result of biased ways of seeking information? Recall from the chapter on the self that one biased way of seeking information at the individual level is through *confirmation bias,* which entails seeking information that confirms an already existing thought or opinion. Schulz-Hardt et al. (2000) conducted three experiments in which they found that confirmation bias also happens when group members are seeking information. In one experiment, they presented participants with a case study regarding a German company that was trying to decide whether to invest in a developing country and relocate some of its production there. Both the investment and no-investment options were described as equally attractive, with identical numbers of opposing and supporting arguments. All participants read the case study alone and decided whether the company should invest. Then some of these participants were placed in homogenous groups, where all participants had previously expressed the same opinion, and told that they would make a preliminary decision after some group discussion. The other participants were told that they would come up with an individual preliminary decision after some more time to deliberate.

Next, the participants were told that in order to prepare the final (group) decision, they would be presented additional information (articles) that were allegedly written by experts in economics. Each article had a thesis statement that made obvious whether the corresponding article favored or opposed an investment. Participants were asked to read the thesis statements and to mark those articles that they wanted to read later on. The results indicated that participants in the individual condition favored the articles that confirmed their original view. Groups in which all five members favored the same alternative or in which only a small minority of one person opposed this choice also showed a significant preference for supporting information. Thus, groups showed the same tendency to seek information that confirms pre-existing biases.

Schulz-Hardt et al. note that most significant decisions (e.g., politics) are made in and by groups. Thus, understanding the ways in which groups seek out biased information is vitally important given the implications of group decision making.

*Groupthink.* As you have read so far, groups can certainly make faulty decisions. Janis (1972) first proposed the concept of *groupthink* as one of the processes by which this faulty decision making occurs. Groupthink occurs in a group that has a high level of cohesiveness, and the majority is favoring one decision over another. This kind of group is generally insulated, resisting external critics and silencing internal dissenters. Individual group members also tend to suppress their own dissenting opinion. The group also tends to be overly optimistic about its decisions, feeling a sense of invulnerability. The group's leadership is opinionated, and group members tend to be loyal to the leader. Even when the group is trying to remain accountable for its decisions, it will often select accountability partners who are part of the in-group (i.e., those who already agree with the group's decisions), resulting in what Tetlock (2007) refers to as an "intellectually incestuous" process. So, does groupthink occur in certain kinds of groups or in all groups that are cohesive?

... There being no other new business, the meeting was adjourned to the parking lot where members said what they really meant.

**Figure 5.2.**

You can imagine a number of situations in which such a process occurs. Consider the history of the church and denominational factions. Think about political decision making. Janis (1972, 1982) reviewed a number of case studies of situations in which groupthink resulted in a fiasco, including the decision-making process for the U.S. military response during the attack on Pearl Harbor and the U.S. involvement in the Vietnam War. He considered cohesion to be the most important antecedent of groupthink.

Yet, the evidence for groupthink is inconsistent. First, group cohesion is not a good predictor of groupthink. Moorhead, Ference and Neck (1991), for example, studied the Challenger disaster, when the shuttle was sent to space despite serious concerns regarding its safety, resulting in an explosion that killed all the astronauts on board ninety seconds after liftoff. The researchers proposed that the group was held together by loyalty to the leader, not group cohesion. Walker and Watson (1994) likewise argue that the evidence of groupthink—from specific case studies to lab experiments—is mixed. Further, Bovens and t'Hart (1996) note that the evidence for groupthink is even less in real-life decision-making situations. Additionally, reliable measures of the components of groupthink have not been well established.

Despite the limitations of the groupthink model, it has inspired much research in the area of group decision making. In addition, it has provided much food for thought regarding the potential dangers of groups that are too like-minded. Consider what possible implications this research on groupthink might have for your own decision making. Moorhead, Neck and West (1998) have outlined ways in which groupthink can be decreased. These strategies include:

- having the leader encourage dissenting opinions within the group,
- inviting experts with contradictory opinions to advise the group and
- considering multiple possible solutions to the task at hand.

I have observed on campus several times in which group leaders have made deliberate attempts to avoid the potential pitfalls of groupthink. In one case, the leader purposely invited outside experts with differing views to attend meetings and offer their perspectives. In another case, the leader encouraged members several times during the meeting to openly disagree with the majority view. In both situations, it seemed to me that individuals (including myself) expressed more openness about their opinions, even when these were minority opinions. Disagreements were expressed in a respectful manner, and successful negotiations were obtained in both cases.

## INTERGROUP RELATIONS

So far, this chapter has been exploring *intragroup* (within-group) processes. You have read about how group membership and allegiance can be a powerful source of social influence, often affecting our performance, our perception of our own attitudes and behavior, and potentially our decision making. On the other hand, the research does not suggest that individuals have no ability to exert influence on their group. Indeed, as will become clearer in the rest of this chapter, the individual and the group mutually influence one another.

Now let us turn our attention to processes involved in the interactions *between* groups. As you have observed, sometimes intergroup relations are positive and productive, whereas at other times, intergroup conflict can arise. Dovidio, Maruyama and Alexander (1998) note that the social psychology of intergroup processes and relations can help inform our understanding of important social issues such as international relations and conflict as well as race relations. You will read about a specific type of intergroup conflict in the prejudice chapter (chap. 8). For now, let us look at other specific intergroup processes and see how these relate to the human condition.

*In-groups vs. out-groups.* We humans often readily identify with our own groups and use terms like *we* and *they* to highlight group differences. Just as individuals can exhibit the self-serving bias, groups can often exhibit *group-serving biases,* which include favorable impressions of one's own group and denigrating the out-group. Consider students' loyalty to their club, school, sports teams and so on. In fact, at times the perceptions of a particular out-group may be so negative that in-group members dehumanize the target group. As you will see in both the aggression and prejudice chapters, there are many instances in which *dehumanization* occurs of the target group. Dehumanization involves seeing the other as less than human and lessening the moral consideration of them. Such dehumanization can result in devastating consequences such as racism, discrimination and genocide, as well as more subtle neglect or refusal to interact with a particular group. Leyens et al. (2000) refer to *infrahumanization* as the belief that one's in-group is more human than an out-group. Leyens et al. have found that people are often more likely to attribute uniquely human emotions such as love and nostalgia to their own group, while they are more likely to attribute emotions that are true of both humans and animals (e.g., joy, anger) to the out-group. This dehumanization increases the probability of aggression between groups.

Aside from the destructive aggressive potential of group-serving biases, everyday group distinctions and favorable preferences for one's own group are a common social phenomenon. Consider examples of this in-group favoritism, such as on dorm floors, in neighborhoods and within political parties. In my own neighborhood, the two book clubs enjoy a playful banter about which group is "better," though sometimes it seems to me that the competition is a bit more fierce than is evident.

**Intergroup vs. interpersonal competition.** One possible result of group-serving biases is increased competition between groups. As we know, there is certainly a significant amount of competition at the interpersonal (individual) level. Yet many experimenters have found that competition between groups is often more intense than is competition between individuals. This is known as the *discontinuity effect*.

Why is there so much competition between groups? Wildschut et al. (2003) conducted a meta-analysis of 130 studies of the discontinuity effect and noted that most social psychological explanations refer to *fear* and *greed* as the two primary motives for competition between groups. Groups are generally perceived as more threatening than are individuals. Also, individual tendencies of greed can be amplified in the group context, with individual tendencies multiplied many times over. In addition, individual accountability is lessened if one is the member of a group.

On the positive side, Wildschut et al. found that competition between groups can be reduced when reciprocal strategies are used. Reciprocal strategies encourage cooperation because you expect cooperation in return for yours. The results suggest that reciprocal strategies discourage selfish seeking of immediate good in favor of longer-term rewards. But cooperative efforts did not seem to decrease competition that is based on greed, since the other group was less likely to be perceived as a threat.

Thus far, you can see that research provides evidence for both the productive as well as destructive facets of group processes. It is interesting to note how variations of the tendencies you read about in the chapter on the self (overconfidence, self-serving tendencies, etc.) as well as in the social perception chapter (cognitive shortcuts, bounded accuracy in mutual perception) also occur in groups. It is helpful to consider how powerful the aggregate effect of these social forces can be in groups. Given their potential, one can appreciate the necessity of understanding groups in order to discover ways in which they can be encouraged toward productive ends.

## GROUPS AND CHRISTIANITY

The preceding discussions about group processes have demonstrated that one of the most powerful aspects of many groups is their sense of uniformity and cohesion. These characteristics speak to the ways in which individuals within the group both contribute and conform to the majority opinion. This is of special interest from a Christian perspective when one considers the modern, Western tendency to emphasize individual faith and personal salvation. This emphasis underestimates the impact of group processes that are inherent in both personal and corporate redemption.

Using the research on such group processes as social facilitation, mere presence, risky and cautious shifts, and so on, one may infer that these processes likely play an important part in how people come to faith as well as how they experience ongoing transformation. It is challenging to consider the delicate balance between an individual's response to God and the social influences that make that response more or less likely. Nevertheless, as Batson and Ventis (1982) noted, "So long as religious experience in all its individuality, transcendence, and mystery leaves observable tracks or symptoms, it is amenable to empirical analysis" (p. 21). Thus, exploring the degree to which faith is the result of adherence to group norms is certainly a reasonable research endeavor and is receiving more emphasis in the psychology of religion. Ysseldyk, Matheson and Anisman (2010), for example, suggest that religiosity offers an "eternal group membership" that transcends identification with other social groups. According to these researchers, religiosity provides a positive social group that offers some measure of certainty about the world, something that is highly valued and consequently deeply integrated into one's identity. Yet, even as we attempt to identify specific group processes involved in developing intrinsic faith, Gorsuch (1997) offers us a legitimate warning: we cannot assume that any one theory regarding the causes of intrinsic religious commitment applies equally well to all believers. In addition, such research must consider both the prosocial and antisocial consequences of religious belief (Batson, 1997).

## CONFORMITY

The American philosopher Eric Hoffer (1959) famously quipped, "When people are free to do as they please, they usually imitate each other.... A society which gives unlimited freedom to the individual, more often than not attains a disconcerting sameness." As we have seen so far in this chapter, a great deal of conformity occurs within groups, and this is one manifestation of the significant amount of social influence that groups can exert. Remember that this chapter is focused on a review of social influence more generally, including intragroup and intergroup processes, and these include conformity. Thus, this section on conformity is obviously relevant to the preceding discussions.

As much as people claim that they have arrived at their own decisions, you do not have to look far to see the influence of others in those decisions. I am often amused by college students who tell me that they want to make

their faith "their own" and then begin to quote with great zeal from a variety of theological readings that have clearly informed their thinking. *Conformity* refers to the act of changing one's behavior in response to real or imagined social pressure. Conformity thus results in a change in behavior and/or attitudes that match the responses of others. Note that a person could conform to behavioral norms without experiencing an actual change in underlying attitudes. Conformity is not in response to a direct order or coercion, but rather to social pressures. One can be aware or unaware of one's conforming behaviors.

In this part of the chapter, we are exploring the various factors involved in conforming to group norms. All groups develop norms. Sometimes these norms are formally and explicitly developed. But most of the time, group norms are implicit (Forsyth, 2006). For example, I belong to a neighborhood book club. When we began the club a few years ago, we explicitly talked about how we wanted to proceed with regard to discussing and rating the books. But other norms for the group are understood more implicitly and reflect broader social norms that we have internalized and applied to this particular group setting. No one has outright said that we should not get up and sing or do acrobatics while someone else is talking about their reactions to the book under discussion, but we don't do those things. This image likely strikes you as absurd, because you, too, have internalized the social norms that inhibit these behaviors in most social contexts.

***Prevalence of conformity.*** Conformity often happens so commonly and in such automatic or implicit ways that we don't notice unless we deliberately pay attention. Consider the *chameleon effect,* which refers to the mostly nonconscious mimicking of others' expressions, mannerisms and movements (Kendon, 1970; LaFrance, 1982). Pay close attention to groups of people talking and notice how often they unconsciously copy each other's movements—for example, crossing their arms or wiping their brow.

This synchronizing of nonverbal cues has been observed in many other forms as well. For example, have you ever found yourself beginning to imitate the accent or vocabulary of another the longer you speak with them? Or have you noticed how quickly moods can spread in a group (Neumann & Strack, 2000)? It happens, whether we notice or not.

Another interesting example of implicit conformity occurs in styles of dress on college campuses. Each year, I ask students in my social psychology class whether they have noted how similar the students on campus dress. When this is pointed out to them, they usually respond with a sort of "aha!" as though they had not ever really thought about it. Yet from my perspective it seems as though there were a dress code at our school that explicitly stated: "You must come to school dressed casually, mostly with jeans and sweatshirts (unless you are giving a group presentation or performing in the choir) and carry a Camelbak water bottle with you at all times." Yet no such explicit policy exists. Instead, students unwittingly absorb social cues from each other's form of dress and generally conform without conscious consideration. This type of conformity gets reinforced by the other students, engendering a sense of collective identity and perpetuating further conformity regarding fashion.

Noticing conformity often takes an outsider's perspective. On a personal note, when I first arrived at Bethel University in Minnesota, I was struck by the difference in dress compared to my previous college in Palm Beach, Florida. I remember attending a computer training workshop just before my first semester, dressed in my customary business-casual attire, complete with jewelry and lipstick. My colleagues, mostly Midwesterners, were dressed in jeans and sweatshirts or T-shirts. If the students from Bethel transferred to a university in South Florida, they would be immediately aware of the different conformity dress cues there.

Chartrand and Bargh (1999) note that in the case of the chameleon effect, mimicking others' expressions and movements is mostly unconscious, increases interpersonal liking and helps facilitate social interaction. To what degree does this same level of social synchronizing occur in simulated, online environments? Bailenson and Yee (2005) note that this is an important question given how prevalent embodied agents are in online games and software applications. Bailemson and Yee suggest that we are, indeed, "digital chameleons." The participants in their study responded to a mimicker that they knew was actually a nonhuman, digital representation controlled by a computer in the same way as we do to a live person who mimics us. Specifically, the researchers studied how the nonhuman agent's mimicry of the participant's slight head movements would affect the participant's response to the persuasive messages presented by the nonhuman agent.

Bailenson and Yee (2005) had participants listen to an embodied agent read a persuasive message about campus security. The agent proposed that a viable way to increase campus security is to require students to carry their identification at all times. The agent either mimicked the participant's head movements or produced head movements that were consistent with a previous participant's head movements. The agent that mimicked the head movements of the participants was viewed as significantly more persuasive and likable than was the agent who simply made seemingly random head movements. Interestingly, most participants in the mimicking condition did not report being consciously aware of the mimicry and were also more likely to look straight at the agent, suggesting greater attention to the agent's message. The researchers refer to earlier research (Moon & Nass, 1996) that suggests that humans attribute personality characteristics to computers and prefer computer personalities that are similar to their own. In any case, a computer image that appeared to be "in sync" with the user was perceived, as the chameleon effect would suggest, more favorably and was more persuasive.

*Is conformity inherently productive or destructive?* Remember that conformity (groupthink) can certainly result in destructive outcomes. Perhaps because of this negative potential, social psychological research has implicitly assumed that conformity itself has a negative connotation or is undesirable (e.g., research on groupthink leading to faulty decision making). Gergen (1973) argued that implied value judgments regarding conformity often leave the conformer with the sense that they are a "second-class citizen," or "a social sheep that forgoes personal conviction to agree with the erroneous opinions of others" (p. 311). He noted that this negative bias hinders our ability to see the potential benefits that occur as a result of conformity, and more recent research on conformity addresses this concern.

A certain amount of conformity is helpful for keeping social order. If you had to redefine the rules for yourself each time you entered a social setting, there would be chaos. Basic conformity to social norms such as rules of etiquette facilitate social interactions and leave cognitive space for contemplating other more difficult social issues and processes. Were there no conformity, parents would have little hope of teaching young children to behave in appropriate and functional ways. Learning how to conduct oneself at a restaurant or theater is a good example of positive conformity.

**Why conform?** The pervasive nature of conformity raises interesting questions about the purposes it might serve. Sometimes we conform to group norms because we truly believe in the group's ideas. This is known as *private conformity*. Other times, however, we conform superficially just to go along with the group. We may have motives such as the desire to be liked or socially included. This is known as *public conformity*. Public conformity often results in a superficial change in observable behavior without an actual internalized change in attitude or belief (Collins, 1973).

Cialdini and Goldstein (2004) specifically note three central motivations for conformity. First, there is the desire to be *accurate*. People want to make decisions that are accurate and either talk with others or look to others to help define the best course of action or to demarcate what is real and true. Bikhchandani, Hirshleifer and Welch (1998) give the example of how people conform to buying a certain kind of car. If others understand that a particular car manufacturer makes a higher-quality car, they are likely to buy it, and so are you based on your assessment of the others' accuracy. Deutsch and Gerard (1955) related the desire for accuracy to what they called *informational influence,* which has to do with the degree to which others provide for us an accurate interpretation of reality that enables us to behave correctly. Often, to save cognitive time and energy, we will look to others, especially high-status others, to define the norms for us. This is an efficient process.

A second motive for conforming is related to the *need for social approval*. In this case, conformity is the result of *normative influence,* which has to do with the degree to which others define norms for us. If we adhere to these norms, we are more likely to be positively viewed by important others (Deutsch & Gerard, 1955). Consider examples from your own interaction with peers.

Cialdini and Goldstein (2004) note a third underlying motive for conformity: the desire to *maintain and protect one's self-concept*. This is related to the other two motives. For example, if you make accurate decisions, others may see you as wise, resulting in social approval. If you behave according to some prescribed norms, others are more likely to affiliate with you and have positive perceptions of you. Both feeling accurate (competent) and well-liked in turn contributes to your own positive sense of self (Cialdini & Trost, 1998; Wood, 2000, as cited in Cialdini & Goldstein, 2004).

*Classic studies of conformity.* Imagine that you are placed in a dark room by yourself and instructed to watch a pinpoint of light and tell the experimenter how far the light has moved. In actuality, the light is not moving at all, but rather appears to be moving. This illusion is called the *autokinetic effect*. You estimate that the light is moving about two to six inches. Now imagine that you are placed in the same room with one or two other participants, and you are all asked to estimate how much the light moved. Sherif (1935) wanted to know whether individual participants' responses would be influenced by the judgments of the other respondents in the group. He found that individuals' responses tended to move toward a consensus with the group norm, often differing about four inches from their initial, independent judgment.

Sherif's (1935) finding that the participants succumbed to group influence when they were uncertain about a judgment suggests that they looked to others for an assessment of reality, or accuracy. A meta-analysis by Bond and Smith (1996) suggests that these results are consistently found.

But what if what you are being asked to judge is not so ambiguous? Solomon Asch (1951, 1955, 1956) conducted another classic series of studies regarding conformity to group influence. He asked college students to take part in an alleged vision test in which they were to match the length of lines. They were shown lines like those in figure 5.3. Participants were grouped with eight other students (all confederates) who gave the wrong answer. The majority of the participants (75 percent) stated they agreed with the others, apparently being led to question their own judgments and to succumb to group influence. Variations of the original Asch study included confed-

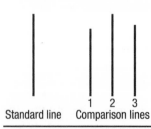

1   2   3
Standard line   Comparison lines

**Figure 5.3. Examples of Lines Used in Asch Studies**

erates who sided with the participant, and in that case, the participant was more likely to resist the group's influence. Regardless of the condition, participants in the Asch studies reported that they were not aware of the influence from others' judgments on their own judgment.

What do early studies suggest about how nonconformers are perceived? Schachter (1951) investigated this by having students participate in one of several groups that differed with regard to how cohesive the group was and the relevance of the task. Across all groups, participants discussed how best to treat a young juvenile delinquent named "Johnny Rocco." Three of the students in the group were confederates: one agreed with the group majority opinion from the outset, another disagreed with the group at first, but then changed their opinion to agree with the group (the "slider"), and the other continually disagreed with the group majority opinion (the "deviate"). Schachter measured the amount of time that the participants spent talking with each group member and also how much they liked the other group members. The results indicated that subjects spent the most time talking to the slider and the deviate until it became clear that the deviate would not change his or her mind. At that point, communication with the deviate dropped sharply, and the deviate was often excluded from the group's communication. Subjects also reported liking the conforming members most, and all reported liking the deviate the least.

Thus, these classic studies of conformity suggest that the pressure to adhere to the group norm can be compelling; individual group members seek information from each other when the decision is related to something ambiguous; dissenting voices are more likely to be expressed if other individuals in the group also dissent; and nonconformers are not viewed positively. Let's now consider what research tells us about other issues related to conformity.

### Factors influencing conformity

*Group size.* What do you think happens to the likelihood of conforming as the size of the group increases? Bond (2005) conducted a meta-analytic review of the research on group size and conformity, and concluded that this relationship is not clear. First, Asch (1951, 1955) proposed that the size of the majority did not have significant influence beyond a minimal number of people. Specifically, he proposed that a majority of three is sufficient for a person to feel the full impact of the group.

Latané (1981; Latané & Wolf, as cited in Bond, 2005), by contrast, proposed *social impact theory* (SIT), which argues that the larger the group, the greater its influence—in other words, the greater the chances of conforming to the group norms. Latané posited that this influence is due to how the majority provides us with information about reality, and also that it has the power to reward and punish individuals (e.g., social approval or social ostracism). Social impact theory holds that a group has a theoretically unlimited capacity to influence the individual because the addition of each new group member will have additional impact.

Tanford and Penrod's (1984) *social influence model* (SIM) makes a different prediction about group size in relation to group influence. These researchers suggest that group size is only important up to a point, beyond which increasing the group size would not have any additional impact. Mullen (1983, 1987, as cited in Bond, 2005) proposed yet another theory of group size and conformity, predicting that group size affects conformity according to a principle called self-attention theory (Carver & Scheier, 1981). *Self-attention theory* maintains that the more attention is focused on the self, the greater the likelihood that the individual will try to match their behavior with the majority standard. Mullen argues that since increasing the majority size increases self-attention, this increased self-attention increases the likelihood of conformity because the individual does not want to stand out in the crowd.

Why are there so many conflicting findings regarding how group size affects conformity? Bond's (2005) meta-analysis suggests several reasons for the conflicting results. First, there are methodological issues, such as the definition of "majority." For example, Asch's research has variously proposed group sizes between three and nine. In addition, Bond notes that the research has generally not differentiated between public and private responses, thus neglecting Insko et al.'s (1985) finding that majority size was more likely to affect public responses than private responses. In addition, other situational and personal variables mediate the power of group size, and these variables are not consistently measured across the studies. For individuals who have a high need for accuracy, for example, they will be more likely to conform to the majority's opinion if that opinion is deemed verifiable and correct than if no correct answer could be obtained. In addition, some individuals are more socially sensitive and self-monitoring, thus more inclined to want to please others. These individuals would be more likely to conform in order to avoid displeasing others or risking social rejection (Lavine & Snyder, 1996).

Bond (2005) further notes that the likelihood of group pressure resulting in conformity also depends on other factors such as who the majority are, the social context, whether private or public responses are required, and whether  the individual has face-to-face interactions with the majority. Until there is a greater consistency of these factors across studies, the effect of group size on conformity is still uncertain.

*Perceived loss of freedom.* Sometimes the social pressures to conform that are imposed by a group can make individual members begin to feel that their freedom is being threatened. Brehm (1966) and others (e.g., Wicklund, 1974; Brehm & Brehm, 1981) proposed that when individuals feel this threat to their freedom, they experience a motivational state known as *reactance* (as cited in Dillard & Shen, 2005). This motivational state leads to behaviors that either *directly* restore freedom (e.g., doing the forbidden act) or *indirectly* restore freedom (e.g., increasing one's liking for the threatened choice, derogating the source of the threat, denying the existence of the threat or exercising a different freedom). Regardless of which of the above-noted outcomes occurs, in each case the individual is seeking some way to restore a sense of personal freedom and choice (Dillard & Shen, 2005).

Reactance can thus reduce the amount of power that a high-pressure group tries to impose because individuals whose freedom feels threatened by the pressure may purposely refuse it. It is also possible that even if an individual secretly agrees with the group's norms, he or she may outwardly disagree with the majority opinion in an effort to assert their freedom. We will explore reactance in more depth in the next chapter on persuasion.

Interestingly, while an individual who displays reactance may seem to be behaving independently, it is possible that this seemingly independent behavior may actually be a response to another norm. For example, consider a person who is an ardent feminist and then refuses to cook just because cooking has traditionally been suggestive of the subordinate role of women. Is this person truly acting independently, or is their seeming reaction against the traditional female role being ironically motivated by a different group's norms?

*Moral convictions.* Most of the research discussed so far could lead one to believe that we have little choice but to conform in cases where we disagree with the majority opinion. Hornsey, Majkut and McKimmie (2003), however, argue that this seeming difficulty with resisting conformity is overemphasized in the literature. This is because the research has focused on conformity in cases where the task was morally neutral (e.g., judging line lengths). In contrast, when people hold strong moral convictions about a matter, the power of group norms is reduced. In such cases, the individual is more likely to show counterconformity. As an example, the researchers cite a study (Shamir, 1997) in which Israelis spoke out their opinions regarding the future of Palestinian territories despite and perhaps because of the opposing position of the prevailing government. Similarly, Jahoda (1959, as cited in Hornsey et al., 2003) said, "To the extent that the experimental literature is largely limited to manipulating conditions of influence with regard to matters in which the individual has no investment, it now becomes understandable why we know in psychology so much more about conformity than about independence" (p. 104).

Hornsey et al. (2003) found that in matters of high moral relevance and importance to the individual (e.g., gay rights), participants were less likely to move toward a group norm with which they disagreed, and in fact, demonstrated nonconformity in both private and public conditions. This nonconformity is different from that which has little cost associated with letting go of one's personal view (as when judging line length). This research suggests that, in matters of moral conscience, the costs to one's personal integrity are higher if one conforms to an opposing group opinion and thus there is less conformity.

Quinn and Schlenker (2002) likewise note that strong moral convictions can increase resistance to the power of a majority who holds a view contrary to one's own. In fact, the strength of one's convictions can grow as the result of attempting to resist the majority. This is true despite perceived lack of social support for one's views. These findings suggest, contrary to those of the classic studies of conformity, that individuals have a greater capacity to act and think independently of the pressure of the majority when the issue at hand is of great importance to the individual.

*Minority vs. majority influence.* Thus far, we have focused on majority influence. It is also true, however, that the voice of a single dissenter can break the power of the group and enable other quiet dissenters to have more confidence to voice their own opinion. A dissenting voice can also be considered an ally who would support another individual's minority position, and then both will be less likely to follow the majority opinion.

A dissenter may reduce the confidence that the group has the only right answer (Morris & Miller, 1975, as cited in Kenrick, Neuberg & Cialdini, 2002). Sherif (1936) explored the effect that a dissenting voice could have on the group's influence by incorporating a dissenting confederate into one of the variations of his autokinetic effect study. This confederate spoke unwaveringly about his significantly higher or lower estimates of the distance the light had moved. In these conditions, he was able to sway the group's judgments accordingly. Sherif notes that this individual's power to influence the group was not based on any special claim of expertise, but on the willingness to hold to one's beliefs unwaveringly as others remain in their uncertainty.

What else can we know regarding how a minority can resist or even influence the majority? The results of earlier research suggested that minority influence is most effective if minority responses are consistent.

For example, Moscovici, Lage and Naffrechoux (1969) revised Asch's approach by having a minority in the group, rather than the majority, act as confederates. One of their studies involved six-member groups participating in a study of "color perception." Participants were shown thirty-six slides and asked to judge the color of each. All slides were blue. However, in one condition, two confederates incorrectly claimed that every slide was green. The results indicated that approximately 32 percent of the real participants said "green" at least once. In another condition, confederates said "green" for only twenty-four of the thirty-six slides. In this condition, the "green" responses by the majority dropped to only 1.25 percent (compared with the previous 32 percent). This minority influence lingered in a later condition in which participants were shown ambiguous blue-green slides; those who had heard a minority say "green" were more likely to answer "green" on occasion.

Majority and minority voices generally have different effects on individual conformity. With regard to majority influence, since individuals often conform in order to seek information and to be well liked, this type of conformity often happens automatically, without much conscious deliberation. Thus, the impact is more like *compliance*, which involves public conformity while privately disagreeing. By contrast, minority influence tends to be strongest when the minority view is portrayed consistently and with assurance of the accuracy of its views. In these circumstances, minority voices can persuade the majority to reexamine its views in a more deliberate manner, and private acceptance is more likely to occur. The minority view can also stimulate the group members to propose new positions or solutions. Clark (1988) thus states that the presence of a minority often helps improve a group's decision-making process.

Trout, Maass and Kenrick (1992) conducted a study that demonstrated the way minority voices can increase the likelihood of exploring alternative positions. Students read arguments that supported comprehensive final exams for all graduating seniors. The argument either proposed that the exam begin in one year (relevant to the student's own graduation) or that it be administered beginning nine years from now (irrelevant to the student's graduation). The arguments were also presented as either representing the majority or the minority viewpoint on campus. Participants then had to rate their own opinion on the issue and to write thoughts they might have about the issue.

The results suggested that the alleged minority opinion appeared to prompt more thinking about the testing proposal: participants who thought they had read the minority position wrote more thoughts down. In the condition in which the testing proposal was not relevant to the student's own graduation, the supposed minority opinion was more likely to persuade the student than was the alleged majority opinion. By contrast, when the issue was personally relevant, the argument that they found most persuasive was the one that supposedly represented the majority of students, not the minority.

Latané (1981, 1996) also investigated the ways in which minority and majority opinions are influential in groups. He reformulated his social impact theory into what he called *dynamic social impact theory*. This theory attempts to explain the give-and-take between minority and majority attitudes within a larger group. This view proposes that groups are not static entities but rather are in a dynamic state of change (Harton & Bullock, 2007, as cited in Forsyth, 2009). Latané proposed a number of specific processes that occur, including:

- Consolidation: diverse attitudes/positions get organized into fewer, smaller minorities and stronger majorities within the group.
- Clustering: subgroups (dyads, triads, etc.) get formed within the larger group; these are drawn together by similar attitudes, etc.
- Continuing diversity: minority group members' opinions linger within a group partly as a result of clustering because minorities within groups find support from one another and are thus often shielded from the majority's influence.

Thus, the research on minority influence in groups suggests that individual dissenters within a group can have a powerful and beneficial effect on the group's decision making. This is especially true if the minority opinions are presented in a consistent and confident manner. In addition, single dissenters who get support from other individual dissenters in the group feel more confident in their opinions and more able to resist the majority's influence.

In applying the research about influence in group decision making, Nemeth (1986) stated that when a group needs to make important decisions, it should allow minority opinions to be expressed and it should encourage the examination of alternative viewpoints. Strauss et al. (2009) also note that minority opinions can be sought by changing the group's structure (member roles, heterogeneous team composition, etc.). In addition, they propose occasionally encouraging members to alternate their individual positions in order to avoid getting stuck in their thinking. Strauss et al. also emphasize the importance of avoiding group formations that are so large that individual members cannot meaningfully interact.

Keep in mind, of course, that not all minority voices are productive. In fact, single voices could certainly change the course of a group toward destructive ends. In addition, there are many cases in which the strongest minority voice comes from those who in other contexts have power or privilege. Nevertheless, this research on the power of minority influence has important implications for us all. It is encouraging to see how powerful our single voices can be because, when used for the good, this power reaffirms humans' capacity for choice and virtue.

*Social contagion.* In addition to social influence within groups, social phenomena can extend to cultures at large, where ideas can sometimes spread quickly across large numbers of people. One example is *urban legends,* in which a partial truth becomes overly exaggerated and spreads quickly. For example, have you heard the story about the woman who went to the gas station where the gas station attendant tried frantically to alert her to the "man" who was hiding in her back seat? Or the story about the people who awaken in a tub of ice with a note that tells them to call 911 because one of their organs has been stolen? These kinds of stories are told and retold, by mouth and social media, until the original version and source is lost but the presumed "truth" of the story remains. Cha et al. (2008) studied how information spreads quickly in online social networks. A new idea has the potential for far-reaching "infecting." Imagine, for example, how quickly a YouTube video can become widely viewed as friends share their new discovery with a friend or two, who then share it with their friends, and so forth in quick succession. This quick generation and spread of social information is called *social cas-*

*cading.* In keeping with their analogy of a virus, the researchers refer to the actors in the social cascading process as "infectors" and "infectees." The researchers studied how quickly it took for one thousand photos posted on Flickr to spread online, and found the relatively quick "infection" time suggestive of the power of social links to disseminate information. This finding is consistent with that of Gladwell's (2000) idea of the *tipping point*, which refers to how ideas and behaviors spread like viruses through certain kinds of people, reaching a critical point when they become very popular with the masses.

Social cascading is an example of the broader concept of *social contagion*, which includes not only the quick spread of ideas, but also of emotions and behaviors. Consider the many examples of social contagion in everyday life. In my community, for example, a high school hockey player was seriously injured during a game. As expected, the local newspaper covered the story the next day. In addition, within moments of the accident, the boy's friends had posted on their Facebook pages their observations and feelings regarding the accident. Within days, I noticed a community-wide response to the events: a highway billboard had an image of the hockey uniform with the boy's number on it, saying, "We're praying for you!" Many of my daughter's friends, who attend a different high school and do not know the boy, changed their profile photos on Facebook to the logo of the injured boy's hockey uniform, with countless postings wishing him well. Several people who did not know the boy or his family established funds to help the family pay for medical expenses. In this case, many in the community were deeply moved, and this translated into helpful behavior on behalf of the boy and his family.

The above example is only one of countless others that affirm the power of social contagion. Both a naturalist and Christian view of persons acknowledge how social contagion can be used both for the good to mobilize people quickly toward some prosocial goal while at other times for very destructive ends. In everyday life, you are probably more likely to see the effects of social contagion in some new trend that is quickly spreading, such as in fashion, music, recreational activities or food. My daughter reminds me of how "boy bands" quickly gain popularity, with swooning fans vowing to marry the lead singer (until, of course, a new band gains popularity several months later). This potential for social contagion to work so quickly and decisively can encourage us to be mindful that many of the ideas, beliefs, emotional reactions and behaviors that we think we arrived at so independently may actually have been our responses to social contagion. Certainly, not all people in all situations equally succumb to this type of social influence. Yet, vulnerabilities exist in our intrinsic relational nature, and history and contemporary life provide ample evidence for both the prosocial and antisocial potential of social contagion. Consequently, it is helpful to be reminded that at least in matters of greater importance, we need to be more conscious and deliberate about what factors are influencing us.

*Christianity and conformity.* The research findings discussed so far regarding conformity are relevant to the Christian perspective of persons presented in this text. The proposed CFR view would see conformity itself as part of our fundamental relational nature, and voluntary conformity to Christ as a positive outgrowth and indicator of our relationship with God. The Scriptures tell us: "Do not be conformed to this world, but be transformed by the renewing of your minds, so that you may discern what is the will of God—what is good and acceptable and perfect" (Rom 12:2). Conforming to the loving and righteous nature of Christ, after whose image we are created, is related to the above-noted positive outcomes of conformity. As the Scriptures suggest, "renewing of your minds" includes greater discernment regarding which social influences to which we conform. We might be more conscious, for example, of how "bad company ruins good morals" (1 Cor 15:33). This is because conforming to Christ is reflected in greater love and other-centeredness. According to Scripture, then, conformity is not a choice, but we can choose to whom or what we wish to conform.

Overall, the conformity research suggests how pervasive social influence is. As previously noted, there are some limitations to this research. Nevertheless, there is empirical evidence for the idea that despite how vulnerable we may be to social pressures to conform to the majority opinion, humans are able to exert their will to varying degrees to resist these pressures. This ability to choose, albeit in a limited fashion, is consistent with Baumeister's (2005) observation that the psychological literature overall does not support a deterministic view of human social behavior. Instead, as noted in chapter two, Baumeister concludes that the view of human nature that emerges is consistent with a Judeo-Christian view, which sees humans as having at least limited agency and therefore accountability.

If we assume that humans have the potential to willfully resist social pressure, the crucial question then becomes: which social pressures should we resist and to which should we conform? As stated earlier, conformity to certain social norms facilitates social interaction, maintains order and leaves cognitive time and space for processing other more complex issues. Other types of conformity result in destructive practices or suboptimal decision making.

Again, some measure of conformity is an integral part of living in other-centered community, according to the CFR view. Arguably, we were created for conformity by virtue of our intrinsic relational nature, and our capacity for other-centeredness is both interpersonal and collective. We must be aware of the power of group influence and the fact that we often conform without knowing it. That awareness can help us make more informed choices about what we do.

For the Christian, the crucial type of conformity includes following Christ's example. It also involves following the example of others who are following Christ, and this helps in the process of discerning to which social forces we should relent. Indeed, the scriptural admonition to be in the world, but not of it (Jn 17:16) suggests discernment regarding conforming. From this view, it is encouraging to see that more recent research supports the idea that humans are indeed capable to varying degrees of resisting negative majority opinion and in some cases influencing the majority in positive ways.

Yet, because of the human condition, there remains a tension in us between self- and group-seeking conformity and other-centered, collective conformity. And as with all social behaviors in real persons, there is likely a combination of these motives when we conform.

While there may be common agreement that conformity is sometimes helpful or at least necessary for socialization and/or positive social functioning, there is very little active inquiry into the benefits of conformity for the well-being of the individual or the group. A specific question is whether conformity can help maintain a balance between the focus on the self and the focus on the group. At least from a CFR perspective, and perhaps from a naturalist one as well, developing this balance of focus is an important developmental task. But research is lacking in this area because of the negative connotations of the concept of conformity. Likewise for obedience, as you will read in the following sections.

## Obedience

As you have read so far in this chapter, conformity is one significant result of the social influence inherent in group processes. Another response to social influence that occurs at both group and interpersonal levels is *obedience* to specific commands. Historically, social psychologists have been especially interested in the factors that tend to increase obedience to commands to harm another. What types of authority figures are we most likely to obey, and under what circumstances?

***What factors contribute to obedience?*** When and whom are you most likely to obey? Does the thought of an authority figure prompt you to be more compliant with their requests? Does an individual with great expertise in some area prompt you to be more likely to follow their orders?

Understanding what factors contribute to obedience is vitally important when one considers its possible implications. Think of different contexts in which obedience can play an important and generally positive role: parenting, school and driving, for example. But then consider cases in which obedience is a significantly destructive process. An example of this destructive potential is what Kelman and Hamilton (1989) refer to as "*crimes of obedience*," where crimes (e.g., torture, genocide) that would be considered immoral or illegal by the larger community occur in direct response to the commands of authority figures.

Thus far, social psychologists have generally focused on obedience that occurs in response to orders to harm another (note that this is much less neutral than many of the conformity studies). Researchers have identified several key factors that increase the likelihood of obeying destructive orders. Hoge (2010) outlines these factors, some of which are based on the research of Milgram (1974), whose study you will read about in the next section:

- When the authority figure is perceived as legitimate and of high status. In this case, individuals may feel intimidated by the prestige of the authority figure. Because the authority figure says, "Do that!" the one who obeys feels they can abdicate personal responsibility for their actions ("I was just following orders!").

- The closeness of the authority figure. When the authority figure is present, visible or close at hand, individuals tend to be more obedient.

- When the distance between the aggressor and the victim is significant. It is easier to dehumanize others and to aggress against them if the victims are either not visible or not at hand. Think of what happens during times of war when people form negative views of the enemy. By contrast, proximity of the victim can help encourage empathy with them as a fellow human being, thereby decreasing the chances of aggressing against them.

- When others in the group obey. If you see others obeying, you may be more likely to conform to the group's normative behavior of obedience. By contrast, if several in the group disobey, an individual's desire to resist the command increases.

*A classic study and its variants: Milgram and others.* Imagine that you are taking part in a research project on learning in which the effects of punishment on learning will be assessed. A researcher explains that your assignment as a "teacher" is to present a "learner"—who is introduced but then seated on the other side of a partition—with a series of paired associates (words) and to deliver electric shocks of increasing intensity every time he gets an item incorrect. If you hesitate, perhaps because the learner is complaining or even screaming, the researcher tells you that you must continue. What do you think you would do in this situation? At what point do you think you would stop and refuse to go on delivering more intense shock?

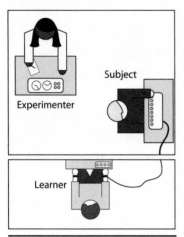

**Figure 5.4. Milgram's Experiment**

Milgram (1963) conducted this study, using graphic recordings of the "learner" once introductions were made, and found that up to 65 percent of the participants delivered the highest possible shock. These individuals continued even after the "learner" complained of a heart condition and became silent. Are these individuals evil? Milgram described the nervous laughter and other behaviors that the participants exhibited. They seemed nervous that they were obeying orders and violating their own conscience. Figure 5.4 shows the position of the subject ("teacher"), experimenter and "learner" (confederate) in the original Milgram study.

Milgram conducted twenty-one variations of this initial experiment, systematically varying different situational factors, as noted in table 5.1. Notice how the rate of obedience declined as specific factors such as nearness of the authority figure and distance from the victim were varied. Note also that the distance from the victim is of special consideration, as distance increases the propensity to dehumanize the other. This dehumanizing then increases the likelihood of destructive social processes such as violent aggression and prejudice, which will be discussed in later chapters.

**Table 5.1. Milgram and Beyond**

| Initial experiment | 65% |
|---|---|
| Low prestige setting | 48% |
| Teacher & learner together | 40% |
| Teacher touches learner | 30% |
| Teacher & experimenter apart | 22% |
| Non-professional gives orders | 20% |
| Two confederates rebel | 10% |

Source: Kilham & Mann, 1971; Milgram, 1963, 1971

Milgram interpreted his results as indicative of the power of the situation to influence the individual. He was especially interested in how Nazi soldiers could have committed such heinous acts of obedience. Milgram also noted that personality variables can influence one's propensity to obey. Blass (1991) agrees that though situational variables can be a significant influence on one's obedience, personality factors are also related to the propensity to obey. These variables include authoritarianism, especially the belief in deferring to authority figures, and religiosity, with people who reported higher levels of religiosity also reporting a greater propensity to obey.

As you can imagine, the results of Milgram's studies stirred a great deal of controversy from an ethical standpoint. In addition, many who read the studies were unnerved at the potential implications of these findings: Are humans really that vulnerable to obeying heinous commands? Do these findings help explain how otherwise normal individuals could obey evil commands? To deal with the ethical concerns of Milgram's study, Burger (2009) partially replicated Milgram's study, changing a few key factors. In Milgram's study, the 150-volt point is where the learner began to call out that he was in pain and begged the teacher to stop. Virtually all subjects who continued to deliver shocks to the 450-volt point continued to ask questions of the learner after receiving prods from the experimenter at the 150-volt point. Burger thus reasoned that he could predict which of his own subjects would continue to the 450-volt point by simply observing whether the subject continued to ask the next question of the learner after receiving the prod from the experimenter. Burger thus stopped the experiment after the 150-volt point without further unnecessarily stressing the subjects. Until that point, all subjects were led to believe that they could deliver shocks all the way up to the 450-volt mark. Burger found similar obedience rates as Milgram. Nevertheless, in one condition where defiant confederates refused to go on beyond the 150-volt mark, Milgram found that only 10 percent of the subjects continued to deliver the full range of voltage, while Burger found that over 54 percent of the male subjects and 68 percent of the female subjects would have continued to give the full range of voltage. This suggests that even having fellow dissidents is not enough to stop some people from obeying grievous orders.

In studies on obedience involving shocking or otherwise "harming" another, the confederates were living humans. Would participants respond similarly if the confederates were simulated beings? Slater et al. (2006) explored this question by using a procedure similar to that used in the original Milgram studies. The researchers had participants read sets of words to a female virtual character (the learner). The learner was then supposed to choose the word she had learned that matched the first word in the sequence. Participants were supposed to shock the learner with increasing intensity each time she got an answer incorrect. In one condition, the learner was presented on a screen, complaining of the increasing shock intensity. In another condition, the learner was hidden behind a partition, never complaining of the shock and only interacting by texting.

Slater et al. (2006) found that participants reported similar empathy for the inanimate learner (virtual human) and distress over harming her as they did in response to real human confederates used in earlier studies of obedience. In fact, several participants withdrew from the experiment before it was completed. This finding is especially interesting, as the researchers note that there is no way the participants could have confused the virtual learner with a real human. This is true even though the visual representation of the learner did have eye movements and facial expressions. In addition, many of the participants, especially those in the condition that allowed them to see and hear the learner, experienced physiological distress (e.g., sweating) and took longer to deliver the shock as they increased the voltage. The researchers conclude that this pattern of responding is similar to that found in the Milgram studies, though at lesser intensity. This was true even though the objections of the virtual learner in this experiment were less severe than in Milgram's.

The findings of the Slater et al. study suggest the human capacity for empathy, which was also observed in the Milgram participants, even among those who delivered the highest level of shock. Despite knowing that they were not actually causing pain to a real person, the participants in the Slater et al. study nevertheless responded with distress. Yet they continued to shock the learner even though it was unpleasant and contrary to their own conscience.

*A Christian view of obedience research.* One thing becomes immediately evident when reviewing the research on obedience: the focus of the overwhelming number of studies is on situations involving negative behavior where the right response would be to disobey. This bias has at least two consequences. First, we are left, as with the research on conformity, with a negative connotation of obedience. Second, we learn more from the research regarding how people succumb to negative commands rather than the processes involved in following the right type of commands. It would thus be helpful for research to focus more on obedience that is healthy and positive, as opposed to the traditional focus on obedience to commands that are tantamount to commands to torture others.

As is the case with conformity, obedience in itself is not a good or bad thing—it becomes so depending on whom/what we are obeying and for what purpose. From a Christian view of persons, obedience has a prominent place in our relationship with God. Obeying God's commands has a direct bearing on our social interactions and is one of the primary ways in which we partake in God's redemptive plan in our interactions with others. Consider the potential for redemption resulting from obedience to God in the matter of forgiveness toward one another (e.g., Mt 6:14; 18:21-22). As you will read in chapter seven on aggression, there is research that suggests that forgiveness of the offender reduces subsequent acts or inclinations toward retaliatory aggression and often increases the likelihood of reconciliation.

The Scriptures also speak of obedience to authority figures (parents, political leaders) that helps to establish and maintain social order. From a Christian view, then, obedience is not merely the process of relenting one's personal freedom. It is also a reflection of our relationship with God and our allegiance to his values and principles, which are expressed in the relationships that occur within loving community. Of course, whether or not to obey can often require great discernment. It would be interesting to explore in future research to what degree the factors involved in obedience to destructive orders are the same as those involved in obedience to prosocial orders. Specifically, looking at how factors such as presence of authority figures, disobedient peers and personality variables work in both types of obedience may help us understand how to better encourage obedience that is prosocial.

## SO FAR . . .

This chapter has presented us with research findings that suggest several key human tendencies. First, human social interaction involves a significant amount of social influence. To varying degrees, we look to each other for cues and information about how to understand our social world and respond to it. The research also suggests that humans seem to be inherently conforming and obedient beings, but not, by design, mindless creatures with no will to resist. Both obedience and conformity can help facilitate social interaction despite their destructive potential. Group membership is of prime importance for our identity and is one defining feature of our social interactions. Indeed, it is within and between groups that most social influence occurs.

Much of this research is consistent with a Christian notion of humans that considers social influence one of the primary ways in which we both learn to be more like God and through which we express the inherent tension between self-serving and other-serving tendencies. As many of my students have noted, it is indeed quite awe-inspiring to think about the potential one has to influence others to work toward both the common good as well as toward destructive ends. Given our common human challenge to deal with this tension, it may be wise to consider in both our personal lives as well as in future research how we can better learn to engage in positive conformity by hanging out with the right people (1 Cor 5:11) and how to engage in positive obedience by *listening* to the right people.

## QUESTIONS TO CONSIDER

1. What factors do you think might be involved in positive versus destructive obedience? How could researchers investigate the difference between the two?

2. In the self chapter, you read about how the self has three different levels or aspects: individual, relational and collective. Researchers (e.g., Brewer, 1996) suggest that the collective self (i.e., the part that identifies with a larger group) is the least likely to make self-sacrifices for the benefit of the larger group. How is this reconcilable with what you read in this chapter regarding the ease with which one might compromise personal convictions to adhere to group norms?

3. What do you think would characterize a person who shows an appropriate balance of conformity, obedience and resistance to both? How might researchers look for these characteristics?

## KEY TERMS

*autokinetic effect*

*brain writing*

*brainstorming*

*cautious shift*

*chameleon effect*

*compliance*

*conformity*

*crimes of obedience*

*dehumanization*

*deindividuation*

*discontinuity effect*

*dynamic social impact theory*

*group polarization*

*groupiness*

*group-serving bias*

*groupthink*

*informational influence*

*infrahumanization*

*intergroup processes*

*intragroup processes*

*mere presence effect*

*normative influence*

*obedience*
*obligatory interdependence*
*private conformity*
*production blocking*
*public conformity*
*reactance*
*risky shift*
*self-attention theory*
*social cascading*
*social contagion*
*social facilitation*
*social identity model of disinhibition effects*
*social impact theory*
*social influence*
*social influence model*
*social loafing*
*urban legend*

# 6

## Attitudes and Persuasion

*Yet More Examples of Social Influence*

*Let the same mind be in you
that was in Christ Jesus, who, though he was
in the form of God, did not regard equality
with God as something to be exploited,
but emptied himself.*

**Philippians 2:5-7**

Suppose you could accurately measure people's views on a wide variety of topics such as smoking, euthanasia, dating, religion and so on. What would that information tell you? Would their attitudes help you predict their behavior? For instance, if you knew how a person felt about integrity, how well would you be able to predict that person's likelihood of telling the truth in any given situation? Is it the attitudes that predict behavior, or is it ever possible that our behavior might actually influence a change in our attitude? And even if we could figure all that out, there would undoubtedly be circumstances under which we might wish to change certain attitudes or behaviors or perhaps even *both*. How are we persuaded to do so? These are the sorts of questions this chapter will explore.

The factors related to both attitudes and persuasion are closely related to the study of social influence more generally. As discussed in the previous chapters, humans significantly influence one another, and persuasion would be one obvious example of the way in which social influence occurs. The development and expression of attitudes is largely the result of persuasion. Thus, it makes sense to consider these two concepts together in this chapter.

In addition to exploring what social psychologists have had to say about the relationship between personal attitudes, behavior and persuasion, here we will together explore how an orthodox Christian perspective of humans might add to this discussion. Attitudes are an integral part of faith, which requires us to discern and make right judgments regarding social interactions and people. Our faith is defined as a relationship with God that includes an attitude of reverence and worship. As Christians, we seek to have attitudes toward one another and the world at large that reflect this loving attitude toward God. Let's see what the research shows us.

## ATTITUDES

**What are attitudes?** *Attitudes* are generally considered to be summary evaluative reactions of a target that include dimensions such as good/bad, harmful/beneficial and likeable/unlikeable (Azjen & Fishbein, 2000). In real life, our attitudes are often complex and ambivalent, consisting of *both* positive and negative reactions (e.g., Priester & Petty, 2001; Thompson, Zanna & Griffin, 1995). Tormala and Petty (2001) note that for some time, social psychologists thought that evaluating is a fundamental part of human nature, and that we have a so-called *need to evaluate* (Bargh, Chaiken, Raymond & Hymes, 1996; Fazio, Sanbonmatsu, Powell & Kardes, 1986; Jarvis & Petty, 1996; Markus & Zajonc, 1985). Uleman et al. (1996) even noted that we automatically evaluate a new person by making inferences regarding his or her traits "as naturally as we extract oxygen from the air" (p. 212).

Other research suggests that there are individual differences in the degree to which people engage in evaluative judgments; we are not all equally inclined to form evaluative attitudes so regularly or so intensely. Jarvis & Petty (1996), for example, showed that when participants were asked to describe their previous day, they differed with regard to how evaluative their descriptions were. High-need-to-evaluate participants made comments like "I really liked the music at the concert," while those with a low need to evaluate gave more neutral responses such as "I woke up at 8 a.m. and went to a concert."

Research also suggests that people differ with regard to whether they emphasize affective information or cognitive information when forming attitudes. Thus, some individuals are more likely to make judgments based on emotional appeals, while others are more inclined to pay attention to cognitive appeals to form their attitudes about a target. In addition, attitudes result in different neurological responses than do nonevaluative judgments (Crites & Cacioppo, 1996, as cited in Ajzen, 2001).

Attitudes often happen automatically and quickly and color our social cognition and perception, often in ways of which we are not even aware (e.g., Bargh & Chartrand, 1999; Eagly & Chaiken, 1998). Ito, Cacioppo and Lang (1998) note that we classify stimuli we encounter as either positive or negative almost immediately. For example, remember from the chapter on social perception that we tend to develop evaluative judgments of others in generally quick and often unconscious ways. Once attitudes are formed, they are often difficult to change, especially if those attitudes are strongly positive or negative. Researchers have found that activating automatic attitudes happens even when there is no explicit need or goal to make an evaluative judgment (Bargh, 1997; Bargh & Chartrand, 1999).

One model of attitudes is the *MODE model* (Fazio, 1990; Fazio & Towles-Schwen, 1999). This view explores how attitudes, which are both conscious and unconscious, are related to the evaluations we make of the target and the subsequent behavior toward that target. This model also focuses on how the positive or negative evaluations of a target are related to how easily the attitude is evoked. This model proposes that one's positive or negative evaluations of some particular target (e.g., race) biases the perceptions of that target, as well as one's behaviors or consequences associated with that target. Positive evaluations result in favorable perceptions of that issue or person in the future. These judgments then affect our behavior toward that target. But, according to this view, only strong (salient and frequent) attitudes, which can be accessed easily and quickly, will affect our behavior.

Regardless of whether the attitude is explicit or implicit, the degree to which attitudes are stable or flexible is a matter of great debate in social psychology. Bohner and Dickel (2010) note that while some researchers (e.g., Fazio, 2007; Petty et al., 2007) see attitudes as enduring memory structures, other researchers (e.g., Schwarz, 2007) see attitudes as fleeting and transient, depending on what each social situation elicits in the perceiver. It is not well established which factors affect a person's ability to alter attitudes, and to what extent former attitudes will continue to affect those that are newly formed about a particular target.

Maio and Haddock (2007) note that attitudes involve such a significant part of our mental life because they affect feelings, beliefs and behaviors. For this reason, research has focused on the influence of attitudes in a wide range of issues such as intergroup relations (e.g., race relations), health-relevant behaviors (e.g., smoking), religious behavior (e.g., church attendance) and humorous stimuli (e.g., cartoons). In general, researchers believe that such issues reflect the important influence of attitudes, and thus researchers often seek how to change destructive attitudes and reinforce positive ones. Maio and Haddock further note that in order to find ways to influence attitudes, the way attitudes are formed, as well as their content, structure and function, must be understood.

***How do we form and change attitudes?*** There are many ways in which we learn attitudes. As noted earlier, some of these ways are more explicit than others. Many attitudes are learned over time through reinforcement and modeling. An attitude to which we are repeatedly exposed is likely to influence our own attitudes regarding the subject (Bandura, 1977).

Researchers have explored many other ways to understand how attitudes develop. One conceptualization is known as the *expectancy-value model* (Fishbein, 1967). From this view, our evaluation of a target arises as the result of the beliefs we form about that target. Each belief becomes associated with an attribute believed to be true of the target. The overall attitude toward that target depends both on the subjective values of the target's attributes as well as the strength of those connections. Thus, we could have different attitudes about the same target, depending on the ease with which the belief is brought to memory.

Let us consider an example of the expectancy-value model to help clarify its basic tenets. Consider a professor toward whom you have developed a favorable attitude. You may have observed that she is witty in class, which you associate with easygoingness, a quality you respect. You may also have observed that she reads a lot, which makes you think she is intelligent. You may have also noticed that she is friendly with students, and you associate this with general kindness. All of these characteristics are attributes that you think are important, thus you develop a positive summary evaluation of the professor. Since you take a number of classes from this professor, you are able to observe the same behaviors again and again, which makes them easily accessible in your memory and further serves to strengthen the positive attitude toward her. This is but one example of how observations become associated with positive or negative attributes, which are then more easily accessed in memory, resulting in an attitude and corresponding behavior.

One model of how attitudes change is presented by Petty et al. (2007). They proposed the *meta-cognitive model* (MCM) and further noted that within the context of changing attitudes, this is called the *"past attitudes are still there" model* (PAST; Petty et al., 2006, as cited in Bohner & Dickel, 2011). These models assume that one can hold more than one summary evaluation of a target. As we are presented with new information about the target, we could alter our attitude, surmising that the previous one was false or incorrect. We then change our attitude, yet we retain some of the old way of thinking. This results in the possibility of varying attitudes toward the target, each dependent on the strength of the association we make. For example, imagine that all your life you have loved and eaten a lot of chocolate. Then you take a nutrition class in college and discover that chocolate is high in fat content and may be associated with a greater risk of heart disease. In this case, the MCM/PAST view would propose that your old positive attitude toward chocolate would be "tagged as false" in your memory and largely replaced by your new, more informed and negative attitude toward chocolate. Yet this does not mean that your previously positive attitude is not also present; in fact, it is still there, just tagged as invalid. Thus, the model predicts that when experiencing attitude changes, people often experience an unconscious ambivalence toward the target. This model suggests why people often have ambivalence when changing attitudes regarding important issues such as race or gender. Wilson et al. (2000) likewise note that while new attitudes may override old ones, they do not totally replace them.

Another way of describing how attitudes change is proposed by researchers (e.g., Schwarz, 2007) who argue that attitudes are in constant flux rather than being a stable personality trait. These researchers propose that attitudes change frequently in response to the information and demands of the environment and situation. As we receive cues from the social setting, we continually alter our attitudes about it.

One longstanding finding has been that attitudes that are very strong tend to be enduring and resistant to change (Petty & Krosnick, 1995). Yet there is other research that suggests that attitude strength changes over the course of life. Contrary to the perception that people become more inflexible with their attitudes as they age, Visser and Krosnick (1998, as cited in Ajzen, 2001) found changes in attitude strength over the life cycle. Their studies found that likelihood of attitude change declined from early adulthood to middle adulthood and then increased again in later life. The researchers noted that attitude certainty and perceived knowledge of attitude-relevant facts actually was higher in middle age than in later years. Perhaps as one gains life experience, one is humbled by the relative ignorance one has as compared to all there is to know.

Attitude strength is a difficult concept to measure because researchers have defined it in different ways. Across studies, attitude strength has been defined in terms of extremity of the attitude, its degree of personal relevance, stability across time, degree of certainty about the attitude and so on (Fazio & Towles-Schwen, 1999). For this reason, it is difficult to conclude how attitude strength is related to changes in attitude across time and susceptibility to persuasive tactics.

In a later section, you will read more about the role that persuasion plays in attitude change. Note so far that regardless of the researcher's perspective, the research suggests that attitude change is a complex process involving cognitive, affective and behavioral dimensions.

***What is the content of attitudes?*** There have been two major theories regarding attitude content. The first of these is called the *three-component model* (Zanna & Rempel, 1988), which posits that attitudes express one's *feelings, beliefs* and *past behaviors* regarding the attitude target. For example, suppose that you, like me, have a positive attitude toward roller coasters. In this case, we may feel exhilarated when riding the roller coaster (affective component), we believe that roller coasters are safe and worth experiencing (belief component), and we are likely to have ridden roller coasters many times in the past (behavioral component).

In real life, there is not always perfect agreement among the three components of attitudes. So, for example, you may ride roller coasters because your children like them, even though you may not believe they are safe and worthwhile and you also find them frightening. The resultant attitude thus may reflect ambivalence both within and among the feelings, beliefs and behaviors regarding the target. Yet there seems to be a tendency to seek coherence among the three attitude components (Eagly & Chaiken, 1993), partly because we generally do not like to experience internal psychological conflict (Festinger, 1957, as cited in Maio & Haddock, 2007).

Maio and Haddock also discuss a second major line of theories of attitude content, which is known as the *theory of reasoned action* (Ajzen & Fishbein, 1980). This view holds that an attitude is the *sum* of all the attitude beliefs regarding the target. The effect of each belief is a function of the degree of certainty with which it is held. So, for example, in the case of the roller coaster, if you strongly believe that it is a fun, worthwhile activity but are only somewhat convinced that the roller coaster is safe, you may experience an overall positive attitude about it.

As previously noted, attitudes can contain both positive and negative evaluations within and between the feelings, beliefs and behaviors associated with the target in question. How are positive and negative evaluations organized? Several researchers (e.g., Cacioppo, Gardner & Berntson, 1997, as cited in Maio & Haddock, 2007) have proposed that positive and negative evaluations are stored along two different dimensions. One dimension refers to whether few or many positive evaluations exist, whereas the other dimension has to do with whether the person has few or many negative evaluations. According to this view, a person could experience ambivalence if they had lots of positive *and* lots of negative feelings about the target, not just by virtue of being halfway between positive and negative feelings. So, for example, you could have an ambivalent attitude toward marriage if you felt *both* a dreadful fear of the responsibilities of marriage *and* a significant excitement about the possible benefits of marriage.

**What functions do attitudes serve?** Given the amount of mental energy we spend on forming and maintaining attitudes, we can surmise that they serve many important functions. Attitudes can help us organize our complex social world because they enable us to interact with it without having to reevaluate the same target person(s) or situation each time we encounter them. Attitudes can also increase our affiliations and connections with others who share similar attitudes. They can be a form of self-expression. Our attitudes can also boost our self-image as we consider them the "right" ones to have.

Attitudes can also serve the function of impression management. For example, presenting the "right" or popular attitudes to others ingratiates us and also increases the likelihood that the other person will form a favorable impression of us. This strategy is more likely to work if the requirements for accuracy are not high (Nienhuis, Manstead & Spears, 2001). Imagine, for example, that you are on a job interview with a publishing company for whom you wish to work as an editor. Imagine that this company is making a strong effort to preserve the environment in all its practices. During the interview, you dress casually, holding a recycled cup of water and making frequent references to the merits of the Environmental Protection Agency. The interviewer smiles and nods at you, obviously having formed a favorable initial impression of you. But then he asks how you as an editor would partake in the company's policies regarding protection of the environment, and all you can do is mention how you would be sure to recycle. Further questions result in continued ignorant responses. In this case, the initial favorable attitude that the interviewer had would likely become less positive as he seeks accurate information regarding your potential to work well within that organization. Figure 6.1 briefly illustrates some of the main purposes of attitudes. Can you think of some others?

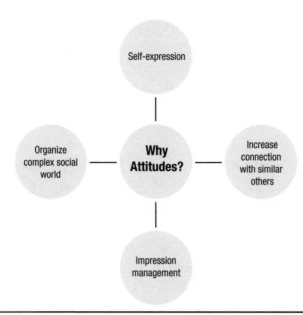

**Figure 6.1. Attitude Functions**

*Are we always aware of our attitudes?* In short, the answer is no. As noted briefly in the previous discussions, attitudes exist on both the conscious (explicit) and unconscious (implicit) level. A change in either explicit or implicit attitudes can affect the other in indirect ways (Gawronski & Bodenhausen, 2006, as cited in Bohner & Dickel, 2011). Measures of attitudes use both explicit and implicit methods in order to address these two levels. These methods each have their strengths and limitations. Explicit measures, where the questions are clearly stated, are based on the assumption that the respondent is both aware of and honest about their attitudes. Often, this is the case. But at other times, the respondent may answer in a way that is deemed socially desirable ("I am not racist"), or they may not be totally aware of the attitude they have. Implicit measures include the *Implicit Association Test* (IAT; Greenwald, McGhee & Schwartz, 1998), which is discussed in more detail in the chapter on prejudice (chap. 8).

Implicit tests assess attitudes in indirect ways, reportedly tapping into unconscious processes. The advantage to this is that the respondent is less likely to be able to guard against reporting negative attitudes. Fazio and Olson (2003) note that implicit measures assess spontaneous attitudes, whereas explicit measures assess more deliberate attitudes. Thus, if an individual is not motivated to deliberate about a particular issue, then implicit measures will assess the spontaneous attitudes and correlate with later behavior. On the other hand, if the person is motivated to deliberate, then deliberate attitudes will be reflected in explicit measures, which would then correlate more with later behavior. Yet some research suggests that the implicit tests also have their disadvantages, including the possibility that they are at least "slightly fakeable," especially if the respondent becomes aware of what attitude it is assessing (Schnabel, Asendorpf & Greenwald, 2008).

One area of research regarding the difference between explicit and implicit attitudes has explored under what conditions religious attitudes are evoked automatically and when they may require more thoughtful and deliberate evoking. Recall that the MODE model proposes that strong attitudes—those that are frequent, salient and connected to broader memory networks—are elicited more automatically than are weaker attitudes. Hill (1994) contends that if religious attitudes are strong, then they should be more easily evoked automatically.

Bassett et al. (2005) used a variation of the Implicit Association Test (IAT) to assess implicit and explicit attitudes regarding spirituality and religiosity. Participants were exposed to either religious words (*holy, communion, God, Bible,* etc.) or spirituality words (*higher being, inner peace, tranquility,* etc.). The results showed significant differences between responses to the two types of words, suggesting that religiosity and the more general, diffuse spirituality were perceived as different constructs by the students. There was also considerable variability between the students' self-report responses on the explicit and implicit measures of religiosity. The researchers suggest that these inconsistencies may reflect either the students' developmental process of faith development or the need to recognize "polarities and paradoxes" within the faith experience. In either case, Bassett et al. call for further research to assess these findings.

Hood, Hill and Spilka (2009) note several other research efforts to use both implicit and explicit measures of religiosity and to assess the connection between these two factors and attitudes toward race (Rowatt

& Franklin, 2004), humility (Powers, Nam, Rowatt & Hill, 2007) and homosexuality (Rowatt et al., 2006). Some researchers have found similarity between self-reported attitudes and implicit measures of those attitudes. For example, Rowatt, Franklin and Cotton (2005) used a mostly Christian sample to assess implicit and explicit attitudes toward Muslims. Participants completed a self-report measure of attitudes toward Muslims and Christians. They also completed the Implicit Association Test, which recorded reaction times as participants categorized Christian and Muslim names and adjectives (pleasant or unpleasant). The results indicated that self-reported attitudes were more positive toward Christians than toward Muslims. The IAT also showed that there was an implicit prejudice against Muslims relative to Christians. This was especially true for those who also scored high on scales measuring *authoritarianism,* the conventional view that highly endorses both authority and aggression that is sanctioned by authority figures.

Other studies of religious individuals have also shown consistencies between self-reported attitudes and implicit attitudes. Rowatt et al. (2006), for example, using a Christian sample, found that self-reported attitudes toward homosexuals were consistent with implicit measures of attitudes. In this study, the IAT recorded reaction times to images of heterosexual and homosexual men and adjectives (good and bad words). The results showed negative explicit and implicit attitudes toward homosexuals relative to heterosexual persons. These results were most prominent in those who self-described as high on *religious fundamentalism.* As you will read in the prejudice chapter, religious fundamentalism refers to the authoritarian manner of holding one's faith as the inerrant truth, and can be characteristic of any religious group. Thus, one must be cautious in assuming that religious faith itself is what encourages negative attitudes toward other religious groups and various marginalized groups. Research suggests that it is the way that faith is held that is more closely related to negative views of out-groups. This will be discussed in more detail in chapter eight on prejudice.

Despite such apparent consistencies between explicit and implicit measures of the relationship between religiosity and attitudes toward specific target groups, Hood, Hill and Spilka (2009) note that much more research is needed in this area. They also caution that with regard to explicit measures, it is not always possible to accurately predict whether the claimed attitudes of religious individuals will be consistent with actual behaviors or beliefs in real life. For example, in one study, religious individuals self-reported negative attitudes toward abortion, but many of those individuals still favored legal abortions (Scott, 1989). One possible explanation of these inconsistencies may be the common problem with self-report measures: they are prone to the social desirability effect. Another possible explanation is that the real life of a person of faith entails many more doubts and ambivalence regarding important moral issues than would be reflected on a questionnaire or in a laboratory setting. Research using implicit measures along with relevant personality variables (e.g., religious fundamentalism) may help to further clarify how the attitudes of religious people relate to actual behavior.

*How are attitudes related to behavior?* It is logical to think that attitudes predict behaviors well. If someone claims a love for animals, you would generally expect that they treat their pet well. Parents who highly value education should likely encourage and participate in their children's education. The relationship between attitudes and behavior is relevant to everyday life as well as to many other areas of inquiry (e.g., racism and discrimination, perceiving others as friend or foe). In our social interactions, we often assume that professed attitudes will be consistent with behavior, but this relationship is not so simple. There are times when attitudes do predict behavior, other times when behaviors influence attitudes, and still other times when professed attitudes and actual behavior seem to be unrelated. The following discussion follows mostly from Ajzen's (2001) review of some of the research in this area.

One theory of the relationship between attitudes and behavior is known as the *theory of reasoned action* (TORA; Fishbein & Ajzen, 1975), which was noted earlier with regard to how attitudes toward a target are the sum of numerous evaluative judgments. Here the focus is on how this theory explains the relationship between attitudes and behavior. This theory proposes that attitude, subjective norms and motivation all predict the likelihood of a behavior. In other words, if a person evaluates a behavior as positive and thinks that significant others want them to perform the behavior, there will be greater intention and consequently a greater chance that the behavior will be performed. Ajzen (1991) later extended this theory to include another factor: *perceived behavioral control,* otherwise known as *self-efficacy,* which refers to how likely an individual thinks it is that he or she would be able to perform the behavior. This is called the *theory of planned behavior* (TPB). From this view, "people act in accordance with their intentions and perceptions of control over their behavior, while intentions are in turn influenced by attitudes toward the behavior, subjective norms, and perceptions of behavior control" (Ajzen, 2001, p. 43). For example, in one study, the participants who were most likely to quit smoking had developed a negative attitude toward smoking, received messages of encouragement from loved ones to quit and believed that they were capable of quitting (Norman, Conner & Bell, 1999). Similar results have been found in a number of studies, including those investigating the likelihood that participants would begin eating low-fat diets (Armitage & Conner, 1999). A meta-analysis reveals that the theory of planned behavior has wide-reaching applications, though there are some criticisms of this theory (Armitage & Conner, 2001). Figure 6.2 depicts the major facets of the theory of planned behavior. Consider how integral is the role of social cues on our forming attitudes and its effect on subsequent behavior.

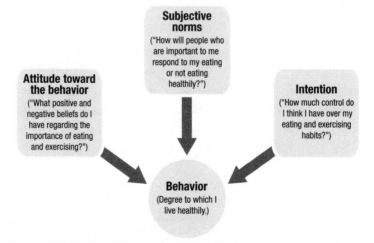

**Figure 6.2. Theory of Planned Behavior**
Source: Fishbein & Ajzen, 1975, 1980

Sometimes, of course, individuals do not behave in accordance with their professed attitudes. You may have observed this inconsistency between what we say and what we actually do any time you have felt surprise or even shock to learn about a friend whose behavior seems to be so at odds with his or her professed beliefs. Indeed, you likely have experienced this yourself: claiming and believing one thing but then doing something that is inconsistent with that value. Media records more extreme examples—stories of seemingly respectable, often churchgoing people who commit shocking or aggressive acts. These can be examples of *moral hypocrisy*, "trying to appear moral, but avoiding the cost of actually being moral" (Batson, Thompson & Chen, 2002, p. 330).

A number of studies have found ample evidence for moral hypocrisy but little evidence of moral integrity (e.g., Batson, Kobrynowicz, Dinnerstein, Kampf & Wilson, 1997; Batson, Thompson, Seuferling, Whitney & Strongman, 1999). Batson, Thompson and Chen (2002) describe this series of studies as follows. Participants assigned themselves and another (fictitious) participant to either an obviously desirable task (chance to win raffle tickets) or a neutral task (no chance of winning tickets). The participants were told that the other would not know that they had been allowed to assign the task, but rather would be led to believe that the assignment had occurred by chance. Most of the research participants assigned themselves the positive task, though most later acknowledged that this was not a moral action. In a related study, participants read instructions that clearly stated that most people would consider flipping a coin to be the most fair way of assigning the task. Though most participants agreed that either flipping a coin or assigning the other participant the positive task was the most just thing to do, only half tossed the coin, and the majority of those who did not assigned themselves the positive task. In these studies, then, self-interest overrode the desire to act morally.

Valdesoso and DeSteno (2007) found moral hypocrisy not only at the individual level but also at the group level. They had participants allot resources (time and energy) either to themselves or to a confederate using a fair (random) process or an unfair process (assigning the more positive resources to themselves). The findings were consistent with moral hypocrisy at the individual level. Further, when subjects witnessed an in-group member (i.e., from their own group) acting in a self-serving manner, they were more likely to judge it as a fair action than if the person was an out-group member.

The preceding discussion has focused on how attitudes affect behavior. Initially, attitude research assumed that this was the direction of causality. Festinger (1964), however, noted a significant concern with this assumption: there was insufficient evidence that changing an attitude changes behavior. He proposed that there are many instances in which behavior actually influences a change in attitude. How does this happen? One possible explanation is based on *consistency theories,* which are based on Heider's (1946) *balance theory.* These propose that we tend to prefer to have consistency among our cognitions, affect and behavior. A discrepancy between any of these causes what Festinger (1957) referred to as *cognitive dissonance,* or dis-ease. When we experience that dissonance, we tend to want to resolve it by bringing cognitions, affect and behavior into alignment. We could change our beliefs or we could change our behavior to restore inner harmony. We could also look for new information that supports or justifies our behavior. Or we could convince ourselves that the discrepancy doesn't really matter because the relevant attitudes and behaviors are not all that important, thereby trivializing them (Simon, Greenberg & Brehm, 1995). Often, we change our attitudes to be consistent with our behaviors, thereby rationalizing our conduct and reducing discomfort.

A classic study that investigated how cognitive dissonance works was conducted by Festinger and Carlsmith (1959). Students were asked to perform a series of very dull tasks, including turning pegs in a board for one hour. Students were paid either one dollar or twenty dollars to convince a waiting participant (actually a confederate) that the task was really interesting. The results indicated that students who were paid one dollar expressed more favorable attitudes toward the task than did students who were paid twenty dollars.

The results of the Festinger and Carlsmith (1959) study seem counterintuitive: you might be inclined to think that the students who were paid more would be more favorable toward the task, as they could at least justify it by their financial gain. But, as the cognitive dissonance theory predicted, though all students had negative attitudes toward the boring task, it was too late to change anything. Further, the students who had been paid only one dollar apparently had an even more negative response to the task (there was no rationalizing it) and thus felt a greater motivation to rationalize their participation in the experiment in order to reduce the dissonance.

The *roles* we play are another powerful factor that affects both behaviors and attitudes. When we are in certain roles, the behaviors associated with that role can be internalized and affect our attitudes as well. Consider military officers. This role entails giving lots of commands and also a great deal of responsibility, including the knowledge that one's decisions could seriously affect subordinates or even result in the loss of many lives. Sometimes, as the officer becomes habituated to being in charge, this can carry over into other aspects of life, including family life. I know a pilot who indicated that part of their training entailed specific instructions about how to transition back into family life where there is no need for such commands.

All right! So they made you chairman of the board . . . but don't you think you're carrying this a bit far?

**Figure 6.3.**

Research suggests that as individuals engage in certain roles or behaviors, they make increasing commitments to the behavior and the attitudes associated with it. One classic and oft-quoted example of this is the *Stanford prison study* conducted by Zimbardo (1971). Zimbardo was interested in what would happen when participants took part in a simulated prison environment where they were randomly assigned the role of prisoner or guard. Would the roles begin to affect attitudes and behaviors?

Zimbardo set up a makeshift prison in a basement at Stanford University. The local police cooperated with the experiment by "arresting" the "prisoners" (who had enrolled in the study), reading them their rights and escorting them to the prison. Here the prisoners were fingerprinted, stripped, deloused, given a prison uniform to wear and then placed in a cell. Prisoners also wore a chain around their ankle as a reminder of their captivity and were only called by their given ID number. Meanwhile, the participants who were assigned the role of guard dressed in guard uniforms, wore a whistle and carried a billy club. They were not given any specific instructions other than to maintain order among the prisoners, within reasonable limits.

As the study continued, both the prisoners and the guards assumed behaviors and attitudes that were consistent with their roles in the study. For example, the guards began by using some fairly innocuous strategies to demonstrate their power (e.g., holding "counts," where the prisoners were required to call out their given ID numbers for attendance). But then beginning on day two of the experiment, the guards escalated their power tactics in response to prisoners' increasingly rebellious attitudes toward them. Prisoners began by refusing to come out of their cells for the count, refusing to eat and spreading a false rumor of an escape plan. Guards, in turn, began to punish prisoners suspected of rebelling, isolating them in cells and refusing to give them food. In addition, the guards forced prisoners to do multiple push-ups and clean toilets with their bare hands. The guards also used strategies to break the solidarity among the prisoners by randomly assigning them to "privilege cells" and isolating cells. The counts also became more arbitrary, waking prisoners in the middle of the night.

The power of this situation became so overwhelming that guards began to assume one of three roles: tough but fair, easygoing or aggressive. The prisoners also assumed different types of roles, from very obedient to continuously rebellious. Several prisoners broke down emotionally, and one even developed a rash all over his body from the stress. Zimbardo (1971), who played the role of prison superintendent, admits that he was so much into his own role that he did not notice how unethical the treatment of the prisoners was until about the sixth day of the study, when a graduate student commented that this was "horrible what you are doing to these boys." At that point, the study was discontinued, even though the original plan was to continue for two weeks.

The surprising and frightening findings of Zimbardo's study suggest not only how powerful certain situations can be, but specifically how the roles played in those situations can powerfully affect our attitudes and behaviors. Zimbardo (2007) notes that this is one primary explanation for how ordinary people can act in evil ways. Interestingly, all the young men in the prison study had been screened and found to be mentally healthy individuals before being allowed to participate in the study. Furthermore, they had all been randomly assigned to their roles. Thus, there is no evidence that psychological problems in either the guards or the prisoners could explain the results. Prison behavior was also not related to personality traits such as authoritarianism, which includes the tendency to highly value deference to authority and to aggress against those who deviate from it (Adorno et al., 1950). Zimbardo concluded that the stress of the situation itself accounted for the behavior of the guards and

prisoners. Look closely at photo 6.1, which depicts a prisoner of war. Consider the relevance of Zimbardo's prison study for such cases in which the guards and prisoners already considered each other enemies before the imprisonment ever took

Photo 6.1

place. How might the behavior of the guards and prisoners in such situations resemble that in regular prisons? How might the situational influences in the two types of prisons differ?

***How do attitudes bias social perception?*** In the chapter on the self, you read about *confirmation bias,* which is the tendency to seek information that confirms our preconceived notions. This tendency is discussed throughout this text regarding many social contexts, including group behavior, race relations and attraction. The study of attitudes likewise suggests that there is a tendency to both seek attitude-consistent information and to rate it as more accurate and reliable than information that refutes our attitudes. A study by Munro et al. (2002) demonstrated this regarding political attitudes and information. Munro and Ditto (1997) also found that participants tended to rate research regarding homosexuality as more accurate if its conclusions were consistent with their own attitudes. Thus, the individual tendency toward confirmation bias can be amplified in a group setting, where it takes on a power that is magnified as group members affirm each other about their mutual viewpoint, as seen in the groupthink discussion.

***CFR view and attitudes.*** Remember from the early discussion on the CFR view that social psychology is better at delineating specific processes underlying social behavior, while the Scriptures describe general tendencies upon which many of these processes are based. The research on attitudes is a good example of this. Attitudes play a central role in both the social world as well as in the life of faith. It is thus possible to explore a number of different ways in which a Christian view of humans relates to the vast research on attitudes and behavior. To that end, let us look first at the ways in which attitudes are understood in both the research and the Scriptures. Then we will discuss the relevance of the distinction between implicit and explicit attitudes, and finally we will examine the issue of moral hypocrisy in the light of creation, fall and redemption.

Attitude research focuses on attitudes as evaluative reactions to many different types of targets, including people (e.g., racial groups) as well as issues or objects (e.g., smoking, diet, consumer goods). The Scriptures speak more broadly about evaluations of moral issues, all of which may be subsumed under the command to "hate evil and love good" (Amos 5:15).

Over and over again, the Scriptures admonish us to have negative attitudes toward every manner of evil that separates us from God and one another, including pride, arrogance and injustice (Prov 8:13). Thus, the Bible is most concerned with promoting righteous attitudes (evaluations) that serve the ultimate end of loving God and our fellow humans rather than attitudes toward different educational pursuits, types of cars and so on, except insofar as these are connected to moral issues.

The Scriptures and the attitude research both speak to the strong propensity we have to evaluate our social world. Though research suggests that people vary with regard to the degree and intensity of their evaluative judgments (e.g., Petty & Jarvis, 1996), there is still ample evidence that attitudes are an integral part of our social world. Evidence of the pervasive nature of attitudes is seen in the research on implicit versus explicit attitudes. Remember that this research shows how evaluative responses occur whether we are aware of them or not, and that implicit attitudes can be elicited rather easily (e.g., Bargh et al., 1996). The concept that we are not aware of our attitudes and that our attitudes can often be self-serving is consistent with Scripture, which refers to the need for God to search our hearts and see if there is any evil way within us (Ps 139:23-24).

Another relevant concept from the attitude research has to do with *moral hypocrisy*, which you recall is the incongruity between professed attitudes and behavior. This research is relevant to the CFR view of personhood, as it relates to the conflict between the created goodness of humans and the fallen condition. Batson and Thompson (2001) note that the research on moral hypocrisy generally suggests two possible motives for acting in a morally hypocritical way. First, people may simply be primarily motivated by self-interest, regardless of the cost. Second, people may be most motivated by wishing to avoid paying too high a price for virtue. In both cases, moral virtue is not seen as an end in itself. These two interpretations of the data suggest that morality is at best a second consideration, as long as it has some practical utility for the self.

Batson and Thompson (2001) discuss how the two motivations noted above can lead to the conclusion that the world is full of moral hypocrites. The authors suggest there may be a third motive for the apparent hypocrisy—they call it *overpowered integrity*—in which morality is seen as an end in itself. In this case, a primary motive for the person is to act morally, but when they see the heavy cost of the action, they may decide to do otherwise. Batson and Thompson note that their research provides evidence for both moral hypocrisy and moral integrity. The researchers distinguish these two experimentally by assessing the initial intent of the person. For example, in the coin toss experiments noted earlier, participants could manipulate the coin toss to their advantage. Batson and Thompson noted that those who are acting out of moral integrity should not really care who tossed the coin, while those who act out of moral hypocrisy (acting morally if it doesn't cost too much) should wish to maintain control over tossing the coin. Batson, Tsang and Thompson (2000) found that 80 percent of the participants opted to have the experimenter toss the coin, consistent with moral integrity.

The researchers also showed how moral integrity could be overpowered by increasing the costs of moral behavior. In one study, they told the participants that they would receive an electric shock if they missed items on the negative learning task. Here, only one-fourth of the students opted to have the experimenter toss the coin. Most of those who tossed it themselves assigned themselves the positive task in order to avoid the shock. Later, those students who had given up even the appearance of moral integrity commented that they knew it was not the right thing to do.

Batson and Thompson (2001) conclude that the data do not support the notion that the world is full of moral hypocrites, but rather that there are plenty of instances in which humans genuinely seem to want to be moral, not just appear moral. The problem is, as the CFR view also suggests, a conflict between a propensity toward moral action on the one hand and a desire to protect self-interest on the other. According to Scripture, this has been the fundamental struggle facing human beings since the fall. To desire to be virtuous while being drawn by self-interest is a conflict that Batson and Thompson say is exemplified in Scripture: "The spirit indeed is willing, but the flesh is weak" (Mt 26:41).

The conclusions drawn by Batson and Thompson (2001) that humans have both moral integrity and moral hypocrisy are at once encouraging and sobering. On the one hand, as the authors suggest, it may be possible to further study under what conditions both moral hypocrisy and integrity are learned such that we may coach individuals to exercise moral integrity, thereby avoiding both minor and sometimes major moral failures. These efforts would be consistent with the Christian view of personhood that acknowledges the created value and goodness in all humans. On the other hand, the finding that moral integrity is often overcome causes us to humbly acknowledge our own vulnerability to forsake moral virtue when the costs are high. As Batson and Thompson note, many atrocious acts are committed by otherwise moral people, not by the "monsters" we typically associate with such crimes. For example, Ted Bundy, the serial killer, noted in an interview the day before his execution that many violent criminals are not the ogres we think they are, but rather brothers and sons.

Can encouraging prosocial, other-centered attitudes possibly reduce moral hypocrisy, a self-centered behavior? Tong and Yang (2010) suggest this is possible. They specifically explored whether encouraging an attitude of gratitude would decrease moral hypocrisy, while encouraging an attitude of pride would increase moral hypocrisy. In previous research gratitude has been associated with many prosocial behaviors such as helping (e.g., Tsang, 2006), empathy and forgiveness (e.g., Bartlett & DeSteno, 2006; McCullough, Emmons & Tsang, 2002, as cited in Tong & Yang, 2010). Conversely, as you read in the self chapter, an attitude of excessive pride generally results in many self-centered, antisocial behaviors such as aggression (Baumeister & Bushman, 1998) and dominating behaviors to obtain personal achievement and prestige (Williams & DeSteno, 2008, 2009, as cited in Tong & Yang, 2010).

In the pride condition, Tong and Yang (2010) induced feelings of pride in the participants by asking them to recall times when they felt really proud of themselves for their accomplishments and to relive that feeling by describing it in detail. In the gratitude condition, participants were instructed to think of times when they had been grateful and to relive them by describing in detail why and how they felt thankful. In a neutral condition, participants were not given any attitude-inducing instructions. All participants were then told that they would have the choice of whether to engage in a fun task (to win a thirty-dollar gift certificate) or in a neutral task (somewhat dull, with no chance of earning a gift certificate). This procedure of task assignment mimics that of Batson et al. (1997), where participants were told that they would be paired with a (fictional) partner. The participant was told they could either decide which task each would complete or flip a coin, which was the fairest way to assign the tasks. The results showed that those in the gratitude condition were significantly more likely to flip the coin, both acknowledging this was the fairest way to assign the tasks and also following through with it. Among those in the gratitude condition who did not toss the coin, a startling 50.5 percent offered their partner the more desirable task. In contrast, those in the pride condition were more likely to assign themselves the more favorable task, but then pretend to the partner that they had flipped a coin, thereby exhibiting moral hypocrisy. The results of Tong and Wang suggest the important connection between attitudes and behaviors. Furthermore, the results provide some additional support for a Christian view of humans that acknowledges how our given capacity for other-centered focus may reduce self-centered concerns. Additional research is needed to explore how other-centered virtues may relate to reduced self-focus and moral hypocrisy in a variety of social situations.

## PERSUASION: *CHANGING ATTITUDES*

Your position as a college student makes you the recipient of numerous persuasive messages. Indeed, one main purpose of this textbook is to persuade you that a Christian view of the human condition can inform our understanding of human social interaction. How many times have your professors tried to convince you (sometimes not successfully) that their lecture material is very interesting and relevant or that one particular theory in the field is more valid than the others? How about group presentations in class where one of your group members needed to be coaxed or persuaded to have a better attitude about the project? Consider the myriad ways in which your peers and you influence one another in forming various opinions of weighty and not-so-weighty matters.

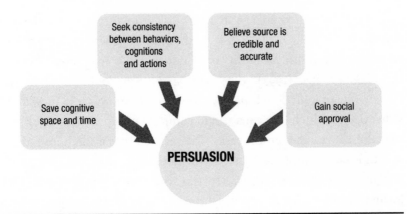

**Figure 6.4. Why Persuasion?**

It is not possible to accurately measure the many ways in which we receive and emit persuasive messages of one form or another. This is because persuasive messages include high-stakes and low-stakes messages, each delivered in both conscious and unconscious ways. You may have had the experience, for example, of being aware that you have a strong conviction about something, yet you cannot recall specifically or without difficulty how you developed this attitude.

While in the previous sections you read mostly about how and why attitudes are formed, this section reviews literature on how attitudes and related behaviors are changed. This distinction helps us better understand the important implications of each facet of attitudes (Crano & Prislin, 2006).

The pervasive nature of persuasion, along with its strong potential for both positive and negative consequences, makes it easy to see why this was one of the early research concerns of social psychologists. Floyd Allport (1937) conducted some of this early research, as did Kurt Lewin (1946), who had escaped Nazi Germany. Lewin studied how war propaganda affected the attitudes of German citizens against Jews. Classic studies of persuasion (e.g., Hovland, Janis & Kelly, 1953) investigated how characteristics of the message, the messenger and the recipient were related to likelihood of persuasion. But, as Ajzen (1992) notes, these earlier studies failed to produce consistent results. More recent research focuses on specific cognitive and affective processes involved in persuasion.

It is obvious that persuasion includes verbal messages that can influence attitudes and behavior. All manner of verbal messages exist, including advertisements, class lectures and peer pressure messages. These messages typically involve a position, arguments in favor of it and evidence to support that position (Ajzen, 1992). Yet research also suggests that nonverbal messages can have a very powerful influence on attitudes and behavior. Chartrand, Maddux and Lakin (2005) review research that has demonstrated that subtle social mimicry—imperceptibly mimicking another's facial gestures, accents or body movements—can convince people to help, buy used cars, and increase positive attitudes of the person who is doing the mimicking. This significant influence of subtle, nonverbal cues is an important consideration for understanding just how vast and often unconscious the persuasive messages we receive can be.

***When does persuasion work?*** We can all recall instances in which the persuasive appeals of another were not the least bit convincing. I remember one such instance with a student who had missed one of my exams; she approached me a few days later to let me know that she was absent due to having contracted mono from using a friend's lip-gloss. In a subdued voice I had never before witnessed in her, she began to mimic the symptoms from which she had suffered, complete with bent-over coughing for added effect. She then handed me an obviously false copy of an ER report, which consisted of some scratched-out text and some "doctor's signature" that I am sure was falsified. I listened intently to this desperate appeal, doing all that I could to refrain from laughing.

Why didn't I find that student convincing? Persuasion research may provide some clues here. Studies suggest that persuasion usually works for several reasons (Petty & Krosnick, 1995). First is when we want *accurate information* about the world and are convinced that the persuader is trustworthy for giving this accurate information to us. In the case of the student, I had a sense that her message was not based in truth, so there would be no advantage in terms of advancing my knowledge of reality. Second, persuasion tends to work when we wish to *gain social acceptance and support*. In my case, I was not motivated to seek the social acceptance of the student; I was more concerned with truth. Needless to say, the student failed to persuade me that she had been ill and deserved special treatment.

Another reason why persuasion works is related to the *consistency theories,* which were discussed earlier. Remember these theories propose that we tend to prefer to have consistency among our cognitions, affect and behavior. A discrepancy between any of these results in *cognitive dissonance,* which we tend to want to resolve by bringing cognitions, affect and behavior into alignment. These strategies involve some measure of persuading the self and may also make us more susceptible to persuasion by others if they can help us reduce the dissonance.

A similar process often occurs when we experience dissonance after a decision is made (Brehm, 1956; Knox & Inkster, 1968). Suppose you could choose between two equally attractive cars to buy. Or suppose you could not afford to buy the car you really wanted, so you had to choose another. In both cases, you may experience dissonance after the decision is made. How might you resolve that dissonance? In either case, you could convince yourself that the other beautiful car was not as good as the one you did buy by downplaying the other car's features and highlighting the features of the one you bought (e.g., "buying this car is really wise because it will help me save money for college bills" or, "I didn't really like the color of that other car after all"). In these ways, we try to persuade ourselves that the decision we made was the best. It seems that seeking accuracy is more important before a decision is made, and then once it is made, reducing dissonance becomes more important. Blanton, Pelham, DeHart and Carvallo (2001) even suggest that one way in which we overcome postdecision cognitive dissonance is by becoming overconfident in the validity of our decisions.

***Dual-process vs. unimodal theories of persuasion.*** *Dual-process models* propose that persuasion occurs through one of two different "routes" (Lavine, 1999). The first of these routes is known as the *heuristic systemic model* (Chaiken, 1987; Chaiken, Liberman & Eagley, 1989). According to this model, persuasive messages are processed either simply and superficially (using heuristics), or more deliberately and thoughtfully (systemically). We tend to process information superficially if we do not have time to process it, we do not find it personally relevant and/or we trust the credibility of the source. This type of processing saves us cognitive time and energy and can be very efficient. We tend to process information more thoughtfully if we are motivated to do so (e.g., if the stakes are high and the issue is personally relevant), though it requires more effort. This type of deliberation is more likely to result in enduring changes in attitude than does superficial processing.

A classic study of the heuristic-systemic model was conducted by Petty and Cacioppo (1984). They gave college students a persuasive argument in favor of the college requiring mandatory final exams for all classes, and students would have to pass these exams in order to graduate. The researchers used various conditions in which they varied the degree of personal relevance (the policy would take effect in ten years, meaning low relevance for the student, or the policy would take effect immediately, meaning high relevance for the student). The researchers also varied the quality of the argument presented. The results indicated that the students for whom the issue had personal relevance thoughtfully considered the high-quality argument in favor of the exam and were generally persuaded in favor of it. By contrast, students for whom the personal relevance was low (i.e., they would not be required to take the exam) did not tend to thoughtfully consider the validity of the argument presented, and were as likely to support it as to oppose it.

A second dual-process model of persuasion is known as the *elaboration likelihood model* (ELM; Petty & Cacioppo, 1986). This view holds that when we have the cognitive capacity or ability and we are motivated to process a persuasive message, we tend to pay close attention to *central* features of the argument—its logic and coherence, for example. But when we do not have sufficient cognitive capacity to comprehend the message and we are not motivated to process the message, we are more easily persuaded by *peripheral* information such as the good looks of the presenter or the humorous strategies used by them. So if you are genuinely concerned about the new curriculum being proposed in your psychology department and are able to process the various proposals, you would intentionally look for information about its pros and cons and take time to consider it. If, on the other hand, your school decided it wanted to persuade students to wear green on St. Patrick's Day, and you are not really interested in the controversy, you would be content to vote in favor of the proposal after having seen the funny posters all around campus and hearing the witty and animated dean speak of his proposal.

In contrast to dual-process models of persuasion, Kruglanski and Thompson (1999) propose a *unimodal approach* to understanding how persuasion works. This view proposes that there really are no different information and processing types as are suggested by the dual-process models. Instead, as Lavine (1999) discusses, this model holds that the primary factor determining the strength of a persuasive message and the amount of processing effort we will put into it has to do with its complexity. *Any* factor involved in persuasion (e.g., a cue given by the presenter, the specific argument made or a feeling associated with an attitude target) varies in processing difficulty. Any evidence that is easier to process, either because it is a short message or presented early on or in a salient way, takes less effort to have a higher likelihood of influencing attitude judgments. By contrast, evidence that is more difficult to process because it is lengthy, complex or presented later, requires a higher level of processing effort to influence attitude judgments.

Despite the differences between dual-processing models and the unimodal approach to persuasion, Bohner and Dickel (2011) note that the two approaches share some important similarities. First, they both assume that persuasion is the result of a continuum of processing effort. Thus, both approaches would suggest that people process more deeply the information that is most relevant to themselves and if they feel like they have the capacity to do so. Second, the models both propose that information that is presented early on can bias the processing of information presented later, assuming the individual is motivated to continue processing information. Table 6.1 summarizes the differences between dual-process and unimodal theories of persuasion.

**Table 6.1. Dual-Process vs. Unimodal Theories**

| DUAL-PROCESS MODELS | Heuristic-Systems Model | Little interest and/or little time leads to superficial processing; high interest/ personal relevance leads to thoughtful deliberate processing |
|---|---|---|
| | Elaboration-Likelihood Model | High motivation to process leads to focus on central features of argument (e.g., logic, consistency, etc.); low motivation leads to focus on peripheral cues (e.g., wit and appearance of persuader) |
| UNIMODAL THEORY OF ATTITUDES | | Little interest and/or little time leads to superficial processing; high interest/ personal relevance leads to thoughtful deliberate processing |

Source: Chaiken, 1982; Petty & Cacioppo, 1986; Kruglanski & Thompson, 1999

*What other factors affect the likelihood of persuasion?* The dual-process models and the unimodal approaches to persuasion follow the early research on persuasion that focused on elements of the message, communicator and audience (Hovland, Janis & Kelly, 1953). In general, the early research made several conclusions that have been supported by later research. First, as already noted, a presenter who seems credible is more likely to be persuasive. In addition, a presenter who gives a two-sided argument and seems to be arguing against his or her own interests often gains the trust of the audience (Chaiken, Wood & Eagly, 1996). Persuasive messages that include repetition of key points often become more easily accessible to memory, making the message seem more valid (Boehm, 1994).

Petty, Brinol and Tomala (2002) claim that the majority of persuasion research, as discussed above, has focused on one of two main aspects of thinking that are related to persuasion. The first of these is the *extent* of thinking, or how much the person engages the persuasive message. The second factor is related to the *content* of the thinking about the persuasive message, most notably whether the message elicits positive, negative or neutral affect. Petty et al. suggest a third way of looking at the power of persuasion. They propose the *self-validation theory*, which posits that the level of confidence in one's own thoughts can increase or decrease persuasion depending on the type of thoughts that the message elicits. When your cognitive responses to a persuasive message are mostly negative, an increase in confidence in those thoughts should increase the chances that you will resist the message. By contrast, if your cognitive responses to the message are mostly positive, increasing confidence in your thoughts should increase the chances that you will be persuaded by the message.

Across three studies, Petty et al. manipulated students' confidence about and emotional reaction to a persuasive message about comprehensive final exams. The results indicated that when thoughts about a message were mostly favorable (e.g., the argument was deemed strong, the topic was seen as important), the student was more likely to be persuaded if their confidence in their thoughts was high than if it was low. The researchers note that these findings raise important questions, as confidence in one's thoughts is not necessarily related to the quality of those thoughts; we can confidently believe in what is not accurate (Metcalfe, 1998, as cited in Petty et al., 2002).

Another powerful factor in persuasion is perceived social norms. Much research suggests that people are more likely to be persuaded if they believe that other people are also behaving or thinking in that particular way. One clever example of this was demonstrated in a study by Goldstein, Cialdini and Griskevicius (2008). A message was left in a hotel room encouraging the customer to reuse their towels because it was good for preservation of the environment. In a different condition, the message said that *most people in that hotel* reused their towels in an effort to save the environment. In that case, reuse of towels increased by an extra 20 percent. In a final condition, the message noted that *most people who stayed in that room* reused towels. In that condition, reuse increased by 33 percent. Thus, more explicit mention that others were complying increased the likelihood of being persuaded to follow suit.

***How is gender related to persuasion?*** Research on the relationship between gender and persuasion has explored both how the two genders may differ in persuasibility as well as what factors impact how persuasive each gender is. Eagly and Carli (1981, as cited in Guadagno & Cialdini, 2002) investigated gender differences related to likelihood of being persuaded. They conducted a meta-analysis of over 140 studies that showed females were more likely to be persuaded than were males.

Yet the researchers noted that this finding was moderated by social factors and how public the response was. Other researchers (Eagly, 1987; Wood & Stanger, 1994) contend that this sex difference in persuadeability is a reflection of different social role expectations for men and women. That is, for males, agency and independence are generally highly valued, and thus they may be more inclined to resist persuasion. Females, on the other hand, are more communally minded and will more often consider the nature of the relationship within which the persuasive argument is made.

Guadagno and Cialdini (2002) assessed whether sex differences in likelihood of persuasion would be found in online persuasive messages as well as in face-to-face encounters. They conducted two studies in which students were told about a policy regarding a comprehensive final exam requirement for graduation. The students were either given this message in an impersonal e-mail or by a confederate after a conversation with that person. In addition, in the second study, the researchers included a series of games varying in competitive level that the student played with the confederate. The results indicated that for female students, prior communication with the persuader increased level of agreement relative to impersonal e-mail interactions. For the male students, less agreement only occurred after they played the competitive game with the confederate. The researchers suggest that these findings are consistent with the social norms explanation offered by Eagly (1987). They also noted that it is not clear how enduring these new attitudes would be, and future research should investigate this.

Other research on sex differences in persuasion have focused on whether there are any differences in factors related to how persuasive an individual can be. For example, remember that competence is an important characteristic in a persuader. Carli (2001) notes that competence works in different ways for male and female persuaders. Carli's research found that women who combine competence cues with warmth in smiling and nodding are as persuasive as their male counterparts and more persuasive than women who show mere competence (Carli, LaFleur & Loeber, 1995, as cited in Carli, 2001). These results suggest that a man can influence others even when they do not particularly like

him, but a woman is more influential if she is likeable. Again, these results do not tell us anything about how enduring these differences are in
terms of changed attitudes in the participants.

*How do emotions affect persuasion?* So far you have read in several
sections of this chapter that affect is an important variable that affects the
likelihood of persuasion. Many times, for example, positive feelings are
associated with greater likelihood of persuasion than are negative feelings,
yet this varies by individual preferences for affective vs. cognitive cues
(Ajzen, 2001). Messages that evoke fear can also be very powerful. This is
true especially if the persuader provides examples of how to avoid the
feared stimulus or consequence. Otherwise, the audience may simply
feel a sense of being overwhelmed with fear and no way to escape the
dreaded consequences (Robberson & Rogers, 1988). Lectures about the
dangers of bad eating habits are thus unlikely to have much effect unless
the audience is offered specific ways to eat a healthful diet and the various

benefits of it. The fears
instilled by a ruthless
leader against an alleged
enemy can have devas-
tating consequences, es-
pecially when the leader
proposes a solution to
dealing with the "enemy."

Cialdini and Goldstein
(2004) review some other
research regarding the relationship between affect and persuasion. They
note that some research (Whatley et al., 1999) shows that once a request is
received, many people use their feelings as cues for avoiding shame and
guilt about complying or not complying with persuasive requests.

Cialdini and Goldstein (2004) also note the research of Forgas's (1998)
*affect infusion model* (AIM), which contends that a target's mood will most
likely greatly affect the processing of a persuasive request if the processing
of that request requires deliberate and thoughtful work. This view thus
holds that the more information processing a request requires, the more the
chances that affect will become an important part of those deliberations.

Thus, research on the relationship between affect and persuasion provides some interesting and inconsistent results. Emotions affect some people's decision making more than other people's. In addition, the type of emotion (happiness, fear, guilt, shame, etc.) interacts in different ways with the likelihood of persuasion depending on the circumstances and the personal relevance that the individual experiences. Future research will continue to explore the complex relationship between mood and persuasion. In any case, this research does alert us to be aware of how much our feelings may impact the effectiveness of efforts to persuade us.

**What are some strategies used in persuasion?** You can well imagine any number of persuasive techniques, some more overt and honest than others. In the preceding sections, you read about how the content of the message, the type of thinking and feelings one has about the message, and the social norms related to that message can all affect the likelihood of persuasion in complex ways. Now let's consider several specific and somewhat deceptive persuasion strategies that are sometimes used in business and that social psychologists have focused on in their research.

*The foot-in-the-door phenomenon.* Imagine making a small request, to which you are certain your friend will gladly comply. Next you make a larger request, which is what you really wanted all along. You find that your friend, having agreed to the smaller request, now more readily agrees to the larger request. How did this happen?

Some research suggests that people tend to agree to perform a larger request once they have agreed to comply with a smaller request. An early study of this *foot-in-the-door phenomenon* was conducted by Freedman and Fraser (1966). The researchers called housewives (an acceptable descriptor in the 1960s) and asked if they could answer a few questions regarding their favorite household products. After a few days, the researchers called again, asking if some men could go to their house to review their closets to take inventory of the household products. The women who had agreed to answer the initial questions were twice as likely to agree to the two-hour inventory than were those who were only asked to comply with the inventory.

Burger and Guadagno (2003) note that the results of more than one hundred studies of the foot-in-the-door compliance technique are not consistent and show small effect sizes. Burger (1999) suggests that some of this inconsistency is due to procedural differences across studies. Burger and Guadagno additionally suggest that some people appear more likely to comply with incremental requests than do other people due to personality variables such as attributional styles, self-concept clarity and self-esteem. Thus, the assumption that making incremental requests will necessarily increase compliance, whether in sales or in everyday life, is not consistently supported. Nevertheless, there is some evidence that committing oneself to a smaller request could increase the chances that one would agree to a larger request.

*Low-ball technique.* Sometimes persuasion occurs when the persuader purposely omits important information from the request in an effort to "trap" the person into agreeing before they realize what they have agreed to do. A classic study by Cialdini, Cacioppo, Bassett and Miller (1978) illustrates this. Students were asked to participate in an experiment, and 56 percent of the students agreed. The students were then told that the study would begin at 7:00 a.m. and that they could withdraw from the study, yet none chose to do so. In fact, the overwhelming majority showed up on time to participate! In the control group, where students were asked to participate and were told the time the experiment would start, only 24 percent agreed to participate. This strategy of getting agreement before important details are presented is often used in sales.

*Door-in-the-face phenomenon.* Sometimes making a request that we know will not be accepted, and then making a smaller request, meets with more success than does the foot-in-the-door technique. Cialdini et al. (1975) suggested that this *door-in-the-face phenomenon* works in part because of reciprocity. That is, if you make a larger request that the other refuses, and then you make a smaller, apparently concessionary request, the other person may feel the need to "meet you halfway," reciprocating with their own concession.

Imagine how the foot-in-the-door, low-ball and door-in-the-face strategies would look in the case of a teenager who asks his parents if he can stay out past his curfew on Saturday night. Imagine that what the teenager wants is to borrow the family car and stay out until about 1 a.m. Figure 6.5 shows an example of how each of the above-noted persuasion techniques could look in this example. This figure shows examples of initial questions the teenager might ask to set his parents up to eventually agree with what he really wants.

Table 6.5. Persuasion Tactics Used by a Teenager Who Wants to Stay Out One Hour Past His Curfew

| Foot-in-the-Door | Low-Ball | Door-in-the-Face |
|---|---|---|
| "Hey, Mom and Dad, can I please go get some ice cream on Saturday night with my friends?" | "Hey, Mom and Dad, remember you agreed to let me take the car out this Saturday. I assume you're still OK with that?" | "Hey, Mom and Dad, can I please take your car out Saturday night and stay out all night long riding through town with my friends?" |

*CFR view and persuasion.* There are a number of interesting connections between the research on persuasion and a Christian view of personhood. Here the focus will be on ways in which persuasive messages speak to the intrinsic relational nature of humans as well as the tension between our created nature and fallen condition. To do this, the discussion will center on the implications of the ubiquitous presence of persuasive messages, resistance to persuasion and the role of social norms in persuasion.

As discussed early in this chapter, our social world is awash in persuasive messages, some subtle and others more blatant, some honest and others more deceptive. The opportunities to persuade also increase with advances in technology. Clearly we are not always moved by efforts to persuade us, yet there are many times when we are. Because persuasive messages seem to be an inescapable part of human social interaction, it is helpful to consider why this might be the case. Certainly, we can imagine many positive reasons for such messages: they help us organize our social world by telling us about what is appropriate or beneficial; they are often helpful in reducing the amount of cognitive energy we need to expend to make decisions or form attitudes (Chaiken, Liberman & Eagly, 1989); they can give us clarity regarding difficult issues, especially when we trust the source of the message (Chaiken, Wood & Eagly, 1996; Petty & Krosnick, 1995); and they can mobilize people into action toward worthy causes such as environmentalism, gender equity and educational reform (Larson, 2010).

From a Christian view, the benefits of persuasion may be seen as one way in which we partake collectively in the redemptive work of Christ. Persuasive messages that instruct us on how to relate to God and to care for one another and for our world are an integral part of the redemptive process. Without persuasion, there would be no way for us to help one another move in the right direction. Indeed, persuasion often plays a major role in our decisions to trust Christ and to share our faith with others. Thus, the capacity and tendency to persuade each other seems to be a key component of our created being, working together with God's grace in mysterious ways to help redeem the human condition.

But, as the CFR view holds, the fallenness of the human condition is also manifested in the process of persuasion. Thus, deceptive and manipulative messages of all sorts are, to greater and lesser extents, also a part of our social world. People will knowingly or unknowingly persuade others for self-serving purposes that come at the expense of the one who is persuaded. So persuasion is also a way in which we collectively partake in fallenness. One need only look at how effective persuasion can serve evil ends such as genocide, cults, discrimination, deception in the marketplace—the list is endless. One important lesson from the research is that we are not invincible to these deceptive ploys, though we tend to underestimate their effect on us (Sagarin, Cialdini, Rice & Serna, 2002).

This vulnerability to being deceived by false or manipulative persuasive messages is spoken of many times in the Scriptures. The numerous warnings against falling prey to such messages are a vivid reminder of just how vulnerable humans can be (e.g., Ps 1:1; Prov 5:3-5; Acts 20:28-31; 1 Cor 15:33; 1 Tim 4:2-4; 2 Tim 4:2-4). Indeed, we are described as having "itching ears" that wish to hear what pleases us (2 Tim 4:3). But the Scriptures do not depict humans in a passive, fatalistic way such that we cannot recognize or resist false messages; rather they call us to exercise discernment and wisdom in the face of persuasive pressures (e.g., Acts 17:11).

Research likewise suggests that we can be active participants in our response to persuasion. Eagly and Chaiken (1993), for example, note that one of the best ways to inoculate ourselves from destructive or otherwise incorrect messages is to consider counterarguments. Sagarin and Cialdini

(2004) additionally found that motivating people to resist destructive, deceptive persuasion often results in making them more receptive to legitimate sources of persuasion. This finding has important implications for our ability to seek God's wisdom and grace regarding whatever issue confronts us (e.g., Jas 1:5; Col 3:16). In any case, both the constructive and destructive potential of persuasive messages suggest the relational nature of humans as well as the tension in the human condition; we work together to give and respond to messages leading to redemption, and we work together to give and respond to those that do not.

As noted, persuasion research also suggests the intrinsic relational nature of humans; persuasion works precisely because we are relational beings. Consider, for example, the finding that social norms significantly affect how likely we are to receive a persuasive message (e.g., Goldstein, Cialdini & Griskevicius, 2008). We often look to each other for cues regarding what attitudes and behaviors are acceptable. Obviously, this has both positive and negative implications. This finding regarding our tendency to look for social cues, considered along with the finding that we are not invincible to false messages (Sagarin, Cialdini, Rice & Serna, 2002), further emphasizes the need to be more intentional in our deliberations about many things, including the choice of social cues. Clearly, there are many persuasive messages (e.g., what toothpaste or shoes to prefer) whose implications are not as far-reaching as those of other messages (e.g., what attitude to have toward people from different groups). In order to continue to partake in the redemptive purposes of Christ, we will need to discern the difference between these two, mindful of the need for his wisdom and that of others.

## So Far . . .

By this point in your readings, you have seen some consistent patterns in the social psychology research discussed thus far. Research on the self, social cognition, group behavior, conformity, obedience, attitudes and persuasion suggests an underlying human condition that is consistent with a Christian view of persons. Specifically, the ways in which we perceive and respond to our social world show both our intrinsic relational nature as well as the tension inherent in our self- and other-centered potential.

The human vulnerabilities and strengths demonstrated by the research can help us to humbly consider how finite we are, especially in relation to God. Nevertheless, the research suggests that there is hope that human social interaction can serve redemptive purposes.

As you have read, the naturalist and Christian views of persons have many points of agreement both in the research as well as in the underlying premises of each. Nevertheless, as discussed throughout the various chapters, a Christian view of persons allows for many additional research questions and interpretations of the findings. In the following chapters, you will consider how both naturalist and Christian views of personhood may be related to the research on aggression, prejudice and racism, helping behavior, and interpersonal attraction. Let us consider together the implications of each of the two views.

## QUESTIONS TO CONSIDER

1. If you were asked to design a study regarding what factors most enable people to acknowledge and resist persuasive messages that are destructive, how would you go about it?

2. Can you think of any ways in which not being totally aware of one's attitudes could be beneficial?

3. What do you think of the disagreement regarding the stability and strength of attitudes? Why is this an important research question, and what relevance could this have to both naturalist and Christian premises about the human condition?

4. What specific factors related to attitudes and persuasion do you see most relevant to advertising?

## KEY TERMS

*affect infusion model*
*attitudes*
*authoritarianism*
*balance theory*
*cognitive dissonance*
*consistency theories*

*door-in-the-face technique*
*dual-process models*
*elaboration likelihood model*
*expectancy-value model*
*foot-in-the-door technique*
*heuristic system model*
*implicit association test*
*low-ball technique*
*meta-cognitive model*
*MODE model*
*moral hypocrisy*
*need to evaluate*
*overpowered integrity*
*PAST model*
*religious fundamentalism*
*self-efficacy*
*self-validation theory*
*theory of planned behavior*
*theory of reasoned action*
*three-component model*
*unimodal approach to persuasion*

# 7

# Aggression

*Let everyone be quick to listen,*
*slow to speak, slow to anger.*

**JAMES 1:19**

If the circumstances were just so, what do you think would be your own potential to commit a seriously aggressive act? This is a difficult question to answer because life has not presented to most of us the full range of incentives to engage in aggressive behavior. You may have had some experiences, however, that have surprised you as to how hostile your own response has been toward another person or specific situation. Perhaps you said more than you had intended, or perhaps you have been violent toward another during a time of conflict or personal threat. What do our responses to such situations suggest to us about the intrinsic relational nature of humans? How does the human capacity for aggressive acts relate to our ability to be other-centered? In this chapter, you will read about:

- how researchers have defined aggression;

- a variety of factors related to the propensity for aggression;

- whether or not the world has become a less aggressive place;

- strategies for reducing aggression; and

- the relevance of Christian ideas regarding forgiveness and honoring the dignity of the other's life to research on aggression.

## WHAT IS AGGRESSION?

As Baron and Richardson (2004) note, formally defining aggression can be difficult because of the wide range of behaviors it entails, and definitions can be quite controversial. They note, for example, that an oft-used definition of aggression includes intent to harm as well as the motivation of the victim to avoid the aggressive behavior. Based on that definition, in the case of suicide where persons aim to die, they are not engaged in an official act of aggression because they are not trying to avoid it. Similarly, Baron and Richardson note, couples whose lovemaking includes sadomasochist behavior are not acting aggressively because both partners find the behaviors sexually arousing. For this chapter let us consider *aggression* to involve behavior, whether verbal, symbolic or physical, that in any way violates the personhood of another (McAfee Brown, 1987). Note that it is of course possible to be aggressive toward nonhuman entities such as animals or inanimate objects. But our focus here is on interpersonal and intergroup aggression among humans within social relationships. Broadly speaking, most aggression can be considered a type of *antisocial behavior*, or behavior that is destructive or not good for the community at large.

Social psychologists generally define the term *aggression* with a focus on *external behaviors* that can be observed, but they are also concerned with possible motives, which include various *cognitions* (e.g., a tendency to interpret hostile intentions in others) as well as *attitudes* (e.g., dehumanizing the other). Thus, aggression, like all other social phenomena, is quite a complex construct.

Note that the term *aggression*, according to the definition noted above, would not include a hurtful act that was not intended to cause harm. Pain that a surgeon "causes" to the patient would not thus be considered aggression, even if the patient thinks so. Nor would an act that includes some unintended harm be considered an act of aggression. For example, when I was in an all-girls high school, my senior class was being coached in football by a boys' high school team for a game with the junior class. While we were in the stands watching a demonstration on the field, one of the boys misthrew a ball into the stands and hit me in the head. It was painful to me and terribly embarrassing to us both, but it was not an aggressive action. (And no, he did not ask me out afterward.)

Baron and Richardson (2004) note that aggressive acts include a wide range of behaviors, including:

- physical assault (e.g., domestic violence)

- verbal assault (e.g., harsh gossip)

- indirect aggression (e.g., destroying someone's property)

- direct aggression (as in the case of physical assault, any behavior that is aimed at the target person directly)

- active or passive aggression (e.g., hitting your classmate or "forgetting" to bring your notes for them to borrow for the upcoming exam, respectively)

Aggression can differ with regard to the perpetrator's *motive*. Specifically, aggression can be *hostile* (i.e., the end goal itself) or *instrumental* (i.e., aggression used as a means to an end; Rule, 1974). Bushman and Anderson (2001) note, however, that this simple distinction between hostile and instrumental aggression is no longer adequate, as it negates the complex mixture of motives that may underlie a single aggressive act.

## WHAT ABOUT VERBAL AGGRESSION?

As noted earlier, aggression can take many forms. One of the most potentially devastating modes involves verbal aggression. This type of aggression includes messages with the intent to inflict psychological pain on the target, and can include insults, teasing, sarcasm and ridicule (Jenkins & Aube, 2002). Stets (1990) noted that approximately 75 percent of men and 80 percent of women in the U.S. admit to engaging in verbal aggression in their interpersonal and/or work contexts.

The devastating psychological effects of verbal abuse have been well documented. For example, there is often a higher proportion of emotional disturbance and hostility in victims of childhood verbal abuse (Kent, Waller & Dagnan, 1999; Miller-Perrin & Perrin, 2007).

In addition to the negative psychological effects of verbal aggression, there is also research that has explored the close connection between verbal and physical aggression. For example, Infante, Sabourin, Rudd and Shannon (1990) found that in their sample of marriages that included verbal aggression between spouses, character attacks specifically were highly correlated with the likelihood of domestic violence.

The research that demonstrates a relationship between verbal and physical aggression is consistent with the view presented in the Scriptures, which speak of how verbal aggression, including slander, false witness and defamation of character, has the capacity to promote distrust and animosity, often leading to physical violence. Consider the following example in Proverbs 16:28-29: "A perverse person spreads strife, and a whisperer separates close friends. The violent entice their neighbors, and lead them in a way that is not good." Or the following from Psalm 140:3, 11: "They make their tongue sharp as a snake's, and under their lips is the venom of vipers. . . . Do not let the slanderer be established in the land; let evil speedily hunt down the violent!"

There have been many developmental studies of the relationship between parents' verbal aggression and children's subsequent aggression. In addition, there is much research on verbal aggression in the domestic violence literature. Yet despite these well-noted negative effects of verbal aggression, social psychology research has nonetheless generally focused more on the motivation and consequences of *physical* aggression. A greater research emphasis on verbal aggression could be helpful for a number of reasons. First, verbal (and symbolic) acts of aggression happen with more regularity than do physical acts of aggression. This may be because many verbally aggressive acts (e.g., anti-Semitic remarks by one citizen to another or malicious gossip spread around a college campus) generally are not illegal, even if they are considered by the culture at large as inappropriate or morally reprehensible. Such verbally aggressive acts are less likely to be reported, and thus are often less understood than are physical acts of aggression. Thus, reports that a community shows a decrease in physical aggression tells us nothing about whether verbal and symbolic acts of aggression have likewise decreased. In fact, we may get an overly hopeful perspective regarding how improved the relationships are among the members of that community. Second, a better understanding of verbal aggression could be helpful for our understanding of the various motivations for aggression (especially those that are provoked).

## How Does Scripture Define Aggression?

The Scriptures are sobering when we read the history of violence that is reported from early on. These aggressive acts include violence committed by humans, including war, rape, theft, social ostracism, genocide, homicide and so on. In addition, we see numerous nonphysical acts of aggression such as social exclusion (remember the Samaritans?). Though the focus in this text, as in social psychology at large, is with social interaction at the human level, a consideration of the role of divinely ordained violence as reported in the Scriptures can be helpful for expanding our understanding of the motives and negative social outcomes of sinful aggression.

Even a casual reading of the Bible can leave us with deep ambivalence regarding the role of aggression in the redemptive work of God. Fretheim (2004) offers a helpful discussion of aggression from the viewpoint of the Scriptures. He notes the difficulty in reconciling two seemingly different views of aggression that the Bible presents. Consider the Old Testament, where there are numerous times where God condemns violence. Fretheim notes that the most common Hebrew word for "violence" refers almost exclusively to human violence, which is almost always condemned, implicitly or explicitly, in the Scriptures. Note the following few examples:

- "The Lord . . . hates the lover of violence" (Ps 11:5).
- "Thus says the Lord: . . . do no wrong or violence to the alien, the orphan, and the widow" (Jer 22:3).
- "The earth was filled with violence" (Gen 6:11), before God brought the judgment of the flood.

Thus, the different kinds of aggression discussed in this chapter would be considered part of the broken, sinful condition of humans. In contrast, though, there are examples in the Scriptures where God both ordains and initiates acts of violence using both imperfect human agents (e.g., the Israelites' genocide of the Canaanites) and nonhuman agents (e.g., the plagues of Egypt, clouds, darkness, etc.). Fretheim (2004) posits that the apparent discrepancy between human-initiated violence and divinely ordained acts of violence can be better understood if one considers the sinfulness of humankind in relation to the perfect nature of God. Specifically, Fretheim proposes that while human aggression is generally self-seeking retaliation ("blind and unbridled anger"), God's uses of violence are associated with two basic purposes: righteous judgment and salvation. For example, violence *against* the Egyptians leads to Israel's salvation *from* Egypt's violence (e.g., Ex 15:1-3). Or, God uses the violence of the Persians under King Cyrus against the enslaving Babylonians as a means to bring salvation to the exiles (e.g., Is 45:1-8).

Thus, Fretheim asserts that God's violence, whether in judgment or salvation, is never an end in itself. Rather it is always exercised in the service of God's more comprehensive *salvific* purposes for creation: the deliverance of slaves from oppression (Ex 15:7; Ps 78:49-50), the righteous from their antagonists (Ps 7:6-11), the poor and needy from their abusers (Ex 22:21-24; Is 1:23-24; Jer 21:12), and Israel from its enemies (Is 30:27-33; 34:2; Hab 3:12-13). Further, "As I live, says the Lord God, I have no pleasure in the death of the wicked, but that the wicked turn from their ways and live" (Ezek 33:11).

Fretheim acknowledges that this view of God working through violence is a controversial one, and Christians have long wrestled with the notion of a violent God. Dietrich Bonheoffer, a theologian and pastor in Germany during World War II, agonized over this before he ultimately joined in a plot to assassinate Adolf Hitler. Taken without critical engagement of the Scriptures, the idea of God-ordained violence can be used to justify "righteous" acts of violence, as you will see in the next section regarding religious extremists.

Despite these difficulties regarding divinely ordained violence, however, the Scriptures are clear about the sinful human use of aggression, which is the primary focus of this chapter. Of prime importance here is the concept of *humanizing* others—considering their dignity and value as humans and treating them with moral consideration. As you will read later in this chapter, humanization is one of the essential elements for reducing aggression. One helpful example of humanizing is seen in the genealogy of Christ in Matthew 1, which surprisingly includes four women who were Gentiles, not Jews, and were either from previously condemned groups or had been involved in personal sin:

- Rahab, a prostitute from Jericho who protected Joshua's spies

- Tamar, daughter-in-law of Judah, who had disguised herself to deceive him and had sexual relations with him

- "the wife of Uriah" (i.e., Bathsheba), with whom King David had an extramarital affair

- Ruth, of the Moabite people who had been condemned for their treatment of the Jews after the exodus

The genealogy of Christ illustrates the importance of humanizing traditionally out-group members. Those whose groups had formerly been condemned by God and were aggressed against by his initiation, or who had sinned themselves, were chosen by God to be in the lineage of Christ. This is instructive, as the inclusion of these four women highlights the redemptive work of Christ and points toward the integral role of humanizing the other and forgiveness. Both of these, as you will see later in this chapter, are essential components of efforts to reduce human aggression.

A biblical definition of human aggression is quite broad, as it is in the social psychology literature, emphasizing physical and verbal assaults, as well as more symbolic aggression such as social exclusion of the other. As noted earlier, if we consider verbal aggression alone, we see numerous Scriptures that speak of the connection between evil and aggressive words, and of the potentially devastating power that aggressive words can have. Indeed, numerous times the Scriptures admonish us to be careful of the way we speak to one another. In Psalm 64:3, we are told that the evil "sharpen their tongues like swords and aim cruel words like deadly arrows" (NIV). Proverbs 12:18 claims that "the words of the reckless pierce like swords, but the tongue of the wise brings healing" (NIV). Thus, a Christian view of the impact of spoken aggression is consistent with the research that suggests this type of aggression can have devastating consequences.

Nevertheless, there is an interesting distinction between the way aggression is conceptualized in the literature and the way it is portrayed in the Scriptures. Considering both of these conceptualizations may help us better understand the complex nature of aggressive behavior. As you will see, research uses an empirical approach that necessitates focusing on specific aspects of aggression and potential motivations and consequences, and it often results in a disjointed overall image of aggression. For example, aggression researchers are likely to focus on a specific context for aggression (e.g., school bullying or domestic violence), or they might focus on specific motivations for aggression (e.g., hostile personality tendencies or crowding and loud noises). The goal of accumulated research over time, then, is to integrate the discrete bits of knowledge regarding the particular topic and to formulate more general theories regarding aggression and its motivators and consequences.

To date, social psychologists have made much progress in understanding how aggression is played out in different contexts. Still there remains considerable disagreement, as you will soon see, regarding many aspects of aggression. Psychology's inability to answer all of these questions is in part a function of the limitations of the empirical method. It is not possible to isolate in any experiment (or combination of experiments) *all* the variables, both explicit and implicit, that are at work in such a complex phenomenon. Nor would you want to—it would be too cumbersome to disentangle all the relative effects of the various factors. In this case, then, one of the strengths of the empirical method (i.e., the ability to isolate both discrete situational and personal factors related to aggressive behavior) is also precisely its weakness (i.e., the relatively narrow focus decreases the ability to construct a broader picture of aggression).

The Scriptures also present a complicated view of aggression, especially when one considers both divinely ordained aggression and human aggression. Nevertheless, Scripture provides at least two general concepts that relate broadly to human aggression, and specifically to reducing aggression. This will be discussed in more detail at the end of this chapter. For now, briefly note that in the Scriptures, inherent in the management of aggression is the call to respond in other-centered ways. From the CFR view, of special interest here are the concepts of *forgiveness* and *valuing the dignity of the other's life* (i.e., humanizing the other). The Scriptures do not distinguish between types of aggression per se in this regard. Thus, for example, forgiveness is an absolute command that is required in *all* situations in which one has been offended. We are to "bless those who persecute" us (Rom 12:14) and not to "repay anyone evil for evil" (Rom 12:17). This often requires the yielding of one's own (often legitimate) right to seek retribution. Scripture also reinforces the dignity of human life, notably in Jesus' interactions with outsiders or "unclean" persons, and the significance in this valuing as a deterrent is clearly played out in his encounter with the woman caught in adultery and her accusers (Jn 7:53–8:11).

Some aggression researchers have focused on the negative effects of dehumanization (e.g., Haslam, 2006) and others emphasize ways in which forgiveness may reduce aggression (e.g., Worthington, 1998). Nevertheless, overall, researchers have understandably concentrated on specific characteristics of the offender and circumstances that elicit aggression. These are indeed helpful pursuits, but from a Christian view one must also consider the characteristics of a transformed heart and mind to understand the motivations for aggression as well as ways to remediate or reduce aggression. This point will be revisited after a more thorough discussion of the research.

## RELIGIOUS EXTREMISTS AND AGGRESSION

As is the case with Christian Scriptures, the sacred writings of other major world religions teach universal love and compassion but sometimes also include references to God-ordained violence. Is it possible that such violent

 references could lead to violence among certain religious followers? Can faith contribute to aggressive tendencies? These are questions being explored by researchers interested in the aggressive behavior of religious extremists.

Bushman et al. (2007) explored the possibility of violent

passages inciting aggressive responses. Specifically, the researchers were interested in whether reading a biblical description of violence might increase the participant's subsequent aggressive behavior more than a secular description of the same type of violence. Bushman et al. also wondered whether greater aggression would result from reading a description of violence that was sanctioned by God (high justification) versus violence not sanctioned by God (low justification).

Bushman et al. (2007) had subjects read the passage from Judges 19 and 20 in which a Levite man's concubine is raped and murdered by a group of men in Gibeah (of the tribe of Benjamin). The Levite then cuts her body into twelve parts and distributes them, one to each tribe of Israel, to represent the horrendous crime. The Israelites meet to decide what to do and to ask of God, who ordains that they "go up against [the Benjamites]" (Judg 20:23). God blesses the army of the Israelites, who, after winning the battles, destroy all remaining animals and households of the Benjamites. Some of the participants in the study were told that the passage originated in an ancient scroll, while the other half were told that the passage came from the Bible.

After this, subjects were engaged in a game with opponents and were given a choice of how loud to blast some noise if they won. As predicted, subjects who thought the passage represented God-ordained violence delivered higher decibels of noise to their losing opponent. Interestingly, the results were consistent among participants from Brigham Young University, who reported high religious belief, as well as a university in the Netherlands, where students reported less belief in God.

Bushman et al. note that when religious extremists engage in selective reading of the Scriptures, often meditating on them for extended periods of time, this can increase the likelihood of aggressive actions. Yet Bushman et al. are careful to note that "violent stories that teach moral lessons or that are balanced with descriptions of victims' suffering or the aggressor's remorse can teach important lessons and have legitimate artistic merit" (p. 207).

## Sexual Violence

Sexual assault is a pervasive criminal and human rights epidemic across the world. The overwhelming majority of victims are females, though more recent research has begun to focus on males who are victims of rape, especially in prison populations. Sexual assault is often underreported, and especially so among male victims (Levinson, 2002). There is currently a better understanding of the possible motivators for and consequences of sexual assault on female victims, partly because victimization of males is less common and so underreported, so this discussion will thus focus on female victims. More research on male victims is certainly needed to address motivators and consequences specific to male victims.

The World Health Organization (WHO, 2005) conducted a study across ten countries in which they investigated the prevalence of sexual violence among intimate partners. Reported incidents ranged from 10 to 50 percent. The report also indicated that when females were given the opportunity to respond anonymously to questions regarding occurrences of sexual abuse before age fifteen, the results were significantly higher than when the women were asked to respond directly to an interviewer's questions. In 2010 the WHO reported that the incidence of sexual violence against women during times of war or emergencies has also increased. These situations often leave women and girls more vulnerable to sexual and gender-based violence (e.g., rape by combatants and sexual exploitation by intimate partners or husbands).

The U.S. Department of Justice reported that in 2007 there were almost 250,000 victims of rape, attempted rape or sexual assault across the United States. This figure does not include victims twelve years old or younger. For rape specifically, in 2009, there were almost 200,000 reported cases, and this figure is considered to be an underestimate. Sexual assaults on college campuses are prevalent. The 2007 Campus Sexual Assault (CSA) study, which was based on surveys of over 6,800 college students, revealed that 19 percent of college women said they had experienced "completed or attempted sexual assault since entering college" (Eberstadt, 2010, p. 56). The risk of sexual assault for these women was significantly related to how often the women got drunk, how often they had sex when they drank and how often they attended fraternity parties. These data are consistent with the significant relationship between alcohol and aggression, which will be discussed later in this chapter (Reiss & Roth, 1994). Humphrey and White (2000) further found in their review of the literature that college women who had experienced sexual victimization earlier in life were significantly more likely to be victimized again during the college years.

Sanday (1997, as cited in Gilovich, Keltner & Nisbett, 2006) explored the cultural norms and contexts of 156 countries that had been described by anthropologists and historians. Sanday identified in these accounts what she referred to as *rape-prone cultures*. These are cultures in which rape is committed against women from enemy groups during times of war, used as part of a ritual (like during an adolescent male's rite of passage into adulthood) and used as a threat against women in order to keep them subservient to men. Sanday noted several characteristics of such cultures. First, they tend to have high levels of violence overall. Second, rape-prone cultures tend to deny women access to education and participation in political decision making.

Sanday offers suggestions for reducing sexual aggression that are consistent with those proposed by the World Health Organization (2010), including:

- Promote gender equality and women's human rights in line with relevant international treaties and human rights procedures, improve women's access to property and assets, and expand educational opportunities for girls and young women.

- Establish, implement and monitor action plans to address violence against women, including violence by intimate partners.

- Enlist social, political, religious and other leaders in speaking out against violence toward women.

- Establish systems for data collection to monitor violence against women and the attitudes and beliefs that perpetuate such violence.

- Develop, implement and monitor programs aimed at primary prevention of intimate-partner violence and sexual violence against women (e.g., sustained public-awareness activities aimed at changing the attitudes, beliefs and values that condone partner violence as normal and prevent it ever being challenged or talked about).

- Give higher priority to combating sexual abuse of girls (and boys) in public health programs, as well as in responses by other sectors such as the judiciary, education and social services.

## WHAT ARE SOME BIOLOGICAL EXPLANATIONS OF AGGRESSION?

Generally, theories regarding the origins of aggression in humans use either biological explanations or psychosocial explanations, and often a combination of the two.

Studies of biological explanations of aggression investigate such factors as brain structure and function, behavioral genetics, and evolutionary traits. It is important to note that biological aspects of aggression cannot be separated from situational, social-cultural and emotional factors for any particular instance. Thus it is important to keep in mind that, just because scientists can identify specific parts of the brain that are related to aggressive responses, one must be careful not to assume that biology is the whole story. Also as you read the following sections wherein specific biological findings are discussed, keep in mind that the brain is actually a complex system where all the parts interact with each other. Hence, the finding that aggression seems related to one brain area also suggests that other related brain areas are likewise involved.

*Prefrontal cortex.* Studies examining the biological aspects of aggression suggest that it is often linked to impairments in the *prefrontal cortex* of the brain. The prefrontal cortex handles what are called *executive cognitive processes,* which include higher-order thinking related to reasoning, impulse control and understanding the consequences of one's behavior (Nelson, 2005). Neurological studies using MRIs and PET scans have demonstrated that aggressive individuals of all ages often have reduced metabolism and less volume in the prefrontal cortex (Raine, 1997, 2002).

Clinical studies of brain-damaged subjects suggest that impairments in the prefrontal cortex may be related to higher levels of aggression. For example, Grafman et al. (1996) demonstrated that Vietnam veterans with prefrontal ventromedial brain injuries displayed more aggression, especially verbal aggression, after the head injury. However, not all individuals with acquired prefrontal ventromedial lesions become aggressive (Ellenbogen et al., 2005).

***The amygdala.*** The *amygdala* plays an important role in emotional learning, response to fear and other emotions, and regulation of emotional reactivity. Davis and Whalen (2001) noted that an aversive stimulus will change the neural transmission to the amygdala, thereby producing significant changes such as somatic, autonomic and endocrine signs of fear. In addition, it will increase attention to the stimulus— the body interprets the threatening stimulus and prepares to respond to it in some way.

The amygdala is also activated in responses to fearful and sad facial expressions (Adolphs et al., 2005). For example, in one study, normal boys and a group of boys who react consistently aggressively to others were shown a picture of threatening faces. The MRIs of the aggressive boys showed more activity in the amygdala and lower activity in the prefrontal cortex.

Blair (2007) has studied the relationship of amygdala dysfunction to psychopathy, or violent criminal activity. He showed threatening stimuli to groups of psychopathic and normal controls. Those with psychopathy (a history of violent aggression) showed a reduction in neural responses, emotional responses in anticipation of punishment, emotional responses to imagined threatening events, and the startle reflex to aversive stimuli. Blair notes that all of these impairments are consistent with general amygdala dysfunction, and that psychopathic persons who experience amygdala dysfunction have a hard time internalizing "right" and "wrong" because they have a difficult time perceiving fear and distress in others.

The role of amygdala dysfunction in aggression is not yet clear, as noted by mixed research results in this area. In one study that compared spousal abusers and nonabusers, Lee, Chan and Raine (2008) showed both groups lists of aggressive words. Functional brain imaging (fMRI) results showed that the brains of the batterers demonstrated increased activation in the right amygdala in response to the aggressive words. The researchers suggest that batterers have an impaired ability in their prefrontal cortex to regulate the excessive activation of the limbic system that was generated by negative stimuli. Hence, in response to anger at their spouse, these individuals would be more likely to react with uninhibited aggression. But another study that compared violent and non-violent males (Tiihonen et al., 2008, as cited in DeLisi, Umphress & Vaughn, 2009) found no differences in regional brain volumes or amygdala function in violent males when compared to healthy males with no history of violence.

As noted earlier, the various brain areas are functionally related to each other. They are also influenced in various ways by the neurotransmitter (neurochemical) systems in the brain. For example, the function of the amygdala is affected by several neurotransmitter systems, including norepinephrine, dopamine, serotonin and acetylcholine. When these are released in the amygdala, they affect how excitatory and inhibitory neurons interact. These neurotransmitters are released and exert effects throughout the forebrain, including within the amygdala (DeLisi, Umphress & Vaughn, 2009). Following is a discussion of one of those neurotransmitters that appears to be related to aggression.

**Serotonin.** The neurotransmitter *serotonin* has been the most widely studied brain chemical. Serotonin has an inhibitory effect in the frontal part of the brain. It also serves to inhibit the firing of the amygdala, which as you just read, controls fear and anger and other emotional responses (Coccaro, 1989). If there is less serotonin present, then when the amygdala is stimulated by potentially threatening cues it becomes overly activated, increasing the chances that the person will act on aggressive impulses.

Yet the role of serotonin is not consistent across types of aggressive acts. Serotonin deficiency seems more related to impulsive, violent aggression rather than to instrumental forms of aggression (Tuinier et al., 1995; Balaban et al., 1996, as cited in Boer & Koolhaus, 2005). Boer and Koolhaus (2005) further note that drugs that increase serotonin levels may not decrease violent aggression per se, but rather they decrease violence as the result of the drug's effect on other important behavioral symptoms; namely, they induce sleep and motor inactivity. Thus the role of serotonin in aggression warrants further study.

**Behavioral genetics.** Another interesting area of research regarding the biological roots of aggression is behavioral genetics. Behavioral geneticists seek to uncover genetic sources of the differences among people with respect to some trait or behavior (Parens, 2004). For example, some studies have explored the heritability of traits found in violent youth. There are a group of traits called the *callous and unemotional traits* (CU) that are considered to be one of the hallmark signs of a budding psychopathy (Frick and White, 2008). These traits are characterized by reduced (constricted) emotional reactivity, low or absent guilt feelings, low empathy with others, and the use of others for one's own benefit. Low emotional reactivity has been found in some studies where participants are shown pictures of graphic portrayals of violent crime. In response to these violent images, psychopaths, when compared to normal samples, show less skin conductance, heart rate changes and contracting of facial muscles that are enacted when one winces when seeing an unpleasant scene. This suggests that violent offenders do not have the same implicit distaste for aggression that normal controls have.

Research suggests that these CU traits are significantly inherited. For example, Viding et al. (2005) studied 3,687 twin pairs and found that 67 percent of variation in extreme CU traits among seven-year-old children was genetic in origin, and even higher (81 percent) for seven-year-olds with psychopathic tendencies. Viding, Frick and Plomin (2007) additionally found that approximately 71 percent of conduct problems in boys and 77 percent in girls were attributable to genes. Larsson, Viding and Plomin (2008) found that about 80 percent of variance in twins with CU traits and antisocial behavior was heritable.

Behavioral genetics seeks to discover differences at the gene level that explain behavior and traits, and it is a highly controversial field of study. This is because behavioral genetics raises questions of human freedom and equality. For example, if one person or type of person is more inclined toward aggressive acts, then how might this affect our interpretation of their accountability for violent crimes? In addition, what if we found that different groups differ with regard to aggressive inclinations? Would we then order society in such a way as to restrain such individuals?

Historically, genetic differences were used as an argument for *eugenics* (literally, "good genes"), which involves trying to improve the genetic composition of a group by discouraging mating with or among those who possess a particular kind of genetic weakness. As an extreme example, consider Hitler's claims that Jews were "feeble minded" and an inferior race. Hitler suggested that the Aryans breed together to improve the human race. Later developments in behavioral genetics have instead explored the complexity of the interplay between genes and environment. For example, Caspi et al. (2002) studied 500 boys, assessing the roles of child abuse and a genetic difference involving a gene for an enzyme (MAOA) that is usually associated with increased aggression in both animal and human studies. MAOA regulates several neurotransmitters, including serotonin. The researchers found that those boys who were *both* the victims of child abuse *and* had the genotype (i.e., low levels of MAOA) were twice as likely to behave antisocially in adulthood as were those who had experienced child abuse but did not have the genotype.

The studies noted in this section may give a false impression regarding how close we really are to understanding genetic influences on any behavior. Parens (2004), for example, notes some significant obstacles for behavioral genetic research. First, suppose researchers find that identical twins (exact genetic match) are more similar on some trait than are fraternal twins. In this case we might have a greater confidence that genes are involved, but these findings do not yet reveal anything regarding which genes are involved and in what ways. Second, suppose a researcher were interested in evaluating the relative effects of genes and environment and compared identical twins raised together with those raised apart for a particular aspect of aggression. The results often will not be informative since, as most of the research suggests, identical twins are likely to be adopted into quite similar environments, which negates the environmental factor.

Thus, it appears that with respect to genetic influences on aggressive behavior, we are nowhere near finding a "criminal gene." Instead, it is more accurate to suggest that some individuals appear to be especially vulnerable to the ill effects of negative environments and may be more inclined toward antisocial behavior, including aggression. The exact mechanisms that explain the complex interplay between genetic/physiological and environmental influences are far from being determined. Additionally, the research to date does not support the notion that people with "vulnerable genes" have no choice regarding aggression.

Indeed, as Parens (2004) notes, to say that something is influenced by genetics is not the same thing as saying that it is unchangeable.

*A brief comment on biological explanations of aggression.* As noted in the literature just discussed, there have been many advances in isolating specific brain structures and neurochemical processes, as well as possible genetic contributions to aggressive behavior. Several words of caution are needed, though. Keep in mind that much of this research has conflicting results. For example, remember that amygdala dysfunction studies have not all demonstrated the same connection between amygdala dysfunction and aggression. In addition, studies on the relationship between aggression and brain function have largely focused either on animal studies or on humans who have displayed extreme violent aggression (usually criminals or violent youth). Thus, generalizability to the general population, who on average display aggression that is more symbolic, verbal or not as violent, may be difficult to do from these studies. It is possible that brain structure may not be as significantly related to "everyday aggression." It may be more helpful to consider that brain abnormalities may predispose some individuals more than others to have difficulty inhibiting aggressive responses.

A correct understanding of the biological underpinnings of aggressive behavior must take into account the limitations of a reductionist stance. *Reductionism* involves reducing a complex process to a few simple laws or explanations. In the case of aggression, focusing exclusively on or overemphasizing biological explanations as the prime causal factor neglects the broad range of motivations and reinforcers for aggression. Remember that researchers are not suggesting that we neglect these other factors. So, for example, even if we can isolate brain areas and genes that are associated with aggressive behavior, it is not clear whether, as in the case of criminals, the brain has been altered with time by some third force such as *desensitization,* which can affect brain function as well as interact with genetic vulnerabilities. In the example of desensitization, repetitive exposure to, or involvement in, aggression alters the brain. For example, an individual who is constantly exposed to violence or engages in violence over an extended period of time may become desensitized to violent images, which means experiencing less psychological or emotional responsiveness to a stimulus after repeated exposure (Bartholow, Bushman & Sestir, 2006). This desensitization may in turn continue to alter the brain and its chemistry such that inhibition of future aggression becomes increasingly difficult. Neglecting this important possibility overlooks the possibility that the brain's function may reflect a consequence, rather than a cause, of aggression.

We may not fully understand the role of biological factors in aggression, but from a Christian view we can at least find in this research a powerful reminder of the fallen condition of humans, even at the physiological level. Yet researchers are careful to note that genetic and other physiological vulnerabilities do not suggest an inevitably aggressive lifestyle. In fact, a clearer understanding of the nature of these biological limitations should increase our hope for finding more specific and effective intervention strategies to reduce aggression.

## EVOLUTIONARY PSYCHOLOGY PERSPECTIVES OF AGGRESSION

An evolutionary psychology perspective of aggression draws on its understanding of the origin of emotions overall. According to Cosmides and Tooby (2000), emotions evolved as superordinate programs that serve to direct the activities of subprograms in the brain. These subprograms regulate a wide variety of functions including learning, perception, attention, memory, goals and categorizing. From this view, anger that results in aggressive behaviors evolved to handle potentially threatening situations.

Buss and Duntley (2003) outline different contexts in which aggression evolved in order to help ensure the reproductive and survival advantage of the individual as well as of the human species at large. They note that aggression is not a unitary concept, but rather context-specific. It is triggered "by adaptive problems that resemble those in which our ancestors confronted specific adaptive problems and reaped particular benefits" (p. 269). Buss and Duntley list the following adaptive motivations for aggression:

- Obtain and protect resources that are essential for survival and reproduction (e.g., land, food, tools)

- Defend against attack
- Rise in social hierarchies (thereby increasing one's status and desirability)
- Deter long-term mates from infidelity
- Regain former mates
- Obtain sexual access to otherwise inaccessible mates

Evolutionary psychologists note that while aggression may have been an adaptive mechanism for our ancestors, many of the vestiges of these adaptations are currently "repugnant," as noted by Buss and Duntley. Some of these destructive outcomes include sexual coercion, domestic abuse, homicide and gang violence.

It is best to consider all the physiological explanations noted above as only one part of several possible explanations, all of which interact in very dynamic ways with each other. Biological, psychological and situational (not to mention spiritual) forces all contribute to and reduce aggression. Now you will read about another level of explanation of the roots of aggression: psychosocial explanations. Remember to keep in mind the intricate relationship of these with the biological ones just mentioned.

## PSYCHOSOCIAL EXPLANATIONS OF AGGRESSION

Psychological explanations of aggression focus on intrapersonal and interpersonal mechanisms. For example, Freud (1929) proposed that aggression is an *instinct,* which means that aggressive tendencies are an inherent part of human nature and are ever present in our unconscious and conscious social interactions. Alternatively, aggression has also been seen as a *drive,* which means that unlike an instinct that is always with us, it is activated when we encounter a situation that impedes our ability to satisfy a need and energizes us to remove whatever is blocking us.

Dollard et al. (1939) used this conceptualization of aggression as a drive to formulate their *frustration-aggression hypothesis,* which posits that aggression serves the purpose of removing some frustration, which is defined as some interference with the individual's goals. According to this view, the person who experiences such frustration would become motivated to act aggressively to remove the obstacle. Berkowitz (1989) later reformulated this hypothesis by suggesting that aggression is only one of a potential number of responses to frustration. Frustration, he also argued, provokes aggression to the degree that it invokes negative emotional arousal. Figure 7.1 illustrates the main features of the frustration-aggression hypothesis.

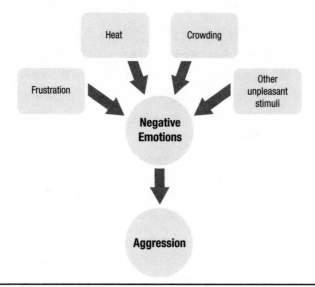

**Figure 7.1. Frustration-Aggression Hypothesis**
Source: Berkowitz, 1989

Berkowitz suggests that there may be other mediating forces such as fear of punishment that may inhibit aggressive responses to frustration and may result in *displaced aggression*. This is the acting out of aggression onto a less powerful and more accessible target than the one who initially frustrated you (Marcus-Newhall et al., 2000). According to this view, when we are frustrated and angry at someone whom we perceive as more powerful than us, we tend to aggress against a less powerful target to vent our anger. For example, a college student who gets angry at a professor due to a low grade received on an exam is more likely to take this anger out by snapping at a roommate or acting rudely at the cafeteria than by directly expressing hostility toward the professor.

Researchers have also explored how individuals learn to be aggressive by observing others. You may recall from earlier studies in psychology

Bandura's (1977) *social learning theory*, which proposes that we learn through observing the example of others and also through reinforcement and punishment. Bandura, Ross and Ross (1961) had children watch models who were either aggressive or not. Children who had seen the aggressive model were more likely later to play aggressively with toys (e.g., the Bobo doll) than were children who had not seen the aggressive model.

From the perspective of the social learning theory, aggressive models can elicit a wide range of aggressive behaviors as well as aggressive schemas where aggression is represented as a legitimate solution to conflict. Interestingly, these models do not have to actually be present to exert their effect, as you will see in the section on the impact of violent media. Aggressive models often come from one's family and friends, one's community (e.g., neighborhood), and media (internet, television, etc.; Bandura, 1978).

Other psychological explanations of aggression emphasize the importance of cognitive processes in the formation of an aggressive response. For example, Berkowitz's (1989, 1990, 1993) *neoassociationist model* of aggression proposes that an aversive event is one that results from being provoked, frustrated or exposed to loud noise, heat, crowding and so on. The aversive event elicits in the person a generalized negative arousal state. The person then either prepares to fight against the aversive event (resulting in aggression) or engages in escape or avoidance tactics. The person engages a host of cognitive resources such as an evaluation of the event, past memories related to this event, potential outcomes of a course of action and social norms related to the potential reactions, in determining how to respond. According to this view, aggression is seen as one of many potential responses to aversive situations.

Zillman's (1983) *excitation transfer model* also emphasizes the cognitive processes entailed when one decides whether or not to engage in an aggressive response. Zillman suggests that the intensity of anger one feels depends on both the strength of the physiological response and the interpretation one makes of the aversive situation. Furthermore, Zillman proposes that a person will look to the environment for cues as to how to interpret their feelings if the emotional arousal is vague and the origin of the feelings is not clear. The person may then attribute the anger to the current situation (misattribution).

The social-cognitive approach expands the focus on underlying cognitive processes in aggression by focusing on the individual differences in social information processing. Heusmann (1998), for example, proposed that individuals develop *scripts,* or cognitive schemas, that help us interpret our social world and respond accordingly. Scripts result from repetitive experiences with situations or from the observations of others' responses to situations. Heusmann stressed the influence of early socialization on our propensity to act aggressively, suggesting that if a child witnessed a parent acting aggressively toward others, the child would develop the cognitive schema that one response to conflict is aggression.

Another cognitive explanation for aggression has to do with how individuals attribute the motives of others. Remember from the social perception chapter that attributions involve making causal explanations for others' behaviors. Research findings suggest that aggressive individuals tend to attribute the behavior of others to hostile motives, even when those behaviors are ambiguous. This so-called *hostile attribution bias* is found in both children and adults (Dodge, 1980; Dodge & Frame, 1982; Geen & Donnerstein, 1998).

Another cognitive bias that relates to aggression is known as the *hostile expectation bias* and refers to the tendency to expect others to react aggressively to conflict (Bushman & Anderson, 2002). In a study that explored how violent media increases aggression, Bushman and Anderson had participants play either a violent or nonviolent video game. Then the participants read an ambiguous story about potential interpersonal conflicts. The subjects were asked what the main character will do, say, think and feel as the story continues. People who played the violent video game were more likely to describe the main characters as behaving more aggressively, having more aggressive thoughts and feeling more angry than did the people who played a nonviolent video game. Interestingly, this reminds us of the availability heuristic that was discussed in the social perception chapter.

Anderson and Bushman (2002) elaborate on what is called the *General Aggression Model* (GAM) in an effort to develop a more concise model of aggression that incorporates various components of those noted above. Specifically, this model's key features include how knowledge structures:

- develop out of experience;

- influence perception at multiple levels, from basic visual patterns to complex behavioral sequences;

- become automated with use;

- contain (or are linked to) affective states, behavioral programs and beliefs;

- are used to guide people's interpretations and behavioral responses to their social (and physical) environment (p. 33).

The General Aggression Model thus incorporates many of the components of earlier theories and specifically considers "the person in the situation" in the following three areas: personal factors (traits, gender, etc.), situational factors (frustration, aggressive cues, etc.) and outcomes (i.e., cognitive appraisals of the situation, affect and arousal).

Anderson and Bushman (2002) note that the General Aggression Model helps explain why interventions with older aggressive individuals are less successful than with younger people. In part, this is because older individuals have had a longer time to rehearse knowledge structures, many of which have become automatic. In addition, Anderson and Bushman note that programs for reducing aggression that have a narrow content focus are not successful because they do not take into account the many possible situations in which people can learn aggressive knowledge structures. An example of an approach that addresses multiple factors that can be influential in an aggressive person's life is known as *multisystemic therapy* (Borduin, 1999). This approach focuses on a wide range of factors in the aggressive individual's life (e.g., family, school, peer interactions) and should be more effective according to a General Aggression Model perspective.

*Personality variables.* Some research in developmental psychology has suggested that children who are seen as having difficult temperaments, including poor impulse control and difficulties with regulating affect, are more inclined to be aggressive (Kingston & Prior, 1995). Calkins and Fox (2002), for example, in their longitudinal study of children, found that the more aggressive children showed difficulty with impulse control on many different levels of functioning, including physiological arousal, emotional responses, attention and behavior. Note that this research is consistent with biological explanations for aggression.

Research with adults suggests that there may be a variety of personality factors characteristic of individuals who display aggression. Carprara, Perugini and Barbaranelli (1994, as cited in Krahé, 2001) noted several such factors. The first is *irritability*, or the tendency to be easily provoked and to react impulsively to provocation. Another personality factor is *emotional susceptibility*, which is the tendency to experience feelings of discomfort, helplessness and inadequacy. A third factor is labeled *dissipation versus rumination*, which is the extent to which people become absorbed with aggressive cognitions. In other words, does the person respond to an aggression-eliciting stimulus by ruminating (obsessing) about the event or by "letting it go" more quickly (i.e., dissipating)?

Bettencourt et al. (2006) conducted a meta-analytic review of studies that explored the relationship between personality variables and aggressive behavior. The researchers hoped to reveal which personality variables predict aggressive behavior only under provocation and which predict aggressive behavior even when situations are relatively neutral. The following personality traits were assessed across studies:

- Trait aggressiveness: the tendency to engage in physical and verbal aggression, to hold hostile cognitions, and to express anger frequently.

- Trait anger: highly correlated with trait aggressiveness; the tendency to feel anger more intensely, more often and for a longer period of time than others; tendency to respond angrily when unfairly criticized or treated unjustly.

- Trait irritability: tendency to be angrier, in general, and take offense to the slightest provocation as well as the propensity to be offensive in the use of aggressive behavior.

- Emotional susceptibility: tendency to feel distressed, inadequate and vulnerable to perceived threats; tendency to experience negative affect and become upset and defensive when confronted with personal attacks and insults.

- Type A personality: feelings of inadequacy regarding self-worth; these fears often result in a need to "prove" oneself through personal accomplishments. When confronted with a threat or challenge to their competence, these individuals become angry, irritated and impatient.

- Narcissism: inflated but vulnerable sense of self-worth; have unstable self-esteem and are thus extremely sensitive to insults and criticism; tend to behave aggressively in conditions of ego threat.

Bettencourt et al. found that there were a few of the above-noted personality variables that were positively correlated with aggressive behavior both when provoked as well as in neutral conditions. Other personality variables were more positively correlated with aggressive behavior only when provoked. Table 7.1 summarizes these results.

**Table 7.1. Personality Variables Associated with Aggression When Provoked**

|  | Provocation Conditions | Neutral Conditions |
|---|---|---|
| Trait Aggressiveness | X | X |
| Trait Anger | X | |
| Trait Irritability | X | X |
| Emotional Susceptibility | X | |
| Type A personality | X | |
| Narcissism | X | |

Source: Bettencourt et al., 2006

The researchers suggest that those who are high on trait aggressiveness and trait irritability (which are highly correlated) may be likely to engage in aggression that is "cold-blooded." In other words, their tendency to engage in aggressive acts even when not provoked suggests that they may be capable of more frequent and violent aggression. In comparison, those with high trait anger, type A personality, emotional susceptibility or narcissism were more likely to aggress under provocation, suggesting that these traits might be associated with a "hot-blooded" style of aggressive behavior—more intense, short-lived aggressive reactions.

One example of a personality variable that helps inhibit aggression is *perspective taking,* or the ability to take the other's perspective, to consider their plight (Richardson, Green & Lago, 1998). In the helping chapter, you will read about how perspective taking enhances one's propensity to help the other. Likewise, the ability to assume the other's perspective seems to decrease the likelihood to act aggressively toward the other.

*Self-esteem.* Bettencourt et al.'s (2006) study suggests that feelings of self-worth are significantly related to one's propensity to engage in aggressive behavior. As you may recall from the chapter on the self, low self-esteem has historically been associated with numerous negative social consequences such as teen pregnancy and trouble with the law. Despite the logic of this association, research has not found a consistent relationship between low self-esteem and aggression. In fact, it seems that excessively *high* and unstable self-esteem, especially when coupled with some threat to the ego, is more likely to lead to aggression than is low self-esteem (Baumeister, Smart & Boden, 1996; Baumeister, Brad & Campbell, 2000).

As noted above, *narcissism,* which is characterized by a grandiose, over-inflated but often vulnerable sense of self-importance, is also related to a greater propensity for aggression. For example, Raskin, Novacek and Hogan (1991) found that narcissism was positively correlated to hostility. The individuals scoring higher in narcissism use hostility as a way to maintain and inflate self-esteem. In addition, Bushman and Baumeister (1998) found that those scoring higher on a narcissism scale had higher emotional reactivity to feedback from others and were more likely to experience "narcissistic rage," consistent with Kernberg's (1976) suggestion. Rhodewalt and Morf (1998) also found that narcissists had higher levels of emotional reactivity. Stucke and Sporer (2002) additionally found that those scoring high in narcissism and low in self-concept demonstrated the highest anger and aggression after failure.

Perez, Vohs and Joiner (2005) found that there was a U-shaped relationship between self-esteem and aggression. That is, they found that both participants with excessively low and excessively high self-esteem, when compared with participants whose self-esteem was more realistic (moderate), scored higher on a self-report measure of aggression. Further, when there was a discrepancy between the subject's self-esteem and the esteem that a roommate had for the subject, scores were higher on the aggression questionnaire for subjects with both excessively high and excessively low self-esteem. The researchers suggest that future research on the relationship between self-esteem and aggression must take into account both extremes as well as the stress of the discrepancy between self-reported self-esteem and others' esteem of the individual.

Other research in this area underscores the complex relationship between self-esteem and aggression. Webster (2007), for example, used a sample size that was twelve times as large as that used by Perez, Vohs and Joiner (2005) and found instead an inverted-U relationship between self-esteem and aggression. That is, excessively high and excessively low self-esteem did not result in higher self-reported levels of aggression. As Webster notes, the relationship between self-esteem and aggression comprises many different mediating variables, "including gender, self-esteem instability, and the type of aggression assessed" (Kernis, Grannemann & Barclay, 1989; Webster, 2006; Webster et al., 2007, as cited in Webster, 2007, p. 981). Thus, in order to better understand how one's level of self-esteem may be related to propensity for aggression, we must consider self-esteem within the context of other contributing factors (e.g., situational stressors, personality variables and biological factors).

***Gender and aggression.*** In general, research suggests that males are more aggressive than females, and this difference begins in preschool (Coie & Dodge, 1998; Maccoby, 1998, as cited in Krahé, 2001). Nevertheless, the gender difference is not as unitary as it might appear. Some research shows that while males show a greater propensity for aggressive assaults, females tend to be more inclined to engage in indirect forms of aggression such as relational aggression, including spreading malicious rumors about someone, gossiping and excluding others (Björkqvist, Osterman & Lagerspetz, 1994). However, Huan Lim and Ang's (2009) review of studies suggests that gender differences in verbal/symbolic acts of aggression are not significant, and at best inconsistent. Thus, males may be as likely to engage in verbal and indirect forms of aggression as are females.

We often assume that husband-to-wife aggression is more frequent than wife-to-husband aggression, especially when it involves hitting and using or threatening with a weapon. Certainly, media attention has highlighted the male's role as aggressor in intimate relationships. Surprisingly, these common perceptions are not substantiated by research. In fact, a number of researchers (e.g., Frye & Karney, 2006) have found a higher rate of wife-to-husband abuse during the early phases of marriage. Archer's (2000, 2002) meta-analyses likewise revealed that the rates of female-to-male aggression in intimate relationships are either similar to or higher than the rates of male-to-female aggression (as cited in Kassin, Fein & Markus, 2010).

As is the case with research on any factor involved in aggression, the gender-related outcomes are affected by the experimental method used. For example, studies using self-report measures can conflict with those using peer- and other-reports as well as observational methods of aggression. Similarly, lab studies of aggression using noise blasts as aggressive measures can differ from those using real-world settings such as prisons or communities. Taking these factors into consideration, Archer (2004) conducted a meta-analysis of over 300 studies to explore gender differences in aggression in real-world settings and across countries in North America, Europe and Asia. The overall findings suggest that males are more physically aggressive than females, beginning as young as age two and continuing throughout childhood and adolescence. There were either no significant differences or a slightly higher incidence among females in verbal aggression. Further, indirect aggression was found to be higher among females, but only in later childhood and adolescence. There were no significant differences between males and females with regard to threshold for feeling anger.

Thus, gender differences in aggression have numerous considerations, including the context, the amount of potential personal cost entailed and the specific measure of aggression used. As far as research suggests, the only consistent finding *overall* is that males tend to be more physically aggressive than females, but this general finding has exceptions (such as the gender differences in spouse abuse).

***Developmental sequence of aggression.*** Researchers have generally found a predictable progression of types of aggression throughout the developmental life span. Generally, as a child matures cognitively, aggressive strategies become more diverse and include more complex

subtle forms (Björkqvist et al., 1992; Cairns & Cairns, 1994). Thus, physical aggression strategies develop first, then verbal aggression and finally more symbolic forms. These findings have important implications for how aggression is measured across the life span. For example, the physically aggressive acts of an older teenager would not generally have the same meaning as the same acts committed by a four-year-old. Similarly, strategies to reduce aggression at all ages need to take into ac-

count the specific developmental factors involved, including psychological as well as biological factors (e.g., brain development).

## FAMILY FACTORS RELATED TO AGGRESSION

We may intuitively expect that, in a home where there is significant verbal and physical aggression, the children are more likely to exhibit aggressive behaviors in their own lives. As noted earlier, this is the trend that researchers have often found, and it is consistent with social learning theory, which posits that aggressive models increase the likelihood of aggression in those who observe them. One caution to note when interpreting these data is that the studies are correlational; one cannot say on the basis of this research that a causal relationship exists between observing domestic abuse and later propensity toward aggression. Even so, it is important to understand which of the many factors in family life might most relate to later aggression in children. The research noted below was cited in Krahé's (2001) extensive overview of aggression.

*Parenting style.* Harsh parental discipline is often associated with higher levels of aggression later in the child's life. This type of discipline includes many forms of aggression (slapping, yelling, etc.) in response to a child's real or perceived disobedience. Weiss et al. (1992) showed a significant relationship between harsh discipline early in life and later aggression in the children. Their analyses suggest that this relationship is not due to possible confounding factors such as child temperament, SES or marital violence, although there was some evidence that these latter variables were related to child aggression. Krahé (2001) notes that one potential reason for this relationship between harsh discipline and aggression is that often the child perceives aggression as an acceptable way to resolve conflict. Thus, one possible effect of harsh discipline may be that the child learns maladaptive social information processing patterns (e.g., aggressive scripts) that are generalized to other social settings.

Pagani et al. (2004) also cite research demonstrating the link between parents' verbal aggression toward their children and subsequent increased levels of aggression in the child. For example, Kubany et al. (1992) observed that when parents use harsh "you" messages with their child, there is a greater likelihood of verbal counterattacks and increasing conflict. Harsh "you" messages can include statements such as "You are no good!" or "You won't amount to anything!"

Dodge, Coie, Pettit and Price (1990, as cited in Pagani et al., 2004) further note that although harsh discipline may result in immediate compliance, strategies such as yelling, threatening or hitting are often associated with peer- and teacher-reported aggression in the short term (six months). Over the long term (at age thirty-two), such disciplining strategies are significantly related to violent and criminal offenses (Farrington, 1991).

*Physical abuse.* It is often difficult to distinguish between harsh physical discipline and outright physical abuse of a child. For the sake of this discussion, harsh physical discipline is used to correct disobedience, while in physical abuse the child's parent(s) or caretaker(s) inflicts harm on the child intentionally, whether or not disobedience has occurred (Remley & Herlihy, 2007). As in the case of harsh discipline, the physical abuse of a child is often associated with subsequent levels of aggressive behaviors in the child. Englander (1997), for example, found that aggressive behavior increases as a function of exposure to abusive physical punishment. This is especially true for boys from age six on. These findings are consistent with those of Prino and Peyrot (1994), who found a significant difference in aggression levels in children depending on whether the child had experienced physical abuse versus physical neglect (e.g., failure to provide food or clothing). Children who had been physically abused showed a higher rate of aggression later on, while children who had been neglected showed more social withdrawal. Gelles (1997) further notes that a *"cycle of violence"* can occur, whereby a minority of physically abused children grow up to become physically abusive toward their own children. Nevertheless, it should be noted that there are other factors or buffers that often interrupt perpetuation of abuse.

## SITUATIONAL FACTORS RELATED TO AGGRESSION

So far in this chapter, you have read about scriptural approaches to understanding aggression, various definitions of aggression, as well as different biological, psychological and familial causes of aggression. Remember that these factors interact with one another, and there is some inconsistency regarding the relative effects of these. Another related type of causal factor has to do with situational cues that may elicit aggressive thoughts, motives and actions. The effects of these situational cues give insight into ways to remediate their negative effects. Generally, the various cues that are discussed in this section are understood to elicit negative affective arousal, which is then believed to lead to an increase in aggression.

**Aggressive cues.** Research suggests that the presence of a weapon can increase a person's aggressive thoughts and behavior. This is known as the *weapons effect*. In a study investigating this phenomenon, Anderson, Benjamin and Bartholow (1998) gave subjects a series of word pairs. The first word in each pair acted as a "prime." The primes were either aggression-related (specifically, weapon words) or neutral (animals). The second word in the pair was also either aggressive or neutral. Subjects were asked to read the second word out loud, and the researchers measured reaction time. As predicted, subjects who read the aggressive prime were much quicker to read the second word in the pair when it was aggressive than when it was neutral. A second study by Anderson et al. (1998) showed subjects visual aggressive cues (e.g., guns) as primes, with similar results.

Along with the weapons effect, other types of cues can likewise act to increase a person's aggressive cognitions and behavior. For example, actors in aggressive films, or violent criminals (e.g., serial killers) whose names are well associated with aggression, can also act as aggressive cues.

*Temperature.* I formerly taught at Palm Beach Atlantic University, which is along the intracoastal waterway in West Palm Beach, Florida. On one of my last days there, I had to walk across campus to the registrar's office. Along the way I could feel the heavy humidity in the air, as if I were walking through a sauna. Sweat ran down my sleeves and back. By the time I arrived in the registrar's office and was greeted by the bright-eyed staff, who had been inside the comfortable air-conditioned office, I was so irritated that I felt ready to snap at the first person who smiled at me. Luckily, I sat quietly for a few minutes to gather my thoughts—and dehumidify—and I was thus able to avoid any undue and potentially career-altering aggressive responses.

Research has found this experience of increased irritability in high temperatures to be quite common. The so-called *heat hypothesis* refers to the finding that "uncomfortably hot temperatures increase aggressive motives and behavior" (Anderson, Bushman & Groom, 1997).When Anderson and his colleagues investigated the relationship between annual average temperature in the fifty largest cities in the U.S. and crime rate between the years 1950 and 1995, they found a positive relationship between temperature and serious or deadly assaults. Interestingly, they found no significant relationship between temperature and property-oriented crime.

Anderson and Anderson (1998), in their review of the literature, similarly noted that rates of violence involving physical assaults, rape and murder are highest in the summer months. These studies take into account the possibility that warmer weather may be associated with increased crime simply because there is more opportunity to interact with others when it is warmer. Yet the studies compared warmer and cooler years, and the results were the same.

Krahé (2001) notes that while the empirical support for the connection between hot temperatures and increased crime is fairly strong, explanations for this relationship between crime and aggression differ. Thus, she notes Anderson et al.'s (1997) proposal to consider heat as just one of many variables that contribute to negative affect.

*Crowding.* Have you ever dreaded the thought of going Christmas shopping? I myself often begin with a great attitude, dressing in the holiday colors and sipping hot chocolate to evoke the right frame of mind. When I then have difficulty finding a parking space, I try to maintain this good attitude, assuring myself that this is "just the season" and that everyone else is putting up with mall madness. Before long, however, I feel overwhelmed by the solicitous salespeople, the long lines, and *other* people's rudeness. One time, I even unplugged one of those annoying Christmas carol machines when it played one song too many! Of course that was not rude of me.

Researchers have found increased violence in situations that are crowded, including inpatient psychiatric units (Ng et al., 2001; Nijman & Henk, 1999), nightclubs (Macintyre & Homel, 1997), prisons (Gaes & Mc-Guire, 1985) and many other places. Crowding is generally defined in terms of density of people in a given space. Generally, the higher the number of people, the less the level of comfort and ease, the greater the opportunity for conflict, the more frustration and the less tolerance for frustration. The relationship between crowding and aggression is not a simple one. The negative effects of overcrowding interact with other factors such as noise, temperature, gender and personality type (Homel et al., 1992).

*Violent media.* As you are probably aware, there has been a long-standing debate regarding the extent to which violent media is associated with subsequent levels of aggressive behavior. This issue has become increasingly salient, given the easy accessibility of violent still and action images on television and movies, video games, and online. Zillmann and Weaver (2007) reviewed literature that explores the relationship between violent media and aggression. For example, they report that Paik & Comstock's (1994) meta-analysis of the literature found consistent agreement that violent media helps facilitate aggression. Nevertheless, as Zillmann and Weaver note, the exact mechanisms by which this relationship occurs has not been understood until more recently. Bushman (1995), for example, noted that those who are the most drawn to violent media are those individuals who score higher on self-report measures of aggression. For those individuals, the violent media may be especially potent as a cue for later aggressive behavior.

Zillmann and Weaver (2007) further explored the question of how, specifically, individuals who receive high scores on aggression questionnaires may be affected by violent images. The researchers distinguished between two subtraits of aggressive individuals. First is *physical aggression*, which has to do with a readiness to hurt or harm others, especially in retaliation or in response to a provocation. The second subtrait is *hostility*— feelings of ill will that emanate from experiences of deprivation and injustice. The researchers suggest that the physical aggression subtype is most relevant in the relationship between media violence and aggression.

One possible way in which violent media increases aggression is by desensitizing the viewer to the effects of violence. Bartholow, Bushman and Sestir (2006) investigated this possibility using male college students who typically played either violent video games or nonviolent video games but not both. Subjects were told that they were in a study investigating the effects of viewing different types of images on performance on a reaction time test. Participants had EEG electrodes placed on their scalp and were shown a series of images that were *negative violent* (e.g., a man holding a gun to another man's head on a subway), *negative nonviolent* (e.g., a baby with a large tumor on her face) and *neutral* (e.g., a man on a bicycle). Participants were then asked to rate the feeling of the image as well as to rate how aroused they felt by the image. The EEG measured their P300 evoked potentials (i.e., brain wave fluctuations that are related to how one evaluates or categorizes a stimulus). Participants were then told that they would be competing with another "participant" (actually a computer controlled by the researchers) in a reaction time test to see who could press a button the fastest after hearing a tone. The loser in each trial would receive a blast of noise through the headphones, and the winner would decide volume (60 decibels to 105 decibels) and duration (.25 seconds to 2.5 seconds) of the noise.

The results demonstrated that those who were frequent violent video game players were significantly more aggressive with the noise blasts during the reaction time phase. They also had lower P300 amplitudes in response to violent images. That is, their brains took longer to categorize (respond to) the image as violent. Interestingly, there was no significant difference in P300 amplitudes for both neutral images and negative, nonviolent images between those who played violent video games and those who did not. The researchers concluded that repeated exposure to violent video games blunts the brain's ability to categorize violent images but not other images.

This concern is likewise expressed by many parents whose children play violent video games. In many cases, the parents cannot monitor or censor the games because the children's proficiency often enables them to reach much higher levels than their parents can. It is at these higher levels where some of the most graphic images are displayed (Biskupic, 2010).

Bartholow, Bushman and Sestir (2006) also reviewed some of the research regarding desensitization and aggression. To become *desensitized* is to experience diminished psychological or emotional responsiveness to a stimulus after repeated exposure to it (Wolpe, 1982). Desensitization can be adaptive because it enables people to ignore irrelevant information and focus instead on relevant information. Surgeons, for example, must have a fair amount of desensitization to blood so that they can perform surgery without being distracted by it. In other contexts, such as for viewers of media, desensitization to blood and gore on television or video games is highly associated with less responsiveness to the effects of real violence (Smith & Donnerstein, 1998) and reduced inhibitions against behaving aggressively (Anderson & Bushman, 2001). Thus, media violence may increase aggression, at least in part, by desensitizing viewers to the effects of real violence (e.g., Griffiths & Shuckford, 1989; Smith & Donnerstein, 1998).

Figure 7.2 lists some of the factors related to aggression that were discussed in the previous sections.

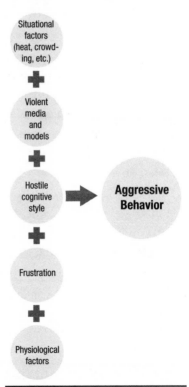

**Figure 7.2. Some Factors Related to Aggression**

## IS AGGRESSION GETTING WORSE?

So far in this chapter, the focus on the many types, causes and outcomes of aggression certainly can leave one with the impression that things are getting worse. The world is in crisis, it seems, and aggression is every-where. Pinker (2007) challenges this view. He argues that the actual in-cidence of overall violence has decreased significantly since the age of the Enlightenment. Specifically, Pinker notes that many violent acts that were common earlier in history (e.g., torture and mutilation as common consequences for crimes, and the sadistic torture of animals as enter-tainment) have decreased substantially.

Pinker (2007) refers to the work of criminologist Eisner, who studied the rate of human-to-human homicides in Europe and North America since 1945. Eisner notes that the death rate due to homicides has de-creased overall. Also, there has been a steep decline in interstate wars, as well as fewer genocides overall. Pinker argues that one of the main reasons we think that aggression is increasing is that we now have better reporting than was available historically.

Graphic images of genocides, homicides and wars are ever present in the media. This greater media attention increases the salience of these memories in our consciousness. We are then inclined to think that the incidence of violence is more common. This would be a good example of the *availability heuristic* you learned about in the social perception chapter. This is where our perception of the likelihood of something is related to the ease with which it is recalled in our memory.

Pinker (2007) suggests several possible reasons for the decline in vi-olent crimes. He notes that a greater consciousness regarding social justice has resulted in policies and regulations that constrain aggressive impulses. Pinker further suggests that violence may have decreased for selfish reasons as well. For example, since trade has increased among groups, aggressing against the other would not be a profitable strategy because then they would not buy your goods. Pinker extends this idea to an evolutionary psychology perspective. He suggests that since our "inner" circle has increased due to an increasing global awareness of our interdependence and perhaps an increased exposure to others, our em-pathy for a broader circle of others has also increased. This increased empathy presumably also increases one's moral consideration of others.

Pinker's (2007) report sounds encouraging. It speaks to the power of collective efforts to decrease lethal aggressive behavior. But there are several reasons why we must be careful not to assume that aggression itself is necessarily decreasing. Assuming that Pinker's data are an accurate representation of the sorts of violence to which he specifically refers, it may be more valid to claim that certain forms of violent aggression are decreasing, but only in some circumstances. Let us consider the data on aggression in the U.S. as an example.

The FBI reports that overall, violent crimes have decreased more than 15 percent from the year 2000 through 2009. Yet the homicide rate specifically is still three times as high as it was in 1960. Additionally, in 2010 in the U.S., the National Coalition for the Homeless reported that over the past eleven years, there has been an increasing rate of violence against homeless individuals, many of whom have been "kicked, set on fire, beaten to death, and even decapitated. Since 1999, there have been 291 deaths of homeless people and 783 homeless victims of violence in 47 states, Puerto Rico and Washington, D.C."

As noted earlier in the chapter, because many forms of aggression (verbal, symbolic, passive, etc.) are generally not reported in official crime statistics, it is difficult to know how much the reduced rates of violent crimes reflect concurrent decreases in all forms of aggression. On the one hand, speaking specifically of the U. S., we see the success of numerous collective preventive efforts (e.g., crime awareness education). On the other hand, we see increases in certain specific kinds of violent crimes (e.g., against the homeless). A cautious optimism regarding violent aggression seems to be warranted, in any case.

## HOW CAN WE REDUCE VIOLENCE?

As you can gather from all the preceding discussions in this chapter, aggression is a complex phenomenon, partly because there are so many different types of aggression and potential causes or motivations for them. There are also many relevant situational and personal factors. It is not a surprise, then, that finding ways to reduce aggression has proven to be quite a complex process. Efforts to reduce aggression must consider the myriad factors outlined already in this chapter and apply them to a particular context. For example, how would interventions for reducing school bullying compare to those used for reducing domestic violence or sexual violence? Would individuals with different personality types or life histories respond differently to these interventions?

Thus far, efforts to reduce aggressive acts have intervened in differing ways, including behavioral reinforcements, cognitive approaches, multisystems approaches, mentoring programs, increasing social support and so on. As noted earlier, the most effective interventions generally include a number of these approaches, addressing the different contexts in which the aggressive person is interacting (e.g., school, work, home, neighborhood, peers; Henggeler et al., 2009). This makes sense given the complexity of the motivations, causes and outcomes of aggression. In this section, you will read a brief summary of these strategies. Then in the following section, you will read about how Christian ideas regarding forgiveness and valuing (humanizing) others may apply to aggression-reducing strategies.

*Social-cognitive approaches.* As noted throughout this chapter, research has generally found a close connection between normative beliefs about aggression and actual aggressive behaviors. So, for example, if an individual believes that aggression is a viable and appropriate way to resolve conflict, then aggressive behaviors are more likely. Guerra et al. (2007) thus recommend that aggression prevention programs in schools address both *general* normative beliefs about aggression (e.g., "aggression is a legitimate way to resolve conflict") as well as more *specific* normative beliefs (e.g., "it is a viable option to retaliate against another male with violence"). Other efforts to address social-cognitive factors in aggression include those aimed at challenging the hostile attribution bias noted earlier. Other related approaches have aimed to teach individuals to activate proactive, helpful thoughts while in hostile contexts, effectively curbing tendencies toward anger and aggression (Wilkowski & Robinson, 2008).

*Prosocial models and norms.* Along with the significant role cognitive processes play in aggression reduction, research has also suggested that role models who demonstrate prosocial problem solving and conflict resolution can have a positive impact on reducing aggression. One effective way to use prosocial models is through various media. Hearold (1986), for example, found that prosocial television programs may produce stronger effects than antisocial television programs. Guerra et al. (2007) also note that in the same way that social norms can encourage prosocial behaviors in males (e.g., helping females; Eagly & Crowley, 1986), social norms that address specific normative beliefs among males regarding retaliatory aggression against other males could also be helpful in reducing violence.

**International peace efforts.** Social psychologists are also interested in aggression between larger groups, including countries. This type of aggression is manifested in a variety of ways, including war, hostility during negotiations and negative portrayals of other nations as "enemies." A group of researchers investigating this type of aggression are involved in a relatively new and growing subdiscipline in the field known as *peace psychology,* a division of the APA. According to its website, this group sees peace as not only the absence of war, but also "the creation of positive social conditions which minimize destructive conflicts and promote human well-being." Thus, peace psychology explores ways to reduce many types of aggression, including sex trafficking, genocides and other basic human rights violations.

Researchers in the area of peace psychology who are interested in reducing international tensions are also interested in many of the social psychological phenomena discussed in this text (e.g., how countries make attributions of one another, how countries perceive themselves as "in-groups," what factors make one country more or less inclined to help another). Often, hostility includes the perception that one side has harmed or will harm the other, and this generally results in self-protective measures to ensure safety. Osgood (1962) introduced one possible strategy that has since been used for reducing potential aggression between nations. This strategy was eventually known as *gradual reduction in tension* (GRIT). In this approach, one side announces that it wants to reduce tensions and then makes a small conciliatory gesture. The other side then makes a gesture. The goal is for the tensions between the two sides to erode as each perceives the other as more trustworthy, eventually hopefully reducing the incidence of aggressive acts. If the first gesture was ignored, Osgood suggests that the first party follow with a second or even third attempt. In the process of increasing cooperation and lessening the adversarial approach, Osgood maintains that the gestures should not be seen as signs of weakness, nor should they be unduly costly. The primary goal is peaceful coexistence.

More recent variations of peace initiatives have moved beyond the goal of peaceful coexistence by emphasizing the humanizing of others, an idea that is central in a Christian approach to reducing violence. In other words, the focus is more on the sort of peace that is based on a rightful regard for the dignity of all humans. The Center for Global Peace at American University (Washington, D.C.) epitomizes this focus. Their study of tribal societies, for example, emphasizes that "civil society, in its broadest sense, seems to imply a society in which the interests, concerns, and dignity of the civilian, the citizen, the 'ordinary person,' are taken seriously."

## A CHRISTIAN VIEW OF REDUCING AGGRESSION: *HUMANIZING AND FORGIVENESS*

The sobering reality of aggressive behavior in its many forms can seem difficult to reconcile with a Christian view of humans as having the capacity for other-centeredness. How might a Christian perspective inform efforts to reduce aggression?

As noted earlier in this chapter, from a Christian view of humans in light of creation, fall and redemption, there are two major topics that seem especially relevant to the research on aggression. Both of these issues are related to humans' capacity for *other-centered concern,* which is an integral part of the CFR view. The first has to do with seeing the value and dignity of the life of the other, a perspective that is often corrupted by the dehumanization that much research links to aggression. As you have read, dehumanization has to do with the process of seeing the other as either animal-like or otherwise lacking in the basic characteristics of human nature. Given the many social implications of the ability to see the common humanity that we share with others, efforts to increase the humanizing of others would seem an integral part of the

healing process that can decrease future aggression. Such efforts are becoming an ever greater focus in peace research and initiatives.

A second important CFR concept related to aggression is *forgiveness,*
which has to do with replacing resentment, bitterness, hatred and anger
with love, compassion, sympathy and empathy (Worthington, 1998).

In the following sections, you will read further about the concepts of
humanizing and forgiving. Then you will see how these were applied to
interventions for the reduction of retaliatory aggression in the case of
the genocide that took place in Rwanda. Implications for the interpersonal level of aggression will also be reviewed.

*Humanizing.* From a Christian view of persons, other-centeredness
has as one of its integral components acknowledging the dignity and
value of the other's life and considering the other from that basic premise.
This humanizing of another person is related to the degree of consideration we give to them and affects our perceptions of the moral consideration the other deserves. One study demonstrated how even more subtle
humanization efforts can increase care for the other. Turner and Hadas-
Halpern (2008, as cited in Waytz, Epley & Cacioppo, 2010) found that
radiologists who viewed x-rays that had a photo of the patient's face attached engaged the patient more, giving extra details regarding their
case and expressing more empathy toward the patient.

Whereas humanizing a person increases our perception of that person's moral worth, you read earlier that dehumanizing others often con-
dones wrongdoing toward them (Haslam, 2006). Waytz, Epley and Cacioppo (2010), for example, reviewed research that demonstrates that
socially different or distant groups—such as homosexuals, drug addicts
and the homeless—are often dehumanized (Harris & Fiske, 2006). The
researchers further note that dehumanization is a central process involved in interethnic discrimination, genocide and slavery.

Haslam (2006) notes that one of the reasons it is difficult to understand
dehumanization is because it targets such a wide range of individuals and
groups. For example, Haslam cites research (e.g., Jahoda, 1999) regarding
ways in which individuals of other races and ethnicities are presented in
popular culture "as barbarians who lack culture, self-restraint, moral sensibility, and cognitive capacity, have brutish appetites for violence and sex, . . .

are impulsive and prone to criminality, and can tolerate unusual amounts of pain" (p. xii). Dehumanization has also been used to help explain acts of genocide (Chalk & Jonassohn, 1990), representations of women in pornography (Check & Guloine, 1989), the characterization and treatment of patients in modern medicine (Barnard, 2001), and the view of people with disabilities (O'Brien, 1999), to name only a few examples.

Haslam (2006) suggests that the research is clear on some of the connections between dehumanization and aggression. For example, it is far easier to kill someone who is seen as somehow not quite human. Yet Haslam notes that the concept of dehumanization has received such varied points of view that it is not well integrated into a formal model that can be applied to both interpersonal and intergroup social interactions. He suggests that this is one of the reasons why the relationship between dehumanization and aggression is not a consistent one.

Haslam proposes that dehumanization occurs not only in aggressive conflict, but also in everyday more subtle ways. Specifically, he suggests that dehumanization involves two specific aspects:

- denying that the other has *uniquely human qualities* that differentiate us from other species (e.g., moral sensibility, civility, rational logic); and

- denying that the other has the characteristics that constitute fundamental *human nature* (e.g., cognitive flexibility, agency, warmth).

Haslam suggests that these two proposed types of dehumanization should result in different types of dehumanization. Specifically, if you see another as lacking *uniquely human qualities* such as civility or rational logic, you would be more likely to see them as animals. The resultant response might be contempt and disgust. If you see another as lacking in a quality related to *human nature* (e.g., lack of cognitive flexibility), then you might see them as "rigid" or "inflexible." A likely response would then be indifference and a lack of empathy toward the other. This difference in responses helps us to see why research on the link between dehumanization and aggression needs to be specific with regard to the type of dehumanizing involved.

One common result of dehumanization in everyday social interactions is *social exclusion,* or isolating the other person. One who is dehumanized is often socially ostracized, neglected or denied participation in social activities. Interestingly, this aggressive act of social exclusion against another often results in an aggressive response from the isolated one. In this way, social exclusion can act to perpetuate aggression of different forms. In fact, social exclusion is one of the most powerful predictors of aggressive behavior. Leary, Twenge and Quinlivan (2006) review the literature that shows a strong positive relationship between feeling socially isolated and anger that leads to aggression. For example, in youth, the strongest predictor of adolescent violence is social exclusion, or "weak social ties" (U.S. Surgeon General's Report on Youth Violence, 2001, as cited in Twenge et al., 2007). In fact, social exclusion is more powerful a predictor than even gang membership, poverty or drug use. Further, many lab experiments have likewise shown that social rejection causes increased aggression, sometimes even against people unrelated to the rejection (Buckley, Winkel & Leary, 2004; Kirkpatrick, Waugh, Valencia & Webster, 2002; Twenge, Baumeister, Tice & Stucke, 2001, as cited in Twenge et al., 2007).

You may recall reading from the chapter on the self that Baumeister and Leary (1995) proposed that humans have an intrinsic need to belong, and are motivated to pursue and maintain connections with others. This is consistent with both the naturalist and Christian views of persons that acknowledges the intrinsically relational nature of humans. Following social rejection or exclusion, a person is likely to make efforts to strengthen weak ties or make new ones. When an individual's desire to reconnect socially is impeded for whatever reasons, this can cause anger and subsequent aggression (Twenge et al., 2001).

In order to explore the possibility that giving a socially ostracized person a chance for social reconnection may result in reduced aggression, Twenge et al. (2007) had participants experience either social inclusion or social isolation, with or without a chance to socially reconnect. Specifically, participants were either excluded from or included in a conversation among peers (confederates). At the end, some subjects who had been excluded were given a chance to reconnect socially by being thanked by the experimenter and given a bag of candy. The other subjects who had been excluded were simply given a receipt for their participation. Then all participants played a noise-blast game against an "opponent" (confederate) who reportedly had arrived late in the study and had not taken part in the previous conversation in which the subjects had been either included or excluded. The subjects all won the game and were directed to deliver a blast of sound to the opponent. Subjects who had been excluded and not been given a chance to socially reconnect (with the experimenter) showed more aggression by delivering the noisy blast for longer periods of time to the losing opponent. A similar study showed that having socially isolated subjects write about a favorite family member after having been rejected decreased their aggression. Apparently, intentional recall of one's strong connections despite being rejected could be a powerful deterrent to aggression.

As noted above, many instances of dehumanization involve more extreme examples of aggressive behavior such as intergroup violence. Other examples of dehumanization involve social exclusion. Remember from the groups chapter that there is often also dehumanization between groups. Leyens et al. (2000) referred to this as *infrahumanization*, the belief that one's in-group is more human than an out-group. Leyens et al. found that people are often more likely to attribute uniquely human emotions such as love and nostalgia to their own group, while they are more likely to attribute emotions that are true of both humans and animals (e.g., joy, anger) to the out-group. This dehumanization is associated with an increased probability of aggression between groups.

Essential to a Christian perspective is the intrinsic value of persons. Christ specifically humanized those who were marginalized out-groups, such as the poor and sick, as well as those who were oppressors. Examples include the Samaritans (Lk 10:25-37), lepers (Lk 17:11-19) and tax collectors (Mk 2:16; Lk 19:9). Christianity combats dehumanization by extending the right of personhood to *all* humans. This is not easy to do, especially when one deals with an aggressor who has committed severe harm. Yet this prominent biblical teaching about humanizing others is consistent with the aggression research just presented. Thus, one could reasonably expect that violations of such a central tenet of the faith would result in many negative social consequences, including aggression. The history of the church provides excellent examples of the link between dehumanization and aggression (e.g., the church's en-dorsement of slavery at various times in history) as well as the link be-tween humanization and reductions in aggression (e.g., efforts to hu-manize those who cannot advocate for themselves: the unborn, the poor and the elderly, among others). In addition, as more recent research suggests, when a nation humanizes their "enemy," chances are better that peace would be more enduring than if the nations had only strived for peaceful coexistence as the end goal.

*Forgiving*. As noted in the preceding section, dehumanization ap-pears to lower the threshold for aggression under any circumstances but the biblically endorsed humanization of all persons helps to counteract aggression. But what of situations in which aggression occurs as a retal-iatory response to a specific harm or perceived harm? In such cases, an-other central biblical concept—forgiveness—has been linked to many positive outcomes. Baskin and Enright (2004) offer a definition of *for-giveness:* "The willful giving up of resentment in the face of another's (or others') considerable injustice and responding with beneficence to the offender even though that offender has no right to the forgiver's moral goodness." It is "an act freely chosen" and is "distinguished from con-doning and excusing, reconciling, and forgetting" (p. 80). Not surpris-ingly, this definition has more to do with the decision of the forgiver than the effects of forgiveness, but it is precisely those effects that are of most interest in this discussion. The majority of forgiveness research has focused on benefits to the forgiver (e.g., improved mental health). But more recently, forgiveness has also been linked to decreased likelihood of retaliation against the offender, whether in the form of a direct physical aggression or in more indirect or symbolic ways that none-theless are destructive.

The important role of forgiveness in reducing violence and other forms of aggression has been documented at the *interpersonal* level. For example, Worthington's (1998) research suggests that forgiveness can relieve psychological distress as well as lessen the perceived need to re-taliate against the offender. Weiner (1995, as cited in Eaton and Struthers, 2006) describes the link between the type of attributions made for the offense and the likelihood of aggression toward the offender. According to Weiner, if a victim attributes the offender's behavior to purposeful actions (i.e., high level of responsibility), there is a greater chance of anger and retaliatory aggression.

Much research (e.g., Karremans, VanLange & Holland, 2005; Crombag, Rassin & Horselenberg, 2003) supports how a victim's attributions regarding the offender's level of responsibility affect the chances of retaliatory aggression. As Eaton and Struthers (2006) note, two factors that can interrupt this process are forgiveness and an apology that is perceived as sincere, expresses repentance and offers reparation (Exline & Baumeister, 2000; Hodgins & Liebeskind, 2003).

At the *group* level, more recent research has also suggested that forgiving and humanizing the "enemy" plays an integral role in the process of reconciliation between groups and reducing future violence. For example, this has been demonstrated in situations involving genocide (e.g., Staub, 1999, 2006).

***Forgiveness and humanizing after genocide.*** Let us look at one example—the genocide in Rwanda—to see how the processes of humanizing and forgiving are playing integral roles in recovery and reconciliation in a land where conflict still exists.

In Rwanda, there are two primary ethnic groups: the Hutus are the majority, and the Tutsis are the minority. There have been ethnic tensions between these two groups since at least 1916, when the Belgian colonists arrived in Rwanda, producing identity cards that classified people according to their ethnicity. The Belgians favored the Tutsis, enabling them to access better educational opportunities and jobs.

As might be expected, resentment among the Hutus grew, and in 1959, there were a series of riots in which more than twenty thousand Tutsis were killed and many others fled the country. In 1962, Belgium relinquished power and granted Rwanda independence. From that point, the Hutus took over power of the country and blamed the Tutsis for whatever problems happened, including a severe economic condition.

The plane of the Rwandan president, Habyarimana, was shot down in April 1994. The presidential guard then instituted an instant retribution plan, which included the slaughter of Tutsis and moderate Hutus, who had helped them. Early on, the killers were military officials, politicians and businessmen, but propaganda encouraged average citizens to be involved. Indeed, military personnel often forced Hutu civilians to kill their Tutsi neighbors and family members. Participants were offered incentives such as money, food and land. From April to July, approximately 700,000 Tutsis were slaughtered, as well as politically moderate Hutus, all killed primarily by knives and machetes. Although the killing in Rwanda later ended, significant conflict continues. How could forgiveness and humanizing possibly offer hope in such a situation?

Staub and his colleagues (2005, 2006) explored how efforts to encourage both forgiveness and humanizing play integral roles within the context of organized efforts toward reconciliation in Rwanda. These organized efforts have included, among other interventions, meetings between Hutu and Tutsi individuals in which speaking the truth about the genocide and learning to empathize with the victim's and the aggressor's perspective has enabled both to experience greater emotional healing and reductions in anger and desire to seek retribution. As Staub (2006) notes, when violence between groups stops, nonviolent relations can begin but violence often resumes (Long & Brecke, 2003). You can well imagine how this occurs: the psychological wounds, fear, mistrust and anger that remain often interfere with peaceful reconciliation efforts. Staub notes that these interruptions in peaceful resolutions also occur because not all parties are satisfied with the solutions that have been reached or how they have been carried out. A significant change in attitudes toward those in the other group is thus a necessary part of the restoration process.

Staub and his colleagues (2005, 2006) worked with community leaders and facilitators in Rwanda by introducing an intervention that could be incorporated into the efforts already taking place there. The participants were 194 rural Rwandese individuals, 61 percent of which were Tutsi, 16 percent Hutu, and 23 percent either did not self-report their ethnicity or else changed their report of their ethnic identity between interviews. They were placed into three groups that met for two hours, twice per week, for three weeks. Group 1 used whatever traditional interventions were already in place in that community, which varied depending on the group facilitator. Some of these aimed to promote healing, while others aimed at building community. Group 2, a control group, had no intervention. Group 3, the experimental group, integrated additional interventions developed by the researchers into the traditional interventions. These additional interventions were designed to increase reconciliation by changing the orientation toward, and degree of acceptance of, the other ethnic group, and by including the following:

- Understanding genocide: Participants were educated about the influences that led to the perpetrators' actions and the bystanders' passivity, with the aim to increase participants' ability to empathize with the human vulnerabilities of the oppressors.

- Understanding the effects of trauma and victimization paths to healing: This part of the intervention educated participants about how they have changed due to the trauma, and how these changes are normal consequences of painful trauma.

- Understanding basic psychological needs: This built upon the above two interventions. Participants were taught about how basic emotional needs like security, trust, esteem, positive identity, feelings of control and positive connections to others can be disrupted by social conditions and instigate groups turning against other groups.

- Sharing painful experiences in an empathic context: Participants drew, talked about or thought about their painful experiences. Then they shared these in small groups, with group members and facilitator responding empathically. This included demonstrations, rehearsal and discussion of empathic responding to another's distress. There was a significant amount of open and emotional sharing of what happened to participants during the genocide.

Participants' emotional distress and orientations toward the other group were measured both right after completion of the group and two months later. In comparison to the control group and the traditional intervention group, those who received the "integrated approach" experienced significantly fewer posttraumatic symptoms and an increased positive orientation to members of the other group. Staub et al. (2005) note that positive orientation to the other (humanizing) is related to an increased readiness to forgive, and consequently a greater chance of reconciliation that maintains peace. The researchers note that reconciliation and decreased violence among groups is an intricate process that features humanizing and forgiving within the context of broader efforts at restorative justice and truth that is empathic with the victims' stories. Further, these sorts of interventions need to be applied and adapted to particular circumstances, such that the specifics of culture, current social conditions and the history of the group relations are taken into consideration.

Before you continue reading, take a moment to absorb the enormity of the forgiveness and reconciliation work that is occurring in places like Rwanda and South Africa. Though these are imperfect efforts and restoration is far from complete, they nevertheless demonstrate that forgiving and humanizing can have great power against aggression and hate in even the worst of situations. It is also a powerful reminder of the relevance of biblical principles for the scientific endeavor to reduce aggression.

*Forgiveness and humanizing in everyday life.* Cases of genocide and other extreme forms of violence are difficult for us to comprehend, but they certainly present a significant challenge in terms of both forgiving and humanizing the aggressor(s). The same is often true with the sorts of aggressive acts that most of us encounter in everyday life (gossip, being cut off in traffic, social ostracizing, etc.). Here also the research discussed throughout this chapter suggests that humanizing and forgiving are essential for reconciliation and reducing aggression, given their relevance for such a wide variety of contexts. The relevance of these two processes could help to integrate various models of aggression such that efforts toward reducing aggressive behavior may become more effective. Indeed, more recent research demonstrates significant findings for youth in schools (Holter et al., 2008), as well as in U.S. cities and Belfast, Ireland (Enright, 2009; Enright et al., 2007).

Forgiving and humanizing are relevant whether one is the aggressor or the victim. Humility with regard to our own transgressions and a willingness to repent when we offend or hurt another is one of the integral parts of reducing at least psychological aggression from the victim as well as reducing the likelihood that we would aggress again against the victim (Rudolph et al., 2004, as cited in Eaton & Struthers, 2006).

When we are the victim of some aggressive act, however, considering the humanity of the aggressor and forgiving them is often not an easy process, and can indeed seem impossible. It is not often easy to be other-centered in the face of hurt. As Worthington (2009) notes, one must remember that forgiveness is not condoning, nor does it necessarily lead to reconciliation of the relationship. It is instead offering mercy to someone who has acted unjustly.

A challenge that the Scriptures present to us is the call to forgiveness and humanizing as absolute commands, even in the absence of repentance on the part of the aggressor (e.g., Mt 6:14; 18:21-35; Mk 11:25). Research suggests that if the transgressor is unrepentant, we are likely to experience negative emotions and that those emotions may result in at least psychological aggression. Meanwhile, forgiveness research indicates that those who forgive experience fewer negative emotions as well as decreased aggression (Enright et al., 2007). In light of this research, Christ's command to forgive is not only consistent with his own character and example but also is in the best interests of both offender and offended.

In summary, approaches intended to reduce aggression have had varying levels of success. The most successful approaches have been narrowly focused on both motivations and outcomes of aggression in a specific behavioral setting (e.g., bullying in school, reducing domestic violence). These results have not usually demonstrated a broad, generalized application of these skills to other settings. Research that continues to explore the roles of humanizing and forgiving could have inestimable value for integrating our understanding of causal factors and strategies for reducing aggression. From a Christian view and from considerable research, the most successful strategies will involve the change of heart and mind that Christ beckons us to when he tells us to forgive and consider the other.

## So Far . . .

As you have read, the study of aggression is replete with difficulties related to defining aggression, the wide array of specific types of aggression, and the relative lack of an organizing theory that leads to interventions that are applicable to the many forms of aggression.

Social psychologists have provided valuable information about aggression. Yet, as noted earlier, using ideas from a Christian view of persons can help provide a more generally applicable set of principles to investigate for reducing aggression in an enduring way. Note in the following chapter on prejudice and racism how the two main biblical principles discussed here (humanizing and forgiving) are distorted or neglected in cases of racial or ethnic hatred.

## Questions to Consider

1. If you were interested in studying humanizing and forgiving, how would you implement and measure these concepts in the following settings: school bullying, domestic violence, gangs?

2. What sort of societal changes need to occur to encourage humanizing and forgiving?

3. If you were going to study situations in which there has been forgiveness but it is not possible for the victim to reconcile with the offender, how would you measure the victim's humanizing of the aggressor?

4. In what ways can you see the relevance of the following specific social psychological concepts in humanizing and forgiving: attributions, in-group bias, overconfidence effect, dual-process persuasion? What other specific concepts do you think are relevant?

## Key Terms

*aggression*
*amygdala*
*antisocial behavior*
*callous and unemotional traits*
*cycle of violence*
*dehumanization*
*desensitization*
*desensitized*
*displaced aggression*
*emotional susceptibility*

*eugenics*

*excitation transfer model*

*executive cognitive processes*

*forgiveness*

*frustration-aggression hypothesis*

*general aggression model*

*heat hypothesis*

*hostile aggression*

*hostile attribution bias*

*hostile expectancy bias*

*humanizing*

*infrahumanization*

*instrumental aggression*

*multisystemic therapy*

*narcissism*

*neoassociationist model*

*perspective-taking*

*prefrontal cortex*

*rape-prone cultures*

*reductionism*

*scripts*

*serotonin*

*social exclusion*

*social learning theory*

*trait aggressiveness*

*trait anger*

*trait irritability*

*weapons effect*

# 8

## Prejudice, Stereotypes
## and Discrimination

*God shows no partiality, but in every nation*
*anyone who fears him and does what is*
*right is acceptable to him.*

ACTS 10:34-35

As I write, and most likely as you read this page, there are in this world (or in the news) numerous examples of hateful crimes and behaviors committed by people of one group against another. The prevalence of hate crimes and everyday acts of vengeance toward dissimilar others is very disturbing. Reports of extreme behaviors like genocide as well as other less obvious and more insidious forms of hatred remind us that antagonism between groups is present to varying degrees in every culture in the world and has always existed in human history. Psychologists have discovered that starting at preschool age, children often show signs of prejudice and ethnocentrism (Aboud, 2003). In-group favor-

**Figure 8.1.**

itism, along with negative perceptions of out-groups, begins at about age five and reaches significant levels thereafter. What happens to these negative perceptions and attitudes as the person grows depends on a number of factors, as we will see in this chapter.

Concurrent with bad news about the existence of racism, prejudice and discrimination are hopeful signs that suggest that in some ways things are getting better. These encouraging signs, though in some measure inconsistent, include more frequent global efforts at racial reconciliation and increased diversity in places of work, college campuses and neighborhoods. There also seems to be a greater consciousness overall regarding matters of social justice, which have become a significant part of public discourse in many parts of the world.

Social psychologists who study negative attitudes about, and behavior toward, dissimilar others are interested in what factors contribute to it, as well as what factors might help remediate such processes. As this chapter will demonstrate, there is a wide range of both personal and interpersonal factors involved.

As with many other social psychological concepts, negative perceptions and behaviors toward different others are intricately related to the overarching social processes between and among groups. For example, consider how negative attributions toward a marginalized group (e.g., the poor) often result in prejudice and discrimination. It may be tempting to think that if an individual just changed their negative attributions about the poor, then their prejudice would almost certainly decrease. Yet this assumption neglects to consider the significant insidious class and power differentials that are present in all human societies. Reducing negative perceptions and actions toward any marginalized group requires acknowledgment of these strong group differentials and efforts to change institutionalized forms of social injustice. Thus, both individual as well as group efforts are essential in the process of remediating hatred. This point will hopefully become clearer as you continue to read.

## SOME RELEVANT QUESTIONS AND KEY TERMS

From both a Christian and naturalist view of persons, the potential for hatred between and among groups is a sad but not unexpected reality of the human condition. The human potential to hate often seems as powerful as the potential to love. How do we reconcile the CFR view of persons as intrinsically relational beings who have the capacity for other-centered concern with the harsh realities of the racial, ethnic and gender conflicts that exist? A Christian understanding of humans is especially relevant to the study of prejudice, stereotypes and discrimination, because these phenomena challenge the heart of the gospel message: "Love the Lord your God with all your heart, and with all your soul, and with all your strength, and with all your mind; and your neighbor as yourself" (Lk 10:27). Further, from the CFR view, the human capacity for these negative social thoughts and behaviors argues against our ability to exemplify other-centered concern.

From a Christian view, then, one crucial question has to do with whether humans have a genuine capacity to embrace dissimilar others. What hope do we have that we can love not just certain neighbors, but *all* our neighbors? Research in this area has explored whether prejudice and negative behavior such as discrimination are inevitable and unchangeable. The findings suggest that there is hope, but it is a tempered hope. That is, ways of reducing prejudice and racism can be successful, but we have yet to see the extent to which this is the case. Given that universal love for all of humankind is an integral part of God's redemptive work in this world, the extent to which we can avoid destructive attitudes and behaviors toward others becomes a central concern.

Before we begin, it is important to define a few terms that are often used interchangeably but actually mean different things. *Prejudice* refers to a categorical judgment, or *attitude,* that can be favorable or unfavorable. It involves judgments made about members of other groups regardless of their individual characteristics. Usually, members of the out-group are judged negatively or are unfavorably stereotyped simply because they belong to the out-group. Prejudice also involves the persistence of this negative bias even when contradictory information is presented (Lyers & Yzerbyt, 1992).

Later in this chapter, you will learn more about different types of prejudice, including those we are aware of (*explicit prejudice*) and those prejudiced attitudes and stereotypes that are not conscious (*implicit prejudice*). In addition, Pettigrew and Mertens (1995) distinguish between more blatant prejudice, which can result in direct hostility toward the out-group, and a more subtle prejudice, which generally involves refraining from outward expressions of negative emotions toward the out-group and perhaps cordially interacting with them in social settings, but generally involves evaluating one's in-group as more positive (the so-called *arms-length prejudice*).

*Stereotypes* are *cognitions*, or thoughts regarding people who belong to various social categories based on such factors as race, sex and age. The *social cognitive approach* is a major theoretical framework for explaining stereotypes (e.g., Hornsey & Hogg, 2002). According to this perspective, stereotypes are belief systems that guide the way we process information. Ashmore and Del Boca (1981) define stereotypes as "a set of beliefs about the personal attributes of a social group" (p. 21, as cited in Jussim et al., 2009). Note that while stereotypes have generally been thought of as inaccurate, leading to negative judgments and overexaggerated, simplistic views of the other, more recent research (e.g., Jussim et al., 2009) suggests that stereotypes can actually often be accurate. And, like prejudice, stereotypes can be both positive (e.g., "All Asian Americans are smart") or negative (e.g., "Men cannot understand emotions").

*Discrimination* involves *behavior* that follows from prejudiced and stereotyped thinking. It can involve, for example, excluding individuals from opportunities for jobs based solely on their out-group membership.

It should be noted that while researchers often find helpful the distinctions among cognitions, attitudes and behavior, in reality these distinctions are not always clear. For example, remember from the discussion in the attitudes chapter that the relationship between attitudes and behavior varies a lot. Furthermore, it can be difficult to separate negative thoughts from negative attitudes or to demonstrate that these are related in any consistent way, as you will see later in this chapter. So while it may make sense to consider negative stereotypes about others (thoughts) as a precursor to prejudice (negative attitudes), which would then result in discrimination (negative behavior), these connections are not clear-cut.

In this chapter, the discussions will focus on stereotypes and prejudice. Though acts of discrimination are, of course, vitally important to understand, a thorough discussion of these is beyond the scope of this chapter. Instead, keep in mind as you read how prejudice and stereotypes often result in discriminatory actions.

## CATEGORIZATION

Earlier in the text you read about how social psychologists have long been interested in how our perceptions of others, and of ourselves for that matter, influence how we feel about and behave toward others. The process known as *categorization*, as you may recall from the chapter on social perception, involves knowing what something is by knowing what things it is like and what things from which it differs (McGarty, 1999). Responses to, and perceptions of, others can be influenced by the various categories that we use to classify them (and ourselves).

As already discussed, the process of categorization is unavoidable and beneficial, enabling us to make sense of the overload of information with which we are constantly confronted. A focus of this chapter is to explore how the process of categorization, along with other processes, is used in *negative* ways. Specifically, we will be looking at how people can form unfavorable perceptions of others based almost entirely on negative perceptions of the group of which that other person is a part. In other words, we will explore "categorization gone awry."

Noted psychologist Gordon Allport (1954) wrote one of the first serious scientific studies of prejudice in his classic book *The Nature of Prejudice*. In it he wrote that the key attributes of prejudice involved the process of categorization and overgeneralization resulting from a lack of sufficient information. Think of the example of making sweeping generalizations about a person you hardly know based solely on their gender or their race. Given the seeming propensity to categorize others based on our experiences, prejudiced ideas and stereotypes can have pervasive and negative consequences. Indeed, the sort of categorization that results in prejudice, racism and discrimination can often be deadly.

One important way of categorizing others is to decide whether they are members of the *in-group* or *out-group*. One important focus of study related to this deals with *in-group bias* (e.g., Mackie & Smith, 1998). As already noted in chapter five on group processes, this is the tendency to evaluate one's own membership group (the in-group) and its members more favorably than a non-membership group (the out-group) or its members. This group-serving tendency can take the form of favoring the in-group and/or derogating the out-group (Wilder & Simon, 2001). Just think, for example, of how much solidarity and in-group bias there can be in the college dorm context. Some students say that they often feel an immediate affinity with other students who live in their dorm, even if they do not know that other student's name! Colleges sometimes make use of this in-group bias when they plan activities for the students that pit one dorm against another in some competition, such as during homecoming week where dorms compete against each other in sports or talent shows.

Interestingly, some students have also said that the in-group bias can even be seen in the relationship among different floors within the same dorm. So, for example, the fifth-floor students may experience group solidarity among themselves and refer to the students on other floors in somewhat derogatory ways (e.g., "Those third-floor students are nerds!" or "How about those fourth-floor dropouts?"). Consider also the in-group bias one sees among many college students when they compare their own school with another. This can be especially intense when schools are near each other geographically or are otherwise similar. Just remember: as you are saying or thinking negative things about the students on other floors in your dorm or about students from other schools, they are also likely to be thinking similar negative things about you!

College life categorization and in-group bias is often relatively harmless (after all, haven't you become friends with students from other dorms?). As we will see, however, these overarching tendencies of categorization and in-group bias can lead to prejudice, stereotyping and discrimination with much more serious consequences.

## WHY STUDY PREJUDICE, STEREOTYPES AND DISCRIMINATION?

There are many reasons why the study of these concepts has significant implications for both social psychologists as well as the public at large. To begin with, these concepts are inherently related to other basic processes that are studied by social psychologists, including social perception, the relationship between attitudes and behavior, group processes, and the proclivity to act toward others in either a prosocial or antisocial manner. Because of this close relationship, the study of prejudice, stereotyping and discrimination can help further clarify how these other processes work, and vice versa.

This area of study is also especially relevant at this unique time in history, when unprecedented global interactions in business, economics and travel result in a greater likelihood of interacting with others from different groups than one's own. For example, never before have so many American college students studied abroad for at least one semester. An article in the *Chronicle of Higher Education* (March 27, 2007) noted that despite our heightened concern about terrorism, the number of American students who study overseas has doubled in the last eight years, and students increasingly report that they wish to study in remote locations all across the globe.

You have probably heard in your own school an increased emphasis on the benefits of study-abroad experiences, which are believed to increase students' appreciation for other cultures and enhance one's global awareness in a way not possible from home. It is yet unclear how this greater likelihood of interaction among culture groups might affect rates of prejudice and discrimination. Could increased interaction among groups facilitate more positive attitudes toward one another? Or might it reinforce negative perceptions and discrimination at even greater levels than before? You will get a hint at the possible answers to these questions later in this chapter.

Another important reason for understanding prejudice, discrimination and stereotyping that is especially relevant to the United States has to do with the changing ethnic makeup of American society. For example, at present, approximately 72.4 percent of the U.S. population is white. The U.S. Census Bureau (2010) estimates that if current trends in immigration and birth rates continue, by the year 2050 less than 53 percent of Americans will be white non-Hispanics, with the fastest growing ethnic group being Hispanics and Asians, doubling from 4 to 8 percent of the overall population. (See table 8.1 for some projections of the U.S. Census Bureau regarding the changing racial and ethnic composition of the U.S.) This unprecedented ethnic diversity will make issues such as racial and ethnic stereotyping, prejudice and discrimination even more relevant. This area of study also has an important bearing on many controversial social and legislative issues such as affirmative action.

Table 8.1. U.S. Census Bureau Projections (percentages of total U.S. population)

|  | 2000 | 2040 |
|---|---|---|
| White alone (non-Hispanic) | 69.4 | 50.1 |
| Black alone | 12.7 | 14.3 |
| Hispanic | 12.6 | 22.3 |
| Asian | 3.8 | 7.1 |

http://www.census.gov/population/www/projections/usinterimproj/natprojtab01a.pdf

The study of prejudice and stereotyping is also very important when one considers the potentially devastating results, which can range anywhere from speaking negatively about a particular group of people (*antilocution;* Allport, 1954), to avoiding them, to acting in a hostile manner toward them, to outright attempts at exterminating them, as during the Nazi era and more recent genocide attempts in Croatia, Kosovo, Rwanda and Iraq. Many researchers (e.g., Davis & Jones, 1960; Worchel & Andreoli, 1978) have noted that people can use negative stereotypes to dehumanize their victims. This can result in a process by which the exploiters avoid seeing themselves as villains and thus also justify further exploitation of their victims. This process is undoubtedly involved in many racial hate crimes.

In addition to the practical aspects noted above, most people consider issues such as prejudice, stereotyping and discrimination to be significant moral and ethical concerns. Christianity, for example, has as one of its central tenets the mandate to love one another. For that reason, in addition to all the others noted above, this area of study has important implications for Christians.

## WHO ARE THE USUAL TARGETS OF PREJUDICE, STEREOTYPES AND DISCRIMINATION?

Since everyone belongs to one particular group or other based on such factors as their age, gender and ethnicity, technically anyone can be the object of another's prejudice. Nevertheless, there are certain groups (e.g., blacks, Asians) who have been more consistently stigmatized than others, and for this reason they have been studied in greater depth by social psychologists. In general, for example, majority groups stigmatize minority groups. But an interesting issue to consider is what happens as a minority group becomes the majority. For example, average age is increasing significantly in the U.S. The Bureau of Labor Statistics estimates that by the year 2040, one in five people in America will be over sixty-five years of age, compared to one in eight in the year 2000. Additionally, the population is aging all over the world. What is likely to happen to current negative stereotypes of the elderly as the population itself becomes more elderly? It will be interesting to observe, for example, how media images of the elderly may change as the population ages.

The vast majority of social psychological research on prejudice, stereotypes and discrimination has focused primarily on racial and ethnic prejudice, so this chapter will devote considerable attention to those areas later on. First, however, let us review some studies on other stigmatized groups. This brief review will help us to examine more closely the powerful relationship between group membership and the likelihood of victimization.

**The obese.** Americans are the most overweight people in the modern, industrialized West (Stearns, 1999). Stereotypes of the overweight have ranged from the positive ("fat people are jolly") to the negative ("fat people are lazy"). In general, however, perceptions of the overweight have been negative, resulting in what some researchers call "anti-fat-attitudes," or AFAs (Crandall et al., 2001). Negative stereotypes of the obese have been demonstrated in a variety of ways, including the perception that when compared to normal-weight individuals, those who are obese are less attractive, more lazy (Jasper & Klassen, 1990) and more weak willed (Lerner, 1969; Taussig, 1994; O'Brien, Hunter & Banks, 2007). Even preschool children have expressed anti-fat attitudes (Holub, 2008).

Rothblum (1992) conducted a review of studies related to perceptions of obese patients by medical students and physicians, and noted that obese patients were more likely to be perceived as ugly, sad, lacking in self-control and more difficult to manage when compared to normal-weight patients. Young and Powell (1985) found that among mental health professionals, there is a tendency to view obesity as a sign of psychopathology.

There are a number of studies that suggest a strong relationship between negative stereotypes of the obese and resultant discrimination. Jasper and Klassen (1990) argue that obese people are often discriminated against because obesity is perceived to be the result of a character flaw. In the area of employment, obesity has been demonstrated to be a source of discrimination. For example, fatter people are often less likely to be hired or promoted than are more normal-weight individuals (Gortmaker, 1993), even if they demonstrate the same qualifications for the job. This may be one reason why Averett and Korenman (1996) found that obese women in general have lower family incomes than do women whose weight is within normal limits.

Bellizzi and Hasty (1998) also noted that overweight workers have been found to be more harshly disciplined for poor work performance than are their normal-weight coworkers. Karris (1977) found that potential renters who were overweight were significantly less likely to be offered housing than were those who were normal weight. In several other studies (e.g., Crandall, 1995), significantly overweight female college students were less likely to be financially supported by their parents, even when parents' educational level, income and family size were taken into consideration.

*The elderly.* Technically, any chronological age can be the target of what is called *ageism,* or the propensity to judge and treat another in negative ways based solely on their age (Barrow & Smith, 1979). For example, older generations engage in ageism when they underestimate the capacity of the younger to either understand particular issues or to be able to assume high levels of responsibility. Judging all youth as irresponsible and then refusing to hire a teenager based on this perception would be another example of ageism. Nevertheless, researchers have focused mostly on ageism as negative perceptions and treatment of older individuals. Another reason why researchers have focused on ageism with reference to the elderly is because, as noted earlier, increased life expectancy leads to an increasing percentage of elderly individuals in the population. Researchers have found a high prevalence of negative stereotypes of the elderly. Banaji (1999), for example, studied the prevalence of *implicit ageism*, or negative attitudes toward the elderly that are subtle and perhaps even unconscious. Responses to questionnaires showed that 95 percent of the participants in the studies held negative views of older people, a proportion significantly higher than for implicit racism and sexism.

Consider this in your own life: how often have you heard any of your peers announce that they can't wait until they turn sixty or seventy years old? Indeed, as Butler (1980) has noted, the youth-obsessed nature of our culture has contributed to "the transformation of aging from a natural process into a social problem" (p. 8).

***Those who are ill or disabled.*** Individuals who are seen as more vulnerable by virtue of their physical infirmity and limitations make up another group that has elicited both positive and negative perceptions and treatment from others. Smart (2001), for example, notes that individuals in wheelchairs have sometimes been characterized as more honest and kinder than those who walk and that individuals with physical infirmities are sometimes given the benefit of the doubt more than those who are not. As with the obese, however, the physically ill have more often been perceived and treated in negative ways, specifically as being more self-pitying, more easily discouraged and more helpless, and expecting special treatment when compared to nondisabled persons (Amsel & Fichten, 1986; Yuker, 1970).

In the U.S., the subject of prejudice and discrimination toward the disabled has become even more relevant since the enactment of the Americans with Disabilities Act (ADA) in 1990. This law bans discrimination toward persons with disabilities in the areas of employment, public accommodations and federally funded programs. In this context, a disability can include any condition that impairs the ability of the individual to interact with their social and physical environment. Thus, it includes a very wide range of medical and psychiatric conditions.

Smart (2001) noted that persons with disabilities are often excluded from the economic and social mainstream due to barriers that are formed as a result of negative attitudes, architectural restraints and policy barriers. These barriers often limit access to employment, education, public transportation and so on. Discrimination and stigmatization of the disabled is especially prevalent with the mentally ill. Golden (1991) recounts a case reported to the U.S. Senate in 1990 involving a New Jersey zoo that refused admittance to a group of children with Down syndrome because it was feared that they would "upset the chimpanzees." A relatively high percentage of people who are homeless also have mental illness. As a result of visual and auditory hallucinations, they may sometimes appear to be conversing with imaginary people. Consider the reactions you have had or have observed in others when this occurs.

One specific medical condition that has elicited much stigmatization research is HIV. As Crandall, Glor and Britt (1994) note, individuals with HIV are often the victims of discrimination in employment, housing and medical care. Often, these negative reactions are related to how much the person with HIV-AIDS is thought to be responsible for contracting the disease. Remember from the social perception chapter that this attribution is the *just-world phenomenon* at work ("They deserve what they get!").

*Gender.* At this point in your life, you likely have developed some relatively consistent and deeply held beliefs regarding males and females. Gender is one of the major criteria used to categorize others (Bem, 1993). This categorization is both habitual and automatic. Imagine how much time it would take you if you had to stop to contemplate the gender of all the people you know. Researchers who have investigated gender stereotyping, prejudice and discrimination have focused on a variety of questions such as the following: Beyond the obvious physical differences, how do we perceive differences between males and females, and to what do we attribute such differences (e.g., social norms or biological differences, or both)? How damaging are gender stereotypes and discrimination? What sorts of institutions or persons contribute to gender stereotypes and discrimination?

Gender stereotypes are related to cognitive processes. As just one example, there are often different expectations for female and male behavior. A classic study focused on adults' interpretations of infants' behavior. Condry and Condry (1976) prepared videotapes of an infant responding to a variety of stimuli. For example, the infant stared and then cried in response to a jack-in-the-box that suddenly popped open.

College students had been led to believe that the infant was either a baby girl or a baby boy. When students watched the videotape with the jack-in-the-box, those who thought the infant was a boy tended to judge that "he" was showing anger. When they thought that the infant was a girl, they decided that "she" was showing fear. Remember that everyone saw the same videotape of the same infant. However, the ambiguous negative reaction of the infant was given a more masculine label (anger, rather than fear) when the infant was perceived to be a boy. There is a considerable body of literature about gender discrimination that is fascinating but beyond the scope of this chapter.

Van Leeuwen (1990, 1994, 2002) argues that fixed negative stereotypes about gender are an expression of our fallen human condition. These stereotypes and prejudice can limit the ability of the genders to relate to each other in the loving, interdependent way that God intended for creation and also limit the expression of individual giftedness.

Recall from an earlier chapter that Van Leeuwen (2002) is also concerned with how beginning with naturalist premises may lead a researcher to interpret common gender differences in social behavior as "natural"—in other words, stemming from our natural state of being. Van Leeuwen says that psychologists need to consider how these social behaviors and prejudices may instead reflect human fallenness, not an inescapable way of being.

Figure 8.2 illustrates the different targets of prejudice discussed above, along with other common targets of prejudice. Please look closely at this figure and consider each group represented here and the vulnerability they possess that makes them "easy targets." What is your response to this image? What groups would you add to this list?

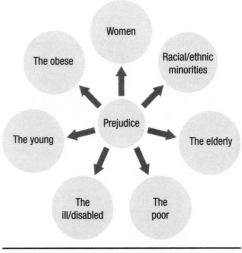

**Figure 8.2. Common Targets of Prejudice**

## How Do Victims of Prejudice, Stereotypes and Discrimination Respond?

Much of the research on prejudice and discrimination, as discussed in the next section, has focused on why or when these occur based on the perspective of the person who holds these views. By contrast, other researchers have focused on the impact of prejudice from the victim's perspective. Spencer, Steele and Quinn (1999), for example, suggest that the victims of prejudice and stereotyping may also be at risk for fulfilling or enacting a negative stereotype about their group. The person does not have to believe the stereotype to be threatened (or influenced) by it. Simple awareness of the stereotype may be sufficient to affect performance, and the more one is vested in a particular domain (e.g., school), the more vulnerable that person may be to the effects of stereotyping. This phenomenon is known as *stereotype threat* (Steele, 1997; Steele & Aronson, 1995).

Dion (2002) notes that perceiving oneself as the object of prejudice and discrimination can have other negative consequences for the victim, including increased stress, lowered self-esteem, and physical and/or psychological symptoms. Dion points out, however, that what may not be so obvious is that perceiving oneself as the object of prejudice and discrimination may also have some positive results as well. For example, prejudice may have a buffering effect on self-evaluation and decrease stress by increasing one's identification with one's own group and receiving support from it. Perceived prejudice may also result in greater efforts to take corrective social action such as collective protest. Consider, for example, the efforts of Martin Luther King Jr. and those who rallied around him against racial discrimination, or more recent efforts by various groups to combat discrimination against physically or otherwise disabled persons.

### Other Relevant Factors

As noted earlier, the occurrence of social categorization has been the focus of much research on these topics. This research focuses on *intergroup differences* (e.g., how in-group bias affects one's judgments of the characteristics of out-groups). Researchers have also tried to understand prejudice, stereotyping and discrimination using an emphasis on *individual differ-*

*ences variables* (e.g., the personality types of those who are more prejudiced in their thinking). In addition, researchers have explored how prejudice is related to efforts at self-esteem enhancement (e.g., assuming the dissimilar other is bad so one can look better). Let us now look at each of these research emphases to see how they might inform and challenge our way of thinking about prejudice and discrimination.

**Approaches emphasizing individual differences.** Are there certain personality types, characteristics or ideologies that are more inclined to have prejudiced thinking than are other types of people? One relevant finding in this line of research is known as *generality of prejudice,* meaning, the tendency of some individuals who are prejudiced against one group to be more likely to also be prejudiced against other groups as well (Duckitt, 1992; Ekehammar & Akrami, 2003, as cited in Duckitt & Sibley, 2007). This generality of prejudice suggests that people can hold enduring beliefs in a stable personality style, and this results in a general tendency either to form favorable impressions of a variety of out-groups or, conversely, to adopt prejudiced and ethnocentric attitudes toward many out-groups (Duckitt, Wagner, du Plessis & Birum, 2002). The main personality style studied by this approach is *authoritarianism.* This term was first proposed by Adorno, Frenkel-Brunswik, Levinson and Sanford (1950) to help explain the rise of fascism in the 1930s.

People high in authoritarianism are those who exhibit high degrees of deference to established authority, aggression toward out-groups when authorities permit that aggression, and support for traditional values when those values are endorsed by authorities. Imagine an overall militant way of thinking. The definition and measures of authoritarianism have evolved during the last sixty years since it was first proposed. It is now generally referred to as *right-wing authoritarianism,* or RWA (Altemeyer, 1981, 1988, 1996, 1998), and it has consistently been associated with prejudice, discrimination and hostility against members of out-groups.

Research cited by Whitley (1999) shows that people high in authoritarianism have been found to be prejudiced against African Americans, Native Americans, women, homosexuals, people with visible handicaps and individuals with AIDS (Altemeyer, 1998; Cunningham, Dollinger, Satz & Rotter, 1991; Duncan, Peterson & Winter, 1997; McFarland &

Adelson, 1996, 1997; Noonan, Barry & Davis, 1970; Peterson, Doty & Winter, 1993; Whitley, 1998).

Another research approach that emphasizes individual differences to help explain prejudice, stereotyping and discrimination looks at an individual's general attitudes or ideologies, especially *social dominance orientation* (SDO; Sidanius & Pratto, 1993, 1999). This concept refers to whether one generally prefers social relations between groups to be equal versus hierarchical, as well as the degree to which one desires that one's in-group dominate and be superior to out-groups.

Altemeyer (1998) presents an evolutionary perspective of social dominance orientation, arguing that humans, as the result of our evolutionary past, have developed a universal drive or predisposition to form "group-based hierarchies" and authoritarianism in which groups try to dominate and oppress subordinate groups. According to this view, because this drive to dominate is biological, it is true of all groups, regardless of the group's status. Hence, low-status groups also work to maintain the hierarchies that oppress them even as they try to climb up in the hierarchy (*behavioral asymmetry;* Sidanius, 1993).

Research conducted by Pratto, Sidanius, Stallworth and Malle (1994) suggests that men are more social-dominance-oriented than are women. In addition, high-SDO people seek hierarchy-enhancing professional roles while low-SDO people seek more collaborative roles. Furthermore, SDO is related to beliefs in a large number of social and political ideologies that support group-based hierarchy (e.g., racism). Individuals with high SDO are described as having less empathy, tolerance and altruism.

If some groups are higher in status than are other groups, then at least some measure of intergroup conflict is inevitable. In order to minimize the chances of intergroup conflict, those supporting a social dominance orientation would propose that societies create ideologies that promote the superiority of one group over others (Sidanius, Pratto, Martin & Stallworth, 1991). To work smoothly, these ideologies must be widely accepted within a society, appearing as self-apparent truths. Historically, policies and social norms that have prevented females and African Americans from entering institutions of higher learning would be an example of this ideological consensus.

Incidentally, if one begins with the premise that any group comprises individuals who are primarily, and even inevitably, self-seeking, then it is only logical to assume that the aggregate (i.e., the group) will also be self-seeking. This conclusion makes sense because one obvious way to self-aggrandize is to enhance the status of one's group at the expense of another's. If humans are wired such that our group membership inevitably leads to attempts to dominate other groups, then reconciliation between groups would be difficult at best and often impossible. From a naturalist view, social dominance attempts could be minimized if the various groups become convinced that it would compromise their own survival (or that of humankind) and impede group-serving interests to engage in such attempts. Challenges to this perspective can be found in the research that is discussed later this chapter.

As already noted, both the right-wing authoritarian (RWA) and the social dominance orientation (SDO) scales have been shown to powerfully predict a wide range of intergroup phenomena such as ethnocentrism and generalized prejudice (Altemeyer, 1988, 1998; Sidanius & Pratto, 1999). More recent research (Duckitt & Sibley, 2007), however, suggests that the reality is more complex than simply considering RWA and SDO as generalized tendencies that both predict negative attitudes and behaviors toward dissimilar others. These researchers instead found that RWA and SDO predicted different dimensions of prejudice, depending on which type of group was the target group. So, persons who were negative toward one out-group were not necessarily negative toward another type of out-group. Specifically, subjects with high authoritarianism were more likely to have prejudiced attitudes regarding groups that are considered "dangerous" (i.e., threatening social order, traditional values and cohesion). Dangerous groups included terrorists, drug dealers and anyone who was deemed a potential threat to the safety of society.

Subjects with high social dominance orientation, by contrast, were more likely to have prejudice against groups that are *derogated*, or considered inferior and low in status and prestige (e.g., the mentally ill, the elderly). Duckitt and Sibley (2007) propose that these groups are often derogated so that they won't challenge the in-group's perceived dominance or the existing social inequalities.

Thus, attempts to find individual differences in propensity toward prejudice have not found uniform results. On the one hand, there is evidence that personality styles are associated with prejudice. On the other hand, a model of a single, prejudice-prone sort of personality that has equally negative attitudes regarding all types of different out-groups seems too simplistic and does not adequately explain the variability in the data. Duckitt and Sibley (2007) further note that research showing the connection between RWA and SDO and other social attitudes has not found a strong predictive relationship for prejudice (Duriez &Van Hiel, 2002; Heaven & Conners, 2001). Thus, authoritarianism and social dominance orientation may not help us predict actual prejudice and discrimination.

*Prejudice as a self-esteem enhancer?* Other research that explores individual processes in prejudice includes assessing the role that self-esteem enhancement can play. Recall from the chapter on the self that humans have a general propensity to maintain their self-esteem. Fein and Spencer (1997) argue that these same self-image maintenance processes play an important role in stereotyping and prejudice. Their studies demonstrated that when individuals evaluated a member of a stereotyped group, they were less likely to evaluate that person negatively if their own self-images had been bolstered through a self-affirmation procedure. Conversely, subjects were more likely to evaluate that other person negatively if their own self-image had been threatened by negative feedback.

In addition, Fein and Spencer (1997) found that among those individuals whose self-image had been threatened, derogating a stereotyped target resulted in an increase in the subject's self-esteem. Based on these results, the researchers suggest that stereotyping and prejudice may be a means to maintain one's self-image; making the other look bad makes you look better, at least in your own eyes. Jordan, Spencer and Zanna (2005) help clarify the possible relationship between self-esteem and prejudice by distinguishing between *explicit self-esteem* ("deliberately reasoned and controlled") and *implicit self-esteem* (efficient and largely unconscious). Those with implicit self-esteem have more stable, healthy self-regard. These authors note that those with fragile (explicit) self-esteem may be more likely to have negative views of different others not only when they feel threatened, but also in general, because denigrating others helps them feel better. Further research will be helpful in better clarifying the possible relationship between self-esteem and prejudice.

**Social-cognitive processes in prejudice.** In addition to research that emphasizes individual differences in prejudice, a number of theories have investigated how cognitive processes may be involved in prejudice and stereotypes. *Social identity theory* (SIT) is one example. This theory begins with several assumptions. First, as noted earlier, it is assumed that people strive to maintain or enhance a positive self-concept. Second, it is assumed that self-concept is largely defined in terms of group affiliations (Tajfel, 1982; Tajfel & Turner, 1979; Turner, 1999). That is, social groups provide their members with an identification that defines their social identity. In this context, social or collective identity refers to the characteristics of one's groups, whether or not those characteristics are true of oneself as an individual.

SIT is primarily concerned with the motivation to maintain a positive social (collective) identity. The theory holds that when confronted with a threat to their social identity, people maintain a positive social identity by viewing the in-group in a more favorable light than they view the out-groups. This theory therefore maintains that the main underlying drive for prejudice is group identification (Crocker & Luhtanen, 1990; Hornsey & Hogg, 2000). This is especially true when social categories are salient, which is when a group would be most likely to try to maintain a sense of in-group superiority.

A classic example of salient social categories leading to in-group perceptions of superiority may be seen when one travels in another country. Suppose that you are from America and traveling throughout Japan. Imagine that one of the local male residents comments to you that his perception of Americans includes the idea that Americans are self-centered, don't care for their families and are very materialistic. According to social identity theory, you would respond by feeling a sense of threat to your social identity as well as to your personal identity by virtue of your affiliation with the group called Americans. In this case, SIT predicts that you would attempt to heighten your self-esteem and your social identity by comparing Americans in a favorable way to the Japanese. For example, you might emphasize that Americans are in fact more thoughtful, honest or considerate than are the Japanese. Thus, you would end up forming negative impressions of the Japanese in an effort to salvage your own group identity.

As noted at the beginning of this section, researchers who study prejudice have been interested in how prejudice results from both individual differences and intergroup dynamics. *Self-categorization theory* (SCT; Reicher, 1987; Turner, Oakes, Haslam & McGarty, 1994) is one attempt to provide a perspective regarding both the possible individual and intergroup effects on prejudice. Like social identity theory, SCT starts from the distinction between collective and personal identity, but according to SCT, these are not seen so much as different forms of identity, but rather as different *levels* of self-categorization. According to this view, both levels of self-categorization are equally valid and authentic definitions of the self. In other words, people are both individual persons and social group members, and self-categorization at both levels is real.

So what is the relevance of the distinction between personal and social identity? According to SCT, it lies in the consequences for perception, evaluation and behavior. Several studies (e.g., Brewer & Miller, 1996) have shown that group perceptions and judgments vary according to whether the personal or social identity is activated. For example, when personal identity is salient and individual differences are accentuated, the in-group appears as more heterogeneous than when social identity is salient and individual differences are minimized or not attended to. So, for example, if you lived in the southern part of the United States your whole life, you are likely to see yourself as an individual within the larger in-group culture of the South, and you are likely to perceive this in-group as comprising many different types of people. Now imagine that you move from Louisiana to New York City, where you are now face to face with the Northern out-group. In this case, SCT predicts that your social identity as a Southerner would be accentuated, and that there would be a heightening of in-group versus out-group comparisons. Thus your sense of group solidarity with Southerners would be heightened, so that you would see Southerners as more of a homogeneous group (and you might, perhaps, exaggerate your own Southern accent). You might find yourself explaining to your New York neighbors that in the South, all neighbors are friendly and know each other by name, whereas in reality when you lived in the South, you observed that some Southerners are friendly, while others are not. This comparison represents an effort on your part to favorably compare your Southern in-group with the Northern out-group.

Verkuyten and Hagendoorn (1998) conducted two experiments in which they varied the emphasis on personal versus national (i.e., social/ collective) identity. They found that when personal identity was made more salient, prejudice appeared to be affected by authoritarianism and not by in-group stereotypes. In contrast, when national identity was made salient, in-group stereotypes and not authoritarianism was related to prejudice. Thus, these experiments suggest that the determinants of prejudice depend on the level of self-categorization. In the personal identity situation, only individual factors, and in particular authoritarianism, were related to prejudice. In the national identity condition, only in-group stereotypes were related to prejudice. Thus, when personal identity is salient, personal standards are relevant; when individuals conceive of themselves as members of a social category, collective standards become more relevant.

Another cognitive approach to understanding prejudice and stereotyping employs the idea that a stereotype functions as a sort of resource-preserving device in mental life (Andersen, Klatzky & Murray, 1990; Bodenhausen & Lichtenstein, 1987; Brewer, 1988). In the social perception chapter, as you may recall, there was a discussion of other mental "shortcuts" such as heuristics and attributions. These tools, while possibly resulting in errors in perception, are used routinely and help us evaluate our social world in efficient ways. In a similar way, some researchers argue that stereotypes are yet another example of a mental shortcut that allows us to respond to the challenges and complexity of our social environment. According to this view, the benefit of such mental tools is that they free up limited cognitive resources so that we can perform other essential tasks.

In an effort to explore this idea that stereotypes free up cognitive space, Macrae, Milne and Bodenhausen (1994) conducted three studies in which they presented subjects with a prose passage. Subjects were told that the experiment was about being able to process two things (forming an impression of a target and understanding a prose passage) simultaneously. Subjects who were given stereotyped descriptions of the target were faster at forming impressions of the target and also showed superior learning of the material in the prose passage, as measured on a multiple choice test of the passage. The results suggest that the stereotype information simplified the impression-formation task by providing a theme to guide or organize impressions of each target. This helped subjects spend more time on learning the prose passage.

The finding that stereotypes save us cognitive space and time has both positive and negative implications. To save cognitive time and space and thereby increase performance on a large number of daily tasks may be good in theory, yet this works only if the stereotypes we hold are accurate. As a simple example, suppose that the task before you is to bring a heavy package into your home. Now suppose you see two people walking toward you: an elderly man and a young college student who is an athlete. You immediately assume that the athlete will be better able to help you lift the package than would the elderly person. To the degree that this stereotype is accurate, you would save not only cognitive time, but time in general, by asking the athlete for help. Most of the time, it is probably true that an athlete has more strength than an elderly person. But, as you will read later on in this chapter, applying a stereotype to *all* people within a group leads to inaccurate assumptions. Suppose that in the case of your needing help with the package, the athlete whom you ask to help you has recently been injured and cannot carry heavy packages. And suppose the elderly person happens to be especially physically fit and strong. Then you would have actually wasted time assuming your stereotypes of athletes and the elderly are always true.

Figure 8.3 outlines some of the main theories regarding the processes that underlie prejudice. Consider how these are related to each other and what other processes you think might be important.

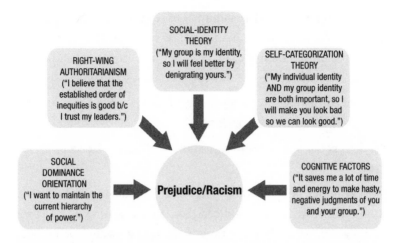

**Figure 8.3. Theories Related to Prejudice and Racism**

## Religiosity and Prejudice

The relationship between prejudice and religiosity is an important one in our society, given that the overwhelming majority of Americans report some affiliation to a higher power or specific religious tradition. In fact, since 1944, when the Gallup Poll began asking Americans whether they "believe in God or a universal spirit," the answers have always been at least 90 percent affirmative.

As noted earlier, the relationship between faith and prejudice is of particular concern to Christians, given God's mandate for universal love and compassion (e.g., Lev 19:17; 1Tim 1:5; 1 Jn 1:7). Does faith help decrease prejudice? The answer to this question depends for Christians on a more basic question: are humans, given our fallen condition, even capable of other-centered, universal compassion and thus of not being prejudiced? In this section, let us see what the research on religion and prejudice suggests, and then in the following section, we can look at the specific question regarding whether prejudice is, as some researchers suggest, inevitable.

The relationship between religiosity and prejudice is one of the most controversial topics in social psychology research. The research results are often mixed, contradictory and, frankly, confusing. According to Allport (1954), "The role of religion is paradoxical. It makes prejudice and it unmakes prejudice. . . . The sublimity of religious ideals is offset by the horrors of persecution in the name of these same ideals. . . . Churchgoers are more prejudiced than the average; they are also less prejudiced than the average" (p. 144). Some of this confusion has to do with:

- a lack of consistent ways to measure religiosity—how, after all, do you accurately measure someone's faith?

- a lack of consistent ways to assess all the different facets of prejudice itself.

Most religious people would likely assume that those who profess a committed faith are less prejudiced than are those who do not profess any faith at all. After all, don't most religions advocate love and acceptance toward others? And, at least for Christians, isn't that love and acceptance supposed to be unconditional and unrelated to the others' race, creed or color?

In reality, although most religious groups officially promote tolerance and love toward members of other groups, the evidence that religiosity is associated with reduced levels of bigotry and prejudice is at best ambiguous (Jacobson, 1998). Let's first review the history of research in the area of religiosity and prejudice to see what patterns emerge.

The first studies of prejudice and religiosity were conducted in the 1940s among Christian church members. In those early studies (e.g., Merton, 1940; Sanford & Levinson, 1948), religiosity was simply measured by whether or not one was a church member. So subjects were divided into one of two groups: those who were church members and those who were not. The results of these early studies consistently showed that church members were found to be more prejudiced than were the nonmembers. Other early studies, such as those conducted by Allport and Kramer (1946) and Rosenblith (1949), also demonstrated that religious involvement correlated positively with racial prejudice. In other words, the more religious you reportedly were, the more likely you were to report prejudiced thinking. In fact, the findings of this early research understandably caused some to speculate that church membership actually either caused or else at least encouraged prejudice (Spilka et al., 1985)!

In the late 1940s and 1950s, research on the relationship between religiosity and prejudice continued to develop and to address the concerns noted with earlier studies. Many researchers (e.g., Parry, 1949; Sanford, 1950) began to examine religiosity in terms of the subjects' level of commitment to faith, not just as a function of church membership. They measured the subjects' involvement with, and loyalty to, their faith by inquiring how often the individual went to church. These findings indicated the following:

- people who never attended church generally exhibited a relatively low level of prejudice, and

- the most highly prejudiced individuals were those who went to church once or twice a month.

Even though these findings seemed to suggest that something about active church membership creates prejudice in people, a closer look at the results of those studies does not support this interpretation. For example, for individuals who attended church more than four times a month, the reported prejudice scores actually decreased (Struening, 1957). This significant decrease in prejudice among highly involved church members indicates that some other factor or factors were at work, but what were those factors?

By the 1960s, some researchers began to make a more sophisticated and also encouraging analysis of the relationship between religion and prejudice. Allport (1966) and Allport and Ross (1967), for example, distinguished between two different motivations for religiosity:

1. Extrinsic religiosity: Religion is a means to an end, such as achieving social status, security or some other personal benefit.

2. Intrinsic religiosity: Religion is an end in itself. It provides a unifying, central motivating role in one's life. In this case, religion is seen as a pathway to truth; God is perceived as a loving, supportive and forgiving figure.

Allport then argued that prejudice would be positively correlated with extrinsic religiosity, but negatively correlated with intrinsic religiosity. That is, people who were "truly religious" would be less prejudiced than those who used religion as a way to obtain some other goal such as respect and social status. Early support for this idea was found by several researchers (e.g., Allport & Ross, 1967; Batson & Ventis, 1982). Later researchers (e.g., Donahue, 1985; Fulton, Gorsuch & Maynard, 1999), however, noted that the research findings did not, in general, provide support for Allport's claims. In fact, many studies seemed instead to demonstrate that extrinsic religiosity, in which religion is used for personal or social gain, is only weakly positively correlated with prejudice, while intrinsic religiosity is generally unassociated with prejudice (Laythe, Finkel, Bringle & Kirkpatrick, 2002). It thus appears that differentiating between the extrinsic and intrinsic motivations for religious faith does not explain the relationship between religiosity and prejudice.

Since Allport's religious orientation model did not find wide support by researchers, subsequent studies attempted to find other possible explanations for the link between religiosity and prejudice. In the late 1960s and early 1970s, many researchers (e.g., Karlins, Coffman & Walters, 1969; Sigall & Page, 1971) pointed out that in virtually all studies of the religion-prejudice relationship, prejudice had been measured overtly (obviously) through the use of questionnaires. Low scores on a prejudice questionnaire could thus easily be the result of the desire not to appear prejudiced rather than the result of a true lack of prejudice.

To address this concern about social desirability on prejudice questionnaires, Batson, Naifeh and Pate (1978) recommended the use of more covert behavioral measures of prejudice, measures that carried real consequences for interaction with out-group members. Batson and his colleagues also recommended the use of a more comprehensive three-dimensional model of religious orientation. That is, in addition to the intrinsic and extrinsic forms of religiosity, they suggested a third form of religiosity called the *quest orientation*. This type of religious orientation includes a tendency to view religious issues as complex and to resist clear-cut answers to the difficult questions raised (Batson, 1976; Batson & Shoenrade, 1991; Batson & Ventis, 1982).

Batson et al. (1978) found that all three factors (intrinsic, extrinsic and quest) correlated negatively with scores on overt measures of prejudice. But when more covert measures were used (e.g., having subjects rate their preference for being interviewed by a white person or a black interviewer), the results were different. Now there was no longer a negative correlation between the intrinsic religiosity perspective and prejudice. In fact, they were nonsignificantly positively correlated. In contrast, individuals who reported a more quest form of religiosity were less prejudiced. Batson et al. note that this overall pattern of results suggests that an intrinsic orientation to religion seems associated more with an increased desire not to appear prejudiced than with a genuine reduction in prejudice. Only the quest orientation appeared to be associated with a genuine reduction in prejudice. Snyder, Kleck, Strenta and Mentzer (1979) discovered a similar pattern of results in their study using confederates who had or did not have a physical disability.

Batson et al. (1989) used a similar approach as Snyder and his colleagues in order to detect covert as well as overt racial prejudice associated with different orientations to religion. They used the following rather complex but fascinating procedure. Forty-four white undergraduate students from the University of Kansas, all of whom reported at least a moderate interest in religion, completed a questionnaire battery that included scales designed to assess religious orientation (intrinsic, extrinsic or quest). At a later session, they were told that they would be participating in a study of factors that affect liking for movies. In the course of that study, subjects were given a choice of whether to watch the movie being shown in a theatre where a black confederate was already seated or in one where a white confederate was seated.

Subjects were either told that both theaters were showing the same movie or that different movies were being shown in each. In the first case, if the subject selected the theater with the white confederate, there was a more obvious racist response as compared to the condition in which the theaters were showing different movies. This is because in the condition where different movies were being shown, the student could claim that the choice of sitting with a white person was really due to the movie being played. The researchers predicted that those scoring highly in intrinsic religiosity scales would be no less prejudiced than those scoring low but would be more concerned about appearing prejudiced. Specifically, the researchers predicted that in the overt (same movie in each theatre) condition, the intrinsically religious subjects would mask their prejudice by choosing to sit with the black person (more than those who were not intrinsically religious). In the covert condition (where the movies were different, so subjects could avoid sitting with the black confederate by claiming that the movie in the other theater was preferable), intrinsically oriented subjects would be no more likely to sit with the black person than would those scoring low on this orientation. The results supported their hypothesis.

More recent research on religious orientation and racism has been conducted with students in Christian colleges who report at least a moderate interest in religion (Batson & Stocks, 2005). In this population, higher *quest* scores may reflect a stage of personal development in the faith journey, with students questioning many of their religious convictions. Hunsberger and Jackson (2005) suggest that these students may show more racial tolerance than do students who demonstrate an intrinsic religious orientation.

Hall, Matz and Wood (2010) conducted a meta-analytic review of fifty-five studies of religiosity and prejudice in order to explore what factors related to religiosity might also facilitate prejudice. The participants in these studies were mostly white and Christian. The researchers note a study by Dougherty and Huyser (2008) that shows how relatively little racial diversity there is in American churches. Specifically, in 1998, "almost half of U.S. congregations were composed of only one racial group, and just 12% of congregations had even a moderate amount of racial diversity" (p. 126).

Hall, Matz and Wood (2010) propose that this racial insularity may inadvertently promote in-group favoritism and out-group derogating. (Consider the distinction between "believers" and "unbelievers" that is often made in Christian circles.) Further, the researchers suggest that two essential components of church communities—social conformity and respect for tradition—also seem related to the perpetuation and acceptance of racial divisions in society. Further, the researchers note, "Although religious people might be expected to express humanitarian acceptance of others, their humanitarianism is expressed primarily toward in-group members" (p. 134). Thus, there was little evidence that religiosity promoted racial tolerance, especially in situations where tolerance was measured in indirect and less controllable ways (e.g., choosing to engage in interracial interactions).

This meta-analysis also suggests that the participants with a quest orientation toward religion were the ones who were more likely to practice racial tolerance. Hall, Matz and Wood (2010), however, distinguish between a quest orientation as it is usually referred to in the literature (i.e., less participation in organized religion and no strong belief in God) and the quest involved when the process of questioning occurs within the context of a strong faith (i.e., when a faith journey acknowledges doubt and complexity). In this meta-analysis, it was the latter form of questioning that was significantly related to increased racial tolerance.

The research presented so far in this section suggests that overall, individuals who have a strong faith (intrinsic religious orientation), participate regularly in church and have strong convictions about God do not demonstrate a higher degree of racial tolerance and are not less likely to avoid prejudice (actually, it mostly shows the opposite). This research presents numerous challenges to Christians who are serious about God's command for universal love and compassion. What use can we make of these results? A distinction between some terms may be of help here.

Often in the literature, terms used to describe different aspects of religiosity are used interchangeably, though they may have different meanings. For example, researchers have differed considerably in how they define and measure religiosity, so it can be difficult to compare one study to another. As a specific instance, the distinction between "quest religiosity" and genuine faith that is open to questions and challenges is important for researchers. One additional and important example involves the terms *orthodoxy* and *religious fundamentalism* (RF), where researchers have often understood orthodox Christian beliefs to belong in the same category as fundamentalism. This seeming mischaracterization is of particular importance, as seen in the research on religious fundamentalism as a link between religiosity and prejudice (Hunsberger, 1995). RF is a belief that is characterized by a militant belief system, a sense of one absolute truth and a sense of a special relationship with God (Altemeyer & Hunsberger, 1992, 2005).

Research has shown a consistent positive relationship between RF and both racism and homosexual prejudice (Hunsberger, 1995, 1996; Laythe et al., 2002). The potential negative effects of religious fundamentalism have been demonstrated for different religious groups. Hunsberger (1996), for example, found that in samples of Muslim, Hindu and Jewish individuals, higher levels of religious fundamentalism were associated with higher levels of right-wing authoritarianism, both of which correlate with negative attitudes about homosexuals.

So, at last, we have the answer: it is the religious fundamentalists who are most likely to have the most prejudice, right? Well, the answer is not so easy. The complexity of this relationship between religious fundamentalism and prejudice has been explored by a number of researchers. Some (e.g., Altemeyer & Hunsberger, 1992) have argued that it is not fundamentalism per se that is highly correlated with prejudice. Instead, they argue, it is the *militant* aspect of fundamentalism, or right-wing authoritarianism (RWA), that is more closely associated with higher levels of prejudice. Recall from earlier this chapter that individuals who demonstrate RWA have a tendency to believe in and exhibit high degrees of deference to established authority, aggression toward out-groups when authorities permit that aggression, and support for traditional, conventional values when those values are endorsed by authorities.

Several studies (e.g., Hunsberger, 1996; Wylie & Forest, 1992) likewise found support for the hypothesis that it is the militant aspect of religious fundamentalism that is most associated with prejudice. These studies demonstrated two main findings: First, RWA and fundamentalism are highly correlated with each other—the more fundamentalist your beliefs, the more likely you are to have militant, dogmatic, RWA beliefs or tendencies. Second, RWA is more strongly associated with prejudice than is fundamentalism itself. Laythe, Finkel, Bringle and Kirkpatrick (2002) further demonstrated from their findings that whereas RWA is a powerful predictor of racism, sexism and homosexual prejudice, fundamentalism was a significant *inverse* predictor of racism. In other words, religious fundamentalism seems to, as Allport suggested, both "make" and "unmake" prejudice. How can this be? If it is the authoritarian part of fundamentalism that "makes" or contributes to racism and prejudice, is there another part of religious fundamentalism that "unmakes" or discourages racism and prejudice?

Laythe et al. (2002) propose that it is the *content* of fundamentalist beliefs that helps discourage prejudice. These researchers specifically address the central beliefs of *Christian orthodoxy* (CO), which is somewhat different from fundamentalism. Researchers refer to Christian orthodoxy as the degree to which one believes in standard teachings of the church (Christ's resurrection, the need to repent of sin, the divine command to love others, including those different from oneself, etc.). In this research, Christian orthodoxy was negatively related to both racism and homosexual prejudice when the effects of both RWA and RF were partialed out. So, Christian orthodoxy seems to "unmake" prejudice against homosexuals as much as it does with racial prejudice. Further, the two different forces of right-wing authoritarianism and Christian orthodoxy explained most of the variance in prejudice. Religious fundamentalism per se did not add any unique explanatory power for racial prejudice, and it did not play a significant role in homosexual prejudice.

The combined research suggests that religiosity has a complex relationship with prejudice. Specifically, religious faith does not necessarily reduce prejudice and may, in some ways, actually encourage it, depending on how the religious views are held (i.e., how militantly). But the research also suggests the promising potential of orthodox Christian beliefs about universal love to help reduce prejudice. At the end of this chapter, we will look more specifically at how the central command of Christ to love one another may relate to what the research findings suggest to us about reducing prejudice.

As noted above, of prime importance in future research on religiosity and prejudice is the need for clarification and distinction of the terms used. Confusion regarding the varying meanings of *religiosity, fundamentalism, Christian orthodoxy* and others often makes it difficult to compare results across studies. Using terms interchangeably (e.g., fundamentalism and authoritarianism) and merging groups together based on supposed similarities (e.g., a general quest orientation to spirituality vs. willingness to explore questions regarding one's enduring and genuine faith) results in erroneous overgeneralizations regarding the relationship between religiosity and prejudice.

One example of difficulty distinguishing relevant terms relates to the concepts of religious fundamentalism versus Christian orthodoxy. Hood, Hill and Williamson (2005) suggest one possible way of distinguishing these two terms. The authors propose that fundamentalism entails looking to the sacred text for meaning and embracing the notion of the inerrancy of the text. Christian orthodoxy, on the other hand, does not require seeing the text as completely inerrant, though orthodoxy acknowledges the authority of Scripture. Hood, Hill and Spilka (2009) further clarify how we might think about the distinction between fundamentalism and nonfundamentalism in terms of how they approach the sacred text.

Let us consider specifically the case of Christianity. The researchers suggest that fundamentalists tend to use an *intratextual approach* whereby the Scriptures are believed to comprise all the truth about the world and how to interact in it. Thus, other sources of knowledge (science, texts, etc.) are relatively neglected in terms of their potential to add to our understanding of truth. In contrast, those with nonfundamentalist beliefs tend to use an *intertextual approach* to the Scriptures. This involves acknowledging how other sources (e.g., historical texts, science, observations in everyday life) can help us in our understanding of Scripture and the nature of reality. Using this distinction, the Christian view of psychology presented in this text could be seen as using an intertextual approach to exploring the truth regarding human social interaction. According to Hood, Hill and Spilka (2009), orthodoxy is not the essential component of fundamentalism, as one could technically be orthodox (conforming, conventional, etc.) using either an intratextual or intertextual approach to Scripture. It will be interesting to see how future research will address these distinctions.

### Is Prejudice Inevitable?

So far in this chapter, you have read about the personal and interpersonal factors related to negative attitudes about dissimilar others. You have also read about examples of targeted groups, their varied responses to prejudice, and the complex relationship between religiosity and prejudice. Early in the chapter, it was noted that the question of the relationship between religiosity and prejudice is related to the broader question of the degree to which humans are capable of other-centered love for dissimilar others. Are we able to overcome prejudice, or is it inevitable?

There are signs of significant reductions in hateful, prejudiced and racist ideology and behavior in the U.S. Increased diversity in many public arenas, as well as in interpersonal relationships, are hopeful signs. Several U.S. surveys (e.g., Schuman, Steeh, Bobo & Krysan, 1997) demonstrate that racism in American society has declined steadily since World War II. From these appearances, it seems that America is indeed becoming "colorblind." What great news!

Before we get too happy, though, we should recall that social psychologists have a knack for uncovering a multitude of unpleasant explanations for seemingly positive results. Accordingly, Arkes and Tetlock's (2004) review of the literature notes that social psychologists are divided with regard to how optimistic they are about the apparent progress in race relations. On the one hand, some psychologists (e.g., Jacoby, 2000; Thernstrom & Thernstrom, 1997) support a more optimistic picture, pointing to the significant economic and educational gains that African Americans have made. These psychologists are of the opinion that the gaps that remain are the result not of whites' racism toward blacks, but rather gaps in social issues such as educational attainment, increase in African American crime and the structure of many African American families.

On the other hand, most social psychologists who study race relations seem to favor a more pessimistic picture of the seeming improvement in race relations. Specifically, they are not convinced that things are as good as they appear to be (e.g., Bell, 1992; Hacker, 1995; Dovidio & Gaertner, 2000). As noted by Arkes and Tetlock (2004), these psychologists remain concerned that prejudice toward African Americans "lies at the center, not the periphery, in the permanent, not in the fleeting, in the real lives of black and white people, not in the caverns of the mind" (Bell, 1992, p. 208, as cited in Arkes & Tetlock, 2004). How can such a pessimistic perspective endure in the face of the observable improvements in race relations? In order to address this question, it would be helpful to review how research on prejudice and stereotyping has developed across time.

Earlier studies of prejudice (i.e., those conducted up through the early 1980s) were more concerned with outright, behavioral expressions (in the forms of sexism, discrimination and hostility toward other groups; Paul, 2003). More recent studies, in contrast, have instead focused on subtle and implicit stereotyping, or those ideas that appear to occur automatically. This latest line of research has produced results that some researchers (e.g., Bargh & Ferguson, 2000) see as particularly distressing because its results suggest that virtually everyone has some hidden negative biases toward members of particular groups and also that people are often not even aware that those biases exist.

Several researchers (e.g., Bargh & Chartrand, 1999; Bargh, Chen & Burrows, 1996; Greenwald & Banaji, 1995) argue that racism and prejudice are caused by automatic processes that are triggered by subtle environmental cues such as the presence of a person of another race or ethnicity. Remember from the social perception chapter that the term *automatic processing* refers to fast, efficient, effortless mental processing. This type of processing does not require or involve any conscious reflection or awareness, even though it can profoundly affect behavior. From an EP perspective, the tendency toward racism presumably became an adaptive mental function and is an inevitable part of our current makeup since there has not yet been time and other conditions to cause humans to evolve away from it. In the meantime, so-called *controlled processes* are necessary to counteract such automatic thoughts. These controlled processes are effortful, conscious and deliberate reflections. The capacity to engage in this type of processing presumably evolved as of the beginning of the human capacity for language and private reflection.

There is, in fact, a great deal of research that suggests that stereotypes are elicited automatically when we encounter a person from another category (group) than our own (e.g., Bargh, Chen & Burrows, 1996; Devine, 1989; Fiske & Neuberg, 1990; Stangor & Lange, 1994). According to this research, these automatic stereotypes are nearly inevitable and often affect our behaviors toward, and judgments of, others. As Lepore and Brown (1997) note, negative group stereotypes are the cognitive component of prejudice. This research is consistent with Billig's (1985) comment that "people will be prejudiced as long as they continue to think" (p. 299, as cited in Lepore and Brown, 1997).

The automatic nature of stereotypes has been demonstrated in a series of studies that use the *implicit association test* (IAT; Greenwald & Banaji, 1995; Greenwald, McGhee & Schwartz, 1998). Recall from the attitudes and persuasion chapter that this test requires participants to make quick judgments about stimuli that appear on the computer screen. While the stimuli have covered a wide range of categories (e.g., gender, age, professions), often the IAT is used to assess racist and preju-diced judgments. In one variation of the IAT that assesses implicit racism, participants are shown either a white face or a black face on the screen and then asked to judge if a word that is presented quickly is re-lated to that face. The words that are presented are either positive (e.g., *friend, loyal, gentle*) or negative (e.g., *murder, tragedy, hatred*). Studies suggest that white Americans generally show an implicit attitudinal preference for white over black by responding faster to the "white plus pleasant" combination than to the "black plus pleasant" combi-nation (Greenwald, McGhee & Schwartz, 1998). Figure 8.4 shows an image similar to the ones used on the implicit association test.

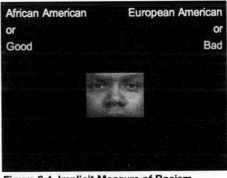

**Figure 8.4. Implicit Measure of Racism**

Blair and Banaji (1996) suggest that the inconsistencies that we see in racial reconciliation may be explained at least in part by the finding that people are not always aware of the negative attitudes they have toward other groups. Specifically, often individuals who are opposed to racism or sexism on explicit surveys demonstrate prejudice toward African Amer-icans or women on implicit measures (Dasgupta, McGhee, Greenwald &

Banaji, 1999). Many researchers believe that the negative affective responses that are elicited during the implicit association test reveal a person's negative judgments of a minority group (Devine et al., 2002, as cited in Arkes & Tetlock, 2004).

So, are we inevitably prejudiced? With so many studies suggesting that white participants hold negative stereotypes of black faces, and that these negative stereotypes often occur outside of one's conscious awareness, can we ever hope to overcome them? Contrary to the majority pessimist view in the field, a number of researchers think it *is* possible to overcome prejudice. They propose that the presence of negative stereotypes about other groups, even those that are implicit, does not necessarily indicate that the person who becomes aware of their own stereotypes will support them and act accordingly. Devine (1989), for example, noted that because our culture is inundated with stereotypes concerning various groups (African Americans, the elderly, etc.), these stereotypes become overlearned and are often automatically activated upon encounters with individuals from those groups, even when the person does not embrace these negative views. Karpinski and Hilton (2001) likewise argue that negative stereotypes (i.e., *cognitions*) elicited by the IAT are not necessarily signs of negative *attitudes* because the respondent might or might not endorse or agree with the cultural stereotypes they have learned over time.

A further challenge to the assumption that implicit racist stereotypes are indicative of unchangeable negative, racist attitudes is seen in studies of the relationship between implicit prejudice and explicit prejudice. These studies have yielded correlations that range from .07 to .60, with most correlations being small (Brauer, Wasel & Niedenthal, 2000). Low correlations between implicit and explicit prejudice have been substantiated in a number of studies cited by Arkes and Tetlock (e.g., Lowery, Hardin & Sinclair, 2001; Wittenbrink, Judd & Park, 2001).

As noted earlier, implicit negative attitudes toward race may be related to the frequent negative stereotypes resulting from exposure to negative cultural stereotypes about blacks. These stereotypes can occur as the result of negative portrayals of African Americans that are passed down from generation to generation in the form of hateful judgments.

Negative cultural stereotypes can also be the result of real existing differences between groups. For example, for some time in the U.S., there has been a significant gap between whites and African Americans in terms of serious crime rates. The U.S. Bureau of Justice Statistics reports that in 2008, blacks were seven times more likely than whites to commit homicide. This gap is often portrayed in the media, and these images of blacks become salient in our culture, perpetuating the stereotype of the aggressive, black male. Hence, on the IAT, when an individual is shown an image of a black face together with the word *crime,* there is likely to be a quick response time in associating these two.

According to Arkes and Tetlock (2004), a crucial question remains regarding what *attributions* (i.e., causal explanations) the participant makes for the real differences in crime rates, and studies of implicit racism have not generally made these finer distinctions. Nevertheless, it is logical to assume that a person who holds racist attitudes may be more inclined to attribute the higher crime rate among black males to the belief that "blacks are naturally more aggressive than whites," rather than to attribute the higher crime rates to the social, environmental pressures such as the stressors associated with poverty that are experienced by many African American families.

So far we have seen that implicit negative stereotypes about other racial groups may not necessarily be indicative of the person's actual attitudes about members of the other group. Rather, these stereotypes may be easily elicited as a result of the high frequency with which such cognitions are encountered in the culture at large. These findings are consistent with research that challenges the traditional belief that stereotyping is both a cause and consequence of prejudice (Allport, 1954). Kawakami, Dion and Dovidio (1998), for example, note that the research on the link between prejudice and stereotyping has suggested only weak or conflicting findings.

Remember also that negative stereotypes can reflect true differences among groups. In fact, some researchers have noted that there seems to be a fair amount of accuracy regarding some stereotypes (Jussim, 1990; Jussim et al., 2009). Ryan (2002) suggests that the degree to which stereotypes may be accurate, although controversial, can help challenge the long-held belief that stereotypes necessarily lead to inaccuracies in social perception.

In addition to the above-noted challenges to the notion that implicit stereotypes are necessarily related to implicit racism, there are other challenges to the presumed inevitability of prejudice. One challenge relates to the various possible outcomes of negative stereotypes. Specifically, if it is true that many people have implicit negative stereotypes about target groups, is there anything that differentiates prejudiced and nonprejudiced people? According to Devine (1989), what differentiates nonprejudiced people from those who hold prejudicial thoughts is not whether or not prejudicial thoughts are activated, but whether those prejudicial thoughts can be inhibited and replaced with more positive, egalitarian thoughts. From this view, nonprejudiced individuals are more likely to reject and subsequently inhibit their negative stereotype cognitions. According to von Hippel, Silver and Lynch (2000), although subsequent research has not provided uniform support for Devine's (1989) model, most researchers have at least agreed that intentional inhibiting of stereotypes and other negative attitudes is an integral part of the process of overcoming prejudice.

If the capacity to inhibit prejudiced thoughts is so important, how exactly do we do this? Bodenhausen and Macrae (1998) note that there are at least two types of inhibition. On the one hand, there are the intentional suppression processes, whereby people consciously and deliberately push a thought from consciousness and prevent it from resurfacing (Wegner & Wenzlaff, 1996). Bodenhasen and Macrae call this type of suppression *hierarchical* or *top-down inhibition*. Some research (e.g., Montieth, Sherman & Devine, 1998) demonstrates that when people are committed to the goal of stereotype suppression, they may be successful at it. In order for this approach to work, however, the person must be both motivated to avoid stereotyping and aware of the prejudiced thoughts to begin with.

On the other hand, in contrast to such effortful, top-down inhibitory processes, there is the type of process that Tipper (1992) described, which entails people unintentionally inhibiting their thoughts in their attempts to focus on others. This process is called *lateral inhibition*. So, for example, one is less likely to hold negative perceptions of Asian Americans if one has several close friends who are Asian American. In this case, the focus is on the other person as a unique individual who possesses a number of different qualities. From this view, that focus on the other person reduces one's focus on the person's minority status per se.

Von Hippel, Silver and Lynch (2000) demonstrated that there are some individuals for whom inhibition of stereotypes is more difficult than for others. For example, they demonstrated that elderly people have a harder time with inhibitory processes overall, and thus reported more stereotypes and prejudiced thought than did younger people, who were presumably more able to inhibit thoughts. This research raises interesting questions about whether, as is often thought, younger generations do in fact have less prejudiced thoughts than do older generations, or whether they are just better able to disguise these.

## RACIAL RECONCILIATION: *Is There Hope?*

Reviewing the research on prejudice can be a humbling experience. It is unsettling to discover the relative persistence of negative attitudes toward target groups. For example, in the U.S., African Americans, Muslims and homosexuals are frequent targets of racism and discrimination (Landrine & Klonoff, 1996). Further, the conflicting results found in the research on the relationship between religiosity and prejudice suggest that though orthodox Christian beliefs are negatively related to prejudice (Laythe et al., 2002), people of all faiths, including Christians, have much work yet to do to grow toward other-centered love of dissimilar others. As noted earlier, the question of the degree to which prejudice is inevitable relates to the central command of Christ to love each other without exception. This includes what researchers refer to as "racial tolerance," but also extends beyond this to include loving kindness, compassion and enduring relationships. From a Christian view, loving relationships among people of different groups have to do with more than merely a peaceful coexistence; such relationships are an integral part of the redemptive work of Christ on earth.

A CFR view of the human condition maintains, as the data suggest, that the human condition is quite vulnerable to succumbing to the potential for racism and prejudice. This is a rather sobering reminder of our brokenness. Hostile divisions of all sorts are destructive social forces that are key deterrents to the central aspect of our existence, which is to live in peace and love with God and others. Nevertheless, just because our other-centered capacity is imperfect in our fallen state, it does not logically follow that any given person will inevitably develop prejudice and racist thoughts and feelings. Other-centered potential still exists in the midst of a troubled world. This hope, of course, needs to be tempered with an honest reckoning of how powerful the influence of hatred can be. Still, as the more recent data suggest, racism is not inevitable. It is advisable, in any case, to be mindful of our own potential vulnerabilities as well as the many specific ways in which racism and prejudice can be overcome.

The challenges noted in the literature about racism and prejudice suggest specific strategies that may help reduce the incidence of these. The *contact hypothesis* (Allport, 1954) is one way in which reduction of negative prejudice can occur. From this view, groups who are treated as equals, work collaboratively on some bigger goal and all have the support of authorities, law or customs can develop a greater appreciation for each other. These interactions help forge deeper relationships and mutual understanding. This would lead to a reduction in prejudice (Rothbart & John, 1985). But this alone is not sufficient. Remember that mere exposure to other groups may help perpetuate negative stereotypes. For example, missions groups who work with disadvantaged minority youth may be expressing love and compassion, but not necessarily challenging narrow stereotypes about that group. In fact, this process might actually be inadvertently reinforcing a negative stereotype of the other group as "needy." Exposure to successful members of that group, however, may help to form new, more positive images of the group's potential.

It is interesting to note that Banaji, a principal researcher and developer of the implicit association test, reported that she herself has negative implicit stereotypes regarding African Americans and other minority groups. In an effort to overcome these, she purchased some postcards that have images of successful and prominent people of color including Ghandi (the nonviolent leader of India's independence from Britain), Nora Zeale Hurston (a famous African American author) and Jackie Robinson (the first African American Major League Baseball player). Banaji has set these images to rotate as screen savers on her computer in order to be reminded on a consistent basis of more positive images that she hopes will instill more positive stereotypes of minorities (Berdick, 2004). This approach can be helpful if those positive images are generalized to other members of the represented groups. Otherwise, it is possible that those high-status individuals will be seen as exceptions to our existing negative stereotypes of that group.

One of the interesting things about Banaji's efforts is that she herself is from India. It may seem logical that being a member of a minority group would make a person more aware of negative stereotypes and attitudes toward dissimilar others, and that this awareness would make the minority person less likely to succumb to them. But this is not necessarily the case. Here I can identify with Banaji. I am Cuban American and have lived in the U.S. for over forty years now. As time progresses and I become more aware of the extent to which stereotypes and prejudice persist, I have become more conscious of my own negative attitudes and judgments about other minority groups. With increasing experience relating with dissimilar others and forming enduring relationships with them, I can attest to how these negative perceptions have been challenged.

Think about the following in your own life: What types of people are your closest friends? Whom do you tend to date? Who are your neighbors? Whom do you consider to be your role models? Now consider how much diversity is represented in your answers. For example, are your closest friends of more than one race or ethnicity? Depending on where you attend school and where you have lived, your responses to the above questions might reflect personal characteristics or choices regarding racial and ethnic diversity, or the demographic variables of diversity that surround you, or both. If the diversity of your personal social network is less than your greater environment (or even if not), you may consider the degree of effort you have made to deliberately befriend peers who are of a different race or cultural group.

Having substantive interaction with members of other racial or ethnic groups seems to be an essential part of the process of racial reconciliation. Part of the way in which this works is that increasing interactions with dissimilar others increases the chances that you will encounter positive images of them, thus reducing even implicit negative attitudes. Along these lines, there is research that suggests that efforts to replace negative stereotypes with more positive images of minorities can help reduce negative implicit stereotypes. Wittenbrink, Judd & Park (2001), for example, showed subjects who had just taken the IAT one of two short movies. One movie showed African American gang members, while the other movie showed an African American family at a barbecue. All participants were then given the IAT again. The results showed that the participants who saw the positive images of a peaceful African American family (in the barbecue movie) showed a significant reduction in negative stereotypes on the second IAT. The findings of this research are consistent with that of Cosmides, Tooby and Kurzban (2003), who showed that categorizing individuals by race is not inevitable and that it is also reversible.

So, how might we work toward racial reconciliation, including broader efforts to love and respect dissimilar others, regardless of age, gender and abilities? Let's consider just a few strategies:

1. DeYoung (1997, 2009) suggests that we begin by humbly considering our own potential for engaging in negative attitudes about other groups. Being willing to face your own vulnerability in this regard is powerful because you begin in a place of truth. Remember that often our negative attitudes about others are implicit (i.e., we are not consciously aware of them). For this reason, some of our negative attitudes may not be "tested" until we find ourselves interacting with a person from another group. Parents who claim to have no racist inclinations, for example, may find themselves surprised by their own negative or cautious reactions when they discover that their child is dating a person from another race or ethnicity.

2. Remember that some of the negative stereotypes you have may actually be accurate (e.g., higher crime rates among African Americans) and based on some social injustices that need to be addressed. Thus, be cautious about automatically trying to dismiss a negative idea; instead be open to examining the possible sources of those ideas and your role in helping to address the broader social inequalities they may represent.

3. Even if the negative stereotype you hold of a group is based on accurate, real-life group differences, be especially careful about applying this stereotype in an absolute way to all members of that group. Jussim (2012), for example, notes that while most stereotypes may have at least a grain of truth in them, any stereotype that is applied to all members of a group are undoubtedly full of error.

4. Consider the importance of reconciliation in terms of God's central command to "love . . . your neighbor as yourself" (Lk 10:27). Consider also the centrality of the concept of reconciliation in our faith. God "reconciled us to himself through Christ, and has given us the ministry of reconciliation" (2 Cor 5:18).

5. Make increasing efforts to befriend and form enduring relationships with individuals from other groups than your own. Remember that the process of lateral inhibition (Tipper, 1992) mentioned earlier suggests that it is more difficult to maintain negative attitudes toward other groups if you have a close relationship with a person from that group. Interestingly, this finding is consistent with the main tenets of the CFR approach. Specifically, the finding that an other-centered focus unintentionally reduces negative stereotypes and attitudes toward the other's group suggests that the intrinsically social nature of humans, when focused on regard for the other person, has some very powerful positive effects.

6. Remember that contact with different others does not necessarily in itself reduce prejudice. Though there have been encouraging results based on the contact hypothesis noted earlier, a Christian view also sees *repentance* and *forgiveness* as key components to any reconciliation effort.

7. Be mindful of media messages that you are exposed to about different target groups. For example, Coltrane and Messineo (2000) suggest that television commercials often give us a set of cognitive stereotypes, and that due to the repetition of these images, these stereotypes become more easily remembered during everyday interaction with others. If you watch a lot of television, remember that television programming reflects and transmits the social values of the prevailing culture. Thus, the images presented on television can have a powerful socializing influence on viewers (Bryant & Zillmann, 2002).

8. Consider what negative messages you may have received so far from relatives or others close to you. Many authors (e.g., Carter & Rice, 1997) have noted that children who are exposed at home to prejudiced and racist thinking are more likely than those who are not to adopt such attitudes.

9. In keeping with the intrinsic social nature of humans, note that efforts at reconciliation are most often effective if done as collective efforts.

It is interesting to note that relative to the general U.S. population, college students on average tend to be less authoritarian and less prejudiced (Laythe et al., 2002). This hopeful finding needs to be considered in the light of a Christian perspective that sees reconciliation as an integral part of God's redemptive work. The good news is that negative social processes such as prejudice and racism are not entirely inevitable. The sobering news is that we are more vulnerable than we might think to fall prey to hateful attitudes about other groups.

## So Far . . .

In addition to all the hopeful strategies that research presents to us about how to reduce negative attitudes about dissimilar others, we must remember that it is God's grace that enables us to use these, and others, to overcome hatred. A heart that values the dignity and worth of all recognizes that reconciliation is an essential part of God's process. From a CFR view, the capacity that humans have to be other-centered is an important part of our work toward reconciliation, yet the fallen human condition reminds us of how imprecise and uneven this process can be. And yet, even if the strategies that research suggests to us for reducing prejudice and racism meet with only limited success, there would be other ways in which God can work. From a naturalist standpoint, possible motives for reconciliation among groups are logically based on group- or self-serving benefits and increased survival value (i.e., there would be more peace and thus less killing). A Christian view acknowledges those motives and also provides an enduring and logical consideration of how humility, forgiveness, repentance and reconciliation are integral parts of God's redemptive work in the world. Accepting both our common humanity as well as our unique cultural identities will be crucial as we move ahead in our efforts at reconciliation (DeYoung, 2003).

## Questions to Consider

1. Consider the list noted above with recommendations for reconciliatory processes. What, if anything, would you add to it?

2. If you were a researcher interested in studying the differences between genuine racial reconciliation and "peaceful coexistence," what specific factors would you measure?

3. There seems to be plenty of evidence of the tendency for intergroup division and hatred. Do you see any evidence of a genuine tendency to embrace others?

## Key Terms

*ageism*
*anti-fat attitudes*
*anti-locution*
*arms-length prejudice*
*authoritarianism*
*automatic processing*
*categorization*
*Christian orthodoxy*
*contact hypothesis*
*controlled processing*
*derogated*
*explicit prejudice*
*explicit self-esteem*
*extrinsic religiosity*
*generality of prejudice*
*hierarchical/top-down inhibition*
*implicit ageism*
*implicit association test*
*implicit prejudice*
*implicit self-esteem*

*in-group bias*
*intertextual approach*
*intratextual approach*
*intrinsic religiosity*
*lateral inhibition*
*prejudice*
*quest orientation*
*religious fundamentalism*
*right-wing authoritarianism*
*self-categorization theory*
*social dominance orientation*
*social identity theory*
*social-cognitive approaches*
*stereotype threat*
*stereotypes*

# 9

# Prosocial Behavior

*Helping*

*No one has greater love than this,
to lay down one's life for one's friends.*

**JOHN 15:13**

Can you imagine an experience in which you are genuinely surprised to see how much someone had gone out of their way to help you with no apparent expectation for you to return the favor? Would you be touched by the act and encouraged to have a greater sense of hope for humanity at large? Or would you suspect that it was too good to be true and that the person had ulterior reasons for helping, such as "looking good" in front of others or expecting something from you in response to his or her charitable act?

Regardless of our responses to those questions, reflecting on helping behavior can be a very sobering experience. This is because it brings to our own minds not only the many instances in which others have helped us and we, too, have helped others, but also the many instances in which

we may not have helped as we should have. In fact, even as you read this, there may be a situation in your own life in which you have felt a nagging pull to help yet you have not done so. This is true for all of us to varying degrees.

## WHY STUDY HELPING?

Social psychologists have been and continue to be very interested in studying helping behavior. In part, this is because of the obvious relevance of such behavior for everyday social interactions. Exploring under which circumstances people are either more or less inclined to assist others may provide clues to the internal motivations for outward displays of helping. Sometimes helping is the result of a long process of deliberation, and at other times it results from a sudden, at-the-moment need. Sometimes it is very heroic helping behavior, while most frequently it is the more mundane, everyday sorts of helping. Always, it is the result of a complex combination of factors, both personal and situational. That sounds interesting, you may be thinking, but after talking in the preceding chapters about so many destructive things of which humans are capable, it is normal to come away with questions about whether there is any real hope for some measure of goodness in us. So much honest thinking about our propensity toward racism and discrimination is enough to dampen anyone's day. How does helping fit alongside the human capacity for hate and savagery?

Even casual observation of social interaction will reveal that many times we *do* help one another, and this is true in every culture. Research on helping behavior has helped to clarify the circumstances in which helping is more likely to occur. If we consider volunteering, for example, we will be heartened to learn that in the year 2009, over 63.4 million Americans volunteered in their communities. These volunteers provided 8.1 billion hours of services, which is roughly equivalent to a dollar value of $169 million (Corporation for National and Community Service, 2010). There are cases, only some of which are publicized, in which individuals actually risk or lose their own lives to save that of another, including strangers. There are also plenty of examples of everyday helping: opening the door for someone, helping another who has fallen, volunteering at soup kitchens or organizations such as Habitat for Humanity, donating money to charitable causes, and the list goes on. Just think about the number of people who have helped you in various ways to get to where you are today as a student.

This chapter will review what the helping research suggests regarding:

- the sorts of persons we are most likely to help,

- under what types of circumstances we are most likely to help others,

- possible motives for helping, and

- why helping behavior even exists at all (both naturalist and Christian views).

You will see shortly that, as elsewhere in the literature, the general results of the helping research are not very encouraging. Numerous studies suggest that humans have primarily, often exclusively, self-centered motives for helping. These studies suggest that the more natural inclination is *not* to help or, when we do help, to still look out for one's own best interests. This chapter will explore both a naturalist and a Christian view of these general findings, and suggest ways in which the complex motives for helping may be understood in light of a Christian view of persons.

Keep in mind that from a CFR approach to understanding humans, helping is considered an integral part of what it means to live in other-centered community and is an essential way in which we reflect the image of God. It is thus important to consider what social psychology tells us about personal and situational factors that are likely to either increase or impede helping behavior. This information allows us to better understand how to address these factors and has the potential to aid us in our goal of striving to live in accordance with God's purposes.

The CFR approach proposes that humans were created with a genuine capacity for other-centered caring and that because of the fall, a tension exists between self-centered motives for helping and other-centered motives for helping. A naturalist approach suggests primarily, or almost exclusively, ultimately self-centered reasons for helping. These differences in perspective will be discussed throughout this chapter.

## Key Terms and Complex Motives

Before we begin the discussion of helping research, it would be beneficial to clarify a few key terms. In addition, a brief introduction regarding the complexity of motives for helping will set the stage for the discussions later in this chapter. Social psychologists refer to any behavior that benefits another as *prosocial behavior* (Aronson, Wilson & Akert, 2004). Note that this is the opposite of *antisocial behavior* as discussed in the previous chapter. Antisocial behavior, as you will recall, harms others. Prosocial behavior refers to a wide diversity of behaviors, essentially anything that benefits another person. Examples of prosocial acts studied by social psychologists include donating blood (e.g., Healy, 2000), participation in civic events such as protests and political campaigns (Skocpol, Ganz & Munson, 2000), organ donation (e.g., Healy, 2004), volunteering, and charitable donations. Prosocial behavior happens universally, but, as Fiske (1991) notes, outward displays of helping behavior tell us nothing about internal motives for helping. This is because any behavior that is intended to help another is officially considered to be prosocial, regardless of the motive.

How can we tell if a prosocial act is primarily intended to help another? What if the giver (or doer) also benefits? This may sound cynical at first, but think of two different scenarios. Ben volunteers time at a local shelter for battered women, feeling deeply moved by the plight of these women. He decides to not tell any of his friends because he reasons that it is not necessary to let others know or be recognized for what he is doing. He simply wishes to help out. Anna volunteers at a local hospital for children, knowing that her peers will probably praise her for what she is doing. She readily tells them about her efforts and perhaps even invites them to help. All the while she consciously realizes that she enjoys the recognition and the positive attributions about her social awareness and overall character.

With the above examples, we will likely perceive that Ben has purer motives for his prosocial behavior than does Anna, who appears to have ulterior motives for her volunteerism. Anna obviously wants to be recognized and praised, so she is engaging in a prosocial act at least partly as a means to an end. In that case, is this really a benevolent act? Ben's actions, on the other hand, seem to represent a more "true" prosocial act because his concern is that others benefit, not him. But wait a minute: What if Ben *does* get something out of his volunteering at the women's shelter? What if, after seeing how he contributes to the women benefiting from the program and starting a new life, he feels good about himself and on some days even skips joyfully home after his time at the shelter? (Okay, the skipping part may be a bit much here, but bear with me in order to see the point.) In other words, Ben gets internal rewards for his benevolence. Conversely, Anna may genuinely care about the children at the hospital even though she gets secondary rewards for helping. One who tells others about their own charitable contributions may simply wish to increase public awareness of the need and not really be seeking out self-centered approval.

As it turns out, social psychologists have long noted the fact that there are a multitude of possible motives for prosocial conduct, and that what benefits another might also benefit the doer or giver. There are internal motives and external motives for prosocial acts. These will be discussed in a later section. At this point, just knowing that helping behavior may have multiple underlying motives makes the study of helping all the more interesting and challenging.

Another important and highly controversial topic in the helping research literature is *altruism*. The word *altruism* originates in the Latin word for "other." Literally, it means to be other-centered, which in this context refers to having unselfish concern for the welfare of another, and at times may include helping behavior that is costly to the helper. Why would the concept of altruism be so controversial in social psychology? As already noted, there is significant disagreement among social psychologists regarding whether humans have a genuine capacity for other-centered behavior or altruism.

There are several potential reasons why there is so much controversy regarding altruism. These will be discussed in more detail later, but for now, consider two possible issues. First, as noted throughout this text, suggestions about how humans are capable of being other-centered strikes at the very core of one's worldview regarding the human condition. People, including researchers, can thus have a lot invested in the answer to what motivates human kindness. A second possible reason for the controversy regarding altruism is the forced and artificial dichotomy of self- and other-centered helping. To suggest that helping behavior must be primarily self- or other-centered makes for cleaner research but also makes it difficult to adequately study the rich complexity of human motives. More on this later.

As Piliavin (2001) notes, research regarding helping behavior has been conducted over a large range of social situations. In these situations, researchers have studied key factors such as age, race and gender of the "victim," the way the victim is dressed, the level of physical attractiveness of the victim, the urgency of the need for help, the level of similarity between the helper and victim, the number of bystanders present, the degree of population density (i.e., smaller towns vs. big cities), and the relationship between religiosity and helping behavior, to name only a few. Such a broad range of factors suggests just how complex the process of helping can be. Despite this complexity, some consistent patterns emerge regarding the propensity to help, and the goal of this chapter, as already noted, is to describe these findings and explore their implications from a Christian view of the human condition.

## WHOM DO WE TEND TO HELP THE MOST?

Consider the type of person(s) whom you have most likely helped. The idea that we help some people more than others may be due to a variety of factors such as opportunity and ability. But the question of who we help also implies that we make some judgments about who is deserving of our help, however unnerving that thought may be. On what basis do we decide whom to help? Let's see what the research findings suggest.

*A just world.* Kay, Jost and Young (2005) review many studies that suggest that in general, we prefer to believe that the social system that affects us is fair and legitimate rather than unfair and full of caprice (e.g., Crosby, Pufall, Snyder, O'Connell & Whalen, 1989; Furnham & Gunter, 1984; Jost & Banaji, 1994; Lerner & Miller, 1978; Martin, 1986; Tyler & McGraw, 1986). Lerner (1965, 1970) first called this the *just-world hypothesis.* As discussed in chapter four on social perception, this term refers to the tendency for people to believe that the world is just and therefore people "get what they deserve." In his initial study investigating this phenomenon, Lerner's (1965) subjects tended to believe that a fellow student whom they were told had won the lottery worked harder than another student who had lost the lottery. What makes this interesting is that, contrary to the opinions of many faithful lottery players, it is pure chance that determines who wins the lottery.

Lerner and Simmons (1966) also investigated the just-world hypothesis in a study in which the subjects watched a film of a female participant (a confederate) allegedly being painfully shocked in a simulated learning experiment. Initially, many of the viewers responded by becoming anxious and upset. Nevertheless, toward the end of the experiment most of the viewers had adopted the "just world" way of thinking. In other words, they formed lower opinions of the "victimized" participant in an apparent effort to bring about some consistency between her fate and her character.

Is there a connection between the just-world hypothesis and actual helping behavior? Apparently so; it seems that this view can both increase and decrease the likelihood of helping. Lipkus, Dalbert and Siegler (1996), for example, suggest that if bystanders see a person who for whatever reasons cannot be helped, the bystanders may often disparage the victim, thus making the world seem like a place in which people get what they deserve. MacLean and Chown (1988) found that British and Canadian university students who believed in a just world were more likely to blame elderly people for poor health or financial circumstances and reported that they would be less likely to help the elderly with social, economic or health needs. Basically, these students had convinced themselves that the elderly "got what they deserved."

It is also possible that the just-world phenomenon may increase helping. For example, De Palma et al. (1999) conducted a study in which they told subjects that a patient had been infected with a (fictitious) blood disease. They varied the patient's level of responsibility for the illness by either telling the subjects that the disease was acquired through unprotected sex (patient responsibility) or that it was a genetic abnormality (no patient responsibility). The results indicated that subjects were overall significantly more likely to report intentions to volunteer if the patient was not perceived as responsible for their condition. In addition, the researchers found that once they perceived that the patient was not responsible, those with a high belief in a just world were more likely to help than were those who did not have such a belief. Thus, those who both hold a strong belief in a just world and perceive a person as not responsible for their plight appeared to be wanting to make things just again.

*Those who are similar to us.* The findings of the helping research suggest that we tend to help those who are most similar to us at an interpersonal level as well as on a group level—in other words, those whom we consider to be part of our in-group (Dovidio et al., 2005). Schroeder et al. (1995), in their review of the literature on the significant effect of similarity on the likelihood of helping, noted that this effect encompasses a broad range of behaviors and characteristics, including race (Glassman, Packel & Brown, 1986), gender (Eagly & Crowley, 1986) and employment status (Wellman & Wortley, 1990). Similarly, passersby seem more inclined to help strangers, give small amounts of money to panhandlers and comply with other types of requests when they were asked by a person with characteristics similar to their own.

The finding that we tend to help those who are similar to us may seem to contradict much of the helping we see in everyday life. For example, what about all the cases of more privileged people helping charitable organizations who tend to the needs of less privileged individuals? And don't older people often help tutor younger people, and healthy people volunteer to work with individuals who are ill? The answer to these questions is, of course, yes. But the research findings suggest that as a general rule, people more often tend to help those who are more similar to themselves.

In fact, the research suggests that it is not just similarity itself, but also the *perception* of similarity to the person in need that increases the would-be helper's desire to act. In various studies, researchers have manipulated similarity in different ways. They have found, for example, that same race, status, apparel appearance or attitude between solicitor and helper is sufficient to produce more compliance to the solicitor request (Gaertner & Bickman, 1971; Wegner & Crano, 1975; Goodman & Gareis, 1993).

In general, the more two people have in common, the stronger the initial bond between them. Cialdini et al. (1997) argue that it is the commonality that is formed between two similar people that leads to subsequent helping behavior. Can you think of examples in your own life about dorm mates or students in the same academic major being more inclined to help one another out as opposed to helping out strangers from other majors? Have you ever been traveling in another state or country and met another person from your own hometown and felt an immediate connection with them? How do you think this feeling of connection could affect your willingness to help them if they suddenly asked you for change or help with directions?

The type of similarity that increases the chances of helping can also be affected by form of dress. Emswiller, Deaux and Willits (1971), for example, found that subjects were more willing to give money to a stranger for a phone call when that stranger was dressed in a manner similar to themselves. (It is likely that we make assumptions about others being similar to us based on the mere fact that they are dressed like us.)

Consider another interesting example of the relationship between helping and similarity. In a study by Furnham (1996), people reported that they would assign higher priorities for life-saving medical treatment for those who shared similar political attitudes! If we take these results at face value, then if you are ever in an emergency situation and need help, be careful about revealing anything about your political affiliations!

More recently, experimenters have begun to explore the relationship between similarity and helping within the context of *computer-mediated interaction* (i.e., online communications). Guéguen, Pichot and Le Dreff (2005) used fifty-two students in their first year of management studies at the University of Bretagne-Sud in France. An e-mail was sent to the subject with the solicitor, who was a confederate, posing as a statistics student at the university who had been assigned to do a survey and statistical analysis of the diet habits of students. The solicitor asked the subject if they would please help out with the project, and the questionnaire was attached. The questionnaire asked fairly routine questions such as, "How many times a week do you eat fresh vegetables?" "What type of drink do you have with lunch?" The researchers created different e-mail addresses that contained either a signature where the surname of the solicitor was the same as the surname of the subject, or in the control condition, five fairly common French surnames such as "Martin," "Durand" and "Rivière." In this condition, the surname employed was deliberately quite different from the surname of the subject.

The results showed that there was a significant difference in response rates between the two conditions, with 96 percent of those in the experimental (same name) situation filling out the questionnaire, as compared to only 52 percent of those in the control situation responding. These results are an interesting example of how it is possible to create similarity between two correspondents in an e-mail interaction, with this similarity leading to an increase in helping. Think of the many possible ways in which this sort of knowledge could be used online to increase compliance with requests for help.

Why does similarity seem to be very powerful in increasing helping? Krebs (1975) and Karylowski (1976) proposed that perceived similarities between two people often enable a potential helper to relate to the victim, and this increases empathy. The potential helper, empathizing with the other, also realizes that he or she would want someone to provide help if they were in the same situation. These feelings may then increase the desire to help. Similarly, Cialdini et al. (1997) have suggested that similarity promotes helping by creating a feeling of oneness or solidarity. Finally, similarity may also create feelings of attraction toward the person in need. Some research suggests that people feel more strongly attracted to others who are similar to themselves, and are nicer to them as a consequence of these feelings of attraction (Byrne, 1971, 1997).

*Those whom we like.* Suppose you had a classmate who was often rude to you, barely acknowledging your existence and rarely responding to your greetings. Then in the middle of the term, she suddenly turned to you and, smiling sweetly for the first time ever in your presence, said that she had noticed that you were doing well in the class and she would really appreciate your help in studying for the upcoming exam. In this case, how likely are you to help the rude fellow student? Given her prior history of rudeness, chances are most people would not like her much, at least not in the context of this classroom situation. In terms of eliciting help from you given her prior history, she might as well have asked you to jump off a cliff for her.

Research suggests a strong, positive relationship between liking and helping. Liking has also been shown to be related to similarity (Byrne, 1978), and since similarity is also related to helping, we see that the various factors interact to produce greater or lesser inclinations to help. Burger et al. (2001), for example, showed that even very subtle cues of similarity can create a fleeting attraction to strangers and increase compliance with a request for help. In each of three studies, the researchers found that small manipulations intended to increase liking of the other (opportunity for interaction, mere exposure to the other and perceived similarity) were enough to significantly increase the chances of subjects agreeing to help the confederate. In one such experiment, subjects were asked by the confederate to read an eight-page essay that the confederate had allegedly written for an English class and to prepare a one-page review by the next day. Subjects who had had the opportunity to interact with the confederate were significantly more apt to both report liking her and to comply with the request. Garrity and Degelman (1990) demonstrated that waitresses in their study received higher tips when they used their first names with their customers. The researchers proposed that the use of first names seemed to ingratiate the waitress to the customers because the use of first names is something we typically associate with friends, whom we like.

*Those whom we find attractive.* Does physical attractiveness increase one's chances of getting help? Often, yes. In a classic series of experiments, Wilson (1978) varied the attractiveness level of two different female confederates. Both were made to look more and less attractive by altering their form of dress, makeup and hairstyles. The two women asked male students who were walking by to mail a letter for them. Wilson found that the male students were significantly more inclined to help the confederates when they were in their attractive appearance as opposed to when they appeared less attractive. Harrell (1978) similarly conducted a field experiment in which female confederates asked 216 male subjects for directions to a health services building. Half of the subjects received self-disclosure information (i.e., the confederate's name), while half received no self-disclosure. In addition, the confederates were either physically attractive or unattractive. Overall, it was found that the male subjects spent more time giving instructions to attractive confederates than to unattractive confederates. The greatest amount of help was given to attractive confederates who self-disclosed, while the least amount of help was received by the unattractive confederates who disclosed their names.

Pomazal and Clore (1973) found that motorists who were perceived as attractive were significantly more likely to receive help than were motorists who were not. Reingen and Kernan (1993) similarly found that when individuals were asked for donations to a charitable cause, they gave more money to physically attractive requesters than to less attractive requesters.

But why are physically attractive people often helped more than those who are perceived as less attractive? Some researchers have suggested that this is due to the link between perceived attractiveness and liking, and the tendency to be more apt to help those whom we like. For example, Hatfield and Sprecher (1986) noted that people often tend to like physically attractive people more than they do less attractive people, at least during initial encounters with them. In addition, there is the possibility of the *physical attractiveness stereotype,* which will be discussed in more detail in the next chapter. This hypothesis proposes that attractive individuals are often evaluated more positively than are unattractive ones on a variety of character traits such as kindness and intelligence (Dion, Berscheid & Walster, 1972). Dion and colleagues found that the effect leads us to perceive that "what is beautiful is good." In other words, we may perceive attractive people as good, like them better and thus perceive them as more deserving of help than individuals whom we perceive as less attractive.

Benson, Karabenick and Lerner (1976) conducted a field study in which they left a stamped, addressed open envelope that contained a graduate school application in a phone booth (in the days well before cell phones!). The picture on the application varied with respect to level of physical attractiveness, race and gender. Results demonstrated that the subjects were more likely to return the graduate application for the attractive candidates.

Langlois et al. (2000) conducted a meta-analytic review of the effects of physical attractiveness on perception of the attributes of an individual and actual social interactions. This research included a number of studies investigating the relationship between attractiveness and the likelihood of receiving help. The researchers concluded that for both adults and children, the effects of facial attractiveness were significant and prevalent. In addition, no sex differences were found, suggesting that the attractiveness of the "victim" is as important for males as for females.

The effects of the physical attractiveness of the *helper* have also been investigated in terms of its effect on another asking for help. Stokes and Bickman's (1974) study, for example, used two confederates who had been rated as attractive or less attractive in photographs. Subjects were generally reluctant to ask for help from the less attractive confederate. Apparently, the attractiveness of the helper can be a distracting or anxiety-provoking experience.

Despite the strong effects of physical attractiveness on the likelihood of receiving help, this effect is mediated by a number of issues. How urgent a situation is deemed to be by the potential helper is an important consideration. West and Brown (1975), for example, found that regardless of the level of physical attractiveness of the female confederate, she was more likely to receive help from a male subject if the severity of the emergency was deemed to be high.

**Kin and other close folks.** All things being equal, do you think that in general you would be most inclined to help a relative or a friend? Social psychologists have generally found that in the case of helping, blood does indeed seem to be thicker than water. The research suggests that people often tend to help family members more than they do unrelated others (Matthews, Batson, Horn & Rosenman, 1981). Similarly, in terms of helping a close friend versus an acquaintance, helping is related to the degree of perceived closeness to the other. Cialdini et al. (1997), for example, found that both the empathic concern for a needy other as well as the amount of costly helping increased significantly as relationship closeness increased from a near stranger to an acquaintance, a good friend and ultimately a family member.

Investigating the relationship between genetic closeness and helping, Essock-Vitale and McGuire (1985) found that the larger the amount of help given, the more likely it was to come from kin; closer kin were more likely sources of help than were more distant kin; childless individuals gave more help to their nieces and nephews; and childless aunts received more help from nieces and nephews. Using an evolutionary model of kin selection, the researchers interpreted the results as an indication of the likelihood of helping primarily as a function of the recipient's expected reproductive potential.

Many of these studies have used interpretations based on evolutionary kin selection models, and we will explore that at greater length later in this chapter. For now, let us briefly explore whether an evolutionary explanation for kin selection is applicable to all cases of helping. If you want to ensure the survival of your genetic heritage, wouldn't it make more sense that the inclination to help would be more pronounced in cases where the situation in which help is needed is a matter of life and death? Or are we as equally likely to help a family member who needs a ride to the airport as we are a family member who needs to be rescued from a fire? Burnstein, Crandall and Kitayama (1994) surveyed U.S. and Japanese college students and asked them how willing they would be to help another either by picking something up for them at the

**Figure 9.1.**

store or rescuing them from a burning building. In general, they found that the closer the relative, the greater the inclination to help, at least on the basis of survey results and not of actual behavior in those situations. But the tendency to help close relatives was much more significant when the situation was life threatening. So when asking a family member for help on a routine, mundane task, you can't be so sure they will comply. Figure 9.1 summarizes some of the factors involved in our helping others. What patterns do you see?

**Whom do we help: A Christian perspective.** To review, the research suggests that we tend to help others who are similar to us, related to us, close friends, people we like and people we find attractive. It also shows that our likelihood of helping each of these groups depends on the severity of the need and the ability of the helper to provide assistance, and on other factors such as time pressure (you will be reading about them in the following sections).

The Scriptures of course record many teachings about helping, some of which seem to support the research that we are considering. For example, James 1 urges Christians to care for other Christians, suggesting that similarity—in faith—should be a powerful motive for helping others. But interestingly, the majority of helping stories in the Bible present scenarios that extend well beyond the factors suggested by current research. Consider Christ himself, who often helped people who were not at all similar to him and whom he didn't necessarily like or find attractive. Jesus' story of the good Samaritan involved helping that today's research would hardly predict. Likewise the apostle Paul describes himself as a servant of all people and urges believers to put others first. Such teachings imply that Christ's redemption of our fallen state enables us to help people we would not ordinarily help. Let's bear this in mind as we review more of the helping research.

## When Do We Tend to Help?

**Emergency situations.** Doesn't it seem logical to think that people would be most likely to help if they witness an emergency situation? Imagine, for example, witnessing an accident that involves a car and bus collision. Certainly, one might guess, *this* is a situation that would evoke in most people an immediate response to help. Cries and screams from people on a burning bus are difficult to ignore, right? Well, the answer is not so simple. It turns out that our likelihood of helping, even during what seems like an obvious emergency situation, depends on a wide variety of things. The famous case of Kitty Genovese prompted the helping research that investigated why people do not help in emergency situations.

Imagine that it is about 3:30 in the morning when you are awakened by a woman's scream outside your bedroom window. Moments later you hear her scream out again, this time yelling, "Oh, my God, he stabbed me! Please help me!" You then hear a neighbor's voice shouting, "Let that girl alone!" A few minutes pass, and again you hear the woman cry out. This time she yells, "I'm dying! I'm dying!" In this case, what would you do? Would you call 911 right away? Would you wait a few moments to be sure you heard what you think you heard and then call 911? Would you not call, assuming that someone else has surely called already? The *New York Times* article from March 1964 about Catherine ("Kitty") Genovese reported that thirty-eight neighbors either heard or otherwise saw the scuffle between Kitty and her assailant, but no one called the police until more than half an hour later, when it was too late. Incidentally, as you will see later this chapter, the details in the news story have been found to have questionable validity. In any case, this is how the story was reported, and many people, including social psychologists, wondered how this apathy among the neighbors could happen.

The story of Kitty Genovese prompted Darley and Latané (1968, 1970) to propose the concept of the *bystander effect*. According to this model, in general, the likelihood that a person will be helped decreases as the number of people present increases. Why does the presence of others often decrease the chances that we will help? One explanation is known as *pluralistic ignorance*. This concept relates to how people look to each other for indications that something is wrong. If the others in the crowd do not seem concerned, then any individual person in that crowd is also likely to assume that nothing is wrong because nobody else looks concerned. This is especially true in ambiguous situations, where one cannot know right away that it is a true emergency.

One example of a study of pluralistic ignorance was conducted by Harrison and Wells (1991). Seventy-two male university students and a confederate, visible through a glass partition in an adjacent room, were completing a questionnaire when an unseen female screamed and the noise of falling objects was heard. Subjects were more likely to offer help when the confederate's behavior appeared agitated than when the confederate exhibited no reactions. Thus, a bystander may use the reactions of others to help define what has happened.

*Diffusion of responsibility* is another possible explanation of the bystander effect. Any single person does not feel as responsible for helping someone if several others are also present, since responsibility is distributed among all those present. You have probably experienced some training in this phenomenon if you have taken a CPR class. Chances are the instructor told you that if you are the one delivering CPR and there is a group of bystanders, you should not randomly call out to the group for someone to call 911. Instead, you should point to a specific person and tell them, "You in the red shirt, call 911." That way there is no confusion about who should take action.

It's my latest invention! This offering plate will ring a little bell if you put in $20 . . . if you don't put in anything, it takes your picture.

**Figure 9.2.**

There are many studies that explore this idea of diffusion of responsibility. Darley and Latané (1968) first demonstrated the bystander effect in the laboratory. In one study, a subject was placed alone in a room and told that he could communicate with other subjects through an intercom. In reality, he was just listening to an audio recording and was told his microphone would be off until it was his turn to speak. During the recording, one "subject" suddenly pretends he is having a seizure. The study found that the length of time the subject waits before alerting the experimenter varies directly with the perceived number of other subjects. In some cases where the subject thought that there were other individuals on the other side of the partition, the subject never told the experimenter about the seizure.

In another study, Darley and Latané (1968) sat a series of college students in a cubicle among a number of other cubicles in which there were tapes of other students playing (the student thought the audiotapes were real people). One of the voices cries for help and makes sounds of severe choking. When the student thought they were the only person there, 85 percent rushed to help. When they thought there was one other person, this dropped to 65 percent. And when they thought there were four other people, this dropped again, to 31 percent.

Gottlieb and Carver (1980) explored a slightly different angle of the bystander effect. They noted that in the studies on the bystander effect, the other witnesses were anonymous others who had no relationship with the subject and with whom the subject probably did not expect to interact again. Gottlieb and Carver examined the possibility that if a person expects to have contact with the others in the group at a later time, they may be more inclined to help significantly more, thereby minimizing the bystander effect. Female college students were led to believe either that they would have no personal contact with the other participants in a group discussion, or that the participants would be involved in a later face-to-face discussion session. Each subject then participated in what she believed to be an anonymous discussion via intercoms, involving either one person or five persons beside herself. During this period, a confederate experienced a supposed choking fit. Help was offered more quickly among subjects who expected future interaction than among those who did not.

The diffusion of responsibility also seems to occur if we experience the virtual presence of others on the Web. Blair, Thompson and Wuensch (2005) sought to explore this question about whether the effect of the virtual presence of others is as powerful as the actual physical presence of others in terms of reducing the tendency to help individuals who need assistance. Participants were sent an e-mail message requesting assistance with an online library search task. Each person received the message along with an indication that 0, 1, 14 or 49 others were also contacted. The results demonstrated partial support for the hypothesis. As expected, the virtual presence of many others significantly reduced e-mail responsiveness; however, nonresponse did not directly increase in proportion with group size. These findings help explain the lack of responsiveness often demonstrated by Internet users who receive e-mail requests sent to multiple people simultaneously. If you know that many others are also being asked to help by filling out an online questionnaire, for example, you may be less likely to fill out the questionnaire, reckoning that "the others will do it."

Incidentally, some researchers (e.g., Levine, 1999; Levine, Cassidy, Brazier & Reicher, 2002) have argued that to better understand helping, researchers should pay more attention to *group* processes instead of focusing so much on how *individuals* are affected by various factors when deciding to help. Levine et al. (2002), for example, suggest that when trying to understand the bystander effect, it is helpful to consider whether the others around were in-group members rather than out-group members. These researchers suggest that it is not just the presence or absence of others that affects a bystander's intervention, but who the bystander perceives those others to be.

Latané and Darley (1970) initially proposed a decision-tree model to explain the steps potential helpers go through in emergency situations. According to this model, at each stage of the process, the inclination to help or not to help can be affected by a number of issues. The model might seem straightforward enough, but as you already know from reading previous chapters, nothing in human social interaction is as simple as it first appears. Consider the list of stages in table 9.1. Notice the challenges that could occur at each stage of the process.

**Table 9.1. Deciding to Help in Emergencies**

| You must notice the situation | Seems simple, but how many potential helping situations do you miss on a given day because you either do not see or hear them? |
|---|---|
| Having noticed the event, you must interpret it as an emergency | Again, sounds simple enough, but could you be over-interpreting the situation? What if you make a fool out of yourself? |
| You must decide that it is your responsibility to help | But what if there are other people around who could help? |
| You have to decide on an appropriate set of actions | But what if you don't think you can do it? |
| Finally, you have to decide to carry out the actions required for helping in this context | But what if it's not in your best interest to help? |

Source: Latané & Darley, 1970

The *arousal/cost-reward model* helps explain helping behavior in emergency situations (Piliavin, Piliavin & Rodin, 1975). Figure 9.3 shows the major components of this model and the likelihood of helping. Note that from this view, the person has already noticed and interpreted the situation as an emergency and is in the position of deciding whether or not to help (Piliavin et al., 1982). The basic premise of this model is that in an emergency situation, observers will feel a significant amount of distress and will be inclined to try to reduce that negative emotional arousal. In this case, helping is one way in which to reduce this personal distress. But, as noted by Kenrick, Neuberg and Cialdini (2002), this model proposes that the need to reduce personal distress usually only results in helping behavior under certain circumstances:

- When the arousal is strong and the subject feels competent to help (Cramer et al., 1988)

- When there is a "we" connection between the victim and the helper (Krebs, 1975)

- When reducing arousal through helping involves small costs and large rewards (Piliavin & Piliavin, 1972)

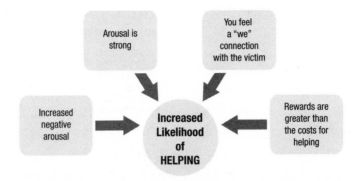

**Figure 9.3. Negative-State Relief Model: After the Emergency and Need for Help Is Detected**

Source: Dovidio, Piliavin, Gaertner, Schroeder & Clark, 1991

Thus, not all situations have an equal capacity to evoke feelings of distress in us such that we feel prompted to help the other person. Furthermore, it seems (once again) that a connection between the victim and the helper facilitates helping, but as long as it doesn't cost too much to do so. At other times, if the negative arousal is strong enough but a person thinks that helping might cost too much in terms of possible danger or time commitment, the person is more likely to reduce the negative arousal through some other means such as leaving the scene (Dovidio et al., 1991, as cited in Kenrick et al., 2002) or perhaps going to call for help.

Despite the apparent consistencies in the findings regarding the bystander effect, there are still many things we don't understand about helping when in groups. For example, our capacity to be apathetic about the plight of others when we are in a group is still not well understood. Consider the story about the neighbors' apathy in the Kitty Genovese case, which inspired the research on the bystander effect. Manning, Levine and Collins (2007) note that transcripts of the murder's trial and other legal documents related to the case do not support the story that thirty-eight witnesses took no action to help the victim. In fact, several of the neighbors called the police, who did not respond immediately. Other neighbors could not see or hear Kitty from their apartment. Still others reported that they could not readily discern the emergency, as lovers' squabbles routinely took place on that street, which was near a local bar.

Manning, Levine and Collins (2007) do not discount the potential power of the bystander effect. Yet the authors' concern is that the negative message in this iconic story has resulted in psychologists being slow to look for ways in which the power of groups can be used in positive ways to promote intervention in bystanders. The research on the bystander effect presents us with valuable information. Nevertheless, this research overemphasizes the apathy of bystanders and the negative influence of others on our likelihood of helping.

*Everyday helping situations.* Research suggests that many of the same factors that are involved in helping during emergency situations are also relevant to everyday helping situations. For example, whether or not a need for help is urgent, potential helpers must decide whether it is their responsibility to provide aid. In addition, they must also decide whether they have the skills to do so, and so forth. Amato (1990) notes that most helping experiments have been conducted either in the lab or in the field, both of which consist of individuals who are usually strangers to each other. But Amato notes that everyday helping, such as helping with homework or the dishes or helping a neighbor start a stalled car, differs in several important respects. First, on the average day, individuals generally provide help to people they know as opposed to strangers. This is because there is generally a greater opportunity for interaction with known others than with strangers. Second, much of the assistance provided in everyday life is planned instead of spontaneous. In real life, helping is usually embedded in long-term relationships. Amato further notes that people generally prefer to get help from those they know rather than from strangers or formal social agencies. In addition, the very definitions that people usually give of "family member" and "friend" include some expectation of mutual helping.

While prior researchers (e.g., Eisenberg & Miller, 1987) had found that personality variables such as empathy are a good predictor of helping, Amato found that such personality variables are more related to planned helping rather than to spontaneous or everyday helping. Thus, according to Amato, it is important to use caution when interpreting the majority of helping research, as it does not focus on situations that are commonplace.

*Geographical area.* Living in a small town or a rural setting is generally more conducive to receiving and offering help than is living in a big city. Levine (2003) studied helpfulness toward strangers in thirty-six cities of various sizes across the United States and twenty-three large cities around the world. He and his colleagues conducted independent field experiments in each city to measure helping in various situations. They had different confederates act as though they had dropped a pen, tried to reach a pile of dropped magazines with a hurt leg, or act as a blind person who needed to cross the street and retrieve a lost letter. Levine and his colleagues observed in which cities help was most likely to be provided. Their first studies were done in the early 1990s. In which large city do you think the passersby were the least helpful? If you guessed New York City, you are almost correct; it placed twenty-second out of twenty-three cities. In this case at least, the stereotype of the rushed, callous New Yorker seems to have at least a grain of truth. Across the results of the five experiments, New York City came out last. Overall, small and medium-sized cities in the southeast were the most helpful, and large northeastern and West Coast cities were the least helpful (Levine et al., 1994; Levine, 1997).

But what is it about the larger cities that discourages helping? Levine et al. (1994) found that the best predictor of helping was population density: the more crowded the city, the less help was generally provided. In fact, population density was more closely tied to the helpfulness of a city than were other important characteristics such as crime rates, economic conditions or environmental stressors like noise and air pollution. Are the people in more densely populated cities indeed more callous and uncaring than those in less densely populated cities? Levine does not think so. As he noted, numerous New Yorkers expressed frustration and anger to the researchers that life seemed to deprive them of the opportunity to help others, for whom they expressed a deep care. Levine noted that this is consistent with how the characteristics of the environment play a key role in influencing helping behavior. He further notes that the size of the place where one was raised has less to do with helping than does the place where one currently lives. In Levine's words, "Brazilians and New Yorkers are both more likely to offer help in Ipanema than they are in Manhattan" (p. 232).

*Mood.* Have you ever had the experience of a resident assistant or some other leader at your school calling a meeting with the students and serving pizza or other snacks before the meeting begins? You smell the scrumptious pizza or popcorn; you enjoy the taste of the food, talk casually with friends, and the next thing you know, you are signing up for some arduous volunteer effort in a remote part of the city. How does this happen? Early studies investigating a possible relationship between mood and helping referred to the *warm-glow hypothesis,* which basically proposes that people who feel good are more likely to help others due to their jubilant mood. Elevated mood was manipulated by such variables as giving subjects success experiences (Berkowitz & Conner, 1966; Isen, 1970), giving them cookies and enabling them to find a dime (the cost of a call) in the phone booth (Isen & Levine, 1972). (Do keep in mind that these studies were done well before cell phones existed, when most everyone used payphones and it was a happy day indeed if one found a dime in the coin return slot.)

Miller (2009) notes that later studies of the effect of finding a dime did not replicate the effects that Isen and Levine had found. Nevertheless, Miller suggests that we not dismiss the effect of good mood on helping altogether. He cites the research of Baron (1997), for example, who found that mall shoppers who were exposed to pleasant smells outside of stores like Mrs. Field's Cookies and Cinnabon were more likely to help a stranger make change for a dollar than were shoppers who were outside of clothing stores where no smell was present. Manucia, Bauman and Cialdini (1984) additionally found that subjects in a positive mood were less concerned with whether helping would maintain or increase their positive mood state.

Batson et al. (1979) further investigated why good mood increases the chances of helping. They proposed that good mood results in a general activation of behavior. In other words, good mood may increase our interest and willingness to do all sorts of things, not just offer help. In their study, Batson et al. elevated half of the subjects' mood by having them find a dime in the coin slot of the payphone (apparently, a popular method back then for enhancing mood without drugs). Subjects whose mood had been enhanced were not only more willing to help, but also were more willing to take an opportunity to acquire more general information about various topics. Think of a time when you have received wonderful news then felt elated and ready to help almost anyone. Be careful what you agree to when you are in a good mood!

If positive mood helps to increase helping behavior, does negative mood *decrease* helping? Or is it possible that people who are experiencing a negative mood might actually increase helping in order to help elevate their mood? This depends on several things, say the researchers, including the nature of the task. Several studies have found that negative mood can increase helping if the task is pleasant, but not if it is unpleasant (Isen & Simmonds, 1978; Forest, Clark, Mills & Isen, 1979; Shaffer & Graziano, 1983). Cunningham, Steinberg and Grey (1980) found that negative mood increased helping only if increased emphasis was placed on the subject's responsibility to help. Positive mood, by contrast, increased helping when the positive outcomes for the victim were emphasized instead of the responsibility of the subject to help.

Other authors (e.g., Cialdini, Kenrick & Baumann, 1982; Schaller & Cialdini, 1990) have further proposed the *negative-state relief model,* which states that one main reason we help others is to reduce sadness or other negative mood states. So, for example, helping can enhance our mood and otherwise have reinforcing consequences, all of which help us to feel better. Think of this possibility in your own life: have you ever felt sad or been in a bad mood and then, after helping someone out, found yourself feeling much better and happy that you had helped?

Mood does appear to affect helping. Generally, the research suggests that a good mood increases the chances of helping. The effects of a negative mood on helping are less clear. Those in a negative mood are more likely than are their happy peers to place more emphasis on the characteristics of the task requested (is it pleasant or unpleasant?) and on the nature of the perceived responsibility to help the other. As an important and interesting point, have you noticed how in the preceding discussions of possible motives for helping, the researchers frequently refer to motivations that are prompted by a significant amount of self-interest? This will be discussed in a later section.

*Empathy.* The capacity to "put yourself in someone else's shoes" is an important social skill that is related to helping behavior. Empathy usually includes such feelings as sympathy, compassion and tenderness. According to Batson (2009), empathy also includes feelings of distress or sadness *for* the person, as distinct from direct personal distress or sadness elicited by witnessing the person's suffering. A number of researchers (e.g., Batson, 1987, 1991; Dovidio, Allen & Schroeder, 1990; Eisenberg & Miller, 1987) have suggested that empathy is an integral part of what motivates people to help. Batson et al.'s (1991, 1998) *empathy-altruism hypothesis* proposes that empathic concern most often produces an altruistic motivation.

Since empathy is so often linked to the likelihood of helping, researchers have naturally been interested in what factors help elicit empathy for another's plight. One significant factor is *perspective-taking,* which as you have read, is the ability to imagine another's situation and especially to imagine the others' feelings in that situation. In numerous studies, increasing subjects' perspective-taking toward a person who is suffering has consistently increased both empathic concern as well as helping behavior (Coke, Batson & McDavis, 1978; Davis, 1999). Despite all the research emphasis on empathy, Eisenberg and Strayer (1987) noted that empathy does not necessarily result in prosocial behavior. "The relationship between the two is neither direct nor inevitable" (p. 11).

Despite the appeal of the empathy-altruism hypothesis, a number of researchers have argued that the ability to take another's perspective is self-centered insofar as it fails to distinguish self from the other. In other words, if one "feels the other's pain," then alleviating that pain is analogous to relieving one's own (Cialdini et al., 1997). Maner et al. (2002) further suggested that when controlling for other egoistic motivators (e.g., feelings of oneness and the relief of negative affect), empathy was not significantly related to higher levels of helping behavior. The researchers suggest that failure to find a consistent link between empathy and helping behavior supports the conclusion that there is no evidence of other-centered helping behavior.

*A Christian view of empathy and helping.* In the helping research, the main controversy regarding whether humans have the capacity for other-centered altruism has focused on whether the capacity to feel empathy for the person in need leads to this altruism. As just noted, several researchers suggest that if increased empathy, especially in the form of perspective-taking, does not significantly relate to increased helping, then other-centered altruism is not present (Cialdini et al., 1997; Maner et al., 2002). This debate regarding the capacity for other-centeredness in helping behavior continues in the field, and a CFR view of persons can help us to address apparent inconsistencies in this literature.

From a CFR perspective, the notion that empathy is a necessary requisite of other-centered altruism is insufficient. A Christian view of persons certainly recognizes the important role that empathy plays in social interactions, especially helping behavior. Nevertheless, from a Christian view, we help others because they are worth helping and need help (*compassion*), not just because we can identify with them (*empathy*). From the CFR view, compassion includes valuing the plight of another on the basis of the other's *personhood*, rather than their position or situation. People are of inherent value. This is an assumption that logically follows from a Christian view of persons, as Christ called for compassion, particularly to those who are disadvantaged. Though efforts at increasing altruism by increasing empathy can be helpful, efforts to increase compassion are likely to be more helpful (along with research that helps guide such efforts). This is because compassion can be exercised toward others even when we feel no connection to them.

In the helping literature, empathy is understood as a quality or ability that a person possesses or can obtain. In contrast, compassion is more a matter of choice or obedience. Certainly, compassion can, and often does, include empathic identification with the other. But ultimately, one does not have to have empathy, or even the ability to empathize, in order to act compassionately. A biblical understanding of compassion is thus applicable to a wider range of social situations (e.g., situations that involve highly dissimilar individuals) than is empathy.

As one colleague noted, current helping research is "conceptually constrained" when it equates empathy with other-centeredness. As noted above, compassion from a biblical view is based on an appreciation of the value and dignity of human life, and is not dependent on perspective-taking per se. Furthermore, the capacity to exercise compassion is an inherent part of our created being. It doesn't rely on one's ability to feel the other's pain, but rather to acknowledge that the pain is worthy of a response.

In fact, while traditionally compassion has not been a focus for social psychologists, there is more recent interest in this topic. Some (e.g., Gilbert, 2005) have identified compassion as feelings of concern and sympathy that prompt people with a desire to help others, especially those who are suffering. Much of this research, however, focuses on the connection between compassion and subjective well-being rather than on the relationship between compassion and helping behavior per se. From this view, compassion may feel good; from a Christian view, we still need to know if it will make you lay down your life for another person. From a biblical view, it isn't truly compassion unless you act on it (Jas 2:16).

Some research that looks at the relationship between compassion and altruism is done in collaboration with Buddhist ideas, which are based on the central tenet of the interconnectedness and interdependence of humankind. Wang (2005), for example, emphasizes the Buddhist view that "compassion is the feeling that arises from the realization of the deeper reality that we are all connected, we are all one" (p. 104). One such collaborative research project is seen on the website for Stanford University's Center for Compassion and Altruism Research and Education, which states that their mission is to "explore ways in which compassion and altruism can be cultivated within an individual as well as within the society on the basis of testable cognitive and affective training exercises."

How to operationally define compassion for research purposes remains a challenge. As happens with any intangible construct, researchers disagree about how best to define and measure compassion. From a Christian perspective, compassionate love "responds directly to the experience of the other as other" (Post, 2002). It is more about helping the other person than deriving benefit for the self. Consequently, the relationship between compassion and subjective well-being would not be an emphasis of this research, even though such secondary benefits often do occur when one demonstrates compassion. The focus would be more on what specific factors are related to the tendency to behave compassionately rather than on what one gets out of it.

## Who Is Most Likely to Offer Help?

*Gender.* Who helps others more: males or females? As noted by Kenrick et al. (2002), in over 90 percent of the countries surveyed, women are perceived as more helpful than men (Williams & Best, 1990). But the real answer to this question about the relationship between gender and helping is complicated. Over the last decades, much research has demonstrated contradictory results. For example, Salminen and Glad (1992) report that in some studies men helped others more than did women, while in other studies women helped more often than did men. Other studies have found no significant gender differences in helping behavior (Benson, Karabenick & Lerner, 1976). Meanwhile, the U.S. Bureau of Labor Statistics notes that women's rate of volunteering increased between 2008 and 2009, while men's rate of volunteering stayed the same.

In trying to understand the apparent inconsistencies in the data, Eagly and Crowley (1986) conducted a meta-analytic review of over 170 studies in the helping literature to assess if there was a significant sex difference in helping behaviors. They reviewed these studies within the framework of their *social-role theory*, which proposes that men and women are greatly influenced by sociocultural norms to assume specific sorts of roles. In terms of helping behavior, Eagly and Crowley suggest that society places a greater pressure on males to help in more heroic, valiant and chivalrous ways, while women are more encouraged to help in ways that are consistent with family caretaking roles.

Because social psychological studies of helping have generally been confined to short-term encounters with strangers, the social-role theory predicted that men should help more than women, and women should receive more help than men. This is because helping strangers is more consistent with the heroic helping emphasis that males receive, whereas women are more encouraged to help within the context of close personal relationships. Consistent with the chivalrous and heroic acts supported by the male gender role, Eagly and Crowley (1986) found that men were indeed more helpful than women to the extent that women perceived helping as more dangerous than men did and an audience witnessed the helping act. The chivalry analysis also suggested that men should direct their helping acts more toward women than men. In general, women received more help than did men.

Thus, gender seems to be most related to the type of helping as opposed to helping per se. Consider the different roles men and women have traditionally played in the helping professions. For example, consider the gender ratios of firefighters versus nurses. In general it seems that strong men are the average "good Samaritans" who perform heroic acts of helping, while women are more inclined to be helpers within the context of family and other close relationships. Eagly and Crowley (1986) suggest that future research examine the extent to which these sex differences in helping are a function of actual physical differences such as upper body strength versus a function of social norms and pressures.

Other researchers have provided support for the notion that different social expectations of males and females is related to the type of helping they each give. For example, who would you guess tends to give more roadside assistance to people with car trouble? Some research (e.g., Gaertner & Bickman, 1971) suggests that it is men, even when the help needed is a simple phone call for assistance. It will be interesting to see what happens to gender differences in helping behaviors as society continues to encourage both men and women to take on roles more traditionally associated with the opposite gender (e.g., stay-at-home dads, female firefighters).

*Social exchange theory.* As you have no doubt noticed in much of the preceding discussion, many social psychologists have investigated the various ways in which people assess how much helping will cost them relative to how much they think they can receive in return. *Social exchange theory* (Blau, 1964), originally offered as an economics theory, proposes that human interactions are transactions that aim to maximize one's rewards and minimize one's costs. In other words, people tend to want an equitable exchange for their efforts. Within the context of helping, this theory would propose that both the likelihood of helping another and the type of helping that one is willing to do are contingent on the potential helper's assessment of how much they will get in return for how much effort they put forth. Basically, this theory proposes that in many instances we conduct a cost-benefit analysis to help us decide whether or not to help.

One way in which potential helpers assess how much helping will cost them is related to experienced time pressures. Research suggests that in general, the more pressed someone is for time, the less likely they are to help another. A classic study that illustrates this point was conducted in 1973 by Darley and Batson. The researchers used an analogy of the story of the good Samaritan (Lk 10:25-37) and helping in real-life circumstances. Recall that in the story of the good Samaritan, a wounded man is passed up on a roadside by both a priest and a Levite (revered by the audience) and is ultimately helped by a Samaritan (disparaged by the audience). Darley and Batson were interested in exploring whether situational factors such as time pressure and personal factors such as religiosity (intrinsic vs. extrinsic) affected propensity to help. They recruited and paid seminary students to prepare either a talk about seminary jobs or a talk about the story of the good Samaritan. The researcher varied the urgency of the task by telling the subjects in one condition that they were late for the next task; in the other condition subjects were told that they had a few minutes before the talk began, but they should head on over anyway.

On the way to the room across campus, all subjects passed by a man in an alleyway who was slumped in a doorway, moaning and coughing as they walked by. Researchers assessed which subjects offered help on a scale that included various levels of helping, such as failing to even notice the victim as in need, perceiving the need but not offering help, offering indirect help by telling the experimenter's aide upon arrival to the room across campus, asking the man if he needed help, and ultimately refusing to leave the man, insisting on taking him somewhere for help.

The results indicated that the most significant factor affecting the likelihood of helping was time pressure. Isn't it ironic that even when consciously thinking about a helping norm (in this case, the good Samaritan idea of social responsibility), the subjects were not more inclined to help if they were in a hurry? And these were seminary students, whom we could reasonably presume had studied that story before and were probably more aware than is the average person about its relevance to real-life helping. Alas, the realities of a hurried existence!

*An altruistic personality?* You have surely noticed in your own interactions with others that some people are consistently kinder, more compassionate, more helpful and more willing to sacrifice for others. For this reason, a number of researchers have explored the idea of an altruistic personality that encompasses such characteristics (Krebs & Von Hesteren, 1992; Oliner & Oliner, 1988; Rushton, 1980, 1981, 1984; Staub, 1974). Jeffries (1998) proposes that the concept of virtue can be useful in our understanding of the altruistic personality. He considers five primary virtues: temperance, fortitude, justice, charity and prudence. Jeffries reviews the evidence, which he argues indicates a possible relationship between each of the virtues and altruistic behavior. The virtues are presented as the personality structure underlying altruistic motivation and behavior.

Despite how logical it may seem that an altruistic personality exists, there is intense debate centering on the degree to which behavior is the result of a consistent trait of altruism. A number of scholars (e.g., Kohn, 1990; Oliner and Oliner, 1988; Eisenberg et al., 1999) are strong advocates of the idea that an altruistic personality style does exist. Central to their thinking is the notion that this type of personality is deeply rooted in childhood and is generally reinforced over the course of the entire life through modeling and practice.

As Eisenberg and Strayer (1987) argued, the development of empathy, or a "sharing of affect," is a chief distinction of the altruistic personality type. In addition, this personality style includes the ability to connect with others in meaningful ways. Daloz, Keen, Keen and Parks (1996) studied 100 individuals whose lives demonstrate a "commitment to the common good." They found one common thread in the life experience of everyone they studied, and they called this "a constructive engagement with otherness." By this they meant an awareness of and sensitivity to a common humanity. This includes encounters or interactions with others who are in some way different from one's family or tribe. Also characteristic of at least half of the individuals in this study was that they had a parental figure who was a mentor and example of concern for others in the wider community.

Kerber and Wren (1982) also investigated the relationship between altruistic personality and reported intentions to help. They used descriptions of situations in which a person was asking for different kinds of help. A sample of 132 college students indicated the amount of help they would provide in each situation and rated the perceived costs and rewards of providing help. They found that highly altruistic subjects viewed identical situations as more rewarding and less costly than did persons low in altruism. Thus, the researchers conclude, it is possible that perceptions of the social situation differ as a function of how naturally altruistic one's personality is.

*Religiosity.* All the major world religions have the concept of prosocial behavior as a key component of their tradition. Such prosocial behavior includes things such as forgiveness, peaceful resolution of conflict and, of course, helping others. Furthermore, as noted by Saroglou et al. (2005), almost all psychological theories of religion assume that religion contributes to prosocial behavior. In numerous self-report studies, religious people perceive themselves as prosocial and helpful (e.g., Batson, Schoenrade & Ventis, 1993). But do they actually behave in prosocial ways? Here the findings are a bit mixed. Some early studies (e.g., Nelson & Dynes, 1976) found that religiosity was significantly related to altruistic behaviors as well as attitudes that demonstrated a social responsibility orientation. Yet other studies (e.g., Glock, Ringer & Babbie, 1967) found that there was no relationship between church attendance and likelihood of charitable acts.

How do we make sense of these contradictory findings? As it turns out, finding whether or not religious people tend toward prosocial behavior depends on a number of factors. In large part, it depends on the specific type of religiosity measured. As you may recall from the racism and prejudice chapter, *intrinsic* religiosity refers to internalized religious affiliation, *extrinsic* religiosity refers to religion as a means to an end (e.g., to gain social approval), and a *quest* religious style refers to a process of questioning and openness to a variety of religious ideas. Another factor that affects the results of research regarding the relationship between religiosity and helping has to do with the type of experimental methodology used (self-report vs. quasi-experimental), the specific sort of helping entailed (e.g., spontaneous vs. planned) and the type of person who needs help (familiar other or stranger).

One example of the importance of the aforementioned factors was illustrated in a study by Hansen, Vandenberg and Patterson (1995). They investigated whether the type of religiosity (intrinsic vs. quest orientation) was related to the type of helping (spontaneous vs. planned volunteering). They asked seventy college students to fill out religiosity scales and also to indicate what sorts of volunteer work they had engaged in (planned helping). Spontaneous helping was assessed by the subjects' responses to a confederate's request for help on a task. Subjects with a quest religious orientation responded more to spontaneous requests for help, while the subjects who adopted an intrinsic religious orientation reported higher levels of volunteering, or nonspontaneous helping. Wilson and Musick (1997) likewise found a positive relationship between likelihood of volunteering and religiosity.

Another study investigating the relationship between religiosity and helping was conducted by Nelson and Dynes (1976). They explored the impact of religious devotion and attendance at religious services on a variety of helping behaviors. The researchers mailed a questionnaire to a sample of adult male residents in a city that had recently been struck by a tornado. The subjects were asked three questions to determine their level of devotion: How often are table prayers said at mealtimes in your home? How often do you pray privately or only with your wife (excluding mealtimes)? How important is prayer in your life? Respondents were also asked how frequently they attended church and to rate their level of religious commitment. The subjects' responses to these questions were then compared with their involvement in both "ordinary" helping behaviors (helping motorists with car trouble, etc.) and emergency helping behaviors (providing relief goods for tornado victims and performing disaster relief services unrelated to regular employment). The researchers found that devotionalism, church attendance and level of religious commitment were positively correlated with levels of helping behavior, both in routine and emergency situations.

Saroglou (2006) discusses an interesting inconsistency in the helping research. While religious people tend to describe themselves as prosocial in studies using self-report measures, when you look at quasi-experimental social psychological studies, there is not a significant effect for religiosity in terms of increased likelihood of helping. Spilka et al. (2003) state that the dominant conclusion in psychology of religion is therefore that (intrinsically) religious people may only *appear* to be helpful and prosocial; in reality they are more preoccupied with their positive self-perception rather than with the needs of others (Batson, Schoenrade & Ventis, 1993). According to this view, religious people are thus "moral hypocrites."

Saroglou et al. (2005) review further research that has also demonstrated that when dealing with people who are perceived as threatening their values (e.g., homosexuals), many religious people—including intrinsically religious types (Batson et al., 1999), religious fundamentalists (Jackson & Esses 1997) and people high in quest religiosity (Batson et al., 2001; Goldfried & Miner, 2002)—are not willing to help targets perceived as representing out-groups. In fact, they are even rather discriminating against them. So, how do we interpret this inconsistency: Are religious people really helpful or not? Are we to conclude that, when it comes to prosocial behavior, religious people are "moral hypocrites," saying one thing but doing another?

Saroglou et al. (2005) further expand on this question by noting that religious people are not necessarily moral hypocrites when they report that they are prosocial. Across four studies the researchers found that religious people were less likely to respond with aggression in response to daily hassles. Similarly, religious subjects were not significantly inclined to respond with aggression or discrimination toward others who were dissimilar to them. In addition, the religious individuals' responses to the self-report measures of helping were consistent with the reports of friends who also rated the subjects. Both of these ratings suggested that religious people were in reality quite helpful.

## SOCIAL NORMS FOR HELPING

Since all cultures have established that helping is a virtue, they have developed ways to ensure that this message gets across. These messages are compelling enough so that we see the continuation of helping, albeit in different forms, across cultures as well as across time. So while it is no longer customary for a man to throw his cloak on a wet street so that his female companion can cross without getting her shoes dirty, various forms of chivalrous helping behavior still exist (although, as some women lament, not enough!). In this next section let us look at two

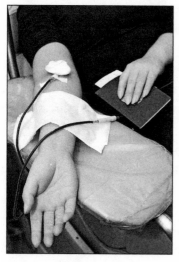

norms related to helping that are believed to be learned through example and instruction.

*Reciprocity norm.* You are no doubt familiar with the concept that you should help those people who have helped you in the past. Sociologist Alvin Gouldner (1960) noted that the idea of "paying back" those who have helped you is a concept that has existed all throughout history. He suggested that a norm of reciprocity is universal and consists of two interrelated, minimal demands: (1) people should help those

who have helped them, and (2) people should not injure those who have helped them. Gouldner further notes that one implication of this norm is that those whom you have helped have an obligation to help you. So, if you want to be helped by others you must help them. Gouldner claims that the norm of reciprocity both helps to maintain a social system once it is in place and also may be what he called a "starting mechanism." That is, as a new social system is forming (e.g., a group), the norm helps to initiate social interaction in the early phases of certain groups before they have developed a set of mutual duties.

The norm of reciprocity has been studied using many different sorts of circumstances, such as expected equity in exchange of personal information (Chaikin & Derlega, 1974). Burger et al. (1997) also found that the norm of reciprocity is affected by the length of time since a favor was done. They found that the obligation to return favors diminishes as the amount of time between the initial favor and the opportunity to reciprocate grows. Participants in the first experiment were given an opportunity to return a favor either five minutes or one week after receiving a free soft drink from a confederate. Participants in the five-minute condition agreed to the confederate's request to deliver an envelope across campus significantly more often than did control group participants receiving only the request (and no free soft drink). However, participants in the one-week condition showed no significant reciprocity effect. In other words, the fact that one week had passed since the request was made seemed to diminish the subjects' sense of obligation to comply with a request, regardless of whether or not the other person had previously done a favor for them. Participants in the second experiment were given hypothetical scenarios in which the length of time to return a favor was varied. These subjects generally reported that they would be less likely to return a favor as the length of time since the favor increased.

*Social responsibility norm.* Another reason for helping is the cultural expectation that we have a moral obligation to help others who really need it, regardless of whether they are able to pay us back someday or if the cost of helping might be significant (Berkowitz & Daniels, 1964; Schwartz, 1975). It is interesting to note that this *social responsibility norm* may be related to the just-world hypothesis noted earlier this chapter. Specifically, some studies have suggested that people feel a sense of responsibility to help a person who is needy to the extent that the person's situation is considered to be not self-imposed. Cialdini and Trost (1998) further suggest that this external social responsibility norm for helping is more likely to increase actual helping behavior to the extent that it coincides with personal norms for helping, which are part of an individual's internalized values.

### OBEDIENCE AS OTHER-CENTEREDNESS

Typically, adherence or obedience to a social norm for helping has not been emphasized in the literature as a possible form of other-centered altruism. And yet the potential for social norms to increase helping is well documented. Some researchers (e.g., Kohn, 1990) note that helping does not imply empathy and may be a response to an internalized moral code or directive from an authority figure. Post (2002) notes that altruism can stem from a rational sense of duty instead of from a genuine care and love for the other. This thinking suggests that if a person is following some social norm for helping (e.g., the social responsibility norm), then the motive is not other-centered. In contrast, from the CFR view, obedience can be a primary way in which other-centered helping is manifested, both in terms of one's relationship with God and with others.

Numerous New Testament Scriptures call us to other-centered behaviors, most often as a matter of choice. For example, the story of the good Samaritan (Lk 10:25-37), which has often been used as an example in the helping literature, demonstrates God's command of a universal care for others. In this passage, Christ commands us to "love your neighbor as yourself." There are times when one may exhibit such behavior as a matter of obedience, even in the absence of either empathy or compassion. Would this behavior then be other-centered or simply compliant? The CFR view suggests that this behavior may also be considered other-centered altruism because it still requires the submission of one's own interests. In the case of a voluntary act of obedience to God's command to "love one another . . . as I have loved you" (Jn 13:34), the individual's response represents, at least in part, a willingness to submit personal interests to the authority of Christ. In this case, the object of one's other-centeredness is God. In a similar fashion, one's obedience to a social norm of altruism could still be other-centered insofar as it represents an acknowledgment of the need to place the interests of the other first. Thus, arguably, both examples of obedience can be considered legitimate components of other-centered altruism, as they both urge the person to extend the focus away from their own interests to those that are for a greater good.

### How Can We Increase Helping Behavior?

*Information.* Some studies have focused on the importance of making people more aware of the factors that tend to inhibit helping, such as perceived dissimilarity or the just-world hypothesis. Beaman et al. (1978), for example, found that subjects were significantly more likely to help a victim later on if they had received information on how the bystander effect can tend to decrease helping. Some studies have found that just talking about helping can increase the tendency to help another. For example, Macrae and Johnston (1998) showed that even a subtle manipulation, such as priming subjects with words related to helping, significantly increased the probability that those subjects would later help a confederate who had dropped a pen.

*Prosocial role models.* As noted earlier, a number of researchers have demonstrated that role models such as parents, mentors, educators and peers can be a powerful influence on modeling altruism (Oliner & Oliner, 1988; Eisenberg & Strayer, 1987). Interestingly, even witnessing complete strangers act in a helpful manner can be enough to prompt some people to help another. For example, in an earlier study, Bryan and Test (1967) showed that L.A. drivers were far more likely to offer help to a female driver with a flat tire if a quarter of a mile earlier they had witnessed someone else helping another woman change a tire. Rushton and Campbell (1977) similarly found that British students were more likely to donate blood if they had just seen a confederate agree to donate blood.

*Reducing ambiguity.* Remember the previous discussion regarding the difficulty of assessing whether a situation is truly in need of help. For example, recall how hard it can sometimes be to discern whether something is a true emergency. Consider also the reality that many people would feel embarrassed if they tried to help in a situation where no help was really needed. After all, running across a restaurant to deliver the Heimlich maneuver to someone who was not really choking, but only laughing, would not really impress a date or a friend. Reducing the ambiguity of a situation by making clear the specific need for help can be a very effective approach for increasing helping. One way to reduce the ambiguity is related to a victim's response. For example, in one study by DeJong, Marber and Shaver (1980), people in a college library saw an experimenter drop a ten-dollar bill, which was then snatched up by a confederate who acted like a thief. Subjects were more likely to notify the victim of the theft when he appeared to know he was missing the cash. In this case, the researchers argued that the victim's actions served to more clearly define the situation as a theft for the subjects.

Batson (1987) also suggests that fostering a helpful self-concept can also increase the likelihood of helping. In addition, other researchers have noted that media efforts to teach norms related to helping can also have a positive effect.

## Complex Motives for Helping: *Two Views*

The research discussed so far exemplifies how complex are the many possible motives for helping. In addition to identifying which factors are most related to helping, at the heart of the helping research is the controversy regarding whether other-centered altruism really exists. One historical example may help us better understand the possible answer to this question.

In 1942, in the midst of war-torn Europe and the devastation and savagery of the Nazi regime, there was a twelve-year-old Jewish boy in Poland named Sam Oliner. The Nazis forced him and his family into the ghetto at Bobowa, which during WWII was made a "concentration village" where the Jews from the surrounding area were imprisoned and ultimately all killed. Several months later as the Nazis were evacuating the ghetto's residents for extermination, Sam managed to escape. He was taken in by a Polish peasant woman named Balwina, who disguised the boy's identity and found him a job. The rest of his family perished. Sam Oliner became a professor of sociology at Humboldt State University in California, and together with his wife, Pearl Oliner, he conducted an extensive study of altruism (Oliner & Oliner, 1988).

Westhues (1996) reviews the Oliners' study, which explored the differences between the thousands of non-Jews who risked their own lives to rescue Jews from the Holocaust from those who stood by and did nothing. How do people who risk personal disaster in order to help others, with no promise of reward, differ from people who do not? What kind of background or upbringing lends itself to altruism? To this end, the Oliners interviewed over 400 German, Polish, Italian, Dutch and French Gentiles whose actions of rescue had been authenticated by Jerusalem's Yad Vashem authority, which is the Holocaust Martyrs' and Heroes' Remembrance Authority. They also interviewed a sample of 126 bystanders, or nonrescuers, a sample matched with the first by age, sex, education and geographic location during the war.

The Oliners found that when compared to bystanders, rescuers were more likely to have experienced close interactions with people different from themselves in social class and religion. Rescuers were more likely to have grown up with Jewish friends and neighbors. The rescuers' ability to empathize, which the Oliners believe was nourished by the diversity of friendships, extended also to Gypsies and people richer or poorer than themselves. Rescuers were also more likely to have come from close, loving families where discipline was based on talking and reasoning as opposed to physical punishment. Rescuers reported having learned the value of caring from their parents. In contrast, bystanders were more likely than rescuers to report having learned values of obedience and economic competence. In terms of their formal religious backgrounds, rescuers and nonrescuers differed little, and the degree of parental religiosity did not differ significantly between the two groups. Rescuers were, however, significantly more likely than nonrescuers to describe themselves as religious.

The Oliners concluded that the rescuers had more of what they call *extensivity*, which is the extension of self to include others, attachment to others and a sense of responsibility for others' welfare. Rescuers showed more trust in people generally, thought more highly both of themselves and of others, and were disinclined to exclude others from the community. Bystanders, on the other hand, had led more constricted lives, and they reserved a sense of obligation to a small circle of people.

Were the rescuers a unique group of people in their ability to extend themselves so much to others? The Oliners conclude that the rescuers were ordinary people, consisting of farmers, teachers, factory workers, entrepreneurs, both single and married folk, Protestants, Catholics, and so forth. Most had done nothing extraordinary before the war nor afterward, and were distinguished only by their sense of connection with others and their commitment to care. Consequently, the Oliners propose that the ability to care deeply about fellow humans is something that can be cultivated in the average person, even though such caring could cost the individual greatly. According to the Oliners, this deep sense of social responsibility that extends broadly to fellow humans instead of to a narrow group of familiar others is possible to learn. In order for this to occur, they propose that homes and schools should model a wide diversity of caring relationships.

Such a story and many others like it certainly have the capacity to inspire hope in the human potential for self-sacrificial caring and helping behaviors. These heroic stories could also help us to consider everyday examples of caring and helping that involve a significant amount of personal sacrifice. On that basis, one might even be persuaded to conclude, consistent with a Christian view of persons, that humans were indeed created with the capacity to genuinely care beyond personal self-interest, to demonstrate compassionate love that is not ultimately or primarily self-focused. But what do social psychologists generally conclude?

First let's review how the term *altruism* is used in the literature. Simmons (1991) notes that although definitions of the term vary across studies, most consider the concept to include the following characteristics:

- it seeks to increase another's welfare, not one's own

- it is voluntary

- it is intentional

- it expects no external reward

Within the social psychological literature, there are a variety of opinions regarding altruism. In general, there are two main streams of thought, often associated with the terms *egoism* (self-interest) and *altruism* (other-centered interest). The first, which is the predominant perspective in social psychology, suggests that altruism ultimately has a self-interested motivation, either in the form of social advantage, self-preservation or survival of one's genes (e.g., Burnstein, Crandall & Kitayama, 1997; Cialdini et al., 1997; Essock-Vitale & McGuire, 1985; Hamilton, 1964; Kruger, 2003; Shavit, Fischer & Koresh, 1994; Trivers, 1971). The second main line of thinking with regard to altruism proposes that, as noted by Sober and Wilson (1998), "people sometimes care about the welfare of others as an end in itself. Altruists have irreducible other-directed ends." (p. 228). This perspective maintains that while there are certainly instances in which humans have ulterior, self-interested motives for helping, it is genuinely possible for humans to care about another and to help without any expectation of benefits to the self. Let's look at both of these assumptions regarding altruism in more detail.

***Naturalism and helping.*** The naturalist perspective on helping typically involves egoism as an ultimate motive for helping. As noted earlier, emphasis is placed on immediate/proximal motives such as social or personal advantage in addition to distal motives such as self-preservation or preservation of one's genetic heritage. Theorists working from both a naturalist and evolutionary approach have considered helping behavior of interest especially because it typically involves the helper's incurring a cost while resulting in a benefit to the recipient. From this view, since helping can risk an individual's life or some aspect of well-being, there must be other possible gains for the helper. This is why we continue to see fairly high levels of helping behaviors among humans (e.g. Schroeder, Penner, Dovidio & Piliavin, 1995) as well as among other species (e.g. Dugatkin, 1997).

Given that helping is often not advantageous for either the survival or the reproductive advantage of the helper, evolutionary theorists have proposed two main explanations for helping. These are known as inclusive fitness and reciprocal altruism. *Inclusive fitness* refers to the process by which an organism's "success" is dependent on leaving behind the maximum number of replicas of its genes within a population (Hamilton, 1964). The term *inclusive fitness* is derived from this idea that a person's evolutionary fitness is in part measured by how "included" their genes remain in the population. So, as noted by McGuire (2003), even if a particular helping situation endangers an individual's survival or reproductive advantage, this self-sacrificing altruism can still perpetuate the helper's genes as long as the recipient shares some of the helper's genes by common descent. So if a parent sacrifices their own life for that of their child, this self-sacrificing altruism is helping to ensure the parent's own genetic "survival" by leaving behind their child, who of course carries the parents' genes.

But what if a person helps an unrelated other? In this case, there is no inclusive fitness gain for the helper because the recipient cannot carry on the unrelated other's genes. Evolutionary theorists then propose a second major motive for helping: *reciprocity.* From this perspective, individuals who are helped are more likely to be available and willing to reciprocate the help later. Thus, the helper gains potential benefits by helping others because he or she is more likely to be helped later on when needed. As McGuire (2003) notes, biological reciprocity models (e.g., Axelrod, 1984; Trivers, 1971) usually include two main assumptions. The first of these is that the benefit to the recipient must exceed the cost to the helper. In other words, the effort put out to help the other must be less than the actual results of helping the recipient. The second assumption of the biological reciprocity models is that helper and recipient recognize each other and have a high probability of future interactions. This is because if the helper expects reciprocity, then obviously the helper and the one helped should be able to interact with each other in the future.

Alexander (1979) also notes that there could be "indirect reciprocity" in cases where there are multiple group members. In those cases, it might not be the specific person whom you helped that would help you back, but the expectation would be that some other person in the same group would. So, for example, if you helped the elderly parent of a friend, you might expect that either that friend or someone else in her family would help you in the future. In this way, your helping was advantageous for you.

But, as McGuire (2003) notes, there are several problems when one considers only inclusive fitness models and reciprocity as the motivators of helping behavior. For one, what about when helping is done by an anonymous stranger? This happens fairly commonly, and from the perspective of both inclusive fitness and reciprocity models, helping strangers who are not related to you and who are not likely to help you in the future is not evolutionarily advantageous. Second, what about instances in which the helper decides to offer aid even when she experiences an immediate cost without any promise or certainty of a future benefit? In order to address these seeming inconsistencies, McGuire proposes that the biological models of altruism must also take into account social cognitive strategies that people use.

These cognitive strategies on the part of the helper essentially distort the cost-benefit analysis in a way that makes it seem favorable for the helper in terms of cost and favorable to the recipient in terms of benefit. So McGuire proposes that it is not just the actual circumstances themselves that we perceive on some level to be advantageous to us for helping. It is also that in circumstances where it seems that it would be evolutionarily disadvantageous for us to help, we somehow cognitively distort the situation to convince ourselves that we have not really done all that much to help and that the recipient's benefits far outweigh the efforts we put into helping them. From this perspective, we still feel that we have not jeopardized our survival or reproductive advantage even though technically we may have.

McGuire (2003) conducted two studies in which she tested what she called the *cognitively enhanced evolutionary model*. Specifically, she looked at how helpers use specific cognitive processes to "fake" themselves into believing that a helpful act was not as costly as it actually was. One of those cognitive processes is what she calls "discounting the labor of love." This strategy is especially relevant when we help relatives, and it involves perceiving helping behavior as less costly as the relationship between parties becomes increasingly close. This "discounting labor of love" cognitive bias would tend to maintain high levels of helping particularly in closer relationships where it is most needed and most likely to be reciprocated. The "labor of love" cognitive distortions of costs and benefits would tend to enhance frequency of helping among familiars, where helping opportunities would be most frequent. So if you help out Uncle Mario for several years, according to this model you would likely convince yourself that you are not actually exerting that much effort. After all, remember that Uncle Mario is related to you and thus is part of your genetic heritage.

A second cognitive bias is known as the *modesty bias*. Say you are the helper. In this case, the modesty bias would involve judging your helping behaviors as less costly to you and less beneficial to the recipient. This would make it seem like you have not really put out all that much energy, and the other person didn't really benefit all that much from what you did ("It was nothing at all"). But say you are the receiver of help. In this case the modesty bias would predict that you would perceive the other's help as a really big deal and you would estimate that you have benefited greatly from their efforts. So it would make it seem like you had come out ahead. But then again, you the recipient would likely feel indebted, and due to the human need to preserve equity, this sense of indebtedness would perpetuate helping behavior (e.g. Walster, Berscheid & Walster, 1973).

In McGuire's study, the modesty bias was found in both men and women and in all three relationships (close friends, acquaintances and strangers). McGuire notes that the modesty bias cannot be explained solely as a way of cementing close relationships because it occurs also between acquaintances and even strangers, suggesting that the modesty bias is a mechanism by which helping may be extended to strangers in modern urban societies (McGuire, 1989). For researchers using a naturalist approach, cognitive processes like the modesty and "labor of love" discounting biases make sense, given the high incidence of helping behavior in human society, for the helping of anonymous strangers (which is insufficiently explained by biological models), and for how the individual helper is motivated to incur an immediate certain cost for a delayed uncertain benefit. McGuire calls for further research and is quick to add that her studies have not provided conclusive evidence for the idea that natural selection shaped the modesty effect or the discounting "labor of love" relationship. Indeed, if these cognitive distortions do exist, it is not clear the degree to which they are causal agents in helping or the results of helping.

Other researchers have focused their efforts on trying to provide a naturalistic explanation for the finding that generally, feelings of empathy are likely to lead a person to help another (Coke, Batson & McDavis, 1978; Eisenberg & Miller, 1987). While at first glance empathic concern seems like a selfless motive, from the naturalist perspective, empathic concern feels distressing to an individual, and that distress prompts the individual to help the victim in order to reduce that uncomfortable feeling (Hoffman, 1981). Remember the negative-state relief model noted earlier? According to this perspective, benefiting the victim is thus simply a means to a self-serving end.

Cialdini et al. (1997) have alternately proposed that it is not empathy per se that motivates helping, but rather what they call the sense of self-other overlap, or "oneness" between the helper and the individual in need. From this perspective, helping others with whom one feels commonality would not be selfless, because it leads to a more favorable mental state. Nevertheless, studies examining whether the effect of empathic concern can be eliminated when the sense of oneness with the target, or "self-other overlap," is accounted for have produced contradictory results (Batson et al., 1997; Cialdini et al., 1997).

Overall the naturalist approach emphasizes the importance of self-seeking goals as the ultimate and primary motivators of helping behavior. Altruism is thus necessarily seen as the result of greater or lesser egoistic motives. Even what appears to be an other-centered empathic concern or compassionate action is really ultimately self-centered. This view is currently the dominant one in the field. Now let us consider a different perspective, which assumes that people are indeed capable of more genuine other-centered helping.

*Altruism as other-centeredness.* There are some researchers who, regardless of their perspective on evolutionary explanations of human social behavior, still maintain that there is the possibility for individuals to feel genuine empathy and other-centered concern that is not ultimately about self-interest. One major contributor to this way of thinking is social psychologist Daniel Batson (1991). According to Batson, those who favor the idea that altruism as genuine other-centeredness does exist generally admit that evolutionary theories have been useful in revealing how self-sacrificial behavior can be consistent with the theory of natural selection. However, advocates for altruism are more concerned with the driving mental motivation of the helper. Batson's empathy-altruism hypothesis was noted earlier in this chapter. Recall that according to this model, when we feel empathy for a person, we will often attempt to help for altruistic reasons. Batson (1990) argues that there is a significant amount of evidence that suggests that, contrary to the naturalist assumption that humans are fundamentally and ultimately egoists, we are actually capable of caring for the welfare of others for the sake of the other and not simply as a more or less subtle way of caring for our own welfare. Thus, from Batson's view, we are not simply social egoists.

Studies comparing the egoistic and altruistic motives for helping have addressed specific egoistic motives such as the relief of personal distress, reducing sadness, increasing a happy mood and escaping public shame for not helping (Batson & Shaw, 1991). These studies have varied whether individuals can only obtain such egoistic goals by helping, or whether they can escape from the situation and obtain the same egoistic goals without helping. The results of those studies suggest that at least some people have helping intentions that are not explained by egoistic motivations (Batson et al., 1989; Batson et al., 1991; Batson, Early & Salvarani, 1997). For example, in one study investigating egoistic versus altruistic motives for helping, Toi and Batson (1982) had students listen to a taped interview with a student who had allegedly broken both legs in an accident and was getting behind in classes. Two factors were manipulated: empathy and the cost of helping. Empathic concern was manipulated by instructions given to participants to either imagine how the victim felt or not. The cost of helping was manipulated by whether or not the injured student was expected to be seen everyday once she returned to class. Consistent with the empathy-altruism hypothesis, subjects in the high empathy condition helped regardless of cost, while those in the low empathy condition helped only if the cost of not helping was high.

Despite the evidence for other-centered altruism, Batson (1990) insists that there are limits to our capacity to truly care for others. For example, though we care for others, we obviously also care for ourselves. In one study, Batson et al. (1983) exposed subjects to a confederate who was allegedly receiving electric shock. The researchers manipulated and assessed the amount of empathy the subjects felt for the "victim." When the cost of helping was high (taking high-level shocks that are "clearly painful but of course not harmful"), the motivation even of individuals who had previously reported high empathy for the person in need appeared to be egoistic, protecting the self. Batson thinks this is not all bad, especially given the realities of having to look out for ourselves in order just to survive.

Batson (1990) also notes that there are many other possible impediments to altruism. Consider the possible effects of dissimilarity between helper and victim and the self-absorption we can experience in some ongoing task. Regardless of these potential roadblocks to altruism, some researchers still maintain that the human capacity for other-centered empathic concern is significant. Like the Oliners mentioned earlier, Fagin-Jones and Midlarsky (2007) investigated what sorts of situational and personal character traits distinguished rescuers of Jews during the Holocaust. They found that rescuers were much more likely than bystanders to possess a high degree of sensitivity to the norm of social responsibility, altruistic moral reasoning and empathic concern. Thus, once again, there is evidence that people genuinely care for others, even when the cost of helping is quite high and the other person is not a relative or close friend.

## CHRISTIANITY AND ALTRUISM

As you can see from the discussions in this chapter, it can be difficult to assess whether humans have a genuine capacity for other-centered motives when helping. The CFR view may enhance our understanding of the rich complexity of helping, and specifically of altruistic behavior. As noted earlier in this chapter, one implication of a Christian view of persons includes an increased focus on compassion (as opposed to empathy) as an example of other-centered motives. Another implication of a Christian view, as noted in the section on cultural norms for helping, is an increased recognition of the valuable role that obedience can play as a legitimate other-centered motive for helping.

These two ideas about compassion and obedience demonstrate how a Christian view can generate research about a greater possible range of explanations for other-centered helping than can a naturalist view alone. Another contribution that a Christian view of persons can make to our understanding of helping behavior is related to the difficulty in assessing ultimate motives or goals for any social behavior. This is a problem that has been noted by numerous researchers. Remember that we do not really see what underlies a person's behavior, but rather infer from that person's behavior what may motivate it. In addition, it is also probably true that any single behavior could have a multitude of motivations, some selfish and some more other-centered. In that case, how can we really tell which is the ultimate goal: egoism or altruism?

Anyone can agree that selfish motives underlie a number of our seemingly altruistic acts. As Clary et al. (1998) have demonstrated, many volunteers, for example, dedicate a significant amount of personal time and effort over extended periods of time to help others. Yet while they may be truly helping others, the volunteers may also themselves experience potential benefits such as gaining increased experience that will help them in the job market, reducing loneliness or increasing positive mood. In fact, as Clary et al. noted, efforts to recruit volunteers based on the potential benefits to the volunteer are very effective. On that basis, how can we tell that people have any genuine other-centeredness?

As noted earlier, it is entirely logical if not essential for a researcher who maintains the naturalist approach to assume that egoist motives ultimately underlie all social behavior, including altruistic acts toward related and unrelated others (Dawkins, 1976; McAndrew, 2002; Rushton, 1991, as cited in Myers, 2005). Many researchers, for example, would agree with Barber (2004), who writes: "Kindness exists, but it struggles to stay afloat on an ocean of cruelty that is the default condition for organisms competing for existence on this planet" (p. 9). To focus so much on egoistic motives is to neglect what Batson and Shaw (1991) call the *pluralism* of motives, which includes other-centered concern. They argue that psychology's focus on finding the most concise theories may impede our ability to explain helping behavior. Specifically, Batson and Shaw suggest that psychology's focus on egoism as an ultimate motive for altruism has not been successful in explaining the majority of data. Thus, in this case, the most concise model, which includes only egoism, must be extended to include other possible motives that may facilitate an explanation of the mixed motives for helping.

This idea of a pluralism of motives is consistent with a Christian view of persons that sees humans as created by God to live in other-centered community. Since the CFR approach proposes that God has created humans to have a capacity for concern not only for those who are similar to themselves or are otherwise related, but also for humankind in general, it is not surprising that research findings provide contradictory results with regard to whether or not empathy is greatest for related others. For example, some studies (e.g., Cialdini et al., 1997; Kruger, 2003) have not found any positive relationship between kinship and empathy, while other studies (e.g., Rushton, 1991) did find this relationship. Furthermore, the finding that people often help strangers with whom they do not expect to have future interactions also presents a significant challenge to a purely naturalist approach, because the expectation of reciprocity is generally not possible in such circumstances.

Researchers who allow for other-centeredness as one of a possible number of motives for helping could develop models that would broaden the range of possible ways to conceptualize other-centeredness. Recall from the earlier discussion that compassion and obedience could be part of this broader understanding of other-centered altruism.

What can be said regarding the finding that helping elevates mood (Seligman, 2003)? Is the improved mood, then, necessarily the ultimate self-serving motive for helping? Maybe so, but what if it were also true that feeling good often accompanies moving *toward* other-centeredness? In other words, what if helping is one of the ways in which we move toward the goodness that God intended for us, and what if one of the possible consequences of engaging in such behaviors is an elevated mood? From this perspective, feeling good after doing good is not necessarily primarily self-centered, but rather one of the beneficial results of living in other-centered community, thus drawing closer to God. Nevertheless, compassionate love as a biblical mandate does not imply any guarantee of personal gain. We are called to other-centeredness partly because that is the way to fulfill our created purpose.

There will likely be an ongoing debate regarding the potential for humans to engage in other-centered helping behaviors. Batson et al. (1983) suggest that even though the capacity for other-centeredness exists, the "concern for others is a 'fragile flower,' easily crushed by self-concern" (p. 718). Kohn (1990), on the other hand, writes, "There is good evidence to suggest that it is as 'natural' to help as it is to hurt" (p. 4). Thus, even among those who support the possibility of genuine other-centered altruism there can be disagreement as to its likelihood or prevalence. But a CFR approach to research would help broaden that dialogue by considering possibilities outside the established lines of thought, including the contributions of compassion and obedience.

## QUESTIONS TO CONSIDER

1. In what ways could a researcher measure the difference between empathy and  compassion? In what ways could this be a difficult distinction to make?

2. Suppose that you were a researcher who specializes in helping behavior and its motives. Someone approaches you with the question regarding what the research can really show us, given our inability to adequately measure underlying motives. What would be your response?

3. Imagine situations in which one's prosocial behavior results in considerable good for society. Does it really matter whether such people act out of primarily self-seeking motives or primarily other-centered motives? Why or why not?

## KEY TERMS

*altruism*

*antisocial behavior*

*arousal-cost reward model*

*bystander effect*

*cognitive-enhanced evolutionary model*

*compassion*

*diffusion of responsibility*

*egoism*

*empathy-altruism hypothesis*

*extensivity*

*inclusive fitness*

*just-world hypothesis*

*kin selection*

*negative-state relief model*

*perspective-taking*

*pluralistic ignorance*

*prosocial behavior*

*reciprocity norm*

*social exchange theory*

*social responsibility norm*

*social role theory*

*warm-glow hypothesis*

# 10

## Interpersonal Attraction
## and Relationships

*Who Likes Whom and When and Why?*

*If you love those who love you, what credit is that to you?*
*For even sinners love those who love them. . . .*
*Love your enemies, do good.*

LUKE 6:32, 35

### THE RELEVANCE OF RELATIONSHIPS AND
### INTERPERSONAL ATTRACTION

How people become attracted to one another is perhaps one of the most
popular topics for university students to explore. As Klohnen and Luo
(2003) note, why we are attracted to some individuals more than others
is one of the fundamental human dilemmas. After all, these initial attractions have important implications for decisions about those with
whom we are most likely to form long-lasting relationships. And, as
Bowlby (1989) noted, these sorts of attachments are an important ingredient of human experience "from the cradle to the grave." Berscheid
(1985) likewise noted the importance of relationships that result from
interpersonal attraction. He found that when people were asked what
makes their life meaningful, most of the answers referred to close relationships with family and friends as well as romantic partners. Thus,
this subject certainly has relevance for everyday life.

Social psychologists are interested in much more than just what attracts people to each other for a date on Saturday night (albeit an important topic in its own right!). The term *interpersonal attraction* is used in a much broader sense to include how people are drawn to one another in different sorts of interactions or relationships: whether romantic, friendship or fleeting encounters.

As you have seen throughout this text, different sorts of social relationships and the factors that impact them are of primary concern to social psychologists. For instance, research on *social perception* helps us understand how the ways in which we perceive others affect our desire to form relationships with them. Likewise, research on *group behavior* investigates both the power of the relationships within groups as well as the relationships between groups. *Helping* research investigates how relationship type can impact the likelihood of offering help, and so forth. Social psychologists have also studied other specific types of relationships such as friendships (e.g., Oswald, Clark & Kelly, 2004) and marriage (e.g., Karney & Bradbury, 2000).

As you will recall, central to an orthodox Christian view of personhood is the value and purpose of relationships. From the perspective of creation, fall and redemption, humans are created as intrinsically relational beings. Remember that this is consistent with the findings of Baumeister and Leary (1995) that humans possess a *fundamental need to belong*. That is, we long to form attachments with individuals and groups, and much of our personal identity is related to those associations. Our very physical and emotional existence depends on this inherently social nature.

Remember that in addition to acknowledging this survival advantage, the CFR approach also assumes that our intrinsically relational nature is a primary way in which God works redemptively among us. Thus, the study of interpersonal relationships is one key factor in a Christian understanding of personhood. So, too, are the factors that attract us to particular others in order to form those relationships in the first place, as well as factors that affect the likelihood of maintaining or dissolving relationships. This chapter thus comes full circle to the original discussion of the importance of relationships from the CFR approach noted in chapter two.

There are, of course, many factors that affect relationship formation and maintenance. The following discussions will focus on four of these factors: *proximity, similarity, physical attractiveness* and *social exchange.* Within these discussions, this chapter will examine the relevance of another central premise of the CFR view. That is, assuming that humans are created with the potential for other-centered relationship and that the human condition is fallen, there is an ongoing tension between self- and other-centered concern in relationships. From this view, we can assume that our created nature and our fallen condition may affect the way in which the four above-noted factors impact our relationships. There will be a brief discussion at the end of the first two sections regarding how a Christian view of personhood relates to the specific research, and then at the end of the chapter, there will be a more lengthy discussion that looks collectively at the four factors in relation to the biblical command to love one another. Figure 10.1 shows these four main factors that research suggests are strongly related to attraction and forming relationships. Think about what other factors seem important when people are drawn together.

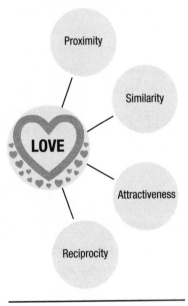

**Figure 10.1. "The Big Four?"**

### PHYSICAL PROXIMITY: *LOVE THY NEIGHBOR*

Imagine that your beloved asks you why you love him/her, and you answer, "The fact that we live only two miles from each other was what sealed it for me." Or, a close friend begins to sentimentally recount the reasons why the two of you have formed such a deep bond, and you say, "Really, the main reason is that we are roommates." These sorts of answers sound unromantic and superficial at best, and for the sake of your relationships I do not recommend using them. But could there be some truth in them? A lot of research in social psychology, sociology and communication studies has long indicated the powerful effect of what is called the *proximity-attraction principle* (e.g., Festinger, Schacter & Back, 1950; Merton, 1948; Sykes, 1983). This refers to how physical proximity is one of the best predictors of who we are attracted to, make friends with, date and marry. Related to this is the concept of *functional proximity*, which refers to the opportunities that proximity brings for interaction.

At first glance, this idea that physical proximity could be such a powerful determinant of our close relationships and initial attractions can sound a bit discomforting. How can an impersonal variable such as geography have that degree of influence on such personal decisions as choosing lifelong friends and romantic partners? But consider your own friends and romantic interests. How many of those relationships would you have missed out on had you attended another college instead of the one you are currently in? Or had you taken different classes? Or had you lived in another state or neighborhood than that in which you were raised?

In both social psychology and sociology, proximity is often referred to as *propinquity* (from the Latin *propinquitas*, meaning "nearness"), so you may encounter either term in this literature. There are many early studies in both fields that explored the effect of proximity on attraction and forming close relationships. Bossard (1932), for example, found that the number of city blocks separating couples was significantly related to the probability of their marrying. (Have you ever heard of the trials that many couples experience when trying to maintain long-distance relationships?)

Sociologist Erbe (1966) found that proximity was related to the probability of graduate students engaging in informal social relationships with other students in their own department. In this case, students with whom one had contact during classes were more likely to be sought out for social activities than were those from other departments. When discussing the factors that influence the likelihood of developing close relationships, Erbe also cites several earlier studies that demonstrated the powerful effect of proximity on the likelihood of developing social relationships. Collectively, the results of those studies suggest the significant effect of proximity in the form of seating arrangements in offices, classrooms and conference tables on likelihood of forming relationships. Segal (1974) also noted that in classrooms where students are seated in alphabetical order, students tend to report more friends whose last names begin with the same letter as theirs.

Nahemow and Lawton's (1975) research suggests that most of our friends live close to where we live, or at least where we lived during the time period the friendship developed. These researchers studied elderly individuals who were living in a city housing project. They found that friendships within the project seemed to be based on proximity in that the subjects tended to interact most with those who lived closest to them. But friendships outside the project tended to be based more on similarity, suggesting that people needed more in common to keep in contact with those farther away. More recent research likewise suggests that close friendships tend to begin with those closest to us geographically. Back, Schmukle and Egloff (2008) suggest that we become friends "by chance" of having lived in close proximity.

One classic study of the effects of propinquity on attraction was conducted by Festinger, Schachter and Back (1950). They observed the friendships of couples who were living in student housing at Massachusetts Institute of Technology (MIT). Consistent with the propinquity effect, they found that 65 percent of friends lived in the same building. In addition, 44 percent of the friends lived next door to one another, 22 percent two doors apart and 10 percent on opposite ends of the hall. Those students who lived near ground-floor staircases and mailboxes were more likely to report having friends on both floors. It seems that their many opportunities for interacting with neighbors who stopped near their apartment to get their mail enhanced their chances of making friends. Consider whether you have observed this in your own housing setting. Based on this and many other studies, it seems that if you want to make new friends or interact with potential dating partners, it would be a good idea that you consider proximity when you are deciding where to sit in class or where to live.

**How does technology affect the relationship between proximity and attraction?**

**Why is proximity so powerful?** One feature of proximity that may enhance liking is the *anticipation of interaction*. That is, just expecting to interact with someone generally seems to increase one's liking of the other. Darley & Berscheid (1967) explored this phenomenon. They gave female subjects a description of two women, one of whom they were told they would meet to discuss appropriate sexual behaviors in dating relationships. The subjects were asked to rate the two women's descriptions using personality traits. The results indicated that the participant rated the person they were expecting to meet as being more likeable than the one they were not expecting to meet. Devine, Sedikides and Fuhrman (1989) also found that anticipated interaction is very powerful, often not only increasing liking for the other, but also affecting our initial impressions of the target person.

Another feature of proximity that enhances liking is the opportunity for repeated exposure to the other. In fact, just being exposed to new stimuli repeated times often increases the chances that you will have a positive reaction to it. This, you may recall, is known as the *mere exposure effect* (Zajonc, 1968, 1970). Bornstein's (1989) meta-analysis found that the mere exposure effect has an impact on a wide variety of objects, from quite meaningless things such as line drawings and nonsense words or syllables to people we encounter in everyday life. Szpunar, Schellenberg & Pliner (2004) have also found that what we are exposed to and then like can be quite meaningful (e.g., music, photographs of objects or people).

In one study of the repeated exposure effect, Moreland and Beach (1992) asked students to respond to a survey regarding their preference for one of four teaching assistants (TA) for a class they were taking. The TAs were actually four female confederates with similar physical appearance. None actually interacted with the students, but each came to class either fifteen times, ten times, five times or never. The findings revealed that the teaching assistant who was in the classroom the most times was best liked by the students, even though no interaction between the students and the TA occurred.

Zajonc (2001) proposed that the exposure effects are more pronounced when the person is not consciously aware that the exposure is intentional. In addition, Zajonc extended his original theory and now refers to it as the *mere-repeated-exposure paradigm* to emphasize the importance of not just initial exposure, but repeated exposure. Repeated exposure, and the familiarity it breeds, can be a powerful factor in liking and attraction to people, ideas or products, as successful advertising demonstrates (Cox & Cox, 2002).

What is it about repeated exposure that tends to increase liking? One possibility is suggested by *affective models of the mere exposure effect*. According to this view, repeated exposure to a stimulus specifically increases positive affect or reduces negative affect toward the stimulus. In other words, this view suggests that you tend to feel happier and more favorable toward a face you recognize. Harmon-Jones and Allen (2001) tested this idea by assessing subjects' facial muscle movement and brain activity while looking at photographs of familiar and unfamiliar female faces. Familiar faces were rated as more likable and prompted more activity in the muscles that are used for smiling (i.e., the zygomatic muscles in the cheeks) than did the unfamiliar faces. In addition, looking at familiar faces tended to increase activity in the subjects' left frontal cortex, which is one area of the brain associated with positive affect and approach.

Could there also be individual difference variables that influence the exposure-liking link? Hansen and Bartsch (2001) studied the relationship between the personal need for structure and the repeated exposure effect. Repeated exposure to words tended to increase all participants' positive responses to those words, and this effect was especially pronounced in those individuals with a higher need for structure (i.e., those who prefer more order and predictability).

**When might proximity not result in liking?** One can well imagine many instances where proximity, repeated exposure and the mere anticipation of meeting another would not necessarily be apt to increase our liking of them. Just think about the idea of meeting a neighbor who has let their ferocious dog run loose and be a menace to your children, your first class with a professor who has a reputation for being harsh and rude with her students, or frequent interactions with an obnoxious classmate. In these situations, proximity, or anticipated proximity, may actually increase *negative* perceptions of the other!

Several researchers have found that the effect of anticipated exposure depends on the initial impression one has of the object. For example, Perlman and Oskamp (1971) found that increased exposure to positive objects (e.g., pictures of scientists or clergymen) or neutral objects (e.g., pictures of a man dressed in a sports suit) increased liking. But repeated exposure to negative objects such as pictures of a police lineup did not. Swap (1977) likewise noted that if you begin with a negative reaction to someone or something, you are not likely to find that stimulus more attractive with repeated exposure, but rather may actually grow to like them less.

So, proximity may also *decrease* your liking of another and increase the chances of hostility. Think of individuals whom you find particularly annoying who seem to get even more annoying with each instance of repeated contact with them. Consider also how many murders and other physical assaults take place between people who live near each other. Bornstein (1989) additionally found that the mere exposure effect is not found after approximately ten to twenty stimulus presentations. Thus, overexposure may result in no effect on liking. Norton, Frost and Ariely (2007) also found that too much knowledge and familiarity with another could also increase one's dislike for the other in cases where the other is perceived as dissimilar to the self. Once a person finds out that she and the other have less in common than originally thought, there can be an increase in negative affect and dislike of the other. Norton et al. therefore propose that in such cases familiarity actually breeds contempt.

Collectively, the studies suggest that proximity, along with the associated repeated exposure and anticipation of interaction effects, are important factors contributing to liking. But is this true regardless of the reason why the people are in close proximity in the first place? Are people who take part in a cancer support group, for example, as likely to initiate and maintain relationships with each other as would a volunteer group that builds houses for Habitat for Humanity? Is an individual who meets frequently with his probation officer as likely to develop fondness for the officer as would a student for their attractive professor? To date, the research has not generally addressed such questions in terms of the mediating effects of the purpose or reason for the relationship on proximity's effect on liking. Thus, the overall results suggest that we are fairly passive recipients of the effects of proximity. Taken at face value, the results imply that the purpose of the closeness is not as relevant as the geographical closeness itself.

It is not clear what future research on the effects of proximity might show, given current technology's impact on ease of contact with distant others. As of the writing of this text, college students all over the world are making and keeping in touch with faraway friends and romantic interests using technology such as Skype and Facebook. As Kraut et al. (1998) note, while strong personal ties are usually initiated and maintained by physical proximity, once those ties are made, they can be and frequently are sustained through technology despite geographical distance. Similarly, Ledbetter, Griffin and Sparks (2007), in their longitudinal study of college friends, found that even despite distances of over eight hundred miles, the closest friends maintained their contact over the years using various forms of technology. Thus, as the researchers note, technology potentially reduces the importance of physical proximity in creating and maintaining strong social ties. Katz and Aspden's (1997) national survey concluded that "far from creating a nation of strangers, the Internet is creating a nation richer in friendships and social relationships" (p. 86, as cited in Krautz et al., 1998). This finding, of course, depends on the motivations of the Internet user; some individuals who use the computer a lot can be otherwise relatively disconnected from family and friends who are nearby.

*A Christian view on proximity and attraction.* As you have read, a lot of the research on proximity looks at liking and relationship building as highly associated with sitting near each other in class, living near each other in the dorm, being from the same neighborhood, working together and so on. There is certainly ample evidence from both empirical studies and everyday life that closeness and familiarity contribute to both the initiation and maintenance of relationships. From a CFR view, one relevant aspect of proximity and liking has to do with the research regarding how to respond to those proximal to us whom we find "unlikeable," yet we have no choice but to interact with them. This is related to what Tyler and Sears (1977) refer to as *no-choice relationships*.

The researchers note that life is full of a series of no-choice relationships, many of which are significant to one's life. Imagine, for example, a sibling or parent whom you find to be particularly annoying, or a coworker who is frustrating. Depending on your level of commitment to a local church body, you may have no-choice relationships at church as well. Research has suggested that one tendency we have is to accommodate our feelings so that we might experience greater liking for individuals with whom we are in a no-choice relationship.

One feature of the research is especially relevant here: as noted earlier, the studies suggest that proximity (along with the factors that are discussed in later sections) is likely to *result* in attraction of some sort. Yet, as noted earlier, most of the research does not directly assess how the *reason* for the proximity could be a moderator of its effect on attraction and liking. In other words, does the reason/purpose of the geographically close relationship impact how that closeness will affect your liking for them? Consider, for example, a person who lives in a particular local neighborhood or a foreign country for the purpose of relational ministry. Does the reason for the proximity increase the likelihood of attraction above the effect of the proximity alone?

How the reason for the proximity may be related to liking has implications for the biblical command to love one another. Some Christian perspectives maintain that God has a reason or purpose for why the people who are proximal to you are there. Those who ascribe to such a theological view propose that these purposes include participation in God's plan for each other's ongoing renewal and sanctification. This process includes those whom we find unlikable. Whether or not one accepts this particular view, the relationship between reason for proximity and liking is a legitimate one that should receive further research.

The practicality of liking and relating to those closest to us is something we can all acknowledge. Nevertheless, this consistent finding alerts us of the need to be cautious about becoming insulated in our friendships and other relationships. Recall from an earlier chapter that having a narrow range of relationships is often associated with negative stereotypes regarding dissimilar others. Keep this in mind as you read the following sections.

## SIMILARITY: *DO WE LIKE PEOPLE WHO ARE LIKE US?*

How similar to us do our friends and romantic partners tend to be, and in what ways? Which characteristics seem to be most important for a married couple to hold in common? In what ways is it all right to be dissimilar? What degree of similarity characterizes the most long-lasting friendships? These questions are of great consequence. For example, the likelihood that a romance or marriage will last and that the couple will express satisfaction with their relationship may depend in large part on how much the couple has in common.

You have probably heard the commonly held belief that opposites often attract, in other words, that people with complementary differences will likely be attracted to each other. In traditional movie portrayals of this notion you would see a couple who is diametrically opposed to one another fall in love. Similarly, you may have heard the argument that in marriage, one partner's strengths can help complement the different strengths of the other, or that friends who are different from one another have more successful relationships in which each helps the other grow.

This notion that opposites are more likely to be attracted to each other is generally not supported by social psychological research (Buss, 1985). In fact, most research supports Byrne's (1961, 1971) *similarity-attraction hypothesis,* which argues that in general, the greater one's perception of similarity with another, the higher the degree of attraction to and liking of the other. Remember from both the helping and prejudice chapters that it is not just actual similarity alone but rather one's *perception* of similarity with another that matters, whether or not that perception is accurate. This hypothesis suggests that you are more likely to choose friends and romantic partners whom you perceive as similar to you along a host of demographic (age, race) and personal (attitudes, values) variables.

Sociologists McPherson, Smith-Lovin and Cook (2001) use the term *homophily principle* for the tendency for similarity to lead to social connections of all sorts, including marriage, friendship, work and other types of relationships. Thus, our personal networks are generally homogeneous with regard to many characteristics. McPherson and colleagues further note that homophily limits people's social worlds in such a significant way that it has powerful implications for the information we receive, the attitudes we form and the interactions we experience. This view predicts that ties between nonsimilar individuals tend to dissolve at a higher rate than do those between similar individuals.

Amodio and Showers (2005) review some of the literature that explores how liking has been associated with similarity along many dimensions in interpersonal relationships. This research suggests that liking is enhanced by similarity in *attitudes* (Byrne, 1971), *personality traits* (Buss, 1985), *similar physical characteristics* such as race and perceived level of physical attractiveness (Berscheid, Dion, Walster & Walster, 1971) and *similar self-concept descriptions* (LaPrelle, Hoyle, Insko & Bernthal, 1990).

In one study that explored the powerful effect of similarity on liking, Veitch and Piccione (1978) told students about a supposed prior subject (the "teacher") who had partaken in an experiment where he/she shocked another subject (the "learner") when he missed an item on a learning task. Students were then given a description of a target (the "teacher") who allegedly held either similar or dissimilar attitudes as themselves. Overall, students rated the similar subject more positively than they did the dissimilar subject. In addition, the students reported viewing the shocking behavior as somehow motivated by better intentions and as being more justified when conducted by the liked teacher as opposed to the unliked teacher. Participants also reported that they thought the person who delivered the shock was somehow less personally responsible if that teacher was similar to themselves. The researchers concluded that similarity leads to liking, which leads to the attribution of more benevolent intentions. In other words, these results suggest that if you feel that you and another are similar, you are more apt to like them and to make excuses for them if they do something that you would otherwise find objectionable.

Griffitt and Vietch (1974) likewise found that even in crowded conditions, similar interests and opinions were related to higher levels of liking. They gave personality assessments to thirteen unacquainted men and then confined them to a fallout shelter. The men reported liking those best who were most like themselves. Other studies have likewise found that the less alike two people are in social characteristics, the less likely they are to be friends (Newcomb, 1956; Verbrugge, 1977).

**Is similarity always real or also just perceived?** Some research suggests that perceived similarity can be more powerful than actual similarity in interpersonal attraction. Montoya, Horton and Kirchner (2008), for example, conducted a meta-analysis of 313 studies that revealed that while both actual similarity and perceived similarity predicted attraction in no-interaction and short-interaction situations, perceived similarity was a more powerful predictor in the context of existing relationships.

Morry (2005, 2007) suggests that the powerful relationship between similarity and attraction works the other way around as well. That is, when we are attracted to someone or are already friends with them, there can be a tendency to overestimate how similar that person is to ourselves. Consider the example of a classmate whom you think is really attractive. You want to go out with them, so why not imagine that they have the same values and interests as you do? In this way, you can validate your reasons for pursuing a possible relationship with them. This is what Morry (2005) calls the *attraction-similarity model,* which proposes that attraction leads to perceptions of similarity between the self and other. In addition, this model proposes that individuals also simultaneously make self- or relationship-serving attributions. This happens in both same-sex friendships (Morry, 2003) and in romantic relationships (Murray, Holmes, Bellavia, Griffin & Dolderman, 2002).

Thus, it seems that individuals may sometimes be attuned to perceiving their own characteristics in others. You may recall reading about a similar concept in the chapter on social perception: *false consensus,* which is the tendency to think that people agree with you. Even in longer-term relationships, where both individuals do tend to establish increasing similarity on a variety of attitudes and behaviors over time, individuals consistently perceived greater similarity than actually exists (Sillars & Scott, 1983).

**What about similarity and marriage?** Are you apt to marry someone who is like you? In what ways is that person most likely to resemble you? In what ways might the two of you differ? To what degree does your similarity with your spouse predict how successful or happy your marriage will be? In the context of marriage, the answers appear to be quite complex because the degree of similarity seen in married couples depends in large part on what specific factor is being measured.

Source: http://www.webdonuts.com/2012/03/status-update/

**Figure 10.2.**

Klohnen and Mendelsohn (1998) and Watson et al. (2004) review much of this literature and come to the following conclusions. First, in general it appears that romantic partners show strong similarity in age and values dealing with politics and religious orientation. Second, couples generally show a moderate similarity in education, general intelligence and values. Third, the level of similarity in the above-noted factors is significantly related to the level of satisfaction that the couple reports about their marriage. Finally, in general, little or no similarity is seen in the couple's individual personality characteristics (e.g., Botwin, Buss & Shackelford, 1997). From these findings it appears that you are most likely to marry someone who shares your political party, religious affiliation and age bracket, as well as your attitudes and values regarding what you consider to be most important in life. The greater the similarity in these factors, the happier the marriage tends to be. Nevertheless, that person may be very different from you with regard to level of extraversion, conscientiousness about details and so on.

Kalmijn (1994) reviews a number of studies that have explored the level of similarity in newlywed couples with regard to their status. In this case, status is defined by social class, occupational prestige and level of education. These researchers have generally found that newlyweds tend to have a great deal of similarity in terms of their status as defined by these variables. This is often referred to as "status homogamy" or similarity, though it might be an artifact of proximity.

Luo and Klohnen (2005) note that studies exploring the connection among similarity, liking and reported satisfaction with the marital relationship have some limitations. One main concern is that the majority of the above-noted studies have used what is called the *variable-centered approach* (VCA). This approach involves researchers computing a correlation between husbands' and wives' scores on the same characteristic (e.g., status, level of extraversion, religious affiliation, intelligence) across *all* couples in a particular sample. A significant positive correlation is interpreted as evidence for similarity, whereas a sizable negative correlation is considered as evidence for complementarity (or opposites). Using this approach to research, the degree of similarity observed depends on the particular individual difference studied. As noted by Luo and Klohnen, this variable-centered approach does not tell you about any *specific* couple's similarity or satisfaction with their relationship because the correlation characterizes the sample rather than any individual couple.

In order to address the concerns with the VCA, some researchers (e.g., Glicksohn & Golan, 2001; Klohnen & Mendelsohn, 1998) have used what is called the *couple-centered approach* (CCA) for studying the relationship between similarity and liking and satisfaction with the marriage. In contrast to the VCA, which focuses on variables (specific characteristics or traits) as the unit of analysis, the CCA focuses explicitly on couples. That is, the CCA is concerned with how similar each husband and wife pair is in terms of their profiles of responses across a number of items. This approach thus offers more specific information regarding each individual couple than does the VCA. In addition, using the couple-centered approach enables researchers to examine the similarity between each husband and wife pair on broad, overarching domains as well as on characteristics that are more narrow and specific. Despite these advantages, the four studies noted above that used the CCA have produced mixed results regarding similarity and satisfaction with the marital relationship. Luo and Klohnen (2005) note that this is because the different studies used different methodologies and examined different levels of traits or characteristics.

Luo and Klohnen (2005) conducted a large-scale study of 291 newlywed couples that was designed to help address some of the concerns with the above-noted studies that used the couple-centered approach. They used a broad range of individual differences variables (e.g., demographics, religious and political orientations) as well as personality variables (e.g., the Big Five personality questionnaire, which measures the five traits of openness to new experience, agreeableness, conscientiousness, neuroticism—a.k.a. anxiety—and extroversion, along with measures of disinhibition, ego resiliency). The couples took part in sessions that typically lasted from two to two and a half hours and included a battery of self-report measures and two videotaped interactions, which were rated by independent raters. The three aspects of relationship quality that were coded were how critical each spouse was of his or her partner, how much in love each spouse appeared to be, and the likelihood of breaking up versus staying together. The couples themselves also filled out self-report measures regarding their level of satisfaction with different aspects of their relationship.

The results of Luo and Klohnen's (2005) study revealed that overall, among newlyweds there was substantial similarity on attitude-related domains (values, religiosity, political attitudes), and these similarities resulted in better reported relationship quality. In addition, there was no support for the contention that couples may just become more similar across time, as the couples in this study were very similar on the issues noted above regardless of how much time they had dated before they married. Hence, as noted earlier, the more a couple shares similar values, the more happy and satisfied they appear to be with their marriage.

Thus, overall, it appears that similarity across various factors is highly correlated with likelihood of developing a relationship as well as with reported satisfaction within the relationship. This powerful effect of similarity has likewise been seen across a vast array of settings, such as in organizational/business settings in which similarity affects hiring practices (Lin, Dobbins & Farh, 1992) and the likelihood of merging companies (Van Oudenhoven & de Boer, 1995). Colleges often employ the same strategy when attempting to increase racial and ethnic diversity on campus. You may have noticed on your own campus how students of different racial and ethnic groups often work in the admissions or recruitment office in order to appeal to potential students of those same backgrounds.

***Why is similarity so powerful?*** There have been a number of different explanations for the relationship between similarity and liking. An obvious possible reason is that similar people just tend to have more opportunities to meet each other by virtue of their taking part in similar activities and hanging out in the same places (Werner & Parmelee, 1979). In addition, as Kalmijn (1991) points out, similar people also have more opportunities to meet each other through third parties such as parents and mutual friends. You have no doubt heard about (or experienced personally) parents wanting to introduce their adult child to a "nice person" who just also happens to be single.

Another explanation of the power of similarity is proposed by the *reinforcement-affect model* (Byrne & Clore, 1967). This model posits that if you have close relationships with others who share your beliefs and values, then you can experience a host of positive consequences such as feeling better understood or feeling less lonely. Similarity thus results in a perceived legitimacy of one's own views and also a sense of a common shared perspective of the world.

Another explanation of the power of similarity is known as the *information integration approach* (e.g., Kaplan & Anderson, 1973). This approach proposes that similarity is only reinforcing when the individual is aware of the relationship between reward and similarity. Montoya and Horton (2004) expand this approach by proposing that interpersonal attraction is guided by a cognitive composite of the available information inferred from target characteristics (attitudes or personality traits) and the cognitive evaluation of this composite.

***Do we tend to like others who look like us?*** Other research that explores the similarity-liking association has focused on the physical attractiveness characteristic and has proposed what is called the *matching hypothesis* (Sprecher & Hatfield, 2009). This view suggests that people tend to be most attracted to, and more likely to form longstanding relationships with, those who are of a similar level of physical attractiveness. Murstein (1972), for example, found that when photos of dating and engaged couples were rated in terms of attractiveness, couples of similar attractiveness levels were more likely to date or be engaged. Folkes (1982) likewise found that couples' similarity in physical attractiveness was related to the likelihood of forming dating relationships. In this study, the subjects were couples who were members of a dating service. It was found that similarity in physical attractiveness was positively correlated with the likelihood of the couple taking steps to pursue a possible relationship (e.g., going out on a second date).

Sprecher and Hatfield (2009) note that some inconsistent findings regarding the matching hypothesis may be due to the actual choices one can make in real life, not just desired outcomes. Thus, they suggest that when it comes time to make a realistic choice, people often settle for "the art of the possible."

**Does similarity always lead to attraction?** Despite the powerful influence of similarity, could there be instances in which differences are also appealing? Klohnen and Mendelsohn (1998) have argued that in terms of personality characteristics, both similarities and dissimilarities can be attractive. Perceiving one's partner as similar to oneself is most appealing if those similarities are aspects of personality that individuals like in themselves. In contrast, when it comes to aspects individuals do not like in themselves, perceived similarity to one's self may be aversive. Newcomb (1956) also notes that attraction often increases between two people whose abilities and talents complement one another such that each possesses some unique ability to contribute to accomplishing some task together. A wife who is very skilled at dealing with details complements a husband who is more inclined to see the "larger picture."

As you might have observed in your own relationships or attractions to others, the degree of influence of similarity can vary. Montoya, Horton and Kirchner (2008) cite a number of studies in which it was found that similarity had a weaker effect on attraction and liking. For example, in one study cited (Montoya & Horton, 2004), they note that the similarity effect is weaker for personality traits than it is for attitudes. It seems that an introvert and an extrovert would be more likely to be attracted to each other than would two people who hold very different political alliances. Similarly, other studies that were cited (e.g., Byrne, London & Griffitt, 1968; Clore & Baldridge, 1968) suggest that similarity is less important for peripheral attitudes compared with central attitudes. For example, similarity regarding attitudes about television shows is likely to be less important than is similarity in religious convictions.

In addition, Montoya and Horton (2004) note research (e.g., Novak & Lerner, 1968) that suggests that similarity in negative traits does not produce interpersonal attraction. Thus, the reinforcement-affect model of attraction that attempts to explain the powerful effects of similarity does not address well these inconsistent effects of similarity on attraction. That is, if similarity is so powerful because it makes us feel validated, then why are there so many examples of our liking people whose ideas are different from our own?

Aboud and Mendelson (1996) also discuss other possible limitations with the similarity-attraction research. They note that since close relationships take time to develop, the characteristics that seemed so important at the beginning of the attraction to one another may not be seen as important as the relationship matures. Thus, the similarities that attracted two friends or lovers to each other initially may be inconsequential over the long run.

*A Christian view on similarity.* The general finding that similarity is such a powerful predictor of relationship initiation and maintenance is consistent with a reading of Scripture in several ways. There are many instances in which the Scriptures speak of the significance of similarity in shaping relationships and community, as well as for leading people to Christ. For example, the apostle Paul talks about his strategy for witnessing within the larger context of what is appropriate for a believer to eat. In this context, he refers to a strategy that consists of appealing to similarity with others ("To the Jews I became as a Jew. . . . To those under the law I became as one under the law"; 1 Cor 9:20). Further, there are some verses that speak directly to avoiding certain types of dissimilarity (e.g., "Do not be mismatched with unbelievers"; 2 Cor 6:14).

The primary similarity with which the Scriptures are concerned has to do with redemption: that we would all share a common love of God. Yet it is reasonable to think that some of the Scriptures can be helpful in our understanding of the role of similarity in interpersonal relationships. The disciples, for example, were different from each other in terms of temperament and occupations. Yet, despite these differences, they were similar in their love for Christ and worked together toward this end (notwithstanding Judas's betrayal of Christ). This is consistent with the finding that when dissimilar people are brought together to work toward a common purpose, that purpose can become more important than the similarity among them (e.g., Devine, Sedikides & Fuhrman, 1989). Further, the Scriptures do not describe the church as a uniform entity, but rather comprising dissimilar people with different roles (e.g., Rom 12:5-9; 1 Cor 12:4-14; Eph 4:11).

The Scriptures can help us better understand the possible limitations of similarity. As noted earlier, too much similarity in our social life would lead to insularity. Remember from the groups chapter that group-think results from a lack of expression of diverse opinions, and this often results in less than optimal consequences.

One other point from the research is relevant here. Recall that most of the research looks at the type of similarity (personality, career, religious preferences, etc.). Yet the research does not generally address how the *degree* of similarity may be relevant to interpersonal relationships. It is possible that while happily married couples have similar faith perspectives, for example, one may find within that similar view a greater deal of dissimilarity regarding the specifics of faith than the research seems to suggest. Thus, it would be interesting to see if close relationships are formed with people who are more dissimilar than the current research suggests. This is an important consideration from a Christian perspective, as it would be more consistent with God's call for us to relate to a wide variety of people.

## PHYSICAL ATTRACTIVENESS: *DO WE TEND TO LIKE BEAUTIFUL PEOPLE?*

You have probably heard the expression that "beauty is only skin deep." This well-known expression assumes that we are prone to give all sorts of

 advantages to beautiful people but that we should be aware that beauty can be deceiving. As noted in the social perception chapter, attractive people do often receive all sorts of social advantages. Greenwald and Banaji (1995) review a number of studies

that show how beauty elicits a halo effect such that attractiveness becomes associated with a number of other positive qualities. Remember that this is called the *physical attractiveness stereotype*. Research suggests that when compared to less attractive individuals, beautiful people are often assumed to be kinder, more sociable, happier and more likely to hold more prestigious jobs (Dion, Berscheid & Walster, 1972). Downs and Lyons (1991) found that more attractive defendants were levied smaller fines and lower bail levels by the judge. The physical attractiveness stereotype has been found in a number of cultural groups such as African American college students (Cash & Duncan, 1984) and Japanese students (Onodera & Miura, 1990), as well as across the lifespan (Adams & Crane, 1980).

In the previous discussion of the physical attractiveness stereotype within the context of social perception, the focus was on how good looks can lead to more favorable impressions of the person and how beautiful people may be afforded more "slack" when they err. Recall the central belief of this stereotype that "what is beautiful is good" (Dion, Berscheid & Walster, 1972). In this chapter, the focus is on exploring whether we tend to be drawn to, and like, attractive people. Do we tend to date, befriend or marry them more often than we do people whom we find less attractive?

There are several early studies that demonstrated the power of physical attractiveness on liking. For example, Hatfield and her associates (1966) gave personality and aptitude tests to a sample of first-year students at the University of Minnesota. The researchers then randomly matched 376 couples for an arranged dance. After spending two and a half hours at the dance with their assigned partners, students were asked to evaluate their dates. Examining a long list of psychological traits, the only significant factor that seemed to predict liking was physical attractiveness. This was true for both men and women.

In terms of defining the ideal romantic partner, one of the most reliable findings in social psychology research on interpersonal attraction is the overwhelming influence of physical attractiveness. Singh (2004) reviews many of these studies whose findings suggest that both men and women express a preference for an attractive partner in noncommitted short-term relationships such as one-night stands or other casual dating relationships (e.g., Hatfield & Sprecher, 1986; Jackson, 1992). What about

for long-term relationships? Buss (1999) notes that for committed relationships, if the male has high social and financial status, females appear
to relax their standards for the partner's attractiveness. Males also tend
to look for various personality qualities (e.g., kindness, good parenting
skills) in potential long-term partners. However, unlike females, males
still assign relatively greater importance to physical attractiveness compared to other personal qualities.

Singh (2004) also cites another study that demonstrates the powerful
effect of physical attractiveness on males' choice of romantic partner. Li,
Bailey, Kenrick and Linsenmeier (2002) gave male subjects a limited
"mating budget" in which they were asked to allocate various characteristics
of a female their respective weights in the equation. The findings showed
that the males allocated the largest proportion of their budget to physical
attractiveness rather than to other attributes such as an exciting personality,
liveliness and sense of humor. Li et al. suggest that in this case, the males had
assessed female attractiveness as a necessity in romantic relationships.

**What is "beautiful"?** If physical attractiveness is such an important
variable in initial liking and relationship building, it is important to explore what physical features contribute to our perceptions of beauty.
There can be, of course, a great deal of variability in what one considers
beautiful. Remember the well-known saying that "beauty is in the eye of
the beholder." It has long been said that notions of beauty vary across
cultures and across time. But are there some characteristics that appear
to be consistently rated as attractive? In order to explore this question, it
is important to distinguish between perceptions of facial beauty versus
perceptions of the beauty of the human figure.

Regarding the perceived attractiveness of facial features, consistent
findings have been seen across cultures. Cunningham et al. (1995) found
that Asian, Hispanic and white subjects were strikingly consistent and
similar in their judgments of the attractiveness of Asian, Hispanic and
white female faces. Fink and Penton-Voak (2002, as cited in Singh,
2004) found that female faces with a thinner jaw and fuller lips are considered attractive. All groups gave higher ratings to female faces with
large eyes, greater distance between the eyes, small noses, expressive,
higher eyebrows, dilated pupils, larger lower lips, larger smiles and well-

groomed, full hair. The researchers suggest that these features may indicate youth and hormonal stability. These features are good indicators of fertility, which increases a female's attractiveness.

Other researchers (e.g., Langlois & Roggman, 1990; Alley & Hildebrandt, 1988) have found that while an average face may be considered good-looking, it is generally not considered ideally attractive. Cunningham, Barbee and Pike (1990) found that the male faces rated the most attractive had exceptionally large eyes, cheekbones and chins. In fact, only noses were rated as most attractive when average sized.

What about perceptions of beauty regarding the body? As noted by Furnham, Dias and McClelland (1998), when compared to crosscultural perceptions of facial beauty, there is more diversity across cultures in terms of what constitutes the most attractive body type. Still, there are many consistencies. For example, in female bodies, the shape is determined by the amount of fat as well as the way it is distributed. Singh (1993, 1994) noted that the distribution of body fat, especially on the waist and hips—the *waist-to-hip ratio* (WHR)—is one of the main features related to perceived attractiveness of women. The WHR is calculated by computing a ratio of the circumference of the waist to the circumference of the hips. Singh found that both male and female subjects systematically used the WHR for inferring attractiveness and healthiness of female figures.

Singh (2004) showed sketches of different female body types to participants and found that the most preferred body type was one with normal weight and low waist-to-hip ratio. This finding is consistent with others that have often found that women choose thin female figures as ideal and perceive their current body as fatter than the ideal. Furthermore, women choose their ideal figure as much thinner than what men's preference generally is (Fallon & Rozin, 1985).

***Is the physical attractiveness stereotype a self-fulfilling prophecy?*** Research suggests that the positive attributions made of attractive people can have a positive influence on their behavior such that many of the positive attributions become reality. Langlois et al. (2000) conducted a meta-analytic review of physical attractiveness studies and found significant behavior differences between less and more attractive children and adults. For example, the attractive children were generally more popular, more socially adept, better behaved and showed better academic performance than less attractive children. Attractive adults also showed specific behavioral advantages such as more occupational success, popularity, dating experiences and strong self-esteem. The meta-analysis further showed that the physical attractiveness stereotype was equally strong in initial encounters as well as in more enduring relationships.

The researchers suggest that many of the behavioral differences between attractive and less attractive individuals may result from the different treatment and opportunities afforded to them. For example, an attractive young woman is likely to be asked on dates more often and to be approached for conversation. This contributes to a sense of self-confidence and opportunities for social engagement, which increase one's social competence. Thus, the perception that more attractive people are more socially competent may be true simply by virtue of opportunity to practice. Similarly, attractive individuals who are perceived as intellectually competent may be offered academic opportunities and extra help in class, thereby increasing the chances of doing well in school. An attractive job candidate may be afforded more positive attributions during the interview than would a less attractive candidate. Nevertheless, Langlois et al. (2000) note that there is a lack of longitudinal studies regarding the effects of the physical attractiveness stereotype. In addition, there need to be more experimental manipulations of these possible effects. Thus, we cannot be sure whether there is a causal link between expectations and behaviors for attractive individuals.

***Is physical attractiveness always a good thing?*** Given all the evidence for the benefits of physical attractiveness, it can be hard to imagine how beauty could work against you. But many researchers have reported on the so-called dark side of physical attractiveness. For example, Singh (2004) reviews research that suggests that attractive people are perceived as less faithful, more snobbish, sometimes less intelligent and more likely to have an extramarital affair and to request a divorce (Dermer & Thiel, 1975). Ashmore, Solomon and Longo (1996) reported similar findings using full-body photographs: Attractive women were perceived to be vain, dishonest, less moral, to have a lack of concern for others and to be more sexually provocative than were less-attractive females. Singh found that college females who perceived themselves as more attractive were more likely to use dating behaviors that increased their chances of attracting a mate, including cosmetics, parading, leaning in, flirting and dressing provocatively.

*Is the physical attractiveness stereotype universal and always so strong?* There is evidence that general preferences and positive evaluations of physically attractive people is a universal phenomenon. And as noted earlier, judgments of what is beautiful are fairly uniform across the world. Yet some researchers propose that this is a simplistic view of the importance of attractiveness. That is, the physical attractiveness stereotype may work differently depending on a number of cultural factors.

Anderson, Adams and Plaut (2008) outline a few ways in which the physical attractiveness stereotype has been understood from a cultural perspective. First, they cite some researchers (e.g., Wheeler & Kim, 1997), who propose that "what is beautiful is culturally good." Wheeler and Kim showed Korean participants photos of Korean individuals who varied in level of physical attractiveness. Participants were asked to judge the individuals in the photos using North American values (e.g., "potency") and traits that are highly valued in Korean culture (e.g., integrity, concern for others). The results indicated that the level of attractiveness of the target photo was significantly related to attributions of positive Korean values, but not North American values. These results suggest that while the physical attractiveness stereotype may be universal, the positive attributions made of attractive people are not uniform.

Second, as Anderson, Adams and Plaut (2008) propose, the impact of the physical attractiveness stereotype may be more highly valued in cultures to the extent that people have a choice about partners. To the extent that people have less choice in relationships, attraction and other personal preferences probably have less impact on life outcomes.

Thus, the physical attractiveness stereotype, while certainly strong, also depends on the specific context and type of inference that is being made. Eagly, Ashmore, Makhijani and Longo (1991) conducted a meta-analysis of the research and concluded that judgments of social competence are where the physical attractiveness stereotype has the strongest effect. The data suggest a weaker effect on judgments of adjustment and intellectual competence, and practically no effect on judgments of integrity and concern for others.

As Riniolo, Johnson, Sherman and Misso (2006) also note, physical attractiveness is based on factors such as the target's personality characteristics, level of similarity between perceiver and target, and the perceiver's sense of self. In addition, Riniolo et al. note that in most of the research on physical attractiveness, it is first impressions that are generally measured. So it is not clear to what degree initial impressions may compare with later impressions following repeated exposure and additional information about the target (Hosoda, Stone-Romero & Coats, 2003).

## SOCIAL EXCHANGE THEORY: *RELATIONSHIPS AND RECIPROCITY*

So far in this chapter, you have read about what attracts us to people and various factors that are related to the maintenance of relationships. One other important factor that affects both the potential of initiating relationships as well as the likelihood of maintaining them has to do with a cost-benefit analysis—how much benefit we think we are getting from the relationship versus how much we are (or would be) putting into it. This cost-benefit analysis, known as *social exchange theory* (Gouldner, 1960; Homans, 1958), was discussed in the helping chapter as well.

Remember that social exchange theory posits that just as the marketplace is based on the exchange of goods and resources, so too are social relationships. In other words, humans rate relationships using markers that are both tangible (e.g., gifts, assets) and intangible (e.g., feelings of security and admiration). From this view, people will be motivated to initiate and maintain relationships where there is a good balance between the costs and the benefits in the relationship. In addition, in this elaborate exchange, *reciprocity* is very important. Generally, there is an expectation that the amount of effort one puts into the relationship will be reciprocated by the other. Partners are expected to abide by certain "rules" of exchange. Some of these rules are explicit, while others are unspoken (Blau, 1964). Uneven effort in a relationship is generally seen in relationships of dominance and increases the chances that the one exerting more effort will leave the relationship.

Lawler (2001) proposes that one way in which the cost-benefit analysis works is that it produces global negative ("punishing") or positive ("pleasant") affect about the relationship. This affect then helps determine the degree to which relationships are pursued, cohesive or terminated. Several researchers (e.g., Gottman & Levenson, 1992; Nakonezny & Denton, 2008) have also argued that this evaluation of the costs and benefits of a marital relationship, along with the emotional picture thereof, contributes to the likelihood of satisfaction with the marriage as well as the likelihood of dissolution of the marriage. From this view, the marital relationship may be seen as a series of transactions of valued resources, whether tangible or intangible, between partners, and the rewards and costs associated with such transactions. This results in overall "profit" or "loss," which in turn results in decisions regarding marriage stability.

Researchers have also explored how social exchange works in friendships. Bleske and Buss (2000), for example, discuss how the value of friendships from an evolutionary standpoint has not been as well understood as the value of mates. Bleske and Buss investigated how both same-sex and opposite-sex friendships may provide certain evolutionary benefits (e.g., providing care for us, introducing us to potential mates) as well as costs (e.g., competing for the same resources). The researchers assessed perceptions of same-sex or opposite-sex friendships of male and female college students. They asked students to rate the top ten benefits and costs of these friendships. The findings suggest that there were common benefits to both same- and opposite-sex friendships, including having a respected friend and being able to talk openly with someone. There were also common costs associated with both types of friendships, such as having to take time to help the other. Additionally, both male and female students reported that getting advice from the opposite-sex friend regarding how to attract potential mates was highly beneficial.

Different patterns emerged, however, between the sexes. For example, for the male students, having access to the opposite sex via their opposite-sex friend was rated as much more important than for the female students. Additionally, the females reported benefiting most from the protection of their male friends (e.g., walking them to the car late at night). The researchers conclude that some of the results support the hypothesis that opposite-sex friendships are an evolved strategy that, on average, had net reproductive payoffs for our ancestors, and thus were adaptive.

Despite the empirical support for social exchange theory, relationship initiation and maintenance is not always based on a mere calculation of costs and benefits. Consider, for example, the important role of *opportunity* for alternatives. Unhappy relationships may remain stable for lack of a better alternative (Thibaut & Kelley, 1959).

Miller (2005) also discusses several areas of weakness of the social exchange theory of interpersonal relationships. For example, she notes that this theory underestimates the impact of other factors besides costs and benefits, such as how one's assessments of previous relationships affects one's assessment of the current relationship. Miller also notes that costs and rewards are difficult to define operationally, as they differ so much from individual to individual. So, for example, financial benefits could be very rewarding for one individual, but only minimally for another. Additionally, it is not the case that relationships necessarily progress in a linear fashion as suggested by social exchange theory, which assumes that as benefits increase, satisfaction, intimacy and maintenance also increase.

Despite the limitations of social exchange theory, it is evident that humans assess, to varying degrees, how much effort relationships entail relative to how much we benefit from them. Nevertheless, as discussed in the chapter on the self, there is growing evidence for what we have observed all along: though people may make the calculations, at the interpersonal relationship level they often make significant sacrifices for those with whom they are in relationship (Gaertner et al., 2008). In various fields, research on seemingly "disadvantageous" relationships has most often focused on them as anomalies or the result of pathology. An interesting research question would be to study the well-being of persons who choose to remain in admittedly disadvantageous relationships, with a focus on their reasons for doing so.

## THE POWER AND MEANING OF RELATIONSHIPS: *A CHRISTIAN VIEW REVISITED*

Throughout this text, you have read about how social psychology helps us understand the complexities of human interaction. Yet social psychology, like any other human endeavor, has its limitations. Some of these limitations are inherent in the empirical approach itself, which you read about in the first chapter. But the major limitation of current social psychological research, from the Christian view presented in this text, is the influence that its naturalist premises has on the range and specific topics of research, the interpretation of that research, and subsequent theory development.

As you have read, naturalism rejects the fundamental truths that humans are created in God's image for loving and meaningful relationship with him and others, are in a fallen condition, yet are redeemable. As a result, social psychology is hindered when exploring human relationships and, of course, ignores entirely the integral part that human relationships play in God's redemptive plan.

The naturalist perspective in social psychology represents an effort to use a unified theory of human nature as a basis for understanding the behavioral specifics research discovers. From this view, having regard for others is beneficial for the species as well as for the individual, thus we all engage in what Kenrick (1991) calls "proximate altruism yet ultimate selfishness." But this view does not explain well the pervasive existence of numerous social behaviors that do not appear to be ultimately self-serving. It also frequently offers a basis for positive social behavior that is not founded on stable, enduring moral ground.

Consider the example of similarity discussed in this chapter. Much social psychological research suggests that increasing a sense of similarity by engendering a common group identity increases mutual liking and helping (e.g., Dovidio et al., 1998; Hewstone, Rubin & Willis, 2002; Vaes et al., 2003). This is true, yet somewhat tenuous as a basis for mutual regard. What if you no longer consider yourself part of a particular group or if a group ostracizes you? What, then, of your regard for the other?

Consider, looking forward, the important distinction between the naturalist and Christian views in terms of the application of research findings. Psychologists may acknowledge all manner of prosocial functioning, but apart from the functional value of this behavior, there is no logical basis for promoting or encouraging it. By contrast, a Christian approach affirms the necessity to love others for their sake, based on the conviction that Christ is the source of the worth and dignity of human life. How that love is best demonstrated with real people in a fallen world is obviously a complex and often difficult matter, but a Christian approach provides a basis to study it.

This type of love can be satisfying or fulfilling, of course, but it is also often difficult, seemingly irrational, and sometimes painful or costly. It can be expressed in many of the behaviors studied by social psychologists such as when we make attributions, help others, form relationships, forgive or partake in racial reconciliation. This is because a Christian worldview acknowledges how these interactions can be an integral part of the redemptive work of Christ and thus, the application of a Christian view of persons is relevant to the broad array of social psychological inquiry.

A Christian perspective, because it embraces transcendent moral values and imperatives, offers a plausible alternative to an exclusively self-centered interpretation of human behavior. It also allows us to explore a wider range of questions and possible explanations of the data, as hopefully you have seen in this text. At the same time, as stated in chapter two, Hill (2005) notes that any approach that integrates psychology and Christianity must recognize both the strengths and limitations of using Scripture as an explanatory model. Hill noted that Scripture is more clear and direct in terms of how we are to live our moral lives and less clear about cognitive and affective psychological processes. Yet Scripture can lend insight into these processes. Because of their central role in our life and in the redemptive work of Christ, social relationships are a moral issue. And as you have seen from the various discussions in this text, many of the basic cognitive and affective processes that underlie these relationships may be informed by an understanding that we are created in God's image for relationship with him and with others.

A scientist who begins with Christian assumptions of personhood must maintain a humble approach to the scientific inquiry of social interactions. We must acknowledge the rich complexity of humans as God's creation. We must also recognize both the strengths and limitations of the empirical approach to explore this complexity. We should also be aware that our own biases might lead us to dismiss accurate interpretations of findings by researchers who have a naturalist worldview. As Worthington (2010) warns, a Christian scholar may also have erroneous interpretations of Scripture, and these biases can unhelpfully restrict both the research questions that we ask and the interpretations that we make of the findings.

From the Christian view presented in this text, in order to most accurately conduct social psychological inquiry and fully make use of the research findings, it is helpful to remember that the process entails more than just integrating faith and reason; it also includes the two other essential features of Christianity: hope and love. If humans are to have true hope for our collective future, then other-centeredness will have to play an integral role. From this Christian view, a central task for social psychologists in the coming years is to explore further how positive, other-centered social behavior can be encouraged, starting from the premise that we are actually capable of genuinely expressing it. Researchers could also further explore the role of faith in promoting and developing genuinely other-centered behavior and, as Batson (1976) reminds us, how faith may also sometimes hinder this.

My hope is that this text has inspired you to see both how scientific findings can enhance your understanding of personhood and how your faith can enrich your scientific endeavors, in social psychology and elsewhere. Cacioppo's (2008) advice to young scientists is that you move forward with modesty, passion and gradualness. That advice is meant to encourage us to stay mindful of how scientific truths are obtained collaboratively and in small increments. Pursuing these efforts from a Christian perspective reminds us of Alister McGrath's (2006) proposal that a theoretical model does not have to try to prove that God exists or that he created us in his image. Rather, a model could "presuppose God's existence so that revelation provides an interpretive framework within which nature can be understood" (p. 7). I wish you blessings as you continue to explore God's created order.

## QUESTIONS TO CONSIDER

1. In what types of relationships have you noticed that similarity has been an important variable for you? When has similarity *not* been an important variable?

2. When do you think that doing a cost-benefit analysis would be a legitimate way to make a decision regarding whether to continue or end a relationship?

3. How has this text affirmed your understanding of human behavior? How has it challenged your view of human behavior?

4. What areas of social psychology research most interest you thus far? Why?

## KEY TERMS

*affective models of the mere exposure effect*
*anticipation of interaction*
*attraction-similarity hypothesis*
*couple-centered approach*
*functional proximity*
*fundamental need to belong*
*homophily principle*
*information integration approach*
*interpersonal attraction*
*matching hypothesis*
*mere exposure effect*
*mere-repeated-exposure effect*
*no-choice relationships*
*physical attractiveness stereotype*
*propinquity*
*proximity-attraction principle*
*reciprocity*
*reinforcement-affect model*
*similarity-attraction hypothesis*
*social exchange theory*
*variable-centered approach*
*waist-to-hip ratio*

# Glossary

**abstract trait knowledge**: when perceiving others, we tend to associate a specific behavior of theirs with some particular trait

**abstraction models**: propose that self-knowledge consists of summary representations that have been abstracted from events and behaviors involving the self (e.g., you would know that you are friendly by accessing a database of previously computed summary representations)

**abstractions**: mental summaries of observations made of another that lead to a conclusion about the other's personality, motives, etc.

**actor-observer bias**: when we observe others, we tend to focus on their internal attributes (e.g., character), while when we observe ourselves, we tend to focus on situational influences on our behavior

**affect**: feeling or emotion

**affect heuristic**: quick perceptual tool that is based on feelings of goodness or badness about some person or situation; these feelings affect our overall perception of the situation/person

**affect infusion model**: suggests that moods influence perceptions, and the more complex the information we need to process, generally the more effect our mood has on our perception

**affective models of the mere exposure effect**: proposes that repeated exposure to a stimulus tends to increase positive feelings toward it and/or decrease negative feelings toward that stimulus

**ageism**: holding prejudices or discriminating against people groups because of their age

**aggression**: verbal, physical or other social acts intended to harm another

**altruism**: an other-centered motive for increasing another's welfare without expectation of benefits in return or regard to one's own welfare

**amotivation**: a stage in self-determination theory that is characterized by diminished willingness to interact and participate

**anchoring effect**: a cognitive bias that involves "anchoring," or over-relying, on a single piece of information when perceiving or making decisions

**anthropocentric approach**: the common tendency in the field of psychology to focus on humans as the central object of study, mostly ignoring possible spiritual implications

**anti-fat attitudes**: generally perceiving overweight individuals negatively

**anticipation of interaction**: the common finding that anticipating having interaction with someone makes them seem more attractive/appealing

**antilocution**: damaging verbal remarks about a person or group; often not directly to the person or group

**antisocial behavior**: any behavior that is destructive to the common good (e.g., violence, discrimination, etc.)

**arms-length prejudice**: treating nongroup members respectfully in social settings, but keeping distant from them otherwise and not forming more intimate relationships with them

**arousal-cost reward model**: used to explain why people do or do not help in emergency situations; once the emergency causes an emotional reaction to the situation, the person will decide whether to help depending on their interpretation of their feelings and how much their helping will "cost" them (time, money, potential danger, etc.)

**attitudes**: positive or negative evaluative reactions one has toward something or someone

**attraction-similarity hypothesis**: the greater the likeness between people, the more likely they will find each other attractive

**attribution theories**: theories of how people explain others' behavior

**attributions**: causal statements and beliefs regarding people's behavior, intentions, etc.

**authoritarianism**: excessive focus on submission to leadership and intolerance of out-groups

**autokinetic effect**: a visual perception distortion in which a stationary point of light in a dark room appears to be moving

**automatic priming**: priming that occurs outside our conscious awareness

**automatic processing**: habitual, effortless, unconscious processing

**availability heuristic**: a cognitive bias that is the tendency to think that something that comes readily to mind is more likely to occur

**balance theory**: a motivational theory of attitude change that emphasizes our desire for consistency between our cognitions and our feelings

**behaviorism**: emphasizes environmental/situational conditioning as the basis of all complex social behavior

**belief perseverance**: the tendency to hold onto one's beliefs or convictions even when there is contrary proof to discredit it

**bounded rationality**: when making decisions, our rationality is limited by the information we have, the cognitive limitations we have and the finite amount of time we have to make the decision

**brainstorming**: used in groups to help facilitate idea generating; group members are encouraged to share all the ideas they can come up with without any evaluation of which ideas are good

**brainwriting**: used in groups to help facilitate idea generating; consists of a group of people writing their individual ideas on paper before the group discussion

**bystander effect**: the tendency to be less likely to offer help when there are other bystanders

**categorization**: sorting others in groups or categories (e.g., by race, age, etc.)

**cautious shift**: when group members make more cautious decisions together than they would alone

**CFR approach**: a Christian view of personhood that is centered on the Christian orthodox tenets of creation, fall and redemption; sees human social interaction in the light of God's purposes

**chameleon effect**: unintentionally mirroring another's gestures, voice inflection, etc.

**Christian orthodoxy**: the core set of Christian doctrine

**cognitive approach**: an approach in psychology that focuses on the processes involved in thinking, memory, learning, etc.

**cognitive dissonance**: the state of tension one feels when holding two or more conflicting cognitions and trying to reconcile them

**cognitive-enhanced evolutionary model**: helpers use specific cognitive processes to "fake" themselves into believing that a helpful act was not as costly as it actually was

**collective self**: the part of our self-concept that represents our relationship with larger groups

**collectivism**: see *sociocentric*

**compassion**: genuine concern for the welfare of others

**compliance**: publicly conforming to a social idea/standard while privately disagreeing with it

**computational models**: suggest that self-knowledge is represented in specific events and behaviors involving the self; a person decides whether a characteristic is self-descriptive by consulting a library of personal memories and computing an answer from whatever episodes are activated

**confirmation bias**: a tendency to look for information that confirms one's preexisting beliefs

**conformity**: a change in beliefs or behavior that is the result of social pressures, whether real or perceived

**consistency theories**: various theories regarding attitudes and behavior that assume that we tend to prefer to have consistency among our cognitions, affect and behavior in order to avoid cognitive dissonance

**contact hypothesis**: the belief that when members of different groups (e.g., racial) have more consistent contact with each other, negative biases and prejudices between them will decrease

**content analysis**: a research method that involves examining social communication (e.g., speeches, television shows, newspaper articles, etc.) and looking for themes or trends

**controlled processing**: effortful, deliberate thinking

**correlational approach**: the research method involving examining how variables co-vary without assuming cause and effect

**correspondence-inference bias**: the tendency to believe that people's behavior reflects their character

**counterfactual thinking**: imagining different possible outcomes to a situation than what actually happened

**couple-centered approach**: a strategy used in research exploring similarity, liking and satisfaction with marriage that focuses on couples as the unit of analysis (compare with variable-centered approach)

**covariation model**: a person will associate a particular behavior with an apparent cause that co-varies with it (e.g., a behavior is attributed to events or conditions that appear at the same time)

**creation**: the orthodox Christian tenet that God is the creator of all things, including humans, and that he was purposeful in his creation

**crimes of obedience**: carrying out an order that violates another's personhood and is contrary to the larger community's moral or legal law

**dehumanization**: any process that degrades people and sees them as being less than human

**deindividuation**: entails a diminished awareness of self and less evaluation apprehension; often results in following group norms, whether positive or destructive

**derogate**: to demean

**desensitization**: the process of decreasing reaction to a certain stimuli after repeated exposure

**diffusion of responsibility**: related to the bystander effect; perceiving that one has less responsibility to act when there are others present who also have some responsibility to respond

**discontinuity effect**: the finding that groups tend to be more competitive with each other than individuals tend to be

**displaced aggression**: hostility toward some other person or object that is not the true source of the person's anger

**door-in-the-face technique**: a way to persuade another to do a lesser favor by first requesting a larger favor one knows will be refused (door in the face); makes the smaller favor seem more reasonable

**downward counterfactuals**: imagining possible outcomes that would have been worse than what actually occurred; often makes one feel better about the actual outcome

**downward social comparison**: a strategy people use to make themselves feel better about their own situation by comparing themselves with others whose situation is worse

**dual-process models**: generally refers to two different routes to persuasion: central (fact-based) and peripheral (superficial)

**dynamic social impact theory**: looks at group phenomena to help predict how beliefs are transmitted through social systems

**ecological rationality**: we determine how accurate our use of heuristics is depending on the environment in which they are used

**effortful processing**: requiring conscious, deliberate thinking when learning and accumulating information

**egocentric**: for cultures, this term refers to those that emphasize personal freedom and autonomy

**egoism**: self-centered concern and motives

**elaboration likelihood model**: when we have the cognitive capacity/ability/ motivation to process a persuasive message, we tend to pay close attention to *central* features of the argument—its logic and coherence, for example; when we do not have sufficient cognitive capacity to comprehend the message or lack motivation to process the message, we are more easily persuaded by *peripheral* information such as the good looks of the presenter or the humorous strategies used by them

**emotional susceptibility**: stable tendency to feel discomfort, inadequacy and vulnerability, especially in response to perceived threats

**empathy-altruism hypothesis**: proposes that the degree to which you experience empathy for another's plight helps determine whether you will help them

**empiricism**: the approach of the sciences that entails systematic observation and hypothesis testing

**eugenics**: literally, "good genes"; involves trying to improve the genetic composition of a group by discouraging mating with or among those who possess a particular kind of genetic weakness

**evolutionary psychology**: approach in psychology that tries to identify which psychological and personality characteristics are evolved adaptations in humans

**excitation transfer model**: leftover excitation from one stimulus will amplify one's response to another stimulus

**executive cognitive processes**: organize and control other cognitive processes such as learning and memory

**exemplars, behavioral**: the specific behaviors observed in another person that we use to form an opinion of the other; we determine whether the other has a specific trait by accessing our memories of trait-specific behaviors we have observed in them

**expectancy-value model**: proposes that attitudes regarding an object or person are a function of the beliefs we form and values we place on those beliefs

**experimental approach**: in research, manipulating one variable to determine if it modifies an outcome in other variables; allows researchers to make cause-effect conclusions

**explicit prejudice**: conscious negative attitudes about dissimilar others

**explicit self-esteem**: a self-evaluation done in an intentional, conscious manner; generally a more fragile self-evaluation

**extensivity**: the extension of self to include others, attachment to others and a sense of responsibility for others' welfare

**extrinsic religiosity**: attending church and participating in religious activities more for social benefit than for spiritual reasons

**eye contact effect**: eye contact elicits activity in the parts of the brain related to social interaction; direction of eye gaze (e.g., averted or forward) affects our perceptions of the other's motives, etc.

**fall**: according to orthodox Christianity, the entrance of sin into the world which caused the separation of humanity and God

**false consensus**: an overestimation of how much other individuals share our behaviors and beliefs

**false modesty**: behavior that is meant to portray humility, but often includes an ulterior motive (e.g., social gain)

**field experiments**: research conducted in real-world settings (e.g., mall, street corner)

**folk-conceptual theory of explanation**: a theory regarding how people make attributions about others' behaviors; focuses on one's perception of whether the other's actions were intentional or not

**foot-in-the-door technique**: a compliance technique that involves making an initial modest request, which often inclines the person to agree to a larger request presented later on

**forgiveness**: the act of pardoning a fault or an offense; often results in less hostile feelings toward the offender as well as a decrease in retaliatory aggression

**frustration-aggression hypothesis**: the view that a state of dissatisfaction or annoyance, resulting from unresolved problems or unfulfilled needs, often leads to aggression in order to remove that annoyance; later revised to suggest that aggression is only one of many possible responses to frustration

**functional proximity**: geographical closeness and resultant opportunities for interaction increase the likelihood of being attracted to an individual

**functional theory of counterfactual thinking**: counterfactual thinking serves the function of managing and coordinating ongoing behavior

**fundamental attribution error**: the tendency to attribute another's negative behavior to internal dispositions (e.g., his/her character) and underestimating environmental factors

**fundamental need to belong**: humans' intrinsic relational nature; the inherent desire to create and maintain stable interpersonal relationships

**general aggression model**: a comprehensive theory of aggression that includes individual, situational and biological variables involved in aggression

**generality of prejudice**: the tendency of some individuals who are prejudiced against one group to be more likely to also be prejudiced against other groups as well

**group polarization**: the tendency of a group to make more extreme decisions than they would make if the individual group members were acting individually

**group-serving bias**: groups tend to make favorable attributions for their own successes and downplay the favorable qualities and successes of other groups; also involves groups attributing their own failures to external or situational factors and vice versa for outsider groups

**groupiness**: the degree to which sets of people freely interact in a wide range of experiences, have a shared history and expect future interaction

**groupthink**: occurs when a homogenous and highly cohesive group is focused on maintaining unanimity, thus failing to evaluate alternatives fairly and suppressing contrary opinions both from within the group and from outside the group

**heat hypothesis**: proposes that a greater incidence of aggression is associated with hotter temperatures

**heuristic system model**: proposes that persuasive messages are processed more simply, using heuristics, or in more complex, deliberate ways; the heuristic approach may be more efficient, but is not as likely to lead to enduring effects of the persuasive message

**heuristics**: cognitive strategies or "rules of thumb" that facilitate quick, efficient judgments

**hierarchical/top-down inhibition**: effort to suppress negative stereotypes by consciously and deliberately pushing those thoughts from consciousness and actively preventing them from resurfacing

**hindsight bias**: the tendency of individuals to view past events as being more predictable then they truly were; the "I-knew-it-all-along" fallacy

**homophily principle**: the tendency of individuals to associate with similar individuals

**hostile aggression**: a type of aggression where the main purpose is inflicting harm on the victim

**hostile attribution bias**: the tendency to falsely interpret another individual's actions as hostile when there is no evidence of that intent

**hostile expectation bias**: the tendency to assume that individuals will respond with aggression to potential conflicts

**humanizing**: honoring the dignity of others' personhood

**hypothesis**: in research, an educated guess that is a testable proposition about a possible relationship between two or more events

**ideograph**: a sign or symbol, rather than words, that represents an idea or concept

**illusion of control**: the perception that events are more controllable than they actually are

**illusory correlations**: perception that a relationship between two things is present when none exists

**imago Dei**: literally, "image of God"; according to Christian orthodoxy, the belief that humans are made in the image of God

**implicit ageism**: one's unconscious prejudice and stereotyping against older individuals

**implicit association test**: a reaction-time test intended to assess implicit (unconscious) attitudes about a variety of issues (e.g., race, age, gender, etc.)

**implicit prejudice**: one's negative prejudice about which one is not consciously aware

**implicit self-esteem**: one's evaluation of self that is largely outside of one's awareness; generally more stable than explicit self-esteem (described above)

**in-group bias**: an appraisal of one's own group as being superior to other groups

**inclusive fitness**: refers to the process by which an organism's "success" is dependent on leaving behind the maximum number of replicas of its genes within a population; in evolutionary psychology, often seen as an ultimate motive for many social behaviors

**individual self**: the part of self-concept that relates to one's unique characteristics (compare with relational self and collective self)

**individualism**: emphasis on individual freedom and potential seen in egocentric cultures

**information integration approach**: suggests that similarity in a relationship is only reinforcing when the individual sees the similarity positively and is aware that it can be rewarding

**informational influence**: in order to save cognitive time and energy, we often look to others (especially those who are high-status) to provide for us an accurate interpretation of reality that enables us to behave correctly

**infrahumanization**: the belief that one's in-group is more human than is an out-group

**instrumental aggression**: aggression as a means to an end; the main goal is not to harm the victim but to attain some other goal, such as access to a valuable resource

**intergroup processes**: having to do with social interactions and perceptions between and among groups

**internalization**: in self-determination theory, a stage that is characterized by the individual choosing to adapt to and accept values and behaviors that are not intrinsically appealing at first

**interpersonal attraction**: finding another person appealing and desiring to form some type of relationship with them (e.g., romantic, friendship, etc.)

**intertextual approach**: an approach to the Scriptures that involves acknowledging how other sources (e.g., historical texts, science, observations in everyday life) can help us in our understanding of Scripture and the nature of reality

**intragroup processes**: social processes that happen within groups

**intratextual approach**: the Scriptures are believed to comprise all the truth about the world and how to interact in it. Thus, other sources of knowledge (science, texts, etc.) are relatively neglected in terms of their potential to add to our understanding of truth.

**intrinsic motivation**: a stage of self-determination theory characterized by a person choosing to engage in an activity for its own sake or for the satisfaction derived from the activity itself rather than from an external reason or reward

**intrinsic religiosity**: authentic faith that is not dependent on the approval or thoughts of others

**introspection**: gaining personal insight by examining one's feelings and thoughts

**just-world hypothesis**: the idea that people will get what they deserve whether it is bad or good; often used to explain why bad things happen to people

**kin selection**: evolutionary strategies that favor the reproduction and offspring of one's relatives, even at the expense of one's own life

**lab experimentation**: experimental research that takes place in a laboratory setting

**lateral inhibition**: in reference to suppression of negative stereotypes this involves the nondeliberate reduction in negative stereotyping that often occurs when one befriends an individual of another race/ethnicity

**looking-glass self**: a person's self mirrors their perception of what others think of them

**low-ball technique**: a persuasive technique in which one gets another to agree to a request that is later revealed to be more costly than was initially presented

**matching hypothesis**: posits that people are more likely to form long-standing relationships with those who are equally matched with them in social attributes such as physical attractiveness

**medical student syndrome**: a form of hypochondriasis in which medical students diagnose themselves with the diseases they are studying

**mere exposure effect** (also known as the familiarity principle): repeated exposure to someone or something enhances our liking for them

**mere presence effect**: the real or imagined presence of others often results in social facilitation effects, i.e., doing better on simple or familiar/well-rehearsed tasks

**meta-cognitive model**: assumes that one can hold more than one summary evaluation of a target; when presented with new information about the target, we could alter our attitude, surmising that the previous one was false or incorrect, then change our attitude, yet we retain some of the old way of thinking, thus the possibility of varying attitudes toward the target, each dependent on the strength of the association we make

**MODE model** (Motivation and Opportunity as DEterminants of the attitude/ behavior relation): proposes that an attitude represents the extent to which a person learns to associate some issue (e.g., race) to positive or negative evaluations. These attitudes bias the perceptions of those issues so that you interpret future encounters with that issue/person in either positive or negative ways. But only strong attitudes, i.e., those that one can easily access in memory, will govern behavior.

**moral hypocrisy**: professing one's agreement with some moral standard, but acting contrary to it

**multisystemic therapy**: collaborative effort treatment program between parents and community to help assist troubled teens

**narcissism**: selfish and self-centered viewpoints that are often associated with higher levels of aggression when provoked

**naturalism**: the belief that all reality comprises material substance and that the immaterial is either false, unknowable or irrelevant

**naturalistic observations**: research performed while not interfering with subject's behavior

**negative-state relief model**: proposes that one main reason we help others is to reduce sadness or other negative mood states

**negativity effect**: the tendency to judge negative information disproportionately greater than the positive information received; thus, the negative information more heavily influences our evaluations/attitudes about the object, person, etc.

**neoassociationist model**: for aggression, an aversive event is one that results from being provoked, frustrated or exposed to loud noise, heat, crowding, etc.; that aversive event elicits in the person a generalized negative arousal state, then the person prepares to fight against the aversive event (resulting in aggression) or engages in escape or avoidance tactics

**no-choice relationships**: involves people whom we must interact with but find unlikable

**normative influence**: conformity to be accepted and approved by others

**obedience**: complying with orders given by an authority

**obligatory interdependence**: an evolutionary perspective that argues that humans must rely on each other for survival

**optimal self-esteem**: a self-evaluation that is well-grounded, stable and includes an honest appraisal of one's strengths and weaknesses

**optimism bias**: believing that one is less at risk of various negative effects than is the general populace

**overconfidence effect**: the tendency to believe that one is more accurate than they actually are; to be more confident than correct

**overpowered integrity**: a primary motive for the person is to act morally, but when they see the heavy cost of the action, they may decide to do otherwise

**PAST model** (Past Attitudes are Still There): see *meta-cognitive model*

**person-centered approach**: a research approach that emphasizes the differences between individuals when analyzing the relationship between the variables

**perspective-taking**: considering other people's circumstances and points of view; often helps reduce aggression and other antisocial behaviors

**physical attractiveness stereotype**: the false idea that more attractive people possess better personality traits like intelligence and kindness, which are actually unrelated to level of attractiveness; the belief that "what is beautiful is good"

**pluralistic ignorance**: a false impression shared in a group

**positive psychology**: focuses on exploring human strengths and virtues and increasing subjective, community and institutional well-being

**prefrontal cortex**: part of the brain that handles higher-order thinking related to reasoning, impulse control and understanding the consequences of one's behavior; aggressive individuals of all ages often have reduced metabolism and less volume in the prefrontal cortex

**prejudice**: usually a negative attitude toward a target object (can also be a positive attitude)

**primacy effect**: information presented first on a list will be better remembered than the middle and last items

**priming**: both explicit and implicit exposure to a stimulus influences one's response to a later stimulus

**private conformity**: an internalized attitude or belief in response to group influence

**probabilistic realism**: regarding the accuracy of our perceptions, reality rarely has all-or-nothing truths, thus our estimation of what is real is accurate much of the time, despite our limitations

**production blocking**: a reduction of idea generation that occurs when individual group members have to wait their turn to provide their answers, thus possibly getting distracted or inattentive due to concentrating on one's own train of thought so as not to forget it

**prosocial behavior**: any behavior that is for the common good

**proximate cause**: the more immediate, obvious cause of any particular social behavior

**proximity-attraction principle**: physical proximity is one of the best predictors of who we are attracted to, make friends with, date and marry

**psychic unity of humankind**: the view in evolutionary psychology that all members of the human species share the same basic, adaptive cognitive capacities and resultant general tendencies in social behavior

**public conformity**: publicly professing belief in the social norms of a group but not truly accepting them; generally results in shorter-lasting conformity

**quest orientation**: an approach to religiosity that is characterized by a tendency to view religious issues as complex and to resist clear-cut answers to the difficult questions raised

**rape-prone cultures**: cultures in which rape is committed against women from enemy groups during times of war, used as part of a ritual (like during an adolescent male's rite of passage into adulthood) and used as a threat against women in order to keep them subservient to men

**reactance**: resisting social pressure when it is perceived that a behavioral freedom is in danger

**recency effect**: information that is received last is more easily recalled

**reciprocity**: exchanging mutual favors

**reciprocity norm**: the expectation that you will help those who have helped you; "paying back"

**redemption**: a core orthodox doctrine related to Christ's salvation of humans as well as the redemptive work that God's grace bestows on humans in this life

**reductionism**: reducing complex issues (e.g., motives for human social behavior) into a few general principles/laws (e.g., survival and reproductive advantage)

**reinforcement-affect model**: posits that if you have close relationships with others who share your beliefs and values, then you can experience a host of positive consequences such as feeling better understood or feeling less lonely

**relational self**: the part of self-concept that has to do with our close, interpersonal relationships

**religious fundamentalism**: rigid obedience to an established set of essential beliefs; authoritarian manner of holding one's faith as the inerrant truth

**representative heuristic**: a cognitive bias used when making judgments about the probability of an event under uncertainty; judging that a person/object, etc., belongs to a particular group/type based on its similarity with that group/type

**right-wing authoritarianism**: high degrees of deference to established authority, aggression toward out-groups when authorities permit that aggression, and support for traditional values when those values are endorsed by authorities

**risky shift**: the tendency for individuals to engage in more risky behavior when in a group than when alone

**rosy retrospection**: past events are viewed as more pleasurable or positive than they actually were

**satisficer**: a person who prefers a satisfactory solution that is good enough rather than finding the optimal answer

**scripts**: cognitive schemas that help us organize our complex social world

**self-attention theory**: maintains that the more attention is focused on the self, the greater the likelihood that the individual will try to match their behavior with the majority standard

**self-categorization theory**: starts from the distinction between collective and personal identity, and sees these as different *levels* of self-categorization, which are both equally valid and authentic definitions of the self; people are both individual persons and social group members

**self-concept**: the idea of "who" one is

**self-determination theory**: concerned with the study of how people can make choices different than what would be expected from the situational influences

**self-esteem**: one's overall sense of self-worth

**self-efficacy**: the sense one has of being effective and competent

**self-handicapping**: sabotaging our efforts at success by creating roadblocks that lessen our chances of success so that we can protect our self-image with behaviors that create an excuse for later failure

**self-monitoring**: being attuned to one's public image and adjusting one's actions according to the needs of the situation

**self-presentation/impression management**: involves trying to control the impressions people have of us

**self-reference effect**: it is easier to remember something when it is related to oneself

**self-regulation**: ability to control and alter one's own behavior

**self-schemas**: beliefs about the self that organize and guide the processing of information that is relevant to the self

**self-serving bias**: tendency to take personal credit for our successes and to blame external factors for our failures

**self-validation theory**: posits that the level of confidence in one's own thoughts can increase or decrease persuasion depending on the type of thoughts that the message elicits

**serotonin**: a neurotransmitter thought to control feelings of well-being or happiness, sleep, mood, learning and vasoconstriction; deficiencies are associated with increased aggression in some cases

**similarity-attraction hypothesis**: comparable traits in others make them more likable

**social cascading**: information disseminating quickly in a social network

**social categorization**: perceiving people as belonging to various groups

**social cognition**: how people interpret social situations, including how we encode, store and retrieve social information to draw conclusions about our social world

**social comparison**: perceiving similarities and differences between the self and others and using those observations to make conclusions regarding the self

**social contagion**: the tendency for ideas, behavior and moods to transfer rapidly from person to person

**social dominance orientation**: a general tendency to perceive one's in-group as dominant or superior to out-groups; generally entails an attitude that intergroup relations are not equal

**social exchange theory**: proposes that social behavior involves weighing the risks and rewards of social interactions/relationships and the tendency to try to maximize the rewards while minimizing the costs

**social exclusion**: when individuals or groups of people are ostracized from social interactions with others; also refers to how one could be blocked from rights, resources or opportunities

**social facilitation**: the tendency, while in the presence of others, to perform better on simple tasks as well as those tasks that one is accustomed to doing

**social identity model of disinhibition effects (SIDE)**: deindividuating settings do not lead to anonymity or a loss of personal identity, rather, they help foster a more social or collective identity, meaning more identification with the group and its norms; even if the group's behavior seems irrational or disinhibited to outsiders, the behavior makes sense to the group members, who do not see themselves as acting mindlessly

**social identity theory**: concerned with the motivation to maintain a positive social (collective) identity; when confronted with a threat to their social identity, people maintain a positive social identity by viewing the in-group in a more favorable light than they view the out-groups, which can result in prejudice

**social impact theory**: argues that the likelihood that you will respond to social influence depends on the perceived strength and immediacy of the impact, as well as the number of forces exerting the impact; the impact tends to increase as the number of sources increases

**social influence**: refers to the many ways in which we impact one another's social behaviors

**social influence model**: group size is only important in social influence up to a point, beyond which increasing the group size would not have any additional impact

**social learning theory**: the theory that people learn from others, especially via modeling and observation

**social loafing**: contributing less effort while in a group than one would if working individually

**social perception**: the process of understanding our social world, including forming impressions of others and of social situations

**social psychology**: the scientific study of human social behavior, including social cognition, social influence and social interaction

**social responsibility norm**: the expectation that those who are in a position to do so will care for those who cannot

**social role theory**: behavioral differences between the genders result from socially constructed roles that are passed down from generation to generation

**sociocentric**: a culture that emphasizes group solidarity and perceives individuals in the light of their part in the whole

**sociometer model of self-esteem**: proposes that self-esteem is contingent upon one's perception of belongingness in a group; self-esteem is enhanced by perceptions of greater belongingness

**spotlight effect**: the assumption that everyone is more aware of you and your behavior than they really are

**stereotype threat**: process whereby a person from a stigmatized group may become anxious/worried about a negative stereotype of their group and act in a way that makes that stereotype a self-fulfilling prophecy

**stereotypes**: a cognition/idea about a group of people; can have varying levels of accuracy

**surveys**: a process for gathering information that is reported by individuals

**theistic evolution**: the belief that God created the universe, and that the natural evolutionary process is a tool used by God to bring about his purposes in creation

**theocentric approach**: in psychology, a view that tries to understand humans from a God-centered approach, i.e., humans in relation to God's nature and purposes

**theories**: broad statements that are based on a hypothesis or group of hypotheses that have received empirical support

**theory of planned behavior**: argues that an individual's likelihood of engaging in a behavior is related to their attitude toward the behavior, subjective norms (the way one perceives that important others view that behavior) and perceived behavioral control

**theory of reasoned action**: proposes that one's likelihood of engaging in a specific behavior depends on one's attitude and one's subjective norms (the way one perceives that important others view that behavior)

**three-component model**: the level of attachment, alleged cost and feeling of duty that form within an individual's commitment to a certain group

**trait aggressiveness**: a tendency toward both verbal and physical aggression that includes hostile cognitions and a tendency to express anger

**trait anger**: a tendency to feel angry more often and more intensely than is usual, including intense anger at being criticized

**trait irritability**: a general tendency to be easily angered, especially at the least provocation; also being easily offended

**ultimate cause**: in evolutionary psychology, generally refers to evolutionary origins/forces of survival and reproductive advantages as the ultimate causes of all social behavior

**unimodal approach to persuasion**: proposes that there really are no different information and processing types as are suggested by the dual-process models; instead, the primary factor determining the strength of a persuasive message and the amount of processing effort we will put into it has to do with its complexity

**upward counterfactuals**: imagining better outcomes to a situation than what actually occurred

**upward social comparison**: comparing oneself to people who are more elite and prestigious than oneself in an effort to see oneself as one of them

**urban legend**: a type of modern folklore that circulates widely and may or may not be true

**variable-centered approach**: a research approach that emphasizes the variables and the relationships among the variables

**waist-to-hip ratio**: proportion of measurement of the waist to that of the hips; a major factor believed to be involved in males' attraction to females

**warm-cold variable**: the phenomenon that first impressions can be drastically influenced by a simple priming of the word *warm* or *cold* used to describe the person one is about to meet

**warm-glow hypothesis**: people who feel good are more likely to help others due to their jubilant mood

**weapons effect**: a higher probability of aggressive behavior that is associated with the mere presence, mention or visual representation of a weapon

# References

Abele, A., & Wojciszke, B. (2007). Agency and communion from the perspective of self versus others. *Journal of Personality and Social Psychology, 93*, 751-63.

Aboud, F. E. (2003). The formation of in-group favoritism and out-group prejudice in young children: Are they distinct attitudes? *Developmental Psychology, 39*(1), 48-60.

Aboud, F. E., & Mendelson, M. J. (1996). Determinants of friendship selection and quality: Developmental perspectives. In W. M. Bukowski, A. F. Newcomb & W. W. Hartup (Eds.), *The company they keep: Friendship in childhood and adolescence* (pp. 87-112). New York, NY: Cambridge University Press.

Adams, G. R., & Crane, P. (1980). An assessment of parents' and teachers' expectations for preschool children's social preferences for attractive or unattractive children and adults. *Child Development, 51*, 224-31.

Adolphs, R., Gosselin, F., Buchanan, T. W., Tranel, D., Schyns, P., & Damasio, A. R. (2005). A mechanism for impaired fear recognition after amygdala damage. *Nature, 433*, 68-72.

Adorno, T. W., Frenkel-Brunswik, E., Levinson, D., & Sanford, R. (1950). *The authoritarian personality*. New York: Harper.

Ainsworth, M. D. S. (1989). Attachments beyond infancy. *American Psychologist, 44*, 709-16.

Ajzen, I. (1982). On behaving in accordance with one's attitudes. In M. P. Zanna, F. T. Higgins & C. P. Herman (Eds.), *Consistency in social behavior: The Ontario Symposium*, vol. 2. Hillsdale, NJ: Erlbaum.

Ajzen, I. (1985). From intentions to actions: A theory of planned behavior. In J. Kuhl & J. Beckmann (Eds.), *Action control: From cognition to behavior*. New York: Springer-Verlag.

Ajzen, I. (1991). The theory of planned behavior. *Organizational Behavior and Human Decision Processes, 50*, 179-211.

Ajzen, I. (1992). Persuasive communication in social psychology: An historical perspective. In M. J. Manfredo (Ed.), *Influencing human behavior* (pp. 1-27). Champaign, IL: Sagamore.

Ajzen, I. (2001). Nature and operation of attitudes. *Annual Review of Psychology, 52*, 27-58.

Ajzen, I. (2002). Perceived behavioral control, self-efficacy, locus of control, and the theory of planned behavior. *Journal of Applied Social Psychology, 32*, 665-83.

Ajzen, I., & Fishbein, M. (1977). Attitude-behavior relatedness: A theoretical analysis and review of empirical research. *Psychological Bulletin, 84*, 888-918.

Ajzen, I., & Fishbein, M. (1980). *Understanding attitudes and predicting social behavior*. Englewood Cliffs, NJ: Prentice-Hall.

Ajzen, I., & Fishbein, M. (2000). Attitudes and the attitude-behavior relation: Reasoned and automatic processes. In W. Stroebe & M. Hewstone (Eds.), *European review of social psychology* (pp. 1-33). San Francisco, CA: John Wiley & Sons.

Albarracin, D., Johnson, B. T., Fishbein, M., & Muellerleile, P. A. (2001). Theories of reasoned action and planned behavior as models of condom use: A meta-analysis. *Psychological Bulletin, 127*, 142-61.

Aldag, R. J., & Fuller, S. R. (1993). Beyond fiasco: A reappraisal of the groupthink phenomenon and a new model of group decision processes. *Psychological Bulletin, 113*, 533-52.

Alexander, R. (1979). *Darwinism and human affairs*. Seattle: University of Washington Press.

Alexander, R. (1998). *The biology of moral systems*. New York, NY: Aldine de Gruyter.

Alhakami, A. S., & Slovic, P. (1994). A psychological study of the inverse relationship between perceived risk and perceived benefit. *Risk Analysis, 14*(6), 1085-96.

Alley, T. R., & Hildebrandt, K. A. (1988). Determinants and consequences of facial aesthetics. Social and applied aspects of perceiving faces. In T. R. Alley and K. A. Hildebrandt (Eds.), *Social and applied aspects of perceiving faces: Resources for ecological psychology* (pp. 101-40). Hillsdale, NJ: Lawrence Erlbaum.

Alloy, L. B., & Clements, C. M. (1992). Illusion of control: Invulnerability to negative affect and depressive symptoms after laboratory and natural stressors. *Journal of Abnormal Psychology, 101*(2), 234-45.

Allport, F. (1926). Social psychology. *Psychological Bulletin, 23*, 285-89.

Allport, F. (1937). Toward a science of public opinion. *Public Opinion Quarterly, 1*(1), 7-23.

Allport, G. (1924). *Social psychology*. Boston, MA: Houghton Mifflin.

Allport, G. W. (1935). Attitudes. In C. Murchinson (Ed.), *Handbook of social psychology* (pp. 798-844). Worcester, MA: Clark University Press.

Allport, G. W. (1954). *The nature of prejudice*. Cambridge, MA: Addison Wesley.

Allport, G. W. (1966). Religious context of prejudice. *Journal for the Scientific Study of Religion, 5*, 447-57.

Allport, G. W., & Kramer, B. M. (1946). Some roots of prejudice. *Journal of Psychology, 22*, 9-39.

Allport, G. W., & Ross, J. M. (1967). Personal religious orientation and prejudice. *Journal of Personality and Social Psychology, 5*, 432-43.

Altemeyer, B. (1981). *Right-wing authoritarianism*. Winnipeg, Canada: University of Manitoba Press.

Altemeyer, B. (1988). *Enemies of freedom: Understanding right-wing authoritarianism*. San Francisco, CA: Jossey-Bass.

Altemeyer, B. (1996). *The authoritarian specter*. Cambridge, MA: Harvard University Press.

Altemeyer, B. (1998). The other "authoritarian personality." In M. P. Zanna (Ed.), *Advances in experimental social psychology* (Vol. 30, pp. 47-92). San Diego, CA: Academic Press.

Altemeyer, B., & Hunsberger, B. (1992). Authoritarianism, religious fundamentalism, quest, and prejudice. *International Journal for the Psychology of Religion, 2,* 113-33.

Altemeyer, B., & Hunsberger, B. (2005). Fundamentalism and authoritarianism. In R. F. Paloutizian & C. L. Park (Eds.), *Handbook of the psychology of religion and spirituality* (pp. 378-93). New York: Guilford Press.

Amato, P. R. (1990). Personality and social network: Involvement as predictors of helping in everyday life. *Social Psychology Quarterly, 53,* 1, 31-43.

Amodio, D. M., & Showers, C. J. (2005). "Similarity breeds liking" revisited: The moderating role of commitment. *Journal of Social and Personal Relationships, 22,* 817-36.

Amsel, R., & Fichten, C. (1986). Trait attributions about college students with a physical disability: Circumplex analyses and methodological issues. *Journal of Applied Social Psychology, 16,* 410-27.

Andersen, S. M., Klatzky, R. L., & Murray, J. (1990). Traits and social stereotypes: Efficiency differences in social information processing. *Journal of Personality & Social Psychology, 59,* 192-201.

Anderson, C.A., & Anderson, K. B. (1998). Temperature and aggression: Paradox, controversy, and a (fairly) clear picture. In R. Geen & E. Donnerstein (Eds.), *Human aggression: Theories, research and implications for policy* (pp. 247-98). San Diego, CA: Academic Press.

Anderson, C. A., Benjamin, A. J., & Bartholow, B. D. (1998). Does the gun pull the trigger? Automatic priming effects of weapon pictures and weapon names. *Psychological Science, 9,* 308-14.

Anderson, C. A., & Bushman, B. J. (1997). External validity of "trivial" experiments: The case of laboratory aggression. *Review of General Psychology, 1*(1), 19-41.

Anderson, C. A., & Bushman, B. J. (2001). Effects of violent video games on aggressive behavior, aggressive cognition, aggressive affect, physiological arousal, and prosocial behavior: A meta-analytic review of the scientific literature. *Psychological Science, 12*(1), 353-59.

Anderson, C. A., & Bushman, B. J. (2002). Human aggression. *Annual Review of Psychology, 53,* 27-51.

Anderson, C. A., Bushman, B. J., & Groom, R. W. (1997). Hot years and serious and deadly assault: Empirical tests of the heat hypothesis. *Journal of Personality and Social Psychology, 73,* 1213-23.

Anderson, K. (2010). *Benign bigotry: The psychology of subtle prejudice.* Cambridge, England: Cambridge University Press.

Anderson, N., & Hubert, S. (1963). Effects of concomitant verbal recall on order effects in personality impression formation. *Journal of Verbal Learning and Verbal Behavior, 2,* 379-91.

Anderson, S. L., Adams, G., & Plaut, V. C. (2008). The cultural grounding of personal relationship: The importance of attractiveness in everyday life. *Journal of Personality and Social Psychology, 95*(2), 352-68.

Archer, J. (2000). Sex differences in aggression between heterosexual partners: A meta-analytic review. *Psychological Bulletin, 126,* 651-80.

Archer, J. (2002). Sex differences in physically aggressive acts between heterosexual partners: A meta-analytic review. *Aggression and Violent Behavior: A Review Journal,* *7,* 313-51.

Archer, J. (2004). Sex differences in aggression in real-world settings: A meta-analytic review. *Review of General Psychology, 8*(4), 291-322. doi:10.1037/1089-2680.8.4.291

Arkes, H. R., & Tetlock, P. E. (2004). Attributions of implicit prejudice, or "Would Jesse Jackson fail the Implicit Association Test?" *Psychological Inquiry, 15*(4), 257-78.

Arkes, H. R., Wortmann, R. L., Saville, P. D., & Harkness, A. R. (1981). Hindsight bias among physicians weighing the likelihood of diagnoses. *Journal of Applied Psychology, 66,* 252-54.

Armitage, C. J., & Conner, M. (1999). Distinguishing perceptions of control from self-efficacy: Predicting consumption of a low-fat diet using the theory of planned behavior. *Journal of Applied Psychology, 29,* 72-90.

Armitage, C. J., & Conner, M. (2001). Efficacy of the theory of planned behavior: A meta-analytic review. *British Journal of Social Psychology, 40*(4), 471-99.

Aron, A., Aron, E., & Smollan, D. (1992). Inclusion of other in the self scale and the structure of interpersonal closeness. *Journal of Personality and Social Psychology, 63,* 596-612.

Aronson, E. (2002). *The social animal* (8th ed.). New York: Wiley.

Aronson, E., Wilson, T., & Akert, R. (2004). *Social Psychology, Media and Research Update* (4th ed.). Upper Saddle River, NJ: Pearson Education.

Asch, S. E. (1946). Forming impressions of personality. *Journal of Abnormal and Social Psychology, 41,* 1230-40.

Asch, S. E. (1951). Effects of group pressure on the modification and distortion of judgments. In H. Guetzkow (Ed.), *Groups, leadership and men* (pp. 177-90). Pittsburgh, PA: Carnegie Press.

Asch, S. E. (1955). Opinions and social pressure. *Scientific American, 193,* 33-35.

Asch, S. E. (1956). Studies of independence and conformity: A minority of one against a unanimous majority. *Psychological Monographs, 70* (Whole no. 416).

Ashmore, R. D., & Del Boca, F. K. (1981). Conceptual approaches to stereotypes and stereotyping. In D. L. Hamilton (Ed.), *Cognitive processes in stereotyping and intergroup behavior* (pp. 1-35). Hillsdale, NJ: Erlbaum.

Ashmore, R. D., Solomon, M. R., & Longo, L. C. (1996). Thinking about fashion models' looks: A mutlidimenaional approach to the structure of perceived physical attractiveness. *Personality and Social Psychology Bulletin, 22,* 1083-1104.

Averett, S., & Korenman, S. (1996). The economic reality of the beauty myth. *Journal of Human Resources, 31*(2), 304-30.

Averett, S., & Korenman, S. (1999). Black-white differences in social and economic consequences of obesity. *International Journal of Obesity, 23,* 166-73.

Axelrod, R. (1984). *The evolution of cooperation.* New York: Basic Books.

Axelrod, R., & Hamilton, W. D. (1981). The evolution of cooperation. *Science, New Series, 2111*(4489), 1390-96.

Back, M. D., Schmukle, S. C., & Egloff, B. (2008). Becoming friends by chance. *Psychological Science, 19*(5), 439-40.

Bailenson, J. N., and Yee, N. (2005). Digital chameleons: Automatic assimilation of nonverbal gestures in immersive virtual environments, *Psychological Science, 16*(10), 814-19.

Balaban, E., Alper, J. S., & Kasamon, Y. L. (1996). Mean genes and the biology of antagonism among adolescents. *Adolescence, 27,* 505-16.

Banaji, M. R. (1999, October 22). *Unconscious isms: Examples from racism, sexism, and ageism.* Paper presented at The Way Women Lead Conference, New Haven, CT.

Bandura, A. (1977). *Social learning theory.* New York, NY: General Learning Press.

Bandura, A. (1978). Social learning theory of aggression. *Journal of Communication, 28*(3), 12-29.

Bandura, A., Ross, D., & Ross, S. A. (1961). Transmission of aggression through imitation of aggressive models. *Journal of Abnormal and Social Psychology, 63,* 575-82. doi:10.1037/h0045925

Banerjee, R. (2002). Individual differences in children's understanding of social evaluation concerns. *Infant and Child Development, 11*(3), 237-52.

Barber, N. (2004). *Kindness in a cruel world: The evolution of altruism.* New York, NY: Prometheus Books.

Bargh, J. A. (1990). Auto-motives: Preconscious determinants of social interaction. In E. T. Higgins and R. M. Sorrentino (Eds.), *Handbook of motivation and cognition* (Vol. 2, pp. 93-100). New York, NY: Guilford Press.

Bargh, J. A. (1997). The automaticity of everyday life. In R. S. Wyer Jr. (Ed.), *Advances in social cognition* (Vol. 10, pp. 1-63). Mahwah, NJ: Erlbaum.

Bargh, J. A. (1999). The cognitive monster: The case against controllability of automatic stereotype effects. In S. Chaiken & Y. Trope (Eds.), *Dual process in social psychology* (pp. 361-82). New York, NY: Guilford Press.

Bargh, J. A. (2004). Being here and now: Is consciousness necessary for human freedom? In J. Greenberg, S. L. Koole & T. Pyszczynski (Eds.), *Handbook of experimental existential psychology* (pp. 385-97). New York, NY: Guilford Press.

Bargh, J. A., Chaiken, S., Raymond, P., & Hymes, C. (1996). The automatic evaluation effect: Unconditional automatic attitude activation with a pronunciation task. *Journal of Experimental Social Psychology, 32,* 104-28.

Bargh, J. A. & Chartrand, T. L. (1999). The unbearable automaticity of being. *American Psychologist, 54,* 462-69.

Bargh, J. A., Chen, M., & Burrows, L. (1996). Automaticity of social behavior: Direct effects of trait construct and stereotype activation on action. *Journal of Personality and Social Psychology, 71*(2), 230-44.

Bargh, J. A., & Ferguson, M. J. (2000). Beyond behaviorism: On the automaticity of higher mental processes. *Psychological Bulletin, 126*(6), 925-45.

Bargh, J. A., & Pietromonaco, P. (1982). Automatic information processing and social perception: The influence of trait information presented outside of conscious awareness on impression formation. *Journal of Personality and Social Psychology, 43,* 437-49.

Barkley, R. A. (1997). Behavioral inhibition, sustained attention, and executive functions: Constructing a unifying theory of ADHD. *Psychological Bulletin, 121*(1), 65-94.

Barkow, J., Cosmides, L., & Tooby, J. (Eds.). (1992). *The adapted mind.* New York, NY: Oxford University Press.

Barnard, A. (2001). On the relationship between technique and dehumanisation. In R. Locsin (Ed.), *Advancing technology, caring and nursing* (pp. 96-105). Westport, CT: Auburn House.

Baron, R. S. (1986). Distraction-conflict theory: Progress and problems. *Advances in Experimental Social Psychology, 19,* 1-40.

Baron, R. (1997). The Sweet smell of . . . helping: Effects of pleasant ambient fragrance on prosocial behavior in shopping malls. *Personality and Social Psychology Bulletin, 23,* 498-503.

Baron, R. A., & Byrne, D. (2003). *Social psychology.* Boston, MA: Allyn & Bacon.

Baron, R. A., & Richardson, D. R. (2004). *Human aggression, 2nd edition.* New York, NY: Plenum.

Barrow, G., & Smith, P. (1979). *Aging, ageism, and society.* St. Paul, MN: West Publishing.

Bar-Tal, D., & Kruglanski, A. W. (Ed.). *The social psychology of knowledge* (pp. 315-34). New York, NY: Cambridge University Press.

Bartholow, B. D., Bushman, B. J., & Sestir, M. A. (2006). Chronic violent video game exposure and desensitization to violence: Behavioral and event-related brain potential data. *Journal of Experimental Social Psychology, 42*(4), 532-39. doi:10.1016/j.jesp.2005.08.006

Bartlett, F. C. (1932). *Remembering: A study in experimental and social psychology.* London, England: Cambridge University Press.

Bartlett, M. Y., & DeSteno, D. (2006). Gratitude and prosocial behavior: Helping when it costs you. *Psychological Science, 17,* 319-25. doi:10.1111/j.1467-9280.2006.01705.x

Baskin, T.W., & Enright, R. D. (2004). Intervention studies on forgiveness: A meta-analysis. *Journal of Counseling and Development, 82,* 79-90.

Bassett, R. L., Thrower, J., Barclay, J., Powers, C., Smith, A., Tindall, M., Tiuch, K., & Monroe, J. (2005). One effort to measure implicit attitudes toward spirituality and religion. *Journal of Psychology and Christianity, 24*(3), 210-18.

Batson, C. D. (1976). Religion as prosocial: Agent or double agent? *Journal for the Scientific Study of Religion, 15,* 29-45.

Batson, C. D. (1987). Prosocial motivation: Is it ever truly altruistic? In L. Berkowitz (Ed.), *Advances in experimental social psychology* (Vol. 20, pp. 65-122). San Diego, CA: Academic Press.

Batson, C. D. (1990). How social an animal? The human capacity for caring. *American Psychologist 45,* 336-46.

Batson, C. D. (1991). *The altruism question: Towards a social-psychological answer.* Hillsdale, NJ: Erlbaum.

Batson, C. D. (1994). Why act for the public good? Four answers. *Personality and Social Psychology Bulletin, 20*(5), 603-10.

Batson, C. D. (1997). Self-other merging and the empathy-altruism hypothesis: Reply to Neuberg et al. (1997). *Journal of Personality and Social Psychology, 73,* 517-22.

Batson, C. D. (2009). Two forms of perspective taking: Imagining how another feels and imagining how you would feel. In K. D. Markman, W. M. P. Klein & J. A. Suhr (Eds.), *Handbook of imagination and mental simulation* (pp. 267-79). New York, NY: Psychology Press.

Batson, C. D., O'Quin, K., Fultz, J., Vanderplas, M., & Isen, M. (1983). Self-reported distress and empathy and egoism versus altruistic motivation for helping. *Journal of Personality and Social Psychology, 45,* 706-18.

Batson, C. D., Batson, J., Griffitt, C., Barrientos, S., Brandt, J., Sprengelmeyer, P., & Bayly, M. (1989). Negative-state relief and the empathy-altruism hypothesis. *Journal of Personality and Social Psychology, 56,* 922-33.

Batson, C. D., Batson, J., Singlsby, J., Harrell, K., Peekna, H., & Todd, R. (1991). Empathic joy and the empathy-altruism hypothesis. *Journal of Personality and Social Psychology, 61,* 413-26.

Batson, C. D., Coke, J. S., Chard, P., Smith, D., & Taliaferro, A. (1979). Generality of the "glow of good will": Effects of mood on helping and information acquisition. *Social Psychology Quarterly, 42,* 176-79.

Batson, C., Dyck, J., Brandt, J., Batson, J., Powell, A., McMaster, M., & Griffitt, C. (1988). Five studies testing two new egoistic alternatives to the empathy-altruism hypothesis. *Journal of Personality and Social Psychology, 55,* 52-77.

Batson, C. D., Early, S., & Salvarani, G. (1997). Perspective taking: Imagining how another feels versus imagining how you would feel. *Personality and Social Psychology Bulletin, 23*(7), 751-58.

Batson, C. D., Eidelman, S. H., Higley, S. L., & Russell, S. A. (2001). "And who is my neighbor?": II. Quest religion as a source of universal compassion. *Journal for the Scientific Study of Religion, 40,* 39-50.

Batson, C. D., Flink, C. H., Schoenrade, P. A., Fultz, J., & Pych, V. (1986). Religious orientation and overt versus covert racial prejudice. *Journal of Personality and Social Psychology, 50,* 175-81.

Batson, C. D., Floyd, R. B., & Meyer, J. M. (1999). "And Who Is My Neighbor?": Intrinsic religion as a source of universal compassion. *Journal for the Scientific Study of Religion, 38*(4), 445-57.

Batson, C. D., & Fultz, J. (1987). Critical self-reflection and self-perceived altruism: When self-reward fails. *Journal of Personality and Social Psychology, 53,* 594-602.

Batson, C. D., Kobrynowicz, D., Dinnerstein, J. L., Kampf, H. C., & Wilson, A. D. (1997). In a very different voice: Unmasking moral hypocrisy. *Journal of Personality and Social Psychology, 72,* 1335-48.

Batson, C. D., Naifeh, S. J., & Pate, S. (1978). Social desirability, religious orientation, and racial prejudice. *Journal for the Scientific Study of Religion, 17,* 31-41.

Batson, C., Sager, K., Garst, E., Kang, M., Rubchinsky, K., & Dawson, K. (1997). Is empathy-induced helping due to self-other merging? *Journal of Personality and Social Psychology, 73,* 495-509.

Batson, C. D., & Schoenrade, P. (1991). Measuring religion as quest: Validity concerns. *Journal for the Scientific Study of Religion, 30,* 416-29.

Batson, C. D., Schoenrade, P., & Ventis, L. (1993). *Religion and the individual.* New York, NY: Oxford University Press.

Batson, C. D., & Shaw, L. (1991). Evidence for altruism: Toward a pluralism of prosocial motives. *Psychological Inquiry, 2,* 107-22.

Batson, C. D., & Stocks, E. L. (2005). Religion and prejudice. In J. F. Dovidio, P. S. Glick & L. A. (Eds.), *On the nature of prejudice: Fifty years after Allport* (pp. 413-27). Malden, MA: Blackwell.

Batson, C. D., & Thompson, E. R. (2001). Why don't moral people act morally? Motivational considerations. *Current Directions in Psychological Science, 10,* 54-57.

Batson, C. D., Thompson, E. R., & Chen, H. (2002). Moral hypocrisy: Addressing some alternatives. *Journal of Personality and Social Psychology, 83,* 330-39.

Batson, C. D., Thompson, E. R., Seuferling, G., Whitney, H., & Strongman, J. (1999). Moral hypocrisy: Appearing moral to oneself without being so. *Journal of Personality & Social Psychology, 77,* 525-37.

Batson, C. D., Tsang, J., & Thompson, E. R. (2000). *Weakness of will: Counting the cost of being moral.* Unpublished manuscript, University of Kansas, Lawrence.

Batson, C., Turk, C., Shaw, L., & Klein, T. (1995). Information function of empathic emotion: Learning that we value the other's welfare. *Journal of Personality and Social Psychology, 68,* 300-313.

Batson, C. D., & Ventis, W. L. (1982). *The religious experience: A social-psychological perspective.* New York: Oxford University Press.

Baumeister, R. F. (1998). The self. In D. T. Gilbert, S. T. Fiske & G. Lindzey (Eds.), *Handbook of social psychology* (4th ed., pp. 680-740). New York: McGraw-Hill.

Baumeister, R. F. (2005). Self and volition. In W. R. Miller & H. D. Delaney (Eds.), *Judeo-Christian perspectives on psychology* (pp. 57-72). Washington, DC: American Psychological Association.

Baumeister, R. F. (2011, September 16). When feeling good isn't good enough: Self-control, not self-esteem, is the key to success. *New York Daily News.* Retrieved from http://articles.nydailynews.com/2011-09-16/news/30182057_1_high-self-esteem-control-psychology.

Baumeister, R. F., Brad, J., & Campbell, W. K. (2000). Self-esteem, narcissism, and aggression: Does violence result from low self-esteem or from threatened egotism? *Current Directions in Psychological Science, 9,* 26-29.

Baumeister, R. F., & Bushman, B. (1998). Threatened egotism, narcissism, self-esteem, and direct and misplaced aggression: Does self-love or self-hate lead to violence? *Journal of Personality and Social Psychology, 75,* 219-29.

Baumeister, R. F., & Bushman, B. (2007). *Social psychology and human nature.* Wadsworth Publishing.

Baumeister, R. F., Campbell, J. D., Kreuger, J. I., & Vohs, K. D. (2003). Does high self-esteem cause better performance, interpersonal success, happiness, or healthier lifestyles? *Psychological Science in the Public Interest, 4*(Whole No. 1), 1-44.

Baumeister, R. F., & Leary, M. R. (1995). The need to belong: Desire for interpersonal attachment as a fundamental human motivation. *Psychological Bulletin, 117,* 497-529.

Baumeister, R. F., Muraven, M., & Tice, D. M. (2000). Ego depletion: A resource model of volition, self-regulation, and controlled processing. *Social Cognition, 18,* 130-50.

Baumeister, R. F., & Newman, L. S. (1994). How stories make sense of personal experiences: Motives that shape autobiographical narratives. *Personality and Social Psychological Bulletin, 20,* 676-90.

Baumeister, R., Smart, L., & Boden, J. (1996). Relation of threatened egotism to violence and aggression: The dark side of high self-esteem. *Psychological Review, 103,* 5-33.

Baumeister, R. F., & Sommer, K. L. (1997). What do men want? Gender differences and two spheres of belongingness: Comment on Cross and Madson (1997). *Psychological Bulletin, 122,* 38-44.

Baumeister, R. F., Tice, D. M., & Hutton, D. G. (1989). Self-presentation motivations and personality differences in self-esteem. *Journal of Personality, 57,* 547-79.

Baumeister, R. F., & Vohs, K. D. (Eds.). (2004). *Handbook of self-regulation: Research, theory, and applications.* New York, NY: Guilford Press.

Beaman, A. L., Barnes, P. J., Klentz, B., & McQuirk, B. (1978). Increasing helping rates through information dissemination: Teaching pays. *Personality and Social Psychology Bulletin, 4,* 406-11.

Beck, A. T., Brown, G., & Steer, R. A. (1989). Prediction of eventual suicide in psychiatric inpatients by clinical ratings of hopelessness. *Journal of Consulting and Clinical Psychology, 57*(2), 309-10.

Bell, D. (1992). *Faces at the bottom of the well.* New York, NY: Basic Books.

Bellizzi, J. A., & Hasty, R .W. (2001). The effects of a stated organizational policy on inconsistent disciplinary action based on a salesperson gender and weight. *Journal of Personal Selling and Sales Management, 21*(3), 189-98.

Bem, D. J. (1972). Self-perception theory. In L. Berkowitz (Ed.), *Advances in experimental social psychology* (Vol. 6, pp. 1-62). New York, NY: Academic Press.

Bem, S. L. (1993). *The lenses of gender: Transforming the debate on sexual inequality.* New Haven, CT: Yale University Press.

Benson, P. L., Karabenick, S. A., & Lerner, R. M. (1975). Pretty pleases: The effects of physical attractiveness, race, and sex on receiving help. *Journal of Experimental Social Psychology, 12,* 409-15.

Berdick, C. (2004, December 19). Invisible bias. Retrieved April 19, 2012 from www .boston.com/news/globe/ideas/articles/2004/12/19/invisible_bias?

Berglas, S., & Jones, E. (1978). Drug choice as a self-handicapping strategy in response to noncontingent success. *Journal of Personality and Social Psychology, 36,* 405-17.

Berkowitz, L. (1989). The frustration-aggression hypothesis: Examination and reformulation. *Psychological Bulletin, 106,* 1, 59-73.

Berkowitz, L. (1990). On the formation and regulation of anger and aggression: A cognitive-neoassociationistic analysis. *American Psychologist.*

Berkowitz, L. 1993. *Aggression—its causes, consequences, and control.* New York: McGraw-Hill.

Berkowitz, L., & Connor, W. (1966). Success, failure and social responsibility. *Journal of Personality and Social Psychology, 4,* 664-69.

Berkowitz, L., & Daniels, L. R. (1964). Affecting the salience of the social responsibility norm: Effects of past help on the response to dependency relationships. *Journal of Abnormal and Social Psychology, 68*(3), 275-81. doi:10.1037/h0040164

Berridge, K. C., & Winkielman, P. (2003). What is unconscious emotion? (The case for unconscious "liking"). *Cognition and Emotion, 17*(2), 181-211.

Berscheid, E. (1985). Interpersonal attraction. In G. Lindzey and E. Aronson (Eds.), *The handbook of social psychology* (Vol. 2, pp. 413-84). New York, NY: Random House.

Berscheid, E., Boye, D., & Walster (Hatfield) E. (1968). Retaliation as a means of restoring equality. *Journal of Personality and Social Psychology*, 10, 370-78.

Berscheid, E., Dion, K., Walster, E., & Walster, W. G. (1971). Physical attractiveness and dating choice: A test of the matching hypothesis. *Journal of Experimental Social Psychology, 7*, 173-89.

Bettencourt, B. A., Talley, A. E., Benjamin, A. J., & Valentine, J. (2006). Personality and aggressive behavior under neutral and provoking conditions: A meta-analytic review. *Psychological Bulletin, 132*(5), 751-77.

Bierhoff, H. W. (2002). *Prosocial behavior.* New York, NY: Taylor & Francis.

Bikhchandani, S., Hirshleifer, D., & Welch, I. (1998). Learning from the behavior of others: Conformity, fads, and informational cascades. *Journal of Economic Perspectives, 12*, 151-70.

Billig, M. (1985). Prejudice, categorization and particularization: From a perceptual to a rhetorical approach. *European Journal of Social Psychology, 15*(1), 79-103.

Birnbaum, M. H. (1974). The nonadditivity of personality impressions. *Journal of Experimental Psychology, 102*(3), 543-61.

Biskupic, J. (2010, October 28). Can states keep kids from violent video games? *USA Today*, pp. 1A-2A.

Björkqvist, K., Lagerspetz, K. M. J., & Kaukiainen, A. (1992). Do girls manipulate and boys fight? *Aggressive Behavior, 18*, 117-27.

Bjorkqvist, K., Osterman, K., & Lagerspetz, K. M. J. (1994). Sex differences in covert aggression among adults. *Aggressive Behavior, 20*, 27-33.

Blair, C. A., Thompson, L. F., & Wuensch, K. L. (2005). Electronic helping behavior: The virtual presence of others makes a difference. *Basic and Applied Social Psychology, 27*(2), 171-78.

Blair, I. V., & Banaji, M. (1996). Automatic and controlled processes in stereotype priming. *Journal of Personality and Social Psychology, 70*, 1142-63.

Blair, R. J. R. (2006). Subcortical brain systems in psychopathy: The amygdala and associated structures. In C. J. Patrick (Ed.), *Handbook of psychopathy* (pp. 296-312). New York, NY: Guilford Press.

Blair, R. J. R. (2007). Aggression, psychopathy, and free will from a cognitive neuroscience perspective. *Behavioral Sciences and the Law, 25*, 321-31.

Blanton, H., Pelham, B. W., DeHart, T., & Carvallo, M. (2001). Overconfidence as dissonance reduction. *Journal of Experimental Social Psychology, 37*, 373-85.

Blass, T. (1991). Understanding behavior in the Milgram experiment: The role of personality, situation, and their interactions. *Journal of Personality and Social Psychology, 60*(3), 398-413.

Blass, T. (1999). The Milgram paradigm after 35 years: Some things we now know about obedience to authority. *Journal of Applied Social Psychology, 29*(5), 889-1109.

Blau, P. (1964). *Exchange and power in social Life.* New York: John Wiley & Sons.

Bleske, A. L., & Buss, D. M. (2000). Can men and women be just friends? *Personal Relationships, 7,* 131-51.

Bobo, L. (1983). White opposition to busing: Symbolic racism or realistic group conflict? *Journal of Personality and Social Psychology, 45,* 1196-1210.

Bodenhausen, G. V., & Lichtenstein, M. (1987). Social stereotypes and information-processing strategies: The impact of task complexity. *Journal .of Personality and Social Psychology, 52*(5), 871-80.

Bodenhausen, G. V., & Macrae, C. N. (1998). Stereotype activation and inhibition. In R. S. Wyer (Ed.), *Stereotype activation and inhibition: Advances in social cognition* (Vol. 11, pp. 1-52). Mahweh, NJ: Lawrence Erlbaum.

Boehm, E. (1994). The validity effect: A search for mediating variables. *Personality and Social Psychology Bulletin, 20,* 285-93.

Boer, S. F., & Koolhaus, J. M. (2005). 5-HT1A and 5-HT1B receptor agonists and aggression: A pharmacological challenge to the serotonin deficiency hypothesis. *European Journal of Pharmacology, 526,* 125-39.

Bohner, G., & Dickel, N. (2011). Attitudes and attitude change. *Annual Review of Psychology, 62,* 391-417.

Boinski, S., & Garber, P. A. (Eds.). (2000). *On the move: How and why animals travel in groups.* Chicago: University of Chicago Press.

Bond, R. (2005). Group size and conformity. *Group Processes and Intergroup Relations, 8*(4), 331-54. doi:10.1177/1368430205056464

Bond, R., & Smith, P. B. (1996). Culture and conformity: A meta-analysis of studies using Asch's line judgment task. *Psychological Bulletin, 119,* 111-37.

Borduin, C. M. (1999). Multisystemic treatment of criminality and violence in adolescents. *Journal of the American Academy of Child and Adolescent Psychiatry, 38,* 242-49.

Bornstein, R. F. (1989). Exposure and affect: overview and meta-analysis of research, 1968-1987. *Psychological Bulletin, 106,* 265-89.

Bossard, J. H. S. (1932). Residential propinquity as a factor in marriage selection. *American Journal of Sociology, 38*(2), 219-24.

Botwin, M. D., Buss, D. M., & Shackelford, T. K. (1997). Personality and mate preferences: Five factors in mate selection and marital satisfaction. *Journal of Personality, 65*(1), 107-36. doi: 10.1111/j.1467-6494.1997.tb00531

Bovens, M., and t'Hart, P. (1996). *Understanding policy fiascos.* New Brunswick, NJ: Transaction.

Bowlby, J. (1989). *Secure and insecure attachment.* New York: Basic Books.

Boyd, R., & Richerson, P. J. (2005). Solving the Puzzle of Human Cooperation. In S. Levinson (Ed.), *Evolution and Culture* (pp. 105-32). Cambridge, MA: MIT Press.

Bradley, M. M.; Codispoti, M., Cuthbert, B. N., & Lang, P. J. (2001). Emotion and motivation: Defensive and appetitive reactions in picture processing. *Emotion, 1*(3), 276-98.

Brauer, M., Wasel, W., & Niedenthal, P. (2000). Implicit and explicit components of prejudice. *Review of General Psychology, 4,* 79-101.

Brehm, J. W. (1956). Postdecision changes in the desirability of alternatives. *Journal of Abnormal and Social Psychology, 52,* 384-89.

Brehm, J. W. (1966). *A theory of psychological reactance.* New York, NY: Academic Press.

Brehm, S. S., & Brehm, J. W. (1981). *Psychological reactance: A theory of freedom and control.* New York, NY: Academic Press.

Brewer, M. B. (1988). A dual process model of impression formation. In R. S. Wyer Jr. & T. K. Srull (Eds.), *Advances in social cognition* (Vol. 1, pp. 1-36). Hillsdale, NJ: Erlbaum.

Brewer, M. B. (1991). The social self: On being the same and different at the same time. *Personality and Social Psychology Bulletin, 17,* 475-82.

Brewer, M. B. (1999). The psychology of prejudice: Ingroup love or outgroup hate? *Journal of Social Issues, 55*(3), 429-44.

Brewer, M. B., & Caporael, L. R. (1990). Selfish genes versus selfish people: Sociobiology as origin myth. *Motivation and Emotion, 14,* 237-42.

Brewer, M. B., & Caporael, L. R. (2006). An evolutionary perspective on social identity: Revisiting groups. In J. A. Simpson, M. Schaller & D. T. Kenrick (Eds.), *Evolution and social psychology* (pp. 143-61). Philadelphia: Psychology Press.

Brewer, M. B., & Chen, Y. (2007). Where (who) are collectives in collectivism? Toward conceptual clarification of individualism and collectivism. *Psychological Review, 114,* 133-52.

Brewer, M. B., & Gardner, W. (1996). Who is this "we"? Levels of collective identity and self representations. *Journal of Personality and Social Psychology, 71,* 83-93.

Brewer, M. B., & Miller, N. (1996). *Intergroup relations.* Buckingham, England: Open University Press.

Brodt, S. E., & Ross, L. D. (1998). The role of stereotyping in overconfident social prediction. *Social Cognition, 16,* 225-52.

Brokner, J., & Chen, Y. R. (1996). The moderating roles of self-esteem and self construal in reaction to a threat to self: Evidence from the People's Republic of China and the United States. *Journal of Personality and Social Psychology, 71,* 603-15.

Brown, R. (1965). *Social psychology.* New York: Free Press.

Brown. R. (1974). Further comment on the risky shift. *American Psychologist, 29,* 468-70.

Brown, V., and Paulus, P. B. (2002). Making group brainstorming more effective: Recommendations from an associative memory perspective. *Current Directions in Psychological Science, 11*(6), 208-12.

Bryan, J. H., & Test, M. A. (1967). Models and helping: Naturalistic studies in aiding behavior. *Journal of Personality and Social Psychology, 6,* 400-407.

Bryant, J., & Zillmann (Eds.). (2002). *Media effects: Advances in theory and research* (2nd ed.). Mahwah, NJ: Lawrence Erlbaum.

Buckley, K., Winkel, R., & Leary, M. (2004). Reactions to acceptance and rejection: Effects of level and sequence of relational evaluation. *Journal of Experimental Social Psychology, 40,* 14-28.

Budesheim, T. L., & Bonnelle, K. (1998). The use of abstract trait knowledge and behavioral exemplars in causal explanations of behavior. *Personality and Social Psychology Bulletin, 24*(6), 575-87.

Bukszar, E., & Connolly, T. (1988). Hindsight bias and strategic choice: Some problems in learning from experience. *Academy of Management Journal, 31*(3), 628-41.

Buller, D. J., & Hardcastle, V. G. (2000). Evolutionary psychology, meet developmental neurobiology: Against promiscuous modularity. *Brain and Mind, 1,* 307-25.

Bureau of Justice Statistics (2011). *Homicide trends in the U.S.* Available at http://bjs.ojp. usdoj.gov/content/pub/pdf/htus8008.pdf

Bureau of Labor Statistics. (2008). "Labor Force Statistics from the Current Population Survey."

Burger, J. M. (1999). The foot-in-the-door compliance procedure: A multiple-process analysis and review. *Personality and Social Psychology Review, 3,* 303-25.

Burger, J. M., Girgis, Z. M., & Manning, C. C. (2011). In their own words: Explaining obedience to authority through an examination of participants' comment. *Social Psychological and Personality Science.* doi:10.1177/1948550610397632

Burger, J. M., & Guadagno, R. E. (2003). Self-concept clarity and the foot-in-the-door phenomenon. *Basic and Applied Social Psychology, 25,* 79-86.

Burger, J. M., Horita, M., Kinoshita, L., Roberts, K., & Vera, C. (1997). The effects of time on the norm of reciprocity. *Basic and Applied Social Psychology, 19,* 91-100.

Burger, J. M., Soroka, S., Gonzago, K., Murphy, E., & Somervell, E. (2001). The effect of fleeting attraction on compliance to requests. *Personality and Social Psychology Bulletin, 27,* 1578-86.

Burnstein, E., Crandall, C., & Kitayama, S. (1994). Some neo-Darwinian decision rules for altruism: Weighing cues for inclusive fitness as a function of the biological importance of the decision. *Journal of Personality and Social Psychology, 67*(5), 773-89.

Burnstein, E., & Vinokur, A. What a person thinks upon learning he has chosen differently from others: Nice evidence for the persuasive-arguments explanation of choice shifts. *Journal of Experimental Social Psychology, 11,* 412-26.

Burnstein, E., & Vinokur, A. (1977). Persuasive argumentation and social comparison as determinants of attitude polarization. *Journal of Experimental Social Psychology, 13,* 315-32.

Bushman, B. J. (1995). Moderating role of trait aggressiveness in the effects of violent media on aggression. *Journal of Personality and Social Psychology, 69,* 950-60.

Bushman, B. J., & Anderson, C. A. (2001). Is it time to pull the plug on the hostile versus instrumental aggression dichotomy? *Psychological Review, 108*(1), 273-79.

Bushman, B. J., & Anderson, C. A. (2002). Violent video games and hostile expectations: A test of the General Aggression Model. *Personality and Social Psychology Bulletin, 28*(12), 1679-86.

Bushman, B. J., & Baumeister, R. F. (1998). Threatened egotism, narcissism, self-esteem, and direct and displaced aggression: Does self-love or self-hate lead to violence? *Journal of Personality and Social Psychology, 75,* 219-29.

Bushman, B. J., Ridge, D. R., Das, E., Key, C. W., & Busath, G. L. (2007). When God sanctions killing: Effect of scriptural violence on aggression, *Psychological Science, 18*(3), 204-7.

Buss, A. H. (1978). *Psychology, behavior in perspective.* New York: Wiley.

Buss, D. M. (1985). Human mate selection. *American Scientist, 73,* 47-51.

Buss, D. M. (1995). Evolutionary psychology: A new paradigm for psychological science. *Psychological Inquiry, 6,* 1-30.

Buss, D. M. (1999). *Evolutionary psychology: The new science of the mind.* Needham Heights, MA: Allyn & Bacon.

Buss, D. M. (2000). The evolution of happiness. *American Psychologist, 55,* 15-23.

Buss, D. M. (2003). The nature of human nature. Review of S. Pinker's The Blank Slate. *Pathways: The Novartis Journal,* Jan.-March, 49.

Buss, D. M. (2005). *The handbook of evolutionary psychology.* Hoboken: Wiley.

Buss, D. M., & Duntley, J. D. (2003). Homicide: An evolutionary perspective and implications for public policy. In N. Dess (Ed.), *Violence and public policy* (pp. 115-28). Westport, CT: Greenwood Publishing Group.

Buss, D. M., & Schmitt, D. P. (1993). Sexual strategies theory: An evolutionary perspective on human mating. *Psychological Review, 100,* 204-32.

Butler, R. N. (1980). Ageism: A forward. *Journal of Social Issues, 36*(2), 8-11.

Byrne, B. M. (1996). On the structure of self-concept for pre-, early, and late adolescents: A test of the Shavelson, Hubner, and Stanton (1976) model. *Journal of Personality and Social Psychology, 70*(3), 599-613.

Byrne, D. (1961). Interpersonal attraction and attitude similarity. *Journal of Abnormal and Social Psychology, 62,* 713-15.

Byrne, D. (1971). *The attraction paradigm.* New York, NY: Academic Press.

Byrne, D. (1978). Separation, integration, or parallel play? *Personality and Social Psychology Bulletin, 4,* 498-99.

Byrne, D. (1997). An overview (and underview) of research and theory within the attraction paradigm. *Journal of Personality and Social Psychology, 14,* 417-31.

Byrne, D., & Clore, G. L. (1967). Affectance arousal and attraction. *Journal of Personality and Social Psychology, 6*(4), 1-18. doi:10.1037/h0024829

Byrne, D., London, O., & Griffitt, W. (1968). The effect of topic importance and attitude similarity-dissimilarity on attraction in the intrastranger design. *Psychonomic Science, 11,* 303-4.

Cabeza, R., & Nyberg, L. (1997). Imaging cognition: An empirical review of PET studies with normal subjects. *Journal of Cognitive Neuroscience, 9,* 1-26.

Cacioppo, J. T. (2008). A letter to young scientists, *Observer, 21,* 39-40.

Cacioppo, J. T., & Berntson, G. G. (1994). Relationship between attitudes and evaluative space: A critical review, with emphasis on the separability of positive and negative substrates. *Psychological Bulletin, 115,* 401-23.

Cacioppo, J. T., Gardner, W. L., & Berntson, G. G. (1997). Beyond bipolar measures: The case of attitudes and evaluative space. *Personality and Social Psychology Review, 1*(1), 3-25. doi:10.1207/s15327957pspr0101_2

Cacioppo, J. T., & Petty, R. E. (1981). Electromyograms as measures of extent and affectivity of information processing. *American Psychologist, 36,* 441-56.

Cairns, R. B., & Cairns, B. D. (1994). *Lifelines and risks: Pathways of youth in our time.* New York, NY: Cambridge University Press.

Calkins, S. D., & Fox, N. A. (2002). Self-regulatory processes in early personality development: A multilevel approach to the study of childhood social withdrawal and aggression. *Development and Psychopathology, 14,* 477-98. doi:10.1017.S0954579402 00305X

Cameron, C. (2005). An introduction to theological anthropology. *Evangel, 23*(2), 53-61.

Campbell, W. K., & Sedikides, C. (1999). Self-threat magnifies the self-serving bias: A meta-analytic integration. *Review of General Psychology, 3,* 23-43.

Cann, A. (1993). Evaluative expectations and the gender schema: Is failed inconsistency better? *Sex Roles, 28,* 667-78.

Caporael, L. R. (1997). The evolution of truly social cognition: The core configuration model. *Personality and Social Psychology Review, 1,* 276-98.

Caporael, L. R. (2001). Evolutionary psychology: Toward a unifying theory and a hybrid science. *Annual Review of Psychology, 52,* 607-28.

Caporael, L. R., & Brewer, M. B. (1995). Hierarchical evolutionary theory: There is an alternative, and it's not creationism. *Psychological Inquiry, 6,* 31-34.

Carli, L. L. (2001). Gender and social influence. *Journal of Social Issues, 57*(4), 725-41.

Carli, L. L., LaFleur, S. J., & Loeber, C. C. (1995). Nonverbal behavior, gender, and influence. *Journal of Personality and Social Psychology, 68,* 1030-41.

Carprara, G. V., Perugini, M., & Barbaranelli, C. (1994). Studies of individual differences in aggression. In M. Potegal & J. F. Knutson (Eds.), *The dynamics of aggression: Biological and social processes in dyads and groups* (pp. 123-53). Hillsdale, NJ: Erlbaum.

Carter, C., and Rice, C. L. (1997). Acquisition and manifestation of prejudice in children. *Journal of Multicultural Counseling and Development, 25,* 185-94.

Carver, C. S., & Scheier, M. F. (1981). *Attention and self-regulation: A control theory approach to human behavior.* New York, NY: Springer-Verlag.

Carver, C. S., & Scheier, M. F. (1998). *On the self-regulation of behavior.* New York: Cambridge University Press.

Cash, T. F., Cash, D. W., & Butters, J. (1983). "Mirror, mirror on the wall . . . ?": Contrast effects and self-evaluations of physical attractiveness. *Personality and Social Psychology Bulletin, 9,* 351-58.

Cash, T. F., & Duncan, N. C. (1984). Physical attractiveness stereotyping among black American college students. *The Journal of Social Psychology, 122,* 71-77.

Caspi, A., McClay, J., Moffitt, T. E., Mill, J., Martin, J., Craig, I. W., Taylor, A., & Poulton, R. (2002). Role of genotype in the cycle of violence in maltreated children. *Science, 297*(5582), 851-54.

Cast, A. D., & Burke, P. J. (2002). A theory of self-esteem. *Social Forces, 80,* 1041-68.

Castano, E., & Kofta, M. (2009). Dehumanization: Humanity and its denial. *Group Processes & Intergroup Relations, 12*(6) 695-97.

Castillo, R. (1997). *Culture and mental illness: A client-centered approach.* Boston: Brook/Cole.

Cha, M., Mislove, A., Adams, B., & Gummadi, K. P. (2008). *Characterizing social cascades in Flickr.* Proceedings of the First Annual Workshop on Online Social Networks. Retrieved from http://portal.acm.org/citation.cfm?id=1397735.1397739

Chaikin, A. L., & Derlega, V. J. (1974). Liking for the norm-breaker in self-disclosure. *Journal of Personality, 42,* 117-29.

Chaiken, S. (1987) The heuristic model of persuasion. In M. P. Zanna, J. M. Olson & C. P. Herman (Eds.), *Social influence: The Ontario Symposium* (Vol. 5, pp. 3-39). Hillsdale, NJ: Erlbaum.

Chaiken, S., Liberman, A., & Eagly, A. H. (1989). Heuristic and systematic information processing within and beyond the persuasion context. In J. S. Uleman & J. A. Bargh (Eds.), *Unintended thought* (pp. 212-52). New York, NY: Guilford Press.

Chaiken, S., Wood, W., & Eagly, A. H. (1996). Principles of persuasion. In E.T. Higgins & A. Kruglanski (Eds.), *Social psychology: Handbook of basic mechanisms and processes.* New York, NY: Guilford Press.

Chalk, F., & Jonassohn, K. (1990). *The history and sociology of genocide: Analyses and case studies.* New Haven, CT: Yale University Press.

Chan, D., Schmitt, N., Jennings, D., Clause, C. S., & Delbridge, K. (1998). Applicant perceptions of test fairness integrating justice and self-serving bias perspectives. *International Journal of Selection and Assessment, 6*(4), 232-39.

Chaplin, W. F., Phillips, J. B., Brown, J. D., Clanton, N. R., & Stein, J. L. (2000). Handshaking, gender, personality, and first impressions. *Journal of Personality and Social Psychology, 79,* 110-17.

Chapman, L. J., & Chapman, J. P. (1967). Genesis of popular but erroneous psychodiagnostic observations. *Journal of Abnormal Psychology, 72*(3), 193-204.

Chartrand, T. L., & Bargh, J. A. (1999). The chameleon effect: the perception-behavior link and social interaction. *Journal of Personality and Social Psychology, 76*(6), 893-910.

Chartrand, T. L., Maddux, W., & Lakin, J. (2005). Beyond the perception-behavior link: The ubiquitous utility and motivational moderators of nonconscious mimicry. In R. Hassin, J. Uleman & J. A. Bargh (Eds.), *The new unconscious* (pp. 334-61). New York, NY: Oxford University Press.

Check, J., & Guloine, T. (1989). Reported proclivity for coercive sex following repeated exposure to sexually violent pornography, non-violent dehumanising pornography, and erotica. In D. Zillmann & J. Bryant (Eds.), *Pornography: Recent research, interpretations, and policy considerations* (pp. 159-84). Hillsdale, NJ: Lawrence Erlbaum.

Chen, N. Y., Shaffer, D. R., & Wu, C. (1997). On physical attractiveness stereotyping in Taiwan: A revised sociocultural perspective. *The Journal of Social Psychology, 137*(1), 117-25.

Cialdini, R. B., Brown, S. L., Lewis, B. P., Luce, C., & Neuberg, S. L. (1997). Reinterpreting the empathy-altruism relationship: When one into one equals oneness. *Journal of Personality and Social Psychology, 73,* 481-94.

Cialdini, R. B., Cacioppo, J. T., Bassett, R., & Miller, J. A. (1978). Low-ball procedure for producing compliance: Commitment then cost. *Journal of Personality and Social Psychology, 36,* 463-76. doi:10.1037/0022-3514.36.5.463

Cialdini, R. B., & Goldstein, N. J. (2004). Social influence: Compliance and conformity. *Annual Review of Psychology*, 55, 591-621.

Cialdini, R. B., Kenrick, D. T., & Baumann, D. J. (1984). Mood as a determinant of prosocial behavior in children and adults. In N. Eisenberg (Ed.), *The development of prosocial behavior* (pp. 339-59). New York, NY: Academic Press.

Cialdini, R. B., & Trost, M. R. (1998). Social influence: Social norms, conformity and compliance. In D. T. Gilbert, S. T. Fiske et al. (Eds.), *The handbook of social psychology, Vol. 2* (4th ed., pp. 151-92). New York, NY: McGraw-Hill.

Cialdini, R. B., Vincent, J. E., Lewis, S. K., Catalan, J., Wheeler, D., & Darby, B. C. (1975). Reciprocal concessions: Process for inducing compliance: The door-in-the-face technique. *Journal of Personality and Social Psychology*, 31(2), 206-15.

Clark, M. S., Ouellette, R., Powell, M. C., & Milberg, S. (1987). Recipient's mood, relationship type, and helping. *Journal of Personality and Social Psychology*, 53, 94-103.

Clark, R. D., III. (1988). On predicting minority influence. *European Journal of Social Psychology*, 18, 515-26.

Clary, E. G., Snyder, M., Ridge, R. D., Copeland, J., Stukas, A. A., Haugen, J., & Miene, P. (1998). Understanding and assessing the motivations of volunteers: a functional approach. *Journal of Personality and Social Psychology*, 74(6), 1516-30.

Clore, G. L., & Baldridge, B. (1968). Interpersonal attraction: The role of agreement and topic interest. *Journal of Personality and Social Psychology*, 9, 340-46.

Coccaro, E. F. (1989). Central serotonin and impulsive aggression. *British Journal of Psychiatry* 155(suppl.), 52-62.

Codol, J. P. (1976). On the so-called superior conformity of the self behavior: Twenty experimental investigations. *European Journal of Social Psychology*, 5, 457-501.

Coie, J. K., & Dodge, K. A. (1998). Aggression and antisocial behavior. In W. Damon (Editor in Chief) & N. Eisenberg (Vol. Ed.), *Handbook of child psychology, 5th edition. Vol. 3. Social, emotional, and personality development.* New York, NY: John Wiley & Sons.

Coke, J., Batson, C., & McDavis, K. (1978). Empathic mediation of helping: A two-stage model. *Journal of Personality and Social Psychology*, 36, 752-66.

Collins, B. E. (Ed.). (1973). *Public and private conformity: Competing explanations by improvisation, cognitive dissonance, and attribution theories.* Andover, MA: Warner Modular Publication.

Coltrane, S., & Messineo, M. (2000). The perpetuation of subtle prejudice: Race and gender imagery in 1990s television advertising. *Sex Roles*, 42, 5, 363-89.

Condry, J. C., & Condry, S. (1976). Sex differences: A study in the eye of the beholder. *Child Development*, 47, 812-19.

Confer, J. C., Easton, J. A., Fleischman, D. S., Goetz, C. D., Lewis, D. M., Perilloux, C., & Buss, D. M. (2010). Evolutionary psychology: Controversies, questions, prospects, and limitations. *American Psychologist*, 65, 110-26.

Cooley, C. H. (1902). *Human nature and the social order.* New York, NY: Scribners.

Cooper, J. (1999). Unwanted consequences and the self: In search of the motivation for dissonance reduction. In E. Harmon-Jones & J. Mills (Eds.), *Cognitive dissonance:*

*Progress in a pivotal theory in social psychology.* Washington, DC: American Psychological Association.

Coopersmith, S. (1967). *The antecedents of self-esteem.* San Francisco, CA: Freeman.

Corporation for National and Community Service, Office of Research and Policy Development. (2010, June). *Volunteering in America 2010: National, state, and city information.* Washington, DC.

Cosmides, L. (1989). The logic of social exchange: Has natural selection shaped how humans reason? Studies with the Wason selection task. *Cognition, 31,* 187-276.

Cosmides, L., & Tooby, J. (1987). From evolution to behavior: Evolutionary psychology as the missing link. In J. Dupre (Ed.), *The latest on the best: Essays on evolution and optimality* (pp. 276-306). Cambridge, MA: MIT Press.

Cosmides, L., & Tooby, J. (1989). Evolutionary psychology and the generation of culture, part II. Case study: A computational theory of social exchange. *Ethology and Sociobiology, 10,* 51-97.

Cosmides, L., & Tooby, J. (1992). Cognitive adaptations for social exchange. In J. Barkow, L. Cosmides, & J. Tooby (Eds.), *The adapted mind.* New York, NY: Oxford University Press.

Cosmides, L., & Tooby, J. (1995). From evolution to adaptations to behavior: Toward an integrated evolutionary psychology. In R. Wong (Ed.), *Biological perspectives on motivated activities.* Norwood, NJ: Ablex.

Cosmides, L., & Tooby, J. (2000). Evolutionary psychology and the emotions. In M. Lewis & J. M. Haviland-Jones (Eds.), *Handbook of emotions, 2nd edition.* New York, NY: Guilford Press.

Cosmides, L., & Tooby, J. (2003). Evolutionary psychology: Theoretical foundations. In *Encyclopedia of cognitive science* (pp. 54-64). London: Macmillan.

Cosmides, L., Tooby, J., & Kurzban, R. (2003). Perceptions of race. *Trends in Cognitive Science, 7*(4), 173-79.

Cottrell, N. B. (1972). Social facilitation. In C. McClintock (Ed.), *Experimental social psychology* (pp. 185-236). New York: Holt, Rinehart & Winston.

Cox, D., & Cox, A. D. (2002). Beyond first impressions: The effects of repeated exposure on consumer liking of visually complex and simple product designs. *Journal of the Academy of Marketing Science, 30*(2), 119-30.

Cramer, R. E., Mcmaster, M. R., Bartell, P. A., & Dragna, M. (1988). Subject competence and minimization of the bystander effect. *Journal of Applied Social Psychology, 18,* 1133-48.

Crandall, C. S. (1995). Do parents discriminate against their own heavyweight daughters? *Personality and Social Psychology Bulletin, 21,* 724-35.

Crandall, C. S., D'Anello, S., Sakalli, N., Lazarus, E., Wieczorkowska, G., & Feather, N. T. (2001). An attribution-value model of prejudice: Anti-fat attitudes in six nations. *Personality and Social Psychology Bulletin, 27,* 30-37.

Crandall, C. S., Glor, J., & Britt, T. W. (1994). AIDS-Related Stigmatization: Instrumental and Symbolic Attitudes. *Journal of Applied Social Psychology, 27*(2), 95-123.

Crano, W. D., & Prislin, R. (2006). Attitudes and persuasion. *Annual Review of Psychology, 57,* 345-74.

Crites, S. L., Jr., & Cacioppo, J. T. (1996). Electrochemical differentiation of evaluative and non-evaluative categorizations. *Psychological Science, 7*, 318-21.

Crocker, J. (2002). The costs of seeking self-esteem. *Journal of Social Issues, 58*(3), 597-615.

Crocker, J., & Luhtanen, R. (1990). Collective self-esteem and ingroup bias. *Journal of Personality and Social Psychology, 58*(1), 60-67.

Crombag, H., Rassin, E., & Horselenberg, R. (2003). On vengeance. *Psychology, Crime and Law, 9*, 333-44.

Crosby, F. J., Pufall, A., Snyder, R. C., O'Connell, M., & Whalen, P. (1989). The denial of personal disadvantage among you, me, and all the other ostriches. In M. Crawford & M. Gentry (Eds.), *Gender and thought: Psychological perspectives* (pp. 79-99). New York: Springer-Verlag.

Cuddy, A. J. C., Fiske, S. T., & Glick, P. (2008). Warmth and competence as universal dimensions of social perception: The stereotype content model and the BIAS map. In M. P. Zanna (Ed.), *Advances in experimental social psychology* (Vol. 40, pp. 61-149). New York, NY: Academic Press.

Cunningham, J., Dollinger, S. J., Satz, M., & Rotter, N. (1991). Personality correlates of prejudice against AIDS victims. *Bulletin of the Psychonomic Society, 29*, 165-67.

Cunningham, M. (1985/1986). Levites and brother's keepers: A sociobiological perspective on prosocial behavior. *Humboldt Journal of Social Relations, 13*, 35-67.

Cunningham, M. R., Barbee, A. P., & Pike, C. L. (1990). What do women want? Facial metric assessment of multiple motives in perception of male facial physical attractiveness. *Journal of Personality and Social Psychology, 56*, 61-72.

Cunningham, M. R., Roberts, A. R., Wu, C. H., Barbee, A. P., & Druen, P. B. (1995). Their ideas of beauty are, on the whole, the same as ours: Consistency and variability in the cross-cultural perception of female attractiveness. *Journal of Personality and Social Psychology, 68*, 261-79.

Cunningham, M. R., Steinberg, J., & Grey, R. (1980). Wanting to and having to help: Separate motivations for positive mood and guilt-induced helping. *Journal of Social Personality and Social Psychology, 38*, 181-92.

Daloz, L. A., Keen, C., Keen, J., & Parks, S. D. (1996). *Common fire: Leading lives of commitment in a complex world.* Boston, MA: Beacon Press.

Darley, J. M., & Batson, C. D. (1973). From Jerusalem to Jericho: A study of situational and dispositional variables in helping behavior. *Journal of Personality and Social Psychology, 27*, 100-108.

Darley, J. M., & Berscheid, E. (1967). Increased liking as a result of the anticipation of personal contact. *Human Relations, 20*(1), 29-40. doi:10.1177/001872676702000103

Darley, J. M., & Latané, B. (1968). Bystander intervention in emergencies: Diffusion of responsibility. *Journal of Personality and Social Psychology, 8*, 377-83.

Darley, J. M., Latané, B., Batson, C. D., Ferrari, J. R., & Leippe, M. R. (1994). Prosocial behavior. In W. A. Lesko (Ed.), *Readings in social psychology: General, classic, and contemporary selections, 2nd edition* (pp. 265-94). Boston, MA: Allyn & Bacon.

Darwin, C. (1859). *On the origin of species by means of natural selection: Or, the preser-*

*vation of favoured races in the struggle for life.* London, England: Murray.

Darwin, C. (1871). *The descent of man and selection in relation to sex.* New York, NY: Appleton.

Dasgupta, N., McGhee, D. E., Greenwald, A. G., & Banaji, M. R. (1999). Automatic preference for White Americans: Eliminating the familiarity explanation. *Journal of Experimental Social Psychology, 36,* 316-28.

Davis, K. E., & Jones, E. E. (1960). Changes in interpersonal perception as a means of reducing cognitive dissonance. *Journal of Abnormal and Social Psychology, 61,* 402-10.

Davis, M. (1980). A multidimensional approach to individual differences in empathy. *Catalog of Selected Documents in Psychology, 10,* 85.

Davis, M. H. (1999). *Empathy: A social psychological approach.* Boulder, CO: Westview Press.

Davis, M., Conklin, L., Smith, A., & Luce, C. (1996). Effect of perspective taking on the cognitive representation of persons: A merging of self and other. *Journal of Personality and Social Psychology, 70,* 713-26.

Davis, M., Luce, C., & Kraus, S. (1994). The heritability of characteristics associated with dispositional empathy. *Journal of Personality, 62,* 369-91.

Davis, M., & Whalen, P. J. (2001). The amygdala: Vigilance and emotion. *Molecular Psychiatry, 6,* 13-34.

Dawkins, R. (1976). *The selfish gene.* New York, NY: Oxford University Press.

De Bruin, E. N. M., & Van Lange, P. A. M. (2000). What people look for in others: Influences of the perceiver and the perceived on information selection. *Personality and Social Psychology Bulletin, 26,* 206-19.

De Vries, N. K., & Van Kippenberg, A. (1987). Biased and unbiased self-evaluations of ability. The effects of further testing. *British Journal of Social Psychology, 26,* 9-15.

Deaux, K., Reid, A., Mizrahi, K., & Ethier, K. A. (1995). Parameters of social identity, *Journal of Personality and Social Psychology, 68,* 280-91.

Deci, E. L., & Ryan, R. M. (1985). *Intrinsic motivation and self-determination in human behavior.* New York: Plenum.

Deci, E. I., & Ryan, R. M. (1991). A motivational approach to self: Integration in personality. In E. Dienstbier (Ed.), *Perspectives in motivation* (Nebraska Symposium on Motivation, Vol. 38, pp. 237-88). Lincoln: University of Nebraska Press.

Deci, E. L., & Ryan, R. M. (1995). Human autonomy: The basis for true self-esteem. In M. Kernis (Ed.), *Efficacy, agency, and self-esteem* (pp. 31-49). New York: Plenum.

Deci, E. I., & Ryan, R. M. (1997). Behaviorists in search of the null: Revisiting the understanding of intrinsic motivation by extrinsic rewards. Unpublished manuscript, University of Rochester.

DeJong, W., Marber, S., & Shaver, R. (1980). Crime intervention: The role of a victims behavior in reducing situational ambiguity. *Personality and Social Psychology, 6,* 113-18.

DeLisi, M., Umphress, Z., & Vaughn, M. G. (2009). The criminology of the amygdala. *Criminal Justice and Behavior, 36,* 1241-52. doi:10.1177/0093854809343119

DePalma, M. T., Madey, S. F., Tillman, T. C., & Wheeler, J. (1999). Perceived patient responsibility and belief in a just world affect helping. *Basic and Applied Social Psychology, 21*(2), 131-37.

Derksen, M. (2005). Against integration: Why evolution cannot unify the social sciences. *Theory and Psychology, 15*(2), 139-62.

Dermer, M., & Thiel, D. L. (1975). When beauty may fail. *Journal of Personality and Social Psychology, 31,* 1168-76.

Deutsch, M., & Gerard, H. B. (1955). A study of normative and informational social influence upon judgment. *Journal of Abnormal and Social Psychology, 51,* 629-36.

Devine, P. G. (1989). Stereotypes and prejudice: Their automatic and controlled components. *Journal of Personality and Social Psychology, 56,* 5-18.

Devine, P. G., Plant, E. A., Amodio, D. M., Harmon-Jones, E., & Vance, S. L. (2002). The regulation of explicit and implicit race bias: The role of motivations to respond without prejudice. *Journal of Personality and Social Psychology, 82,* 835-48.

Devine, P. G., Sedikides, C., & Fuhrman, R. W. (1989). Goals in social information processing: The case of anticipated interaction. *Journal of Personality and Social Psychology, 56*(5), 680-90.

DeYoung, C. (1997). *Reconciliation: Our greatest challenge—our only hope.* Valley Forge, PA: Judson Press.

DeYoung, C. (2003). *United by faith. The multiracial congregation as an answer to the problem of race.* New York: Oxford University Press.

DeYoung, C. (2009). *Coming together in the 21st century: The Bible's message in an age of diversity.* Valley Forge, PA: Judson Press.

Diekman, A. B., Eagly, A. H., & Kulesa, P. (2002). Accuracy and bias in stereotypes about the social and political attitudes of women and men. *Journal of Experimental Social Psychology, 38,* 268-82.

Diener, E. (1980). Deindividuation: The absence of self-awareness and self-regulation in group members. In P. B. Paulus (Ed.), *The psychology of group influence* (pp. 209-42). Hillsdale, NJ: Lawrence Erlbaum.

Diener, E., & Diener, C. (1996). Most people are happy. *Psychological Science, 7*(3), 181-85.

Diener, E., & Suh, E. (1997). Measuring quality of life: Economic, social, and subjective indicators. *Social Indicators Research, 40,* 189-216.

Diener, E., & Wallburn, M. (1976). Effects of self-awareness on antinormative behavior. *Journal of Research on Personality, 10,* 107-11.

Dijksterhuis, A., & Bargh, J. A. (2001). The perception-behavior expressway: Automatic effects of social perception on social behavior. *Advances in Experimental Social Psychology, 33,* 1-40.

Dillard, J. P., & Shen, L. (2005). On the nature of reactance and its role in persuasive health communication. *Communication Monographs, 72*(2), 144-68.

Dion, K. L. (2002). The social psychology of perceived prejudice and discrimination. *Canadian Psychology,* 1-10.

Dion, K. L., Berscheid, E., & Walster, E. (1972). What is beautiful is good. *Journal of Personality and Social Psychology, 24,* 285-90.

Dion, K. L., Dion, K. K., & Pak, A. W. (1992). Personality-based hardiness as a buffer for discrimination-related stress in members of Toronto's Chinese community. *Canadian Journal of Behavioural Science, 24,* 517-36.

Dion, K. L., & Earn, B. M. (1975). The phenomenology of being a target of prejudice. *Journal of Personality and Social Psychology, 32,* 944-50.

Dion, K. L., Earn, B. M., & Yee, P. H. N. (1978). The experience of being a victim of prejudice *International Journal of Psychology, 13,* 197-214.

Dion, K. L., & Kawakami, K. (1996). Ethnicity and perceived discrimination in Toronto: Another look at the personal/group discrimination discrepancy. *Canadian Journal of Behavioural Science, 28,* 203-13.

Dion, K. L., & Kawakami, K. (2000, June 18). *Predictors of collective action among women.* Symposium presentation to the Third Biennial Meeting of the Society for the Psychological Study of Social Issues, Minneapolis, MN.

Dodge, K. A. (1980). Social cognition and children's aggressive behavior. *Child Development, 51,* 162-70.

Dodge, K. A., Coie, J. D., Pettit, G. S., & Price, J. M. (1990). Peer status and aggression in boys' groups: Developmental and contextual analyses. *Child Development, 61,* 1289-1309.

Dodge, K. A., & Frame, C. L. (1982). Social cognitive biases and deficits in aggressive boys. *Child Development, 53,* 620-35.

Dollard, J., Doob, L., Miller, N., Mowrer, O., & Sears, R. (1939). *Frustration and Aggression.* New Haven, CT: Yale University Press.

Donahue, M. (1985). Intrinsic and extrinsic religiousness: Review and meta-analysis. *Journal of Personality and Social Psychology, 48*(2), 400-419.

Dougherty, K. D., & Huyser, K. R. (2008). Racially diverse congregations: Organizational identity and the accommodation of differences. *Journal for the Scientific Study of Religion, 47,* 23-43.

Dovidio, J. F., Allen, J. L., & Schroeder, D. A. (1990). The specificity of empathy-induced helping: Evidence for altruistic motivation. *Journal of Personality and Social Psychology, 59,* 249-60.

Dovidio, J. F., Eller, A., & Hewstone, M. (2011). Improving intergroup relations through direct, extended and other forms of indirect contact. *Group Processes and Intergroup Relations, 14,* 147-60.

Dovidio, J. F., & Gaertner, S. L. (2000). Aversive racism and selection decisions: 1989 and 1999. *Psychological Science, 11,* 315-19.

Dovidio, J. F., Glick, P., & Rudman, L. (2005). *On the nature of prejudice.* Malden, MA: Blackwell.

Dovidio, J. F., Maruyama, G., & Alexander, M. G. (1998). A social psychology of national and international group relations. *Journal of Social Issues, 54,* 831-46.

Dovidio, J. F., Piliavin, J. A., Gaertner, S. L., Schroeder, D. A., & Clark, R. D., III. (1991). The arousal/cost-reward model and the process of intervention: A review of the evidence. In M. S. Clarck (Ed.), *Review of personality and social psychology* (Vol. 12, pp. 86-118). Newbury Park, CA: Sage.

Downs, A. C., & Lyons, P. M. (1991). Natural observations of the links between attractiveness and initial legal judgments. *Personality and Social Psychology Bulletin, 17*, 541-47.

Duckitt, J. (1992). Psychology and prejudice: A historical and integrative framework. *American Psychologist, 47*, 1182-93.

Duckitt, J., & Sibley, C. G. (2007). Right wing authoritarianism, social dominance orientation and the dimensions of generalized prejudice. *European Journal of Personality, 21*, 113-30.

Duckitt, J., Wagner, C., du Plessis, I., & Birum, I. (2002). The psychological bases of ideology and prejudice: Testing a dual process model. *Journal of Personality and Social Psychology, 82*, 75-93.

Duffy, M. K., & Shaw, J. D. The Salieri syndrome: Consequences of envy in groups. *Small Group Research, 31*, 3-23.

Dugatkin, L. A. (1997). *Cooperation among animals: An evolutionary perspective*. New York, NY: Oxford University Press.

Duncan, L. E., Peterson, B. E., & Winter, D. G. (1997). Authoritarianism and gender roles: Toward a psychological analysis of hegemonic relationships. *Personality and Social Psychology Bulletin, 23*, 41-49.

Dunning, D., Griffin, D. W., Milojkovic, J. D., & Ross, L. (1990). The overconfidence effect in social prediction. *Journal of Personality and Social Psychology, 58*, 568-81.

Duriez, B., & Van Hiel, A. (2002). The march of modern fascism: A comparison of social dominance orientation and authoritarianism. *Journal of Personality and Individual Differences, 32*(7), 1199-1213.

Duvall, N. S. (1998). From soul to self and back again. *Journal of Psychology and Theology, 26*, 6-15.

Eagly, A. H. (1987). *Sex differences in social behavior: A social role interpretation*. Hillsdale. NJ: Erlbaum.

Eagly, A. H., Ashmore, R. D., Makhijani, M. G., & Longo, L. C. (1991). What is beautiful is good, but . . . : A meta-analytic review of research on the physical attractiveness stereotype. *Psychological Bulletin, 100*, 109-28.

Eagly, A. H., & Carli, L. L. (1981). Sex of researchers and sex-typed communications as determinants of sex differences in influenceability: A meta-analysis of social influence studies. *Psychological Bulletin, 90*, 1-20.

Eagly, A. H. & Chaiken, S. (1993). *The psychology of attitudes*. Fort Worth, TX: Harcourt Brace Jovanovich.

Eagly, A. H., & Chaiken, S. (1998). Attitude structure and function. In D. T. Gilbert, S. T. Fiske & G. Lindzey (Eds.), *The handbook of social psychology* (4th Ed., Vol. 1, pp. 269-322). Boston, MA: McGraw-Hill.

Eagly, A. H., & Crowley, M. (1986). Gender and helping behavior: A meta-analytic review of the social psychological literature. *Psychological Bulletin, 100*, 283-308.

Eagly, A. H., & Wood, W. (1999). The origins of sex differences in human behavior: Evolved dispositions versus social roles. *American Psychologist, 54*, 408-23.

Eaton, J., & Struthers, C. W. (2006). The reduction of psychological aggression across varied interpersonal contexts through repentance and forgiveness. *Aggressive Behavior, 32*(3), 195-206.

Ebbinghaus, H. (1885). *Memory: A contribution to experimental psychology.* New York: Teachers College, Columbia University.

Eberstadt, M. (2010). Bacchanalia unbound. *First Things, 207,* 55-60.

Eck, B. E. (1996). Integrating the integrators: Framework for a multifaceted process of integration. *Journal of Psychology and Christianity, 15*(2), 101-13.

Eisenberg, N., Guthrie, I., Cumberland, A., & Murphy, B. (2002). Prosocial development in early adulthood: A longitudinal study. *Journal of Personality and Social Psychology, 82,* 993-1006.

Eisenberg, N., Guthrie, I. K., Murphy, B. C., Shepard, S. A., Cumberland, A., & Carlo, G. (1999). Consistency and development of prosocial dispositions: A longitudinal study. *Child Development, 80*(6), 1360-72.

Eisenberg, N., & Miller, P. A. (1987). Empathy, sympathy and altruism: Empirical and conceptual links. In N. Eisenberg & J. Strayer (Eds.), *Empathy and its development* (pp. 292-316). New York, NY: Cambridge University Press.

Eisenberg, N., & Strayer, J. (Eds.). (1987). *Empathy and its development.* Cambridge: Cambridge University Press.

Eisenberger, N. I., Lieberman, M. D., & Williams, K. D. (2003). Does rejection hurt? An fMRI study of social exclusion. *Science, 302,* 290-92.

Ekehammar, B., & Akrami, N. (2003). The relation between personality and prejudice: A variable- and a person-centred approach. *European Journal of Personality, 17,* 449-64.

Elkind, D., & Bowen, R. (1979). Imaginary audience behavior in children and adolescents. *Developmental Psychology, 15*(1), 38-44.

Ellenbogen, J. M., Hurford, M. O., Liebeskind, D. S., Neimark, G. B., & Weiss, D. (2005). Ventromedial lobe trauma. *Neurology, 64*(4), 757.

Emler, N. (2001). *Self-esteem: The costs and causes of low self worth.* Layerthorpe, England: York Publishing Services.

Emswiller, T., Deaux, K., & Willits, J. (1971). Similarity, sex, and requests for small favors. *Journal of Applied Social Psychology, 1,* 284-91.

Englander, E. (1997). *Understanding violence.* Mahwah, NJ: Erlbaum.

Enright, R. (2009, February). Forgiveness: The missing piece to the peace puzzle. Presented to the Bascom Hill Society, Madison, Wisconsin.

Enright, R. D., Knutson, J. A., Holter, A. C., Baskin, T., & Knutson, C. (2007). Waging peace through forgiveness in Belfast, Northern Ireland: A review and proposal for mental health improvement of children. *Journal of Research in Education, 13,* 51-61.

Epstude, K., & Roese, N. J. (2008).The functional theory of counterfactual thinking. *Personality and Social Psychology Review, 12*(2), 168-92.

Erbe, W. 1966. Accessibility and informal social relationships among American graduate students. *Sociometry, 29*(3), 251-64.

Erikson, E. H. (1959). *Identity and the life cycle: Selected papers, with a historical introduction by David Rapaport.* New York: International University Press.

Esser, J. K. (1998). Alive and well after 25 years: A review of groupthink research. *Organizational Behavior and Human Decision Processes, 73*(2), 116-41.

Esser, J. K., & Lindoerfer, J. L. (1989). Groupthink and the space shuttle Challenger accident:

Toward a quantitative case analysis. *Journal of Behavioral Decision Making, 2,* 167-77.

Essock-Vitale, S., & McGuire, M. (1985). Women's lives viewed from an evolutionary perspective. II. Patterns of helping. *Ethology and Sociobiology, 6,* 155-73.

Evans, C. S. (1979). *Preserving the person: A look at the human sciences.* Downers Grove, IL: InterVarsity Press.

Evans, C. S. (2005). The relational self: Psychological and theological perspectives. In W. R. Miller & H. D. Delaney (Eds.), *Judeo-Christian perspectives on psychology: Human nature, motivation, and change* (pp. 73-94). Washington, DC: American Psychological Association.

Evans, C. S. (2006). Is there a basis for loving all people? *Journal of Psychology and Theology, 34*(1), 78-90.

Exline, J. J., & Baumeister, R. F. (2000). Expressing forgiveness and repentance: Benefits and barriers. In M. E. McCullough, K. I. Pargament & C. E. Thoresen (Eds.), *Forgiveness: Theory, research, and practice* (pp. 133-55). New York, NY: Guilford Press.

Fagin-Jones, S., & Midlarsky, E. (2007). Courageous altruism: Personal and situational correlates of rescue during the Holocaust. *Journal of Positive Psychology, 2*(2), 136-47.

Falbo, T., Poston, D. L., Triscari, R. S., & Zhang, X. (1997). Self-enhancing illusions among Chinese school children. *Journal of Cross-Cultural Psychology, 28,* 172-91.

Fallon, A., & Rozin, P. (1985). Sex differences in perceptions of desirable body shape. *Journal of Abnormal Psychology, 94*(1), 102-5.

Farrington, D. P. (1991). Childhood aggression and adult violence: Early precursors and later-life outcomes. In D. J. Pepler & K. H. Rubin (Eds.), *The development and treatment of childhood aggression* (pp. 5-29). Hillsdale, NJ: Erlbaum.

Fazio, R. H. (1990). Multiple processes by which attitudes guide behavior: The MODE model as an integrative framework. In M. P. Zanna (Ed.), *Advances in experimental social psychology* (Vol. 23, pp. 75-109). New York, NY: Academic Press.

Fazio, R. H. (1995). Attitudes as object-evaluation associations: Determinants, consequences, and correlates of attitude accessibility. In R. E. Petty & J. A. Krosnick (Eds.), *Attitude strength: Antecedents and consequences* (pp. 247-82). Hillsdale, NJ: Erlbaum.

Fazio, R. H. (2007). Attitudes as object-evaluation associations of varying strength. *Social Cognition, 25,* 603-37.

Fazio, R. H., & Olson, M. A. (2003). Implicit measures in social cognition research: Their meaning and uses. *Annual Review of Psychology, 54,* 297-327.

Fazio, R. H., Sanbonmatsu, D. M., Powell, M. C., & Kardes, F. R. (1986). On the automatic activation of attitudes. *Journal of Personality and Social Psychology, 50,* 229-38.

Fazio, R. H., & Towles-Schwen, T. (1999). The MODE model of attitude-behaviour processes. In S. Chaiken & Y. Trope (Eds.), *Dual-process theories in social psychology* (pp. 97-116). New York, NY: Guilford.

FBI Bureau of Justice Statistics-Criminal Victimization (2009). http://bjs.ojp.usdoj.gov/index.cfm?ty=pbdetail&iid=2217

FBI National Crime Statistics. www2.fbi.gov/ucr/cius2009/data/table_01a.html

Feather, N. T. (1983). Causal attributions for good and bad outcomes in achievement and affiliation situations. *Australian Journal of Psychology, 35,* 37-48.

Fehr, E., & Fischbacher, U. (2003). The nature of human altruism. *Nature, 425*, 785-91.

Fein, S., & Spencer, S. (1997). Prejudice as self-image maintenance: Affirming the self through derogating others. *Journal of Personality and Social Psychology, 73*(1), 31-45.

Fessler, D. M. T. (2004). Shame in two cultures: Implications for evolutionary approaches. *Journal of Cognition and Culture 4*, 207-62.

Festinger, L. (1954). A theory of social comparison processes. *Human Relations, 7*, 117-40.

Festinger, L. (1957). *A theory of cognitive dissonance.* Stanford, CA: Stanford University Press.

Festinger, L. (1964). *Conflict, decision, and dissonance.* Stanford, CA: Stanford University Press.

Festinger, L., & Carlsmith, J. M. (1959). Cognitive consequences of forced compliance. *Journal of Abnormal and Social Psychology, 58*(2), 203-10.

Festinger, L., Pepitone, A., & Newcomb, T. (1952). Some consequences of de-individuation in a group. *Journal of Abnormal and Social Psychology, 47*, 382-89.

Festinger, L., Riecken, H. W., & Schachter, S. (1956). *When prophecy fails.* Minneapolis, MN: University of Minnesota Press.

Festinger, L., Schachter, S., & Back, K. (1950). *Social pressures in informal groups: A study of human factors in housing.* Palo Alto, CA: Stanford University Press.

Fink, B., & Penton-Voak, I. (2002). Evolutionary psychology of facial attractiveness. *Current Directions in Psychological Science, 11*, 154-58.

Fischhoff, R. (1975). Hindsight ≠ foresight: The effect of outcome knowledge on judgment under uncertainty. *Journal of Experimental Psychology, Perception & Performance, 1*, 288-99.

Fischhoff, B., & Beyth, R. (1975). "I knew it would happen": Remembered probabilities of once-future things. *Organizational Behavior and Human Performance, 13*, 1-16.

Fischhoff, B., Slovic, P., Lichtenstein, S., Reid, S., & Coombs, B. (1978). How safe is safe enough? A psychometric study of attitudes towards technological risks and benefits. *Policy Sciences, 9*, 127-52

Fishbein, M. (1967). Attitude and the prediction of behaviour. In M. Fishbein (Ed.), *Readings in attitude theory and measurement.* New York: Wiley.

Fishbein, M., & Ajzen, I. (1975). *Belief, attitude, intention, and behavior: An introduction to theory and research.* Reading, MA: Addison-Wesley.

Fiske, A. P. (1991). The cultural relativity of selfish individualism: Anthropological evidence that humans are inherently sociable. In M. S. Clark (Ed.), *Review of personality and social psychology: Vol. 12, Prosocial behavior* (pp. 176-214). Newbury Park, CA: Sage.

Fiske, S. T. (1980). Attention and weight in person perception: the impact of negative and extreme behavior. *Journal of Personality and Social Psychology, 38*(6), 889-906.

Fiske, S. T., & Neuberg, S. L. (1990). Automaticity of social behavior: Direct effects of trait construct and stereotype activation on action. *Advances in Experimental Social Psychology, 23*, 1-74.

Fiske, S. T., & Taylor, S. (1991). *Social cognition.* New York: Random House.

Fitzgerald, C. J., & Colarelli, S. M. (2009). Altruism and reproductive limitations. *Evolutionary Psychology, 7*, 234-52.

Flowers, M. L. (1977). A laboratory test of some implications of Janis's groupthink hypothesis. *Journal of Personality and Social Psychology, 35,* 888-96.

Folkes, V. S. (1982). Forming relationships and the matching hypothesis. *Personality and Social Psychology Bulletin, 8,* 631-36.

Forest, D., Clark, M., Mills, J., & Isen, A. (1979). Helping as a function of feeling state and nature of the helping behavior. *Motivation and Emotion, 3,* 161-69.

Forgas J. P. (1998). Asking nicely? The effects of mood on responding to more or less polite requests. *Personality and Social Psychology Bulletin, 24,* 173-85.

Forgas, J. P., & von Hippel, W. (Eds.). *The social outcast: Ostracism, social exclusion, rejection, and bullying* (pp. 279-95). New York, NY: Psychology Press.

Forsyth, D. R. (2006). *Group Dynamics* 4e [International Student Edition]. Belmont, CA: Thomson Wadsworth Publishing.

Forsyth, D. R. (2009). *Group Dynamics* (5th ed.). Belmont, CA: Wadsworth Cengage Learning.

Forsyth, D. R., & Kerr, N. A. (1999). *Are adaptive illusions adaptive?* Poster presented at the annual meeting of the American Psychological Association, Boston, MA.

Foucault, M. (1977). *Language, counter memory, practice.* Ithaca, NY: Cornell University Press.

Frankenberger, K. D. (2000). Adolescent egocentrism: A comparison among adolescents and adults. *Journal of Adolescence, 3,* 343-54.

Freedman, D. G. (1964). Smiling in blind infants. *Journal of Child Psychology and Psychiatry* 5(3-4), 171-84.

Freedman, J. L., & Fraser, S. C. (1966). Compliance without pressure: The foot-in-the-door technique. *Journal of Personality and Social Psychology, 4,* 195-202.

Fretheim, T. E. (2004). God and violence in the Old Testament. *Word and World, 24*(1), 18-28. www2.luthersem.edu/word&world/Archives/24-1_Violence/24-1_Fretheim.pdf

Freud, S. (1929). *Civilization and its discontents.* In *The Works of Sigmund Freud,* Britannica Great Books (Vol. 54, 1989). Chicago: William Benton.

Frick, P. J., & White, S. F. (2008). Research review: The importance of callous-unemotional traits for developmental models of aggressive and antisocial behavior. *Journal of Child Psychology and Psychiatry, 49,* 359-75.

Friedrich, J. (1996). On seeing oneself as less *self*-serving than others: The ultimate *self*-serving bias? *Teaching of Psychology, 23,* 107-9.

Fritz, H. L. (1998). Distinctions of unmitigated communion from communion: Self-neglect and overinvolvement with others. *Journal of Personality and Social Psychology, 75*(1), 121-40.

Frye, N. E., & Karney, B. R. (2006). The context of aggressive behavior in marriage: A longitudinal study of newlyweds. *Journal of Family Psychology, 20,* 12-20.

Fulton, A. S., Gorsuch, R. L., & Maynard, E. A. (1999). Religious orientation, anti-homosexual sentiment, and fundamentalism among Christians. *Journal for the Scientific Study of Religion, 38,* 14-22.

Funder, D. C. (1999). *Personality judgment: A realistic approach to person perception.* San Diego, CA: Academic Press.

Furnham, A. (1996). Factors relating to the allocation of medical resources. *Journal of Social Behavior and Personality, 11*, 615-24.

Furnham, A., Dias, M., & McClelland, A. (1998). The role of body weight, waist-to-hip ratio, and breast size in judgments of female attractiveness. *Sex Roles, 34*, 311-26.

Furnham, A., & Gunter, B. (1984). Just world beliefs and attitudes towards the poor. *British Journal of Social Psychology, 23*, 265-69.

Gable, S., & Haidt, J. (2005). Positive psychology. *Review of General Psychology, 9*, 1089-2680. (Introduction to special issue on positive psychology).

Gabriel, S., & Gardner, W. L. (1999). Are there "his" and "her" types of interdependence? The implications of gender differences in collective and relational interdependence for affect, behavior, and cognition. *Journal of Personality and Social Psychology, 75*, 642-55.

Gaertner, L., & Bickman, L. (1971). Effects of race on the elicitation of helping behavior: The wrong number technique. *Journal of Personality and Social Psychology, 20*, 218-22.

Gaertner, L., & Iuzzini, J. (2005). Rejection and entitativity: A synergistic model of mass violence. In K. D. Williams, J. P. Forgas & W. von Hippel (Eds.), *The social outcast: Ostracism, social exclusion, rejection, and bullying*. New York, NY: Psychology Press.

Gaertner, L., Sedikides, C., & Chang, K. (2008). On pancultural self-enhancement: Well-adjusted Taiwanese self-enhance on personally-valued traits. *Journal of Cross-Cultural Psychology, 39*, 463-77.

Gaertner, L., Sedikides, C., Luke, M., & Iuzzini, J. (2008). Hierarchy among selves: An implication for relations with persons versus groups. In H. A. Wayment, & J. J. Bauer (Eds.), *Quieting the ego: Psychological benefits of transcending egotism* (pp. 127-35). Washington, DC: American Psychological Association.

Gaes, G. G., & McGuire, W. J. (1985). Prison violence: The contribution of crowding versus other determinants of prison assault rates. *Delinquency, 22*(1), 41-65.

Garrity, K., & Degelman, D. (1990). Effect of server introduction on restaurant tipping. *Journal of Applied Social Psychology, 20*, 168-72.

Gawronski, B. (2007). Editorial: Attitudes can be measured! But what is an attitude? *Social Cognition, 25*, 573-81.

Gawronski, B., & Bodenhausen, G. V. (2006). Associative and propositional processes in evaluation: An integrative review of implicit and explicit attitude change. *Psychological Bulletin, 132*, 692-731.

Gecas, V., & Schwalbe, M. (1983). Beyond the looking glass self: Social structure and efficacy-based self-esteem. *Social Psychology Quarterly, 46*, 77-88.

Geen, R. G., & Donnerstein, E. I. (Eds.). (1998). *Human aggression: Theory, research, and implications for social policy*. San Diego, CA: Academic Press.

Geertz, C. (1973). Person, time, and conduct in Bali. In C. Geertz (Ed.), *The interpretation of cultures* (pp. 360-411). New York, NY: Basic Books.

Gelles, R. J. (1997). *Intimate violence in families* (3rd ed.). Thousand Oaks, CA: Sage.

Gergen, K. J. (1973). Social psychology as history. *Journal of Personality and Social Psychology, 26*(2), 309-20.

Gergen, K. J. (1991). *The saturated self: Dilemmas of identity in contemporary life*. New York: Basic Books.

Gergen, K. J. (1992). The decline and fall of personality. *Psychology Today*, November/December, pp. 59-63.

Gibson, R., and Sachau, D. (2000). Sandbagging as a self-presentational strategy: Claiming to be less than you are. *Personality and Social Psychology Bulletin, 26*, 56-70.

Gigerenzer, G. (2008). Why heuristics work. *Perspectives on Psychological Science, 3*(1), 20-29.

Gigerenzer, G., Todd, P. M., & ABC Research Group. (1999). *Simple heuristics that make us smart.* Oxford, England: Oxford University Press.

Gigerenzer, G., & Selten, R. (Eds.). (2002). *Bounded rationality: The adaptive toolbox.* Cambridge, MA: MIT Press.

Gilbert, D. T., & Malone, P. S. (1995). The correspondence bias. *Psychological Bulletin, 117*(1), 21-28.

Gilbert, D. T., Pelham, B. W., & Krull, D. S. (1988). On cognitive busyness: When person perceivers meet persons perceived. *Journal of Personality and Social Psychology, 54*, 733-40.

Gilbert, P. (Ed.). (2005). Compassion: Conceptualisations, research, and use in psychotherapy. New York, NY: Routledge.

Gilovich, T. (1991). *How we know what isn't so: The fallibility of human reason in everyday life.* New York, NY: The Free Press.

Gilovich, T., Keltner, D., & Nisbett, R. (2006). *Social psychology* (2nd ed.). New York, NY: W. W. Norton.

Gladwell, M. (2000). *The tipping point: How little things can make a big difference.* New York, NY: Little, Brown & Co.

Glassman, R. B., Packel, E. W., & Brown, D. L. (1986). Green beards and kindred spirits: A preliminary mathematical model of altruism toward non-kin who bear similarities to the giver. *Ethology and Sociobiology, 7*, 107-15.

Glicksohn, J., & Golan, H. (2001). Personality, cognitive style and assortative mating. *Personality and Individual Differences, 30*, 1199-1209.

Glock, C., Ringer, B., & Babbie, E. (1967). *To comfort and to challenge: A dilemma of the contemporary church.* Berkeley, CA: University of California Press.

Golden, M. (1991). The Americans With Disabilities Act (ADA) of 1990: An activist's perspective. Paper presented at the Independent Living Institute. Retrieved from http://www.independentliving.org/cib/cibbudapest11.html

Goldfried, J., & Miner, M. (2002). Quest religion and the problem of limited compassion. *Journal for the Scientific Study of Religion, 41*, 685-95.

Goldstein, N. J., Cialdini. R. B., & V. Griskevicius, V. (2008). A room with a viewpoint: Using social norms to motivate environmental conservation in hotels. *Journal of Consumer Research, 35*, 472-82.

Goodman, M. D., & Gareis, K. C. (1993). The influence of status on decisions to help. *Journal of Social Psychology, 133*(1), 23-31.

Gorsuch, R. L. (1997). Toward a motivational theory of intrinsic relational commitment. In B. Spilka & D. N. McIntosh (Eds.), *The psychology of religion: Theoretical approaches* (pp. 11-22). Boulder, CO: Westview Press.

Gorsuch, R. L., & Aleshire, D. (1974). Christian faith and ethnic prejudice: A review and interpretation of research. *Journal for the Scientific Study of Religion, 13*, 281-307.

Gortmaker, S. L. (1993). Social and economic consequences of overweight in adolescence and young adulthood. *New England Journal of Medicine, 329*(14), 1008-12.

Gottlieb, J., & Carver, C. S. (1980). Anticipation of future interaction and the bystander effect. *Journal of Experimental Social Psychology, 16*, 253-60.

Gottman, J. M., & Levenson, R. W. (1992). Marital processes predictive of later dissolution: Behavior, physiology, and health. *Journal of Personality & Social Psychology, 63*, 221-33.

Gouldner, A. W. (1960). The norm of reciprocity: A preliminary statement. *American Sociological Review, 25*, 161-78.

Grafman, J., Schwab, K., Wardne, D., Prigden, A., Brown, H. R., & Salazar, A. M. (1996). Frontal lobe injuries, violence, and aggression: A report of the Vietnam Head Injury Study. *Neurology, 46*(5), 1231-38.

Green, L., & Mehr, D. R. (1997). What alters physicians' decisions to admit to the coronary care unit? *The Journal of Family Practice, 45*, 219-26.

Greenberg, J., Koole, S. L., & Pyszczynski, T. (2004). *Handbook of experimental existential psychology*. New York, NY: Guilford Press.

Greenwald, A. G., & Banaji, M. R. (1995). Implicit social cognition: Attitudes, self-esteem, and stereotypes. *Psychological Review, 102*(1), 4-27. doi:10.1037/0033-295X.102.1.4

Greenwald, A. G., McGhee, D. E., & Schwartz, J. K. L. (1998). Measuring individual differences in implicit cognition: The Implicit Association Test. *Journal of Personality and Social Psychology, 74*(6), 1464-80.

Griffin, G. E., Gorsuch, R. L., & Davis, A. (1987). A cross-cultural investigation of religions orientation, social norms, and prejudice. *Journal for the Scientific Study of Religion, 26*(3), 358-65.

Griffiths, M. D., & Shuckford, G. L. J. (1989). Desensitization to television violence: A new model. *New Ideas in Psychology, 7*, 85-89.

Griffitt, W., & Veitch, R. (1974). Preacquaintance, attitude similarity and attraction revisited: Ten days in a fall-out shelter. *Sociometry 37*(2), 163-73.

Grenz, S. J. (1994). *Theology for the community of God*. Nashville, TN: Broadman & Holman.

Guadagno, R .E., & Cialdini, R. B. (2002). Online persuasion: An examination of gender differences in computer-mediated influence. *Group Dynamics: Theory, Research, Practice, 6*(1), 38-51.

Guéguen, N., Pichot, N., & Le Dreff, G. (2005). Similarity and helping behavior on the web: The impact of the convergence of surnames between a solicitor and a subject in a request made by e-mail. *Journal of Applied Social Psychology, 35*(2), 423-29.

Guerra, N., Henry, D., Huesmanrt, L. R., & Tolan, P. (2007). Changing the way children "think" about aggression: Social-cognitive effects of preventive intervention. *Journal of Consulting and Clinical Psychology, 75*, 160-67.

Hacker, A. (1995). *Two nations: Black and White, separate, hostile, and unequal*. New York, NY: Ballantine.

Hagan, J., Krivo, L. J., & Peterson, R. D. (2006). *The many colors of crime: Inequalities of race, ethnicity, and crime in America.* New York, NY: New York University Press.

Hagen, E. (2005). Controversial issues in evolutionary psychology. In D. M. Buss (Ed.), *The handbook of evolutionary psychology.* New York, NY: Wiley.

Hall, D., Matz, D. C., & Wood, W. (2010). Why don't we practice what we preach? A meta-analytic review of religious racism. *Personality and Social Psychology Review, 14*(1), 126-39.

Hamilton, D. L. (1981). *Cognitive processes in stereotyping and intergroup behavior.* New York: Erlbaum & Associates.

Hamilton, D. L., Katz, L. B., & Leier, V. O. (1980). Cognitive representations of personality impressions: Organizational processes in first impression formation. *Journal of Personality and Social Psychology, 19*(6), 1050-63.

Hamilton, D. L., & Rose, T. L. (1980). Illusory correlation and the maintenance of stereotypic beliefs. *Journal of Personality and Social Psychology, 39*(5), 832-45.

Hamilton, D. L., & Trolier, T. K. (1986). Stereotypes and stereotyping: An overview of the cognitive approach. In J. Dovidio & S. Gaertner (Eds.), *Prejudice, discrimination, and racism* (pp. 127-163). Orlando, FL: Academic Press.

Hamilton, W. (1964). The evolution of altruistic behavior. *The American Naturalist, 97,* 354-56.

Hancock, J. T., & Dunham, P. J. (2001). Impression formation in computer-mediated communication revisited: An analysis of the breadth and intensity of impressions. *Communication Research, 28*(3), 325-47.

Haney, C., Banks, W. C., & Zimbardo, P. G. (1973). A study of prisoners and guards in a simulated prison. *Naval Research Review, 30,* 4-17.

Hansen, D. E., Vandenberg, B., & Patterson, M. L. (1995). The effects of religious orientation on spontaneous and nonspontaneous helping behavior. *Personality and Individual Differences, 19,* 101-4.

Hansen, T., & Bartsch, R. A. (2001). The positive correlation between personal need for structure and the mere exposure effect. *Social Behavior and Personality: An International Journal, 29*(3), 271-76. doi:10.2224/sbp.2001.29.3.271

Hardcastle, V. G., & Stewart, C. M. (2002). What do brain data really show? *Philosophy of Science, 69*(3 Supplement), S72, S82.

Harmon-Jones, E., & Allen, J. J. B. (2001). The role of affect in the mere exposure effect: Evidence from psychophysiological and individual differences approaches. *Personality and Social Psychology Bulletin, 27*(1), 889-98.

Harrell, W. A. (1978). Physical attractiveness, self-disclosure, and helping behavior. *Journal of Social Psychology, 104*(1), 15-17.

Harris, L. T., & Fiske, S. T. (2006). Dehumanizing the lowest of the low: Neuroimaging responses to extreme outgroups. *Psychological Science, 17*(10), 847-53.

Harrison, J. A., & Wells, R. B. (1991) Bystander effects on male helping behavior: Social comparison and diffusion of responsibility. *Representative Research in Social Psychology, 19*(1), 53-63.

Harter, S. (1993). Causes and consequences of low self-esteem in children and adolescents. In R. F. Baumeister (Ed.), *Self-esteem: The puzzle of low self-regard.* Plenum

Series in Social/Clinical Psychology (pp. 87-116). New York, NY: Plenum Press.

Harton, H. C., & Bullock, M. (2007). Dynamic social impact: A theory of the origins and evolution of culture. *Social and Personality Psychology Compass, 1*.

Haselton, M. G., & Funder, D. C. (2006). The evolution of accuracy and bias in social judgment. In M. Schaller, J. A. Simpson & D. T. Kenrick (Eds.), *Evolution and social psychology* (pp. 189-210). New York, NY: Psychology Press.

Haslam, N. (2006). Dehumanization: An integrative review. *Personality and Social Psychology Review, 10*(3), 252-64.

Haslam, N., Bain, P., Douge, L., Lee, M., & Bastian, B. (2005). More human than you: Attributing humanness to self and others. *Journal of Personality and Social Psychology, 89*, 973-50.

Hatfield, E., Aronson, E., Abrahams, D., & Rottman, L. (1966). The importance of physical attractiveness in dating behavior. *Journal of Personality and Social Psychology, 4*, 508-16.

Hatfield, E., & Sprecher, S. (1986). *Mirror, mirror: The importance of looks in everyday life*. Albany, NY: SUNY Press.

Healy, K. (2000). Embedded altruism: *Blood* collection regimes and the European Union's donor population. *American Journal of Sociology, 105*, 1633-57.

Healy, K. (2004). Altruism as an organizational problem: The case of organ procurement. *American Sociological Review, 69*, 387-404.

Hearold, S. (1986). A synthesis of 1043 effects of television on social behaviour. In G. Comstock (Ed.), *Public communications and behavior* (Vol. 1, pp. 65-133). New York, NY: Academic Press.

Heatherton, T. F., & Polivy, J. (1991). Development and validation of a scale for measuring state self-esteem. *Journal of Personality and Social Psychology, 60*, 895-910.

Heaven, P., & Conners, J. (2001). A note on the value correlates of social dominance orientation and right-wing authoritarianism. *Personality and Individual Differences, 31*, 925-30.

Heider, F. (1946). Attitudes and cognitive organization. *Journal of Psychology, 21*, 107-12.

Heine, S. H., Takata, T., & Lehman, D. R. (2000). Beyond self-presentation: Evidence for self criticism among Japanese. *Personality and Social Psychology Bulletin, 26*, 71-78.

Heine, S. H., Takata, T., Lehman, D. R, Markus H. R., & Kitayama, S. (1996). Is there a universal need for positive self regard? *Psychological Review, 106*, 766-94.

Held, B. S. (2004). The negative side of positive psychology. *Journal of Humanistic Psychology, 44*, 9-46.

Henggeler, S. W., Clingempeel, W. G., Brondido, M. J., & Pickerel, S. G. (2002). Four-year follow-up of multisystemic therapy with substance-abusing and substance dependent juvenile offenders. *Journal of Child and Adolescent Psychiatry, 41*(7), 868-74. doi:10.1097/00004583-200207000-00021

Henggeler, S. W., Letourneau, E. J., Chapman, J. E., Borduin, C. M., Schewe, P. A., & McCart, M. (2009). Mediators of change for multisystemic therapy with juvenile sexual offenders. *Journal of Consulting Clinical Psychology, 77*(3), 451-62. doi:10.1037/a0013971

Huesmann, L. R. (1998). The role of social information processing and cognitive schema in the acquisition and maintenance of habitual aggressive behavior. In R. G. Geen & E. Donnerstein (Eds.), *Human aggression: Theories, research, and implications for policy* (pp. 73-109). New York, NY: Academic Press.

Hewstone, M., Rubin, M., & Willis, H. (2002). Intergroup bias. *Annual Review of Psychology, 53*, 575-604.

Hill, P. C. (1994). Toward an attitude process model of religious experience. *Journal for the Scientific Study of Religion, 33*, 303-14.

Hill, P. C. (2002). Spiritual transformation: Forming the habitual center of personal energy. *Research in the Social Scientific Study of Religion, 13*, 87-108.

Hill, P. C. (2005). Living on the boundary; Scriptural authority and psychology. *Journal of Psychology and Theology, 33*(2), 98-112.

Hill, P. C., & Hood, R. W., Jr. (Eds.). (1999). *Measures of religiosity*. Birmingham, AL: Religious Education Press.

Hilton, D. J., & Slugoski, B. R. (1986). Knowledge-based causal attribution: The abnormal conditions focus model. *Psychological Review, 93*, 75-88.

Hodgins, H. S., & Liebeskind, E. (2003). Apology versus defense: Antecedents and consequences. *Journal of Experimental Social Psychology, 39*, 297-36.

Hoekema, A. (1986). *Created in God's image*. Grand Rapids, MI: Eerdmans.

Hoffer, E. (1959). *The passionate state of mind, and other aphorisms*. New York: Buccaneer Books.

Hoffman, M. L. (1981). Is altruism part of human nature? *Journal of Personality and Social Psychology, 40*(1), 121-37.

Hoffrage, U., Hertwig, R., & Gigerenzer, G. (2000). Hindsight bias: A by-product of knowledge updating? *Journal of Experimental Psychology: Learning, Memory, and Cognition, 26*(3), 566-81.

Hofstadter, Douglas. (1979). *Godel, Escher, Bach: The Eternal Braid*. New York, NY: Basic Books.

Hoge, M. A. (2010). Influence and leadership. In S. T. Fiske, D. T. Gilbert & G. Lindzey (Eds.), *Handbook of social psychology* (5th ed., Vol. 2, pp. 1166-1207). Hoboken, NJ: Wiley.

Holmes, A. (1992). The closing of the American mind. In A. Walker (Ed.), *Integrating faith and academic discipline: Selected H. I. Hester Lectures*. Nashville, TN: Education Commission, Southern Baptist Convention.

Holter, A. C., Magnuson, C., Knutson, C., Knutson Enright, J.A., & Enright, R. D. (2008). The forgiving child: The impact of forgiveness education on excessive anger for elementary-aged children in Milwaukee's central city. *Journal of Research in Education 18*, 82-93.

Holub, S. C. (2008). Individual differences in the anti-fat attitudes of preschool-children: The importance of perceived body size. *Body Image, 5*(3), 317-321.

Homans, G. C. (1958). Social behavior as exchange. *American Journal of Sociology, 63*, 597-606.

Homel, R., Tomsen, S., & Thommeny, J. (1992). Public drinking and violence: Not just an alcohol problem. *The Journal of Drug Issues, 22*, 679-97.

Hood, R. W., Jr., Hill, P. C., & Williamson. W. P. (2005). *The psychology of religious fundamentalism.* New York, NY: Guilford Press.

Hood, R. W., Jr., Hill, P. C., & Spilka, B. (2009). *The psychology of religion: An empirical approach* (4th ed.). New York, NY: Guilford Press.

Hornsey, M. J., & Hogg, M. A. (2000). Assimilation and diversity: An integrative model of subgroup relations. *Personality and Social Psychology Review, 4,* 143-56.

Hornsey, M. J., Majkut, L., Terry, D. J., & McKimmie, B. M. (2003). On being loud and proud: Non-conformity and counter-conformity to group norms. *British Journal of Social Psychology, 42*(3), 319-35.

Hosoda, M., Stone-Romero, E. F., & Coats, G. (2003). The effects of physical attractiveness on job-related outcomes: A meta-analysis of experimental studies. *Personnel Psychology, 56*(2), 431-62.

Hovland, C. I., Janis, I. L., & Kelley, H. H, (1953).*Communication and persuasion: Psychological studies of opinion change.* New Haven, CT: Yale University Press.

Hsee, C. K., & Kunreuther, H. (2000). The affection effect in insurance decisions. *Journal of Risk and Uncertainty, 20,* 141-59.

Hsee, C. K., & Menon, S. (1999). *Affection effect in consumer choices.* Unpublished study, University of Chicago.

Huan Lim, S., & Ang, R. P. (2009). Relationship between boys' normative beliefs about aggression and their physical, verbal, and indirect aggressive behaviors. *Adolescence, 44,* 175, 635-49.

Huesmann, L. R. (1998). The role of social information processing and cognitive schema in the acquisition and maintenance of habitual aggressive behavior (pp. 73-109). In R. G. Geen & E. Donnerstein (Eds.), *Human Aggression: Theories, Research, and Implications for Policy.* New York, NY: Academic Press.

Humphrey, J. A., & White, J. W. (2000). Women's vulnerability to sexual assault from adolescence to young adulthood. *Journal of Adolescent Health, 27,* 419-24.

Hunsberger, B. (1995). Religion and prejudice: The role of religious fundamentalism, quest, and right-wing authoritarianism. *Journal of Social Issues, 51*(2), 113-29.

Hunsberger, B. (1996). Religious fundamentalism, right-wing authoritarianism, and hostility toward homosexuals in non-Christian religious groups. *International Journal for the Psychology of Religion, 6*(1), 39-49.

Hunsberger, B., & Jackson, L. M. (2005). Religion, meaning, and prejudice. *Journal of Social Issues, 61,* 807-26.

Huston, T., Ruggiero, M., Conner, R., & Geis, G. (1981). Bystander intervention into crime: A study based on naturally-occurring episodes. *Social Psychology Quarterly, 44,* 14-23.

Hyden, M. (1995). Verbal aggression as prehistory of woman battering. *Journal of Family Violence, 10*(1), 55-75. doi:10.1007/BF02110537

Infante, D. A., Sabourin, T., C., Rudd, J. E., & Shannon, E. A. (1990). Verbal aggression nonviolent marital disputes. *Communication Quarterly, 38*(4), 361-71.

Insko, C. A., Smith, R. H., Alicke, M. D., Wade, J., & Taylor, S. (1985). Conformity and group size: The concern with being right and the concern with being liked. *Personality and Social Psychology Bulletin, 11,* 41-50.

Isen, A. M. (1970). Success, failure, attention, and reaction to others: The warm glow of success. *Journal of Personality and Social Psychology, 15,* 294-301.

Isen, A. M., & Levin, P. (1972). Effect of feeling good on helping: Cookies and kindness. *Journal of Personality and Social Psychology, 21*(3), 384-88.

Isen, A. M., & Simmonds, S. (1978). The effect of feeling good on a helping task that is incompatible with good mood. *Social Psychology Quarterly, 41,* 345-49.

Isen, A. M., & Simmonds, S. (1979). The effect of feeling good on a helping task that is incompatible with good mood. *Social Psychology, 14,* 341-46.

Isenberg, D. J. (1986). Group polarization: A critical review and meta-analysis. *Journal of Personality and Social Psychology, 50*(6), 1141-51.

Ito, T .A., Cacioppo, J. T., & Lang, P. J. (1998). Eliciting affect using the International Affective Picture System: Trajectories through evaluative space. *Personality and Social Psychology Bulletin, 24,* 855-79.

Iyengar, S. S., & Lepper, M. R. (2002). Choice and its consequences: On the costs and benefits of self-regulation. In A. Tesser, D. A. Stapel & J. V. Wood (Eds.), *Self and motivation: Emerging psychological perspectives* (pp. 71-96). Washington, DC: American Psychological Association.

Jackson, L. A. (1992). *Physical appearance and gender: Sociobiological and sociocultural perspectives.* Albany, NY: SUNY Press.

Jackson, L. M., & Esses, V. M. (1997). Of Scripture and ascription: The relation between religious fundamentalism and intergroup helping. *Personality and Social Psychology Bulletin, 23,* 893-906.

Jacobson, C. (1998). Religiosity and prejudice: An update and denominational analysis. *Review of Religious Research, 39*(3), 264-72.

Jacoby, T. (2000). *Someone else's house: America's unfinished struggle for integration.* New York, NY: Basic Books.

Jahoda, G. (1999). *Images of savages: Ancient roots of modern prejudice in western culture.* London, England: Routledge & Kegan Paul.

Jahoda, M. (1959). Conformity and independence. *Human Relations, 12,* 99-120.

Jain, U. (1990). Social perspectives on causal attribution. In G. Misra (Ed.), *Applied social psychology in India.* New Delhi, India: Sage.

James, F. (1996). On seeing oneself as less self-serving than others: The ultimate self serving bias? *Teaching of psychology, 2,* 107-9.

James, W. (1890). *Principles of psychology.* New York: Holt.

Janis, I. L. (1971). Groupthink. *Psychology Today,* November, 43-46, 74-76.

Janis, I. L. (1972). *Victims of groupthink.* New York, NY: Houghton Mifflin.

Janis, I. L. (1982). *Groupthink: Psychological studies of policy decisions and fiascoes* (2nd ed.). New York, NY: Houghton Mifflin.

Jarvis, W. B. G., & Petty, R. E. (1996). The need to evaluate. *Journal of Personality and Social Psychology, 70,* 172-94.

Jasper, C. R., & Klassen, M. L. (1990). Stereotypical beliefs about appearance: Implications for retailing and consumer issues. *Perceptual and Motor Skills, 71*(2), 519-28.

Jeeves, M. (1997). *Human nature at the millennium: Reflections on the integration of psychology and Christianity*. Grand Rapids, MI: Baker Books.

Jeffries, V. (1998). Virtue and the altruistic personality. *Sociological Perspectives, 41*(1), 151-66.

Jenkins, S., & Aube, J. (2002). Gender differences and gender-related constructs in dating aggression. *Personality and Social Psychology Bulletin, 28*, 1106-18.

Johnson, E. (2011). The three faces of integration. *Journal of Psychology and Christianity, 30*(4), 339-55.

Johnson, P. (2002). *The right questions: Truth, meaning and public debate*. Downers Grove, IL: InterVarsity Press.

Johnson, R. D., & Downing, L. L. (1979). Deindividuation and valence of cues: Effects on prosocial and antisocial behavior. *Journal of Personality & Social Psychology, 37*, 1532-38. doi:10.1037//0022-3514.37.9.1532

Jonas, E., Schulz-Hardt, S., Frey, D., & Thelen, N. (2001). Confirmation bias in sequential information search after preliminary decisions: An expansion of dissonance theoretical research on selective exposure to information. *Journal of Personality and Social Psychology, 80*, 557-71.

Jones, E. E. (1990). *Interpersonal perceptions*. New York: W. H. Freeman.

Jones, E. E., & Baumeister, R. F. (1976), The self-monitor looks at the ingratiator. *Journal of Personality, 44*, 654-74.

Jones, E. E., & Davis, K. E. (1965). From acts to dispositions: The attribution process in person perception. In L. Berkowitz (Ed.), *Advances in experimental social psychology* (Vol. 2, pp. 219-66). New York, NY: Academic Press.

Jones, E. E., & Goethals, G. R. (1972). Order effects in impression formation: Attribution context and the nature of the entity. In E. E. Jones, D. E. Kanouse, H. H. Kelley, R. E. Nisbett, S. Valins & B. Weiner (Eds.), *Attribution: Perceiving the causes of behavior* (pp. 27-46). Morristown, NJ: General Learning Press.

Jones, E. E., & Harris, V. A. (1967). The attribution of attitudes. *Journal of Experimental Social Psychology, 3*, 1-24.

Jones, E. E., & Nisbett, R. E. (1971). *The actor and the observer: Divergent perceptions of the causes of behavior*. New York: General Learning Press.

Jones, E. E., & Nisbett, R. E. (1972). The actor and the observer: Divergent perceptions of the causes of behavior. In E. E. Jones et al. (Eds.), *Attributions: Perceiving the causes of behavior*. Morristown, NJ: General Learning Press.

Jones, M. (1991). Gender stereotyping in advertisements. *Teaching of Psychology 18*, 231-33.

Jones, S. L., & Butman, R. E. (1991). *Modern psychotherapies: A comprehensive Christian appraisal*. Downers Grove, IL: InterVarsity Press.

Jordan, C. H., Spencer, S. J., & Zanna, M. P. (2005). Types of high self-esteem and prejudice: How implicit self-esteem relates to ethnic discrimination among high explicit self-esteem individuals. *Personality and Social Psychology Bulletin, 31*, 693-702. doi:10.1177/0146167204271580

Jost, J. T., & Banaji, M. (1994). The role of stereotyping in system justification and the production of false consciousness. *British Journal of Social Psychology, 22*, 1-27.

Jost, J. T., Glaser, J., Kruglanski, A. W., & Sulloway, F. (2003). Political conservatism as motivated social cognition. *Psychological Bulletin, 129*, 339-75.

Jost, J. T., & Kruglanski, A. W. (2002). The estrangement of social constructionism and experimental social psychology: History of the rift and prospects for reconciliation. *Personality and Social Psychology Review, 6*, 168-87.

Jowett, G., & O'Donnell, V. (1992). *Propaganda and persuasion* (2nd ed.). Newbury Park, CA: Sage Publications.

Jussim, L. (1990). Social reality and social problems: The role of expectancies. *Journal of Social Issues, 46*(2), 9-34.

Jussim, L. (2005). Accuracy: Criticisms, controversies, criteria, components, and cognitive processes. *Advances in Experimental Social Psychology, 37*, 1-93.

Jussim, L. (2010). Social reality and social problems: The role of expectancies. *Journal of Social Issues, 46*(2), 9-34.

Jussim, L. (2012). *Social perception and social reality: Why accuracy dominates bias and self-fulfilling prophecy.* New York, NY: Oxford University Press.

Jussim, L., Cain, T. R., Crawford, J. T., Harber, K., & Cohen, F. (2009). The unbearable accuracy of stereotypes. In T. Nelson (Ed.), *The handbook of prejudice, stereotyping, and discrimination* (pp. 199-225). New York, NY: Psychology Press.

Kahneman, D., & Ritov, I. (1994). Determinants of stated willingness to pay for public goods: A study in the headline method. *Journal of Risk and Uncertainty, 9*, 5-38.

Kahneman, D., & Tversky, A. (1982). The simulation heuristic. In D. Kahneman, P. Slovic, & A. Tversky (Eds.), *Judgment under uncertainty: Heuristics and biases* (pp. 201-8). New York, NY: Cambridge University Press.

Kalmijn, M. (1991). Status monogamy in the United States. *American Journal of Sociology, 97*(2), 496-523.

Kalmijn, M. (1994). Assortative mating by cultural and economic occupational status. *American Journal of Sociology, 100*(2), 422-52.

Kanouse, D. E., & Hanson, L. R., Jr. (1971). Negativity in evaluations. In E. E. Jones et al. (Eds.), *Attribution: Perceiving the causes of behavior.* Morristown, NJ: General Learning Press.

Kaplan, H. (1975). The self-esteem motive. In H. Kaplan (Ed.), *Self-attitudes and deviant behavior.* Pacific Palisades, CA: Goodyear.

Kaplan, M. F. (1977). Discussion polarization effects in a modified jury decision paradigm: Informational influences. *Sociometry, 40*, 262-71.

Kaplan, M. F., & Anderson, N. H. (1973). Information integration theory and reinforcement theory as approaches to interpersonal attraction. *Journal of Personality and Social Psychology, 28*, 301-12.

Karlins, M., Coffman, T. L., & Walters, G. (1969). On the fading of social stereotypes: Studies in three generations of college students. *Journal of Personality and Social Psychology, 13*, 1-16.

Karlsson, L., Juslin, P., & Olsson, H. (2008). Exemplar-based inference in multi-attribute decision making: Contingent, not automatic, strategy shifts? *Judgment and Decision Making, 3*(3), 244-60.

Karney, B. R., & Bradbury, T. N. (2000). Attributions in marriage: State or trait? A growth curve analysis. *Journal of Personality and Social Psychology, 78*, 295-309.

Karoly, P. (1993). Mechanisms of self-regulation: A systems view. *Annual Review of Psychology, 44*, 23-52.

Karpinski, A., & Hilton, J. L. (2001). Attitudes and the implicit association test. *Journal of Personality and Social Psychology, 81*, 774-88.

Karremans, J. C., Van Lange, P. A. M., & Holland, R. W. (2005). Forgiveness and its associations with prosocial thinking, feeling, and doing beyond the relationship with the offender. *Personality and Social Psychology Bulletin, 31*, 1315-26.

Karris, L. (1977). Prejudice against obese renters. *Journal of Social Psychology, 101*, 159-60.

Karylowski, J. (1976). Self-esteem, similarity, liking and helping. *Personality and Social Psychology Bulletin, 2*, 71-74.

Kasimatis, M., & Wells, G. L. (1995). Individual differences in counterfactual thinking. In N. J. Roese & J. M. Olson (Eds.), *What might have been: The social psychology of counterfactual thinking* (pp. 80-102). Mahwah, NJ: Erlbaum.

Kassin, S. M., Fein, S., & Markus, H. R. (2010). *Social psychology* (8th ed.). Boston, MA: Houghton Mifflin.

Katz, J. E., & Aspden, P. (1997). Motivations for and barriers to internet usage: Results of a national public opinion survey. *Internet Research: Electronic Networking Applications and Policy, 7*(3), 170-88.

Kawakami, K., Dion, K. L., & Dovidio, J. F. (1998). Racial prejudice and stereotype activation. *Personality and Social Psychology Bulletin, 24*, 407-16.

Kay, A. C., Jost, J. T., & Young, S. (2005). Victim derogation and victim enhancement as alternate routes to system justification. *Psychological Science, 16*, 240-46.

Kelley, H. H., (1950). The warm-cold variable in first impressions of persons. *Journal of Personality, 18*, 431-39.

Kelley, H. H. (1967). Attribution theory in social psychology. In D. Levine (Ed.), *Nebraska symposium on motivation*. Lincoln, NE: University of Nebraska Press.

Kelley, H. H. (1973). The processes of causal attribution. *American Psychologist, 28*(2), 107-28.

Kelman, H. C., & Hamilton, V. L. (1989). *Crimes of obedience: Toward a social psychology of authority and responsibility*. New Haven, CT: Yale University Press.

Kendon, A. (1970). Movement coordination in social interactions. *Acta Psychologica, 32*, 101-25.

Kenrick, D. (1991). Proximate altruism and ultimate selfishness. *Psychological Inquiry, 2*, 135-37.

Kenrick, D. T., Neuberg, S. L., & Cialdini, R. B. (2002). *Social psychology: Unraveling the mystery* (2nd ed.). Boston, MA: Allyn & Bacon.

Kenrick, D., & Simpson, J. (1997). Why social psychology and evolutionary psychology need one another. In J. Simpson & D. Kenrick (Eds.), *Evolutionary social psychology* (pp. 1-20). Mahwah, NJ: Lawrence Erlbaum Associates.

Kent, A. Waller, G., & Dagnan, D. (1999). A greater role of emotional than physical or sexual abuse in predicting disordered eating attitudes: The role of mediating variables. *International Journal of Eating Disorders, 25*(2), 159-67.

Kerber, K. W. (1984). The perception of non-emergency helping situations: Costs, rewards, and the altruistic personality. *Journal of Personality, 52,* 177-87.

Kerber, K. W., & Wren, R. W. (1982, April 15-18). *Helping in non-emergency situations: Costs, rewards, and the altruistic personality.* Paper presented at the 53rd Annual Meeting of the Eastern Psychological Association, Baltimore, MD.

Kernberg, O. (1976). *Borderline conditions and pathological narcissism.* New York, NY: Jason Aronson.

Kernis, M. H. (2003). Toward a conceptualization of optimal self-esteem. *Psychological Inquiry, 14*(1), 1-26.

Kernis, M. H., Grannemann, B. D., & Barclay, L. C. (1989). Stability and level of self-esteem as predictors of anger arousal and hostility. *Journal of Personality and Social Psychology, 56,* 1013-22.

Kidwell, R. E., & Bennett, N. (1993). Employee propensity to withhold effort: A conceptual model to intersect three avenues of research. *Academy of Management Review, 18,* 429-56.

Kihlstrom, J. F., & Klein, S. B. (1994). The self as a knowledge system. In. R. S. Wyer & T. K. Srull (Eds.), *Handbook of cognition* (Vol. 1, pp. 153-208). Hillsdale, NJ: Erlbaum.

Kilham, W., & Mann, L. (1974). Level of destructive obedience as a junction of transmitter and executant roles in the Milgram Obedience Paradigm. *Journal of Personality and Social Psychology, 29,* 696-702.

Kilner, J. F. (2010). Humanity in God's image: Is the image really damaged? *Journal of the Evolutionary Theological Society, 53*(3), 601-17.

King, K., Vidourek, R., Davis, B., & McClellan, W. (2002). Increasing self-esteem and school connectedness through a multidimensional mentoring program. *Journal of School Health, 72*(7), 294-99.

Kingston, L., & Prior, M. (1995). The development of patterns of stable, transient, and school-age onset aggressive behavior in young children. *Journal of the American Academy of Child and Adolescent Psychiatry, 34,* 348-58.

Kirkpatrick, L. A., Waugh, C. E., Valencia, A., & Webster, G. D. (2002). The functional domain specificity of self-esteem and the differential prediction of aggression. *Journal of Personality and Social Psychology, 82,* 756-67.

Kitayama, S., Takagi, H., & Matsumoto, H. (1995). Cultural psychology of Japanese self: Causal attributions of success and failure (in Japanese). *Japanese Psychological Review, 38,* 247-80.

Klaaren, K. J., Hodges, S. D., & Wilson, T. D. (1994). The role of affective expectations in subjective experience and decision making. *Social Cognition, 12,* 77-101.

Klein, S. B., & Loftus, J. (1993). The mental representation of trait and autobiographical knowledge about the self. In T. K. Srull & R. S. Wyer (Eds.), *Advances in social cognition* (Vol. 5). Hillsdale, NJ: Erlbaum.

Klein, S. B., Rozendal, K., & Cosmides, L. (2002). A social-cognitive neuroscience analysis of the self. *Social Cognition, 20*(12), 105-35.

Klohnen, E. C., & Luo, S. (2003). Interpersonal attraction and personality: What is attractive—self similarity, ideal similarity, complementarity or attachment security? *Journal of Personality and Social Psychology, 85*(4), 709-22.

Klohnen, E. C., & Mendelsohn, G. A. (1998). Partner selection for personality characteristics: A couple-centered approach. *Personality and Social Psychology Bulletin, 24,* 268-78.

Knox, R. E., & Inkster, J. A. (1968). Postdecision dissonance at post time. *Journal of Personality and Social Psychology, 8*(4), 319-23.

Kobrynowicz, D., & Branscombe, N.R. (1997). Who considers themselves victims of discrimination? Individual difference predictors of perceived gender discrimination in women and men. *Psychology of Women Quarterly, 21,* 347-63.

Kohn, A. (1990). *The brighter side of human nature: Altruism and empathy in everyday life.* New York, NY: Basic Books.

Kolak, D. (1997). *Lovers of wisdom: A historical introduction to philosophy.* Florence, KY: Wadsworth.

Koole, S. L., & T. Pyszczynski (Eds.). *Handbook of experimental existential psychology* (pp. 385-99). New York, NY: Guilford Press.

Koriat, A., Lichtenstein, S., & Fischhoff, B. (1980). Reasons for confidence. *Journal of Experimental Psychology: Human Learning and Memory, 6,* 107-18.

Krahé, B. (2001). *The social psychology of aggression.* Philadelphia, PA: Taylor & Francis.

Kraut, R., Patterson, M., Lundmark, V., Kiesler, S., Mukopadhyay, T., & Scherlis, W. (1998). Internet paradox. A social technology that reduces social involvement and psychological well-being? *American Psychologist, 53*(9), 1017-31.

Krebs, D. (1975). Empathy and altruism. *Journal of Personality and Social Psychology, 32,* 1134-46.

Krebs, D. (1998). The evolution of moral behaviors. In C. Crawford & D. Krebs (Eds.), *Handbook of evolutionary psychology: Issues, ideas, and applications* (pp. 337-68). Mahwah, NJ: Lawrence Erlbaum Associates.

Krebs, D., & Denton, K. (1997). Social illusions and self-deception: The evolution of biases in person perception. In J. Simpson & D. Kenrick (Eds.), *Evolutionary social psychology.* Mahwah, NJ: Lawrence Erlbaum Associates.

Krebs, D. L., & Van Hesteren, F. (1992). The development of altruistic personality. In P. M. Oliner, S. P. Oliner, L. Baron, L. A. Blum, D. L. Krebs, & M. Z. Smoleneska (Eds.), *Embracing the other: Philosophical, psychological, and historical perspectives on altruism* (pp. 142-69). New York, NY: New York University Press.

Krueger, J., & Clement, R. W. (1994). The truly false consensus effect: An ineradicable and egocentric bias in social perception. *Journal of Personality and Social Psychology, 67*(4), 596-610.

Kruger, D. (2001). Psychological aspects of adaptations for kin directed altruistic helping behaviors. *Social Behavior and Personality, 29,* 323-30.

Kruger, D. J. (2003). Evolution and altruism: Combining psychological mediators with naturally selected tendencies. *Evolution and Human Behavior, 24,* 118-25.

Kruger, J., & Dunning, D. (1999). Unskilled and unaware of it: How difficulties in recognizing one's own incompetence lead to inflated self-assessments. *Journal of*

*Personality and Social Psychology, 77*(6), 1121-34.

Kruglanski A. W., & Thompson, E. P. (1999). Persuasion by a single route: A view from the unimodel (Target article). *Psychological Inquiry, 10,* 83-109.

Kubany, E. S., Richard, D. C., Bauer, G. B., & Muraoka, M. Y. (1992). Impact of assertive and accusatory communication of distress and anger: A verbal component analysis. *Aggressive Behavior, 18,* 337-47.

Kuhl, J., & Koole, S. (2004). Workings of the will: A functional approach. In J. Greenberg, S. L. Koole & T. Pyszczynski (Eds.), *Handbook of experimental existential psychology* (pp. 411-30). New York, NY: Guilford Press.

Kurman, J. (2001). Self-enhancement: Is it restricted to individualistic cultures? *Personality and Social Psychology Bulletin, 27*(12), 1705-16.

Kurzban, R., & Aktipis, C. A. (2007). Modularity and the social mind: Are psychologists too selfish? *Personality and Social Psychology Review, 11*(2), 131-49.

La France, M. (1982). Posture mirroring and rapport. In M. Davis (Ed.), *Interaction rhythms: Periodicity in communicative behavior* (pp. 279-98). New York, NY: Human Sciences Press.

LaFrance, M., & Hecht, M. A. (1995). Why smiles generate leniency. *Personality and Social Psychology Bulletin, 21,* 207-14.

Ladd, G. E. (1974). *A theology of the New Testament.* Grand Rapids, MI: Eerdmans.

Ladd, G. W. (1985). Documenting the effects of social skills training with children: process and outcome assessment. In B. H. Schneider, K. H. Rubin, & J. E. Ledingham (Eds.), *Children's peer relations: Issues in assessment and intervention.* New York, NY: Springer-Verlag.

Lakin, J. L., & Chartrand, T. L. (2005). Exclusion and nonconscious behavioral mimicry. In K. D. Williams, J. P. Forgas & W. von Hippel (Eds.), *The social outcast: Ostracism, social exclusion, rejection, and bullying* (pp. 279-95). New York, NY: Psychology Press.

Lambert, A. J., Payne, B. K., Jacoby, L. L., Shaffer, L. M., Chasteen, A. L., & Khan, S. R. (2003). Stereotypes as dominant responses: On the "social facilitation" of prejudice in anticipated public contexts. *Journal of Personality and Social Psychology, 84*(2), 277-95.

Landrine, H., & Klonoff, E.A. (1996). The schedule of racist events: A measure of racial discrimination and a study of its negative physical and mental health consequences. *Journal of Black Psychology, 22,* 144-67.

Langer, E. J. (1975). The illusion of control. *Journal of Personality and Social Psychology, 32*(2), 311-28.

Langlois, J. H., Kalakanis, L. Rubenstein, A. J., Larson, A., HaUam, M., & Smoot, M. (2000). Maxims or myths of beauty? A meta-analytic and theoretical review. *Psychological Bulletin, 126*(3), 390-423.

Langlois, J. H., & Roggman, L. A. (1990). Attractive faces are only average. *Psychological Science, 1,* 115-21.

Langlois, J. H., Roggman, L. A., Casey, R. J., Ritter, J. M., Rieser-Danner, L. A., & Jenkins, V. Y. (1987). Infant preference for attractive faces: Rudiments of a stereotype. *Developmental Psychology, 23,* 363-69.

LaPiere, R. T. (1934). Attitudes vs. action. *Social Forces, 13*, 230-37.

LaPrelle, J., Hoyle, R. H., Insko, C. A., & Bernthal, P. (1990). Interpersonal attraction and descriptions of the traits of others: Ideal similarity, self similarity, and liking. *Journal of Research in Personality, 24*, 216-40.

Larson, L. U. (2010). *Persuasion: reception and responsibility*. Boston, MA: Wadsworth, Cengage Learning.

Larsson, H., Viding, E., & Plomin, R. (2008). Callous-unemotional traits and antisocial behavior: Genetic, environmental and early childhood influences. *Criminal Justice and Behaviour 35*, 197-211.

Latané, B. (1981). Psychology of social impact. *American Psychologist, 36*, 343-56.

Latané, B. (1996). Dynamic social impact: The creation of culture by communication. *Journal of Communication, 4*, 13-25.

Latané, B., & Darley, J. (1970). *The unresponsive bystander: Why doesn't he help?* New York, NY: Appeleton-Century-Crofts.

Latané, B., Williams, K., & Harkins, S. (1979). Many hands make light the work: The causes and consequences of social loafing. *Journal of Personality and Social Psychology, 37*, 822-32.

Latané, B., & Wolf, S. (1981). The social impact of majorities and minorities. *Psychological Review, 88*, 438-53.

Laughlin, P. R. (1980). Social combination process of cooperative problem-solving groups at verbal intellective tasks. In M. Fishbein (Ed.), *Progress in social psychology* (Vol. 1, pp. 127-55). Hillsdale, NJ: Erlbaum.

Lavine, H. (1999). Types of evidence and routes to persuasion: The unimodel versus dual-process models. *Psychological Inquiry, 10*(2) 141-44.

Lavine, H., & Snyder, M. (1996). Cognitive processing and the functional matching effect in persuasion: The mediating role of subjective perceptions of message quality. *Journal of Experimental Social Psychology, 32*, 580-604.

Lawler, E. J. (2001). An affect theory of social exchange. *American Journal of Sociology, 107*(2), 321-52. doi:10.1086/324071

Laythe, B., Finkel, D. G., Bringle, R. G., & Kirkpatrick, L. E. (2002). Religious fundamentalism as a predictor of prejudice: A two-component model. *Journal for the Scientific Study of Religion, 41*(4), 623-35.

Leary, M. R. (2007). Motivational and emotional aspects of the self. *Annual Review of Psychology, 58*, 317-44.

Leary, M. R., & Cox, C. (2007). Belongingness motivation: A mainspring of social action. In J. Shah & W. Gardner (Eds.), *Handbook of motivation science* (pp. 27-40). New York, NY: Guilford Press.

Leary, M. R., & Downs, D. L. (1995). Interpersonal functions of the self-esteem motive: The self-esteem system as a sociometer. In M. H. Kernis (Ed.), *Efficacy, agency, and self-esteem* (pp. 123-44). New York, NY: Plenum Press.

Leary, M. R., Haupt, A. L., Strausser, K. S., & Chokel, J. T. (1998). Calibrating the sociometer: The relationship between interpersonal appraisals and state self-esteem. *Journal of Personality and Social Psychology, 74*, 1290-99.

Leary, M. R., Tambor, E., Terdal, S., & Downs, D. (1995). Self-esteem as an interpersonal monitor: The sociometer hypothesis. *Journal of Personality and Social Psychology, 68*(3), 518-30.

Leary, M. R., Twenge, J. M., & Quinlivan. E. (2006). Interpersonal rejection as a determinant of anger and aggression. *Personality and Social Psychology Review, 10*, 111-32.

Ledbetter, A. M., Griffin, E. M., & Spark, G. (2007). Forecasting "friends forever": A longitudinal investigation of sustained closeness between best friends. *Personal Relationships, 14*, 2, 343-50.

Lee, T. M. C., Chan, S. C., & Raine, A. (2008). Strong limbic and weak frontal activation to aggressive stimuli in spouse abusers. *Molecular Psychiatry, 13*, 655-60.

Lefebvre, L. M. (1979). Causal attributions for basketball outcomes by players and coaches. *Psychological Beligica, 19*, 109-15.

Lepore, L., & Brown, R. (1997). Category and stereotype activation: Is prejudice inevitable? *Journal of Personality and Social Psychology, 72*(2), 275-87.

Lepore, L., & Brown, R. (1999). Exploring automatic stereotype activation: A challenge to the inevitability of prejudice. In D. Abrams & M. Hogg (Eds.), *Social identity and cognition* (pp. 141-63). Malden, MA: Blackwell.

Lerner, M. J. (1965). Evaluation of performance as a function of performer's reward and attractiveness. *Journal of Personality and Social Psychology, 1*, 355-60.

Lerner, M. J. (1966). Observer reaction to the "innocent victim": Compassion or rejection? *Journal of Personality and Social Psychology, 4*(2), 203-10.

Lerner, M. J. (1970). The desire for justice and reactions to victims. In J. Macaulay & L. Berkowitz (Eds.), *Altruism and helping behavior* (pp. 205-29). New York, NY: Academic Press.

Lerner, M. J. (1980). *The belief in a just world: A fundamental delusion.* New York, NY: Plenum Press.

Lerner, M. J., & Miller, D. T. (1978). Just world research and the attribution process: Looking back and ahead. *Psychological Bulletin, 85*, 1030-51.

Lerner, M. J., & Simmons, C. H. (1966). Observer's reaction to the "innocent victim": Compassion or rejection? *Journal of Personality and Social Psychology, 4*, 203-10.

Lerner, R. M. (1969). The development of stereotyped expectancies of body build-behavior relations. *Child Development, 40*, 137-41.

Lerner, R. M., & Gellert, E. (1969). Body build identification, preference, and aversion in children. *Developmental Psychology, 1*(5), 456-62. doi:10.1037/h0027966

Levine, J., & Moreland, R. L. (2006). *Small groups: Key readings in psychology.* New York, NY: Psychology Press.

Levine, R. (1997). *A geography of time.* New York, NY: Basic Books.

Levine, R. M. (1999). Rethinking bystander non-intervention: Social categorisation and the evidence of witnesses at the James Bulger murder trial. *Human Relations, 52*, 1133-55.

Levine, R. M. (2003). Measuring helping behavior across cultures. In W. J. Lonner, D. L. Dinnel, S. A. Hayes & D. N. Sattler (Eds.), *Online readings in psychology and culture* (Unit 15, Chapter 9). Center for Cross-Cultural Research, Western Washington University, Bellingham, Washington. Retrieved from www.wwu.edu/~culture

Levine, R. M., Cassidy, C., Brazier, G., & Reicher, S. (2002). Self-categorisation and by-stander intervention: Two experimental studies. *Journal of Applied Social Psychology*, 7, 1452-63.

Levine, R., Martinez, T., Brase, G., & Sorenson, K. (1994). Helping in 36 U.S. cities. *Journal of Personality and Social Psychology, 67*, 69-81.

Levinson, D. (2002). *The encyclopedia of crime and punishment.* Thousand Oaks, CA: Sage.

Lewin, K. (1946). Action research and minority problems. *Journal of Social Issues, 2*(4), 34-46.

Lewin, K. (1952). Group choice and social change. In G. E. Swanson, T. M. Newcomb & E. L. Hartley (Eds.), *Readings in social psychology* (pp. 459-73). New York: Holt.

Leyens, J. Ph., Paladino, M. P., Rodriguez, R. T., Vaes, J., Demoulin, S., Rodriguez, A. P., & Gaunt, R. (2000). The emotional side of prejudice: The attribution of secondary emotions to ingroups and outgroups. *Personality and Social Psychology Review, 4*, 186-97. doi:10.1207/S15327957PSPR0402_06

Li, N. P., Bailey, J. M., Kenrick, D. T., & Linsenmeier, J. A. W. (2002). The necessities and luxuries of mate preference: Testing the tradeoffs. *Journal of Personality and Social Psychology, 82*, 947-55.

Li, Y. J., Johnson, K. A., Cohen, A. B., Williams, M. J., Knowles, E. D., & Chen, Z. (2012). Fundamental(ist) attribution error: Protestants are dispositionally focused. *Journal of Personality and Social Psychology, 102*(2), 281-90.

Lichtenstein, S., Slovic, P., Fischhoff, B., Layman, M., & Combs, B. (1978). Judged frequency of lethal events. *Journal of Experimental Psychology: Human Learning and Memory, 46*(6), 551-78.

Liddle, J. R., & Shackelfrod, T. K. (2011). Teaching the evolution of the mind: Current findings, trends, and controversies. *Teaching of Psychology, 38*(2), 128-32.

Liebrand, W., Messick, D. M., & Wolters, F. J. (1986). Why we are fairer than others: A cross-cultural replication and extension. *Experimental Social Psychology, 22*, 590-604.

Lin, T. R., Dobbins, G. H., & Farh, J. L. (1992). A field study of race and age similarity effect on interview ratings in conventional and situational interviews. *Journal of Applied Psychology, 77*, 363-71.

Lingle, J. H., & Ostrom, T. M. (1981). Principles of memory and cognition in attitude formation. In R. Petty, T. Ostrom & T. Brock (Eds.), *Cognitive responses to persuasion.* Hillsdale, NJ: Lawrence Erlbaum.

Lipkus, I. M., Dalbert, C., & Siegler, I. C. (1996). The importance of distinguishing the belief in a just world for self versus for others: Implications for psychological well-being. *Personality and Social Psychology Bulletin, 22*(7), 666-77.

Lipton, P. (2004). What good is an explanation? In J. Cornwell (Ed.), *Understanding explanation* (pp. 1-22). Oxford, England: Oxford University Press.

Long, W. L., & Brecke, P. (2003). *War and reconciliation: Reason and emotion in conflict resolution.* Boston, MA: MIT Press.

Lord, C. G., Ross, L., & Lepper, M. R. (1979). Biased assimilation and attitude polarization: The effects of prior theories on subsequently considered evidence. *Journal of Personality and Social Psychology, 37*(11), 2098-2109.

Lowenstein, G., Weber, E. U., Hsee, C. K., & Welch, N. (2001). Risk as feeling. *Psychological Bulletin, 127*(2), 267-86.

Lowery, B. S., Hardin, C. D., & Sinclair, S. (2001). Social influence effects on automatic racial prejudice. *Journal of Personality and Social Psychology, 81,* 842-55.

Luo, S., & Klohnen, E. C. (2005). Assortative mating and marital quality in newlyweds: A couple-centered approach. *Journal of Personality and Social Psychology, 88*(2), 304-26.

Lyers, Ph., & Yzerbyt, V. Y. (1992). The in-group overexclusion effect: The impact of valence and confirmation on stereotypical information search. *European Journal of Social Psychology, 22,* 549-69.

Maccoby, E. E. (1998). *The two sexes: Growing up apart, coming together.* Cambridge, MA: Belknap Press.

MacGregor, D. G., Slovic, P., Dreman, D., & Berry, M. (2000). Imagery, affect, and financial judgment. *Journal of Psychology and Financial Markets, 1*(2), 104-10.

MacIntyre, A. (2007). *After virtue: A study in moral theory* (3rd ed.). Notre Dame, IN: University of Notre Dame Press.

Macintyre, S., & Homel, R. (1997). Danger on the dance floor: A study of interior design, crowding, and aggression in nightclubs." In R. Homel (Ed.), *Policing for prevention: Reducing crime, public intoxication, and injury* (Vol. 7). Crime Prevention Studies. New York, NY: Criminal Justice Press.

Mackie, D. M., & Smith, E. R. (1998). Intergroup relations: Insights from a theoretically integrative approach. *Psychological Review, 105,* 499-529.

MacLean, M. J., & Chown, S. M. (1988). Just world beliefs and attitudes toward helping elderly people: A comparison of British and Canadian university students. *International Journal of Aging and Human Development, 26*(4), 249-60.

Macrae, C. N., & Bodenhausen, G. V. (2000). Social cognition: Thinking categorically about others. *Annual Review of Psychology, 51,* 93-120.

Macrae, C. N., Hewstone, M., & Griffiths, R. J. (1993). Processing load and memory for stereotype-based information. *European Journal of Social Psychology, 23,* 77-87.

Macrae, C. N., Hood, B. M., Milnes, A. B., Rowe, A. C., & Mason, M. F. (2002). Are you looking at me? Eye gaze and person perception. *Psychological Science, 13*(5), 460-64.

Macrae, C. N., & Johnston, L. (1998). Help, I need somebody: Automatic action and inaction. *Social Cognition, 16,* 400-417.

Macrae, C. N., Milne, A. B., & Bodenhausen, G. V. (1994). Stereotypes as energy-saving devices: A peek inside the cognitive toolbox. *Journal of Personality and Social Psychology, 66*(1), 37-47.

Maeher, M. (2005). The meaning that religion offers and the motivation that may result. In W. R. Miller & H. D. Delaney (Eds.), *Judeo-Christian perspectives on psychology* (pp. 133-44). Washington, DC: American Psychological Association.

Magnuson, C. M., & Enright, R. D. (2008). The church as forgiving community: An initial model. *Journal of Psychology and Theology, 36*(2), 114-23.

Maio, G. R., & Haddock, G. (2007). Attitude change. In A. W. Kruglanski & T. Higgins (Eds.), *Social psychology: Handbook of basic principles* (Vol. 2, pp. 565-86). New York, NY: Guilford Press.

Malamuth, N. M., & Heilmann, M. F. (1998). Evolutionary psychology and sexual aggression. In C. Crawford & D. Krebs (Eds.), *Handbook of evolutionary psychology: Issues, ideas, and applications* (pp. 515-42). Mahwah, NJ: Lawrence Erlbaum Associates.

Malle, B. F. (1999). How people explain behavior: A new theoretical framework. *Personality and Social Psychology Review, 3*(1), 23-48.

Malle, B. F. (2004). *How the mind explains behavior: Folk explanations, meaning, and social interaction.* Cambridge, MA: MIT Press.

Malle, B. F. (2006). The actor-observer asymmetry in causal attributions: A (surprising) meta-analysis. *Psychological Bulletin, 132,* 895-919.

Malle, B. F., Knobe, J. M., & Nelson, S. E. (2007). Actor-observer asymmetries in explanations of behavior: New answers to an old question. *Journal of Personality and Social Psychology, 93*(4), 491-514.

Malle, B. F., Knobe, J., O'Laughlin, M., Pearce, G. E., & Nelson, S. E. (2000). Conceptual structure and social functions of behavior explanations: Beyond person-situation attributions. *Journal of Personality and Social Psychology, 79,* 309-26.

Mandel, D. R., & Lehman, D. R. (1996). Counterfactual thinking and ascriptions of cause and preventability. *Journal of Personality and Social Psychology, 71*(3), 450-63.

Maner, J. K., Luce, C. L., Neuberg, S. L., Brown, S., & Sagrin, B. J. (2002). The effects of perspective taking on motivations for helping: Still no evidence for altruism. *Personality and Social Psychology Bulletin, 28*(11), 1601-10.

Manning, R., Levine, M., & Collins, A. (2007). The Kitty Genovese murder and the social psychology of helping: The parable of the 38 witnesses. *American Psychologist, 62,* 555-62.

Manucia, G. K., Baumann, D. J., & Cialdini, R. B. (1984). Mood influences on helping: Direct effects or side effects? *Journal of Personality and Social Psychology, 46,* 357-64. doi:10.1037/0022-3514.46.2.357

Marcus-Newhall, A., Pedersen, W. C., Carlson, M., & Miller, N. (2000). Displaced aggression is alive and well: A meta-analytic review. *Journal of Personality and Social Psychology, 78*(4): 670-89.

Markman, K. D., Gavanski, I., Sherman, S. J., & McMullen, M. N. (1993). The mental simulation of better and worse possible worlds. *Journal of Experimental Social Psychology, 29,* 87-109.

Marks, G., & Miller, N. (1987). Ten years of research on the false consensus effect: An empirical and theoretical review. *Psychological Bulletin 102,* 72-90.

Markus, H., & Kitayama, S. (1991). Culture and the self: Implications for cognition, emotion, and motivation. *Psychological Bulletin, 98,* 224-53.

Markus, H., & Wurf, E. (1987). The dynamic self-concept: A social psychological perspective. In M. R. Rosenzweig & L. W. Porter (Eds.), *Annual Review of Psychology, 38,* 299-337.

Markus, H., & Zajonc, R. B. (1985). The cognitive perspective in psychology. In G. Lindzey & E. Aronson (Eds.), *Handbook of social psychology* (3rd ed., Vol. 1, pp. 137-230). New York, NY: Random House.

Marsh, H. W. (1993). Relations between global and specific domains of self: Importance of individual importance, certainty, and ideals. *Journal of Personality and Social Psychology, 65,* 975-92.

Martin, J. (1986). The tolerance of injustice. In J. M. Olson, C. P. Herman & M. P. Zanna (Eds.), *Relative deprivation and social comparison: The Ontario Symposium* (Vol. 4). Hillsdale, NJ: Erlbaum.

Massimini, F., & Delle Fave, A. (2000). Individual development in a bio-cultural perspective. *American Psychologist, 55*(1), 24-33. doi:10.1037/0003-066X.55.1.24

Matthews, K., Batson, C., Horn, J., & Rosenman, R. (1981). The heritability of empathic concern for others. *Journal of Personality, 49,* 237-47.

McAdams, D. P. (1988). Personal needs and personal relationships. In S. Duck (Ed.), *Handbook of personal relationships: Theory, research and interventions* (pp. 7-22). New York, NY: Wiley.

McAfee Brown, R. (1987). *Religion and violence* (2nd ed.). Philadelphia, PA: Westminster Press.

McAndrew, F. T. (2002). New evolutionary perspectives on altruism: Multilevel selection and costly signaling theories. *Current Directions in Psychological Science, 11,* 79-82.

McCullough, M. E., Bellah, C. G., Kilpatrick, S. D., & Johnson, J. L. (2001). Vengefulness: Relationships with forgiveness, rumination, well-being, and the big five. *Personality and Social Psychology Bulletin, 27,* 601-10.

McCullough, M. E., Emmons, R. A., & Tsang, J. A. (2002). The grateful disposition: A conceptual and empirical topography. *Journal of Personality and Social Psychology, 82,* 112-27. doi:10.1037/0022-3514.82.1.112

McFadyen, A. I. (1990). *The call to personhood: A Christian theory of the individual in social relationships.* Cambridge, England: Cambridge University Press.

McFarland, S. G., & Adelson, S. (1996). *An omnibus study of personality, values, and prejudice.* Paper presented at the annual meeting of the International Society for Political Psychology, Vancouver, British Columbia.

McGarty, C. (1999). *Categorization in social psychology.* Thousand Oaks, CA: Sage.

McGrath, A. (2006). *The order of things: Explorations in scientific theology.* Oxford, England: Blackwell.

McGrath, A., & McGrath, J. C. (1992). *Self-esteem: The cross and Christian confidence.* Wheaton, IL: Crossway Books.

McGrath, A., & McGrath, J. C. (2007). *The Dawkins delusion? Atheist fundamentalism and the denial of the divine.* London, England: SPCK.

McGrew, W. (1981). The female chimpanzee as a human evolutionary prototype. In F. Dahlberg (Ed.), *Woman the gatherer.* New Haven, CT: Yale University Press.

McGuinness, D. (1976). Perceptual and cognitive differences between the sexes. In B. Lloyd and J. Archer (Eds.), *Explorations in sex differences.* New York, NY: Academic Press.

McGuire, A. M. (1989). The compatibility of self-sacrifice and self-interest: Social and psychological supports of helping in social relationships. Unpublished doctoral dissertation. University of Michigan, Ann Arbor, MI.

McGuire, A. M. (2003). "It was nothing": Extending evolutionary models of altruism by two social cognitive biases in judgment of the costs and benefits of helping. *Social Cognition, 21*(3), 363-94.

McKenna, F. P., & Myers, L. B. (1997), Illusory self-assessments—can they be reduced? *British Journal of Psychology, 88*, 39-51.

McMinn, M. R., & Campbell, C. D. (2007). *Integrative psychotherapy: Toward a comprehensive Christian approach.* Downers Grove, IL: InterVarsity Press.

McPherson, M., Smith-Lovin, L., & Cook, J. M. (2001). Birds of a feather: Homophily in social networks. *Annual review of Sociology, 27*, 415-44.

Mecca, A. M., Smelser, N. J., & Vasconcellos, J. (1989). *The social importance of self-esteem.* Los Angeles, CA: University of California Press.

Medcof, J. W. (1990). PEAT: A new model of attribution processes. *Advances in Experimental Social Psychology, 23*, 111-35.

Mellers, B. A., Richards, V., & Birnbaum, M. H. (1992). Distributional theories of impression formation. *Organizational Behavior and Human Decision Processes, 51*, 313-43.

Merton, R. K. (1940). Facts and factitiousness in ethnic opinionnaires. *American Sociological Review, 5*, 13-28.

Merton, R. K. (1948). The self-fulfilling prophecy. *The Antioch Review, 8*, 193-210.

Metcalfe, J. (1998). Cognitive optimism: Self-deception or memory-based heuristics. *Personality and Social Psychology Review, 2*, 100-110.

Middleton, J. R., & Walsh, B. J. (1995). *Truth is stranger than it used to be: Biblical faith in a postmodern age.* Downers Grove, IL: InterVarsity Press.

Milgram, S. (1963). Behavioral study of obedience. *Journal of Abnormal and Social Psychology, 67*, 371-78.

Milgram, S. (1974). *Obedience to authority: An experimental view.* New York: HarperCollins.

Miller, C. (2009). Social psychology and helping: Mixed results for virtue ethics. *Journal of Ethics, 13*, 145-73.

Miller, D. T., & Ross, M. (1975). Self-serving biases in the attribution of causality: Fact or fiction? *Psychological Bulletin, 82*, 213-25.

Miller, D. T., Taylor, B., & Buck, M. L. (1991). Gender gaps: Who needs to be explained? *Journal of Personality and Social Psychology, 61*, 5-12.

Miller, G. F. (1998). How mate choice shaped human nature: A review. In C. Crawford & D. Krebs (Eds.), *Handbook of evolutionary psychology: Issues, ideas, and applications* (pp. 87-130). Mahwah, NJ: Lawrence Erlbaum Associates.

Miller, K. (2005). *Communication theories.* New York, NY: McGraw-Hill.

Miller, N., Sears, R. R., Rosenzweig, S., Bateson, G., Levy, D. M., Hartmann, G. W., & Maslow, A. H. (1941). Symposium on the frustration-aggression hypothesis. *Psychological Review, 48*, 337-66.

Miller, W. R. (2005). What is human nature? Reflections from Judeo-Christian perspectives. In W. R. Miller & H. D. Delaney (Eds.), *Judeo-Christian perspectives in psychology* (pp. 11-30). Washington, DC: American Psychological Association.

Miller-Perrin, C. L., & Perrin, R. D. (2007). *Child maltreatment: An introduction* (2nd ed.) Thousand Oaks, CA: Sage.

Mitchell, T. R., & Thompson, L. (1994). A theory of temporal adjustments of evaluation of events: Rosy prospection and rosy retrospection. In *Advances in managerial cognition and organizational information processing* (Vol. 1, pp. 85-114). Greenwich, CT: JAI Press.

Mitchell, T. R., Thompson, L., Peterson, E., & Cronk, R. (1997). Temporal adjustments in the evaluation of events: The "rosy view." *Journal of Experimental Social Psychology,* 33(4), 421-48.

Molden, D. C., & Dweck, C. S. (2006). Finding "meaning" in psychology: A lay theories approach to self-regulation, social perception, and social development. *American Psychologist, 61,* 192-203.

Montada, L., & Lerner, M. J. (Eds.). (1998). *Responses to victimization and belief in a just world.* New York, NY: Plenum Press.

Montleith, M., Sherman, J. W., & Devine, P. G. (1998). Suppression as a stereotype control strategy. *Personality and Social Psychology Review, 2,* 63-82.

Montoya, R. M., & Horton, R. S. (2004). On the importance of cognitive evaluation as a determinant of interpersonal attraction. *Journal of Personality and Social Psychology,* 86(5), 696-712.

Montoya, R. M., Horton, R. S., & Kirchner, J. (2008). Is actual similarity necessary for attraction? A meta-analysis of actual and perceived similarity? *Journal of Social and Personal Relationships* 25(6), 889-922.

Mook, D. G. (1991). Why can't altruism be selfish? *Psychological Inquiry,* 2(2), 139-41.

Moon, Y., & Nass, C. (1996). How "real" are computer personalities? Psychological responses to personality types in human-computer interaction. *Communication Research, 23,* 651-74.

Moorhead, G., Ference, R., & Neck, C. P. (1991). Group decision fiascoes continue: Space shuttle Challenger and a revised groupthink framework. *Human Relations, 44*(6), 539-50.

Moorhead, G., Neck, C. P., & West, M. S. (1998). The tendency toward defective decision making within self-managing teams: The relevance of groupthink for the 21st century. *Organizational Behavior and Human Decision Processes, 73*(2-3), 327-51.

Moreland, R. L. (1987). The formation of small groups. In C. Hendrick (Ed.), *Review of personality and social psychology* (Vol. 8, pp. 80-110). Newbury Park, CA: Sage.

Moreland, J. P., & Rae, S. B. (2000). *Body and soul: Human nature and the crisis of ethics.* Downers Grove, IL: InterVarsity Press.

Moreland, R. L., & Beach, S. (1992). Exposure effects in the classroom: The development of affinity among students. *Journal of Experimental Social Psychology, 28,* 255-76.

Morell, V. (1996). Genes vs. teams: Weighing group tactics in evolution. *Science, 273,* 739-40.

Morenoff, J. D. (2005). Racial and ethnic disparities in crime and delinquency in the United States. In M. Rutter & M. Tienda (Eds.), *Ethnicity and causal mechanisms* (pp. 139-73). Cambridge, England: Cambridge University Press.

Morris, W. M., & Miller, R. S. (1975). The effects of consensus-breaking and consensus-preempting partners on reduction in conformity. *Journal of Experimental Social Psychology, 11,* 215-23.

Morry, M. M. (2003). Perceived locus of control and satisfaction in same-sex friendships. *Personal Relationships, 10,* 495-509.

Morry, M. M. (2005). Relationship satisfaction as a predictor of similarity ratings: A test of the attraction-similarity hypothesis. *Journal of Social and Personal Relationships, 22*(4), 561-84.

Morry, M. M. (2007). Relationship satisfaction as a predictor of perceived similarity among cross-sex friends: A test of the attraction-similarity model. *Journal of Social and Personal Relationships, 24,* 117-38.

Morse, S. J., & Gergen, K. J. (*1970*). Social comparison, self-consistency and the concept of self. *Journal of Personality and Social Psychology, 16,* 148-56.

Morton, J., & Johnson, M. (1991). CONSPEC and CONLEARN: A two-process theory of infant face recognition. *Psychological Review, 98,* 164-81.

Moscovici, S., Lage, E., & Naffrechoux, M. (1969). Influence of a consistent minority on the responses of a majority in a color perception task. *Sociometry, 32*(4), 365-80.

Moscovici, S., & Zavalloni, M. (1969). The group as a polarizer of attitudes. *Journal of Personality and Social Psychology, 12,* 125-35.

Mullen, B. (1983). Operationalizing the effect of the group on the individual: A self-attention perspective. *Journal of Experimental Social Psychology, 19,* 295-322.

Mullen, B. (1987). Self-attention theory: Effects of group composition on the individual. In B. Mullen & G. R. Goethels (Eds.), *Theories of group behavior* (pp. 125-146). New York: Springer-Verlag.

Mullen, B., & Goethals, G. R. (Eds.). (1995). *Theories of group behavior* (pp. 125-46). New York, NY: Springer-Verlag.

Munro, G. D., & Ditto, P. H. (1997). Biased assimilation, attitude polarization, and affect in reactions to stereotyped-relevant scientific information. *Personality and Social Psychology Bulletin, 23,* 636-53.

Munro, G. D., Ditto, P. H., Lockhart, L. K., Fagerlin, A., Gready, M., & Peterson, E. (2002). Biased assimilation of sociopolitical arguments: Evaluating the 1996 U.S. presidential debate. *Basic and Applied Social Psychology, 24,* 15-26.

Murphy-Berman, V., Berman, J. L., Singh, P., Pachauri, A., & Kumar, P. (1984). Factors affecting allocation to needy and meritorious recipients: A cross-cultural comparison. *Journal of Personality and Social Psychology, 46,* 1267-72.

Murray, S. L., Holmes, J. G., Bellavia, G., Griffin, D. W., & Dolderman, D. (2002). Kindred spirits? The benefits of egocentrism in close relationships. *Journal of Personality and Social Psychology, 82,* 563-81.

Murstein, B. I. (1972). Physical attractiveness and marital choice. *Journal of Personality and Social Psychology, 22*(1), 8-12.

Murstein, B. I., Cerreto, M. G., MacDonald, M., & Mac, G. (1977). A theory and investigation of the effect of exchange-orientation on marriage and friendship. *Journal of Marriage and the Family, 39*(3): 543-48. doi:10.2307/350908

Myer, C. (2000). Academic procrastination and self-handicapping: Gender differences in response to noncontingent feedback. *Journal of Social Behavior and Personality*, 15(5), 87-102.

Myers. D. G. (1978). Polarizing effects of social comparison. *Journal of Experimental Social Psychology*, 14, 554-63.

Myers. D. G. (1982). Polarizating effects of social interaction. In H. Brandstatter, J. H. Davis & G. Stocher-Kreichgauer (Eds.), *Contemporary problems in group decision making* (pp. 125-61). New York, NY: Academic Press.

Myers, D. G. (2005). *Social psychology* (8th ed.). Boston, MA: McGraw-Hill.

Myers, D. G., & Lamm, H. (1975). The polarizing effects of group discussion. *American Scientist*, 63, 297-303.

Myers, D. G., & Ridl, J. (1979). Can we all be better than average? *Psychology Today*, August.

Mysterud, I., & Poleszynski, D. V. (2003). Expanding evolutionary psychology: Toward a better understanding of violence and aggression. *Social Science Information*, 42(1), 5-50. doi:10.1177/0539018403042001791

Nahemow, L., & Lawton, M. P. (1975). Similarity and propinquity in friendship formation. *Journal of Personality and Social Psychology*, 32, 205-13.

Nakonezny, P. A., & Denton, W. H. (2008). Martial relationships: A social exchange theory perspective. *The American Journal of Family Therapy*, 36, 402-12.

Nelson, L. D., & Dynes, R. R. (1976). The impact of devotionalism and attendance on ordinary and emergency helping behavior. *Journal for the Scientific Study of Religion*, 15(1), 47-59.

Nelson, R. J. (Ed.). (2005). *The biology of aggression*. London, England: Oxford University Press.

Nemeth, C. J. (1986). Differential contributions of minority and majority influence. *Psychological Review*, 93, 23-32.

Neumann, R., & Strack, F. (2000). Mood contagion: The automatic transfer of mood between persons. *Journal of Personality and Social Psychology*, 79(2), 211-23.

Neuberg, S., Cialdini, R., Brown, S., Luce, C., & Sogarin, B. (1997). Does empathy lead to anything more than superficial helping? Comment on Batson et al. *Journal of Personality and Social Psychology*, 73, 510-16.

Newcomb, T. M. (1956). The prediction of interpersonal attraction. *American Psychologist*, 11, 575-86.

Ng, B., Kumar, S., Ranclaud, M., & Robinson, E. (2001). Ward crowding and incidents of violence on an acute psychiatric inpatient unit. *Psychiatric Services*, 52(4), 521-25.

Nickerson, R. S. (1998). Confirmation bias: A ubiquitous phenomenon in many guises. *Review of General Psychology*, 2, 175-220.

Niebuhr, R. (1941). *The nature and destiny of man* (Vol. 1). London, England: Nisbet.

Nienhuis, A. E., Manstead, A. S. R., & Spears, R. (2001). Multiple motives and persuasive communication: Creative elaboration as a result of impression motivation and accuracy motivation. *Personality and Social Psychology Bulletin*, 27(1), 118-32. doi: 10.1177/0146167201271010

Nijman, H. L. I., & Rector, G. (1999). Crowding and aggression on inpatient psychiatric wards. *Psychiatric Services, 50,* 830-31.

Nisbett, R. E., & Ross, L. D. (1980). *Human inference: Strategies and shortcomings of social judgment.* Englewood Cliffs, NJ: Prentice-Hall.

Noonan, J. R., Barry, J. R., & Davis, H. C. (1970). Personality determinants in attitudes toward visible disability. *Journal of Personality, 38,* 1-15.

Norman, P., Conner, M., & Bell, K. (1999). The theory of planned behavior and smoking cessation. *Health Psychology, 18,* 89-94.

Norton, M. I., Frost, J. H., & Ariely, D. (2007). Less is more: The lure of ambiguity, or why familiarity breeds contempt. *Journal of Personality and Social Psychology, 92*(1), 97-105.

Novak, D. W., & Lerner, M. J. (1968). Rejection as a consequence of perceived similarity. *Journal of Personality and Social Psychology, 9,* 147-52.

O'Brien, K. S., Hunter, J. A., & Banks, M. (2007). Implicit anti-fat bias in physical educators: Physical attributes, ideology, and socialization. *International Journal of Obesity, 31,* 308-314. doi:10.1038/sj.ijo.0803398.

O'Brien, M. (1999). *How I became a human being: A disabled man's quest for independence.* Madison, WI: University of Wisconsin Press.

O'Collins, G. (1999). *The tripersonal God: Understanding and interpreting the trinity.* New York, NY: Paulist Press.

O'Keeffe, J. (1993). Disability, discrimination & the Americans With Disabilities Act. *Journal of Consulting Psychology, 45*(2), 3-9.

O'Laughlin, M. J., & Malle, B. F. (2002). How people explain actions performed by groups and individuals. *Journal of Personality and Social Psychology, 82*(1), 33-48.

Oliner, S., & Oliner, P. (1988). *The altruistic personality.* New York, NY: Free Press.

Onodera, T., & Miura, M. (1990). Physical attractiveness and its halo effects on a partner: "Radiating beauty" in Japan also? *Japanese Journal of Psychological Research, 32,* 148-53.

Osgood, C. E. (1962). *An alternative to war or surrender.* Urbana, IL: University of Illinois Press.

Oswald, D. L., Clark, E. M., & Kelly, C. M. (2004). Friendship maintenance: An analysis of individual and dyad behaviors. *Journal of Social and Clinical Psychology, 23*(3), 413-41. doi:10.1521/jscp.23.3.413.35460

Oudenhoven, J. P., & de Boer, T. (1995). Complementarity and similarity of partners in international mergers. *Basic and Applied Social Psychology, 17*(3), 343-56.

Pagani, L. S., Tremblay, R. E., Nagin, D., Zoccolillo, M., Vitaro, F., & McDuff, P. (2004). Risk factor models for adolescent verbal and physical aggression toward mothers. *International Journal of Behavioral Development, 28*(6), 528-37.

Paik, H., & Comstock, G. (1994). The effects of television violence on antisocial behavior: A meta-analysis. *Communication Research, 21*(4), 516-46.

Panksepp, J. (2003). Feeling the pain of social loss. *Science, 10*(3), 237-39.

Papps, B. P., & O'Carrol, R. E. (1998). Extremes of self-esteem and narcissism and the expression of anger and aggression. *Aggressive Behavior, 24,* 421-38.

Parens, E. (2004). Genetic differences and human identities: On why talking about behavioral genetics is important and difficult. *The Hastings Center Reports, 34*(1), S1-S36.

Parry, H. J. (1949). Protestants, Catholics and prejudice. *International Journal of Opinion and Attitude Research, 3*, 205-13.

Paul, A. M. (2003). Where bias begins: The truth about stereotypes. In W. Lesko (Ed.), *Readings in social psychology: General, classic, and contemporary selections* (5th ed., pp. 158-62). Boston, MA: Allyn & Bacon.

Paulus, P. B., Larey, T. S., & Ortega, A. H. (1995). Performance and perceptions of brainstormers in an organizational setting. *Basic and Applied Social Psychology, 18*, 3-14.

Paulus, P. B., & Yang, H. C. (2000). Idea generation in groups: A basis for creativity in organizations. *Organizational Behavior and Human Decision Processes, 82*, 76-87.

Payne, J. W., Bettman, J. R., & Johnson, E. J. (1993). *The adaptive decision maker*. Cambridge, England: Cambridge University Press.

Pearcey, N. R., & Thaxton, C. B. (1994). *The soul of science: Christian faith and natural philosophy*. Wheaton, IL: Crossway Books.

Penner, L. A., Dovidio, J. F., Piliavin, J. A., & Schroeder, D. A. (2005). Prosocial behavior: Multilevel perspectives. *Annual Review of Psychology, 56*, 14.1-14.28.

Penner, L. A., & Finkelstein, M. A. (1998). Dispositional and structural determinants of volunteerism. *Journal of Personality and Social Psychology, 74*, 525-37.

Pennington, D. C. (1981). Being wise after the event: an investigation of hindsight bias. *Currents in Psychological Research, 1*, 271-82.

Perdue, C. W., Dovidio, J. E., Gurtman, M. B., & Tyler, R. B. (1990). Us and them: Social categorization and the process of intergroup bias. *Journal of Personality and Social Psychology, 59*(3), 475-86.

Perez, M., Vohs, K. D., & Joiner, T. E., Jr. (2005). Self-esteem, self-other discrepancies, and aggression: The consequences of seeing yourself differently than others see you. *Journal of Social and Clinical Psychology, 24*(5), 607-20.

Perlman, D., & Oskamp, S. (1971). The effects of picture content and exposure frequency on evaluations of negroes and whites. *Journal of Experimental Social Psychology, 7*(5), 503-14.

Peters, E., & Slovic, P. (1996). The role of affect and worldviews as orienting dispositions in the perception and acceptance of nuclear power. *Journal of Applied Social Psychology, 26*(16), 1427-53.

Peterson, B. E., Doty, R. M., & Winter, D. G. (1993). Authoritarianism and attitudes toward contemporary social issues. *Personality and Social Psychology Bulletin, 19*, 174-84.

Peterson, C., & Seligman, M. (2004). *Character strengths and virtue: A handbook for classification*. Oxford, England: Oxford University Press.

Pettigrew, T. F., & Mertens, R. W. (1995). Subtle and blatant prejudice in Western Europe. *European Journal of Social Psychology, 25*, 57-75.

Pettijohn, T. F. (1994). *Sources: Notable selections in social psychology*. Guilford, CT: Dushkin Publishing Group.

Petty, R. E., Brinol, P., & DeMarree, K. (2007). The meta-cognitive model: Implications for attitude measurement, change, and strength. *Social Cognition, 25*(5), 657-87.

Petty, R. E., Brinol, P., & Tomala, Z. (2002). Thought confidence as a determinant of persuasion: The self-validation hypothesis. *Journal of Personality and Social Psychology, 82*(5), 722-41.

Petty, R. E., & Cacioppo, J. T. (1984). The effects of involvement on responses to argument quantity and quality: Central and peripheral routes to persuasion. *Journal of Personality and Social Psychology, 46*, 69-81.

Petty, R. E., & Cacioppo, J. T. (1986) *Communication and persuasion: Central and peripheral routes to attitude change.* New York, NY: Springer-Verlag.

Petty, R. E., & Jarvis, W. G. B. (1996). An individual differences perspective on assessing cognitive processes. In N. Schwartz & S. Sudman (Eds.), *Answering questions: Methodology for determining cognitive and communicative processes in social research* (pp. 221-57). San Francisco, CA: Jossey-Bass.

Petty, R. E., & Krosnick, J. A. (Eds.). (1995). *Attitude strength: Antecedents and consequences.* Hillsdale, NJ: Lawrence Erlbaum.

Petty, R. E., Zakary, L. T., Briñol, P., & William, B. G. J. (2006). Implicit ambivalence from attitude change: An exploration of the PAST Model. *Journal of Personality and Social Psychology, 90*(1), 2.

Phelps, M. P. (2004). Imago Dei and limited creature: High and low views of human beings in Christianity and cognitive psychology. *Christian Scholar's Review, 33*(3), 345-66.

Piaget, J., & Inhelder, B. (1969). *The child's conception of space.* (F. J. Langdon & J. L. Lunzer, Trans.). New York, NY: W. W. Norton.

Pieters, R. G. M., & Verplanken, B. (1995). Intention-behavior consistency: Effects of consideration set size, involvement and need for cognition. *European Journal of Social Psychology, 25*, 531-43.

Piliavin, I. M., Piliavin, J. A., & Rodin, J. (1975). Costs, diffusion, and the stigmatized victim. *Journal of Personality and Social Psychology, 32*, 429-38.

Piliavin, J. A., & Piliavin, I. M. (1972). The effect of blood on reactions to a victim. *Journal of Personality and Social Psychology, 23*, 353-61.

Piliavin, J. A. (2001). Sociology of altruism and prosocial behavior. In N. J. Smelser & P. B. Baltes (Eds.), *International encyclopedia of the social and behavioral sciences* (pp. 411-15). New York, NY: Elsevier.

Piliavin, J. A., Dovidio, J., Gaertner, S., & Clark, R. D., III. (1982). Responsive bystanders: The process of intervention. In V. Derlega and J. Grzelak (Eds.), *Cooperation and helping behavior: Theories and research.* New York, NY: Academic Press.

Pinker, S. (2007). The myth of violence. Speech delivered on March 7, 2007 at the Ted Institute. Accessed on October 3, 2010, at www.ted.com/talks/steven_pinker_on_the_myth_of_violence.html

Pinker, S. (2007, March 19). A history of violence. *The New Republic, 236*(12), 18.

Plantinga, A. (1984). Advice to Christian philosophers. *Faith and philosophy: Journal of the Society of Christian Philosophers, 1*(3), 253-71. Accessed online at www.faithandphilosophy.com/article_advice.php

Plantinga, A. (1994). On Christian scholarship. In T. Hesburgh (Ed.), *The challenge and promise of a Catholic university*. Notre Dame, IN: University of Notre Dame Press. Retrieved from www.veritas-ucsb.org/library/plantinga/ocs.html

Pomazal, R., & Clore, G. (1973). Helping on the highway: The effects of dependency and sex. *Journal of Applied Social Psychology, 3*, 150-64.

Porter, R., Cernoch, J., & Balogh, R. (1984). Recognition of neonates by facial-visual characteristics. *Pediatrics, 74*, 501-4.

Post, S. G. (2002). Altruism and altruistic love: The tradition of agape. In S. G. Post, L. G. Underwood, J. P. Schloss & W. B. Hurbut (Eds.), *Altruism and altruistic love: Science, philosophy, and religion in dialogue*. New York, NY: Oxford University Press.

Postmes, T., & Spears, R. (1998). Deindividuation and anti-normative behavior: A meta-analysis. *Psychological Bulletin, 123*(3), 238-59.

Postmes, T., & Spears, R. (2002). Behavior online: Does anonymous computer communication reduce gender inequality? *Personality and Social Psychology Bulletin, 28*, 1073-83.

Postmes, T., Spears, R., & Cihangir, S. (2001). Quality of decision making and group norms. *Journal of Personality and Social Psychology, 80*(6), 918-30.

Powers, C., Nam, R., Rowatt, W. C., & Hill, P. (2007). Associations between humility, spiritual transcendence, and forgiveness. In R. Piedmont (Ed.), *Research in the Social Scientific Study of Religion* (pp. 74-94). Herndon, VA: Brill Academic Publishers.

Powlishta, K. K., Serbin, L. A., & Doyle, A. (1994). Gender, ethnic, and body-type biases: The generality of prejudice in childhood. *Developmental Psychology, 30*(4), 526-36.

Pratto, F., Sidanius, J., Stallworth, L., & Malle, B. (1994). Social dominance orientation: A personality variable predicting social and political attitudes. *Journal of Personality and Social Psychology, 67*, 741-63.

Presson, P. K., & Benassi, V. A. (1996). Illusion of control: A meta-analytic review. *Journal of Social Behavior & Personality, 11*(3), 493-510.

Presson, P. K., & Benassi, V. A. (2003). Are depressive symptoms positively or negatively associated with the illusion of control? *Social Behavior and Personality: An International Journal, 31*(5), 483-95.

Priester, J. R., & Petty, R. E. (2001). Extending the bases of subjective attitudinal ambivalence: Interpersonal and intrapersonal antecedents of evaluative tension. *Journal of Personality and Social Psychology, 80*(1), 19-34. doi:10.1037/0022-3514.80.1.19

Prino, C., & Peyrot, M. (1994). The effect of child physical abuse and neglect on aggressive, withdrawn, and prosocial behavior. *Child Abuse and Neglect, 18*(10), 869-82.

Pruitt, D. G. (1967). Reward structure and cooperation: The decomposed prisoner's dilemma game. *Journal of Personality and Social Psychology, 7*(1), 21-27. doi:10.1037/h0024914

Pyszczynski, T., & Greenberg, J. (1987). Self-regulatory perseveration and the depressive self-focusing style: A self-awareness theory of the development and maintenance of reactive depression. *Psychological Bulletin, 102*, 122-38.

Pulakos, J. (1989). Young adult relationships: Siblings and friends. *Journal of Psychology, 123*, 237-44.

Quinn, A., & Schlenker, B. R. (2002). Can accountability produce independence? Goals as determinants of the impact of accountability on conformity. *Personality and Social Psychology Bulletin, 28,* 472-83.

Raine, A. (2002). The biological basis of crime. In J. Q. Wilson and J. Petersilia (Eds.), *Crime: Public policies for crime control* (pp. 43-74). San Francisco, CA: ICS Press.

Raine, D. (1997). Biosocial studies of antisocial and violent behavior in children and adults: A review. *Journal of Abnormal Child Psychology, 30*(4), 311-26. doi:10.1023/A:1015754122318

Raskin, R., Novacek, J., & Hogan, R. (1991). Narcissism, self-esteem, and defensive self-enhancement. *Journal of Personality, 59,* 19-38. doi:10.1111/j.1467-6494.1991.tb00766.x

Ray, J. J., & Lovejoy, F. H. (1986). The generality of racial prejudice. *Journal of Social Psychology, 126*(4), 563-64.

Reeder, G. D., & Brewer, M. B. (1979). A schematic model of dispositional attribution in interpersonal perception. *Psychological Review, 86,* 61-79.

Reeve, H. (1998). Acting for the good of others: Kinship and reciprocity with some new twists. In C. Crawford & D. Krebs (Eds.), *Handbook of evolutionary psychology: Issues, ideas, and applications* (pp. 43-83). Mahwah, NJ: Lawrence Erlbaum Associates.

Reicher, S. D. (1984). Social influence in the crowd: Attitudinal and behavioural effects of de-individuation in conditions of high and low group salience. *British Journal of Social Psychology, 23,* 341-50.

Reicher, S. D. (1987). Crowd behaviour as social action. In J. C. Turner, M. A. Hogg, P. Oakes, S. D. Reicher & M. S. Wetherell (Eds.), *Rediscovering the social group: A self-categorisation theory* (pp. 171-202). Oxford, England: Basil Blackwell.

Reicher, S., Spears, R., & Postmes, T. (1995). A social identity model of deindividuation phenomena. In W. Stroebe & M. Hewstone (Eds.), *European Review of Social Psychology* (Vol. 6, pp. 161-98). Chichester, England: Wiley.

Reingen, P. H., & Kernan, J. B. (1993). Social perception and interpersonal influence: Some consequences of the physical attractiveness stereotype in a personal selling setting. *Journal of Consumer Psychology, 2*(1), 25-38.

Reiss, A. J., Jr., & Roth, J. A. (Eds.). (1994). *Understanding and preventing violence* (Vol. 3). Washington, DC: National Academy Press.

Remley, T. P., & Herlihy, B. (2007). *Ethical, legal, and professional issues in counseling* (Updated 2nd ed.). Upper Saddle River, NJ: Merrill/Prentice-Hall.

Rhodewalt, F., & Morf, C. (1998). On self-aggrandizement and anger: A temporal analysis of narcissism and affective reactions to success and failure. *Journal of Personality and Social Psychology, 74,* 672-85.

Richardson, D. R., Green, L., & Lago, T. (1998). The relationship between perspective taking and nonaggressive responding in the face of attack. *Journal of Personality, 66,* 235-56.

Riniolo, T. C., Johnson, K. C., Sherman, T. R., & Misso, J. (2006). Hot or not: Do professors perceived as physically attractive receive higher student evaluations? *The Journal of General Psychology, 133*(1), 19-36.

Robberson, M. R., & Rogers, R. W. (1988). Beyond fear appeals: Negative and positive personal appeals to health and self-esteem. *Journal of Applied Social Psychology, 18*(3), 277-87.

Roese, N. J. (1994). The functional basis of counterfactual thinking. *Journal of Personality and Social Psychology, 66*(5), 805-18.

Roese, N. J. (1997). Counterfactual thinking. *Psychological Bulletin, 121*(1), 133-48.

Roese, N. J., Hur, T., & Pennington, G. L. (1999). Counterfactual thinking and regulatory focus: Implications for action versus inaction and sufficiency versus necessity. *Journal of Personality and Social Psychology, 77*, 1109-20.

Roizen, J. (1997). Epidemiological issues in alcohol-related violence. In M. Galanter (Ed.), *Recent developments in alcoholism* (Vol. 13, pp. 7-40). New York, NY: Plenum Press.

Rokeach, M. (1967). Attitude change and behavioral change. *Public Opinion Quarterly, 30*, 529-50.

Rosenberg, M. (1976). Beyond self-esteem: The neglected issues in self-concept research. Paper presented at the Annual Meeting of the American Sociological Association.

Rosenberg, M. (1979). *Conceiving the self.* New York, NY: Basic Books.

Rosenberg, M., Schooler, C., & Schoenbach, C. (1989). Self-esteem and adolescent problems: Modeling reciprocal effects. *American Sociological Review, 54*, 1004-18.

Rosenberg, M., Schooler, C., & Schoenbach, C. (1995). Global self-concept and specific self-esteem. *American Sociological Review, 60*, 141-56.

Rosenblith, J. F. (1949). A replication of "Some roots of prejudice." *Journal of Abnormal Psychology, 44*, 470-89.

Ross, L. (1977). The intuitive psychologist and his shortcomings: Distortions in the attribution process. In L. Berkowitz (Ed.), *Advances in experimental social psychology* (Vol. 10, p. 84). New York, NY: Academic Press.

Ross, L. (1990). Recognizing the role of construal processes. In J. Rock (Ed.), *The legacy of Solomon Asch: Essays in social and cognitive processes* (pp. 72-96). Hillsdale, NJ: Erlbaum.

Ross, L., Amabile, T. M., & Steinmetz, J. L. (1977). Social roles, social control, and biases in social-perception processes. *Journal of Personality and Social Psychology, 35*, 485-94.

Ross, L., Greene, D., & House, P. (1977). The false consensus effect: An egocentric bias in social perception and attribution processes. *Journal of Personality and Social Psychology 13*, 279-301.

Ross, L., & Lepper, M. R. (1980). The perseverance of beliefs: Empirical and normative considerations. In R. A. Shweder & D. Fiske (Eds.), *New directions for methodology of behavioral science: Fallible judgments in behavioral research* (pp. 17-36). San Francisco, CA: Jossey-Bass.

Ross, L., & Nisbett, R. E. (1991). *The person and the situation.* New York, NY: McGraw-Hill.

Rothbart, M., & John, O. P. (1985). Social categorization and behavioral episodes: A cognitive analysis of the effects of intergroup contact. *Journal of Social Issues, 41*, 81-104.

Rothblum, E. D. (1992). The stigma of women's weight: Social and economic realities. *Feminism and Psychology, 2*, 61-73.

Rovai, A. P. (2001). Building and sustaining communication in asynchronous learning networks. *Internet and Higher Education, 3*, 285-97.

Rowatt, W. C., & Franklin, L. (2004). Christian orthodoxy, religious fundamentalism, and right-wing authoritarianism as predictors of implicit racial prejudice. *The International Journal for the Psychology of Religion, 14*, 125-38.

Rowatt, W. C., Franklin, L. M., & Cotton, M. (2005). Patterns and personality correlates of intrinsic and extrinsic attitudes toward Christians and Muslims. *Journal for the Scientific Study of Religion, 44*(1), 29-43.

Rowatt, W. C., Tsang, J., Kelly, J., LaMartina, B., McCullers, M., & McKinley, A. (2006). Associations between religious personality dimensions and implicit homosexual prejudice. *Journal for the Scientific Study of Religion, 45*(3), 397-406.

Rudolph, U., Roesch, S. C., Greitemeyer, T., & Weiner, B. (2004). A meta-analytic review of help giving and aggression from an attributional perspective: Contributions to a general theory of motivation. *Cognition and Emotion, 18*, 815-48.

Rule, B. G. (1974). The hostile and instrumental functions of human aggression. In J. DeWit & W. Hartup (Eds.), *Determinants and origins of aggressive behavior.* The Hague, Netherlands: Mouton.

Rushton, J. P. (1980). *Altruism, socialization, and society.* Englewood Hills, NJ: Prentice Hall.

Rushton, J. P. (1981). The altruistic personality. In J. P. Rushton & R. M. Sorrentino (Eds.), *Altruism and helping behaviour: Social, personality, and developmental perspectives* (pp. 251-66). Hillsdale, NJ: Erlbaum.

Rushton, J. P. (1984). Sociobiology: Toward a theoretical understanding of individual and group differences in personality and social behavior. In J. R. Royce & L. P. Moss (Eds.), *Annals of Theoretical Psychology* (Vol. 2, pp. 1-48). New York, NY: Plenum Press.

Rushton, J. P. (1991). Is altruism innate? *Psychological Inquiry, 2*, 141-43.

Rushton, J. P., & Campbell, A. C. (1977). Modeling, vicarious reinforcement and extraversion on blood donating in adults: Immediate and long-term effects. *European Journal of Social Psychology, 7*(3), 297-306.

Rushton, J. P., Russell, R. J. H., & Wells, P. A. (1984). Genetic similarity theory: Beyond kin selection. *Behavior Genetics, 14*, 179-92.

Ryan, C. S. (2002). Stereotype accuracy. *European Review of Social Psychology, 13*, 75-109.

Ryan, R. M., Kuhl, J., & Deci, E. L. (1997). Nature and autonomy: An organizational view of social and neurobiological aspects of self-regulation in behavior and development. *Development and Psychopathology, 9*, 701-28.

Sagarin, B. J., & Cialdini, R. B. (2004). Creating critical consumers: Motivating receptivity by teaching resistance. In E. S. Knowles & J. A. Linn (Eds.), *Resistance and persuasion* (pp. 259-82). Mahwah, NJ: Lawrence Erlbaum.

Sagarin, B. J., Cialdini, R. B., Rice, W. E., & Serna, S. B. (2002). Dispelling the illusion of invulnerability: The motivations and mechanisms of resistance to persuasion. *Journal of Personality and Social Psychology, 83*, 526-41.

Sagiv, L., & Schwartz, S. H. (2000). Values priorities and subjective well-being: Direct relations and congruity effects. *European Journal of Social Psychology, 30*, 177-98.

Salminen, S., & Glad, T. (1992). The role of gender in helping behavior. *Journal of Social Psychology, 132*, 131-33.

Sanbonmatsu, D. M., Sherman, S. J., & Hamilton, D. L. (1987). Illusory correlation in the perception of individuals and groups. *Social Cognition, 5*(1), 1-25.

Sanday, P. R. (1997). The socio-cultural context of rape: A cross-cultural study. In L. L. O'Toole (Ed.), *Gender violence: Interdisciplinary perspectives.* New York, NY: New York University Press.

Sanford, R. N. (1950). Ethnocentrism in relation to some religious attitudes and practices. In T. W. Adorno, E. Frankel-Brunswik, D. Levinson & R. Sanford. *The authoritarian personality* (pp. 208-21). New York, NY: Harper Books.

Sanford, R. N., & Levinson, D. J. (1948). Ethnocentrism in relation to some religious attitudes and practices. *American Psychologist, 3,* 350-51.

Saroglou, V. (2006). Religion's role in prosocial behavior: Myth or reality? *Psychology of Religion Newsletter.* American Psychological Association, Division 36, *31,* 1-8.

Saroglou, V., Pichon, I., Trompette, L., Verschueren, M., & Dernelle, R. (2005). Prosocial behavior and religion: New evidence based on projective measures and peer rating. *Journal for the Scientific Study of Religion, 44,* 323-48.

Sassenberg, K., & Postmes, T. (2002). Cognitive and strategic processes in small groups: Effects of anonymity of the self and anonymity of the group on social influence. *British Journal of Social Psychology, 41,* 3, 463-80.

Saucier, G. (2000). Isms and the structure of social attitudes. *Journal of Personality and Social Psychology, 78,* 366-85.

Sawatsky, R. (2004). Prologue: The virtue of scholarly hope. In D. G. Jacobsen & R. H. Jacobsen (Eds.), *Scholarship and Christian faith: Enlarging the conversation* (pp. 3-14). New York, NY: Oxford University Press.

Schachter, S. (1951). Deviation, rejection, and communication. *Journal of Abnormal and Social Psychology, 46,* 190-208.

Schaller, M., & Cialdini, R. (1990). Happiness, sadness, and helping: A motivational integration. In E. Higgins & R. Sorrentino (Eds.), *Handbook of Motivation and Cognition* (pp. 265-96). New York, NY: Guilford Press.

Schaller, M., Simpson, J. A., & Kenrick, D. T. (Eds.). (2006). *Evolution and social psychology.* Madison, CT: Psychosocial Press.

Schlenker, B. R., & Weingold, M. F. (1990). Self-consciousness and self-presentation: Being autonomous versus appearing autonomous. *Journal of Personality and Social Psychology, 59,* 820-28.

Schnabel, K., Asendorpf, J. B., & Greenwald, A. G. (2008). Assessment of individual differences in implicit cognition: A review of IAT measures. *European Journal of Psychological Assessment, 24*(4), 210-17.

Schroeder, D. A., Penner, L. A., Dovidio, J. F., & Piliavin, J. A. (1995). *The psychology of helping and altruism.* New York, NY: McGraw-Hill.

Schulz-Hardt, S., Frey, D., Lüthgens, C., & Moscovici, S. (2000). Biased information search in group decision making. *Journal of Personality and Social Psychology, 78*(4), 655-69.

Schuman, H., Steeh, C., Bobo, L., & Krysan, M. (1997). *Racial attitudes in America: Trends and interpretations* (Rev. ed.). Cambridge, MA: Harvard University Press.

Schwartz, S. H. (1975). The justice of need and the activation of humanitarian norms. *Journal of Social Issues, 31*(3), 111-36.

Schwarz, N. (2007). Attitude construction: Evaluation in context. *Social Cognition, 25*, 638-56.

Scott. J. (1989). Conflicting beliefs about abortion: Legal and moral doubts. *Social Psychology Quarterly, 52*(4), 319-26.

Sedikides, C., & Brewer, M. B. (Eds.). (2001). *Individual self, relational self, collective self.* Philadelphia, PA: Psychology Press.

Sedikides, C., Campbell, W. K., Redder, G. D., & Elliot, A. J. (1998). The self-serving bias in relational context. *Journal of Personality and Social Psychology, 74*(2), 378-86.

Sedikides, C., Oliver, M. B., & Campbell, W. K. (1994). Personal benefits and costs of romantic relationships for women and men: Implications for social exchange theory. *Personal Relationships, 1*, 5-21.

Sedikides, C., Skowronski, J. J., & Dunbar, R. I. M. (2006). When and why did the human self evolve? In M. Schaller, J. A. Simpson & D. T. Kenrick (Eds.), *Evolution and social psychology: Frontiers in social psychology* (pp. 55-80). New York, NY: Psychology Press.

Sedikides, C., & Strube, M. (1997). Self-evaluation: To thine own self be good, to thine own self be sure, to thine own self be true, and to thine own self be better. In M. P. Zanna (Ed.), *Advances in experimental social psychology, 29* (pp. 209-69). New York, NY: Academic Press.

Seeley, E. A., Gardner, W. L., Pennington, G., & Gabriel, S. (2003). Circle of friends or members of a group? Sex-differences in relational and collective attachment to groups. *Group Processes and Intergroup Relations, 6*, 251-64.

Segal, M. W. (1974). Alphabet and attraction: An unobtrusive measure of the effect of propinquity in a field setting. *Journal of Personality and Social Psychology, 30*, 654-57.

Seligman, M. E. P. (2002). Positive psychology, positive prevention, and positive therapy. In C. R. Snyder & S. J. Lopez (Eds.), *The handbook of positive psychology* (pp. 3-12). New York, NY: Oxford University Press.

Seligman, M. E. P. (2003). Positive psychology: Fundamental assumptions. *American Psychologist,* 126-27.

Seligman, M. E. P., & Csikszentmihalyi, M. (2000). Positive psychology: An introduction. *American Psychologist, 55*, 5-14.

Seligman, M. E. P., Parks, A., & Steen, T. (2004). A balanced psychology and a full life. The Royal Society, Philosophical Transactions. *Biological Sciences, 359*, 1379-81.

Senju, A., & Johnson, M. A. (2009) The eye contact effect: Mechanisms and development. *Trends in Cognitive Sciences, 13*(3), 127-34. doi:10.1016/j.tics.2008.11.009

Shaffer, D., & Graziano, W. (1983). Effects of positive and negative moods on helping tasks having pleasant or unpleasant consequences. *Motivation and Emotion, 7*, 269-78.

Shamir, J. (1997). Speaking up and silencing out in face of a changing climate of opinion. *Journalism and Mass Communication Quarterly, 74*(3), 602-14.

Sharpley, C. F., & Rodd, J. (1985). The effects of real versus hypothetical stimuli upon preschool children's helping behavior. *Early Child Development and Care, 22*, 303-13.

Shavelson, R. J., Hubner, J. J., & Stanton, G. C. (1976). Self-concept: Validation of construct interpretations. *Review of Educational Research, 46,* 407-41.

Shavit, Y., Fischer, C. S., & Koresh, Y. (1994). Kin and nonkin under collective threat: Israeli networks during the gulf war. *Social Forces, 72,* 1197-1215.

Sheppard, J. A., Ouellette, J. A., & Fernandez, J. K. (1996). Abandoning unrealistic optimism: performance estimates and the temporal proximity of self-relevant feedback. *Journal of Personality and Social Psychology, 70,* 844-55.

Shepperd, J. A., & Taylor, K. M. (1999). Social loafing and expectancy-value theory. *Personality and Social Psychology Bulletin, 25,* 1147-58.

Sherif, M. (1935). A study of some social factors in perception: Chapter 2. *Archives of Psychology, 27*(187), 17-22.

Sherif, M. (1936). *The psychology of social norms.* New York, NY: Harper.

Sherman, D. A., Kim, H., & Zajonc, R. B. (1998, August). *Affective perseverance: Cognitions change but preferences stay the same.* Paper presented at the annual meeting of the American Psychological Society, San Francisco.

Sherman, S. J., & McConnell, A. R. (1995). Dysfunctional implications of counterfactual thinking: When alternatives to reality fail us. In N. J. Roese & J. M. Olson (Eds.), *What might have been: The social psychology of counterfactual thinking* (pp. 199-232). Hillsdale, NJ: Erlbaum.

Showers, C. J., & Ryff, C. D. (1996). Self-differentiation and well-being in a life transition. *Personality and Social Psychology Bulletin, 22,* 448-60.

Shweder, R. A., & Bourne, E. J. (1984). Does the concept of person vary cross culturally? In R. Shweder & R. A. Levine (Eds.), *Culture theory: Essays on mind, self, and emotion* (pp. 158-99). New York, NY: Cambridge University Press.

Sidanius, J. (1993). The psychology of group conflict and the dynamics of oppression: A social dominance perspective. In S. Iyengar & W. J. McGuire (Eds.), *Explorations in political psychology* (pp. 183-219). Durham, NC: Duke University Press.

Sidanius, J., & Pratto, F. (1993). The dynamics of social dominance and the inevitability of oppression. In P. Sniderman & P. Tetlock (Eds.), *Prejudice, politics, and race in America today* (pp. 173-211). Stanford, CA: Stanford University Press.

Sidanius, J., & Pratto, F. (1999). *Social dominance: An intergroup theory of social hierarchy and oppression.* Cambridge, England: Cambridge University Press.

Sidanius, J., Pratto, F., Martin, M., & Stallworth, L. M. (1991). Consensual racism and career track: Some implications of social dominance theory. *Political Psychology, 12,* 691-720.

Sigall, H., & Page, R. (1971). Current stereotypes: A little fading, a little faking. *Journal of Personality and Social Psychology, 18,* 247-55.

Sillars, A. L., & Scott, M. D. (1983). Interpersonal perception between intimates: An integrative review. *Human Communication Research, 10,* 153-76.

Silverman, I., & Eals, M. (1992). Sex differences in spatial abilities: Evolutionary theory and data. In J. H. Barkow, L. Cosmides & J. Tooby (Eds.), *The adapted mind* (pp. 533-49). New York, NY: Oxford University Press.

Silverman, I., & Phillips, K. (1998). The evolutionary psychology of spatial sex differences. In C. Crawford & D. Krebs (Eds.), *Handbook of evolutionary psychology: Issues, ideas, and applications* (pp. 595-612). Mahwah, NJ: Lawrence Erlbaum Associates.

Simmons, R. G. (1991). Presidential address on altruism and sociology. *The Sociological Quarterly, 32,* 1-22. doi:10.1111/j.1533-8525.1991.tb00342.x

Simon, H. A. (1956). Reply: Surrogates for uncertain decision problems. Reprinted in 1982 in H. A. Simon (Ed.), *Models of bounded rationality, Vol. 1: Economic analysis and public policy* (pp. 235-44). Cambridge, MA: MIT Press.

Simon, L., Greenberg, J., & Brehm, J. (1995). Trivialization: the forgotten mode of dissonance reduction. *Journal of Personality and Social Psychology, 68*(2), 247-60.

Singh, D. (1993). Adaptive significance of female physical attractiveness: Role of waist-to-hip ratio. *Journal of Personality and Social Psychology, 65,* 292-307.

Singh, D. (1993). Body shape and women's attractiveness: The critical role of waist-to-hip ratio. *Human Nature, 4,* 297-321.

Singh, D. (1994). Is thin really beautiful and good? Relationship between physical attractiveness and waist-to-hip ratio. *Personality and Individual Differences, 16,* 123-32.

Singh, D. (2004). Mating strategies of young women: Role of physical attractiveness. *Journal of Sex Research, 41*(1), 43-54. doi:10.1080/00224490409552212

Skaalvik, E. M., & Hagtvet, K. A. (1990). Academic achievement and self-concept: An analysis of causal predominance in a developmental perspective. *Journal of Personality and Social Psychology, 58*(2), 292-307. doi:10.1037/0022-3514.58.2.292

Skinner, B. F. (1971). *Beyond freedom and dignity.* New York, NY: Alfred Books.

Skocpol, T., Ganz, M., & Munson, Z. (2000). A nation of organizers: The institutional origins of civic voluntarism in the United States. *American Political Science Review. 94*(3), 527-46.

Slater, M., Antley, A., Davison, A., Swapp, D., Guger, C., Barker, C., Pistrang, N., & Sanchez-Vives, M. V. (2006). A virtual reprise of Stanley Milgram obedience experiments, *PLoS ONE.* Retrieved from www.plosone.org/article/info%3Adoi%2F10.1371%2Fjournal.pone.0000039

Slovic, P. (1987). Perception of risk. *Science, 236,* 280-85.

Slovic, P., & Fischhoff, B. (1977). On the psychology of experimental surprises. *Journal of Experimental Psychology: Human Perception and Performance, 3,* 544-51.

Slovic, P., Finucane, M., Peters, E. R., & MacGregor, D. G. (2002). The affect heuristic. In T. Gilovich, D. Griffin & D. Kahneman (Eds.), *Heuristics and biases: The psychology of intuitive judgment* (pp. 397-420). New York, NY: Cambridge University Press.

Smart, J. (2001). *Disability, society, and the individual.* Gaithersburg, MD: Aspen Publishers.

Smith, E. R., & Zarate, M. A. (1992). Exemplar-based models of social judgment. *Psychological Review, 99,* 3-21.

Smith, S. L., & Donnerstein, E. (1998). Harmful effects of exposure to media violence: Learning of aggression, emotional desensitization, and fear. In R. G. Geen & E. Donnerstein (Eds.), *Human aggression: Theories, research, and implications for social policy* (pp. 167-202). San Diego, CA: Academic Press.

Sniderman, P. M., & Piazza, T. (1993). *The scar of race.* Cambridge, MA: Belknap Press.

Snyder, M. (1980). The many me's of the self-monitor. *Psychology Today, 13*, 33-40.

Snyder, M. (1987). *Public appearances, private realities: The psychology of self-monitoring.* New York, NY: Freeman.

Snyder, M. L., Kleck, R. E., Strenta, A., & Mentzer, S. J. (1979). Avoidance of the handicapped: An attributional ambiguity analysis. *Journal of Personality and Social Psychology, 37*, 2297-2306.

Sober, E., & Wilson, D. S. (1998). *Unto others: The evolution and psychology of unselfish behavior.* Cambridge, MA: Harvard University Press.

Spears, R., Doosje, B., & Ellemers, N. (1997). Self-stereotyping in the face of threats to group status and distinctiveness: The role of group identification. *Personality and Social Psychology Bulletin, 23*, 538-53.

Spencer, S. J., Steele, C. M., & Quinn, D. M. (1999). Stereotype threat and women's math performance. *Journal of Experimental Social Psychology, 3*, 4-28.

Spilka, B., Hood, R. W., Jr., & Gorsuch, R. L. (1985). *The psychology of religion: An empirical approach.* Englewood Cliffs, NJ: Prentice-Hall.

Spilka, B., Hood, R., Hunsberger, B., & Gorsuch, R. (2003). *The psychology of religion: An empirical approach* (3rd ed.). New York, NY: Guilford Press.

Sprecher, S., & Hatfield, E. (2009). Matching hypothesis. In H. Reis & S. Sprecher (Eds.), *Encyclopedia of human relationships.* New York, NY: Sage.

Stangor, C., & Lange, J. E. (1994). Mental representations of social groups: Advances in understanding stereotypes and stereotyping. In M. P. Zanna (Ed.), *Advances in experimental social psychology* (Vol. 26, pp. 357-99). San Diego, CA: Academic Press.

Staub, E. (1974). Helping a distressed person. In L. Berkowitz (Ed.), *Advances in experimental social psychology* (Vol. 7). New York, NY: Academic Press.

Staub, E. (1999). The roots of evil: Personality, social conditions, culture and basic human needs. *Personality and Social Psychology Review, 3*, 179-92.

Staub, E. (2006), Reconciliation after genocide, mass killing, or intractable conflict: Understanding the roots of violence, psychological recovery, and steps toward a general theory. *Political Psychology, 27*, 867-94. doi:10.1111/j.1467-9221.2006.00541.x

Staub, E., Pearlman, L. A., Gubin, A., & Hagengimana, A. (2005). Healing, reconciliation, forgiving, and the prevention of violence after genocide or mass killing: An intervention and its experimental evaluation in Rwanda. *Journal of Social and Clinical Psychology, 24*(3), 297-334.

Stearns, S. (Ed.). (1999). *Evolution in health and disease.* Oxford, England: Oxford University Press.

Steele, C. M. (1988). The psychology of self-affirmation: Sustaining the integrity of the self. In L. Berkowitz (Ed.), *Advances in experimental social psychology* (Vol. 21, pp. 261-302). New York, NY: Academic Press.

Steele, C. M. (1997). A threat in the air: How stereotypes shape the intellectual identities and performance of women and African-Americans. *American Psychologist, 52*, 613-29.

Steele, C. M., & Aronson, J. (1995). Stereotype threat and the intellectual test performance of African-Americans. *Journal of Personality and Social Psychology, 69*, 797-811.

Stets, J. E. (1990). Verbal and physical aggression in marriage. *Journal of Marriage and Family*, 52(2), 501-14.

Stewart, T. L., Latu, I. M., Kawakami, K., & Myers, A. C. (2010). Consider the situation: Reducing automatic stereotyping through situational attribution. *Journal of Experimental Social Psychology*, 46, 221-25.

Stewart-Williams, S. (2011, Jan. 8). *The nature-nurture-Nietzsche blog: The meaning of life revealed: Evolution and the purpose of life.* Retrieved from www.psychologytoday .com/blog/the-nature-nurture-nietzsche-blog/201101/the-meaning-life-revealed

Stokes, S. J., & Bickman, L. (1974). The effect of the physical attractiveness and role of the helper on help-seeking. *Journal of Applied Social Psychology*, 4(3), 286-94.

Strauss, S. G., Parker, A. M., Bruce, J .B., & Dembosky, J. W. (2009). The group matters: A review of the effects of group interaction on processes and outcomes in analytic teams. Working paper, Rand Corporation. Retrieved from www.rand.org/pubs/ working_papers/2009/RAND_WR580.pdf.

Struening, E. L. (1957). The dimensions, distribution, and correlates of authoritarianism in a midwestern university faculty population. Unpublished doctoral dissertation. Accessed at www.religioustolerance.org/chr_prej.htm

Stucke, T. S., & Sporer, S. L. (2002). When a grandiose self-image is threatened: Narcissism and self-concept clarity as predictors of negative emotions and aggression following ego threat. *Journal of Personality*, 70, 509-32.

Suls, J., Martin, R., & Wheeler, L. (2002). Social comparison: Why, with whom and with what effect? *Current Directions in Psychological Science*, 11(5), 159-63.

Sutton, R. I., & Hargadon, A. (1996). Brainstorming groups in context. *Administrative Science Quarterly, 41*, 685-718.

Swap, W. C. (1977). Interpersonal attraction and repeated exposure to rewarders and punishers. *Personality and Social Psychology Bulletin*, 3(2), 248-51.

Sykes, R. E. (1983), Initial interaction between strangers and acquaintances: A multivariate analysis of factors affecting choice of communication partners. *Human Communication Research, 10*, 27-53. doi:10.1111/j.1468-2958.1983.tb00003.x

Symons, C. S., & Johnson, B. T. (1997). The self-reference effect in memory: A metaanalysis. *Psychological Bulletin*, 371-94.

Szpunar, K. K., Schellenberg, E. G., & Pliner, P. (2004). Liking and memory for musical stimuli as a function of exposure. *Journal of Experimental Psychology: Learning, Memory, and Cognition, 30*, 370-81.

Tajfel, H. (1982). Social psychology of intergroup relations. *Annual Review of Psychology, 33*, 1-39.

Tajfel, H., & Turner, J. C. (1979). An integrative theory of intergroup conflict. In S. Worchel & W. G. Austin (Eds.), *The social psychology of intergroup relations* (pp. 33-47). Monterey, CA: Brooks/Cole.

Takata, T. (1987). Self-depreciative tendencies in self-evaluation through social comparison. *Japanese Journal of Experimental Social Psychology, 27*, 27-36.

Tanford, S., & Penrod, S. (1984). Social influence model: A formal integration of research on majority and minority influence processes. *Psychological Bulletin, 95*, 189-225.

Tangney, J. P., Baumeister, R. F., & Luzio Boone, A. (2004). High self-control predicts good adjustment, less pathology, better grades, and interpersonal success. *Journal of Personality, 72*(2), 271-322.

Taussig, W. C. (1994). Weighing in against discrimination: Cook v. Rhode Island Department of Mental Health, Retardation, and Hospitals and the recognition of obesity as a disability under the Rehabilitation Act and the Americans with Disabilities Act. *Boston College Review, 35,* 927-63.

Taylor, D. M., & Doria, J. R. (1981). Self-serving bias and group-serving bias in attribution. *Journal of Social Psychology, 113*(2), 201-11.

Taylor, S. E., & Gonzaga, G. C. (2006). Evolution, telationships, and health: The social shaping hypothesis. In M. Schaller, J. A. Simpson & D. T. Kenrick (Eds.), *Evolution and Social Psychology* (pp. 211-36). New York, NY: Psychology Press.

Tesser, A. (1988). Toward a self-evaluation maintenance model of social behavior. In L. Berkowitz (Ed.), *Advances in experimental social psychology* (Vol. 21, pp. 181-227). New York, NY: Academic Press.

Tesser, A., & Martin, L. (1996). The psychology of evaluation. In E. T. Higgins & A. W. Kruglanski (Eds.), *Social psychology: Handbook of basic principles* (pp. 400-432). New York, NY: Guilford Press.

Tesser, A., Martin, L. L., & Cornell, D. P. (1996), On the substitutability of self-protective mechanisms. In P. M. Gollwitzer & J. A. Bargh (Eds.), *The psychology of action: Linking cognition and motivation to behavior* (pp. 48-68). New York, NY: Guilford Press.

Tesser, A., Wood, J. V., & Stapel, D. A. (2006). *On building, defending, and regulating the self: A psychological perspective.* New York, NY: Taylor & Francis.

Tetlock, P. E. (2007). Psychology and politics: The challenges of integrating levels of analysis in social science. In A. W. Kruglanski & E. T. Higgins (Eds.), *Social psychology: Handbook of basic principles* (2nd ed., pp. 695-715). New York, NY: Guilford Press.

Thernstrom, S., & Thernstrom, A. (1997). *America in black and white.* New York, NY: Simon & Schuster.

Thibaut, J. W., & Kelley, H. H. (1959). *The social psychology of groups.* New York, NY: John Wiley & Sons.

Thoits, P. A. (1994). Stressors and problem-solving: The individual as psychological activist. *Journal of Health and Social Behavior, 35*(2), 143-60.

Thompson, M. M., Zanna, M. P., & Griffin, D. W. (1995). Let's not be indifferent about (attitudinal) ambivalence. In R. E. Petty & J. A. Krosnick (Eds.), *Attitude strength: Antecedents and consequences* (pp. 361-86). Mahwah, NJ: Erlbaum.

Thornhill, R., & Palmer, C. T. (2000). *Rape: A natural history.* Cambridge, MA: MIT Press.

Tiihonen, J., Rossi, R., Laakso, M. P., Hodgins, S., Testa, C., & Perez, J. (2008). Brain anatomy of persistent violent offenders: More rather than less. *Psychiatry Research: Neuroimaging, 163,* 201-12.

Tipper, S. P. (1992). Selecting for action: The role of inhibitory mechanisms. *Current Directions in Psychological Science, 1,* 105-9.

Todd, P. M., & Gigerenzer, G. (2007). Mechanisms of ecological rationality: Heuristics and environments that make us smart. In R. I. M. Dunbar & L. Barrett (Eds.), *The Oxford handbook of evolutionary psychology* (pp. 197-210). Oxford, England: Oxford University Press.

Toi, M., & Batson, C. D. (1982). More evidence that empathy is a source of altruistic motivation. *Journal of Personality and Social Psychology, 43*, 281-92.

Tong, E. M. W., & Yang, Z. (2010). Moral hypocrisy of proud and grateful people. *Social Psychological and Personality Science, 2*(2), 159-65.

Tooby, J., & Cosmides, L. (1992). The psychological foundations of culture. In J. Barkow, L. Cosmides & J. Tooby (Eds.), *The adapted mind: Evolutionary psychology and the generation of culture.* New York, NY: Oxford University Press.

Tooby, J., & Cosmides, L. (2005). Conceptual foundations of evolutionary psychology. In D. M. Buss (Ed.), *The handbook of evolutionary psychology* (pp. 5-67). Hoboken, NJ: John Wiley & Sons.

Tooby, J., Cosmides, L., & Barrett, H. C. (2005). Resolving the debate on innate ideas: Learnability constraints and the evolved interpenetration of motivational and conceptual functions. In P. Carruthers, S. Laurence & S. Stich (Eds.), *The innate mind: Structure and content.* New York, NY: Oxford University Press.

Tooby, J., & DeVore, I. (1987). The reconstruction of hominid behavioral evolution through strategic modeling. In W. Kinzey (Ed.), *Primate Models of Hominid Behavior.* Albany, NY: SUNY Press.

Tormala, Z. L., & Petty, R. E. (2001). On-line vs. memory-based processing: The role of need to evaluate in person perception. *Personality and Social Psychology Bulletin, 27*(12), 1599-1612.

Townsend, J. M. (1989). Mate selection criteria: A pilot study. *Ethology and Sociobiology, 10*, 173-206.

Triandis, H. C. (1995). *Individualism and collectivism.* Boulder, CO: Westview Press.

Trivers, R. L. (1971). The evolution of reciprocal altruism. *Quarterly Review of Biology, 46*, 35-37.

Trivers, R. L. (1972). Parental investment and sexual selection. In B. H. Campbell (Ed.), *Sexual selection and the descent of man, 1871-1971* (pp. 136-79). Chicago: Aldine.

Trivers, R. L. (1974). Parent-offspring conflict. *American Zoologist, 14*, 249-64.

Trivers, R. L. (1985). *Social evolution.* Menlo Park, CA: Benjamin Cummings.

Trobst, K. K., Collins, R. L., & Embree, J. M. (1994). The role of emotion in social support provision: Gender, empathy and expressions of distress. *Journal of Social & Personal Relationships, 11*, 45-62.

Trope, Y. (1986). Self-assessment and self-enhancement in achievement motivation. In R. M. Sorrentino & E. T. Higgins (Eds.), *Handbook of motivation and cognition: Foundations of social behavior* (Vol. 1, pp. 350-78). New York, NY: Guilford Press.

Trout, M. R., Maass, A., & Kenrick, D. T. (1992). Minority influence: Personal relevance biases cognitive processes and reverses private acceptance. *Journal of Experimental Social Psychology, 28*, 234-54.

Tsang, J. (2006). Gratitude and prosocial behaviour: An experimental test of gratitude. *Cognition and Emotion, 20*, 138-48. doi:10.1080/02699930500172341

Tuinier, S., Verhoeven, W. M., & van Praag, H. M. (1995). Cerebrospinal fluid 5-hydroxy-indolacetic acid and aggression: A critical reappraisal of the clinical data. *International Journal of Clinical Pharmacology, 10*, 147-56.

Turner, J. C. (1999). Some current directions in social identity. In N. Ellmers, R. Spears & B. Doosje (Eds.), *Social identity: Context, commitment, content.* Malden, MA: Blackwell.

Turner, J. C., Oakes, P. J., Haslam, S. A., & McGarty, C. (1994). Self and collective: Cognition and social context. *Personality and Social Psychology Bulletin, 20*, 454-63.

Turner, Y., & Hadas-Halpern, I. (2008, December 3). The effects of including a patient's photograph to the radiographic examination. Paper presented at Radiological Society of North America, Chicago, IL.

Tversky, A., & Kahneman, D. (1974). Judgment under uncertainty: Heuristics and biases *Science, 185*(4157), 1124-31.

Twenge, J. M., Baumeister, R. F., Tice, D. M., & Stucke, T. S. (2001). If you can't join them, beat them: Effects of social rejection on aggressive behavior. *Journal of Personality and Social Psychology, 81*, 1058-69.

Twenge, J. M., Shang, L., Catanese, K. R., Dolan-Pasce, B., Lyche, L. F., & Baumeister, R. F. (2007). Replenishing connectedness: Reminders of social activity reduce aggression after social exclusion. *British Journal of Social Psychology, 46*(1), 205-24.

Tyler, T. R., & McGraw, K. M. (1986). Ideology and the interpretation of personal experience: Procedural justice and political quiescence. *Journal of Social Issues, 42*, 115-28.

Tyler, T. R., & Sears, D. O. (1977). Coming to like obnoxious people when we must live with them. *Journal of Personality and Social Psychology, 35*(4), 200-211.

Uleman, J. S., Newman, L. S., & Mosowitz, G. B. (1996). People as flexible interpreters: Evidence and issues from spontaneous trait inference. In M. P. Zanna (Ed.), *Advances in experimental social psychology* (Vol. 28, pp. 211-79). San Diego, CA: Academic Press.

Urdan, T., & Midgley, C. (2001). Academic self-handicapping: What we know, what more there is to learn. *Educational Psychology Review, 13*, 115-38.

Vacera, S., & Johnson, M. (1995). Gaze detection and the cortical processing of faces: Evidence from infant and adults. *Visual Cognition, 2*, 59-87.

Vaes, J., Paladino, M. P., Castelli, L., Leyens, J. Ph., & Giovanazzi, A. (2003). On the behavioral consequences of infra-humanization: The implicit role of uniquely human emotions in intergroup relations. *Journal of Personality and Social Psychology, 85*, 1016-34.

Valdesoso, P., & DeSteno, D. (2007). Moral hypocrisy: Social groups and the flexibility of virtue. *Psychological Science, 18*(8), 689-90.

Van Hiel, A., & Mervielde, I. (2001). Explaining conservative beliefs and political preferences: a comparison of social dominance orientation and authoritarianism. *Journal of Applied Social Psychology, 32*(5), 965-76.

Van Hiel, A., & Mervielde, I. (2005). Authoritarianism and social dominance orientation: Relationships with various forms of racism. *Journal of Applied Social Psychology, 35*, 2323-44.

Van Leeuwen, M. S. (1985). *The person in psychology: A contemporary Christian appraisal.* Grand Rapids, MI: Eerdmans.

Van Leeuwen, M. S. (1990). *Gender and grace: Love, work, and parenting in a changing world.* Downers Gorve, IL: InterVarsity Press.

Van Leeuwen, M. S. (1994). The challenge of gender relations. In J. B. Nelson & S. P. Longfellow (Eds.), *Sexuality and the sacred: Sources for theological reflection* (pp. 120-30). Louisville, KY: John Knox Press.

Van Leeuwen, M. S. (2002). *My brother's keeper: What the social sciences do & don't tell us about masculinity.* Downers Grove, IL: InterVarsity Press.

Van Leeuwen, M. S. (2002). Of hoggamus and hogwash: Evolutionary psychology and gender relations. *Journal of Psychology and Theology, 30,* 101-11.

Van Oudenhoven, J. P., & de Boer, T. (1995). Complementarity and similarity of partners in international mergers. *Basic and Applied Social Psychology, 17,* 343-56.

VanBeest, I., & Williams, K. D. (2006). When inclusion costs and ostracism pays, ostracism still hurts. *Journal of Personality and Social Psychology, 91*(5), 918-28.

Veitch, R., & Piccione, A. (1978). The role of attitude similarity in the attribution process. *Social Psychology, 41*(2), 165-69.

Verbrugge, L. M. (1977). The structure of adult friendship choices. *Social Forces, 56,* 576-97.

Verkuyten, M., & Hagendoorn, L. (1998). Prejudice and self-categorization: The variable role of authoritarianism and in-group stereotypes. *Personality and Social Psychology Bulletin, 24*(1), 99-110.

Viding, E., Blair, R. J. R., Moffitt, T. E., & Plomin, R. (2005). Evidence for substantial genetic risk for psychopathy in 7-year-olds. *Journal of Child Psychology and Psychiatry, 46,* 592-97.

Viding, E., Frick, P. J., & Plomin, R. (2007). Aetiology of the relationship between callous-unemotional traits and conduct problems in children. *British Journal of Psychiatry, 190,* 33-38.

Visser, P. S., & Krosnick, J. A. (1998). Development of attitude strength over the life cycle: Surge and decline. *Journal of Personality and Social Psychology, 75,* 1389-1410.

Vitz, P. (1997). A Christian theory of personality. In R. Roberts & M. R.Talbot (Eds.), *Limning the psyche: Explorations in Christian psychology.* Grand Rapids, MI: Eerdmans.

Vohs, K. D., Baumeister, R. F., & Ciarocco, N. J. (2005). Self-regulation and self-presentation: Regulatory resource depletion impairs impression management and effortful self-presentation depletes regulatory resources. *Journal of Personality and Social Psychology, 88,* 632-57.

Vohs, K. D., & Heatherton, T. F. (2001). Self-esteem and threats to self: Implications for self construals and interpersonal perceptions. *Journal of Personality and Social Psychology, 81,* 1103-18.

Vohs, K. D., & Schooler, J. W. (2003). The value of believing in free will: Encouraging a belief in determinism increases cheating. *Psychological Science, 19,* 49-54.

Volf, M. (2006). *Free of charge: Giving and forgiving in a culture stripped of grace.* Grand Rapids, MI: Zondervan.

Von Hippel, W., Silver, L. A., & Lynch, M. E. (2000). Stereotyping against your will: The role of inhibitory ability in stereotyping and prejudice among the elderly. *Personality and Social Psychological Bulletin, 26*(5), 523-32.

Wade, N. G. (2010). What works best: Whether explicit forgiveness treatment or not remains unclear: Introduction to Special Issues on Forgiveness in Therapy. *Journal of Mental Health Counseling, 32*, 1-4.

Walker, S. G., & Watson, G. I. (1994). Integrative complexity and British decisions during the Munich and Polish crises. *Journal of Conflict Resolution, 38*, 3-23.

Walster, E., Aronson, V., Abrahams, D., & Rottman, L. (1966). Importance of physical attractiveness in dating behavior. *Journal of Personality and Social Psychology, 4*(5), 508-16.

Walster, E., Berscheid, E., & Walster, G. W. (1973). New directions in equity research. *Journal of Personality and Social Psychology, 25*, 151-76.

Wang, S. (2005). A conceptual framework for integrating research related to the physiology of compassion and the wisdom of Buddhist teachings. In P. Gilbert (Ed.), *Compassion: Conceptualisations, research and use in psychotherapy*. New York, NY: Psychology Press.

Ward, T., & Siegert, R. (2002). Rape and evolutionary psychology: A critique of Thornhill and Palmer's theory. *Aggression and Violent Behavior, 7*(2), 145-68. doi:10.1016/S1359-1789(00)00042-2

Ward, T., & Siegert, R. (2002). Toward a comprehensive theory of child sexual abuse: A theory knitting perspective. *Psychology, Crime and Law, 8*(4), 319-51.

Watson, D., Klohnen, E. C., Casillas, A., Nus, S. E., Haig, J., & Berry, D. S. (2004). Match makers and deal breakers: Analyses of assortative mating in newlywed couples. *Journal of Personality, 72*(5): 1029-68. doi:10.1111/j.0022-3506.2004.00289.x

Waytz, A., Epley, N., & Cacioppo, J. T. (2010). Social cognition unbound: Insights into anthropomorphism and dehumanization. *Current Directions in Psychological Science, 19*, 58-62. doi:10.1177/0963721409359302

Webster, E. C. (1964). *Decision-making in the employment interview*. Montreal, Canada: Industrial Relations Center, McGill University.

Webster, G. D. (2006). Low self-esteem *is* related to aggression, but especially when controlling for gender: A replication and extension of Donnellan et al. (2005). *Representative Research in Social Psychology, 29*, 12-18.

Webster, G. (2007). Is the relationship between self-esteem and physical aggression necessarily U-shaped? *Journal of Research in Personality, 41*(4), 977-82. doi:10.1016/j.jrp.2007.01.001

Webster, G. D., Jonason, P. K., & Orozco, T. (2010). Hot topics and popular papers in evolutionary psychology: Analyses of title words and citation counts in *Evolution and Human Behavior*, 1979-2008. *Evolutionary Psychology, 7*, 348-62.

Webster, G. D., Kirkpatrick, L. A., Nezlek, J. B., Smith, C. V., & Paddock, E. L. (2007). Diverent slopes for diferent folks: Self-esteem instability and gender as moderators of the relationship between self-esteem and attitudinal aggression. *Self and Identity, 6*, 74-94.

Wegner, D., & Crano, W. (1975). Racial factors in helping behavior: An unobtrusive field experiment. *Journal of Personality and Social Psychology, 32*, 901-5.

Wegner, D. M., & Wenzlaff, R. M. (1996). Mental control. In E. T. Higgins & A. Kruglanski (Eds.), *Social psychology: Handbook of basic mechanisms and processes* (pp. 466-92). New York, NY: Guilford Press.

Wegner, D. M., & Wheatley, T. (1999). Apparent mental causation: Sources of the experience of will. *American Psychologist, 54,* 480-92.

Weiner, B. (1995). *Judgments of responsibility: A foundation for a theory of social conduct.* New York, NY: Guilford Press.

Weisbuch, M., Ivcevic, Z., & Ambady, N. (2009). On being liked on the web and in the "real world": Consistency in first impressions across personal webpages and spontaneous behavior. *Journal of Experimental Social Psychology, 45,* 573-76.

Weiss, B., Dodge, K. A., Bates, J. E., & Petit, G. S. (1992). Some consequences of early harsh discipline: Child aggression and a maladaptive social information processing style. *Child Development, 63*(6), 1321-35.

Weiss, R. F., Buchanan, W., Altstatt, L., & Lombardo, J. P. (1971). Altruism is rewarding. *Science, 171,* 1262-63.

Wellman, B., & Wortley, S. (1990). Different strokes from different folks: Community ties and social support. *American Journal of Sociology, 96,* 558-88.

Wells, G. L., & Turtle, J. W. (1987). Eyewitness testimony: Current knowledge and emergent controversies. *Canadian Journal of Behavioral Science, 19,* 363-88.

Werner, C., & Parmelee, P. (1979). Similarity of activity preferences among friends: Those who play together stay together. *Social Psychology Quarterly, 42,* 62-66.

West, S. G., & Brown, T. J. (1975). Physical attractiveness, the severity of the emergency and helping: A field experiment and interpersonal simulation. *Journal of Experimental Social Psychology, 11*(6), 531-38.

Westhues, K. (1996, April 28). Review of Samuel P. Oliner and Pearl M. Oliner, *The Altruistic Personality: Rescuers of Jews in Nazi Europe. Catholic New Times.*

Whatley, M. A., Webster, M. J., Smith, R. H., & Rhodes, A. (1999). The effect of a favor on public and private compliance: How internalized is the norm of reciprocity? *Basic Applied Social Psychology, 21,* 251-59.

Wheeler, L., & Kim, Y. (1997). What is beautiful is culturally good: The physical attractiveness stereotype has different content in collectivistic cultures. *Personality and Social Psychology Bulletin, 23,* 795-800.

Wheeler, L., & Miyake, K. (1992). Social comparison in everyday life. *Journal of Personality and Social Psychology, 62*(5), 760-73.

White, P. A. (1991). Ambiguity in the internal/external distinction in causal attribution. *Journal of Experimental Social Psychology, 27,* 259-70.

Whitley, B. E. (1998, August). *Authoritarianism and social dominance orientation as independent dimensions of prejudice.* Paper presented at the 106th Annual Convention of the American Psychological Association, San Francisco, CA.

Whitley, B. E. (1999). Right-wing authoritarianism, social dominance orientation, and prejudice. *Journal of Personality and Social Psychology, 77*(1), 126-34.

Wicklund, R. A. (1974). *Freedom and reactance.* Potomac, MD: Lawrence Erlbaum Associates.

Widemeyer, W. N., & Loy, J. W. (1988). When you're hot, you're hot! Warm-cold effects on first impressions of persons and teaching effectiveness. *Journal of Educational Psychology, 80*(1), 118-21.

Wilder, D., & Simon, A. F. (2001). Affect as a cause of intergroup bias. In R. Brown & S. Gaertner (Eds.), *Blackwell Handbook of Social Psychology: Intergroup Processes* (pp. 153-72). Malden, MA: Blackwell.

Wilder, D., & Simon, A. F. (2008). Affect as a cause of intergroup bias. In R. Brown & S. L. Gaertner (Eds.), *Blackwell handbook of social psychology: Intergroup processes.* Oxford, England: Blackwell. doi:10.1002/9780470693421

Wildschut, T., Pinter, B., Vevea, J. L., Insko, C. A., & Schopler, J. (2003). Beyond the group mind: A quantitative review of the interindividual-intergroup discontinuity effect. *Psychological Bulletin, 129*(5), 698-722.

Wilkowski, B. M., & Robinson, M. D. (2008). Guarding against hostile thoughts: Trait anger and the recruitment of cognitive control. *Emotion, 8*(4), 578-83. doi:10.1037/1528-3542.8.4.578

Williams, J. E., & Best, D. L. (1990). *Measuring sex stereotyping: A multination study.* Newbury Park, CA: Sage.

Williams, K. D. (2001). *Ostracism: The power of silence.* New York, NY: Guilford Press.

Williams, K. D., Forgas, J. P., & von Hippel, W. (Eds.). (2005). *The social outcast: Ostracism, social exclusion, rejection, and bullying.* New York, NY: Psychology Press.

Williams, K. D., Harkins, S., & Latané, B. (1981). Identifiability as a deterrent to social loafing: Two cheering experiments. *Journal of Personality and Social Psychology, 40*, 303-11.

Williams, K. D., Harkins, S. G., & Karau, S. J. (2003). Social performance. In M.A. Hogg & J. Cooper (Eds.), *The Sage handbook of social psychology* (pp. 327-46). Thousand Oaks, CA: Sage.

Williams, L. E., & Bargh, J. A. (2008). Keeping one's distance: The influence of spatial distance cues on affect and evaluation. *Psychological Science, 19*, 302-8.

Williams, L., & DeSteno, D. (2008). Pride and perseverance: The motivational role of pride. *Journal of Personality and Social Psychology, 94*, 1007-17.

Willis, J., & Todorov, A. (2006). First impressions: Making up your mind after a 100-ms exposure to a face. *Psychological Science, 17*(7), 592-98.

Wilson, D. S. (1997). Human groups as units of selection. *Science, 276*, 1816-17.

Wilson, D. W. (1978). Helping behavior and physical attractiveness. *Journal of Social Psychology, 104*(2), 313-14.

Wilson, E. O. (1975). *Sociobiology: The New Synthesis.* Cambridge, MA: Harvard University Press.

Wilson, E. O. (1998). *Consilience: The unity of knowledge.* New York, NY: Alfred A. Knopf.

Wilson, J. (2000). Volunteering. *Annual Review of Sociology, 26*, 215-40.

Wilson, J. W., & Musick, P. (1997). Who cares? Toward an integrated theory of volunteerism. *American Sociological Review, 62*, 694-713.

Wilson, T. D., Lindsey, S., & Schooler, T. Y. (2000). A model of dual attitudes. *Psychological Review, 107*, 101-26.

Winkielman, P., Zajonc, R. B., & Schwarz, N. (1997). Subliminal affective priming resists attributional interventions. *Cognition and Emotion, 11,* 433-65.

Wittenbrink, B., Judd, C. M., & Park, B. (2001). Spontaneous prejudice in context: Variability in automatically activated attitudes. *Journal of Personality and Social Psychology, 81,* 815-27.

Wojciszke, B. (2005). Morality and competence in person and self perception. *European Review of Social Psychology, 16,* 155-88.

Wojciszke, B., Bazinska, R., & Jaworski, M. (1998). On the dominance of moral categories in impression formation. *Personality and Social Psychology Bulletin, 24,* 1251-63.

Wolpe, J. (1982). *The practice of behavior therapy.* New York, NY: Pergamon Press.

Wood, W., & Stagner, B. (1994). Why are some people easier to influence than others? In S. Shavitt & T. C. Brock (Eds.), *Persuasion* (pp. 149-74). Boston, MA: Allyn & Bacon.

Wood, E. (2000). Attitude change: Persuasion and social influence. *Annual Review of Psychology, 51,* 539-70.

Woods, S., Matterson, J., & Silverman, J. (1966). Medical students' disease: Hypocondriasis in medical education. *Journal of Medical Education, 41,* 785-90.

Worchel, S., & Andreoli, V. M. (1978). Facilitation of social interaction through deindividuation of the target. *Journal of Personality and Social Psychology, 36,* 549-56.

World Health Organization. (2005). *Multi-country study on women's health and domestic violence against women: Initial results on prevalence, health outcomes and women's responses.* Retrieved from www.who.int/gender/violence/who_multicountry_study/en/

World Health Organization. (2010). *Sexual violence.* Retrieved from www.who.int/gender/violence/sexual_violence/en/index.html

Worthington, E. L., Jr. (1998). *Dimensions of forgiveness: Psychological research and theological perspectives.* Philadelphia, PA: Templeton Foundation Press.

Worthington, E. L., Jr. (2003). *Five steps to forgiveness: The art and science of forgiving: Bridges to wholeness and hope.* Downers Grove, IL: InterVarsity Press.

Worthington, E. L., Jr. (2009). *A just forgiveness: Responsible healing without excusing injustice.* Downers Grove, IL: InterVarsity Press.

Worthington, E. L., Jr. (2010). *Coming to peace with psychology: What Christians can learn from psychological science.* Downers Grove, IL: InterVarsity Press.

Wulff, D. M. (1991). *Psychology of religion: Classic and contemporary views.* New York, NY: John Wiley & Sons.

Wylie, L., & Forest, J. (1992). Religious fundamentalism, right-wing authoritarianism, and prejudice. *Psychological Reports, 71,* 1291-98.

Yik, M. S., Bond, M. H., & Paulhus, D. L. (1998). Do Chinese self-enhance or self-efface? It's a matter of domain. *Personality and Social Psychology Bulletin, 24,* 399-406.

Young, L., & Powell. B. (1985). The effects of obesity on the clinical judgments of mental health professionals. *Journal of Health and Social Behavior, 26*(3), 233-46.

Ysseldyk, R., Matheson, K., & Anisman, H. (2010). Religiosity as identity: Toward an understanding of religiosity from a social identity perspective. *Personality and Social Psychology Review, 14*(1), 60-71.

Yuker, H. E. (1970). *Attitudes toward persons with disabilities.* New York, NY: Springer Publishing.

Zajonc, R. B. (1968). Attitudinal effects of mere exposure. *Journal of Personality and Social Psychology,* Monongraph supplement 9, 1-27.

Zajonc, R. B. (1970, February). Brainwash: Familiarity breeds comfort. *Psychology Today,* 33-35, 60-62.

Zajonc, R. B. (1980). Feeling and thinking: Preferences need no inferences. *American Psychologist, 35,* 151-75.

Zajonc, R. B. (2000). Feeling and thinking: Closing the debate over the independence of affect. In J. P. Forgas (Ed.), *Feeling and thinking: The role of affect in social cognition.* New York, NY: Cambridge University Press.

Zajonc, R. B. (2001). Mere exposure: A gateway to the subliminal. *Current Directions in Psychological Science, 10,* 224-28.

Zanna, M. P., & Rempel, J. K. (1988). Attitudes: A new look at an old concept. In D. Bar-Tal & A. Kruglanski (Eds.), *The social psychology of knowledge* (pp. 315-34). New York, NY: Cambridge University Press.

Zillmann, D. (1983). Transfer of excitation in emotional behavior. In J. T. Cacioppo & R. E. Petty (Eds.), *Social psychophysiology: A sourcebook* (pp. 215-40). New York, NY: Guilford Press.

Zillmann, D., & Weaver, J. B. (2007). Aggressive personality traits in the effects of violent imagery on unprovoked aggression. *Journal of Research in Personality, 41*(4), 753-71.

Zimbardo, P. G. (1969). The human choice: Individuation, reason, and order vs. deindividuation, impulse and chaos. In W. J. Arnold & D. Levine (Eds.), *Nebraska Symposium on Motivation* (Vol. 17, pp. 237-307). Lincoln, NE: University of Nebraska Press.

Zimbardo, P. G. (1971, October 25). *The power and pathology of imprisonment.* Congressional Record. (Serial No. 15). Hearings before Subcommittee No. 3 of the Committee on the Judiciary, House of Representatives, Ninety-Second Congress, First Session on Corrections, Part II, Prisons, Prison Reform and Prisoner's Rights: California. Washington, DC: U.S. Government Printing Office.

Zimbardo, P. G. (2007). *The Lucifer effect: Understanding how good people turn evil.* New York, NY: Random House.

# Image Credits and Permissions

Photo 1.1. © Chantalnathalie/Dreamstime.com

Figures 1.2, 3.1, 4.4, 10.2. © Mike Gruhn/WebDonuts. Used by permission.

Photo 2.1. © Odyssei/Dreamstime.com

Photo 3.1. © kycstudio/iStockphoto.com

Figures 3.2, 3.3, 4.3, 5.1, 5.2, 6.3, 9.2. © Mary Chambers, *Church Is Stranger Than Fiction*. Downers Grove, IL: InterVarsity Press, 1990.

Photo 5.1. © Scott Griessel/Dreamstime.com

Photo 5.2. © Yuri_Arcurs/iStockphoto.com

Photo 5.3. © Arenacreative/Dreamstime.com

Photo 6.1. © Sergey Kamshylin/123RF Stock Photos

Photo 6.2. Bundesarchiv, Bild/Wikimedia Commons

Photo 7.1. © zerocattle/iStockphoto.com

Photo 7.2. © Monkey Business Images Ltd/iStockphoto.com

Photo 8.1. © mstay/iStockphoto.com

Figure 8.3. Source: the Implicit Association Tests (IAT). Used by permission.

Photo 9.1. © Ongap/Dreamstime.com

Photo 9.2. © Withgod/Dreamstime.com

Photo 10.1. © Rebecca Abell/Dreamstime.com

Photo 10.2. © Monkey Business Images Ltd/Dreamstime.com

# Author Index

Aboud, F. E., 329, 445
Abrahams, D., 447
Adams, G. R., 447, 451
Adelson, S., 343-44
Adolphs, R., 289
Adorno, T. W. E., 33, 343
Ainsworth, M. D. S., 110
Ajzen, I., 143, 159, 239, 242-43, 248-49, 268
Akert, R., 378
Akrami, B., 343
Aktipis, C. A., 135
Alexander, M. G., 208
Alexander, R., 208, 418
Alhakami, A. S., 170
Alicke, M. D., 218
Allen, J. J. B., 433
Allen, J. L., 400
Alley, T. R., 449
Alloy, L. B., 174
Allport, F., 192, 260
Allport, G., 156, 333, 351-54, 365, 368
Alper, J. S., 290
Altemeyer, B., 343-45, 357-58
Amabile, T. M., 160
Amato, P. R., 396
Ambady, N., 152
Amodio, D. M., 438
Amsel, R., 339
Andersen, S. M., 349
Anderson, C. A., 278, 298-99, 307-8, 311
Anderson, K. B., 50, 308
Anderson, N. H., 443
Anderson, N., 173
Anderson, S. L., 451
Andreoli, V. M., 336
Ang, R. P., 303
Anisman, H., 211
Antley, A., 232-33
Archer, J., 304
Ariely, D., 434
Arkes, H. R., 172, 361, 364-65
Armitage, C. J., 249
Aronson, E., 160, 342, 378, 447
Asch, S. E., 33, 150, 173, 216-17
Asendorpf, J. B., 246
Ashmore, R. D., 332, 450-52
Aspden, P., 435

Aube, J., 278
Averett, S., 338
Axelrod, R., 110, 418
Babbie, E., 404
Back, M. D., 431
Bailenson, J. N., 213-14
Bailey, J. M., 162, 448
Bain, P., 104
Balaban, E., 290
Baldridge, B., 444
Banaji, M. R., 339, 362-64, 380
Bandura, A., 240, 296-97
Banerjee, R., 113
Banks, M., 337
Barbaranelli, C., 300
Barbee, A. P., 448, 449
Barber, N., 424
Barclay, J., 246
Barclay, L. C., 303
Bargh, J. A., 128, 143, 151-52, 167, 213, 238-39, 362
Barker, C., 232-33
Barkley, R. A., 129
Barkow, J., 40
Barnard, A., 318
Baron, R. A., 144, 202, 277-78, 398
Barrett, H. C., 40
Barrientos, S., 422
Barrow, G., 338
Barry, J. R., 344
Bartell, P. A., 394
Bartholow, B. D., 294, 307, 310-11
Bartlett, F. C., 175
Bartlett, M. Y., 258
Bartsch, R. A., 433
Baskin, T. W., 326, 371
Bassett, R. L., 246, 270
Bastian, B., 104
Bates, J. E., 305
Bateson, G., 33
Batson, C. D., 250, 256-58, 354, 387, 398-400, 413, 422-24
Batson, J., 400, 422
Bauer, G. B., 306
Baumann, D. J., 39-99
Baumeister, R. F., 32, 68, 100-102, 106-7, 112, 120, 127, 171, 302, 319

Bayly, M., 422
Bazinska, R., 145, 151
Beach, S., 432
Beaman, A. L., 412
Beck, A. T., 129
Bell, D., 361
Bell, K., 249
Bellah, C. G., 124
Bellavia, G., 439
Bellizzi, J. A., 338
Bem, D. J., 92, 159
Bem, S. L., 340
Benassi, V. A., 174
Benjamin, A. J., 300, 307, 310
Benson, P. L., 386, 403
Berdick, C., 369
Berglas, S., 121, 126
Berkowitz, L., 295-97, 398, 411
Bernthal, P., 438
Berntson, G. G., 145, 243-44
Berridge, K. C., 147
Berry, D. S., 440
Berscheid, E., 148, 386, 419, 427, 432, 447
Best, D. L., 403
Bettencourt, B. A., 300, 310
Bettman, J. R., 184
Beyth, R., 172
Bickman, L., 382, 387, 404
Bierhoff, H. W., 34
Bikhchandani, S., 215
Billig, M., 363
Birnbaum, M. H., 169, 173
Birum, I., 343
Biskupic, J., 311
Björkqvist, K., 303, 305
Blair, I. V., 363-64
Blair, R. J. R., 289, 291
Blanton, H., 262
Blass, T., 231
Blau, P., 404, 452
Bleske, A. L., 453-54
Bobo, C., 361
Boden, J., 302
Bodenhausen, G. V., 156-57, 245, 349-50, 366
Boehm, E., 265
Boer, S. F., 290
Bohner, G., 240-41, 245
Boinski, S., 195

Bond, R., 216-18
Bonnelle, K., 149
Borduin, C. M., 299, 314
Bornstein, R. F., 432, 434
Bossard, J. H. S., 430
Botwin, M. D., 440
Bourne, E. J., 98
Bovens, M., 207
Bowen, R., 125
Bowlby, J., 427
Boyd, R., 42
Brad, J., 302
Bradbury, T. N., 428
Bradley, M. M., 157
Brandt, J., 422
Branscombe, N. R., 250
Brase, G., 397
Brauer, M., 364
Brazier, G., 393
Brecke, P., 323
Brehm, J. W., 219, 251, 262
Brewer, M. B., 44, 93, 96, 159, 195, 348
Bringle, R. G., 354, 358
Brinol, P., 240-41, 265-66
Britt, T. W., 340
Brodt, S. E., 184
Brown, D. L., 382
Brown, G., 129
Brown, H. R., 288
Brown, J. D., 148
Brown, R., 204, 364, 363
Brown, S. L., 35, 383, 400
Brown, T. J., 387
Brown, V., 197-99
Bruce, J. B., 224
Bryan, J. H., 413
Bryant, J., 371
Buchanan, T. W., 289
Buckley, K., 319
Budesheim, T. L., 149
Bukszar, E., 172
Buller, D. J., 43
Bullock, M., 223
Bureau of Justice Statistics, 365
Bureau of Labor Statistics, 337
Burger, J. M., 269-70, 231-32, 385, 410
Burke, P. J., 106
Burnstein, E., 204, 388-89
Burrows, L., 362

Bushman, B. J., 102, 106-7, 294, 298-99, 302, 309-11
Buss, A. H., 27, 40, 41, 44, 46, 68, 163, 294-95, 437-38, 448, 453-54
Butler, R. N., 339
Butman, R. E., 61, 127
Butters, J., 105
Byrne, B. M., 95
Byrne, D., 144, 177, 384-85, 437-38, 443
Cabeza, R., 43
Cacioppo, J. T., 145, 239, 243-44, 264, 270, 317, 457
Cain, T. R., 332
Cairns, B. D., 305
Calkins, S. D., 299
Cameron, C., 76
Campbell, A. C., 413
Campbell, C. D., 63
Campbell, J. D., 100-101
Campbell, W. K., 32, 116, 125, 302
Caporael, L. R., 44, 111, 195
Carli, L. L., 266-67
Carlo, G., 406
Carlsmith, J. M., 251-52
Carlson, M., 296
Carprara, G. V., 300
Carter, C., 372
Carvallo, M., 262
Carver, C. S., 129, 218, 392
Casey, R. J., 449-50
Cash, D. W., 105
Cash, T. F., 105, 447
Casillas, A., 440
Caspi, A., 292
Cassidy, C., 393
Cast, A. D., 106
Castelli, L., 455
Castillo, R., 98
Catalan, J., 270
Catanese, K. R., 319
Chaiken, S., 238-39, 262-63, 265, 271
Chaikin, A. L., 410
Chalk, F., 318
Chan, S. C., 289
Chang, K., 119
Chaplin, W. F., 148
Chapman, J. E., 314
Chapman, J. J., 178

Chard, P., 398-99
Chartrand, T. L., 112, 213, 239, 261, 362
Chasteen, A. L., 203
Check, J., 318
Chen, H., 96, 98, 250, 362
Chown, S. M., 381
Cialdini, R. B., 120, 201, 215-16, 221, 266-68, 272-73, 394, 403
Ciarocco, N. J., 128
Clanton, N. R., 148
Clark, E. M., 428
Clark, M., 399
Clark, R. D., 222
Clary, E. G., 423
Clement, R. W., 116
Clements, C. M., 174
Clore, G. L., 386, 443-44
Coats, G., 452
Coccaro, E. F., 290
Codispoti, M., 157
Coffman, T. L., 354
Cohen, F., 332
Coie, J. D., 306
Coke, J. S., 398-99, 420
Colarelli, S. M., 42
Collins, A., 395-96
Collins, B. E., 215
Coltrane, S., & Messineo, M., 371
Combs, B., 170
Comstock, G., 309
Condry, J. C., & Condry, S., 340-41
Confer, J. C., 40
Conner, M., 249
Conner, R., 30
Conners, J., 346
Connolly, T., 172
Connor, W., 398
Cook, J. M., 437-38
Cooley, C. H., 93
Coopersmith, S., 105
Copeland, J., 423
Cornell, D. P., 105
Corporation for National and Community Service, Office of Research and Policy Development, 376
Cosmides, L. 27, 40, 42-43, 94-95, 154, 184-85, 370

Cotton, M., 247
Cottrell, N. B., 202
Cox, A. D., 433
Cox, C., 32, 46
Cox, D., 433
Craig, I. W., 292
Cramer, R. E., 394
Crandall, C. S., 337-38, 340, 388-89
Crane, P., 447
Crano, W. D., 260, 382
Crawford, J. T., 332
Crites Jr., S. L., 239
Crocker, J., 104, 126, 347
Crombag, H., 332
Cronk, R., 175
Crosby, F. J., 380
Crowley, M., 382
Csikszentmihalyi, M., 34, 81
Cuddy, A. J. C., 150-51
Cumberland, A., 406
Cunningham, J., 343, 399, 448-49
Cuthbert, B. N., 157
D'Anello, S., 337
Dagnan, D., 278
Dalbert, C., 381
Daloz, L. A., 406
Damasio, A. R., 289
Daniels, L. R., 411
Darby, B. C., 270, 392, 394, 405, 432
Darwin, C., 40
Dasgupta, N., 363-64
Davis, B., 100
Davis, H. C., 344
Davis, K. E., 159, 289, 336, 400
Davison, A., 232-33
Dawkins, R., 424
Dawson, K., 259
de Boer, T., 442
De Bruin, E. N. M., 144-45
Deaux, K., 93, 383
Deci, E. L., 129-31
Degelman, D., 385
DeHart, T., 262
DeJong, W., 413
Del Boca, F. K., 332
DeLisi, M., 290
Delle Fave, A., 82
DeMarree, K., 240-41
Dembosky, J. W., 224

Demoulin, S., 209
Denton, W. H., 453
DePalma, M. T., 381
Derksen, M., 40
Derlega, V. J., 410
Dermer, M., 450
Dernelle, R., 407, 409
DeSteno, D., 250-51, 258
Deutsch, M., 215
Devine, P. G., 203, 362, 364, 366, 432, 446
DeVore, I., 42
DeYoung, 370, 373
Dias, M., 449
Dickel, N., 240-41, 245
Diekman, A. B., 184
Diener, C., 175
Dijksterhuis, A., 143
Dillard, J. P., 219
Dinnerstein, J. L., 250
Dion, K. L., 148, 342, 365, 438
Ditto, P. H., 255
Dobbins, G. H., 442
Dodge, K. A., 298, 303, 305, 306
Dolan-Pasce, B., 319
Dolderman, D., 439
Dollard, J., 295
Dollinger, S. J., 343
Donahue, M., 351
Donnerstein, E. I., 298, 311
Doob, L., 295
Doosje, B., 158-59
Doria, J. R., 194
Doty, R. M., 334
Douge, L., 104
Dougherty, K. D., 356
Dovidio, J. E., 35, 50, 157, 208, 361, 365, 394, 400, 417
Downing, L. L., 199
Downs, A. C., 447
Downs, D., 102-4
Dragna, M., 394
Druen, P. B., 448
du Plessis, I., 343
Duckitt, J., 343
Duffy, M. K., 201
Dugatkin, L. A., 417
Dunbar, R. I. M., 135
Duncan, L. E., 343
Duncan, N. C., 447
Dunham, P. J., 152-53

Dunning, D., 116
Duntley, J. D., 294-95
Duriez, B., 346
Duvall, N. S., 90
Dweck, C. S., 38
Dynes, R. R., 408
Eagly, A. H., 184, 239, 262-63, 266-67, 271, 382, 451-52
Eals, M., 47
Early, S., 422
Easton, J. A., 40
Eaton, J., 321-22
Ebbinghaus, 173
Eberstadt, M., 286
Eck, B. E., 58
Egloff, B., 431
Eidelman, S. H., 409
Eisenberg, N., 400, 406, 413, 420
Eisenberger, N. I., 111
Ekehammar, N., 343
Elkind, D., 125
Ellemers, N., 158-59
Ellenbogen, J. M., 288
Eller, A., 38
Elliot, A. J., 116
Emler, N., 101
Emmons, R. A., 258
Emswiller, T., 383
Englander, E., 306
Enright, J. A., 325
Enright, R. D., 58, 325-26, 371
Epley, N., 317
Epstude, K., 177
Erbe, 430
Erikson, 68
Esses, V. M., 409
Essock-Vitale, S., 387-88
Ethier, K. A., 93
Evans, C. S., 54, 67, 133-34
Exline, J. J., 322
Fagerlin, A., 255
Fagin-Jones, S., 422
Fallon, A., 449
Farh, J. L., 442
Farrington, D. P., 306
Fazio, R. H., 34, 81, 83, 203, 238-40, 445-46
FBI Bureau of Justice Statistics-Criminal Victimization, 365
Feather, N. T., 337

Fehr, E., 124
Fein, S., 304
Ferguson, M. J., 362
Fernandez, J. K., 175
Fessler, D. M. T., 44
Festinger, L., 117, 199, 251-52, 343, 431
Fichten, C., 339
Fink, B., 448-49
Finkel, D. G., 354, 358
Finucane, M., 168
Fischbacher, U., 124
Fischer, C. S., 416
Fischhoff, B., 170, 172, 179
Fishbein, M., 143, 159, 240, 243, 248-49
Fiske, A. P., 145, 378
Fiske, S. T., 150-51, 317, 362
Fitzgerald, C. J., 42
Fleischman, D. S., 40
Floyd, R. B., 409
Folkes, V. S., 443
Forest, D., 399
Forest, J., 358
Forgas, J. P., 112, 268
Forsyth, D. R., 106-7, 193, 212, 223
Foucault, M., 91
Fox, N. A., 299
Frame, C. L., 298
Frankenberger, K. D., 117-18
Franklin, L., 246-47
Fraser, S. C., 269
Freedman, J. L., 173, 269
Frenkel-Brunswik, E., 33, 343
Fretheim, T. E., 280-82
Freud, S., 27, 48, 295
Frey, D., 205-6
Frick, P. J., 291
Friedrich, J., 116
Fritz, H. L., 67
Frost, J. H., 434
Frye, N. E., 304
Fuhrman, R. W., 432, 446
Fulton, A. S., 354
Fultz, J., 422
Funder, D. C., 155, 383
Furnham, A., 449
Gable, S., 34, 81, 83
Gabriel, S., 113-14
Gaertner, L., 112, 119, 126-27, 361, 382, 404, 454

Gaes, G. G., 309
Ganz, M., 378
Garber, P. A., 195
Gardner, W. L., 96, 113-14, 243-44
Gareis, K. C., 382
Garrity, K., 385
Garst, E., 259
Gaunt, R., 209
Gavanski, I., 177
Gawronski, B., 245
Gecas, V., 99
Geen, R. G., 298
Geertz, C., 98
Geis, G., 30
Gelles, R. J., 307
Gerard, H. B., 215
Gergen, K. J., 91, 104, 214
Gibson, R., 121
Gigerenzer, G., 70, 140-41, 172, 184-85
Gilbert, D. T., 158, 159
Gilbert, P., 402
Gilovich, T., 287
Giovanazzi, A., 455
Girgis, Z. M., 385
Gladwell, M., 225
Glassman, R. B., 382
Glick, P., 50, 150-51
Glicksohn, J., 441
Glock, C., 407
Glor, J., 340
Goethals, G. R., 173
Goetz, C. D., 40
Golan, H., 441
Golden, M., 340
Goldfried, J., 409
Goldstein, N. J., 215-16, 273
Gonzaga, G. C., 123
Goodman, M. D., 382
Gorsuch, R. L., 211, 352, 354, 409
Gortmaker, S. L., 338
Gosselin, F., 289
Gottlieb, J., 392
Gottman, J. M., 453
Gouldner, A. W., 410
Grafman, J., 288
Grannemann, B. D., 303
Graziano, W., 399
Gready, M., 255
Green, L., 185, 301

Greenberg, J., 179, 251
Greenwald, A. G., 246, 362-64
Greitemeyer, T., 325
Grenz, S. J., 63-64
Grey, R., 399
Griffin, D. W., 116, 238, 439
Griffin, E. M., 435
Griffiths, M. D., 311
Griffitt, C., 422, 438, 444
Griskevicius, V., 273
Groom, R. W., 308
Guadagno, R. E., 266-70
Gubin, A., 323
Guéguen, N., 383
Guerra, N., 314
Guger, C., 232-33
Guloine, T., 318
Gunter, B., 380
Gurtman, M. B., 157
Guthrie, I. K., 406
Hacker, A., 361
Hadas-Halpern, I., 317
Haddock, G., 240
Hagan, J., 184
Hagen, E., 43
Hagendoorn, L., 349
Hagengimana, A., 323
Hagtvet, K. A., 101
Haidt, J., 34, 81, 83
Haig, J., 440
Hall, D., 356
Hamilton, D. L., 153, 157, 179, 238, 416
Hamilton, V. L., 228
Hamilton, W. D., 110, 417
Hancock, J. T., 152-53
Hansen, D. E., 408
Hansen, T., 433
Hanson, L. R., Jr., 145
Harber, K., 332
Hardcastle, V. G., 43
Hardin, C. D., 364
Hargadon, A., 198
Harkins, S. G., 201-2
Harkness, A. R., 172
Harmon-Jones, E., 433
Harrell, K., 400
Harrell, W. A., 385-86
Harris, L. T., 317
Harris, V. A., 77
Harrison, J. A., 391
Harter, S., 105

Hartmann, G. W., 33
Harton, H. C., 223
Haselton, M. G., 155
Haslam, N., 104, 284, 318, 348
Hasty, R. W., 338
Hatfield, E., 386, 443-44, 447
Haugen, J., 423
Healy, K., 378
Hearold, S., 315
Heatherton, T. F., 100
Heaven, P., 346
Hecht, M. A., 147
Heider, F., 251
Heine, S. H., 119
Held, B. S., 83
Henggeler, S. W., 314
Henry, D., 314
Herlihy, B., 306
Hertwig, R., 172
Heusmann, L. R., 298
Hewstone, M., 38, 156-57, 455
Higley, S. L., 409
Hildebrandt, K. A., 449
Hill, P. C., 59, 170, 246-47, 360, 456
Hilton, D. J., 159
Hilton, J. L., 364
Hirshleifer, D., 215
Hodgins, H. S., 322
Hodgins, S., 290
Hoffer, E., 211
Hoffman, M. L., 420
Hoffrage, U., 172
Hofstadter, D., 177
Hogan, R., 302
Hoge, M. A., 229, 332, 347
Holland, R. W., 322
Holmes, A., 54
Holmes, J. G., 439
Holter, A. C., 325-26
Holub, S. C., 337
Homans, G. C., 452
Homel, R., 309
Hood, B. M., 146, 156
Hood, R. W., Jr., 352, 360, 409
Horita, M., 410
Horn, J., 387
Hornsey, M. J., 220-21, 332, 347
Horselenberg, R., 332
Horton, R. S., 439, 443
Hosoda, M., 452

Hovland, C. I., 260
Hoyle, R. H., 438
Hsee, C. K., 169
Huan Lim, S., 303
Hubert, S., 173
Hubner, J. J., 95-97
Huesmanrt, L. R., 314
Humphrey, J. A., 287
Hunsberger, B., 356-58, 400
Hur, T., 177-78
Hurford, M. O., 288
Huston, T., 30
Hutton, D. G., 99, 108
Huyser, K. R., 356
Hymes, C., 238
Infante, D. A., 279
Inhelder, B., 117
Inkster, J. A., 262
Insko, C. A., 209-10, 218, 398-99, 422, 438
Isenberg, D. J., 204
Ito, T. A., 239
Iuzzini, J., 112, 126-27, 454
Ivcevic, Z., 152
Iyengar, S. S., 127
Jackson, L. A., 447
Jackson, L. M., 356, 409
Jacobson, C., 352
Jacoby, L. L., 203
Jacoby, T., 361
Jahoda, G., 220, 317
James, W., 458
Janis, I. L., 206-7, 260
Jarvis, W., 238-39, 256
Jasper, C. R., 337
Jaworski, M., 145, 151
Jeffries, V., 406
Jenkins, S., 278
Jenkins, V., 449-50
John, O. P., 368
Johnson, B. T., 117
Johnson, E. J., 184
Johnson, E., 131
Johnson, J. L., 124
Johnson, M. A., 146
Johnson, P., 55
Johnston, L., 412-13
Joiner, T. E., Jr., 302-3
Jonason, P. K., 45-46
Jonassohn, K., 318
Jones, E. E., 77, 120-21, 126, 159, 173, 336

Jones, S. L., 61, 127, 159-60
Jordan, C. H., 346-47
Jost, J. T., 183, 380
Jowett, G. S., 33
Judd, C. M., 364, 370
Juslin, P., 149
Jussim, L., 183-84, 332, 365, 371
Kahneman, D., 166-68, 177
Kalakanis, L., 386-87
Kalmijn, M., 440, 443
Kampf, H. C., 250
Kang, M., 259
Kanouse, D. E., 145
Kaplan, H., 106
Kaplan, M. F., 205, 443
Karabenick, S. A., 386, 403
Karau, S. J., 202
Kardes, F. R., 238
Karlins, M., 354
Karlsson, L., 149
Karney, B. R., 304, 428
Karpinski, A., 364
Karremans, J. C., 322
Karris, L., 338
Karylowski, J., 384
Kasamon, Y. L., 290
Kasimatis, M., 177
Kassin, S. M., 304
Katz, J. E., 435
Katz, L. B., 153
Kaukiainen, A., 305
Kawakami, K., 114, 365
Kay, A. C., 380
Keen, C., 406
Kelley, H. H, 33, 150, 159, 164-65, 260, 454
Kelly, C. M., 428
Kelly, J., 247
Kelman, H. C., 228
Keltner, D., 287
Kendon, A., 212
Kenrick, D. T., 120, 162, 201, 221-23, 394, 403, 448, 455
Kent, A., 278
Kerber, K. W., 406-7
Kernan, J. B., 386
Kernberg, O., 302
Kernis, M. H., 106, 108-9, 303
Kerr, N. A., 106-7
Khan, S. R., 203
Kiesler, S., 435
Kilham, W., 230

Kilner, J. F., 72
Kilpatrick, S. D., 124
Kim, H., 168-69
Kim, Y., 451
King, K., 100
Kingston, L., 299
Kinoshita, L., 410
Kirchner, J., 439
Kirkpatrick, L. A., 303, 319
Kirkpatrick, L. E., 354, 358
Kitayama, S., 118, 388-89
Klassen, M. L., 337
Klatzky, R. L., 349
Kleck, R. E., 355
Klein, S. B., 94-95
Klohnen, E. C., 427, 440-42
Klonoff, E. A., 36
Knobe, J. M., 163-64
Knox, R. E., 262
Knutson, C., 325-26
Kobrynowicz, D., 250
Kohn, A., 406
Kolak, D., 41
Koole, S., 128
Koolhaus, J. M., 290
Korenman, S., 338
Koresh, Y., 416
Koriat, A., 179
Krahé, B., 300, 303, 305-6, 308
Kramer, B. M., 352
Kraut, R., 435
Krebs, D., 384, 394, 406
Kreuger, J. I., 100-101
Krivo, L. J., 184
Krosnick, J. A., 242, 261, 271
Krueger, J., 116
Kruger, D., 82-83, 416, 424
Kruglanski A. W., 183, 264-65
Krull, D. S., 158
Krysan, M., 361
Kubany, E. S., 306
Kuhl, J., 128, 130
Kulesa, P., 184
Kumar, S., 309
Kunreuther, H., 169
Kurman, J., 119
Kurzban, R., 135, 370
La France, M., 147, 212
Laakso, M. P., 290
LaFleur, S. J., 267-68
Lage, E., 222
Lagerspetz, K. M. J., 303, 305

Lago, T., 301
Lakin, J. L., 112, 261
LaMartina, B., 247
Lambert, A. J., 203
Lamm, H., 204
Landrine, H., 367
Lang, P. J., 157, 239
Lange, J. E., 362
Langer, E. J., 174
Langlois, J. H., 386-87, 449-50
LaPrelle, J., 438
Larey, T. S., 198
Larson, A., 386-87
Larson, L. U., 271
Larsson, H., 291
Latané, B., 201, 218, 223, 390, 392-94
Latu, I. M., 114
Laughlin, P. R., 201
Lavine, H., 219, 264
Lawler, E. J., 452-53
Lawton, M. P., 431
Layman, M., 170
Laythe, B., 354, 358
Lazarus, E., 337
Le Dreff, G., 383
Leary, M. R., 32, 46, 89, 102-4, 109, 113, 319, 428
Ledbetter, A. M., 435
Lee, M., 104
Lee, T. M. C., 289
Lehman, D. R., 119, 400
Leier, V. O., 153
Lepore, L., 363
Lepper, M. R., 117, 125, 127
Lerner, M. J., 162, 337, 380-81, 386, 403, 444
Letourneau, E. J., 314
Levenson, R. W., 453
Levin, P., 398
Levine, J., 192-93
Levine, M., 395-96
Levine, R. M., 393, 397
Levinson, D., 33, 286, 343, 352
Levy, D. M., 33
Lewin, K., 127, 260
Lewis, B. P., 35, 383
Lewis, D. M., 40
Lewis, S. K., 270
Leyens, J. Ph., 209, 455
Li, N. P, 162, 448
Liberman, A., 262-63, 271

Lichtenstein, M., 349
Lichtenstein, S., 170, 179
Liddle, J. R., 41
Lieberman, M. D., 111
Liebeskind, D. S., 288
Liebeskind, E., 322
Lin, T. R., 442
Lindsey, S., 242
Lingle, J. H., 173
Linsenmeier, J. A. W., 162, 448
Lipkus, I. M., 381
Lipton, P., 87
Lockhart, L. K., 255
Loeber, C. C., 267-68
Loftus, J., 95
London, O., 444
Long, W. L., 323
Longo, L. C., 450-52
Lord, C. G., 117
Lowenstein, R., 169
Lowery, B. S., 364
Loy, J. W., 150
Luce, C. L., 35, 383, 400
Luhtanen, R., 347
Luke, M., 126-27, 454
Lundmark, V., 435
Luo, S., 427, 441-42
Lüthgens, C., 205-6
Luzio Boone, A., 132
Lyche, L. F., 319
Lyers, Ph., 331
Lynch, M. E., 367
Lyons, P. M., 447
Maass, A., 222-23
Maccoby, E. E., 303
MacGregor, D. G., 168
MacIntyre, A., 20, 74
Macintyre, S., 309
Mackie, D. M., 334
MacLean, M. J., 381
Macrae, C. N., 146, 156-57, 350, 366, 412-13
Maddux, W., 261
Madey, S. F., 381
Magnuson, C. M., 58, 325
Maio, G. R., 240
Majkut, L., 220-21
Makhijani, M. G., 451-52
Malle, B. F., 163-65, 344
Malone, P. S., 159
Mandel, D. R., 178

Maner, J. K., 400
Mann, L., 230
Manning, C. C., 385
Manning, R., 395-96
Manstead, A. S. R., 244
Manucia, G. K., 398
Marber, S., 413
Marcus-Newhall, A., 296
Markman, K. D., 177
Markus, H. R., 93, 118, 238, 304
Marsh, H. W., 97
Martin, J., 292, 380
Martin, L. L., 105
Martin, M., 344
Martin, R., 94
Martinez, T., 397
Maruyama, G., 208
Maslow, A. H., 33
Mason, M. F., 146, 156
Massimini, F., 82
Matheson, K., 211
Matsumoto, H., 118
Matterson, J., 179-80
Matthews, K., 387
Matz, D. C., 356
Maynard, E. A., 354
McAfee Brown, R., 278
McAndrew, F. T., 424
McCart, M., 314
McClay, J., 292
McClellan, W., 100
McClelland, A., 449
McCullers, M., 247
McCullough, M. E., 124, 258
McDuff, P., 306
McFadyen, A. I., 65, 73-74
McFarland, S. G., 343-44
McGarty, C., 348
McGhee, D. E., 363-64
McGrath, A., 56, 60, 77, 107, 457
McGrath, J. C., 56, 60, 77, 107
McGraw, K. M., 380
McGuire, A. M., 83, 417-18
McGuire, M., 387-88
McGuire, W. J., 309
McKenna, F. P., 116, 125
McKimmie, B. M., 220-21
McKinley, A., 247
McMinn, M. R., 63
McMullen, M. N., 177

McPherson, M., 437-38
Medcof, J. W., 159
Mehr, D. R., 185
Mellers, B. A., 169
Mendelsohn, G. A., 440
Mendelson, M. J., 445
Menon, S., 169
Mentzer, S. J., 355
Mertens, R. W., 332
Merton, R. K., 352, 430
Metcalfe, J., 266
Meyer, J. M., 409
Middleton, J. R., 92
Midgley, C., 122
Midlarsky, E., 422
Miene, P., 423
Milgram, S., 229-31
Mill, J., 292
Miller, C., 398
Miller, D. T., 32, 380
Miller, J. A., 270
Miller, K., 454
Miller, N., 33, 295-96, 348
Miller, P. A., 420
Miller, R. S., 221
Miller, W. R., 57, 77-78
Miller-Perrin, C. L., 278
Mills, J., 399
Milne, A. B., 350
Milojkovic, J. D., 116
Miner, M., 409
Mitchell, T. R., 171, 175
Miura, M., 447
Miyake, K., 105
Mizrahi, K., 93
Moffitt, T. E., 291, 292
Molden, D. C., 38
Monroe, J., 246
Montada, L., 162
Monteith, M., 366
Montoya, R. M., 439, 443
Moon, Y., 214
Moorhead, G., 207
Moreland, J. P., 62, 193
Moreland, R. L., 192-93, 432
Morf, C., 302
Morris, W. M., 221
Morry, M. M., 439
Morse, S. J., 104
Morton, J., 146
Moscovici, S., 204-6, 222
Mosowitz, G. B., 238

Mowrer, O., 295
Mukopadhyay, T., 435
Mullen, B., 218
Munro, G. D., 255
Munson, Z., 378
Muraoka, M. Y., 306
Muraven, M., 129
Murphy, B. C., 406
Murray, J., 349
Murray, S. L., 439
Murstein, B. I., 439
Musick, P., 408
Myers, A. C., 114
Myers, D. G., 38, 116, 120, 204, 424
Myers, L. B., 116, 125
Naffrechoux, M., 222
Nagin, D., 306
Nahemow, L., 431
Naifeh, S. J., 354
Nakonezny, P. A., 453
Nam, R., 247
Nass, C., 214
Neck, C. P., 207
Neimark, G. B., 288
Nelson, L. D., 408
Nelson, R. J., 285
Nelson, S. E., 163, 164
Nemeth, C. J., 244
Neuberg, S. L., 35, 120, 201, 221, 362, 383, 394, 400, 403
Neumann, R., 212
Newcomb, T. M., 199, 439
Newman, L. S., 171, 238
Nezlek, J. B., 303
Ng, B., 309
Nickerson, R. S., 179
Niebuhr, R., 72
Niedenthal, P., 364
Nienhuis, A. E., 244
Nijman, H., 309
Nisbett, R. E., 159-60, 173, 183, 287
Noonan, J. R., 344
Norman, P., 249
Norton, M. I., 434
Novacek, J., 302
Novak, D. W., 444
Nus, S. E., 440
Nyberg, L., 43
O'Brien, K. S., 337
O'Brien, M., 318

O'Collins, G., 64
O'Connell, M., 380
O'Donnell, V. J., 33
O'Laughlin, M. J., 163
O'Quin, K., 422
Oakes, P. J., 348
Oliner, P., 413-15
Oliner, S., 406, 413-15
Oliver, M. B., 47
Olson, M. A., 445-46
Olsson, H., 149
Onodera, T., 447
Orozco, T., 45-46
Ortega, A. H., 198
Osgood, C. E., 315-16
Oskamp, S., 434
Osterman, K., 303
Ostrom, T. M., 173
Oswald, D. L., 428
Oudenhoven, J. P., 442
Ouellette, J. A., 175
Packel, E. W., 382
Paddock, E. L., 303
Pagani, L. S., 306
Page, R., 354
Paik, H., 309
Paladino, M. P., 209, 455
Parens, E., 290-93
Park, B., 364, 370
Parker, A. M., 224
Parks, A., 34
Parks, S. D., 406
Parmelee, P., 443
Parry, H. J., 353
Pate, S., 354
Patterson, M., 435, 408
Paul, A. M., 362
Paulus, P. B., 197-99
Payne, B. K., 203
Payne, J. W., 184
Pearlman, L. A., 323
Pedersen, W. C., 296
Peekna, H., 400
Pelham, B. W., 158, 262
Penner, L. A., 35, 417
Pennington, D. C., 172
Pennington, G. L., 113-14,
    177-78
Penrod, S., 218
Penton-Voak, I., 448-49
Pepitone, A., 199
Perdue, C. W., 157

Perez, J., 290
Perez, M., 302-3
Perilloux, C., 40
Perlman, D., 434
Perrin, R. D., 278
Perugini, M., 300
Peters, E. R., 168
Peterson, B. E., 343-44
Peterson, E., 175, 255
Peterson, R. D., 184
Petit, G. S., 305-6
Pettigrew, T. F., 332
Petty, R. E., 238-42, 261,
    265-66, 271
Peyrot, M., 306-7
Phelps, M. P., 70, 187
Phillips, J. B., 148
Piaget, J., 117
Piccione, A., 438
Pichot, N., 383
Pietromonaco, P., 167
Pike, C. L., 449
Piliavin, I. M., 394
Piliavin, J. A., 35, 380, 394, 417
Pinker, S., 312-13
Pinter, B., 209-10
Pistrang, N., 232-33
Plantinga, A., 56
Plaut, V. C., 451
Pliner, P., 432
Plomin, R., 291
Polivy, J., 100
Pomazal, R., 386
Post, S. G., 402
Postmes, T., 199-200
Poulton, R., 292
Powell, B., 338
Powell, M. C., 238
Powers, C., 246-47
Pratto, F., 344-45
Presson, P. K., 174
Price, J. M., 306
Priester, J. R., 238
Prigden, A., 288
Prino, C., 306-7
Prior, M., 299
Prislin, R., 260
Pruitt, D. G., 47
Pufall, A., 380
Pyszczynski, T. 179
Quinlivan, E., 319
Quinn, A., 221

Quinn, D. M., 342
Rae, S. B., 62
Raine, A., 288-89
Ranclaud, M., 309
Raskin, R., 302
Rassin, E., 332
Raymond, P., 238
Redder, G. D., 116, 159
Reicher, S. D., 200, 348, 393
Reid, A., 93
Reingen, P. H., 386
Remley, T. P., 306
Rempel, J. K., 243
Rhodes, A., 268
Rhodewalt, F., 302
Rice, C. L., 372
Rice, W. E., 272-73
Richard, D. C., 306
Richards, V., 169
Richardson, D. R., 277, 278,
    301
Richerson, P. J., 42
Ridge, R. D., 423
Ridl, J., 116, 120
Riecken, H. W., 117
Rieser-Danner, L. A., 449-50
Ritter, J. M., 449-50
Robberson, M. R., 268
Roberts, A. R., 448
Roberts, K., 410
Robinson, E., 309
Robinson, M. D., 314
Rodin, J., 394
Rodriguez, A. P., 209
Roesch, S. C., 325
Roese, N. J., 177-78
Rogers, R. W., 268
Roggman, L. A., 449-50
Rosenberg, M., 99, 102
Rosenblith, J. F., 352
Rosenman, R., 387
Ross, D., 297
Ross, L. D., 116-17, 125, 160-61,
    173, 183-84, 353-54
Ross, M., 32
Ross, S. A., 297
Rossi, R., 290
Rothbart, M., 368
Rothblum, E. D., 337-38
Rotter, N., 343
Rottman, L., 447
Rovai, A. P., 148-49

Rowatt, W. C., 246-47
Rowe, A. C., 146, 156
Rozendal, K., 94-95
Rozin, P., 449
Rubenstein, A. J., 386-87
Rubin, M., 455
Rudd, J. E., 279
Rudman, L., 50
Rudolph, U., 325
Ruggiero, M., 30
Rule, B. G., 278
Rushton, J. P., 46, 413, 424
Russell, S. A., 409
Ryan, R. M., 129-31
Ryan, C. S., 184, 365
Ryan, R. M., 130
Ryff, C. D., 129
Sabourin, T. C., 279
Sachau, D., 121
Sagarin, B. J., 272-73, 400
Sager, K., 259
Sagiv, L., 124
Sakalli, N., 337
Salazar, A. M., 288
Salvarani, G., 422
Sanbonmatsu, D. M., 238
Sanchez-Vives, M. V., 232-33
Sanday, P. R., 287
Sanford, R. N., 33, 343, 352-53
Saroglou, V., 407-9
Satz, M., 343
Saville, P. D., 172
Sawatsky, R., 57, 61, 73
Schachter, S., 117, 217, 431
Schaller, M., 399
Scheier, M. F., 129, 218
Schellenberg, E. G., 432
Scherlis, W., 435
Schewe, P. A., 314
Schlenker, B. R., 97, 221
Schmukle, S. C., 431
Schnabel, K., 246
Schoenbach, C., 99, 102
Schoenrade, P., 354, 407, 409
Schooler, C., 99, 102
Schooler, J. W., 132
Schooler, T. Y., 242
Schopler, J., 209-10
Schroeder, D. A., 35, 400, 417
Schulz-Hardt, S., 205-6
Schuman, H., 361
Schwab, K., 288

Schwalbe, M., 99
Schwartz, J. K. L., 363
Schwartz, S. H., 124, 411
Schwarz, N., 146-47, 240
Schyns, P., 289
Scott, J., 248
Scott, M. D., 439
Sears, D. O., 435-36
Sears, R. R., 33, 295
Sedikides, C., 32, 36, 116, 119,
  126-27, 135, 454
Seeley, E. A., 113-14
Segal, M. W., 430-31
Seligman, M. E. P., 34, 81, 124
Selten, R., 70, 140-41
Senju, A., 146
Serna, S. B., 272-73
Sestir, M. A., 294, 310-11
Seuferling, G., 250
Shackelford, T. K., 41, 440
Shaffer, D., 399
Shaffer, L. M., 203
Shamir, J., 220
Shang, L., 319
Shannon, E. A., 279
Shavelson, R. J., 95-97
Shaver, R., 413
Shavit, Y., 416
Shaw, J. D., 201
Shaw, L., 424
Shen, L., 219
Shepard, S. A., 406
Shepperd, J. A., 175, 202
Sherif, M., 216, 221
Sherman, D. A., 168-69
Sherman, J. W., 366
Sherman, S. J., 177, 238
Showers, C. J., 129, 438
Shuckford, G. L. J., 311
Shweder, R. A., 98
Sibley, C. G., 343
Sidanius, J., 344-45
Siegert, R., 41
Siegler, I. C., 381
Sigall, H., 354
Sillars, A. L., 439
Silver, L. A., 366-67
Silverman, I., 47
Silverman, J., 179-80
Simmonds, S., 399
Simmons, C. H., 381
Simmons, R. G., 416

Simon, A. F., 334
Simon, H. A., 140, 185
Simon, L., 251
Simpson, J. A., 39
Sinclair, S., 364
Singh, D., 204, 447-50
Skaalvik, E. M., 101
Skinner, B. F., 27
Skocpol, T., 378
Skowronski, J. J., 135
Slater, M., 232-33
Slovic, P., 168, 170, 172
Slugoski, B. R., 159
Smart, J., 339
Smart, L., 302
Smelser, N. J., 169
Smith, A., 246
Smith, C. V., 303
Smith, D., 398-99
Smith, P. B., 216, 338
Smith, R. H., 218, 268
Smith, S. L., 311
Smith-Lovin, L., 437-38
Smoot, M., 386-87
Snyder, M. L., 97, 120, 126, 219,
  355, 423
Snyder, R. C., 380
Sober, E., 416
Solomon, M. R., 450-51
Sommer, K. L., 114
Sorenson, K., 397
Sparks, G. G., 435
Spears, R., 158-59, 199-200, 244
Spencer, S. J., 342, 346-47
Spilka, B., 352, 360, 409
Sporer, S. L., 302
Sprecher, S., 386, 443-44
Sprengelmeyer, P., 422
Stagner, B., 264
Stallworth, L. M., 344
Stangor, C., 362
Stanton, G. C., 95-97
Stapel, D. A., 93
Staub, E., 206, 322-25
Stearns, S., 337
Steeh, L., 361
Steele, C. M., 105, 342
Steen, T., 34
Steer, R. A., 129
Stein, J. L., 148
Steinberg, J., 399
Steinmetz, J. L., 160

Stets, J. E., 278
Stewart, C. M., 43
Stewart, T. L., 114
Stewart-Williams, S., 48
Stocks, E. L., 356
Stokes, S. J., 387
Stone-Romero, E. F., 452
Strack, F., 212
Strauss, S. G., 224
Strayer, J., 400, 406, 413
Strenta, A., 355
Strongman, J., 250
Strube, M., 36
Struening , E. L., 353
Struthers, C. W., 321-22
Stucke, T. S., 112, 302
Stukas, A. A., 423
Suh, E., 83
Suls, J., 94
Sutton, R. I., 198
Swap, W. C., 434
Swapp, D., 232-33
Sykes, R. E., 430
Symons, C. S., 117
Szpunar, K. K., 432
t'Hart, P., 207
Tajfel, H., 347
Takagi, H., 118
Takata, T., 118-19
Taliaferro, A., 398-99
Talley, A. E., 300, 310
Tambor, E., 102-4
Tanford, S., 218
Tangney, J. P., 132
Taussig, W. C., 337
Taylor, A., 292
Taylor, D. M., 194
Taylor, K. M., 202
Taylor, S. E., 123, 218
Terdal, S., 102-4
Terry, D. J., 220-21
Tesser, A., 93, 105-6
Test, M. A., 413
Testa, C., 290
Tetlock, P. E., 206, 361, 364-65
Thernstrom, A., 361
Thibaut, J. W., 454
Thiel, D. L., 450
Thoits, P. A., 106
Thommeny, J., 309
Thompson, E. P., 250, 256-58, 264-65, 393

Thompson, L., 171, 175
Thompson, M. M., 238
Thrower, J., 246
Tice, D. M., 99, 108, 112, 129
Tiihonen, J., 290
Tillman, T. C., 381
Tindall, M., 246
Tipper, S. P., 366-67, 371
Tiuch, K., 246
Todd, P. M., 184-85
Todd, R., 400
Todorov, A., 146
Toi, M., 422
Tolan, P., 314
Tomala, Z., 265-66
Tomsen, S., 309
Tong, E. M. W., 258-59
Tooby, J., 27, 42-43, 154, 184-85, 294, 370
Tormala, Z. L., 238
Towles-Schwen, T., 239, 242
Tranel, D., 289
Tremblay, R. E., 306
Triandis, H. C., 98
Trivers, R. L., 46-47, 416, 418
Trolier, T. K., 157
Trompette, L., 407, 409
Trope, Y., 159
Trost, M. R., 216
Trout, M. R., 222-23
Tsang, J. A., 247, 257-58
Tuinier, S., 290
Turner, J. C., 347
Turner, Y., 317
Tversky, A., 166-68, 177
Twenge, J. M., 112, 319
Tyler, R. B., 157
Tyler, T. R., 380, 435-36
Uleman, J. S., 238
Umphress, Z., 290
Urdan, T., 122
Vacera, S., 146
Vaes, J., 209, 455
Valdesoso, P., 250-51
Valencia, A., 319
Valentine, J., 300, 310
Van Hiel, A., 346
Van Lange, P. A. M., 144-45, 322
Van Leeuwen, M. S., 54, 59, 77, 341
Van Oudenhoven, J. P., 442
van Praag, H. M., 290

VanBeest, I., 112-13
Vance, S. L., 364
Vandenberg, B., 408
Vanderplas, M., 422
Vasconcellos, J., 100
Vaughn, M. G., 290
Veitch, R., 438
Ventis, L., 354, 407, 409
Vera, C., 410
Verbrugge, L. M., 439
Verhoeven, W. M., 290
Verkuyten, M., 349
Vevea, J. L., 209-10
Viding, E., 291
Vidourek, R., 100
Vincent, J. E., 270
Vinokur, A., 204
Visser, P. S., 242
Vitaro, F., 306
Vitz, P., 61, 65
Vohs, K. D., 100-101, 127-28, 132, 302-3
Volf, M., 65
Von Hesteren, A., 406
von Hippel, W., 112, 366-67
Wade, J., 218
Wade, N. G., 58-59
Wagner, C., 343
Walker, S. G., 207
Waller, G., 278
Walsh, B. J., 92
Walster, E., 148, 386, 419, 438, 447
Walster, G. W., 354, 419, 438
Wang, S., 402
Ward, T., 41
Wardne, D., 288
Wasel, W., 364
Watson, D., 440
Watson, G. I., 207
Waugh, C. E., 319
Waytz, A., 317
Weaver, J. B., 309-10
Webster, E. C., 173
Webster, G. D., 45-46, 303, 319
Webster, M. J., 268
Wegner, D. M., 128, 366, 382
Weiner, B., 321-22, 325
Weingold, M. F., 97
Weisbuch, M., 152
Weiss, B., 305

Weiss, D., 288
Weiss, R. F., 305
Welch, I., 215
Wellman, B., 382
Wells, G. L., 177
Wells, R. B., 391
Wenzlaff, R. M., 366
Werner, C., 443
West, M. S., 207
West, S. G., 387
Westhues, K., 414-15
Whalen, P. J., 289, 380
Whatley, M. A., 268
Wheatley, T., 128
Wheeler, D., 270
Wheeler, J., 381
Wheeler, L., 94, 105, 451
White, J. W., 287
White, P. A., 163
White, S. F., 291
Whitley, B. E., 343-44
Whitney, H., 250
Wicklund, R. A., 219
Widemeyer, W. N., 150
Wilder, D., 334
Wildschut, T., 209-10

Wilkowski, B. M., 314
Williams, J. E., 403
Williams, K. D., 111-13, 201-2
Williams, L. E., 151-52, 258
Williamson, W. P., 360
Willis, H., 455
Willis, J., 146
Willits, J., 383
Wilson, A. D., 250
Wilson, D. S., 416
Wilson, D. W., 385-86
Wilson, E. O., 49
Wilson, J. W., 242, 408
Wilson, T. D., 242, 378
Winkel, R., 319
Winkielman, P., 146-47
Winter, D. G., 334, 343
Wittenbrink, B., 364, 370
Wojciszke, B., 143, 145, 151
Wolf, S., 218
Wolpe, J., 311
Wood, E., 216
Wood, J. V., 93
Wood, W., 264-65, 271, 356
Woods, S., 179-80
Worchel, S., 336

World Health Organization, 286-88
Worthington, E. L., Jr., 67, 80, 284, 317, 321-22, 456-57
Wortley, S., 382
Wortmann, R. L., 172
Wren, R. W., 406-7
Wu, C. H., 448
Wuensch, K. L., 393
Wurf, E., 93
Wylie, L., 358
Yang, Z., 198, 258-59
Yee, N., 214
Young, L., 338
Young, S., 380
Ysseldyk, R., 211
Yuker, H. E., 339
Yzerbyt, V. Y., 331
Zajonc, R. B., 143, 146-47, 168-69, 238, 432-33
Zanna, M. P., 238, 243, 346-47
Zarate, M. A., 95, 149
Zavalloni, M., 204
Zillmann, D., 297, 309-10, 371
Zimbardo, P. G., 253-54
Zoccolillo, M., 306

## Subject Index

abstract trait knowledge, 149
abstractions, 149
actor-observer bias, 159-60
affect, 168-70
  and affect infusion model,
    268
  persuasion and, 268-69
  *See also* emotion
ageism, 338-39
aggression
  age and, 304-5
  biological explanations of,
    288-94
  callous and unemotional
    traits (CU), 291
  cognitive processes in,
    297-98
  desensitization and,
    293-94, 311
  displaced, 296
  emotions and, 300-301,
    324, 326
  executive cognitive
    processes and, 288
  family factors and, 305
  frustration-aggression
    hypothesis, 295-96
  General Aggression
    Model (GAM), 298-99
  genetic influences and,
    291-92
  gradual reduction in
    tension (GRIT) strategy,
    315-16
  hostile, 278
  instinct and, 295
  instrumental, 278
  media and, 309-11
  multisystemic therapy of,
    299
  neoassociationist model
    of, 297
  reductionism and, 293
  religious extremists and,
    284-85
  situational factors and,
    307-11
  social learning theories of,
    296-97
  verbal, 278-80

weapons effect, 307
altruism, 42, 59, 124, 379-80,
  400-407, 411-18, 421-25
  and altruistic personality,
    406-7
  Christianity and, 423-25
  reciprocal, 46-47
  *See also* empathy; helping
anchoring effect, 167-68
anthropocentric view of
  humans, 75-76
anti-fat attitudes, 337-38
anticipation of interaction,
  432
antilocution, 336
antisocial behavior, 26, 277,
  378. *See also* aggression;
  prejudice; prosocial
  behavior
attitudes, 238-59
  behavior and, 248-55
  biasing of social
    perception and, 255
  content of, 243-44
  functions of, 244-45
  *See also* persuasion
attraction, 26, 80, 427-52
  matching hypothesis of,
    443-44
  physical attraction,
    446-52
  physical attractiveness
    stereotype, 148, 386,
    447-51
  proximity-attraction
    principle, 430, 432-35
  similarity and, 384-85,
    437-45
  similarity-attraction
    hypothesis, 437
  *See also* proximity
attributions, 158-66
  actor-observer hypothesis,
    159-60
  aggression and, 298
  covariation model of,
    164-66
  folk-conceptual model of,
    163-65
  fundamental attribution

    error, 77, 160-62
  internal and external
    forces, 159
authoritarianism, 343-46, 349,
  351, 358-59
  right-wing authoritari-
    anism (RWA), 343,
    345-46, 358-59
autokinetic effect, 216
automatic processing, 143, 362
autonomy, 96, 129-30
balance theory, 251
behavioral exemplars, 149-50
behaviorism, 39
bias
  accuracy of, 181-85
  confirmation bias, 179-80,
    255
  correspondence inference
    bias, 161
  hindsight bias, 172
  hostile attribution bias,
    298, 314
  hostile expectancy bias,
    298
  illusion of control, 174
  optimism bias, 175
  rosy prospection, 175-76
  rosy retrospection, 175-76
  *See also* attribution;
    self-centered tendencies
bounded rationality, 140-42
brainstorming, 197-99
  brainwriting, 198
bystander effect, 390-96
  diffusion of responsibility,
    391-93
  pluralistic ignorance,
    390-91
categorization, 156-58, 333-34,
  342
chameleon effect, 212-14
Christian view of human
  condition
  accuracy in social
    judgment and, 186-88
  aggression and, 280-84,
    316-26
  altruism and, 423-25
  attitudes and, 255-59

attraction and, 428,
435-36, 445-46
conformity and, 226-28
creation, fall, redemption
(CFR) and, 60-75
empirical approach and,
76-78
groups and, 195-97, 210-11
helping and, 389, 400-402,
411-12, 423-25
integration with social
psychology and, 55-60
intrinsic relational nature
and, 63-68, 114-15,
122-25
limited beings and, 62-63,
69-70, 142, 182, 186-88
no-choice relationships
and, 435-36
obedience and, 233-34
other-centered potential
and, 57-59, 64-68, 125-27,
368, 377-80, 411, 457
persuasion and, 271-73
prejudice/racism and, 367,
372-73
relationships and, 454-58
scientific method and,
78-80
self-esteem and, 106-8
self-regulation and, 132-34
theistic evolution and, 41
theocentric approach,
75-76
cognitive dissonance, 251-52,
262
collectivism, 98, 118-20, 126
competence, 99-100, 129-30,
143-45, 151, 267
social, 450-52
compliance, 222, 306, 382, 385
conformity, 192-94, 212-22,
226-28
autokinetic effect and, 216
informational influence,
215
minority influence, 221-23
normative influence, 215
public and private, 215
contact hypothesis, 368
content analysis. *See*
psychological research,

content analysis
correlational approach. *See*
psychological research,
correlational
counterfactual thinking,
176-78
couple-centered approach
(CCA), 441-42
creation, fall, redemption
(CFR) approach, 60-87. *See
also* Christian view of
human condition
culture, 42, 91-92, 97-98,
118-19, 129, 317, 335, 409,
448-49, 451
egocentric, 98, 118-19
rape-prone, 287
sociocentric, 98, 118-19
dehumanization, 208-9,
230, 284, 316-21. *See also*
groups; infrahuman-
ization
domestic violence, 279, 314,
326
egocentrism, 68, 117-18, 124
egocentric cultures, 98,
118-19
egoism, 416-17, 423-24
elaboration likelihood model,
263
emotion, 268-69, 289-91, 294,
296, 320
emotional susceptibility,
300-301
empathy, 34, 229, 232, 312-13,
317-18, 400-402, 406, 421-24
empathy-altruism
hypothesis, 400, 421-22
naturalistic explanation
for, 420
*See also* altruism; helping
empiricism. *See* psychological
research, empirical
approach to
evaluation, 143-54
automatic processing, 143,
362
effortful processing,
143-44, 149
evolutionary psychology (EP),
40-47, 72, 86, 123, 362
aggression and, 294-95

groups and, 196
helping behavior and,
417-21
and ultimate and
proximate causes, 41, 86
expectancy-value model,
240-41
experimental approach. *See*
psychological research,
experimental
extensivity, 415
eye contact effect, 146, 157
forgiveness, 58-59, 82, 233,
283-84, 316-17, 321-26
fundamentalism, 247-48,
357-60
gender
aggression and, 303
helping and, 403-4
persuasion and, 266-68
relational nature and,
113-14
groups, 96, 192-211
brainstorming, 197-99
dehumanization, 208-9
deindividuation, 199-201
discontinuity effect, 209
evolutionary view of, 195
groupiness, 193
group-serving bias, 194,
208-9
groupthink, 206-8
in- and out-group, 157-58,
208-9, 251, 282, 315, 320,
329-34, 342-49, 356, 382,
393, 409
infrahumanization, 209
polarization of, 204
religion and, 210-11
risky shift, 204
social facilitation, 202-4
social loafing, 201-2
*See also* conformity
heat hypothesis, 308
helping, 375-426
arousal/cost-reward
model, 394
bystander effect, 390-96
gender and, 403-4
genetic relatedness and,
387-89
mood and, 398-99

population density and,
397
*See also* empathy
heuristics, 141, 166-68, 180
accuracy of, 182-85
affect and, 168-70
affect heuristic, 168, 180
anchoring effect and,
167-68
availability heuristic,
166-67, 170, 180
representative heuristic,
167, 170, 180
hypotheses, 28-29, 37, 46-47,
58-59, 78-79
ideograph, 147
illusory correlations, 178-79
Implicit Association Test
(IAT), 245, 363-64
impression management,
120
informational influence, 215
infrahumanization, 209, 320.
*See also* groups
introspection, 92-93
irritability. *See* trait irritability
just-world hypothesis, 161-62,
340, 380-81, 411
kin selection, 42, 388
mere exposure effect, 432-34
affective models of, 433
and mere-repeated-
exposure paradigm, 433
mere presence effect, 202
meta-cognitive model
(MCM), 241-42
minority influence, 221-23
moral hypocrisy, 80, 250-51,
255-59
overpowered integrity
and, 257-258
narcissism, 101-2, 301-2
naturalism (naturalistic
model), 27, 40-41, 47-50
Christian view and, 75,
84-87
empathy and, 420
negative-state relief model,
395, 399, 420
negativity effect, 144-45
normative influence, 215
obedience, 228-33

crimes of, 228
obligatory interdependence,
195-96
"past attitudes are still there"
model (PAST), 241-42
peace psychology, 315-16
persuasion, 259-74
door-in-the-face
phenomenon, 270-71
dual-process models of,
262-65
foot-in-the-door
phenomenon, 269-71
heuristic systemic model
of, 262-63, 265
low-ball technique,
270-71
unimodal theories of, 262,
264-65
positive psychology, 34,
80-84, 124
prejudice, 33, 50, 80-81, 158,
180, 230, 247, 329-72
arms-length, 332
explicit and implicit types
of, 364-67
generality of, 343
inevitability of, 360-67
*See also* categorization;
race
primacy effect, 172-74
priming, 167
probabilistic realism, 183
production blocking, 198
prosocial behavior, 26, 378.
*See also* altruism; antisocial
behavior; helping
proximity
functional, 430
propinquity, 430-31
proximity-attraction
principle, 430, 432-35
*See also* mere exposure
effect
psychic unity of humankind,
43
psychological research
content analysis, 31
correlational, 29-31, 305
empirical approach to
(empiricism), 27, 31-32,
37-39, 76-78, 455-56

experimental, 28-30, 80,
304, 407
race
racial reconciliation, 38,
196, 363, 367-72
racism, 38, 84, 351-52,
358-59, 361-68, 372
rape, 286-87
reactance, 219-20
recency effect, 172-74
reciprocity, 270, 410-11, 417-18,
429, 452
relatedness, 75, 129-30
relational nature, 67-69, 72,
96, 109-15
religiosity
aggression and, 284-85
Christian orthodoxy and,
85, 359-60
extrinsic and intrinsic,
353-55, 407
helping and, 405, 407-9
intertextual approach to,
360
intratextual approach to,
360
prejudice and, 351-59
quest orientation, 354-57,
359, 407
religious fundamentalism
(RF). *See* fundamentalism
research. *See* psychological
research
right-wing authoritarianism.
*See* authoritarianism
risky shift, 204
satisficer, 140-41
scientific method, 27-32. *See
also* psychological research
self-attention theory, 218
self-categorization theory
(SCT), 348
self-centered tendencies,
115-22, 126, 416-17, 423-24
belief perseverance, 116-17,
172
collectivism and, 126
culture and, 118-20
egocentrism, 117-18
false consensus, 115-16,
439
false modesty, 121

overcPrev overconfidence effect,
115-17, 141-42
self-handicapping, 121-22
self-reference effect, 117
self-serving bias, 115-16
spotlight effect, 115, 117
*See also* bias; egoism
self-concept, 92-98
abstraction models of, 95
collective self, 96, 126
components of, 95-96
computational models of,
94
individual self, 96, 126
relational self, 96, 126
self-schemas and, 93
*See also* self-perception
self-control. *See* self-regulation
self-determination theory
(SDT), 129-32
self-esteem, 96-109
benefits and limitations
of, 100-102
enhancement and mainte-
nance of, 102-4
excessive levels of, 102
explicit, 346-47
implicit, 346-47
optimal, 106
*See also* competence;
narcissism; self-per-
ception; worth
self-monitoring, 120
self-perception, 88-93, 97, 143.
*See also* social perception
Christian view of, 90-92
self-presentation, 120-22
self-regulation, 127-34
Christian view of, 132-34
self-validation theory of,
265-66
self-worth. *See* worth
similarity. *See* attraction
social cascading, 224-25
social categorization. *See*
categorization

social cognition, 138-43, 149,
152-58, 170-71, 180-88
accuracy of, 181-86
Christian view of, 186-88
social comparison, 93-94,
104-5
downward social
comparison, 94
upward social com-
parison, 94
social contagion, 224-26
social dominance orientation
(SDO), 344-46, 351
social exchange theory, 404-5,
454-58
social exclusion, 103, 280,
318-320
social facilitation, 202-4
Social Identity Model of
Disinhibition (SIDE), 200
social identity theory (SIT),
347-48
social impact theory (SIT),
218
social influence, 26, 80,
191-92, 226-28, 234, 237-38
social influence model
(SIM), 218
*See also* attitudes;
conformity; groups;
obedience; persuasion
social loafing, 201-2
social perception, 26, 80,
139, 151, 156, 180, 194,
255, 428. *See also* social
cognition
social psychology
defined, 24
focuses of, 24-25
history of, 32-33
negative bias of, 32-34, 36,
37
social responsibility norm,
411
social-role theory, 403-4
sociocentric cultures, 98,
118-19

sociometer theory, 103
stereotypes, 179-80, 183-84,
203, 329
automatic, 362-63
benefits of, 349-50
cultural, 364-66
defined, 332
disabled and, 339-40
elderly and, 338-39
gender and, 340-41
hierarchical/top-down
inhibition of, 366
in-group, 349
lateral inhibition of,
366-367
negative implicit, 364-66,
368-71
obesity and, 337-38
physical attractiveness
stereotype, 148, 386,
447-51
stereotype threat, 342
surveys, 30-31
technology, 152-53, 435
theocentric view of humans,
75-76
theories, 28
theory of planned behavior
(TPB), 249
theory of reasoned action
(TORA), 243, 248
three-component model, 243
trait aggressiveness, 300-301
trait anger, 300-301
trait irritability, 300-301
Type A personality, 301
urban legends, 224
variable-centered approach
(VCA), 441-42
video games, 309-11
waist-to-hip ratio (WHR),
449
warm-cold variable, 150-52
weapons effect, 307
worth, 99, 107-8, 301-2